The Southern Ghors and Northeast 'Arabah Archaeological Survey

The Southern Ghors and Northeast 'Arabah Archaeological Survey

by

B. MacDonald

with major contributions by

K. 'Amr, N. H. Broeder and H. C. W. Skinner
C. Meyer, M. P. Neeley, D. S. Reese and D. S. Whitcomb

Sheffield Archaeological Monographs 5

J.R. Collis Publications
Department of Archaeology and Prehistory
University of Sheffield
1992

© Individual Authors 1992
Publisher: J.R. Collis
Editor: R.B. Adams
Cover design: K. Slater

This book has been published with the help of a grant from the
Social Science Federation of Canada, using funds provided by
the Social Sciences and Humanities Research Council of
Canada.

A catalogue record of this book is available from the British
Library.

ISBN 0 906090 43 1

Copies of this volume and a catalogue of other
publications by the Department of Archaeology & Prehistory,
University of Sheffield can be obtained from:

    J.R. Collis Publications
    Department of Archaeology & Prehistory
    University of Sheffield
    Sheffield   S10 2TN

Printed in Great Britain by

    The Dorset Press
    Dorchester

Contents

List of Figures

List of Tables

List of Photographs

List of Plates

Contributors

K. 'Amr	Dept. of Antiquities of Jordan Amman, Jordan
N.H. Broeder	Research Fellow, Yale University New Haven, Connecticut
B. MacDonald	Dept. of Theology, St. Francis Xavier University, Antigonish, Nova Scotia
C. Meyer	Oriental Institute, University of Chicago Chicago, Illinois
M.P. Neeley	Dept. of Anthropology, Arizona State University Tempe, Arizona
H.C.W. Skinner	Dept. of Geology and Geophysics, Yale University New Haven, Connecticut
D.S. Reese	Dept. of Anthropology, Field Museum of Natural History Chicago, Illinois
D.S. Whitcomb	Oriental Institute, University of Chicago Chicago, Illinois

Archaeological Periods and Dates *

Lower Palaeolithic Period (ca. 500,000 – 90,000 B.C.)

Middle Palaeolithic Period (ca. 90,000 – 45,000 B.C.)

Upper Palaeolithic Period (ca. 45,000 – 18,000 B.C.)

EpiPalaeolithic Period (ca. 18,000 – 8500 B.C.)

Neolithic Period (ca. 8500 – 4500 B.C.):

    Prepottery Neolithic (ca. 8500 – 5500 B.C.)
    Pottery Neolithic (ca. 5500 – 4500 B.C.)

Chalcolithic Period (ca. 4500 – 3300 B.C.):

    Early Chalcolithic (ca. 4500 – 3750 B.C.)
    Late Chalcolithic (ca. 3750 – 3300 B.C.)

Early Bronze Period (ca. 3300 – 1950 B.C.):

    Early Bronze I (ca. 3300 – 2900 B.C.)
    Early Bronze II (ca. 2900 – 2700 B.C.)
    Early Bronze III (ca. 2700 – 2300 B.C.)
    Early Bronze IV (ca. 2300 – 1950 B.C.)

Middle Bronze Period (ca. 1950 – 1550 B.C.)

Late Bronze Period (ca. 1550 – 1200 B.C.):

    Late Bronze I (ca. 1550 – 1400 B.C.)
    Late Bronze II (ca. 1400 – 1200 B.C.)

Iron I Period (1200 – 918 B.C.):

    Iron IA (1200 – 1000 B.C.)
    Iron IC (1000 – 918 B.C.)

Iron II Period (918 – 539 B.C.):

    Iron IIA (918 – 721 B.C.)
    Iron IIB (721 – 605 B.C.)
    Iron IIC (605 – 539 B.C.)

Persian Period (539 – 332 B.C.)

Hellenistic Period (332 – 63 B.C.):

    Early Hellenistic (332 – 198 B.C.)
    Late Hellenistic (198 – 63 B.C.)

Roman and Nabataean Periods (63 B.C. – A.D. 324):

    Early Roman (63 B.C. – A.D. 135)
    Late Roman (A.D. 135 – 324)

Byzantine Period (A.D. 324 – 640):

    Early Byzantine (A.D. 324 – 491)
    Late Byzantine (A.D. 491 – 640)

Early Islamic Period (ca. A.D. 630 – 1174):

    Umayyad (A.D. 661 – 750)
    Abbasid (A.D. 750 – 969)
    Fatimid (A.D. 969 – 1171)
    (Crusader A.D. 1099 – 1291)

Late Islamic Period (A.D. 1174 – 1918):

    Ayyubid (A.D. 1174 – 1263)
    Mamluk (A.D. 1250 – 1516)
    Turkish/Ottoman (A.D. 1516 – 1918)

Modern (A.D. 1918 – Present)

* These dates are given for the sake of convenience. There is, of course, the realization that there is not complete agreement among scholars on the dating of the various periods (cf. Homès–Fredericq and Hennessy 1986:10). For the Islamic Periods, compare also Whitcomb's archaeological periodization in Chapter 10, especially Table 57, of this report.

Abbreviations and Symbols

Abb	Abbasid	Mod	Modern
Ayy	Ayyubid	N	north/Neolithic
approx	approximately	Nab	Nabataean
ASTM	American Society for Testing Materials	NL	Neolithic
Ayy	Ayyubid	no(s).	number(s)
B	Bronze	nyp	not yet published
beg	beginning	opal	opalescent (a shimmer like a white opal.
Byz	Byzantine		'Iridescent' is much more brilliant, like a
c	century		peacock tail or oil film.)
C/Chal	Chalcolithic	Ott	Ottoman
chap(s)	chapter(s)	pl(s).	plate(s)
D/dia	diameter	pll	parallel
dec	decoration	PN/PNL	Pottery Neolithic
decomp	decomposition	PPNL	Prepottery Neolithic
dk	dark	PL	Palaeolithic
E	Early/east	poss	possible
EB	Early Bronze	prob	probable/probably
EB–MB	Intermediate Early Bronze–Middle	R. I.	refractive index
	Bronze	Reg. No.	registration number
EPL	EpiPalaeolithic	Rom	Roman
est	estimated	S	south
ext	exterior	SEM	Scanning Electron Microscopy
Fat	Fatimid	S. G.	specific gravity
fig(s).	figure(s)	SGNAS	Southern Ghors and Northeast 'Arabah
gr	green		Archaeological Survey
H	hardness	TH	Thickness
Hell	Hellenistic	turq	turquoise
horiz	horizontal	U	Upper
ID	identification	Um	Umayyad
impur	impurities	Ud	undetermined
int	interior	unpub	unpublished
Isl	Islamic	v	very
JVA	Jordan Valley Authority	W	west/width
Kh.	Khirbet	w/	with
L	Late/Length/Lower	wt	white
lg	large	WHS	Wadi al-Hasa Archaeological Survey
lt	light	x-section	cross section
M	Middle	Y	yellow
Mam	Mamluk	/	either/or
max	maximum	–	through
MB	Middle Bronze	+	plus

Acknowledgements

The director, Burton MacDonald, of the Southern Ghors and Northeast 'Arabah Archaeological Survey (SGNAS), acknowledges first of all those who participated in the 1985 and 1986 infield seasons. These include R. Adams; N. Bega'in; G. A. Clark; J. M. Ferguson; M. Gregory; F. L. Koucky; E. C. Lapp; Z. Al Muheisen; and Abu Yousef, camp cook. Without such help, the field work would not have been possible.

The College of Wooster and the University Council for Research of St. Francis Xavier University financed the 1985 season. Grants from the Social Sciences and Humanities Research Council of Canada (Leave Fellowship Programme); the University Council for Research of St. Francis Xavier University; The Kyle-Kelso Foundation, Inc., Holland, Michigan; the National Science Foundation; the National Geographic Society; and Arizona State University made the 1986 season possible.

Several contributors facilitated both the preparation for and the actual, infield work of the 1986 season   Dr.   A. Hadidi, former Director General, Department of Antiquities of Jordan, and his staff, especially Dr. F. Zayadine; Mr. D. Cimiotti, Impresit Construction Company; Mr. A. I. Ghandour, former Chairman and Chief Executive Officer, Royal Jordanian Airlines; Dr. M. Haddadin, former Director, Jordan Valley Authority; and Dr. D.W. McCreery, former Director, American Center of Oriental Research, Amman. To these individuals and their associates the SGNAS expresses sincerest gratitude.

During both infield seasons, the project was licenced by the Department of Antiquities of Jordan and affiliated with the American Schools of Oriental Research (ASOR). It was also affiliated with ASOR for its publication phases.

The director of the SGNAS would like to extend a very sincere expression of gratitude to those who helped in many ways in the preliminary and final analysis of the collected materials. Some of these individuals have written chapters in this report. Others, especially those mentioned at the end of Chapter 1, however, gave their time and their expertise in an attempt to understand better the occupational prehistory and history of the survey territory. Still others visited the area with the director and made many helpful comments about the archaeological remains in the area. The comments of R. G. Khouri; N. L. Lapp; C. D. Politis; W. E. Rast; and R. T. Schaub helped the director understand these remains more clearly.

The director owes a special debt of gratitude to his wife, R. Sampson, whose interest in the SGNAS was always high. She was always ready to accompany him and scale even the highest mountains where archaeological remains are present.

M. Gillis typed the manuscript. She also made many helpful suggestions about grammar and clarity of expression.

This book has been published with the help of a grant from the Social Science Federation of Canada, using funds provided by the Social Sciences and Humanities Research Council of Canada.

1. Introduction

by B. MacDonald

Introduction

The name of the project, the Southern Ghors and Northeast 'Arabah Archaeological Survey (SGNAS), is taken from the modern designation for the area. The Southern Ghors includes the area from Wadi Ibn Hammad, at the northern edge of the Lisan Peninsula, to Ghor Khuneizir. Wadi 'Arabah extends from this point to 'Aqaba (Khouri 1981: 216–18). The survey, as the subsequent discussion will make clear, did not cover the entire Southern Ghors and the northeast Wadi 'Arabah.

Topography

The survey territory extends from the agricultural fields just to the north of al-Safi southward to Wadi Fidan. The distance from north-to-south is approximately 40 kilometres. The width of the territory investigated is considerably less due to the international border to the west and an increasingly rugged terrain, the western edge of the Jordan Graben, to the east (Figure 1). For practical purposes, the survey area can be divided into two topographical regions: 1) the region from just north of al-Safi to a major east–west escarpment; and 2) from the escarpment south to Wadi Fidan.

The northern portion of the survey territory, i.e., from just north of al-Safi to the escarpment, ranges in elevation from ca. -390 m to ca. -300 m in a north-south direction and from ca. -390 m to ca. -200 to -180 m in a west-east direction. There are agricultural fields, alluvial fans, and sandy areas within this low-lying, western area. To the east and higher in elevation, there are heavily dissected, barren piedmont, wadi beds, and cuesta ridges. A number of major wadi systems feed this part of the survey area with the major perennial source of water being Wadi al-Hasa. The other wadis, though often containing active springs, flow seasonally.

The escarpment is characterized by a sharp rise in elevation, from -300 m to -200 m, over a very short distance. The terrain at the south end of the escarpment is heavily eroded and dissected. Toward the west, the mouth of Wadi 'Arabah can be seen as it enters this low lying plain, the Southern Ghors. Formation of the escarpment may be due to tectonic activity, differential erosion, or receding lake levels.

The southern portion of the survey area, from the top of the escarpment to Wadi Fidan, is characterized by elevations from ca. -230 m to 0 m, north to south, and ca. -230 to +10-50 m, west-to-east. The western portion of this area is a barren, heavily dissected flood plain/fan that extends into Wadi 'Arabah. The eastern area is characterized by dissected piedmont, sand dunes, rugged hills, wadi beds, and associated ridges. The wadi ridges appear to have experienced less downcutting and erosion than those in the northern portion. As a result, better preserved terraces are found along the wadis, a phenomenon which is largely absent in the north. As in the north, several springs are found in the wadi systems but the SGNAS observed no perennial flows of water into Wadi 'Arabah.

History of exploration in the area

The Southern Ghors and Northeast 'Arabah have been of interest to explorers and archaeologists for almost 200 years. This interest has resulted in visits to and reports on the area beginning as early as the first decades of the 19th century.

In 1812 Burckhardt (1822) went from Damascus to Karak on his way to Petra. He was delayed in Karak for a few days. He did not visit the area of the Dead Sea but he provides some information, which he collected from the people of Karak, on the area. He speaks about the fertility of the ghors and gives a description of its vegetation on its east side (1822: 392–93). He locates the principal settlement of the inhabitants at the southern extremity of the sea near the mouth of Wadi al-Hasa. He writes that its situation corresponds to that of Zoar. He places the ruins of an ancient city, which he calls Tawahin al-Sukkar, about the middle of the Dead Sea on its eastern side (1822: 391). After his visit to Petra he passed from there through the 'Arabah on his way to Egypt.

Irby and Mangles (1823; 1844) passed along the south end of the Dead Sea in 1817–18. There is nothing of great interest archaeologically in the report of their visit to al-Safi.

Lynch carried out a United States' expedition, mainly by boat, to the Dead Sea in 1848. He crossed to Mazra'a and went down along the eastern side of the Dead Sea by horseback. He went as far south as what he believed to be the Zoar visited by Irby and Mangles (Lynch 1849: 345–46).

De Saulcy (1853) passed around the south end of the Dead Sea in January 1851. He has very little to say about the archaeological ruins in the area.

Seetzen (1854–55) visited Syria and Transjordan in the years 1805 and 1806. He passed along the King's Highway as far as Karak. From there he passed around the southern extremity of the Dead Sea to Jerusalem.

Tristram (1866) undertook an examination of the geology and natural history of Palestine in 1863–64. In the account of his travels, he provides a description of the vegetation in the Southern Ghors

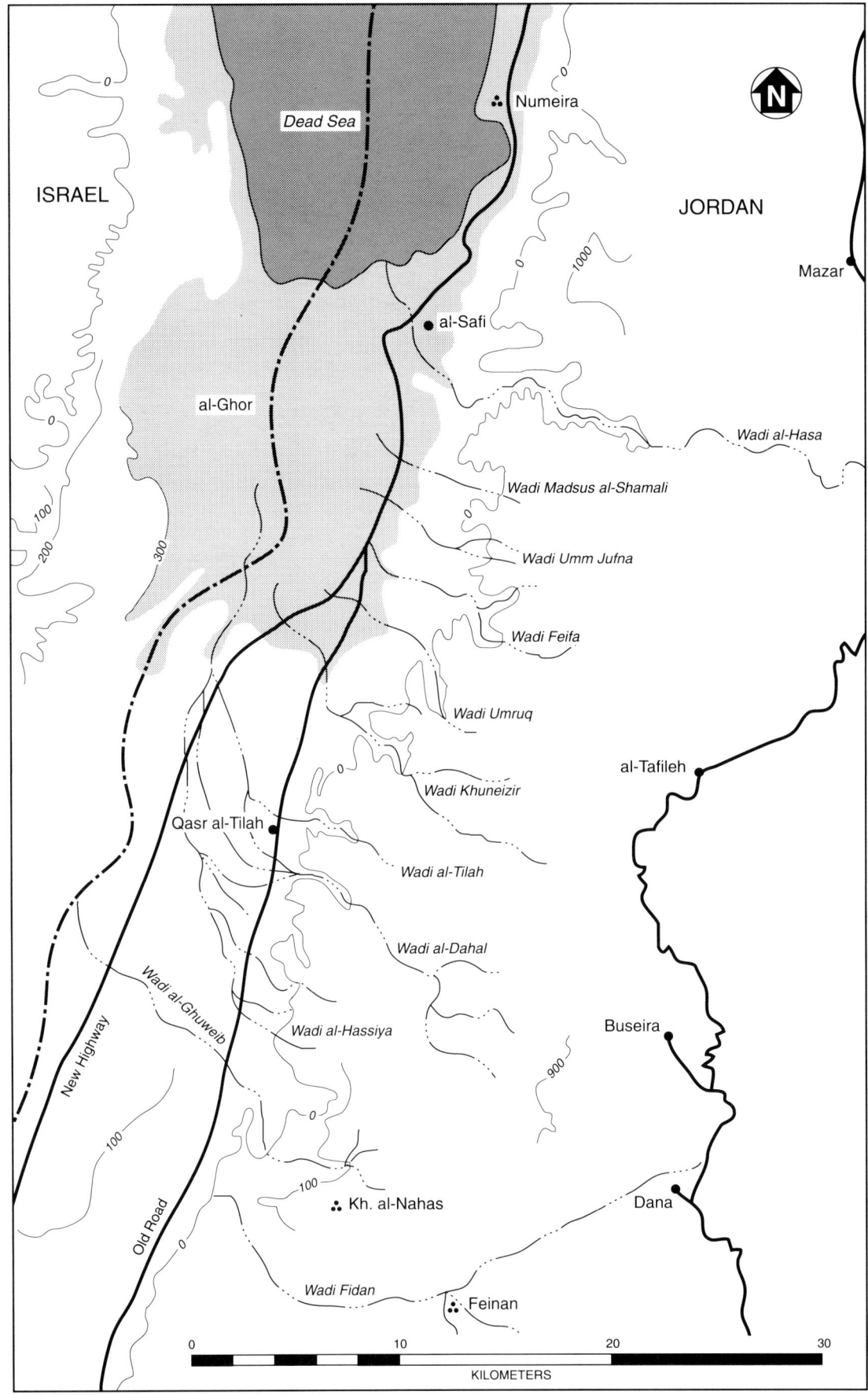

Figure 1   Southern Ghors and Northeast 'Arabah Archaeological Survey territory.

(1866: 339–40). Moreover, he gives a description of a fine ruin, which he calls Tawahin-es-Sukkar. He dates it to the Crusader Period. He writes: 'The ruins exactly resembled those of the sugar mills at Jericho....' (1866: 345). Just above this ruin, he locates a coarsely-built chapel which he also dates to the period of the Crusaders (1866: 345).

The expedition of de Luynes (1874) passed Ghor al-Safi in May 1864 and continued through the 'Arabah to the Red Sea. De Luynes examined Khirbet Sheikh 'Isa. He recognized in the ruins Arabic sherds and pottery. He saw the site as the Sogar of the Arabs and the Ségor of the Crusaders. He went further and identified the site as the biblical Zoar (Mallon 1924: 438, note 2).

Palmer (1871) provides a very interesting and positive description of the Southern Ghors as a result of his visit to the area in the spring of 1870. He visited Tawahin al-Sukkar and Khirbet Sheikh 'Isa. Moreover, he speaks of the ruins of a small town/village on the hills above these sites (1871: 463).

Klein (1880) journeyed from Jerusalem around the south end of the Dead Sea in January-February 1873. He camped at Ghor al-Safi in February of that year and examined the ruins of Khirbet Sheikh 'Isa and Tawahin al-Sukkar. Above the latter site he reported a ruined hut which he called El-Mashnaka (1880: 253).

Major Kitchener (1884) passed on a surveying trip from 'Aqaba to the south end of the Dead Sea in 1883. He visited many areas in the 'Arabah including Wadis Fidan, al-Ghuweib, and al-Dahal. After a visit to Qasr al-Tilah, he descended into the ghors and encamped at Ghor al-Feifa for one day (December 16, 1883) and then passed on to Ghor al-Safi where he camped from December 17–26. Of interest in his report are his comments on the archaeological sites in Ghor al-Safi. Hart served as botanist on the expedition. He provides valuable information on the natural resources of the region (Hart 1885).

In 1895, Hill (1896) desired to visit Petra from the north. However, he was not given permission to proceed to Petra. He, thus, proceeded from Karak to the Southern Ghors and passed around the south end of the Dead Sea on his return to Jerusalem. He also makes valuable comments on the natural resoures of the area.

Musil made a very important expedition of discovery in the area beginning in 1896 (1907). His findings will be referred to repeatedly in this report.

Brünnow and von Domaszewski (1904) did archaeological survey work in Jordan in 1897 and 1898. However, they only passed through the area under discussion on their journey from Jerusalem via Ghor al-Safi to Karak. They make very few comments of value about the area (1904: 15–18).

There was a stop to visits to the area from the end of the 19th century until 1924 when Albright undertook the first archaeological excavations in the area (1924; 1926; Mallon 1924; Kyle 1924; 1928). His expedition visited the districts of al-Safi and Feifa. He carried out excavations, by way of a trench, at Khirbet Sheikh 'Isa. The findings of this work will be referred to in subsequent discussions of sites, especially in Ghor al-Safi.

Frank (1934; Alt 1935; Alt and Wickert 1935) in 1932 and Glueck (1935) in 1934 carried out important expeditions of discovery in the Southern Ghors and the Northeast 'Arabah. Glueck (1937) followed his pedestrian explorations of the area by an aerial reconnaissance in 1937. No one can write about the archaeological remains in the area without reference to these two explorers.

After working with Lapp at Bab al-Dhra' in the late 60's (Schaub and Rast 1989), Rast and Schaub carried out a survey of the southeastern plain of the Dead Sea in 1973. The area covered extended from the modern settlement of Haditha, 6 km north of Bab al-Dhra' to Wadi Khuneizir, approximately 45 km to the south, at the southern end of the Southern Ghors, just east of the entrance to the 'Arabah (Rast and Schaub 1974: 5). In the territory under discussion, they made important discoveries at al-Safi, Feifa, and Khuneizir. Their survey resulted in the inauguration of The Southeastern Dead Sea Plain Expedition (Rast and Schaub 1978; 1981: 1–5). The expedition carried out excavations at both Feifa and in the area of Wadi Khuneizir in December 1989 – January 1990. The writer was a participant in this work. This work will be returned to later in this report.

The work of Raikes (n.d.; 1980; 1985) added a great deal to the archaeological inventory in the area. Raikes was the first to deal seriously with the lithic materials in the Northeast 'Arabah and to report unobtrusive sites. Previous explorers had confined their descriptions to the highly obtrusive, architectural sites in the area. Raikes, however, found a large number of sites not as the result of systematic search but in his six-years of work between 1967–69 and 1975–79 on the construction of the al-Safi to 'Aqaba and al-Safi to Mazra'a Highways. He found new sites in the course of normal activities: road construction; examination of floods and river beds; and, especially in the summer, in the course of looking for shade for the mid-day break. The SGNAS owes a great deal to the work of Raikes in the area as well as to conversations with him and his wife both before and during the actual, infield work.

McCreery (1979) did a survey in Ghor al-Safi for the JVA in 1979 in preparation for the building of a townsite.

In 1982 King *et al.* (King 1985; 1986; King *et al.* 1987; 1989) searched for Byzantine and Islamic sites along the eastern and southern coasts of the Dead Sea and Wadi 'Arabah as far as Gharandel in the south. From their work they concluded that there was extensive settlement in this area in the Byzantine period, while there is evidence of Roman and Nabataean occupation at an earlier date. They state, moreover, that there is not a great deal of evidence for settlement during the Umayyad period. They also found that there is evidence of later Islamic settlement in the Ghor, 'culminating in an efflorescence that came in Ayyubid and Mamluk times' (King 1986: 252). They report a decrease in activity, in the Northeast

'Arabah, during the Islamic Periods.

Frohlich and Lancaster carried out a survey of five settlement sites, namely, Bab al-Dhra'; Numeira; al-Safi; Feifa; and Khuneizir, in January 1985 with several objectives, related to The Southeastern Dead Sea Plain Expedition, in mind (1985: 1). Their comments on the sites of al-Safi, Feifa, and Khuneizir are of importance.

Donner and Knauf (1986) searched for the Church of Saint Lot in Ghor al-Safi in 1983. They saw the hermitage on the north bank of Wadi al-Hasa which Frank (1934; Alt and Wickert 1935) discovered in 1932 as its possible location.

Hauptmann *et al.* of the German Mining Museum, Bochum, West Germany, began a series of archaeometallurgical explorations and mining-archaeological studies in the Wadi Feinan region with a preliminary investigation in 1983 (Bachmann and Hauptmann 1984). The first survey season took place in 1984 (Hauptmann, Weisgerber, and Knauf 1985) while the second (Hauptmann 1986; Hauptmann and Weisgerber 1987) and third seasons were in the field in 1986 and 1988. This work has resulted in a vastly increased knowledge of the periods when this area was mined, the sites used for mining and smelting activities, and the technology employed, especially during the earliest periods (Hauptmann 1989).

Finally, Politis worked recently at SGNAS Site 46, Deir 'Ain 'Abata (1988; 1989; and 1990). Adams carried out explorations and excavations of several of the SGNAS sites in Wadi Fidan in 1989 and 1990 (1991). Specific references will be made to these explorations and excavations in subsequent chapters.

Recent economic developments in the area

In 1977 the government of Jordan made a decision to develop the southern half of the Jordan Rift Valley, from the Dead Sea to 'Aqaba, which Khouri refers to as Jordan's 'last frontier' (1981: 216). Up until that time the area was totally cut off from the rest of the country; it lacked a paved road; and it was also sealed off as a military area. Since then a two-lane paved highway was built linking 'Aqaba with Ghor al-Safi, the Lisan Peninsula, and the road to Karak. In the early 1980's the Arab Potash Company, located along the southern coastline of the Dead Sea, began to extract potash from the mineral-rich brine of the Dead Sea. A drip irrigation system in the Southern Ghors is now in operation. Water to feed this system comes from a few springs and nine side wadis. Farming is also developing in the Wadi 'Arabah. However, it depends more on underground water reserves than on perennial spring or side wadi flows. These developments have truly revolutionized life in the Southern Ghors and, to a lesser extent, in Wadi 'Arabah (Khouri 1981: 219–21). This development, which includes quarrying, the building of dams, roads, and flood diversion devices, the clearing of land for agricultual purposes, and the building of housing for the increasing population, has led to a destruction of archaeological remains in the area. This destruction of archaeological sites has continued since 1986. Some of the sites which the SGNAS surveyed are no longer in existence. Thus, the SGNAS was able to recover some of the cultural resources of the area before they are further destroyed by economic development.

The present survey

MacDonald *et al.* (1988) completed the Wadi al-Hasa Archaeological Survey (WHS) in 1983 after four infield seasons. The writer, director of the WHS, then wished to shift to the east in the Southern Ghors and Northeast 'Arabah to compare the archaeological remains in both areas and to attempt to draw parallels between the two (Figure 2). Several early explorers, e.g., Burckhardt (1922: 391) and Hart (1885: 267), had reported transhumance between the two areas in the 19th century. Was such the practice in previous centuries? If so, which wadis were used for such activity? The present writer also wanted answers to the following questions. What is the evidence for prehistoric settlement in the Southern Ghors and Northeast 'Arabah relative to the level of Lake Lisan? How far south in the Northeast 'Arabah must one survey before picking up evidence of Lower, Middle, and Upper Palaeolithic remains? Are the main, known sites in the Southern Ghors, especially at al-Safi, Feifa, and Khuneizir, predominantly one period, namely, Early Bronze Age sites? There was very little evidence of Middle Bronze Age and Late Bronze Age occupation on the plateau to the east (MacDonald *et al.* 1988). Is such the case in the Southern Ghors and Northeast 'Arabah? What is the relationship between the so-called 'Edomite' occupation on the plateau to the east and of that in both the Southern Ghors and Northeast 'Arabah and the area to the west of the 'Arabah in southern Judaea and the Negev? Are the Nabataean/Roman sites in the area part of a north–south route through the 'Arabah to 'Aqaba or are they merely east–west routes? Or, was there a line of fortresses/caravanserai throughout the 'Arabah in Nabataean/Roman times (Rothenberg 1971)? Where are biblical and Byzantine Zoar located? Are such sites as al-Safi, Feifa, and Qasr al-Tilah the location of Roman Zoara, Praesidium, and Toloah respectively? Where is the Church of Saint Lot of the Madaba Map located? What evidence is there for Islamic Period presence in the survey territory? The SGNAS was an attempt to provide at least preliminary answers to some of these questions.

The SGNAS comprised two in-field seasons. Koucky and MacDonald (1985; MacDonald and Koucky 1986) carried out an archaeological reconnaissance survey of the Southern Ghors and Northeast 'Arabah in May–June 1985. They were assisted in the field by two of Koucky's students, namely, J. M. Ferguson and E. C. Lapp, and Z. al Muheisen, Department of Antiquities. The purpose of the survey was to acquire a first-hand knowledge of the area between al-Safi in the north and Wadi Fidan

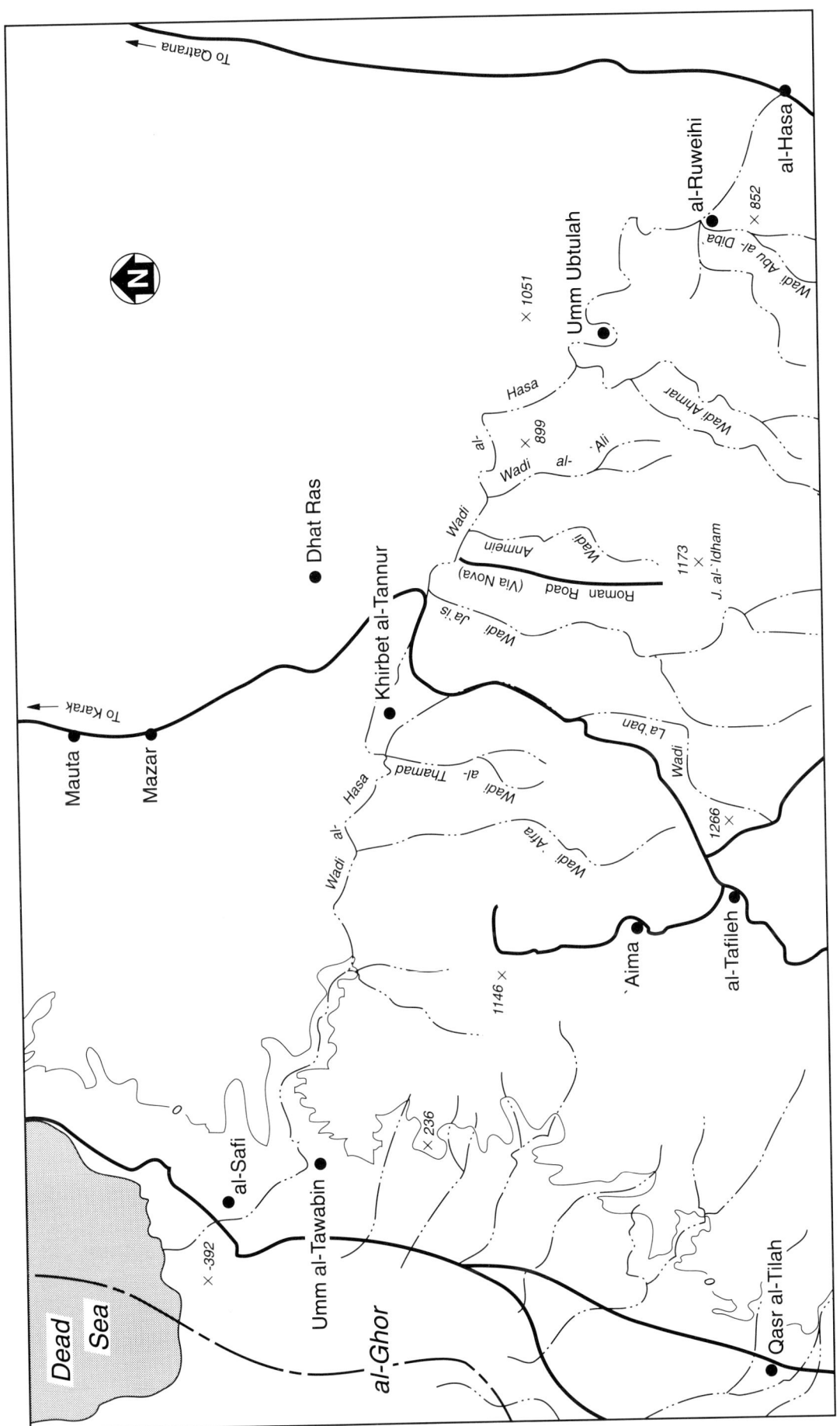

Figure 2 Wadi al-Hasa and Southern Ghors and Northeast 'Arabah Archaeological Surveys Territories.

in the south (Figure 1) and to assess the feasibility of carrying out an intensive and systematic survey of the area. The 10 days in the field, during which they visited 26 sites, most of them previously known (Table 1), acquainted Koucky and MacDonald with the area and led them to the conclusion that an intensive and systematic survey of the area was warranted. The intensive and reconnaissance survey, which resulted from the 1985 season, was in the field from October to December 1986 (MacDonald 1986; MacDonald *et al.* 1987; MacDonald, Clark, and Neeley 1988). The SGNAS spent a total of 39 days in actual infield work. The survey team was located in a JVA housing complex in Mazra'a (Photo 1) to the north of the survey territory. The team consisted of G.A. Clark, Department of Anthropology, Arizona State University, Tempe; two graduate students, namely, M. Gregory and M. Neeley, of the same department and university; R. Adams, graduate student, Department of Religion and Culture, Wilfrid Laurier University, Waterloo, Ontario; N. Beqa'in, Department of Antiquities; Abu Yousef, cook; and the writer, director.

The 1985 reconnaissance survey examined some sites in the Wadi Feinan region. However, the southern limit of the 1986 season was further to the north, namely, about 0.50 km north of 'Ain Fidan. During both seasons, however, the northern limit of the survey was Ghor al-Safi.

The SGNAS surveyed a total of 240 sites during the 1986 season (Figure 3 – in pocket at end of book). The 26 sites of the 1985 season are included in this total with the exception of several sites in Wadi Feinan. Of the 240 sites surveyed, 42.5% are located in the Southern Ghors while 57.5% are located on the escarpment and southward. The SGNAS collected both ceramics and lithics at 60 (25%) sites; ceramics at 123 (51%) additional sites; and lithics at 34 (14%) additional sites. It collected neither ceramics nor lithics at 23 (10%) architectural sites. Thus, the SGNAS collected ceramics at 183 sites and lithics at 94 sites.

The writer, helped by a number of ceramic specialists, did the preliminary analysis of the ceramic materials. These specialists included Z. Kafafi, Yarmouk University; N. Khairy, University of Jordan; N. Lapp, Pittsburg Theological Seminary; M. Piccirillo, Studium Biblicum Franciscanum; and F. Zayadine and K. 'Amr, Department of Antiquities. The writer along with K. 'Amr and D. S. Whitcomb, Oriental Institute, University of Chicago, carried out further analysis of the ceramics materials between 1987 and 1989 (Table 2). Whitcomb concentrated on the Islamic Periods ceramics from SGNAS Sites 1; 4; 45; and 91 (chapter 10). He prepared Plates 29–36. 'Amr did the drawings on Plates 6–28, ware analysis, exterior and interior descriptions, and the search for parallels in the literature. The local pottery traditions are not as well known in the south as they are in the north of Jordan. 'Amr searched for pottery parallels which were geographically close to the survey territory. However, often she had to look further afield

for parallels.

Neeley studied the lithic materials of the survey (chapter 4) for his M.A. thesis (1989) under the supervision of Professor Clark who, along with Neeley, participated in the 1986 season of the survey. Neeley prepared Plates 1–5.

Several specialists, who had not participated in the infield work, agreed to do the analyses of other materials which the SGNAS collected. C. Meyer, Oriental Institute, University of Chicago, studied the glass fragments (chapter 12); N. H. Broeder and H. C. W. Skinner, Yale University, did an analysis of the bead material (chapter 13); and D. S. Reese, Field Museum of Natural History, studied the shells (chapter 14). Meyer prepared Plates 37–38.

M.J. Westland prepared the settlement pattern maps. She also did Figures 10 and 25 from sketches based on the infield work of the survey team. Moreover, she drew Figures 12; 13; 15; 17; 18; 19; 20; 26; 27; 28; 29; and 30 based on aerial photographs at a scale of 1:25,000 which the writer had blown up 10 times to a scale of ca. 1:2,500. N. Hagen prepared Figures 22 and 23 (MacDonald and Politis 1988). I. Deeb prepared the map at the scale of 1:50,000 on which the SGNAS sites are located (Figure 3 – in pocket at end of book). Adams and the writer are responsible for Photos 1–30.

The settlement pattern maps indicate where sites from a specific period are located. There is no intention to indicate that all the sites from a given period were in existence at the same time. The

Table 1   Sites in the survey territory known previous to 1985 *

	SGNAS Site No.
Al-Rujoum	(45)
Khirbet Sheikh 'Isa	(4)
Hermitage on north bank of Wadi al-Hasa	(7)
Tawahin al-Sukkar/Qasr al-Tuba	(1)
Umm al-Tawabin	(6)
al-Safi	(2)
Feifa – ancient and medieval	(75,76)
Aqueduct on north bank of Wadi Feifa	(77)
Qasr al-Feifa	(91)
Rujm Umruq	(94)
Rujm Khuneizir	(108)
Aqueduct on east bank of Wadi Khuneizir	(112)
Qasr al-Tilah	(155)
Khirbet al-Dahal	(211)
Khirbet al-Hassiya	(229)
Tell Rabet al-dschamuse	(228 [?])
Rechemat al-bed	(215 [?])
Khirbet al-Nahas	(159)
Khirbet al-Ghuweib	(161)
Khirbet al-Jariyeh	(no SGNAS Site)
al-Munbateha/Khirbet Hamr Ifdan	(30)
Raikes' sites along the route of the new Mazra'a-'Aqaba road	
Raikes' sites in the Wadi Fidan gorge	

* Sites are listed in a north-to-south direction.

likelihood is that they were not since most of the periods cover at least several centuries. However, the artifactual evidence indicates that they belong to a specific time-stratigraphic unit.

The ceramics from the survey are stored at the Department of Antiquities Museum, Karak; the glass is at the Oriental Institute; and the lithics are at Arizona State University.

The spelling of place names follows, for the most part, that set forth in Zaghloul (1988). However, the article is written 'al-', rather than using the spoken form. Moreover, diacritics are not used, except where the name is taken as an Arabic word.

Appendix 1 contains a description of the 240 sites of the survey. It will provide the reader with more detailed information on each site as well as the periods represented. The 'Periods represented' are based on the analyses of the ceramics, glass, and lithics which the SGNAS collected at the site. The map references were not determined from an instrumental survey of the site. They are based on the SGNAS team members' estimation of the site's location in relation to available landmarks.

Appendix 2 is a sample of the Site, Ceramic, Lithic, and Inventory Rating Sheets the SGNAS used. (The SGNAS coloured these sheets for easier identification.) SGNAS team members completed in the field some or all of these sheets for each site. They added further information after preliminary and final analyses of the collected materials.

As noted above, one of the most compelling reasons for making this research available to scholars was that economic developments within the area, in the form of quarrying, construction, and agricultural land-clearance, were leading to the destruction of archaeological remains inclusive of several sites which the SGNAS surveyed. Moreover, this destruction is continuing.

Table 2   Ceramic sites of the SGNAS*

Period	#	%
NL	6	3.28
NL–Chal	7	3.83
Chal	14	7.65
Chal/EB	27	14.75
EB I and IB	5	2.73
EB IIB	1	0.55
EB II–III	3	1.64
EB III	2	1.09
EB IV; IVA; IVB	22	12.02
EB IV–MB I	1	0.55
EB	29	15.85
Iron IA and IC	11	6.01
Iron I–II	3	1.64
Iron II and A–C	26	14.21
Iron	26	14.21
Hell	7	3.83
Nab **	27	14.75
Nab/Rom	2	1.09
Rom	24	13.66
LRom	2	1.09
LRom–Byz	4	2.19
Byz (E and L)	64	34.97
LByz–Um	2	1.09
EIsl	8	4.37
Ayy/Mam	12	6.56
Ott	15	8.20
Isl	18	9.84
Ott/Mod	9	4.92
Mod	21	11.48

* Sites at which the field reading for a particular period was possible, probable, or questionable are not included in the table. Moreover, sites at which all the collected ceramics were Ud are not included in the table. Many of the sites, as mentioned in the text, are multiperiod.

** This is a combination of Nab (=LHell–ERom), Nab (=ERom), and Nab, without further specification, sites.

2. Methodology

by B. MacDonald

Introduction

As outlined in the previous chapter, the area which the SGNAS covered extends from Ghor al-Safi in the north to Wadi Fidan in the south (Figures 1 and 3). For the purposes of actual infield work, the SGNAS stratified the territory on the basis of the Jordan 1:50,000 scale maps (Series K737) into five regions: 1) agricultural land, farms, orchards, and plantations; 2) gravels, gravel/cobble veneer, and colluvium; 3) sandy areas, including dunes; 4) piedmont (the dissected slopes of the western edge of the Graben); and 5) wadi beds and their cuesta ridges. The strata frequently determined the methodology used. For example, pedestrian transects can be employed quite easily in strata one, two, and three. However, such is not the case for strata four and five. In these strata, the topography determined the areas surveyed. Thus, for reasons which will be outlined below, the SGNAS did not survey all areas of the territory in the same manner or with the same intensity.

Within these five strata the SGNAS used a combination of pedestrian transects and purposive surveying techniques. Because of time constraints and wadi washouts in December 1986, aerial photographs were used to pick out the major, architectural sites along the 'Old Road' between Wadi al-Dahal and to the area just north of Wadi al-Ghuweib (Figures 1 and 3). Once identified, the SGNAS visited these sites.

Within the Southern Ghors, between al-Safi and Wadi Khuneizir, the SGNAS used maps at the scale of 1:10,000 and 1:50,000. Hansa Luftbild (German Air Surveys) in cooporation with the Royal Jordanian Geographic Center (Aerial Photography June 1977) prepared the former for The Hashemite Kindgom of Jordan, Jordan Valley Authority, Mujib and Southern Ghors Irrigation Project (Palestine Grid). The latter were prepared for the Ministry of Economy and the United States Agency for International Development to Jordan; they are compiled by photogrammetric methods from aerial photography dated 1961 and from existing data furnished by the Jordan Department of Lands and Surveys, Series K737 (Universal Transverse Mercator Grid, Zone 36, International Spheroid). However, in the Northeast 'Arabah the only available maps were those at the scale of 1:50,000. Sheets at this scale which the SGNAS used for both the Southern Ghors and the Northeast 'Arabah were: Sheet 3152 III (Karak); Sheet 3052 II (Es-Safi); Sheet 3051 I (Fifi); and Sheet 3051 II (Jebel Hamrat Fidan).

Site definition

The definition of what constitutes a 'site' is not something upon which all archaeological surveyors and those who use the results of their work agree. It is, therefore, important to specify what this report understands by a 'site'. The SGNAS, like the WHS (MacDonald *et al.* 1988), called all scatters of sherds or artifacts, and all architectural remains, which appeared to date earlier than A.D. 1918 a 'site' (Banning 1988: 15–17). This would, of course, include sites which were in use after A.D. 1918 as long as these sites had more ancient remains present. For example, caves and rockshelters which are still being used, at least sporadically, as animal pens are called sites if there are sherds and/or lithics present. On the other hand, most field clearances, stone fences, and terrace walls which are still in use are excluded from the samples. A potbust, for the purposes of this study, qualifies as a site. In the opinion of the SGNAS, not to record such archaeological remains would be to miss some of the cultural resource material in the survey territory.

Visibility and obtrusiveness

The visibility in stratum 1, i.e., in the agricultural land; farms; orchards; and plantations, was not good, especially if a crop was being grown at the time of the SGNAS's visit. The only way to locate a site of low obtrusiveness in such a stratum would be for a team member to walk directly over the artifactual remains. Visibility in the other four strata was generally good since all the 240 sites were surveyed during the fall of the year.

The majority of the sites recorded were very unobtrusive. These included, for the most part, sherd and lithic scatters, which were generally only detected when a team member walked over them. Even in this category, however, Raikes, due to the nature of his work in the Southern Ghors and Northeast 'Arabah, had previously recorded some of these (n.d.; 1980; 1985). The majority of the obtrusive sites, with several important exceptions, which the SGNAS recorded were already known from the work of previous explorers in the area (Table 1). Some of the obtrusive sites, e.g., stone enclosures, had not been previously recorded because of lack of interest on the part of previous surveyors.

The location of sites

The sites which the SGNAS recorded came as a result of the study of the work of previous surveyors in the territory, by pedestrian transcects, by the study of aerial photographs, and by conversations with those living and/or working in the area.

Chapter 1 of this report outlines the work of those who had visited the area in search for archaeological remains prior to 1985. The SGNAS attempted to visit, record, and 'sherd' all these previously located sites (Table 1). This is generally referred to as purposive surveying. Following is a list of sites which the SGNAS purposively surveyed along with the person-hours spent: i) purposive survey of known sites in the al-Safi area: Site 1, Tawahin al-Sukkar (site partitioned for sampling purposes into three areas); Site 2, al-Safi, Early Bronze Age cemetery; Site 3, tomb; Site 4, Khirbet Sheikh 'Isa (the SGNAS covered by means of transects about 50% of the plowed field in which the site is located); Site 5, camp; Site 6, Umm al-Tawabin (site partitioned for sampling purposes); and Site 7, hermitage on north bank of Wadi al-Hasa (36 person-hours); ii) survey of sites previously sampled by Raikes (n.d.; 1980; 1985) in the Wadi Fidan gorge (72 person-hours); iii) survey of Sites 75 and 76, ancient Feifa (both sites partitioned for sampling purposes) (18 person-hours); iv) survey of modern and medieval Feifa, Site 91 (site partitioned for sampling purposes) (three person-hours); v) Site 155, Qasr al-Tilah, (site partitioned for sampling purposes) (five person-hours); vi) major sites along Wadi al-Ghuweib, e.g., Site 159, Khirbet al-Nahas, and Site 161, Khirbet al-Ghuweib (sites partitioned for sampling purposes (30 person-hours); vii) area around the new Police Post at Wadi al-Dahal east and west of the main Mazra'a–'Aqaba Highway where Raikes (n.d.; 1980; 1985) had reported lithic sites (27 person-hours); and viii) survey of a number of sites in the Wadi Feifa bed and Wadi Madsus al-Shamali (10 person-hours).

Most of the sites which the survey discovered were by means of pedestrian transects, the location of which can be easily identified on Figures 1 and 3. Pedestrian transects carried out in each stratum is given in detail below along with the time spent:

Stratum 1 (agricultural land, farms, orchards, plantations)

i) Small tract of plowed fields immediately north of the Wadi al-Hasa gorge and immediately northeast of Site 65; three persons spaced ca. 10 m apart; the SGNAS found neither lithics nor sherds (three person-hours).

ii) North of the main Mazra'a–'Aqaba Highway and north of Site 36: three transects in cultivated fields (in east–west and west–east directions) by six persons spaced ca. 10 m apart; the transects covered 41 fields (each field measures 150 x 200 m); 45% of the fields in the area covered; 33% of each field covered; the SGNAS found a total of six isolated, body sherds – no sites (36 person-hours).

iii) South of the main Mazra'a–'Aqaba Highway and north of Wadi al-Hasa: three transects in cultivated fields (in east–west and west–east directions) by six persons spaced ca. 10 m apart; the transects covered 23 fields; 33% of

each field covered; the SGNAS found one sherd scatter, Site 36, in the area (36 person-hours).

iv) South of the main Mazra'a–'Aqaba Highway and immediately southwest of Wadi al-Hasa: one transect (in a north–south direction) by six persons spaced ca. 10 m apart; 33% of each field covered; the SGNAS surveyed a total of five sites (Sites 27, 58, 59, 65 and 66); however, most of these sites are located immediately west of major architectural sites or where the remains of modern houses had been (30 person-hours).

v) From the Wadi Feifa bridge for a distance of 4 km to the north and ca. 50–75 m west of the main Mazra'a–'Aqaba Highway; through strata 1, 2, and 3; four persons spaced ca. 15 m apart; Sites 157, 181, and 182 surveyed (12 person-hours).

Stratum 2 (gravels, gravel/cobble veneer, colluvium)

i) From Wadi Umruq to Wadi Khuneizir; east of main Mazra'a–'Aqaba Highway; between the highway and the western edges of the Graben; eventually the western segment of the transect met the highway; five team members spaced 20 m apart; Sites 111D–G surveyed (12 person-hours).

ii) Through Al Naqa village, south of Wadi al-Hasa; five team members spread ca. 5 m apart; no sites (three person-hours).

Stratum 3 (sandy areas, including dunes)

i) The transects in this strata are combined with those in stratum 2.

Strata 2 and 3 (combination)

i) From 5.30 km north of the Wadi Feifa bridge to 6.70 km north of bridge; west of main Mazra'a–'Aqaba Highway a distance of ca. 50–75 m; four team members spaced ca. 15 m apart; part of the area had been cleared recently (1986) of shrubs for agricultural purposes; no sites (four person-hours).

ii) From south bank of Wadi Feifa to north bank of Wadi Umruq; east of main Mazra'a'Aqaba Highway a distance of ca. 75 m; five team members ca. 20 m apart; Sites 92, 93, 95, 106, 111A–C, and 158 surveyed (12 person-hours); and iii) on plateau south of the JVA camp at Khuneizira to Wadi al-Tilah; east of the main Mazra'–'Aqaba Highway; five team members spread ca. 15 m apart; Sites 148A–C, 154A–H, 163A–C, 166 surveyed (60 person-hours).

Stratum 4 (piedmont – the dissected footslopes of the western edge of the graben)

i) Between main mound at Site 2, al-Safi, to

Wadi Madsus al-Shamali; two transects – one in each direction; five team members spread ca. 10–10–50–10–10; north-directed transect spaced ca. 0.25 km west of the south-directed transect; Sites 17, 18, 19, 22, 23, 24, 25, 26 surveyed (36 person-hours).

ii) Along the dissected slopes east of the modern village of al-Safi as far south as Wadi al-Hasa; six team members spaced ca. 15 m apart; Sites 61, 62, 63, 64, 79A–H, 80, and 81 surveyed (30 person-hours).

iii) West and east terraces of Wadi al-Ghuweib; three team members transected the west terrace spread over an area of ca. 40 m; two team members transected the east terrace spread over an area of ca. 40 m; each team going in a northerly direction; Sites 96, 97A–F, 98–102, 42, 43, 82, 83, and 85–88 surveyed (30 person-hours).

iv) Three team members from mouth of the Wadi Fidan gorge to Wadi al-Ghuweib; two team members along the north bank of Wadi al-Ghuweib; spacing for each team was ca. 30 m (30 person-hours).

v) Southern segment of plateau and dissected slopes between Wadi Feifa and Wadi Umm Jufna; five team members spaced ca. 10 m apart (50 person-hours).

vi) From Wadi Khuneizir to Wadi Feifa; west of main Mazra'a'Aqaba Highway; ca. 100 m west of the highway; two team members spread over a distance of ca. 40 m; no sites (four person-hours).

Strata 2 and 4 (combination)

i) From flood diversion dams east of the main Mazra'a–'Aqaba Highway towards Wadi Madsus al-Shamali and then along the north and south ridges of Wadi Madsus al-Shamali for a distance of ca. 4.50 km; six team members spread ca. 10 m apart; Site 8 surveyed (36 person-hours).

Stratum 5 (wadi beds and their cuesta ridges)

i) Two teams comprised of three persons each along the north and south sides of Wadi Fidan; spacing ca. 15 m between each person (30 person-hours).

ii) Area between Wadi Fidan and Wadi al-Ghuweib – one team going in a northeasterly direction; a heavy concentration of sites; the second team going in a southwesterly direction; Sites 114–117; each team comprised of three persons (30 person-hours).

iii) Along the north and south ridges of Wadi Umm Jufna; two teams comprised of three persons each; transect began ca. 4 km southeast of the main Mazra'a–'Aqaba Highway (36 person-hours).

iv) Checking terraces along the north and south sides of Wadi Feifa; two teams of two members each (30 person-hours).

v) Checking terraces along the north and south ridges of Wadi Umruq; two team of two members each; Sites 132–134, 137–139, 145–146 surveyed (24 person-hours).

vi) Checking terraces along the north and south ridges of Wadi al-Tilah; two team of two members each; Sites 156 and 167 surveyed (16 person hours); and vii) two teams – one comprised of two members and one comprised of three members – checking terraces for a distance of ca. 6 km east of the old Police Post at al-Dahal along the north and south ridges of Wadi al-Dahal; a heavy concentration of sites (60 person-hours).

Strata 4 and 5 (combination)

i) Checking terraces to the east and west of Wadi Khuneizir; two teams comprised of two members each (42 person-hours).

ii) Checking terraces to the east of Wadi al-Nukhbar (12 person-hours).

The SGNAS carried out two transects from the area of the so-called 'Edomite' plateau north of al-Tafileh to the Southern Ghors (Figures 1 and 3). Two teams, consisting of two persons each, went by vehicle to the northwestern segment of the plateau. A guide showed each team where to begin the descent from the plateau to the Southern Ghors. One team descended between Wadi al-Hasa and Wadi Madsus al-Shamali while the other team descended between Wadi Madsus al-Shamali and Wadi Umm Jufna.

The descent, which involves a change in elevation of ca. 1,300 m over a distance of ca. 10 km, was extremely difficult and arduous for both teams. The time required to complete the descent was between five and six hours. The descent followed goat paths for the most part since no better paths could be found. There is no direct descent. One team ended up at Site 6, Umm al-Tawabin, while the other ended up at Site 73, Rujm Umm Jufna (Figure 3).

Shepherds use the region today to pasture their flocks of sheep and goats. It is also an area frequented by hunters. During the descent, the SGNAS noted sherd and lithics. However, it recorded only two sites, namely, Sites 177 and 196. These two sites are not accurately indicated on the survey maps since it is almost impossible to tell with any degree of accuracy just where one is once one gets into the mountains. The carrying of more collected sherds and lithics would have made the descent even more arduous.

To survey the mountainous area between the Southern Ghors and the Northeast 'Arabah and the Edomite plateau would require a great deal of preparation, time, and energy. Logistics for such work would have to be carefully worked out. Anyone carrying out such work would have to camp out at times. And even with this, there would be the problem of carrying collected artifacts to a place where they could be picked up by a vehicle. Accurate plotting of the location of sites on a map would be very difficult. (The only maps available for the area are at a scale of 1:50,000.)

There are foot paths along Wadis Feifa, Umruq, Khuneizir, and al-Tilah which lead from the Southern Ghors and Northeast 'Arabah towards the area to the north and south of al-Tafileh. However, time-constraints did not permit the following of these paths to the plateau. A survey of each path would have required the hiring of a knowledgeable guide. A minimum of one day per path would be needed for such an undertaking. These paths could have been used by shepherds and their flocks going seasonally from the Southern Ghors to the plateau and vice-versa. The best route to the plateau leads through Wadi al-Dahal. It comes out near Buseira. There is evidence in this wadi of a dirt road. However, the rains of previous winters had cut it at the time of the SGNAS' visit. (As mentioned previously, the SGNAS surveyed the terraces of this wadi for a distance of ca. 6 km from the old Police Post at al-Dahal.)

The SGNAS used the 'Old Road' from Wadi al-Dahal and Wadi al-Ghuweib only sparingly since the sand dunes, Stratum 3, between these two wadis make vehicular and pedestrian travel extremely difficult. At times, however, vehicular traffic was virtually impossible. The area on both sides of the road, which is very poorly indicated in places, is mostly sand. Thus, the SGNAS carried out no pedestrian transects in this region.

Because of time-constraints, coupled with the difficulty of reaching the area by either foot or vehicle, the SGNAS used aerial photographs to locate architectural sites along the 'Old Road' between Wadi al-Dahal and just north of Wadi al-Ghuweib (Stratum 2) (42 person-hours). The SGNAS recorded several important architectural sites, namley, Sites 216; 228; 229; 232; and 233 in this way (Figure 3). The SGNAS also discovered Sites 239 and 240 immediately north of Wadi Madsus al-Shamali (Figure 3) using aerial photographs. The walk by team members to and from these sites resulted in the discovery of other sites.

As Figure 3 clearly indicates, the SGNAS generally stayed away from the territory close by the international border. One reason for this was to avoid drawing undue attention to ourselves from the military in the region. Secondly, in the Southern Ghors' segment of the survey territory there are agricultural fields in this area. Since the SGNAS had discovered so little, archaeologically-speaking, in the agricultural fields further to the east, it thought that it would be unproductive to spend more time and energy to the west. Furthermore, some of this territory would have been covered by the waters of the Dead Sea at various periods in the past. In the Northeast 'Arabah, there is a vast area of desert between the Southern Ghors and Wadi Fidan. Here again, as indicated in the previous paragraph, we concentrated our efforts along the regions closer to the 'Old Road'.

Due to several factors, the SGNAS did not visit Khirbet al-Jariyeh. However, Hauptmann *et al.* have recently carried out extensive investigations at this site

Table 3 Types of survey, time, and percentages

Type of Survey	Person* Hours	Percentage
1 Pedestrian transects	726	70.83
2 Purposive	207	20.20
3 As a result of conversation with locals	50	4.88
4 As a result of the study of aerial photographs	42	4.10
Total	1025	100.00

* Person-hours represents the actual time spent in the field. It does not represent the time driving to and from the place of survey.

(Hauptmann, Weisgerber, and Knauf 1985; Hauptmann 1986; Hauptmann and Weisgerber 1987).

The SGNAS discovered a number of sites due to conversations with people living in and/or working in the area. For example, employees of the Impresit Construction Company pointed out Site 46, Deir 'Ain 'Abata, which is located above the site of their camp. Residents in the area indicated the location of Sites 205 and 223. The latter site is located in the present wadi bed of Wadi Feifa. It is hardly a place where one would carry out a pedestrian transect or expect to find a site. Moreover, it is too small to be located by means of the aerial photographs available.

The above-described, surveying techniques are summarized in Table 3.

Conclusions from sampling procedure

Stratum 1 (agricultural land, farms, orchards, and plantations)

The SGNAS discovered very few sites and artifacts in agricultural fields. The only exceptions are the sherd and lithic scatters in this environmental zone which are most probably associated with major architectural sites such as Site 1, al-Safi, and Sites 75 and 76, ancient Feifa. Further attempts to find sites in this stratum would probably produce little in the way of significant results.

Stratum 2 (gravels, gravel/cobble veneer, and colluvium)

As for Stratum 1, there are very few sites located in this stratum. However, if this stratum is adjacent to stratum 4 there is the chance of locating additional, albeit, small sites.

Stratum 3 (sandy areas, including dunes)

As for Stratum 2, there are very few sites located in this zone. Here again, as for stratum 2, if this stratum is adjacent to Stratum 4 then there is the possibility of locating additional sites.

Stratum 4 (piedmont [dissected slopes of the western edge of the graben])

Major architectural sites, graves, stone piles, and stone lines (also probably graves and/or field clearances), as well as sherd and lithic scatters, are located in this zone. Further surveying in this stratum would lead to the location of more sites. These sites would probably be small in size since the SGNAS has pruposively surveyed all major architectural sites in this zone.

Stratum 5 (wadi beds and their cuesta ridges)

The wadi beds and their ridges, and epecially the terraces along these wadis, are places where archaeological sites are located. Further surveying in this zone beyond the limites of the SGNAS, namely, to the east and southeast, would lead to the location of many more sites. These site would be look-out and/or communication points, camp sites, and tombs, for the most part. Moreover, as one surveyed into the higher elevations there would be present earlier lithic sites. This is especially true where the elevations are above the level once covered by Lake Lisan (MacDonald, Clark, and Neeley 1988: 42–43). This is also borne out by the WHS which located early lithic sites in the western extremity of the survey territory (MacDonald *et al.* 1988).

Collection and recording techniques

The SGNAS surveyed 240 sites during the 1986 infield season. At all but 23 (10 %) of these sites, the SGNAS collected some artifactual remains such as ceramics, glass, lithics, shells, and/or slag. The 23 sites at which the SGNAS did not find such artifacts were architectural sites.

Some of the architectural sites had very few associated artifacts. In such cases the SGNAS made a total collection, i.e., all that could be located on the site at the time of the visit, of associated artifacts. The SGNAS partitioned for collecting purposes some of the very large architectural sites which had low-to-high density of artifacts. This partitioning involved taking separate samples from several different segments of the site, e.g., from the top, slopes, lower elevations, etc. Team members made transects across these segments of the site. Each sample was labelled accordingly. For non-architectural sites such as lithic and sherd scatters, the decision to partition the site for collecting purposes was made on the basis of the density and size of the site. The SGNAS made no attempt to collect only diagnostic lithics, sherds, and/or glass fragments. Thus, the attempt was to avoid bias in favour of diagnotics. However, it must be admitted that the tendency on the part of collectors is to pick rims, bases, handles, and decorated sherds as well as lithic tools and cores. These diagnostic materials are more helpful for dating purposes than are body sherds and flakes.

Team members filled out a site sheet and an inventory rating sheet for each site.[1] Each site was plotted on the 1:10,000 and/or the 1:50,000 scale maps. If there were glass, lithics, sherds, and/or other artifactual material collected at the site then this material was labelled and appropriate sample sheets completed. If appropriate, the SGNAS made a sketch of each architectural site for reference and/or publication purposes. A team member took photographs of the main architectural sites. Artifactual materials were returned to base camp where they were washed and preliminarily 'read'. The 'reading' was used for dating the sites and, if possible, for indicating the type of activity that took place at the site at various periods in the past. Following the infield seasons, the authors of this report and their associates carried out further analyses of the materials. The results of these analyses are the subject of this report.

Note

1   For a sample of the SGNAS site sheets, see Appendix 2.

3. Natural Resources

by B. MacDonald

Introduction

Harlan (1981; 1982; 1985; 1988) has carried out the most systematic study of the natural resources, especially the water and vegetation, of the Southern Ghors. He did his study in association with his work at Bab al-Dhra' between 1977 and 1981. Moreover, McCreery (1980), who analyzed paleobotanical remains retrieved by means of a simple water flotation operation during the 1975, 1977, and 1979 excavation seasons at Bab edh-Dhra' and Numeira, has made an archaeological reconstruction of the nature and cultural implications of Early Bronze Age agriculture in the Southern Ghors of Jordan. There is little information, however, on the natural resources of the area immediately to the south, namely, the Northeast 'Arabah.

For his study, Harlan makes use of the accounts of the 19th century visitors to the Southern Ghors to get some idea of what the vegetation/natural resources were like at the time of their visits. On the basis of this information he extrapolates to an earlier age (1982: 71; 1985: 125).

The information in this chapter is based, for the most part, on Harlan's work.[1] It is included here for the reader's convenience. Besides the natural resources which Harlan discusses, bitumen and copper-manganese ores were also important resources of the area in antiquity. Both of these resources will be treated briefly at the end of this chapter.

Present environment

As a general rule, the climate of the Southern Levant deteriorates as one moves from the north to the south, with a more Mediterranean climate present in the north and a desert climate present in the south where the survey territory is located. Rainfall within the survey area is infrequent.

Zohary (1962; 1982) describes the soils in the area of the survey as hammadas, sands, regs, and salines while Horowitz (1979) describes them as hammadas, salines, and sebkhas. All of these are characteristic of desert environments or the result of the shrinking and deposition of the Lisan Lake/Dead Sea. Alluvial sediments are rare except where there are flowing waterways, e.g., Wadi al-Hasa.

Zohary (1962) and Horowitz (1979) describe the vegetation as Saharo-Sindian with small pockets of Sudano-Deccan. The Saharo-Sindian vegetation association is usually characteristic of a desert environment. Some species manage to survive on rocky hill slopes in which water is retained among the rocks (Zohary 1982) while other species survive in the sands. Most of the vegetation, however, is found in the dry wadi beds where runoff from higher elevations passes through, and in depressions where the water can be retained. In areas that are slightly better watered than the dry wadi beds, Sudano-Deccan vegetation, similar to that found in the dry regions of tropical Africa, may be found.

The fauna of this region is of course adapted to its xeric flora (Horowitz 1979). Animals tend to be crepuscular or nocturnal, remaining sheltered during the day in burrows, emerging only during the night hours. They are most active at dawn and dusk. Their major desert adaptation is in their ability to survive without being tied to a fixed source of water as they often absorb it from their food.

It is apparent from this brief characterization of the present environment that this is a marginal environment in which, for humans, a reliable water source is a necessity. However, environmental variations in the past, in conjunction with the different nature of the Dead Sea, may have made this area more attractive for subsistence and settlement purposes, than the present.

Present water resources

The most critical resource of the survey area is water. The water supply also determines the abundance and distribution of other resources such as plants and animals available for hunting-gathering cultures, the crops that can be grown by farmers, and the animals that can be reared by nomads (Harlan 1988: 40).

Rainfall

Rainfall is the primary source of water. Secondary sources are springs, wells, flowing streams, and moisture stored in the soil. All of these are dependent ultimately on rainfall (Harlan 1981: 162–63; 1988: 40).

Jordan has a winter rainfall regime. In the Southern Ghors and the adjacent highlands no rains have been recorded from June through September inclusive, and they are relatively rare in May and October. In 26 years in Ghor al-Safi there were three rains recorded in May and four in October. In the highlands, stations at Kerak, al-Tafileh, and Mazar show a somewhat higher frequency of May and October rains, but they occur on the average of only one year in three. Thus, the effective rainy season is from November through April (Harlan 1981: 155).

Table 4 gives the rainfall at two of the Southern Ghors and three of the adjacent highland stations. The table shows that the 65 mm yearly average recorded at both Ghor Mazra'a and Ghor al-Safi is approximately

Table 4 Rainfall at two of the Southern Ghors and adjacent highland stations (from data sheets of the Natural Resources Authority. The Hashemite Kindgom of Jordan)*

Location and recording period		Range (mm)
Ghor Mazra'a 1939/1940–1973/1974		
Ave. 28 seasons:	65.6	(6.5–149.0)
Ave. first 10 years:	63.5	(12.5–100.2)
Ave. last 10 years:	73.6	(22.0–149.0)
Ghor Safi 1939/1940–1973/1974		
Ave. 26 seasons:	65.2	(18.0–151.5)
Ave. first 10 years:	70.3	(35.0–109.6)
Ave. last 10 years:	57.2	(18.0–151.5)
Karak 1937/1938–1973/1974 no missing data		
Ave. 37 seasons:	360.7	(101.9–661.0)
Ave. first 10 years:	414.7	(122.8–540.6)
Ave. last 10 years:	411.5	(187.1–661.0)
Mazar 1937/1938–1973/1974 one season missing		
Ave. 36 seasons:	339.8	(119.8–610.0)
Ave. first 10 years:	414.6	(171.0–491.0)
Ave. last 10 years:	315.7	(136.5–610.0)
Tafileh 1937/1938–1973/1974 no missing data		
Ave. 37 seasons:	280.6	(82.7–751.1)
Ave. first 10 years:	310.8	(131.0–463.5)
Ave. last 10 years:	315.2	(82.7–751.1)

* Taken from J. R. Harlan, Natural Resources of the Southern Ghor. P. 156, Table 1 in *The Southeastern Dead Sea Plain Expedition: An Interim Report of the 1977 Season*, eds. W. E. Rast and R. T. Schaub. The Annual of the American Schools of Oriental Research 46 (1979). Cambridge, MA: American Schools of Oriental Research, 1981.

2.6 inches and is negligible from an agricultural point of view. Crops must be raised under irrigation, although rainfall may replace one or two irrigations during the winter growing season.

Sources of irrigation water for the Southern Ghors are shown in Table 5.

Streams and springs

There is not a great dependence on springs in the Southern Ghors for the purposes of irrigation. However, springs are necessary in the Northeast 'Arabah for the watering of animals in the region of such wadis as al-Dahal, al- Hassiya, al-Ghuweib, and Fidan (Figures 1 and 3).

Wadi al-Hasa is a perennial stream considered more stable and reliable than other wadis flowing to the Dead Sea Rift (Table 6). As noted in Table 5 the base flow at al-Safi has been rated at 810 l/s based on a limited number of measurements. Most of the discharge is used for irrigation in the Ghor al-Safi. Fluctuation in the stream flow is greater than that of spring flow. Wadi al-Hasa, however, is less subject to disastrous floods than other wadis of the eastern rift escarpment (Harlan 1988: 42). However, the waters from Wadis Feifa, Umruq, and Khuneizir, and to a much lesser extent, from Wadi al-Tilah, are also used for irrigation purposes. There is even a present plan to

bring water from Wadi Mujib to irrigate segments of the Southern Ghors (Khouri 1981: 220).

Bringing water for irrigation purposes out of the wadis of the Southern Ghors has been a problem for millennia because the wadis are subject to violent and destructive floods. Heavy rains in the highlands commonly cause flash floods; walls of water come crashing down through the canyons rolling boulders and cutting away the banks. Harlan and the SGNAS found broken and abandoned irrigation ditches along the sides of each of the wadis examined. The struggle to maintain irrigation systems against destructive floods has gone on as long as humans have farmed the Southern Ghors (Harlan 1981: 156–57).[2]

The frequency of floods varies greatly among the several wadis with the largest, Wadi al-Hasa, being by far the safest. According to estimates of Hunting Technical Services (Anonymous 1973), the predicted flood frequencies per century are: al-Hasa 2; Feifa 460; and Khuneizir 512. Harlan notes that not all of these will cut the banks and destroy canals, but many of them do, and maintenance of the systems has been a perennial struggle (1981: 157).

Data for monthly changes in base flow have been assembled for most of the water sources by Binnie and Jouzy Arup Bookers (Anonymous 1977). Peak flows are recorded in February in all cases and the lowest flows July–October inclusive (Harlan 1981: 157).

Hunting Technical Services (Anonymous 1973) have done water analyses on six of the Southern Ghors sources. The waters are generally similar and fall in the same quality class (C3–S1). Salinity, as measured by conductivity at 25°C, ranges from 0.83 millimhos per centimetre (Feifa) to 1.17 mmhos/cm

Table 5 Sources of irrigation water for Southern Ghors (adapted from Binnie Jouzy Arup Bookers Report, 1977)*

Location irrigable*	Ave. yearly *base flow (l/s)	Hectares
Wadi Dhra'a	40	68
'Ain Sikkin (at Ghor Mazra'a)	65	110
'Ain Maghara (Haditha)	300	510
Wadi Ibn Hammad	150	255
Wadi Isal	30	51
Wadi Numeira	30	51
Wadi Hasa	810	1,377
Wadi Feifa	110	187
Wadi Khanzira	40	68

*Taken from J. R. Harlan, Natural Resources of the Southern Ghor. P. 157, Table 2 in *The Southeastern Dead Sea Plain Expedition: An Interim Report of the 1977 Season*, eds. W. E. Rast and R. T. Schaub. The Annual of the American Schools of Oriental Research 46 (1979). Cambridge, MA: American Schools of Oriental Research, 1981.

**Based on 250 M /irrigation, 10 day irrigation schedule and 50% water loss, 10 l/s can irrigate 17 ha.; or approximately 0.6 l/s can water one hectare.

Table 6 Discharge of Wadi al-Hasa at al-Safi in millions of cubic metres (from data sheets of Natural Resources Authority. The Hashemite Kingdom of Jordan) *

Season	Mm
63/64	29.8
64/65	26.2 (record rains)
65/66	25.1
66/67	38.4
67/68	42.6 (record discharge)
xx	xxxx (no records)
72/73	26.4
73/74	25.6

* Taken from J. R. Harlan, Natural Resources of the Southern Ghor. P. 158, Table 3 in *The Southeastern Dead Sea Plain Expedition: An Interim Report of the 1977 Season*, eds. W. E. Rast and R. T. Schaub. The Annual of the American Schools of Oriental Research 46 (1979). Cambridge, MA: American Schools of Oriental Research, 1981.

('Ain Sikkin). Total dissolved salts is fairly high, ranging from 531 parts per million (Feifa) to 749 ppm ('Ain Sikkin). The calcium/sodium ratio is favorable and pH runs from 8.0 (Feifa) to 8.3 (Wadi 'Isal). In conclusion Harland states: 'Without getting very technical about it, we can say that the waters carry more salts that we would like, but they are usable' (1981: 158).

Present plant resources

Harlan notes that 'the apparent barrenness of the landscape is misleading. There is actually a rich flora in the Dead Sea Rift as indicated by the short list in Table 7' (1981: 160). However, he 'made no attempt to obtain a complete collection; only the more common plants were sampled in order to characterize the vegetation in a general way. Yet the casual collection turned up representatives of 40 different families. Adaptation to desert conditions has apparently evolved many times from numerous and diverse plant groups' (1981: 160).

Harlan points out that many of the species are dependent upon rainfall in the highland rather than in the Southern Ghors (1981: 160). In conclusion he writes:

> Despite the richness of the flora, the yield is inevitably low. The Ghors are in a desert zone and plants cannot grow without water. The vegetation is fragile, easily overgrazed and easily overexploited. For many species survival depends on tapping moisture supplied by running streams, living springs or infiltrating from the highlands to the alluvial fans of the Ghors (1981: 162).

The Highlands and the Southern Ghors

Harlan makes important comments about the relationship between the highlands to the east and the Southern Ghors and Northeast 'Arabah:

> From the foregoing it is evident that much of the life in the Ghors depends on rains in the highlands. Man and his livestock are not exceptions. The ecological ties between the two zones are intimate, fragile, and sensitive. An understanding of the natural resources of the Ghors must depend to some extent on an understanding of the ecology of the highlands...
>
> Water delivery in the Ghors depends not only on rain in the highlands but on water retention. How much of the rainfall is trapped and allowed to percolate slowly to the springs below or is released slowly from the upland soils to the perennial streams and how much runs off to come crashing down the canyons in destructive floods depends to a considerable extent on the vegetational cover in the highlands...
>
> Whatever the history of the upland vegetation may have been, it was important to the Ghors and needs much more careful study. The distance between the two ecological zones is not great, and one can presume a good deal of social contact among the people, exchange of agricultural produce and trading in goods. The Ghors should not be considered as isolated from the highlands (1981: 162–63).

Human occupation

The earliest evidence of human occupation in the Southern Ghors is during the Epipaleolithic/Neolithic Period (Chapter 4). However, in the Northeast 'Arabah the evidence indicates occupation from as early as the Lower/Middle Paleolithic Period (chap. 4). There is evidence from the Neolithic Period onwards, with some gaps which will be mentioned below, of human occupation in both areas.

The first evidence of urbanization of the region began about 3100–3000 B.C. with the Early Bronze site of Bab al-Dhra '(Harlan 1985: 125). The generally held opinion is that this system collapsed about 2300 B.C. and was replaced by an EB IV civilization throughout the entire region of the Southern Ghors and the Northeast 'Arabah. The relation between the EB II–III and EB IV peoples of the area is debated (Rast 1981: 32). There does not appear to have been much in the way of human occupation of the area during the Middle and Late Bronze Periods. However, with the beginning of the Iron Age there is evidence of human presence, especially in the mining and smelting areas of Wadis al-Ghuweib and al-Jariyeh. Human occupation appears, on the basis of the

Table 7   Short plant list for the Ghors of Jordan *

Filicales
    Polypodiaceae
        Adiantum capillus-veneris
Gymnospermae
    Cupressaceae
        Juniperus phoenica (Highlands near Dana)
    Ephedraceae
        Ephedra sp.
Angiospermae-Dicotyledones
    Acanthaceae
        Blepharis ciliaris
    Aizoaceae
        Mesembryanthemum nodiflorum
    Amaranthaceae
        Aerva tomentosa
    Anacardiaceae
        Pistacia palaestina (Highlands near Dana)
        P. vera (Highlands cult.)
    Apocynaceae
        Nerium oleander
    Asclepiadaceae
        Calotropis procera
    Boraginaceae
        Echium sp.
    Capparidaceae
        Capparis spinosa
    Caryophyllaceae
        Sclerocephalos arabicus
    Chenopodiaceae
        Anabasis setifera
        Atriplex halimus
        Bassia eriophora
        Haloxylon salicornicum
        Salsola tetrandra
        Suaeda palaestina
    Compositae
        Artemisia inculta=herba-alba
        Centaurea calcitrapella
        C. pallescens
        Cichorium intybus
        et alia. unidentified
    Crucifereae
        Anastatica hierochuntica
        Hirschfeldia incana
        Matthiola parviflora
    Fagaceae
        Quercus calliprinos (Highlands near Dana)
    Malvaceae
        Malva sp
    Mimosaceae
        Acacia raddiana
        A. tortilis
    Moraceae
        Ficus carica (cult.)
        Ficus sp. (Petra)
    Oleaceae
        Olea europaea (cult.)
    Orobanchaceae
        Orobanche sp.

    Papaveraceae
        Papaver sp.
    Papilionaceae
        Retama raetam
    Plumbaginaceae
        Limonium thouini
    Resedaceae
        Ochradenus baccatus
        Reseda sp.
    Rhamnaceae
        Zizyphus lotus
        Z. spina-christi
    Rosaceae
        Amygdalus communis (Highlands, cult.)
        Amygdalus sp. (Highlands near Dana)
    Rutaceae
        Haplophyllum blanchi
    Salicaceae
        Salix sp.
    Salvadoraceae
        Slavadora persica
    Scrophulariaceae
        Verbascus syriacum
    Tamaricaceae
        Reaumuria hirtella
        Tamarix maris-mortui
    Umbelliferae
        Ammi majus
    Urticaceae
        Forsskaolea tenacissima
    Vitaceae
        Vitis vinifera (cult.)
    Zygophyllaceae
        Fagonia mollis
Anglospermae-Monocotyledones
    Palmae
        Phoenix cactylifera (cult. and spontaneous)
    Juncaceae
        Juncus acutus
    Gramineae
        Cynodon dactylon
        Desmostachya bipinnata
        Dichanthium annulatum
        Elyonurus argentea
        Erianthus (=Saccarum) ravenae
        Hyparrhenia hirta
        Panicum turgidum
        Pennisetum ciliare
        P. orientale
        P. sp.
        Phragmites australe=communis
        Polypogon monspeliensis

* Taken from J. R. Harlan, Natural Resources of the Southern Ghor. Pp. 161–62, Table 4 in *The Southeastern Dead Sea Plain Expedition: An Interim Report of the 1977 Season*, eds. W. E. Rast and R. T. Schaub. The Annual of the American Schools of Oriental Research 46 (1979). Cambridge, MA: American Schools of Oriental Research, 1981.

available evidence, to have increased during the Iron II Period. Little is known about the area during the Persian Period. There was a strong human presence in the area from the Nabataean through to the end of the Byzantine Periods. The archaeological evidence appears to support a decrease in human population in both the Southern Ghors and Northeast 'Arabah during the Early Islamic Period. However, there is archaeological evidence for human presence in the Southern Ghors during both the Early and Late Islamic Periods and especially during the Ayyubid/Mamluk Period. Due to recent development, there has been a steady growth in population in the area during the past decade.

Natural resources during the 19th century

During the 19th century, in particular, many travellers passed through the Southern Ghors and made comments on the natural resources of the area. Among these travellers whose comments are helpful in reconstructing the natural resources during this century are Irby and Mangles (1823); De Saulcy (1853); Tristram (1866; 1873); Palmer (1871); Hayne (1873); Klein (1880); Kitchener (1884); Hart (1885); and Hill (1896) (Harlan 1985: 126).

The picture presented by these travellers is very different to that of today. In the 19th century the land was not heavily populated. There were small Gawarani villages at Mazra'a–Haditha and al-Safi. Some of the people lived in tents while others lived in reed-mat huts. The waters of Wadi al-Hasa were diverted by a system of small canals to irrigate arable patches cleared of thicket (Harlan 1985: 126). Each of the Ghors supported massive canebrakes near the shores of the Dead Sea where the underground flow of the wadis kept the soil permanently moist. These canebrakes, which were of considerable extent at Ghor al-Safi, were virtually impenetrable to humans and domestic animals, but abounded in wild pigs. In turn, the swine population supported a few leopards, and jackals were common. The travellers write of enormous numbers of pigeons and other birds. Grass and pasture land were abundant. The streams swarmed with fish. Hayne (1873) was especially impressed by the palms that grew at the edge of the Dead Sea and which dotted the steep slopes above as far as the eye could see. The shores of the Dead Sea were heaped high with driftwood, mostly composed of trees eroded from the banks of the Jordan River to the north (Harlan 1985: 126).

Today, the thickets are nearly all cleared away for fields, orchards, and vineyards; only occasional specimen trees remain. The canebrakes are all but gone with only small clumps of reeds remaining (Harlan 1985: 126).

Resources in the Neolithic and Early Bronze Periods

On the basis of the remarks on the part of the 19th century commentators, Harlan attemtps to reconstruct the natural resources for both the Neolithic and Early Bronze Periods. About the Neolithic Period he writes:

With the last century as a point in the trajectory one may reconstruct the probable state of natural resources in pre-urban times with some confidence. The disturbance to the vegetation would surely be less than in the 19th century. The settled communities were small and widely scattered. The herds were probably smaller and less destructive. Hull (65), for example, reported sighting a herd of some 200 camels at Safiyeh, and Tristram (66) commented on the number of animals grazing at Ghor Mazra'a (67). There were nomadic winter herds that would leave the Ghors for the hill country when hot weather came. The resident flocks were much less extensive. It seems most likely that the primary effect of the winter transients, both man and beast, was on the form and stature of the woody vegetation. The browsing and hacking for fire wood would tend to form thicket out of solitary specimens. The pre-urban woodland should have consisted of rather evenly spaced trees with grassy herbage beneath. The teaming (sic) bird and fish life and the canebrakes full of wild boar would have been much as described a hundred years ago (1982: 76–77).

And about the Early Bronze Period Harlan writes:

The concensus seems to be that Early Bronze opened during a minor pluvial and favorable climate. Conditions began to change about 3500 B.C. with a slight drop in temperature and increased rainfall. The oak woodland spread rapidly in the Zagros...

There is also general agreement that a sharp climatic crisis occurred about 2300 B.C. The temperature rose and rainfall decreased; droughts and crop failures became common...

There is evidence of people moving out of the Sahara as shown by the abandonment of sites and the cessation of rock painting....Hordes of nomadic herdsmen were forced from their desiccating steppes and invaded settled agricultural lands. Towns, cities and villages throughout Palestine were sacked and burned including Jericho, Bab edh-Dhra and Numeira...(1985: 127).

More specifically, using the descriptions of the 19th century travellers, Harlan extrapolates in an attempt to understand the conditions in the Southern Ghors in the Early Bronze Period. He admits that we do not know how much more rainfall the region received at the onset of the period. However, he does not think that it could possibly have been sufficient for dryland farming in the Southern Ghors. Agriculture depended on springs and streams fed by rains in the highlands. Stream and spring flows were surely stronger and more stable than now. This, in turn, would lead to an increase in the frequency of destructive floods but not to the present level (1982: 77). Tree growth should have been well developed to thickets as dense as those of the 19th century A.D. Harlan continues:

> The Dead Sea side of each fan was, no doubt, covered by a dense candbrake of reeds and rushes and inhabited by wild pigs in abundance. Not only leopards but lions as well preyed on them and jackals and hyenas helped to scavenge the kills. Birds and fish would have been no less numerous than 100 years ago and were probably even more abundant. The Ghors were ripe for settlement and exploitation...

> Judging from last century descriptions, even the upper slopes of the Ghors were studded with acacia trees and dwarf palms were scattered up the steep slopes. The banks of the wadis were bordered by dense stands of oleander and willow. Ibex should have been common on the slopes of the rift (1985: 128).

He continues:

> The picture of a fat and pleasant land must have changed with the drastic climatic reversal toward the end of the 3rd millenium. A sudden rise in temperature and decrease in rainfall can have a shocking effect on the vegetation as well as the people. Trees on the upper slopes of the alluvial fan probably died; the thickets receded to areas of most reliable water supply. Grazing lands suffered sharply reduced productivity. Crops failed and wells dried up. The ecology suddenly favored tent dwellers of the semi-arid steppes and desert fringes. Temporarily, the fertile crescent was fertile no more (1985: 128).

Other natural resources

A number of other natural resources played a role in the development of the area. These include bitumen, copper, manganese, salt, and gypsum. Only the first three are treated.

Bitumen

The Dead Sea was one of the major sources of commercial bitumen in the ancient Near East (Hammond 1959: 40; Forbes 1964: 29–30; Sperber 1976: 138–39). Its specific product is true bitumen. This justifies the classical references to 'asphalt,' and the application of the name 'asphaltic lake' to the Dead Sea.

Hammond writes that 'the appearance of bitumen in the Dead Sea is recorded by Diodorus in detail. It is said to spring forth from the center of the sea as a solid mass. . . . This mass floats on the surface, and is chopped up into workable size with axes and loaded into boats' (1959: 41). He concludes that Diodorus is correct in reference to the quantity of bitumen present and, thus, to the extent of the industry in the first century B.C. which was of some importance financially (1959: 42).

Diodorus and Strabo (Sperber 1976: 138) indicate that bitumen was used by the Egyptians for embalming purposes.[3] However, it did have other important uses, e.g., waterproofing for coffins and other articles among the Egyptians, as a cement or binding agent, for the manufacture of imitation gems, in the colouring and production of metals, and for the manufacture of masks for the preservation of mummy faces (Hammond 1959: 43–44; Forbes 1964: 56–109). Evidence from 'Ain Ghazal in Jordan indicates that its inhabitants used bitumen both on their statues and in their burial practices. Rollefson specifies that bitumen was used on the statues 'as an eyeliner around a strikingly white eye bearing a circular iris of bitumen' (1986: 46; Tubb 1985) and that one of the human skulls 'bore a thin coating of black pigment, possibly bitumen' (1986: 51). Both of these uses date to the end of the 8th and in the first half of the 7th millenia B.C. (Rollefson 1986: 47).

There is evidence for the use of bitumen as a building material at Jericho. Garstang found a thick wall enclosing a large area. The wall was built by cementing large bricks with bituminous earth. The wall can be dated to the Early Bronze Age (Forbes 1964: 27). Forbes cites evidence from the Ophel in Jerusalem and from Tell Beith Mirsim for the use of bitumen during the second and first millennia (1964: 27). De Vaux notes the presence of bitumen during the Hellenistic and/or Roman Periods at both Qumran and 'Ain Fashkha at the northwest end of the Dead Sea (1961: 68– 69).[4]

It appears that the Nabataeans had, at least for a time, a monopoly on the bitumen industry of the Dead Sea. For them, the industry had both economic and political importance (Hammond 1959: 47; Forbes 1964: 30). The Nabataeans, thus, emerge not only as a group of caravaners and agriculturists, but also as the one of the entrepreneurs of a basic industry in the economy of the eastern reaches of the Fertile Crescent (Hammond 1959: 47). However, there was also an interest in the industry on the part of the Ptolemies of Egypt and the Seleucids of Syria (Forbes 1964: 29–30).

Copper and manganese

There are two different ore horizons, namely, mixed manganese and copper ores and only copper ores, in the Feinan area (Hauptmann 1986: 415; Hauptmann and Weisgerber 1987: 421) which is located immediately south of the SGNAS territory. These resources and their associated technologies, during the different archaeological periods, are presently under study by a team from the German Mining Museum, Bochum, West Germany (Bachmann and Hauptmann 1984; Hauptmann, Weisgerber, and Knauf 1985; Hauptmann 1986; Hauptmann and Weisgerber 1987; and Hauptmann 1989). To date, Hauptmann *et al.* have posited that copper production in the area extends from the Chalcolithic Period up into the 13th century A.D. The periods specifically posited for this production are: the Chalcolithic (4500–3100 B.C.); Early and Middle Bronze (3100–1900 B.C.); Iron I (1200–1000 B.C.); Iron IIC (800–400 B.C.); Roman (1st–4th century A.D.); and the Mamluk Periods (A.D. 1260–1516) (Hauptmann and Weisgerber 1987: 421–24). In the estimate of these researchers, the Feinan region may represent the oldest, large-mining area for copper in the Near East so far known (Hauptmann 1986: 416). Not only was copper produced in the area but there is evidence, according to Hauptmann (1989), for the export of copper ores from the region during the Neolithic and Chalcolithic Periods.

Notes

1 The present writer informed Harlan of his intention to use Harlan's published material on the natural resources of the area.

2 Even the recently installed systems to harness the waters of these wadis are plagued by damage caused by flash floods.

3 For a contrary position see Sperber 1976: 139

4 De Vaux also notes the exloitation of salt by the Qumran community (1961: 68).

4. Lithic Period Sites

by M. P. Neeley

Statement of data problems

Nature of the lithic samples

The samples used for this study represent a total of 87 sites. Sites comprised of only lithic scatters account for 50 of the samples, while the remaining 37 are found in association with ceramics. Although the association of lithics with ceramics does not necessarily demonstrate contemporaneity in the occupation or occupations of the site, in the absence of absolute dates this contextual information may be useful in refining the chronological placement of the samples.

Collection of the lithic samples by the survey was done in a rather random, haphazard manner. In nearly every instance, no part of the site was segregated or subdivided prior to collection. Thus, discrete areas of the sites cannot be associated with various lithic samples, i.e., no activity areas within the samples are discernible. The collections represent the whole site, as well as it was defined, and any division of the collections in the field into different samples is by-and-large arbitrary and purely for convenience. The amount of material collected per site varied according to the density of material present. Where large amounts of material were present, a large sample was collected in order to obtain a somewhat representative sample. Smaller densities of materials were more exhaustively collected in an attempt to obtain a more workable sample and in some instances all of the visible pieces were collected from the surface. The collection strategy described above precludes any spatial differentiation of the samples within the sites. While limiting particular site specific conclusions, the focus of this study is oriented towards regional time-space systematics rather than intrasite problems. The problem with the lithic sample collections more directly related to the task at hand, is that of discerning different culture-stratigraphic groups from these collected samples. Also, the objective of the SGNAS was to sample all sites in the area which precluded taking large samples from the lithic period sites of interest here.

Problems with the SGNAS survey data

One problem is that of small sample size for a given site. Samples range from as few as three pieces to several hundred pieces. The difference in the number of items per sample from site to site makes culture-stratigraphic identification very tenuous in many instances, especially for those sites containing non-diagnostic debitage and retouched pieces. In an attempt to overcome this sampling problem, those sites consisting of larger collections or containing obvious temporal diagnostics are the main focus of the lithic analysis.

Another problem concerns the representativeness of the collections for a given time period and whether the culture-stratigraphic period can be determined from the available material. The success or failure of this often depends on the presence or the recognition of various 'diagnostic elements' in both the retouched and the debitage components. Underlying this process is the traditional or normative view of lithic assemblages representing discrete entities both spatially and temporally. Such is the case for the cultural chronology for the Levant in which temporal periods are separable according to certain discrete/ discontinuous types. While these discontinuities may exist in an arbitrarily defined ideal sense, much of the continuity through time and space along these types is dismissed in order to facilitate chronology building. Often small collections and even larger collections may not contain these supposed temporally sensitive diagnostics in which case the sample is classified as unknown or assigned to a broader temporal span based upon the available contextual evidence, e.g., ceramics.

A related problem is the validity of diagnostics as dating implements and the limited temporal span in which they can be used. Diagnostic elements, which in an ideal situation are indicative of only one culture-stratigraphic group, i.e., they do not crosscut different 'cultures' or time periods, more often than not are somewhat continuous over time. The difficulty in separating temporal units from small surface collections may be further exacerbated by the reappearance of various diagnostic elements. An example of such a case is the reappearance of chopping implements during the Neolithic and Chalcolithic that resemble diagnostic implements of the Lower Palaeolithic (Solecki 1985). Temporal ambiguity may exist with the presence of this type of diagnostic unless related site information is used. Another problem with diagnostics is that the temporal sequences are largely derived from northern coastal contexts, i.e., Israel, and it is uncertain whether these schemes are valid for the inland areas of Jordan.

A diagnostic type of a limited time range in the Levant is the arrowpoint. These points are generally a component of the various Neolithic cultures (PPNA, PPNB, Yarmoukian, PNA) though they overlap slightly with bracketing periods (Natufian, Chalcolithic). Various temporal schemes have been proposed for these diagnostics in which the Neolithic is divided into Pre-Pottery and Pottery groups, yet the diagnostics often crosscut these divisions (Burian and

Friedman 1979; Bar-Yosef 1981; Crowfoot Payne 1983). This problem is magnified for sites represented by small sample sizes.

Collection biases may also affect the nature of the lithic samples. This includes (1) unfamiliarity with the general observable morphological characteristics of lithics as well as (2) the visibility of smaller pieces relative to larger ones. The first problem results in the collection of non-cultural lithics due to the lack of experience in recognizing these pieces. This problem was encountered as the survey teams were comprised of individuals with little to no lithic experience. However, the subsequent lab work was able to 'weed out' these non-cultural pieces. The second problem may not be the fault of the collector but most certainly results in a different characterization of the assemblage. This may lead to an underrepresentation of certain assemblages, especially Epi-Palaeolithic ones, based upon the collected sample. Unlike the first problem, which is resolved through experience, only excavation or intensive collecting will rectify the second problem.

Similarly, the environment in which these samples are found will affect the state or character of the assemblages. The survey area is situated in a rather dynamic environment in which certain landforms are not necessarily stable over time. Examples of the active environment include the fluctuating levels of the Lisan Lake and the continuous downcutting of the wadi systems. Such an active environment may select for certain pieces to remain visible and/or *in situ* while others are rendered inaccessible through survey or are missing.

Last, the problem of the discreteness of site occupation may affect the samples when attempting to identify culture-stratigraphic affinities. Sites occupied several different times by different temporal groups may hinder the chronological determination, especially when ambiguous diagnostics that crosscut different time periods are present. In addition, the later re-use of earlier materials may make identification problematic.

To summarize, the samples to be used for this study are in no way ideal. Many problems exist within this particular data set and with survey collections in general. It is noted that assigning lithic samples a chronological position based on various morphological attributes is often somewhat tenuous when working with small samples and contextual information limited by survey data. While I am not particularly fond of the present system for classifying undated material, it is recognized that these are of some use as crude temporal markers when other information is lacking. For these reasons, it is expected that a fair portion of the samples may be placed in an unknown category or in broader time periods encompassing more variability than a single discrete period. However, it is believed that some of the samples, despite these limitations, can be accurately assigned a temporal affiliation based on the lithic characteristics. Contextual information from the survey forms will be used to further secure these assignments.

The Lisan Lake

The one factor that may be most responsible for the presence or absence of lithic sites (Lower Palaeolithic through Early Bronze) in the area is the Lisan Lake and its present day remnant, the Dead Sea. The Lisan Lake/Dead Sea is part of the Rift Valley system, a series of faults extending south into Africa and north into Asia. The lake/sea is located in a graben, a narrow tectonic valley, with fault systems on the east and west borders as well as transverse faults to the north and south. These latter faults are somewhat smaller in magnitude.

The present Dead Sea consists of two basins, a deep north basin, and a shallow south basin. The south basin forms the northern boundary of the survey area. As a result of the changing shoreline over time during both the Lisan Lake and Dead Sea phases, several geomorphological/topographical features are apparent in the form of plains. Most pertinent here is the Amatsyahu Plain, located just south of a major east/west escarpment. Like the Lisan Peninsula to the north, it is believed to be the remnant of the Lisan Lake floor (Neev and Emery 1967). This conclusion is based upon the present areal extent, southward, of marls deposited during the Lisan Lake phase.

The escarpment to the south of the Dead Sea, which forms an arbitrary boundary point for the survey, is an east west running transverse fault called the Amatsyahu Fault (Neev and Emery 1967: 23). Neev and Emery divide this fault into two parts: a low straight cliff and an upper portion rising to the Amatsyahu Plain in the south. The escarpment is approximately 100 m high but is somewhat lower at its western extremity than the eastern. The formation of this feature has been hypothesized as the result of water abrasion by the Lisan Lake/Dead Sea, but is more likely the combined result of faulting in which the north portion has slipped down below the south portion and erosion of the marls from water run-off.

The Lisan Lake, like the present Dead Sea, was a variably alkaline lake and began ca. 70,000 BP lasting until ca. 18,000 BP (Neev and Emery 1967). Begin, Ehrlich, and Nathan (1974) also place the end of the Lisan Formation around 18,000 BP though high lake levels may have persisted to ca. 12–11,000 BP. Roberts (1982) suggests that the lake may have lasted until ca. 16,000 BP while Edwards *et al.* (1988) believe the lake lasted to ca. 12,000 BP. As these various schemes indicate, the precise dating of the termination of the Lisan Lake is uncertain, a point which is still unresolved by both geologists and archaeologists (Schuldenrein 1983: 298). Unlike the present Dead Sea in which the shore line lies ca. -400 m, the Lisan Lake's most recent shore maximum appears to have been ca. -180 m on the western side (Neev and Emery 1967) and -160 m on the eastern side (Clark 1988). At this elevation, the whole Southern Ghor basin (area north of the Amatsyahu escarpment) would have been inundated as well as much of the Amatsyahu Plain to the south. It is estimated that the Lisan Lake may have extended approximately 30 km further south than the present southward extension of the Dead Sea. This event alone is certainly a major, if not the major, force affecting the location and discovery of prehistoric sites (pre 18,000 BP) and possibly affecting sites during the Post-Lisan Lake periods as well.

The formation of the Dead Sea between sometime after 16,000 BP was the result of a rapid decrease in size of the Lisan Lake. A climatic drying trend in which the runoff to evaporation ratio declined is seen as a possible cause during this time (Neev and Emery 1967). Climatic evidence from the Negev (Clark 1984) suggests that a drying trend peaked ca. 16,000 BP. Also suggested is the possible role of tectonic activity in which the lake basin was lowered, thus lowering the water line. In any case, the area occupied by the lake/sea was greatly reduced at this time.

Following the formation of the Dead Sea (which was a 'process' rather than a discrete 'event'), sea levels continued to fluctuate but there is some disagreement as to when these changes occurred and the magnitude of change. Neev and Emery (1967) identify a high runoff to evaporation ratio at the end of the Lisan Lake phase (ca. 20,000 BP) followed by a sharp decline in this ratio lasting to ca. 14–13,000 BP when this ratio then increases. Begin, Ehrlich, and Nathan (1974) see a high runoff to evaporation ratio beginning ca. 18,000 BP (a 'pluvial'), coinciding with the end of the Lisan Lake, and lasting to ca. 12–11,000 BP when the ratio decreases. Exactly how these schemes affected the lake levels for this time period is uncertain since no evidence concerning lake levels for these time periods is available. Perhaps more important is the effect that such a discrepancy might have on human occupation/settlement in the area. If a pluvial is associated with the onset of the Dead Sea, ca. 18,000 BP, then lake levels must have remained high unless other processes, such as tectonic activity, acted to lower the waterline. If the waterline was not drastically lowered, then human occupation prior to 12,000 BP might be confined to the upper elevations deep within the wadi systems (to the east) in the Ghor area and restricted to the southern portion of the survey area. Since the lake was increasing in salinity as the size decreased, this process may have made large, long term occupation impractical unless freshwater sources, e.g., springs, wadi run-off, were available. Evidence from the Lower Jordan Valley (Schuldenrein and Goldberg 1981) indicates that late Epi-Palaeolithic settlement (Natufian) is not found below the recent maximum (-180 m) suggesting high water levels which agrees with Begin, Ehrlich, and Nathan (1974) termination of the pluvial (also see Edwards *et al.* 1988). The model of the Dead Sea formation proposed by Neev and Emery (1967) suggests that with the decreasing ratio, lake levels also decreased. If so, then the earlier Epi-Palaeolithic sites, in the higher elevations of the area, should increase in

frequency as well as move down in elevation, assuming that the area was habitable.

These two interpretations of the termination of the Lisan Lake by Neev and Emery (1967) and Begin, Ehrlich, and Nathan (1974) are in some senses diametrically opposed (Figure 4). The acceptance of one over the other is bound to effect one's interpretation of the archaeological record for the Late Pleistocene. Consequently, it is probably more prudent to examine the available archaeological evidence and then ascertain which of these interpretations best fits the data.

SGNAS data – a synthesis

The aim of this synthesis is to make some intra-regional (SGNAS) generalizations within the various culture-stratigraphic units represented in the area. From these generalizations, a tentative diachronic model for the survey area can be constructed and compared with other regional surveys.

Lithic characteristics by period

The following section is intended to be a brief characterization of the lithic assemblages according to temporal periods. The focus of this characterization or summary includes both the debitage and the retouched pieces of the samples for these periods. For the most part, the samples to be summarized are limited to those designated as 'large' samples (>50 pieces) though a few of the smaller collections will be mentioned where relevant. The debitage characterization will emphasize the percentage of flakes, blades, and bladelets between collections of the same period with the aim of identifying the presence of general trends in these collections. Where possible, the debitage percents will be compared with debitage percents from other sites of the same period in the southern Levant. As a cautionary note, this sort of comparison will entail the use of excavated material in which the samples are often much larger and more temporally discrete. These different recovery techniques are apt to result in different percentages from the survey samples. The decision to look for general trends at a low level of resolution, e.g., percentage of flakes, blades, bladelets which provide an indication of technological trends, rather than a more comprehensive metrical analysis is tempered by the varying sample sizes along with the questionable representativeness of the survey sample assemblages for these time periods. Such a labor intensive undertaking as a metrical analysis for somewhat biased samples might result in misleading conclusions. Furthermore, comparable metrical data from large assemblages representative of many of these time periods, especially the recent ones (Neolithic through Early Bronze Age), is either unavailable or has not been attempted.

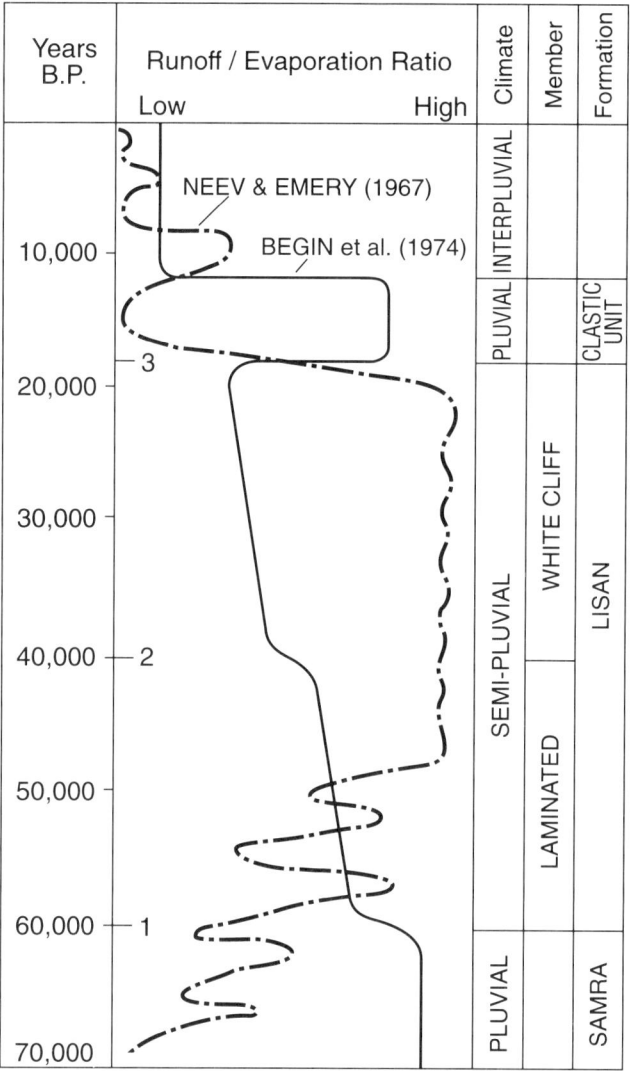

Figure 4   Competing Palaeoclimatic models for the Lisan Lake (from Schuldenrein 1983: 289).

Following this simple comparison of the debitage portions of these samples, the retouched pieces are also treated with an equally low level of resolution. Very basic retouched forms are the units of comparison between similar period sites as well as the general blank morphology of the piece (flake, blade, bladelet). Sample sizes for the retouched pieces are smaller than the debitage fraction and are expected to be more variable in terms of the percentage values. In addition to comparison among the survey sites, retouched pieces from outside areas are used as another comparative device. Patterns or trends from these additional areas are identified and serve as a general model against which the survey collections can be tentatively tested. The possible problems associated with the debitage comparisons mentioned above also apply here.

Lower and Middle Palaeolithic

Sites representing either of these periods (or these periods combined) are very rare in the survey area. Due to the small number of these assemblages and the difficulty in separating them into one period or the other based upon paltry collections, they are treated as a single time unit for the lithic characterization. Both sites (32, 33) are comprised of diffuse scatters of lithics from which one or two diagnostic forms are recognized. There exists a real possibility that both collections are not representative of just one culture-stratigraphic period and may include 'background noise' from a variety of time periods. Site boundaries are somewhat arbitrary as a continuous light scatter of material characterizes much of the area around these sites (Wadi Fidan). These samples consist of fewer than 50 pieces and after separating the retouched pieces, they are quite small and susceptible to small counts of items creating a notable percentage difference. For these reasons, the comparisons of debitage and retouched pieces do not include outside assemblages as any pattern in the survey samples is

Table 8   Debitage percentages from Lower/Middle and Middle Palaeolithic SGNAS sites

Site	Flakes	Blades	Bladelets *
32	87.1	12.9	0.0
33	90.9	9.1	0.0
28	81.4	18.5	0.0

* Bladelet percentages are included in the blade percentages (blades = % blades + % bladelets).

Table 9   Lower/Middle and Middle Palaeolithic tool class percentages

	32	33	28
Notches	–	14.3	33.3
Denticulates	18.1	21.4	11.1
Endscrapers	9.1	–	5.5
Scrapers	18.1	14.3	–
Borers	–	–	–
Picks	–	–	–
Choppers	9.1	–	–
Burins	18.1	–	–
Ret. Blades	–	14.3	–
Ret. Bladelets	–	–	–
Ret. Flakes	27.2	35.7	38.8
Miscellaneous	–	–	11.1

Table 10   Flake, blade, and bladelet percentages of retouched tools from SGNAS sites

Lower/Middle and Middle Palaeolithic

Site	Flakes	Blades	Bladelets *	Misc.
32	90.9	–	–	9.1
33	78.5	21.4	–	–
28	83.3	16.6	–	–

Neolithic

Site	Flakes	Blades	Bladelets *	Misc.
12	56.3	40.3	2.1	3.1
15	43.3	54.9	31.6	1.6
44	51.5	39.0	1.5	9.3
Dhra'	31.6	68.2	3.7	–

Chalcolithic

Site	Flakes	Blades	Bladelets *	Misc.
87	86.9	13.0	–	–
185	92.0	4.0	–	4.0
186	64.3	35.7	–	–

Chalcolithic/Early Bronze

Site	Flakes	Blades	Bladelets *	Misc.
10	94.1	5.9	–	–
14	78.5	21.4	3.6	–
20	62.7	37.2	–	–
86	76.3	18.4	2.6	5.2
82	91.7	8.3	–	–
137	80.0	20.0	20.0	–
84	100.0	–	–	–
171	94.7	5.3	–	–
135	82.6	17.4	–	–
217	91.7	8.3	8.3	–
227	66.6	33.3	–	–
30	50.0	50.0	–	–

Early Bronze Age

Site	Flakes	Blades	Bladelets *	Misc.
105	90.0	9.1	–	–

* Bladelet percentages are included in the blade percentages (blades = % blades + % bladelets).

likely to be biased. Site 28, which contains some Levallois type debitage, is excluded from the discussion because it is uncertain if this is representative of the Middle Palaeolithic or the much later Chalcolithic. Both of the samples are flake oriented (87% to 90%) (Table 8) and heavily patinated. Bladelets are absent from both of these samples. The most frequently occurring retouched pieces are retouched flakes, followed by denticulates and scrapers. These are tools that generally require low manufacture inputs, i.e., expedient tools and probably meet a wide range of functional requirements. Differences in retouched pieces (Table 9) between the two samples are noted in terms of choppers, burins, and retouched blades (Plate 1). Site 32 contains a chopper, allegedly 'diagnostic' of Lower/Middle Palaeolithic assemblages, along with several burins. In comparison, retouched blades are present at Site 33, while absent from Site 32. It is impossible to determine whether these retouched tool differences represent functional differences, temporal differences, or are intrusive and overrepresented in such a small sample. The retouched blank percentages (Table 10) indicate the absence of blade tools at Site 32 while Site 33 shows a higher percentage of blade tools than represented in the blade debitage. This difference suggests blade forms were utilized despite the technological trend favoring the manufacture of flakes.

Neolithic

A total of nine sites represent the Neolithic period in the survey area (including Dhra'). Of this number, four (21, 76, 92, and 95) are represented by Neolithic ceramics with small, essentially non-diagnostic lithic samples. Due to the deficiencies of the lithic samples, as well as the presence of later period ceramics, e.g., Chalcolithic and Early Bronze Age, these four sites will be excluded from the summary of Neolithic samples. A fifth site (239) is also excluded as the sample is small (N=6) and the Neolithic period is represented by a single broken projectile point. These omissions leave four Neolithic samples (12, 15, 44, and Dhra') for comparison.

The site of Dhra' is not in the actual survey area and is located east of the Lisan Peninsula on the road to Kerak. It is included in this study for the purpose of providing comparable material for the other Neolithic sites. Previous work on the Dhra' material is very cursory, focusing largely on gross chronology (Bennett 1980; Raikes 1980). While chronology is still an issue here, an attempt is made to compare Dhra' and the other Neolithic survey samples with other sites in the region.

The percentages of flakes from these samples (Table 11) indicate some consistency, ranging between 40% and 50%, in the collections from Dhra', 44, and 15. On the other hand, Site 12 deviates from this trend with a high percentage (72.2%) of flakes in the debitage. Likewise, the blade percentages from Dhra', 44, and 15 are between 50% and 59% while Site 12 is represented by 27.7% blades. It has been noted elsewhere that there is an apparent trend through time for Neolithic assemblages to move from a blade oriented technology, e.g., PPNB, to a flake oriented one, e.g., PN, Yarmoukian (Rollefson and Simmons 1988). The percentages given here suggest the possibility of such a trend in the survey region; however, several problems hamper the direct application of such an interpretation. These include the ubiquitous sampling bias along with evidence indicating the presence of multiple components for these sites, a problem which cannot be controlled in a grab surface collection. Thus, the observed surface collection trend and its possible culture-stratigraphic explanation should be considered highly tentative in light of these problems.

Bladelets have been considered a subset of the blade class, that is, blade percents represent a combined blade/bladelet total. The bladelet percentages (Table 11) are remarkably similar among Dhra' and Sites 12 and 44 (5–6%). A low percentage of these forms is not unusual for Neolithic sites (Rosen 1984; Rollefson and Simmons 1988; Gebel *et al.* 1988). The bladelet percentage from Site 15 is markedly different (21.4%) from these other sites. Concentrations of bladelets come from two of the three collection areas on the site and might represent areas of manufacture. The possibility of the high frequency representing a pre-Neolithic component, e.g., Epi-Palaeolithic, is possible but the absence of traditional Epi-Palaeolithic diagnostics, e.g., geometric microliths and lunates, tend to weaken this conclusion.

For comparative purposes, the debitage percentages from six Neolithic sites outside the SGNAS territory, ranging from PPNA through Late Neolithic in date, are used. The sites represented are Nahal Lavan 108 (Noy, Friedman, and Burian 1981), 'Ain Ghazal (Rollefson and Simmons 1988), Basta (Gebel *et al.* 1988), Mushabi VI (Mintz and Ben-Ami 1977), Sha'ar Hagolan (Stekelis 1972), and Kvish Harif (Rosen 1984). The comparison focuses on the percentages of flakes, blades, and bladelets (when available) in the debitage. Because these sites represent excavated material, the debris and core elements are excluded from the debitage percents and the figures used here have been re-calculated based upon the information available in the literature.

This small sample of Neolithic sites indicates that the trend for Neolithic assemblages to change from a blade oriented to a flake oriented technology through time, suggested by Rollefson and Simmons (1988: 399), appears to hold true (Table 11). All of the PPN sites (Nahal Lavan 108, 'Ain Ghazal, Basta, and Mushabi VI) are characterized by blade percentages between 53% and 64%. The later Neolithic sites (PPNC and Yarmoukian levels at 'Ain Ghazal and Kvish Harif) show the blade percents to be 40% or less. The dominance of flakes over blades in a Late Neolithic context is also evident from the coastal region where flakes are the most frequent debitage category (Epstein 1984). The fit of this debitage pattern is offset somewhat by the percentages from Sha'ar Hagolan (Stekelis 1972). This is the type site

Table 11 Debitage percentages from selected Neolithic sites and SGNAS sites

Site	Flakes	Blades	Bladelets *
Nahal Lavan 108 (PPNA)	37.6	62.3	51.7
Basta (PPN)	35.7	64.2	5.5
'Ain Ghazal			
PPNB	43.6	56.3	10.8
PPNC	61.4	38.5	5.4
Yarmoukian	57.0	42.9	7.9
Mushabi VI (PPN)			
F	41.5	58.4	–
G	46.6	53.3	–
H(i)	39.6	60.3	–
K	36.9	63.0	–
Sha'ar Hagolan(PN)	34.3	65.6	41.4
Kvish Harif (PN)	96.5	3.4	1.5
SGNAS sites			
12	72.2	27.7	6.0
15	49.4	50.5	21.4
44	45.9	54.0	5.1
Dhra'	40.7	59.2	6.0

* Bladelet percentages are included in the blade percentages (blades = % blades + % bladelets).

for the Yarmoukian culture (PN) and according to the notion of technological change through time (Rollefson and Simmons 1988), the debitage should be flake dominated. The opposite is the case here, however, as 65.6% of the debitage consists of blades. A possible explanation for this deviation might be found in Moore's observation (1973: 49) that some of the material is indicative of an earlier PPN occupation at Sha'ar Hagolan. This earlier occupation might account for the high percentage of blades in the debitage. Also, the bladelet percentage (41.4%) at Sha'ar Hagolan is rivaled only by Nahal Lavan 108 (51.7%), a PPNA site. The other Neolithic assemblages contain 10% or less of this form.

In comparison with this general Neolithic trend, the SGNAS survey sites of this time frame display some variability. The sites of Dhra' and 44 fall within the debitage parameters suggested for the PPN periods. The debitage frequencies from Site 12 certainly fall within the range of PN sites, in which a flake oriented debitage is more prominent. The position of Site 15 is less certain in this scheme as the flake and blade percentages are nearly equal and a large percentage of the blades are comprised of bladelets, much like Nahal Lavan 108 and Sha'ar Hagolan. It is tempting to posit that the apparent technological transition from blade technology to flake technology is represented by a gradual continuum in which an assemblage like Site 15, with an even flake and blade debitage frequency, is a transitional assemblage. Unfortunately, evidence supporting this technological change is only available from a limited number of sites and the smoothness of this transition has not yet been demonstrated nor has any particular reason been adduced as to why the change should take place. Finally, the effect of multiple components on the survey collections is not understood and the trends observed are very tentative in light of the possible bias due to this factor.

	1	2	3	4	5	6	7	8	9	10	11	12	Dhra'	15	12	44
Scrapers	7.59	12.64	2.0	5.5	25.80	5.2	7.7	7.8	4.7	8.0	27.1	1.82	11.3	2.5	15.9	4.6
Burins	3.79	1.26	8.0	3.7	2.30	39.0	29.3	30.3	23.4	16.8	–	7.29	3.7	2.5	7.4	–
PPT	6.32	13.90	4.4	18.5	1.21	0.5	3.4	3.4	7.4	5.0	12.9	44.06	–	–	–	3.1
Sickles	29.11	–	–	–	14.67	9.2	0.6	1.6	23.6	16.1	15.1	–	–	0.8	–	40.6
Borers	6.32	1.26	8.8	9.2	0.47	8.3	8.5	9.4	4.1	4.4	8.3	2.12	12.6	50.0	9.5	6.2
Notches	11.39	11.39	6.0	16.2	3.65	10.4	17.9	12.6	–	–	12.6	12.46	18.9	6.6	14.8	7.8
Denticulates	–	–	–	–	1.47	5.6	7.1	5.6	2.5	3.2	–	–	12.6	6.6	4.2	9.3
Ret. Flakes	7.59	6.32	18.0	–	2.08	–	–	–	3.4	11.7	–	2.43	13.9	14.1	15.9	3.1
Ret. Blades	12.65	21.48	23.6	18.5	4.91	–	–	–	–	–	2.2	9.42	15.1	6.6	8.5	–
Ret. Blt.	–	13.87	24.4	3.8	1.26	–	–	–	–	–	1.8	–	1.2	1.7	1.0	–
Ret. Points	–	6.32	–	–	–	–	–	–	–	–	–	2.12	–	–	–	–
Axes	5.06	5.04	–	–	3.82	–	–	–	0.1	0.4	2.8	–	–	1.7	1.0	–
Hammerstone	–	1.26	–	–	–	–	–	–	–	–	0.3	–	–	–	–	–
Drills	–	–	–	–	–	–	–	–	–	–	2.2	–	–	–	–	–
Tab. Scrapers	–	–	–	–	–	–	–	–	–	–	9.8	–	–	–	–	–
Choppers	–	–	–	–	0.65	–	–	–	–	–	0.9	–	1.2	0.8	1.0	1.5
Picks	–	–	–	–	0.56	–	–	–	–	–	–	–	–	–	–	1.5
Bif. Ret.	–	–	–	–	1.52	5.4	8.2	8.5	–	1.0	–	–	1.2	–	2.1	1.5
Truncations	–	–	–	–	–	4.1	8.5	7.4	–	–	–	3.34	–	1.7	–	–
Backed Pieces	–	–	–	–	–	1.3	–	2.7	0.9	1.0	–	3.34	–	–	–	–
Knives	–	–	–	–	–	1.2	1.4	2.0	–	–	–	–	–	–	–	–
Tanged Blades	–	–	–	–	–	1.6	0.3	0.2	2.8	2.4	–	–	–	–	–	–
Spear Pts.	–	–	–	–	–	5.2	2.0	2.5	–	–	–	–	–	–	–	–
Awls	10.12	–	4.4	11.1	33.59	–	–	–	–	–	–	–	–	–	2.1	–
Varia	–	1.26	–	13.0	2.01	3.1	5.1	6.1	27.4	30.5	4.0	11.54	7.5	4.1	15.9	20.3

1 Epstein (1984).
2 Noy, Friedman, and Burian (1981).
3 Noy, Schuldenrein, and Tchernov (1980) (slope).
4 Noy, Schuldenrein, and Tchernov (1980) (excavation).
5 Stekelis (1972).
6 Rollefson and Simmons (1988) (PPNB).
7 Rollefson and Simmons (1988) (PPNC).
8 Rollefson and Simmons (1988) (Yarmoukian).
9 Crowfoot Payne (1983) (Table 14 Square M).
10 Crowfoot Payne (1983) (Table 16 Trench III).
11 Rosen (1984).
12 Mintz and Ben-Ami (1977) (Mushabi VI H(i)).

Table 12 Retouched Piece Percentages from Neolithic Sites

Underlying all of this is the assumption that the technological trend for the Neolithic observed by Rollefson and Simmons (1988) can be generalized. For the most part, data available from other Neolithic sites concur with this scenario. While the relative percentage of these debitage categories may facilitate the temporal ordering of assemblages within the Neolithic, the assignment of a temporal affiliation based solely on debitage frequencies is most certain to be fraught with errors as temporal markers must be identified prior to testing the possible utility of this trend. In other words, for this pattern to be useful it must follow the general dating of the assemblage to the Neolithic as the percentages alone are certain to be found in assemblages from other temporal periods. Working within these limitations, the SGNAS material, excluding the sampling problem for the moment, suggests possible temporal ties extending from the Early Neolithic (PPN) through the Late Neolithic (PN). This observation is in contrast with the supposed age of some of the diagnostic materials as well as conclusions from previous reports for these sites (Raikes 1980; Bennett 1980).

The Neolithic retouched tool components (Table 12) show a much more mixed character than that of the debitage. For example, of the eight sites represented, excluding for the moment the four survey sites, the burin tool class comprises a major component of the retouched pieces at 'Ain Ghazal, PPNB through Yarmoukian (Rollefson and Simmons 1988) and Jericho, PPNB (Crowfoot Payne 1983), only. Similarly, sickles are prominent only at PPNB Jericho (Crowfoot Payne 1983), PN Sha'ar Hagolan (Stekelis 1972), and PN Tel Qatif (Epstein 1984). These examples demonstrate that tool frequencies within the Neolithic do not exhibit any sort of directional change through time akin to that of the debitage frequencies. This lack of a pattern is expected when one considers the possible different functional activities at these sites, i.e., not all sites represent the same range of activities. To a lesser degree, patterning may be partially masked by the varying number of retouched classes used by different authors. Some classes may distinguish sites functionally, while other tool classes seem to be redundant or too fine, which make comparison with other assemblages difficult because of a lack of standardized retouched categories.

A brief summary of the SGNAS retouched collections (Table 12) indicate some general trends. The most frequent retouched pieces at Dhra' are notches, retouched blades, retouched flakes, borers, denticulates, and scrapers. Site 12 is characterized by retouched flakes, scrapers, notches, and borers, while both Site 15 and 44 contain predominantly borers and retouched flakes (Plates 1–2). In terms of so called formal tool types, i.e., those that are not expedient forms, only borers and scrapers are represented in moderately high percentages (>9.0%) with borers represented at all four sites. Of the less formal types, e.g., expedient tools, retouched flakes are present in all four assemblages followed by notches, denticulates, and retouched blades.

From a functional point of view, Sites 15 and 44, containing high percentages of borers, (50.0% and 40.6% respectively), suggest some sort of specialized or intensive activity involving these forms at these sites. These two sites differ from Dhra' and 12 where a less skewed and wider range of retouched forms are present.

The blank morphology data for retouched pieces (blade, flake, bladelet) is only available for the SGNAS sites. In addition to these three forms, a fourth category, miscellaneous, covers tools not made on any of the above, e.g., core tools. A comparison of the retouched blank form percentages (Table 10) with the unretouched debitage percentages indicates an increase in the use of blade forms for retouch over the debitage blade percentage in every site but one. Only Site 44 shows a decrease in the retouched blade percentage. While this trend suggests a general preference of blade forms over flake forms for retouching, this may also represent a collection bias favoring the more visible and often more aesthetically attractive blade tools at the expense of flake tools. This trend of blank preference should be considered very tentative in light of these possible collection biases. In contrast to this trend of increasing blade retouch is a decline in the percentage of retouched bladelets from their debitage proportion. This trend might suggest that bladelets were not a desired end product, as was the case with Epi-Palaeolithic industries. Site 15, however, containing the largest debitage bladelet percentage in the entire survey region, shows an increase in bladelet percents for the retouched portion. A possible implication is that bladelet forms were a desired end product to be further retouched rather than an incidental by-product of manufacture. Of the retouched bladelet pieces for Site 15 (N=38), 84.2% are borers. This evidence indicates that the bladelet forms were primarily used for this one tool form rather than a wider range of forms.

The observed trend that debitage percentages from Neolithic assemblages may be indicative of a temporal position is generally supported by the evidence from other Neolithic sites. The applicability of this pattern to the SGNAS sites is hindered by the fact that these are survey collections and not necessarily single component sites. Given these drawbacks, conclusions related to the debitage pattern are tentative at best. While the debitage percents may possibly be related to chronology, the retouched piece percents probably are not, as there exists the problem of differential site function. Even percentages of gross diagnostic forms, e.g., sickles and arrowheads, are tied to site function[1] and operate best to separate Neolithic sites from other periods rather than within the Neolithic itself. Finally, the trend for the use of blades over flakes for retouching may be a construct of the collection samples rather than a demonstrable cultural trend.

Chalcolithic

Only three sites (87, 185, 186) are attributed to the Chalcolithic due in part to the large number of sites that fall in the Chalcolithic/Early Bronze range. Unlike the Neolithic sites, unambiguous diagnostics are not present for these collections, hence the creation of a Chalcolithic/Early Bronze category. The debitage percentages (Table 13) from these three Chalcolithic sites are remarkably similar. All of them are flake oriented with percentages between 71% and 77% for flakes. Blades account for 22% to 28% of the debitage and the bladelet contribution is between 3% and 6%. This sort of debitage 'clustering' suggests some technological consistency, possibly along similar lines of those posited for the Neolithic by Rollefson and Simmons (1988). However, better control in sample collection is required before such a proposition is considered to accurately reflect a regional pattern. One of the Neolithic collections in the preceding section, Site 12, a flake dominated assemblage, also falls within the percentage range of these Chalcolithic sites suggesting a possible mixed component site.[2]

While these three Chalcolithic sites appear to be closely related in terms of debitage production, it might be useful to compare them with other Chalcolithic assemblages from the Levant. The assemblages chosen represent several different areas; Southern Jordan (Henry 1982), the Jordan Valley (Dollfus *et al.* 1988), and the Northern Negev (Levy and Rosen 1987; Rosen 1987).

From Table 13, it is apparent that these few samples show some variability in terms of Chalcolithic debitage percents. Based on the flake and blade percents, this variability can be divided into two groups. The first group contains flake percentages of 90% or greater and less than 2% bladelets. The sites in this group include Abu Hamid (Dollfus *et al.* 1988), Shiqmim (Levy and Rosen 1987), Horvat Beter (Rosen 1987), and Har Queren (Rosen 1987). The second group is represented by lower flake percentages (71% to 76%) and in one case, Wadi Gaza Site A (Rosen 1987), by an increase in bladelets. Only two sites comprise this group, Jebel al-Jill (Henry 1982) and Wadi Gaza Site A (Rosen 1987). It is recognized that a sample of two sites is woefully inadequate for regional generalizations. Interestingly, the flake and blade percentages from this latter group are within the range of the survey site percentages. Whether these different debitage percentages reflect a different range of activities requiring a different technology, as suggested for Wadi Gaza Site A (Rosen 1987: 299), or are evidence of regional technological variation, is uncertain.

It has been suggested by Rosen (1987: 297–300) that Chalcolithic sites, primarily in the Northern Negev region, are divisible into specialized and generalized types based upon tool class frequencies. While this scheme seems plausible from the perspective of tool classes, it raises the question as to whether this functional difference is directly reflected in the debitage classes as well. Following his criteria (Rosen 1987: 298) for occupational sites, e.g., general site functions, he places Shiqmim and Horvat Beter into this class to which Abu Hamid (Dollfus *et al.*

Table 13 Debitage percentages from selected Chalcolithic and SGNAS sites

Site	Flakes	Blades	Bladelets*
Jebel al-Jill	76.0	23.9	–
Abu Hamid	90.8	9.2	1.6
Shiqmim	98.7	1.2	0.1
H. Beter	95.6	4.3	0.2
H. Qeren	96.4	3.5	0.3
Gaza A	71.6	28.3	12.1
SGNAS sites			
87	71.4	28.5	3.0
185	77.9	22.0	5.8
186	76.0	24.0	6.0

* Bladelet percentages are included in the blade percentages (blade = % blades + % bladelets).

1988) might also be added. These three sites are characterized by flake debitage in excess of 90%. Conversely, Wadi Gaza Site A (Rosen 1987) contains evidence of large scale blade and bladelet production as the higher debitage frequencies for these products indicate (Table 13). Functionally, this site is considered to be a specialized activity site rather than an occupational site with a generalized range of activities. This division in the debitage frequencies is not always black and white as Har Queren (Rosen 1987) is interpreted as a primary manufacture site, i.e., it exhibits specialized activities, yet the flake debitage is greater than 90% and a wide range of tool classes are present.

Expanding Rosen's model (1987) for differentiating site types to areas out of the Northern Negev, one finds that Jebel al-Jill (Henry 1982) contains a high frequency of blades (comparable to Wadi Gaza Site A). The general tool forms (scrapers, notches, and retouched pieces) are present in medium to high percentages (Table 14) along with architecture indicating an occupational rather than a specialized site. However, lunates and microliths are also present which tend to indicate specialized activity in Rosen's model (1987: 298). It is possible that these forms represent a different regional technology than that characteristic of the Northern Negev, e.g., bladelet rather than flake production for the most common kinds of 'toolkits'.

Three Chalcolithic sites from the Sinai (Oren and Gilead 1981) also differ from the Northern Negev occupational sites as blade and bladelet tools are more prevalent. In terms of Rosen's (1987) Negev criteria, these would be classified as specialized sites as special tools like sickles and micrograttoirs along with retouched blades and bladelets are present (Table 14). Although debitage frequencies are not given, the tool forms indicate more use of a specialized blade technology than a general flake technology. Whether this represents a regional technological difference might only be testable at occupation sites in which a more general 'toolkit' of this region (if one exists) could be compared to similar sites in the Northern Negev (assuming occupation sites in different areas entail the same range of processing and maintenance activities).

The samples from the Chalcolithic SGNAS sites, as mentioned previously, contain higher percentages of blades than the Northern Negev occupational sites, e.g., Shiqmim and Horvat Beter. The retouched frequencies (Table 14) contain medium to high frequencies of some combination of scrapers, notches, borers, and retouched flakes (Plates 3–4) indicating, in terms of Rosen's (1987) site function model, an occupational site.[3]

Specialized activities, as inferred from tool types, do not appear to have been the main focus here and assuming that the surface collection is representative of the assemblage, a technology favoring an increasing blade component is represented. This difference might represent a regional technological variation during the Chalcolithic (or possibly a temporal technological variation). Certainly, the few sites further south, Jebel al-Jill (Henry 1982) and in the Sinai (Oren and Gilead 1981), suggest the possibility of regional technological variation and the SGNAS sites might be more 'related' to these sites in this respect than they are to the Northern Negev sites. In assessing the effectiveness of Rosen's (1987) model, it seems to be limited to the Northern Negev, possibly the Jordan Valley, as the other areas mentioned seem to contain technological variations (flake, blade, bladelet) for sites of similar 'function'

than the pattern found in the Negev, i.e., the same gross 'function' is implied but the technology of production seems to be different.

The tool blanks used (Table 10), representing the three survey sites, are different from their debitage counterparts. Both Site 87 and 185 contain tools on flakes in a higher percentage (86.9 and 92.0 respectively) than flakes are represented in the debitage. Based on this sample, though debitage blades are produced at reasonably high levels, the selection of tool blanks favors flakes suggesting blades were not the desired end product (one might argue for blade 'curation', however, no evidence, e.g., numerous blade cores, is available to support this argument). In contrast to this pattern of blank use, at Shiqmim blades and bladelets account for 1.2% of the debitage but comprise 19.3% of the retouched pieces indicating a preference for lamellar blanks when they were available (Rosen 1987). The last survey site, 186, also follows this pattern of a higher percentage of retouched blades than debitage blades suggesting these were preferred forms. Taken at face value, two of the sites (87 and 185), while indicating technological differences from the Northern Negev sites, e.g., more blade production, seem to contradict this technological pattern by using flake tools more frequently than blade tools. The limited evidence from the survey samples, suggests this trend of blade

Table 14 Retouched piece percentages from selected Chalcolithic and SGNAS sites

	1	*2*	*3*	*4*	*5*	*6*	*87*	*185*	*186*
Fan Scrapers	3.08	–	1.48	0.9	–	0.5	–	–	–
Scrapers	–	1.54	4.85	2.22	6.8	29.1	15.1	17.3	8.0
Perforated Disks	–	–	–	0.6	–	–	–	–	–
Endscrapers	2.46	3.88	7.40	13.0	–	–	13.0	16.0	–
Ret. Bladelets	11.41	3.88	8.14	1.5	–	1.4	–	–	–
Sickles	–	14.19	13.50	2.96	18.2	–	2.3	–	–
Axe/Adze/Chisel	0.92	2.91	2.22	5.9	–	5.7	–	4.0	–
Transverse PPT	0.30	–	–	0.6	–	–	–	–	–
Burins	3.70	0.97	1.48	1.5	1.8	–	–	12.0	7.1
Truncations	2.46	2.91	5.92	4.3	1.8	–	4.3	–	–
Borers	5.24	2.91	7.40	10.5	12.7	–	17.3	4.0	21.4
Notches	11.11	8.73	9.62	4.6	7.3	10.5	13.0	8.0	28.6
Choppers	0.92	0.97	–	0.3	–	–	–	–	–
Ret. Pieces–	–	–	23.8	25.5	42.6	–	–	–	–
Ret. Blades	8.64	23.33	9.62	–	–	–	–	–	14.3
Denticulates	7.71	10.67	13.33	–	–	0.7	8.6	8.0	–
Ret. Flakes	5.55	8.73	11.85	–	–	–	21.7	40.0	21.4
Microgratt.	16.04	4.85	9.62	–	–	10.2	–	–	–
PPT	–	–	0.74	–	–	–	–	–	–
Lunates	–	–	–	–	7.3	5.8	–	–	–
Nongeo micro.	–	–	–	–	9.1	–	–	–	–
Bifaces	–	–	–	–	3.6	–	–	–	–
Massive Pieces	–	–	–	–	1.8	–	–	–	–
Backed Blades	–	–	–	–	–	–	–	–	7.1
Varia	4.62	6.79	5.92	–	–	–	4.3	–	–

1   Oren and Gilead (1981) (R48).   **4**   Dollfus *et al.* (1988).
2   Oren and Gilead (1981) (R45).   **5**   Henry (1982). 5.2
3   Oren and Gilead (1981) (A301).   **6**   Levy and Rosen (1987).

Table 15 Debitage percentages from selected and SGNAS Early Bronze sites

Site	Flakes	Blades	Bladelets *
Sheikh 'Awad	77.0	22.9	–
Feiran	95.6	4.3	–
En Shadud	91.4	8.5	–
Jericho			
Trench 1	71.1	28.8	–
Trench 2	71.1	28.8	–
Trench 3	44.0	55.9	–
Arad			
Stratum IV	94.4	5.5	–
Stratum III	91.1	8.8	–
Stratum II	92.3	7.6	1.0
Stratum I	94.5	5.4	–

Survey Sites

105	93.6	6.3	1.0

* Bladelet percentages are included in the blade percentages (blades = % blades + % bladelets).

production may not have been intentional, i.e., not the desired endproduct, and as such creates a misleading impression of the character of the assemblage. These are small samples, however, that are compared with excavated assemblages in order to discern some possible rudimentary patterns.

Early Bronze Age

The Early Bronze Age in the survey region is represented by only one site (Site 105) containing more than fifty pieces. Rather than compare this single site with other Early Bronze Age assemblages, a general review of selected Early Bronze Age sites will follow. Then, the single Early Bronze Age SGNAS site, along with the twelve Chalcolithic/Early Bronze survey sites, are compared to Early Bronze Age and Chalcolithic assemblages from other areas of the Southern Levant. The Early Bronze Age sites selected for comparison are Sheikh 'Awad (Beit-Arieh 1981), Feiran (Beit-Arieh 1982), En Shadud (Rosen 1985), Jericho (Crowfoot Payne 1983), and Arad (Schick 1978). The size range represented by these sites varies from small scale occupations to larger 'urban' locales.

The flake percentages from Early Bronze Age sites (Table 15) fall into two groups, much like the Chalcolithic Period assemblages previously discussed. These groups represent flake oriented technologies with percentages of flakes between 71% to 77% and 91% to 95%. The one exception to this trend is trench III at Jericho where flakes comprise only 44% of the debitage (Crowfoot Payne 1983). The two debitage percent groups do not appear to reflect regional variation as the first group (71% to 77%) includes one site from the Sinai (Beit-Arieh 1981) and two Jericho trench assemblages (Crowfoot Payne 1983). The second group includes material from the Sinai (Beit-Arieh 1982), northwest Israel (Rosen 1985), and the

Table 16 Retouched piece percentages from selected and SGNAS Early Bronze sites

	1	2	3	4	5	6	7	105
Tabular Scrapers	–	70.65	0.5	28.5	19.1	30.0	30.4	–
Scrapers	55.0	–	23.6	4.7	2.1	1.1	8.7	9.1
Borers	10.0	7.72	7.8	4.7	–	1.1	4.3	6.1
Harvest Knife	–	0.38	–	–	–	–	–	–
Notches	–	2.70	–	–	–	–	–	24.2
Denticulates	–	1.93	–	–	–	–	–	3.0
Pieces esquillees	10.0	1.93	–	–	–	–	–	–
Nose Scrapers	–	1.15	–	–	–	–	–	–
Endscrapers	5.0	0.38	–	–	–	–	–	–
Truncations	10.0	0.77	–	–	–	–	–	–
Burins	–	0.38	1.8	–	–	–	–	9.1
Lunates	–	0.38	–	–	–	–	–	–
Ret. Blt.	–	1.15	–	–	5.3	–	4.3	–
Ret. Blades	–	4.63	5.5	–	14.9	–	–	3.0
Ret. Flakes	10.0	3.47	–	16.6	13.8	7.7	43.5	36.3
Sickles	–	–	9.8	23.8	29.8	43.3	8.7	–
Notch/Denticulate	–	–	33.6	21.4	14.9	11.1	–	–
Misc. trimmed	–	–	15.8	–	–	–	–	–
Choppers	–	–	–	–	–	3.3	–	–
Celts	–	–	–	–	–	1.1	–	–
Pick	–	–	–	–	–	–	–	3.0
Varia	–	2.31	1.8	–	–	1.1	–	6.1

1 Beit-Arieh (1982) (Feiran).
2 Beit-Arieh (1981) (Sheikh 'Awad).
3 Rosen (1985).
4 Schick (1978) (Stratum IV EB I).
5 Schick (1978) (Stratum III EB II).
6 Schick (1978) (Stratum II EB II).
7 Schick (1978) (Stratum I EB II).

Negev (Schick 1978). These debitage flake percentages might possibly represent functional differences (as suggested for the Chalcolithic earlier) rather than different regional technologies, i.e., different frequencies of blade production. A comparison of the Early Bronze Age debitage percentages against the Chalcolithic percentages indicate similar ranges for flakes and blades, but bladelets are conspicuously absent from the Early Bronze Age debitage. This difference may be the result of a technological shift, with a different emphasis placed upon the flint implements in Early Bronze Age contexts where metal is believed to be used more than in preceding Chalcolithic contexts. It is also possible that with the rise of more complex social networks, there is a declining interest archaeologically in the recovery of 'primitive' flint tools resulting in biased collections favoring the formal types, e.g., sickle blades and tabular scrapers.

The retouched piece percentages used here (Table 16) represent the Sinai (Beit-Arieh 1981, 1982), the Negev (Schick 1978), and northwest Israel (Rosen 1985). The Jericho retouched pieces were too few in number and have been dropped from the analysis.

The traditional Early Bronze Age diagnostic tool forms are the tabular scraper and sickle blade (Hanbury-Tenison 1986; Schick 1978). These two tool types are the focus of a comparison of Early Bronze Age tool assemblages. At Arad (Schick 1978), tabular scrapers in stratum I–IV (EB I–EB II) represent from 19% to 30% of the retouched assemblage per stratum (Table 16). Further north and west, at En Shadud (Rosen 1985), this tool comprises only 0.5% of the retouched pieces. Rosen (1985) contends that distance to the tabular raw material is generally reflected in the frequency of this tool form in an assemblage, i.e., sites further from the source have fewer tabular scrapers. Although tabular scrapers tend to be more

standardized, i.e., less ad hoc, than most of the Early Bronze Age tools, it is suggested that functionally these tools might perform the same functions as other scrapers. If this is the case, then in areas where tabular scrapers are few, regular scrapers should be more numerous, assuming the range of activities to be comparable. In the Arad collections, scrapers comprise 1% to 8% of the retouched percentage per stratum, while at En Shadud, where tabular scrapers are rare, scrapers account for 23.6% of the retouched pieces. The percentage differences might indicate that this form is the functional equivalent of the tabular scraper.

In the Sinai, at Sheikh 'Awad (Beit-Arieh 1981), tabular scrapers comprise 70.65% of the retouched pieces while only 1.53% of the total is represented by scrapers (Table 16). At Feiran (Beit-Arieh 1982), no tabular scrapers are present but scrapers account for 60.0% of this small (N=20) collection. The distance from these sites to tabular flint sources is unknown but they seem to fit the pattern of assemblages with either a high tabular scraper index or a high scraper index. Admittedly, these samples are very small and this pattern must be demonstrated at a wider range of sites before it is accepted.

Sickle blades are absent from the Sinai assemblages (Beit-Arieh 1981; 1982) and this absence may reflect a different, less sedentary type of adaptation than in the Negev where sickles are relatively common (Schick 1978). The En Shadud assemblage (Rosen 1985), while containing sickles, is represented by lower percentages of this tool than Arad. If the assumption that sickles were used for harvesting grasses (Rosen 1985: 155) is correct, then the absence of these tools suggest this activity was not part of the economic system or that other tools provided the same function as sickles. These few sites suggest that southern assemblages (Sinai) contain few sickle

Table 17 Retouched piece percentages from SGNAS Chalcolithic/Early Bronze sites

	10	*14*	*20*	*86*	*82*	*137*	*84*	*171*	*135*	*217*	*227*	*30*
Backed Pieces	–	3.6	4.6	2.6	–	–	–	–	–	–	4.2	–
Notches	23.5	10.7	13.9	13.1	50.0	–	16.6	15.8	21.7	16.6	8.3	8.3
Denticulates	5.9	–	2.3	15.8	8.3	–	8.3	21.0	4.3	16.6	12.5	–
Endscrapers	5.9	10.7	18.6	7.9	–	–	8.3	5.2	4.3	8.3	4.2	8.3
Scrapers	5.9	14.3	20.9	15.8	–	–	–	21.0	26.1	–	8.3	25.0
Borers	11.7	–	2.3	5.3	8.3	20.0	33.3	5.2	8.7	8.3	16.6	–
Picks	–	3.6	–	–	–	20.0	–	–	–	–	–	–
Choppers	5.9	–	2.3	–	–	–	–	–	–	–	–	–
Axe/adze/chisel	–	–	–	5.3	–	–	–	–	–	–	–	–
PPT	–	–	–	–	–	–	–	–	–	–	–	–
Biface ret.	–	–	–	–	–	–	–	–	–	–	–	–
Sickles	–	3.6	4.6	–	–	–	–	–	–	–	–	16.6
Truncations	–	3.6	–	–	–	–	–	–	–	–	4.2	–
Burins	11.7	17.8	4.6	5.3	16.6	20.0	16.6	5.2	8.7	–	–	–
Ret. Blades	–	3.6	7.0	5.3	–	–	–	–	4.3	–	4.2	16.6
Ret. Blts.	–	–	–	–	–	–	–	–	–	8.3	–	–
Ret. Flakes	23.5	21.4	13.9	13.1	16.6	40.0	8.3	21.0	21.7	41.7	25.0	25.0
Tabular Scrapers	–	–	2.3	2.6	–	–	–	–	–	–	–	–
Varia	5.9	7.1	2.3	7.9	–	–	8.3	5.2	–	–	12.5	–

blades, for whatever reason, e.g., economic, environmental, while elsewhere this tool was often a major component of the tool kit. A larger number of reported Early Bronze Age chipped stone assemblages, along with viable environmental data, are necessary to further test this hypothesis.

An examination of the SGNAS Chalcolithic/Early Bronze assemblages with regard to tabular scraper and sickle blade trends is, therefore, inconclusive. Tabular scrapers (Plates 3–5) are present at only two sites, namely, Sites 20 and 86, and they comprise less than 2.6% of the total retouched component (Table 17). End and sidescraper percentages from these two sites are high, 39.5% and 23.7% respectively. These tend to conform to the non-local tabular source trend of En Shadud (Rosen 1985). The remainder of the survey sites contain no tabular scrapers but scraper percentages fluctuate and sample sizes are very small in some cases. In general, the SGNAS survey sites appear most like assemblages that are located at a distance from tabular flint sources.

Sickle blades (Plate 3), found at only three of the sites (14, 20, 30) are represented in low percentages (Site 30 contains a small sample size). Perhaps more telling about these tools is not the frequency but the location of these sites within the survey area-all in Wadi Fidan. If the functional use of these tools suggested by Rosen (1985) is correct, then these assemblages indicate the cutting of plant materials, e.g., grasses/cereals, only in Wadi Fidan. The rest of the assemblages, with an absence of this tool, may represent different sorts of adaptations to the environment.

The remainder of the Early Bronze Age toolkit has been characterized as being *ad hoc*, i.e., non-standardized, in nature (Rosen 1985: 153; Hanbury-Tenison 1986: 149). The general tool forms meeting this criteria are notches, denticulates, retouched flakes and blades, crude borers, and most of the scrapers. These pieces are frequently produced on poorer quality lithic materials than that used for the sickles and tabular scrapers.

Within the survey region, the Chalcolithic/Early Bronze debitage percentages show a continuum in the

flake percentages (Table 18) from 64.2% to 97.2%. Unlike the few Chalcolithic or Early Bronze Age assemblages reviewed from other areas of the southern Levant, no dichotomous groups are observable. Assuming that the survey samples are representative of the time periods in question and the sampling bias is minimal, these percentage values suggest that while these assemblages are flake oriented technologically, there is some variability in the degree to which flakes are produced. The bladelet percentages for these sites are low, generally 3% or less with several (N=7) containing no bladelet debitage. The exception is Site 137 where bladelets comprise 12.5% of the blade debitage. When this collection (137) is compared to Early Bronze Age assemblages from outside areas, there is a stark contrast as those Early Bronze Age assemblages are characterized by very few bladelets in the debitage. Similarly, Chalcolithic assemblages are also characterized by few bladelets in the debitage except for Wadi Gaza Site A (Rosen 1987). The bladelet percentage from Site 137 suggests that, in terms of Rosen's (1987) site function model, this would represent a specialized activity site. Unfortunately, retouched pieces are so few (N=5) that specific 'functional' evidence is absent. This bladelet percentage is higher than many of the Neolithic debitage collections and is only topped by Site 15 (21.4%). In terms of the possible Chalcolithic pattern of regional technological variation, the uncertain date of these Chalcolithic/Early Bronze sites in relation to the Chalcolithic sites makes it difficult to discern.

The retouched pieces for these 13 sites (12 Chalcolithic/Early Bronze and one Early Bronze) indicate a dominance of tool forms that tend to reflect domestic activities (Rosen 1987: 298). Tool classes (Plates 3–5) that represent 10% or more of the total retouched portion were recorded for each of these 13 survey sites. The most frequently occurring classes are retouched flakes (12 of 13), notches/denticulates (11 of 13), scrapers (6 of 13), borers and burins (both 3 of 13). Specialized tools, e.g., celts, sickles, tabular scrapers, and retouched bladelets (Rosen 1987: 298) are present at five sites (10, 14, 20, 30, 86) but only at Site 30 do they represent greater than 10% of the total percentage (sickle blades). It may be of some importance that three (10, 14 and 20) of these sites represent three of the four lowest flake debitage percentages and four (14, 20, 30, and 86) account for four of the five lowest flake percents for retouched blank forms. These differences might be indicative of functional differences between these sites and the others containing none of these specialized tools. The low percentage of these specialized forms suggest specialized activities were not the sole function of the site and a wider range of activities occurred at these sites, as indicated by the high percentage of domestic tools. With the possible exception of Site 137, and maybe Site 30, very few of these sites appear to have been strictly specialized sites based on inferences from the retouched and debitage portions.

Table 18 Debitage percentages from Chalcolithic/Early Bronze SGNAS sites *

Site	Flakes	Blades	Bladelets
10	84.2	15.7	0.0
14	75.0	25.0	0.0
20	69.3	30.6	2.6
86	89.7	10.2	1.0
82	97.2	2.7	0.0
137	64.2	35.7	12.5
84	90.9	9.0	0.0
171	86.4	13.5	0.0
135	92.0	8.0	2.0
217	95.1	4.8	0.0
227	85.7	14.2	3.1
30	90.5	9.4	0.0

* Bladelet percentages are included in the blade percentages (blades = % blades + % bladelets).

Using Rosen's (1987) model of retouched pieces to characterize site function outside of the survey area, one finds specialized Chalcolithic sites in the Sinai, R48, R45 (Oren and Gilead 1981) and to a lesser degree at Abu Hamid (Dollfus *et al.* 1988). Occupational sites would include Shiqmim (Levy and Rosen 1987), Jebel al-Jill (Henry 1982), and A301 (Oren and Gilead 1981). When this pattern is applied to the Early Bronze Age sites, only En Shadud (Rosen 1985) and Feiran (Beit-Arieh 1982) fit the occupation criteria while Sheikh 'Awad (Beit-Arieh 1981) and Arad (Schick 1978) represent specialized activity sites. It appears that conclusions based solely on this criteria are somewhat misleading as a site as large as Arad is likely not to have been only a limited activity station. The development of non-lithic technology, e.g., metallurgy, which likely replaces some of the lithic functions, may make the pattern appear to be specialized as the commonplace use of chipped stone tools becomes obsolete.

The retouched blank form percentages (Table 10) from the survey collections show some variation from the debitage percentages. Part of this is due to smaller sample sizes for the retouched portions. Other fluctuations seem to reflect a preference for certain blank forms, especially blades. This variation in blank forms is similar to that observed for the few Chalcolithic SGNAS collections.

Summary

To recapitulate, the low level of resolution selected here precludes the generation of any definitive conclusions concerning technological or functional/behavioral trends. Generalizations arising from previous research in the Levant have been presented for comparison with the SGNAS collections.

Survey sites from the Lower and Middle Palaeolithic are compared with one another because these sites are few in number and collection sizes are small. It is suggested that while functional activities are essentially the same, based upon the tool types present, some variation between the retouched pieces may correspond to different functional or temporal episodes.

The focus of the Neolithic comparison is the changing technology within this period (Rollefson and Simmons 1988). Functional activities, based on tool type percentages, appear to vary during the PPN and PN but the technology within each of these periods is largely homogeneous. The SGNAS assemblages tend to follow these general technological/temporal trends though some of the variability may reflect different on-site activities.

Chalcolithic assemblages are viewed in terms of the debitage (technology) and retouched pieces, especially as these may apply to specialized/generalized site functions (Rosen 1987). The results indicate that this model tends to work best in the area, i.e., the Northern Negev, in which it was designed. Because of the lack of broad regional applicability, the conclusions

derived from this model for the SGNAS are very tentative.

Early Bronze Age assemblages, which are not well known, are examined in terms of two specific tool types, the sickle blade and the tabular scraper (Rosen 1985; Hanbury-Tenison 1986). Since discrete Early Bronze Age survey assemblages are rare, the Chalcolithic/Early Bronze SGNAS assemblages are compared with both the Early Bronze Age and Chalcolithic models with mixed results. Rosen's model (1987) exhibits the same problem here as with the Chalcolithic sites while the diagnostic tool types from the SGNAS sites are few in number, resulting in weak generalizations.

Problems with comparison include sample size, methods of recovery, temporal discreteness, as well as the different focus per period of the models used (Rosen 1985; Hanbury-Tenison 1986; Rosen 1987; Rollefson and Simmons 1988). The regional applicability of these models is unknown as varying data bases have yet to be tested along these lines. Given the incompleteness of our knowledge, the comparison with the SGNAS material, albeit crude, is intended to suggest tentative trends that may be tested by more rigorous data.

Settlement patterns by period

Lower/Middle Palaeolithic

The earliest occupational evidence in the survey area is attributed to the Lower/Middle Palaeolithic (Table 19). This period is represented by one site (32) located in the southern-most portion (Wadi Fidan) of the survey area (Figure 5). The absence of comparable sites in the northern portion as well as the diffuse nature of the lithic scatter suggest that the Lower/Middle Palaeolithic settlement of the survey area was restricted in space and probably in time, i.e., very short period of time represented by the small amount of material. This is probably due in part to the size of the Lisan Lake during this period.

Middle Palaeolithic

Middle Palaeolithic sites are also few in number and are limited in space. The number of identified Middle Palaeolithic sites (Table 19) is two (33, 28) but the second (28) is somewhat equivocal (since it is based on the occurrence of Levallois technique) and might be Chalcolithic in age (see Hanbury-Tenison 1986 for an example of Levallois elements in Chalcolithic contexts). The sites are restricted to terraces along Wadi Fidan (Figure 5) at elevations of 0-20 m above sea level. The scarcity of Middle Palaeolithic sites along with the apparent low artifact density indicates a very limited Middle Palaeolithic occupation of the survey area.

Other sites present in the Wadi Fidan area, especially those on the Wadi Fidan/Wadi Ghuweib interfluve, e.g., Sites 51, 53, might contain Middle Palaeolithic material but the lack of identifiable diagnostics makes such a conclusion highly speculative. These sites are best considered unknown.

No other areas of the survey have Middle Palaeolithic-like samples which supports the argument of a localized occupation in the south segment.

Upper Palaeolithic/Epi-Palaeolithic

Sites of an Upper Palaeolithic or Epi-Palaeolithic character are absent from the entire survey region. The absence of Upper Palaeolithic sites in the survey area is not surprising given the extent of the Lisan Lake but the absence of identifiable Epi-Palaeolithic sites is somewhat unexpected. Several sites in the Fidan area, namely, Sites 14, 15, and 44, all in the Neolithic to Early Bronze Age range, contain a few pieces that might represent an unknown Palaeolithic component. Except for Dhra', which might contain a Late Natufian/PPNA component (Bennett 1980; Raikes 1980) and is out of the survey area proper, none of the sites north of the Fidan contain any evidence of an Upper Palaeolithic or Epi-Palaeolithic occupation. Possible reasons for this gap in the cultural history will be explored in the tentative diachronic model for the Southern Ghors and Northeast 'Arabah.

Neolithic

Eight sites in the SGNAS region plus Dhra' contain Neolithic components. Of the nine, seven contain later components of either Chalcolithic or Early Bronze Age. Not surprisingly, Neolithic sites are present in Wadi Fidan (12, 15, 21, and 44) and three (12, 15, 44) appear to represent substantial occupations, both in size and duration (possible associated architecture and a high density of chipped stone). It appears that areas north of the Wadi Fidan region are occupied for the first time during the Neolithic (Figure 5). Neolithic

Table 19 List of the Sites by Period.

LPL /MPL	MPL	NL	Chal	Chal/EB	EB
32	33	12	12	3	12
	28	15	15	9	21
		21	28	10	35
		44	30	14	76
		76	44	15	78
		92	76	20	105
		95	84	30	108
		239	87	82	118
		Dhra'92	83	119	
			108	84	121
			129	86	124
			137	95	131
			185	116	141
			186	117	154D
				129	174
				135	194
				137	224
				138	
				140	
				171	
				189	
				208	
				217	
				227	

components are found in Wadi Feifa (76, 92, 95), further north in Wadi Madsus al-Shamali (239), and at Dhra', east of the Lisan Peninsula. Except for Site 239, which is dated from a single point fragment, the Neolithic sites in Wadis Fidan and Feifa are clustered together.[4] Additionally, both Wadis Feifa and Fidan presently contain springs or running water which in antiquity might have made settlement in these areas more attractive than other wadis in the region. The Neolithic sites in Wadi Feifa are the first sites located in areas considerably below sea level, ca. -295 metres.

The site 'types' represented include architectural feature sites (4), cemeteries (2), wall alignments (1), and lithic scatters (no features, 1). Three of the architectural sites are in Wadi Fidan. The median site size is 5000 m² and terraces (3) are the most frequent landforms used for settlement. All of the Neolithic sites, except Site 239, are situated at or near the mouth of a wadi.

A topic of some debate in Neolithic studies is the continuity (or lack thereof) between PPN and PN occupations. Obviously, the question of PPN/PN continuity cannot be resolved from survey material alone but the presence of temporal markers from one phase or the other may be useful in determining which 'phase' of the Neolithic is represented in the region. In dividing these Neolithic sites into aceramic and ceramic components, four of the sites (21, 76, 92, 95) contain pottery without lithic diagnostics and are considered to be later developments. Of the remaining sites, Dhra', 12, and 15 have been attributed to the PN by Raikes (1980) though the point diagnostics could be either late PPNB or early PN (Bar-Yosef 1981; Burian and Friedman 1979). The same situation is true for Site 44. The final Neolithic site, i.e., Site 239, contains an ambiguous point fragment which could be either PPN or PN. Based on this scant evidence, an unequivocal PPN occupation in the survey region is not supported. More certain, however, is the presence of PN settlements. The Neolithic settlement around Wadi Feifa appears to be a later episode, i.e., PN, while those in the Fidan and at Dhra' might represent periods on either side of the transition based upon projectile point morphology. Also, an earlier occupation at Dhra' is indicated by the presence of El-Khiam points which might be of an early PPNA phase (Bar-Yosef 1981; Noy, Schuldenrein, and Tchernov 1980; Noy, Friedman, and Burian 1981).

Chalcolithic

The isolation of Chalcolithic sites, *sensu stricto* in the survey is difficult due to apparent multiple components, small lithic samples, and temporal ambiguities inherent in both lithics and ceramics. For these reasons, only the sites with positive Chalcolithic ceramics or lithics will be included under this heading (Table 12). Those sites in which the Chalcolithic component is less certain, i.e., those assigned to the Chalcolithic/Early Bronze category, will be addressed separately.

Fourteen sites meet the criteria for Chalcolithic settlements (12, 15, 28, 30, 44, 76, 84, 87, 92, 108,

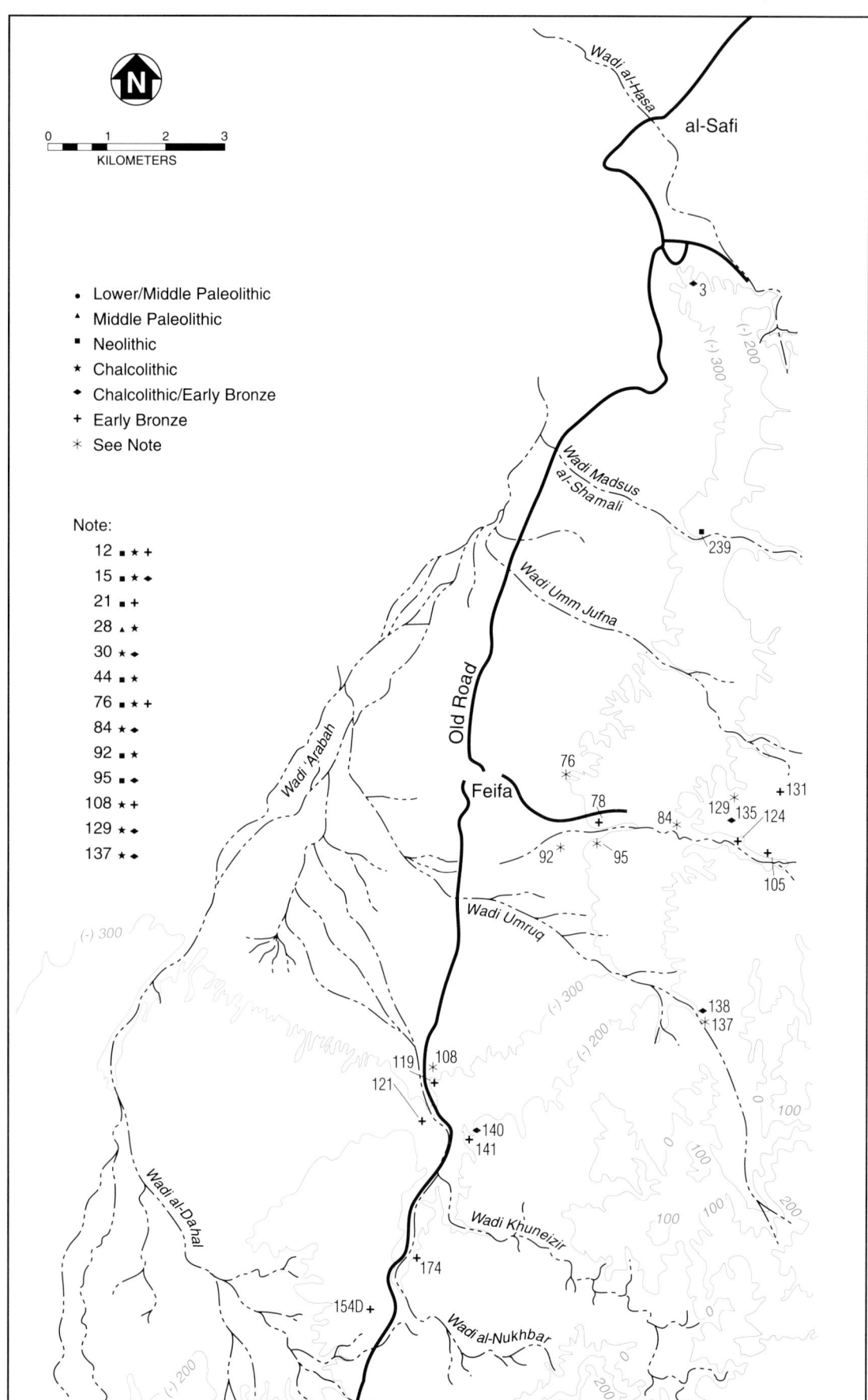

Figure 5   Lower/Middle Palaeolithic, Middle Palaeolithic, Neolithic, Chalcolithic, Chalcolithic/Early Bronze, and Early Bronze
Period lithic sites settlement pattern map (northern portion).

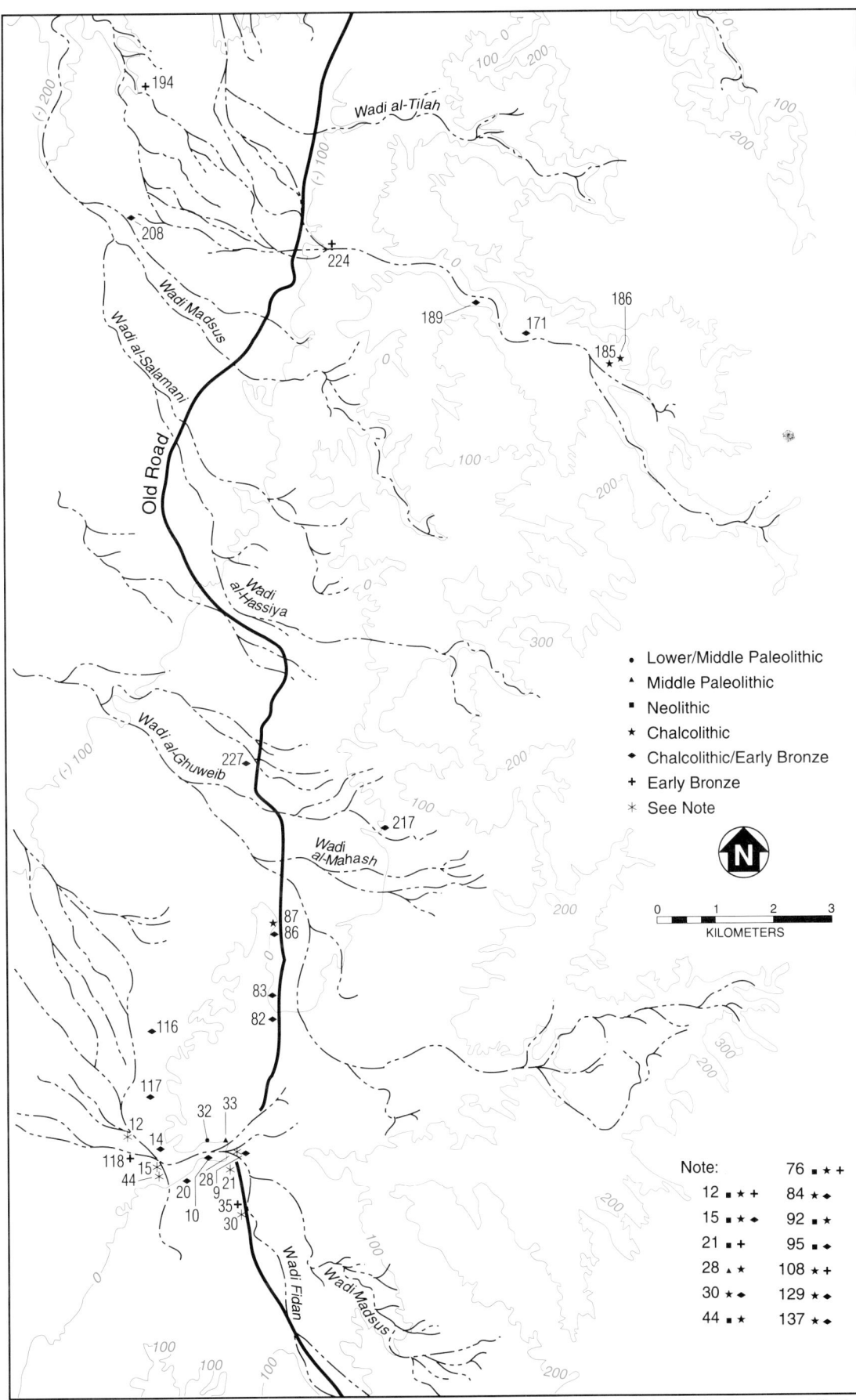

Figure 5 Lower/Middle Palaeolithic, Middle Palaeolithic, Neolithic, Chalcolithic, Chalcolithic/Early Bronze, and Early Bronze
Period lithic sites settlement pattern map (southern portion).

129, 137, 185, 186). Five of these sites (12, 15, 44, 76, and 92) also contain Neolithic components while three (87, 185, 186) contain elements suggestive of the Late Neolithic/Early Chalcolithic and one (28) might be of a Middle Palaeolithic age (see Middle Palaeolithic). The remaining sites (30, 84, 108, 129, 137) are somewhat ambiguous (Chalcolithic/Early Bronze) according to the lithics but contain some Chalcolithic ceramics. Part of the Neolithic/Chalcolithic uncertainty may rest in the placement of the temporal 'break' between the two, as some archaeologists put this division late, e.g., Moore 1982, ca. 3750 BC, while others place the break earlier in time, ca. 4500–4400 BC (Gilead 1988) and overlapping with the Late Neolithic. Regional variation in the stone tool assemblages suggests that certain Neolithic 'markers' persist into the Chalcolithic while they are absent at other contemporaneous Chalcolithic sites, e.g., Rosen 1984, giving Chalcolithic age sites a Neolithic flavor.

Chalcolithic settlement is concentrated in three areas (Figure 5), Wadis Feifa, Dahal, and Fidan but sites are also found in Wadis Umruq (137) and Khuneizir (108). In addition to being represented by more sites than the Neolithic, the Chalcolithic sites are found in a greater variety of areas over the survey landscape. Most of the sites are located at the mouth of the wadi or on a low terrace next to the wadi. This site location pattern is the same as the previous Neolithic period sites. Two Chalcolithic sites differ from this pattern as one (129) is located on a plateau between Wadis Feifa and Umm Jufna while the other (137) is situated high above Wadi Umruq. Both sites are still reasonably close to a potential water source, as most sites are since the wadi courses were purposefully surveyed, but these site locations are not necessarily dependent upon the immediate proximity of water. This hint of a change in the settlement patterns/systems based on different locations of sites is provocative but it should be noted that site character, i.e., presence of architecture or an artifact scatter which may directly reflect the range and duration of activities, differs from site to site and is not assumed to be necessarily comparable. As an example, lithic scatter sites from periods with known sedentary and semi-sedentary activities, e.g., Neolithic through Early Bronze Age, while expressing the range of variability within the settlement system, are not comparable to architectural sites in terms of their dependence on critical resources, e.g., water, because of the assumed transitional nature of lithic scatter occupations. However, site assessment based upon surface remains, even in deflated land surfaces, is not always a reliable indicator of sub-surface remains (see Lewarch and O'Brien 1981).

Architectural feature sites (8) are the most numerous for the Chalcolithic sites, followed by surface scatters (3), cemeteries (2), and wall alignments (1). These numerous architectural features suggest a degree of sedentism for this area and time. Median site size is smaller than the Neolithic at 2500 m² suggesting smaller groups spread across the landscape. The landforms occupied are mostly

terraces (6) but as noted above, plateaux and plains away from the wadis are utilized more during this period.

Chalcolithic/Early Bronze

This temporal category is represented by twenty-four sites (3, 9, 10, 14, 15, 20, 30, 82, 83, 84, 86, 95, 116, 117, 129, 135, 137, 138, 140, 171, 189, 208, 217, 227), very few of which are actually transitional, i.e., Late Chalcolithic/Early Bronze. This is more of a residual category due to the inadequacies of diagnostics previously mentioned (see Chalcolithic) and because this is an artificial construct, it may create a misleading settlement peak during this period in the area. Sites from both the preceding Chalcolithic and succeeding Early Bronze Age are fewer in number (Table 19).

Despite the problems of temporal differentiation, site location over the survey area continues to be variable (Figure 5). Evidence of Chalcolithic/Early Bronze occupations are found from Wadi al-Hasa in the north to Wadi Fidan in the south. During this period the entire range of the survey area contains evidence of settlement for the first time. Nearly every major wadi drainage contains at least one site of this period but the major concentration is in Wadis Ghuweib and Fidan where 50% (12) of these sites are situated. Sites are still situated along the wadi banks and mouths as well as away from the easy water access locations.

New developments that probably affect the settlement systems include metallurgical processing and increasing population aggregations. Concerning the former, two sites (10, 30) in Wadi Fidan contain evidence of smelting activities in the form of slag residuals. To the south and east of this area is Wadi Feinan which has been identified as a source of copper objects found at Palestinian sites to the west and north (Shalev and Northover 1987). Beit-Arieh and Gophna (1977) have suggested that a Chalcolithic site in Wadi 'Arabah may have been involved in the movement of copper materials into the Northern Negev. It is possible that routes from Feinan passed through Wadi Fidan as copper material was moved westward. The presence of a number of Chalcolithic (12, 15, 28, 30, 44) and Chalcolithic/Early Bronze sites (10, 14, 15, 20, 30) in Wadi Fidan further suggests possible involvement in this network.

The second development, that of increasing population centers, is most closely associated with the development of Early Bronze Age cities, e.g., Arad, Bab al-Dhra', but evidence from the Northern Negev, e.g., Bir al-Safadi, Shiqmim, and the Jordan Valley (Teleilat Ghassul, Abu Hamid) indicate the presence of large populations during the Chalcolithic. While some larger Chalcolithic sites are known, it is only in the Early Bronze Age that fortified settlements appear (Gilead 1988: 430). Excavation data is absent from the survey area and the determination of when multiple component sites actually became larger is unknown, i.e., during the Chalcolithic or Early Bronze Age. If the general Chalcolithic settlement pattern from the

Northern Negev area is applied here, there is a notable absence of a large Chalcolithic village that seems to characterize the Negev systems (Levy and Alon 1987). Most of the Chalcolithic and Chalcolithic/Early Bronze sites from the survey are represented by a few architectural features or a lithic scatter and are in close proximity to other Chalcolithic/Early Bronze sites.

The main site 'types' present are architectural feature sites (9), lithic scatters (9), and graves (3). Other 'types' are represented by one or fewer occurrences. Eight of the ten architectural sites are in the southern half of the survey region, all in the Ghuweib/Fidan area. Assuming that these features represent at least a semi-sedentary settlement system, the differences in site 'types' between the north and south areas of the survey may reflect seasonal settlement patterns, e.g., pastoralists, or resource differences. Median site size is 1200 m^2 and the largest sites are found in the southern area. A rank sum t-test indicates that there is no significant difference in site size between the north and south areas for this period. Sites are most often found on terraces (12) and plateaus (6) followed by slopes (2), plains (2), hills (1), and ridges (1). This landform preference is an extension of the pattern identified in the Chalcolithic but with an increase in the number of sites further away (plateaux, plains, hills) from the wadi beds.

Early Bronze

The Early Bronze (Table 19) is represented by seventeen lithic sites (12, 21, 35, 76, 78, 105, 108, 118, 119, 121, 124, 131, 141, 154D, 174, 194, 224) though this number probably underrepresents the total number of Early Bronze Age sites in the region for two reasons. First, because of the catchall Chalcolithic/Early Bronze category, some Early Bronze Age sites are likely to be in that middle group rather than the Early Bronze Age group because of 'fuzzy' or ambiguous temporal diagnostics. And second, a number of sites in the survey region contain Early Bronze Age ceramics but no lithics and have been omitted from this discussion. Only a few large Early Bronze Age sites excluded by these parameters will be mentioned as they pertain to the general settlement pattern of the area.

Settlement evidence spans the region from Wadi al-Hasa to Wadi Fidan but the area between the escarpment (Wadis Khuneizir and Nukhbar area) and Wadi Fidan is relatively empty of Early Bronze Age sites (Figure 5). Two Early Bronze Age sites in this area are situated in the Wadi Dahal region, one at the wadi mouth and the other along a minor drainage emptying into Wadi 'Arabah. The areas of the most intensive occupation are along Wadis al-Hasa, Feifa, Khuneizir, Nukhbar, and Fidan. Sites are still situated along wadi courses, though the trend of site location deeper, i.e., further east, into the wadis and further from the water course established in the Chalcolithic continues into the Early Bronze Age.

Examining the areas of intensive occupation, settlement along Wadi Fidan appears to have changed little in the Early Bronze Age from the earlier Neolithic and Chalcolithic pattern as sites are situated on or near previous sites. The continuity in site location may be due in part to the availability and transport of ore from the Wadi Feinan region (see Chalcolithic/Early Bronze). Continuity in the Chalcolithic settlement pattern is also apparent along Wadi Feifa as both the water course and inter-wadi plateaux are still utilized. New settlements along the Wadi Khuneizir/Nukhbar system appear during the Early Bronze Age, e.g., a large site (141) in the eastern hills. A number of smaller sites are present in this area but contain no lithic evidence and are dated according to the ceramic collections.

Possibly the most dramatic settlement development during the Early Bronze Age, in a broad context, is the appearance of large villages, some of which might approach 'urban' dimensions. Some larger sites are present within the survey area but confined to the Southern Ghors region of the survey area, i.e., not south of the Nukhbar. Large architectural sites, possibly fortified, are present in Wadi Khuneizir (108), Wadi Feifa (75 with an associated cemetery, 76)[5], and possibly Wadi al-Hasa where a large cemetery (2) is present but the settlement has not been located (possibly razed by construction). This regional confinement of larger sites roughly corresponds to the areas with the greatest density of Early Bronze sites, except for the Wadi Fidan region. In addition to these larger sites, further north are the Early Bronze sites of Numeira (Coogan 1984) and Bab al-Dhra' (Rast and Schaub 1978; 1980; 1981). The most frequent site 'types' for the Early Bronze Age lithic sites are graves (6), surface scatters (5), architectural features (3), wall alignments (2), and cemeteries (2). This departs from the patterns of Neolithic, Chalcolithic, and Chalcolithic/Early Bronze sites in which architectural features were the most numerous site 'type'. Several schemes may account for this change: (1) environmental change might require an adaptive strategy in which mobility is more productive than sedentism, thus more non-feature and small feature sites appear while architectural sites decline; (2) an economic change to full-fledged pastoralism from a semi-sedentary Chalcolithic strategy resulting in fewer architectural feature sites; and (3) an increase in sedentism in which semi-sedentary ways are abandoned and larger, long term sites appear, but are few in number, while small, activity specific sites increase, i.e., non-feature sites.

The Early Bronze site size median is 15,000 m^2 which is an enormous increase over the site sizes of the preceding periods. This figure may be misleading as many of these sites are diffuse scatters of material over the surface rather than compact, clusters of artifacts, and include a number of grave and cemetery sites rather than architectural sites. Terraces are still the most common areas of settlement (6), though plateaux (5), further from the wadis, are also utilized.

Summary

A summary of the various lithic periods along the lines of the variables used for the general settlement patterns reveals several trends. The horizontal or spatial location of lithic sites is confined to the extreme southern portion of the survey area during the early periods, e.g., Lower and Middle Palaeolithic. Only during the Neolithic and subsequent Chalcolithic and Early Bronze Age periods do site locations encompass the entire survey region from north to south. The vertical location/elevation of sites are tied to the spatial location given the effects of the Lisan Lake on area available for settlement, i.e., only above -160 m/-180 metres.

In terms of settlement site 'types', there appears to be an increase in the number of architectural feature sites from the Neolithic through the Chalcolithic/Early Bronze and then a dropoff in the Early Bronze Age (Figure 6). A similar pattern is observed for sites containing no surface features. While these general trends suggest a different settlement pattern/system during the Early Bronze Age, it should be stressed that the Chalcolithic/Early Bronze group is an arbitrary one that has no real temporal or cultural significance. Due to the absence of precise temporal indicators, the sites comprising the Chalcolithic/Early Bronze group could be Chalcolithic, Early Bronze Age or both. Among the other site 'types', cemeteries are fairly constant from Neolithic to the Early Bronze Age, as are sites with wall alignments. Graves are absent prior to the Chalcolithic/Early Bronze group and increase in frequency in the Early Bronze Age. The difference between grave and cemetery trends, rather than necessarily indicating different mortuary practices prior to the Chalcolithic/Early Bronze, may be a result of the cemeteries containing surface material representing the Neolithic through the Early Bronze Age which may or may not contain burials representative of this entire span. The presence of Neolithic material culture does not necessarily designate these as Neolithic cemeteries.

Table 20 Wilcoxen rank sum test results for site size between periods.

Pair	n	Z score	p-value *
Neolithic	6		
Chalcolithic	12	.46	.3192
Neolithic	6		
Chal/Early Bronze	23	1.29	.0985
Neolithic	6		
Early Bronze	17	.56	.2877
Chalcolithic	12		
Chal/Early Bronze	23	.74	.2266
Chalcolithic	12		
Early Bronze	17	1.66	.0485
Chal/Early Bronze	23		
Early Bronze	17	2.63	.0043

* p-values less than .05 are considered significant in this instance.

A comparison of site size through time indicates some differences. A visual representation of the site sizes by periods in the form of a box plot (Figure 7) shows that Chalcolithic and Chalcolithic/Early Bronze sites are very similar in size range while Neolithic sites are somewhat larger and Early Bronze Age sites are vastly larger. All four of these groups contain right tails (skewed) indicating a few larger values affecting the rest of the sample. This visual representation indicates some differences which can be further tested using a Wilcoxen rank sum test (Table 20). The results of this test (.05 level) indicate that site sizes for the Chalcolithic and Chalcolithic/Early Bronze are significantly smaller than Early Bronze Age site sizes. Neolithic site sizes, which visually appear to be different, were not significantly different from any of the groups when tested. Excluding the site 'types' represented by Early Bronze Age sites, e.g., graves, non-features, and architecture, this site size 'explosion' might be the product of an influx and agglomeration of people into the survey area during the Early Bronze Age resulting in larger sites, e.g., the beginning of 'urbanism'. Regional evidence supporting such an increase includes large Early Bronze Age sites Bab al-Dhra' (Rast and Schaub 1978; 1980; 1981), Numeira (Coogan 1984), SGNAS Sites 30, 75 (no lithics) and cemeteries (Bab al-Dhra' cemetery, SGNAS Sites 76, 141, and 2 (no lithics). Prior to the Early Bronze Age, 'very large' sites are rare, though the Neolithic boxplot suggests an earlier 'mini-explosion' in site size. Unfortunately, evidence of pre-Neolithic settlement, except for the two early sites, is highly equivocal.

The graphs of the landforms (Figure 8) on which sites occur through time show that terraces are the most desired location for settlement. During every period, more of the sites are situated on terraces along the wadis than anywhere else. This may reflect the importance or need to be near a reliable water source in this environment. Another trend, which seems to begin in the Chalcolithic and expand in the Early Bronze Age, is the use of plateaux, generally further from the water courses, for settlement. The sites of the Neolithic and earlier periods are generally closely tied to a water source. Given the incomplete record of the Holocene Palaeoenvironment and climate, the use of areas away from the wadis in the Early Bronze Age might correspond to a period of increasing moisture (Goldberg and Rosen 1987), but some other factor(s) may also be responsible. These could possibly include changing economic and adaptive strategies and population increases. Other areas of site location show less marked trends through time, though the use of hill sites shows a slight increase. Some of these patterns might be more clearly defined if those sites in the Chalcolithic/Early Bronze category were separable according to one period or the other.

Tentative diachronic model for the SGNAS

The following summarizes the preceding sections with an emphasis on the diachronic aspects of the

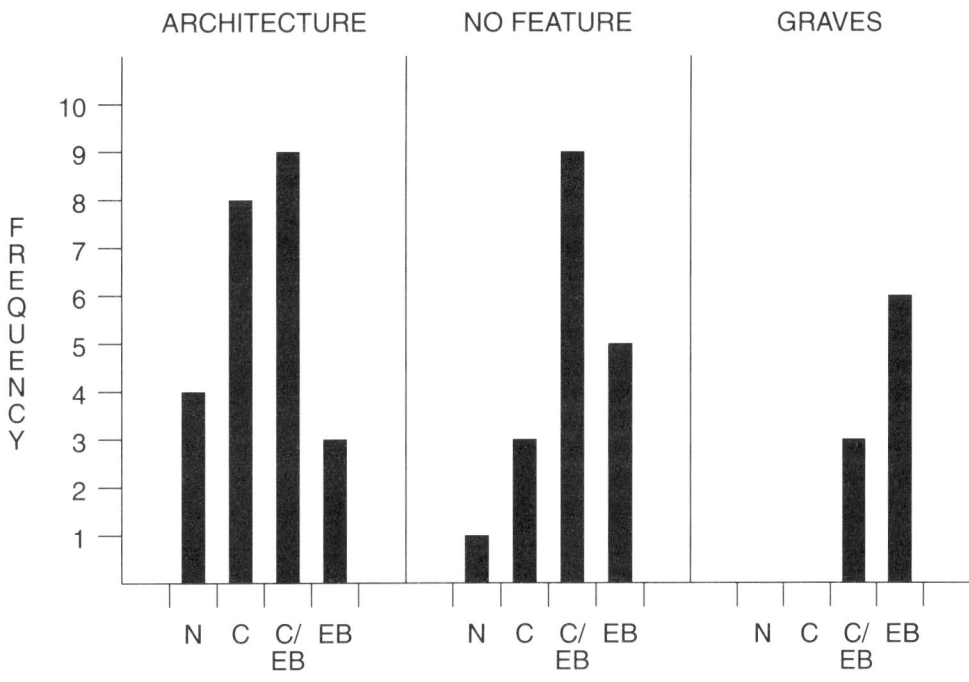

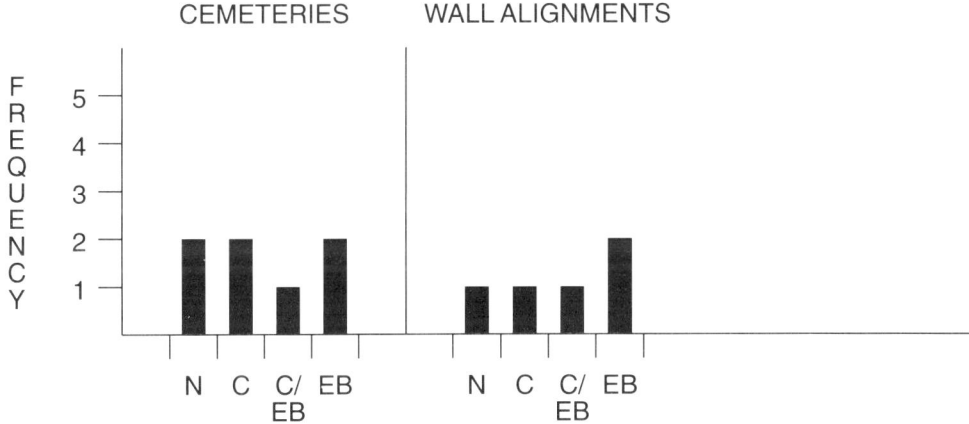

Figure 6 Histogram of site types by period.

prehistoric lithic periods in the Southern Ghors and Northeast 'Arabah. In constructing a diachronic model, evidence pertaining to settlement patterns, Palaeoenvironment, the Lisan Lake/Dead Sea, and the lithic samples are used. Each of the major culture-stratigraphic units is characterized based upon this evidence with tentative suggestions of possible 'causes' of changes through time. The tentative nature of this model is stressed given the patchy and coarse grained data from which it is derived.

Lower/Middle Palaeolithic

The Lower/Middle and Middle Palaeolithic are represented by two, possibly three sites, all in the southern extremity of the survey area with elevations ranging from -20 m to 0 metres. These are low density lithic scatters suggesting an ephemeral occupation during this time. The Lisan Lake, which occupied the

Dead Sea Basin and the Jordan Valley from ca. 70,000 BP to at least 16,000 BP (and probably later), probably limited the location of sites and activity during much of the Late Pleistocene. It is possible that sites from these periods were at one time found further north during periods of water level fluctuation but the recent maximumm of -160 m below sea level, ca. 20–16,000 BP and constant sediment deposition and erosion during the later phases has probably hidden any evidence of these occurrences.

Palaeoenvironmental evidence for this period has not been previously discussed due to the primary focus of this study on the Late Pleistocene/Early Holocene time frame. Data of this sort from Jordan is largely unavailable and must be extrapolated from elsewhere. For the coarse grained focus of this study, Clark's (1984) synopsis of the Negev Palaeoenvironment is used, based on Marks' (1976; 1977; 1983) work in the

Central Negev highlands. In gross temporal terms, the formation of the Lisan Lake, ca. 70,000 BP, roughly corresponds to a period of increased humidity, i.e., wet. From 65–45,000 BP, roughly the end of the Middle Palaeolithic, there is an apparent drying trend. The effect of this climatic episode in terms of human settlement may have been dramatic, especially in light of the present marginal environment. The areal extent of the Lisan Lake coupled with a less favorable (increasingly xeric) environment may have resulted in a sporadic settlement of the survey area. Additionally, environmental dynamics, such as erosion, associated with the drying trend, may have acted in a manner to destroy the integrity of Lower/Middle and Middle Palaeolithic deposits, especially sites located in the immediate vicinity of springs and wadis. The retouched pieces available are too few to offer any conclusions, but the absence of dense concentrations of Lower/Middle and Middle Palaeolithic lithics suggest a casual rather than intensive occupation in the area.

Upper Palaeolithic

Settlement during the Upper Palaeolithic, ca. 45–20,000 BP, is not found anywhere in the survey area. The absence of Upper Palaeolithic sites is unusual as other regional surveys have yielded some results in regard to this underrepresented period (MacDonald *et al.* 1983; Henry 1988; Garrard *et al.* 1985; 1988). Much of the area was still covered by the Lisan Lake during the Upper Palaeolithic and a brief humid interval, following the drying trend that began in the Middle Palaeolithic, may have increased the size of the Lisan Lake (see Clark [1984] for a summary of the climatic sequences used here). This type of lake level fluctuation may be partly responsible for the absence of Late Pleistocene sites. After a brief wet interval ca. 32–27,000 BP, the drying trend continued and accelerated until the latter part of the Epi-Palaeolithic. It is during the end of the Upper Palaeolithic/Early Epi-Palaeolithic that the Lisan Lake is believed to have reached its most recent maximum of -160 m below sea level. During this episode, the northern half of the survey region was under water as

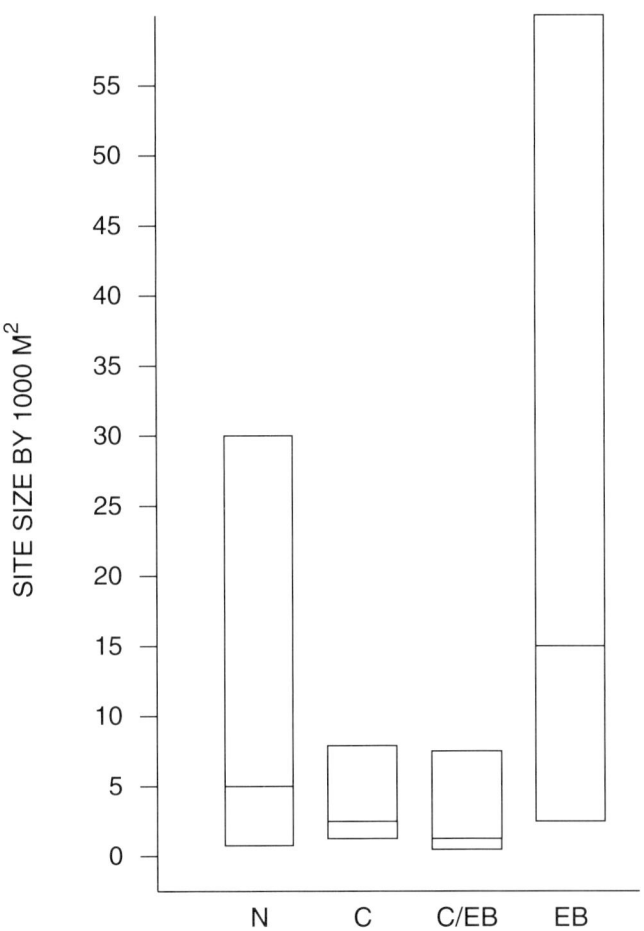

Figure 7   Boxplot of site size by period.

was a good portion of the southern half, especially the lower western reaches near Wadi 'Arabah.

Epi-Palaeolithic

The Epi-Palaeolithic and Natufian, beginning ca. 20,000 BP and lasting to ca. 10,500 BP, are also not represented in the lithic samples from the survey area. The drying trend at the end of the Upper Palaeolithic continues and appears to have reached its maximum ca. 16,000 BP roughly corresponding to the end of the Lisan Lake (Begin, Ehrlich, and Nathan 1974; Roberts 1982). This time period is characterized by the reduction in size of the Lisan Lake from its most recent maximum to the point in which separate lakes (Dead Sea, Lake Tiberias) were formed. The drying trend also appears to have resulted in renewed erosion which may be responsible for the absence of Upper Palaeolithic and Early Epi-Palaeolithic sites, not to mention later Middle Palaeolithic sites (Clark 1984). In a marginal environment such as this, the drying trend may have been magnified to the extent that extended human occupation was not feasible. The latter portions of the Epi-Palaeolithic through the Natufian are characterized by brief wet and dry intervals. The absence of sites from the Late Epi-Palaeolithc and Natufian in the survey area is puzzling as the climatic episodes, at least periodically, favor movement into more marginal zones. This sort of movement can be seen by the distribution of sites on a regional level for the Southern Levant during the Epi-

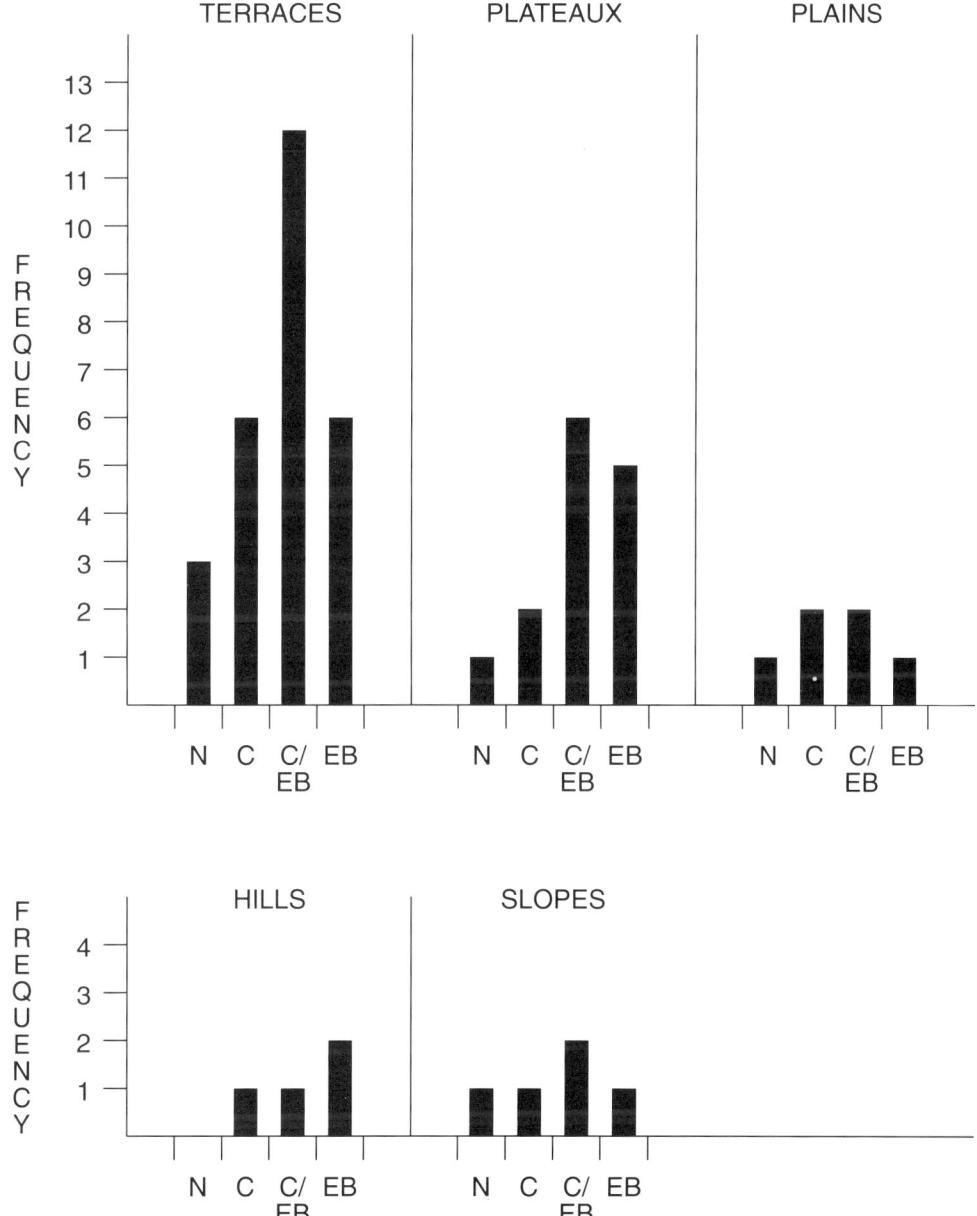

Figure 8   Histogram of site locations by period.

Palaeolithic (Goldberg and Bar-Yosef 1982; Olszewski 1986). It is suggested that this absence in the SGNAS area is due to the Lisan Lake. In the Lower Jordan Valley, Schuldenrein and Goldberg (1981) found that sites pre-dating 13–12,000 BP are all above -180 m, the recent maximum, suggesting that the termination of the Lisan Lake occurred later than the 18–16,000 BP date that has been widely accepted. Also, Edwards *et al.* (1988) suggest a late termination (ca. 12,000 BP) of the lake from their work in the Wadi al-Hammah. If the termination of the Lisan Lake can be pushed forward to this date, 13–12,000 BP, then the absence of Epi-Palaeolithic sites may be the result of the lake levels rather than other environmental factors. Uncertain, are any residual effects of the Lisan Lake in terms of subsistence potentials, i.e., whether plants and animals could relatively rapidly recolonize the newly exposed marls.

Palaeoenvironmental data from the Late Natufian in the Southern Levant indicates a drying trend which may have lasted into the Early Neolithic (PPNA). At some point during the Early Neolithic (PPNA to PPNB) there appears to be an amelioration of the climate, the length of which seems to vary regionally. Some of the environmental variability may depend upon the data from which it is derived, i.e., different sorts of data yield different results. Neev and Emery (1967), using the Lisan Lake sediments, place this wetter period between 10,000 and 6500 BP (roughly the entire Neolithic period) while Henry (1986), in a more regional overview suggests this wet phase was shorter in duration from ca. 9000–8500 BP. As discussed elsewhere, the different kinds of Palaeoenvironmental data are often at odds with one another (Neeley 1989). The unevenness of this data is greatly magnified when applied to the Southern Ghors and Northeast 'Arabah area where independent information of this sort is not available.

Neolithic

Neolithic settlement in the survey territory, represented by nine sites, is concentrated in two areas, one within the Southern Ghors and the other at the southern extremity of the territory. The sites in the Ghors proper are the earliest evidence of human occupation in this area. The lowest elevation of a Neolithic site, ca. -300 m below sea level, indicates that the Dead Sea was below this level sometime between ca. 10,000–6,000 BP. Unless Dead Sea levels were much lower prior to this wet Neolithic phase, rising sea levels probably had little effect on settlement in the Southern Ghors from the Neolithic to the present. The effect of the Dead Sea during the later periods is markedly different than the span from the Middle Palaeolithic through the Early Epi-Palaeolithic when settlement in the Southern Ghors and part of the Northeast 'Arabah was removed or impossible because of high or fluctuating lake levels.

The small number of sites from the Neolithic suggest that the regional settlement density was low. The southern sites (Wadi Fidan) indicate fairly intensive occupations, based upon amount of surface lithic material[6], while the northern sites (Wadi Feifa), except for Dhra', contain far less surface material. The retouched pieces include tool types that may indicate function as it applies to economic activity, e.g., projectile points and sickle blades, or other functions, e.g., axes/adzes for woodworking. Projectile points are found in both the north and south areas indicating the economic importance of hunting. No unequivocal Neolithic sickle blades were recovered, so the reaping/cutting of plants is unknown. The presence of a few axes/adzes suggest a more wooded environment during the Neolithic than that of the present. This is also tentatively supported by the Palaeoenvironmental data indicating a wet Neolithic. The location of sites on or near wadi beds and springs stress the importance of this resource. These areas may also have been richer environmental niches with more Mediterranean vegetation and fauna than those of the surrounding areas. This is certainly the case in the area today as the springs are characterized by dense vegetation while the surrounding areas are literally devoid of vegetation.

Chalcolithic

The Chalcolithic spans the time period from ca. 6000–5200/5000 BP. Like the preceding Neolithic, Palaeoenvironmental data is somewhat conflicting according to the region and the data used. A drying trend encompassing the Late Neolithic/Early Chalcolithic is suggested by Goldberg and Rosen (1987), Danin (1985), and Neev and Emery (1967) while Horowitz (1979), Goldberg and Bar-Yosef (1982), Schuldenrein and Goldberg (1981), and Tsukada (in Bottema and Van Zeist 1981) see a Late Neolithic/Early Chalcolithic moist phase which dries out at the end of the Chalcolithic. These interpretations represent different types of data and different geographic zones. The contradictory nature of Palaeoenvironment data is recognized by Gilead (1988: 407–8) and only when more regional Holocene data is collected can some of these inconsistencies be resolved.

The Chalcolithic sites increase in number over the Neolithic and different areas within the survey region are occupied at this time. This pattern is a departure from the Neolithic, in which sites are concentrated in two wadis. The location of sites away from wadi courses also differs from the previous Neolithic pattern. This might indicate the greater availability of water, e.g., moister climate than the Neolithic, some form of water control, or site location nearer some other resource at the expense of the wadi resources. Site size for the Chalcolithic is smaller than the previous Neolithic (though the Neolithic sample is small and possibly biased by later occupations) and may represent smaller sized groups.

Economic/subsistence evidence consists of sickle blades and axes/adzes. Projectile points are absent suggesting a decrease in the emphasis on hunting. The number of architectural features suggests some degree of sedentism, possibly including some agricultural

Years BP	Period	Settlement Location	Climate[1]	Lisan Lake[2]	Size	No.
3900	Early Bronze Age	on wadis and plateau, less architecture, more sites in the north half	dry? wet	probably no effect	larger than 15,000m^2	18
5200/5000	Chalcolithic	on wadis and plateau, more architecture, more spread out	wet dry	little effect	smaller than 2500m^2	14
6000	Neolithic	in wadis Feifa and Fidan	dry wet	receding, sites as low as -300m	fairly large, Median 5000m^2	9
10,500	Natufian	no sites	dry wet	shrinking	–	0
12,500	Epi-Palaeolithic	no sites	dry wet (erosion) dry	termination of lake ca. 13,000 BP, no sites below -180m in Lower Jordan Valley	–	0
20,000	Upper Palaeolithic	no sites	dry wet dry	possible recent maximum of -180m increase in size shrinking	–	
45,000 65,000	Middle Palaeolithic	near wadis in the south (Wadi Fidan)	dry (erosion)	shrinking or fluctuating levels	diffuse	2–3
70,000	Middle Palaeolithic	?	wet	probably high levels formation of the Lisan Lake	–	?

Table 21 Summary of the Diachronic model for the SGNAS.

activities (based on the presence of sickles). If sickle blades are indicators of agriculture, which of course may or may not be true, then an increase in the amount of water would be necessary for successful agriculture. Currently in this area, the natural flow of water is sporadic requiring some form of water control for agriculture. Based on this present situation, Chalcolithic agriculture may have benefitted from conditions wetter than the present or utilized some form of water control. At this time the effects of the Dead Sea on settlement are likely to be minimal.

Early Bronze Age

The Early Bronze Age, from ca. 5200–3900 BP, is characterized by a climatic drying trend, though the earlier portion may include a wet carryover from the Chalcolithic (Horowitz 1979; Goldberg and Rosen 1987; Neev and Emery 1967). The change to a drier climate probably affected adaptations to this marginal environment.

The settlement pattern evidence indicates an increase in Early Bronze Age sites over Chalcolithic ones (excluding the undifferentiated Chalcolithic /Early Bronze sites). The trend for site location to be further from wadi courses continues as sites away from the wadis are almost equal in frequency to those associated with them. There is also, however, a great increase in mean site size when the Early Bronze Age is compared to the Chalcolithic. Whether this 'population explosion' (assuming increased site size equals more people) is the result of an increasingly favorable environment during the Early Bronze Age, increased use of water control devices, e.g.,

aqueducts, or some combination of these and other factors is uncertain given the coarseness of the available data. Spatially, Early Bronze Age settlement appears to be more dense in the Ghors region than on the 'Arabah plain further south. This settlement pattern represents a shift from the previous periods when settlement was densest in the southern region. Settlement in the Ghors may be a result of the large Early Bronze Age sites present, e.g., Bab al-Dhra', Numeira, and Sites 75, 108, and 141, whose counterparts in the south are largely absent, though some of the Early Bronze Age sites in the Wadi Fidan area may be comparable in size.

During the Early Bronze Age, several of the diagnostic tool types disappear, probably replaced by metal functional counterparts. Absent from Early Bronze Age assemblages are projectile points, a trend noted by Rosen (1987), and celts (Hanbury-Tenison 1986). Sickle blades, in the traditional Early Bronze Age sense, e.g., Canaanean sickle blades, are absent which suggests a decline in reaping activities from the Chalcolithic. However, this conclusion may be somewhat misleading of Early Bronze Age subsistence in the SGNAS area as only one Early Bronze Age lithic site with >50 pieces has been identified. The presence of large Early Bronze Age sites within the SGNAS area and to the north certainly suggest that some form of large scale subsistence activity was necessary to support these large settlements.

Summary

The above information is summarized in Table 21. The most dominating factor effecting settlement in the survey region during the Late Pleistocene appears to be the Lisan Lake. Added to the effect of the lake may have been the periodic dry spells which, while reducing the lake levels, may have made this environment somewhat inhospitable. Subsequent rising levels associated with wetter periods may have obscured earlier occupations. The temporal placement of the most recent lake level maximum, -180 m/-160 m is uncertain. Neev and Emery (1967) place this maximum ca. 20,000 BP, Begin *et al.* (1974) suggest a later date, ca. 18–16,000 BP, and archaeological evidence from the Lower Jordan Valley (Schuldenrein and Goldberg 1981) and Wadi al-Hammah (Edwards *et al.* 1988) suggest high levels as late as 13–12,000 BP. Based on the archaeological evidence at hand, a later termination is suspected.

The best evidence for regional settlement in the survey territory comes from the Holocene in the form of Neolithic sites. Several settlement trends are apparent beginning in the Neolithic and extending into the Early Bronze Age. First, is the spread of sites over the survey area. Confined to a few core areas during the Neolithic, more areas are represented in the Chalcolithic and Early Bronze Age. Second, site location exhibits a change from being 'tied' to wadi courses to being situated further away on the plateaux and interfluves. Third, median site size decreases from the Neolithic to the Chalcolithic but then makes a significant leap during the Early Bronze Age. Fourth, the number of sites per period increases steadily through time. And fifth, general spatial trends indicate the southern portion of the survey was favored during the Middle Palaeolithic, Neolithic, and Chalcolithic, but in the Early Bronze Age settlement appears to be more concentrated in the north.

The tentative nature of the diachronic model is intended to suggest trends or patterns observed from the data. The coarseness of the data prevents any of the statements from being in any way definitive. The absence of previous research in this area of Jordan requires that certain assumptions be made in order to reach any conclusions. The aim of this model is to provide a general framework against which other models/hypotheses pertaining to this area can be tested. It is only through the acceptance, modification, or rejection of these tentative conclusions by other work that the relationship of the SGNAS with the rest of the Southern Levant can be established.

Other regional surveys

The preceding sections, with the exception of the lithic characterization by period, have been oriented toward the SGNAS area without placing the results in any sort of larger pan-Jordanian context. Comparison of the SGNAS results with other areas is important for understanding the prehistoric relationship of this area with other areas. As a result of the recent number of

systematic surveys in Jordan, four surveys from around the country are available for comparison. They are the Azraq Basin (Garrard *et al.* 1985; 1988), the Black Desert (Betts 1988), the Hisma region (Henry 1988), and Wadi al-Hasa (MacDonald *et al.* 1983; Coinman *et al.* 1986; Clark *et al.* 1988). Each of these surveys will be summarized in terms of the culture history, settlement pattern trends, and Palaeoenvironment. The information available for each of these aspects is variable so comparisons will proceed at a very elementary level.

Azraq Basin

The Azraq Basin survey results (Garrard *et al.* 1985; 1988) indicate a prehistoric presence in the area from the Lower Palaeolithic through the Neolithic. The periods represented by the most number of sites are the Epi-Palaeolithic and Neolithic. Upper Palaeolithic sites are rare and the Lower and Middle Palaeolithic sites consist primarily of derived materials (Garrard *et al.* 1988: 333). In terms of settlement location, sites appear to be located along the wadis leading into the basin during the Lower and Middle Palaeolithic. In contrast, site settlement during the Epi-Palaeolithic and Neolithic is concentrated near springs and basalt outcrops as well as along the wadis. Palaeoenvironmental evidence indicates a wetter period between ca. 23–15,000 BP possibly corresponding to the maximum levels of the Azraq Lake which subsided during the drier periods following 15,000 BP.

The Black Desert

Settlement evidence in the Black Desert area is not continuous (Betts 1988). Lower Palaeolithic and Upper Palaeolithic sites are not present and the Middle Palaeolithic evidence is largely from derived contexts. Epi-Palaeolithic sites include some Early Epi-Palaeolithic scatters and Natufian occupations. The Neolithic is represented by numerous PPNB sites and several Pottery Neolithic locales. Settlement pattern information indicates Middle Palaeolithic sites are situated near the open gravel plains and hills. Epi-Palaeolithic sites are found in the vicinity of hills in the basalt hammada and near a source of water (Betts 1988: 389). Neolithic sites also tend to be situated near hills in the basalt hammada but not necessarily near a water source. The 'burin sites' (PPNB?) are situated near the open country along the gravel plains, i.e., not in the basalt hammada. Settlement, in general, is most evident in the western area around the edge of the basalt hammada and along wadis and mudflats. These western sites also tend to be larger in size than sites in the basalt hammada to the east (Betts 1988: 389). A Palaeoenvironmental reconstruction is not presented but the absence of sites from the Lower Palaeolithic and Upper Palaeolithic might be related to a less favorable environment during these periods. Dry conditions may have persisted during at least the latter part of the Middle Palaeolithic as sites are found in the gravel plains to the west rather than in the basalt hammada. A climatic amelioration may coincide with the Epi-Palaeolithic and PPNB as there are more sites for these periods. The general similarity of species exploited at a few Epi-Palaeolithic and Neolithic sites, e.g., gazelle, sheep/goat, hare, suggest some continuity in environmental conditions during these periods.

Hisma Region

The survey results for this region indicate the presence of sites from the Lower Palaeolithic through the Chalcolithic (Henry 1988). The most frequent sites are Epi-Palaeolithic and Chalcolithic while Upper Palaeolithic and Neolithic occurences are less frequent. The settlement evidence indicates that during the Middle, Upper, and early Epi-Palaeolithic, sites at lower elevations, i.e., ca. below 1000 m, are larger and possibly represent winter encampments. Sites above 1000 m are smaller, possibly more specialized, and relate to summer occupations. This settlement system changes during the Natufian and Chalcolithic when the higher elevation sites are larger with deeper deposits and the lower sites are smaller and less intensively occupied. The Palaeoenvironmental sequence indicates a drying trend during the late Middle Palaeolithic and a change from slightly more humid conditions to a drier episode in the Late Upper Palaeolithic (these are similar to the Negev trends summarized in Clark (1984). The Epi-Palaeolithic is characterized by succeeding intervals of wet and dry culminating with a drying trend in the Late Natufian. Data for the Neolithic is unavailable and the later Chalcolithic appears to be similar to today's dry climate.

Wadi al-Hasa

Settlement evidence from Wadi al-Hasa indicates sites dating from the Lower Palaeolithic through the Early Bronze Age and beyond (MacDonald *et al.* 1983; MacDonald *et al.* 1988; Coinman, Clark, and Lindly 1986; Clark *et al.* 1988). The prehistoric settlement of the Wadi al-Hasa area is addressed by Coinman, Clark, and Lindly (1986) and these results are briefly recapitulated. Examining the variables of site size and elevation through time, sites from the Middle Palaeolithic, Upper Palaeolithic, Upper Palaeolithic/Epi-Palaeolithic combined samples, and PPN exhibit some similarity as they are fairly small in size and located at medium to high elevations (Coinman, Clark, and Lindly 1986: 163). Differences are noted for the Lower/Middle Palaeolithic combined sample, where more larger sites are found at medium elevations, the Middle/Upper Palaeolithic combined sample, where smaller sites range from low to high elevations, and the Epi-Palaeolithic/PPN combined sample, where small sites are clustered at high elevations. These patterns are compared to idealized models of circulating and radiating settlement patterns. Except for the Lower/Middle Palaeolithic, marked site size differentiation, which is characteristic of a radiating system, is not present suggesting that a circulating settlement system was in use most of the time (see also Clark 1992).

The settlement patterns for the later periods, i.e., Pottery Neolithic through Early Bronze, are treated by MacDonald (1988a, b) and breakdown as follows. Pottery Neolithic sites are relatively few in number and with a few exceptions, situated in close proximity to a source of water, i.e., near the wadi beds. Chalcolithic sites are slightly more numerous and in addition to sites being situated down near the wadi beds, they are also located higher up on the surrounding ridges and plateaux. The Early Bronze Age settlement is characterized by a sedentary occupation, i.e., dense concentration of material, in the western portion of Wadi al-Hasa while the eastern portion, with more ephemeral sites, is believed to represent a mobile/pastoral settlement system (MacDonald 1988b: 166).

The Palaeoenvironmental evidence for Wadi al-Hasa, like much of the Levant contains some conflicting interpretations. Donahue and Beynon (1988) suggest a humid interval from ca. 65–16,000 BP, a drying out until 12,000 BP when another humid interval begins lasting until 8000 BP. This interval is followed by a short dry period 8000–6500 BP after which more humid conditions persist until 5500 BP (Donahue and Beynon 1988: 35). Associated with the more humid intervals is the aggradation (filling up) of the wadi channels and terraces. In contrast to this interpretation is that of Clark *et al.* (1988) in which following a 'climatic optimum' in the Early Middle Palaeolithic, conditions generally dry out during the late Middle Palaeolithic and Upper Palaeolithic with the dry peak ca. 16,000 BP. This is essentially compatible with Clark's (1984) synopsis of the Negev sequence. Part of the difference may be the point of reference for these interpretations. Following Goldberg (1981) and Horowitz (1979), Clark *et al.* (1988) suggest the Middle Palaeolithic and Upper Palaeolithic are dry intervals, yet they also note that it still was probably moister than the present conditions.

Comparison with the SGNAS

Comparing the culture history of these four surveys with the SGNAS, nearly all of them contain sites representative of the periods from the Lower Palaeolithic through the Neolithic, Chalcolithic, or Early Bronze Age (the cut off point depends on the goals of the project). Only the Black Desert Survey (Betts 1988) is lacking in Lower and Upper Palaeolithic sites. The SGNAS, to date, is represented by Lower/Middle Palaeolithic combined sites, Middle Palaeolithic, Neolithic and later period sites but lacks Epi-Palaeolithic sites which are represented in moderate to high frequencies in these other areas. The scarcity of Palaeolithic sites in the SGNAS in comparison to these other areas strongly suggests some factor(s) involved in the absence or disappearance of these sites. One of the most likely reasons for a lack of Palaeolithic settlement is that large portions of the SGNAS area were covered by the transgressive phases of the Lisan Lake. The only Palaeolithic evidence to date comes from the southern tip of the area where the lake was least likely to extend. Some of the other survey areas, e.g., Azraq, Wadi al-Hasa, appear to have contained Pleistocene lakes as well but these were freshwater or slightly alkaline bodies which likely would enhance settlement due to the richer environment, unlike the hypersaline Lisan Lake.

Settlement patterns for the various prehistoric periods are of limited comparability with the SGNAS as most of these other surveys stop at the Neolithic or Chalcolithic. The SGNAS, on the other hand, contains very few Palaeolithic occurrences and essentially begins with the Neolithic. The SGNAS Lower/Middle Palaeolithic combined sites are situated in close proximity to a wadi which is likely to be the most diverse environment. Middle Palaeolithic sites from the Azraq Basin (Garrard *et al.* 1985; 1988) and the Black Desert (Betts 1988) are similarly located along wadis (Azraq Basin) or the open plains of the Black Desert. The placement of these assemblages as either Early or Late Middle Palaeolithic is uncertain, but the drying trend of the Late Middle Palaeolithic may have made settlement near water sources more important. The Upper Palaeolithic and Epi-Palaeolithic settlement patterns for the SGNAS are unknown and the other areas will not be summarized for these periods.

Neolithic sites in the SGNAS basically are tethered to a secure source of water. This pattern is also duplicated for the Pottery Neolithic in Wadi al-Hasa (MacDonald 1988a). Neolithic settlement in the Black Desert and Azraq Basin are slightly different. In the Black Desert, sites are found in the basalt hammada away from sources of water (Betts 1988). Similarly, Neolithic sites in the Azraq Basin, while still apparently closely tied to water, are found in a wider variety of areas than the Palaeolithic sites. It is suggested that during the Neolithic (possibly Late Neolithic) larger settlements in Wadi al-Hasa, Azraq Basin, and SGNAS were constrained to reliable water sources. The location near water during this time may also reflect a need of water for subsistence activities as some of the Azraq sites show evidence of domesticated grains and possible water channelling (Garrard *et al.* 1988: 334). The Black Desert Neolithic, possibly associated with 'kite' sites, i.e., wall lines, hunting traps, may reflect a different kind of adaptation. This dichotomy in Neolithic site location may reflect the relative importance of nomadic pastoralists and foragers, on the one hand, and more sedentary agriculturalists, on the other.

The Chalcolithic settlement patterns in the SGNAS area indicate a general decrease in site size with site location more variable as areas away from the wadi beds are more utilized. Wadi al-Hasa Chalcolithic sites mirror this pattern as they too are located at greater distances from the wadi courses (MacDonald 1988a). Whether this different settlement pattern represents a different adaptation, e.g., pastoralism, or is the result of environmental change, e.g., wetter

Palaeoenvironments, is not certain. In the Hisma region, Henry (1988) suggests that in such an arid region, the settlement pattern of intensively exploiting the higher elevations is indicative of pastoralism. The testing of this proposition in the SGNAS region is not possible given the lack of marked elevational differences in the region associated with different environmental zones. More plausible would be a comparison with Chalcolithic sites in the mountains to the east.

The Early Bronze Age settlement in the SGNAS continues the pattern of site location away from the wadis and in addition to an increase in the number of sites and site size, the concentration of sites shifts to the northern region, the Southern Ghors. Early Bronze Age settlement in the Wadi al-Hasa area is dichotomized into a sedentary west and mobile/pastoral east (MacDonald 1988b). A certain amount of sedentism in the Ghors is evident by the large Early Bronze Age villages (e.g., Bab al-Dhra' and Numeira), but the numerous non-architectural sites may also indicate a less sedentary population. Although no temporal control is available, the difference in sedentary and mobile sites may reflect the variations within a single adaptation to this environment. It is generally believed that the Early Bronze Age (I–II) was a period of early proto-urban centers which developed during a relatively unstable interval and the later Early Bronze Age, which saw a decline in these centers corresponding to the dry period.

The Palaeoenvironmental sequences for the Hisma (Henry 1988), Wadi al-Hasa (Clark 1984), and the SGNAS are essentially the same. The Black Desert Palaeoenvironment is currently unknown. In the Azraq Basin (Garrard *et al.* 1988) the available evidence suggests a wet period ca. 23–15,000 BP which is generally considered a dry period in the other areas. This may indicate a different environmental history for the eastern part of Jordan than the west. The extrapolation of the western Palaeoenvironmental data may be inappropriate as a result.

The comparison of the SGNAS with other survey areas has attempted to point out some basic similarities and differences. In the absence of fine grained and equally comparable data, this has resulted in a descriptive overview rather than an in depth study of the survey areas. The aim of the descriptive comparison is to provide a first approximation of patterns for these areas and to see how the SGNAS area 'fits in' with them. Future area surveys may benefit by stressing the recovery of Palaeoenvironmental data and the isolation of settlement systems in an attempt to better understand regional adaptive strategies.

Notes

[1] Percentages of different arrowhead types form the basis of the Neolithic temporal divisions for this diagnostic, see Bar-Yosef 1981; Burian and Friedman 1979.

2   The SGNAS found Early Bronze Age ceramics at Site 12.

3   Site 87 and 185 also contain surface architecture.

4   The area around Dhra' was not surveyed and information pertaining to the settlement patterns of that area is unavailable.

5   Recent excavations in December 1989–January 1990 at Site 75 have indicated that this dates to the Iron II and not the Early Bronze Age (see Rast and Schaub, forthcoming). There is also a strong possibility that Site 108, designated as Early Bronze Age, may also be Iron Age with a scattering of Early Bronze Age IV tombs (MacDonald, personal communication).

6   The intensity of occupation includes later and possibly earlier material as well.

5. Pottery Neolithic–Chalcolithic / Early Bronze Period Sites

by B. MacDonald

Introduction

This chapter will treat the Pottery Neolithic, Neolithic–Chalcolithic, Chalcolithic, and Chalcolithic /Early Bronze Period sites. The presentation will follow a time-stratigraphic sequence. The sites for each period will be studied, for the most part, in a north to south direction. Some of the sites treated in this chapter are ones which Neeley, in the previous chapter, has studied as lithic period sites since they yielded both lithics and sherds.

Pottery Neolithic

The SGNAS collected Neolithic sherds at six sites, namely, Sites 21; 29; 75; 76; 92; and 95 (Table 22) (Figure 9). Four of these sites, namely, Sites 75; 76; 92; and 95, are located in the Wadi Feifa region. The remaining two, namely, Sites 21 and 29, are located along the south and north sides of Wadi Fidan respectively.

Among the drawn sherds, Kenyon and Holland (1982) designate several of them as either Pottery Neolithic A or B. Kafafi (1982), however, calls some of the same sherds Late Neolithic 2–beginning of Chalcolithic. Sites 75 and 76, the western and eastern segments respectively of ancient Feifa, are generally associated with the Early Bronze Period (Rast and Schaub 1974; Frolich and Lancaster 1985). However, sherds from earlier (and later) periods are also present at the sites.

Sites 75 yielded a small number of Neolithic sherds. Site 76, the eastern and/or cemetery segment of the site, yielded Neolithic Period sherds from two separate areas, namely, from the southern ridge and from the area of a robbed tomb located ca. 100 m west of what is believed to have been a tower at the southeastern extremity of the site. Sites 75 and 76 will be treated in more detail in relation to the Early Bronze Period sites of the survey.

Site 92, which consists of a heavy sherd and light lithic scatter in a plowed field just south of Wadi Feifa and immediately east of the main Mazra'a–'Aqaba Highway, is located ca. 1 km to the southeast of the two previously-discussed sites. There are small piles of stones in the area where the SGNAS collected the artifacts. These stone piles could be the site of an ancient cemetery or more recent field clearance. Plowing has probably destroyed a large portion of the site. Recent (1987–89) construction of a school, houses, and an army camp in the area has probably caused further disturbance to the site.

Site 95, which also consists of a sherd and lithic scatter, may have been one with Site 92 in antiquity. It is located in a gravely area immediately to the northeast of Site 92. There were signs of bulldozing activity in the area at the time of the SGNAS's 1986 visit. Moreover, since the SGNAS's 1986 visit to the site, it, like Site 92, has been further disturbed and possibly obliterated by building activity. Both Sites 92 and 95 will be returned to in the discussion of the Neolithic–Chalcolithic and Chalcolithic/Early Bronze Period sites respectively.

Site 21 is a low density sherd scatter located in what maybe ancient agricultural fields along the south side of Wadi Fidan. There appears to be retaining and/or terrace walls along with remnants of an aqueduct associated with the fields. What may be the remnants of water dams are present in a small side wadi coming from the south. It is impossible to say, based on the available evidence, whether or not all these features are contemporaneous.

Sites 21, 29, 75, 76, 92, and 95 will appear more impressive when seen in relationship to the other periods discussed in this chapter. They are all located where Neolithic–Chalcolithic, Chalcolithic, and/or Chalcolithic/Early Bronze sites are present.

Pottery Neolithic–Chalcolithic Period Sites

The SGNAS collected Pottery Neolithic–Chalcolithic sherds at seven sites, namely, Sites 29; 75; 76; 92; 134; 177; and 182 (Table 23) (Figure 9). We have discussed four of these sites, namely, Sites 29; 75; 76; and 92, in relation to the Pottery Neolithic Period sites.

The pottery from these sites falls somewhere in the Neolithic through Chalcolithic Periods. The SGNAS follows Kafafi's (1982) dating for most of the drawn sherds (Table 23).

The SGNAS collected a large number (52) of sherds from this period in association with an enclosure, Site 177, high in the mountains to the east of the Southern Ghors between Wadis Madsus al-Shamali and Umm

Table 22: Pottery Neolithic Period sites

Site No.	Sample No.	No. of Sherds	Plate No (if any)
21	71	2	
29	73	1	6 (1)
75	117	3	7 (2;3)
76	119	4	8 (1)
76	129	31	
76	228	8	9 (4)
92	137	4	10 (1;8)
95	146	1	

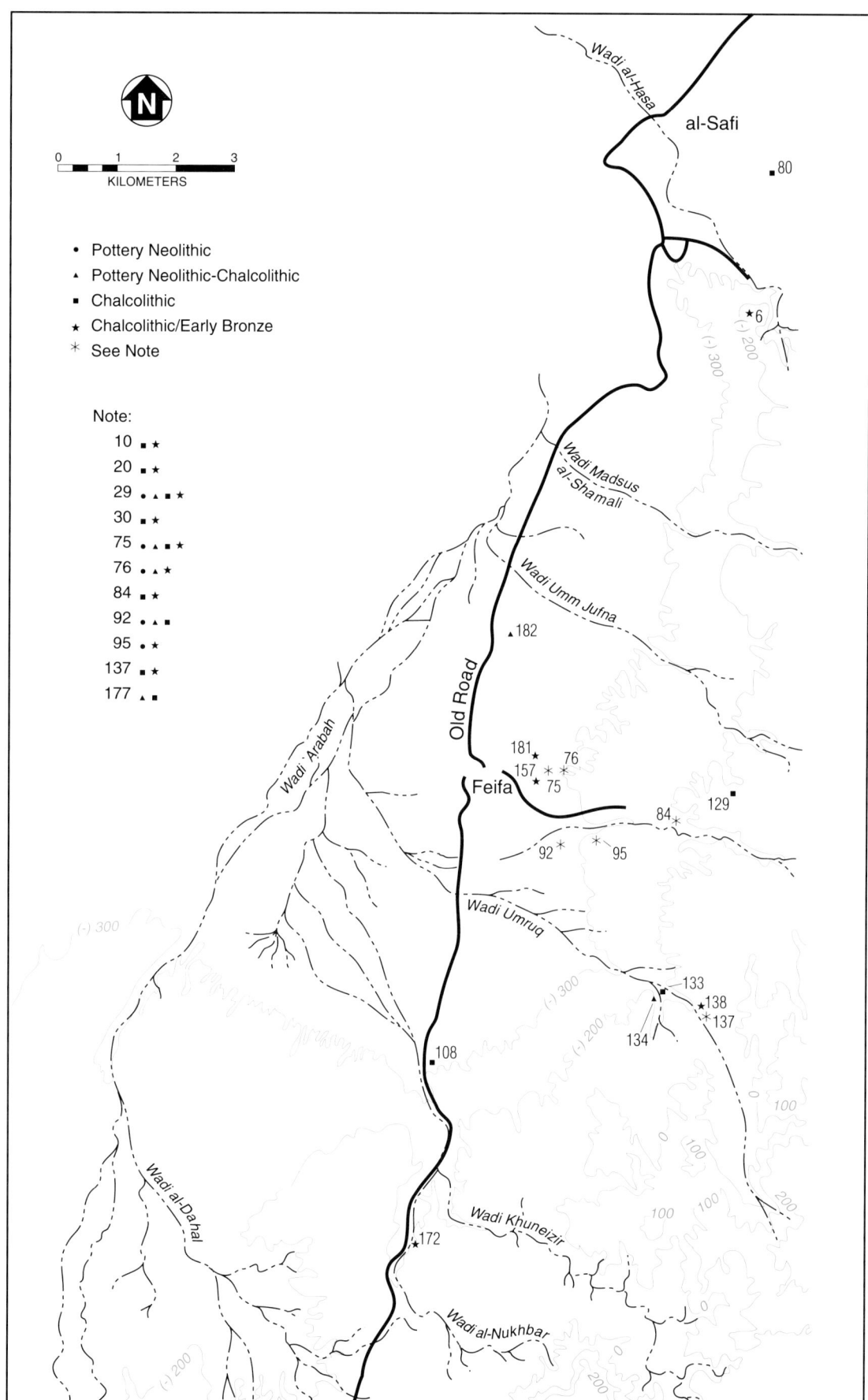

Figure 9 Pottery Neolithic, Neolithic–Chalcolithic, Chalcolithic, and Chalcolithic/Early Bronze settlement pattern map (Northern portion).

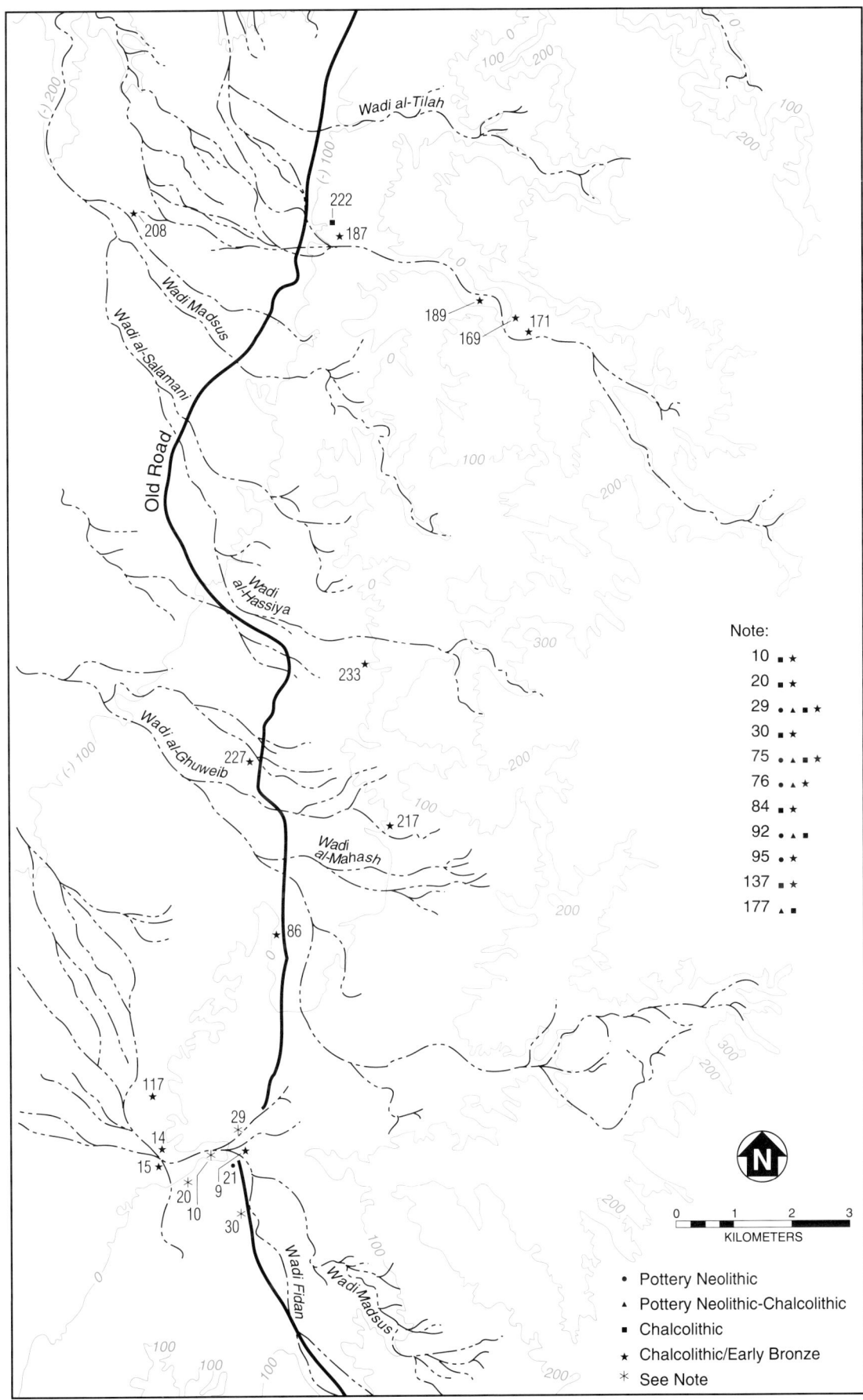

Figure 9 Pottery Neolithic, Neolithic–Chalcolithic, Chalcolithic, and Chalcolithic/Early Bronze settlement pattern map (Southern portion).

Table 23   Pottery Neolithic–Chalcolithic Period Sites

Site No.	Sample No.	No. of Sherds	Plate No. (if any)
29	74	1	6 (4)
75	116	1	7 (4)
75	117	1	7 (1)
76	119	2	8 (2;3)
76	128	12	
92	137	69	9 (3;7)
134	232	13	
177	309	52	
182	285	9	

Jufna. The enclosure, which measures ca. 15 x 15 m, is typical of such sites found throughout the survey area. Neolithic Chalcolithic sherds were the only ones which the SGNAS found in association with the enclosure. Further surveying in the mountains to the east of the Southern Ghors would undoubtedly lead to the discovery of more sites from the periods under discussion. However, as noted in Chapter 2, surveying in this area would require serious logistic preparation plus the expenditure of a great deal of both time and energy.

Site 182 is a sherd scatter in a sandy area to the northwest of Sites 75 and 76. It is located to the west of the main Mazra'a–'Aqaba Highway.

The SGNAS collected a small number (2) of Neolithic Chalcolithic sherds from the southern ridge of Site 76. This is the same area from which it collected Neolithic Period sherds. Moreover, it collected 12 body and base sherds of this period from the northern segment of the same site.

As mentioned previously in relation to the Neolithic Period sites, Site 92 is a sherd and lithic scatter in a plowed field. The SGNAS also collected a large number (69) of Neolithic Chalcolithic sherds at the same site.

Site 134 is a poorly preserved enclosure which measures ca. 8 x 5 metres. It is located on a plateau on the south side of Wadi Umruq.

Chalcolithic Period

The SGNAS collected Chalcolithic Period sherds at fourteen sites, namely, Sites 10; 20; 29; 30; 75; 80; 84; 92; 108;129; 133; 137; 177; and 222 (Table 24) (Figure 9). At the majority of these sites, however, the density of Chalcolithic sherds collected was low (n=1–3). Several of these sites, namely, Sites 29; 75; 92; and 177, are also listed as Pottery Neolithic Chalcolithic Period sites.

Site 80 appears to be a camp-site in a cleared area on the west-facing slope to the east of the modern village of al-Safi. The cleared area measures ca. 22 x 5–6 metres. Chalcolithic Period pottery was the only identifiable pottery which the SGNAS collected at the site.

Circular enclosures are common throughout the survey area. Site 129 is comprised of two such enclosures. One of the enclosures measures ca. 12 m while the other measures ca. 8m in diameter. There is an associated lithic and sherd scatter. The site is located on a plateau between Wadis Umruq and Feifa. There are two raised areas, ca. 0.50 m high, adjoining the larger enclosure.

Site 84 is a lithic and sherd scatter along with the remnants of what appears to be an aqueduct on the southeast edge of a terrace along the north side of Wadi Feifa. The area is disturbed by bulldozing caused by the recent water reclamation development in the wadi. However, the lithics and sherds which the SGNAS collected were from a seemingly, undisturbed area. There is the possibility that the site extended to the southwest but this area has been disturbed by erosion as well as by bulldozing activity. It is in this area that the remnants of what appears to be an aqueduct, measuring ca. 10 m long by 0.40 cm wide, are present.

Site 92 has been mentioned in the discussion of both the Neolithic and Neolithic Chalcolithic Period sites. It also yielded Chalcolithic sherds (n=7). Thus, this site is certainly a Neolithic Chalcolithic Period site.

Site 137 is a lithic and sherd scatter located on a plateau just north of Wadi Umruq. It is situated just above an open area in the wadi where there is much vegetation and water. It was probably a camp-site.

The SGNAS found a heavy concentration of Chalcolithic sherds at Site 133, a well-preserved, cluster of structures (Figure 10). The site is located on a difficult to get to plateau on the south side of Wadi Umruq, a distance of ca.0.50 km northwest of Site 137. There is an enclosure measuring ca. 16 m in diameter on the north side of the plateau. A rectangular structure is located ca. 55 m to the south. It measures ca. 17 x 4 m and has what appears to be an entrance-way facing north. Both structures are constructed of two lines of stone filled with smaller stones. There are at least two-other, smaller structures located between the two, above-mentioned structures. Chalcolithic Period sherds were the only ones which

Table 24   Chalcolithic Period Sites

Site No.	Sample No.	No. of Sherds	Plate No. (if any)
10	17	1	6 (3)
20	70	1	9 (4;6)
29	73	2	6 (2;5)
30	410	1	
75	117	1	7 (6)
80	124	2	
84	140	1	
92	137	7	9 (2;9)
108	148	3	10 (3)
129	224	3	
129	225	2	
133	231	55	9 (5)
137	233	2	
177	309	1	10 (2)
222	386	11	

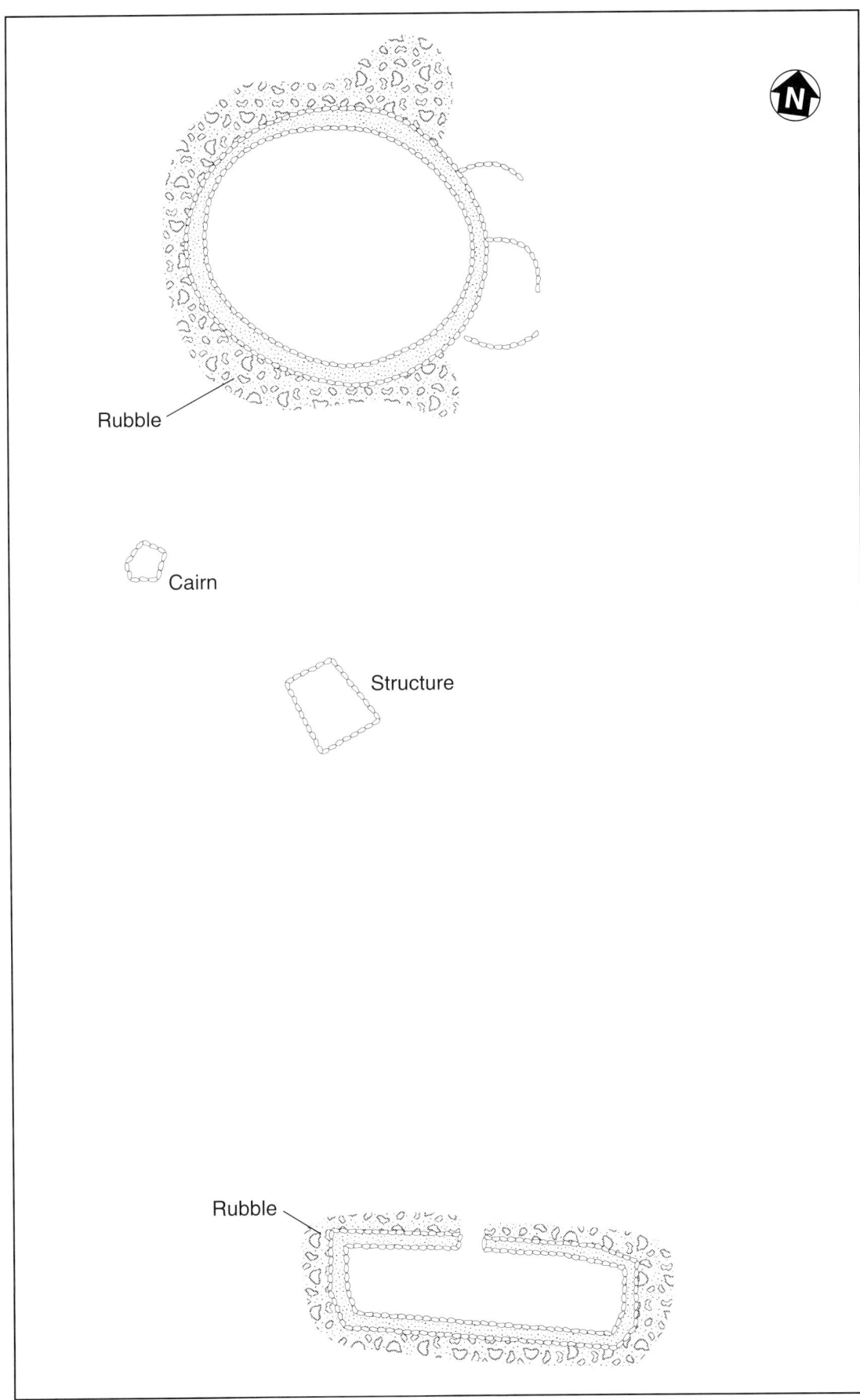

Rubble

Cairn

Structure

Rubble

Figure 10 Site 133.

the SGNAS found at the site. The architecture and dating of the site bear some resemblance to the Chalcolithic shrine/temple at Ein Gedi across the Dead Sea to the northwest (Ussishkin 1971; 1980). However, the function of the site will probably only be discovered through excavation.

Rujm Khuneizir (Frank 1934; Glueck 1935; Rast and Schaub 1974; Raikes n.d.; Frolich and Lancaster 1985), Site 108, is known as an important Early Bronze site at the southern extremity of the Southern Ghors. We will deal with it in detail later. However, at this point it is sufficient to mention that the SGNAS collected a small quantity of Chalcolithic sherds (n=3), the possible remnants of a cornet, at the site.

Site 222 is a sherd scatter in what appears to be a cemetery along the north bank of Wadi al-Dahal close to its mouth. The SGNAS noted approximately 10–15 graves which seem to be recent and undisturbed. The area is apparently a Bedouin camping site as well. The sherd scatter appears to be the remains of a single vessel.

One Chalcolithic Period sherd was among the many sherds which the SGNAS collected at Site 30, al-Munbateha/Khirbet Hamr Ifdan (Frank 1934; Glueck 1935; Raikes n.d.; 1980; Bachmann and Hauptmann 1984; Hauptmann; Weisgerber; and Knauf 1985; Knauf and Lenzen 1987). The site is an important smelting site and will be returned to later in the treatment of the Chalcolithic/Early Bronze Period sites.

Chalcolithic/Early Bronze Period Sites

The SGNAS collected Chalcolithic/Early Bronze Period sherds at 27 sites (Table 25) (Figure 9). Analysis of the sherds could not determine if they were Chalcolithic or Early Bronze. Thus, the designation Chalcolithic/Early Bronze. We have at least referred to several of these sites, e.g., Sites 10; 29; 75; 76; 84; and 137, above.

Site 6, Umm al-Tawabin, is the most northerly located site at which the SGNAS collected Chalcolithic/Early Bronze Period sherds. The collected sherds from the periods under discussion came from two different, but associated, locations at the site. These locations are the southwest segments of the site within the enclosure wall and the ridge immediately above it. It is impossible to determine if the sherds are associated with the structures along the enclosure wall or if they are washed down from the ridge above. Whatever the case, it appears that the area at which Umm al-Tawabin is located presently was used for some purpose during the Chalcolithic/Early Bronze Period. However, the predominant pottery which the SGNAS collected at the site comes from the Nabataean Period. Therefore, it will be treated in detail along with other Nabataean Period sites of the survey.

In the area of Wadi Feifa, the SGNAS collected Chalcolithic/Early Bronze sherds at six sites, namely, Sites 75; 76; 84; 95; 157; and 181. All of these sites, with the exception of Sites 157 and 181, have been treated previously in relation to the discussion on the

Neolithic, Neolithic Chalcolithic, and/or Chalcolithic sites of the survey.

Site 181 is a sherd scatter located in a sandy area northwest of Sites 75 and 76, ancient Feifa, and west of the main Mazra'a–'Aqaba Highway. Site 157 is another sherd scatter less than 0.50 km to the south. It is, however, located in an agricultural field. Both sites could have been closely related to Sites 75 and 76 during the periods under discussion.

Sites 137 and 138 are lithic and sherd scatters located ca.100 m apart along the north side of Wadi Umruq. The former has been discussed in the treatment of the Chalcolithic Period sites. Both sites yielded Chalcolithic/Early Bronze sherds.

On a terrace, ca. 6 m above the bed of Wadi al-Nukhbar, is a sherd scatter, Site 172, which covers an area of ca. 25 x 15 metres. A small number (7) of Chalcolithic/Early Bronze sherds were among those collected at the site.

Along Wadi al-Dahal, Chalcolithic/Early Bronze sherds were found at Sites 169; 171; 187; and 189. Site 169 is a cemetery, camp-site, and sherd scatter on the north side of the wadi. The SGNAS collected a moderate concentration of Chalcolithic/Early Bronze sherds at the site. However, neither the cemetery nor camp-site need be from the period under discussion. Site 171 is located immediately to the east, a distance of ca. 0.25 kilometres. It is a very dense lithic and sherd scatter. Sites 187 and 189 appear to be cemeteries with associated indications of recent camping. The former is located on the north side of the wadi near its mouth. The graves appear recent and the SGNAS noted modern artifacts nearby. The latter is located on the south side of the wadi. It consists of graves, a rock alignment, and a lithic and sherd scatter.

Site 208 is a lithic and sherd scatter located in the flood plain along the north side of Wadi Madsus. The only identifiable pottery which the SGNAS found at the site is dated to the Chalcolithic/Early Bronze Period.

Khirbet al-Hassiya South, Site 233, is essentially a Byzantine hamlet or village and, as such, it will be described later. Down slope from the structures, a distance of ca. 40 m, 48 Chalcolithic/Early Bronze sherds were collected in an area measuring only ca. 5 x 5 metres. This sherd scatter was not given a separate site number because of its proximity to the structures.

There are two robbed tombs and a light, lithic and sherd scatter located just northeast of Wadi al-Ghuweib and west of the 'Old Road'. This is Site 227. The SGNAS collected 10 Chalcolithic/Early Bronze sherds at the site.

Site 217 is comprised of two, interconnected enclosures, each measuring ca. 10 x 13 metres. It is located to the northeast of Wadi al-Ghuweib. The only identifiable pottery which the SGNAS collected at the site was Chalcolithic/Early Bronze.

Site 86 consists of two more stone enclosures south of Wadi al-Ghuweib. One measures ca. 25 m while the other ca. 15 min diameter. The SGNAS collected lithics from both enclosures while it collected

Chalcolithic/Early Bronze sherds from the smaller. The site is not unlike Site 129, located between Wadi Umruq and Wadi Feifa, discussed as a site at which the SGNAS collected Chalcolithic Period sherds. Most of Henry's Chalcolithic Period sites in the Ras al-Naqb vicinity contained one or more circular or semi-circular stone structures in association with thick ash lenses and refuse pits (1981: 117). However, enclosures of this type, which the SGNAS found throughout the survey area, are probably not dated only to the Chalcolithic Period.

There are a large number of Chalcolithic/Early Bronze sites, namely, Sites 9; 10; 14; 15; 20; 29; 30; and 117, along the terraces of Wadi Fidan. Raikes (n.d.; 1980;1985) studied some of these sites previous to the visit of the SGNAS to the wadi. A number of these Chalcolithic/Early Bronze sites, namely, Sites 15; 20; 10; and 30, are located along the south side of Wadi Fidan. Many of them are related. It appears that the entire south bank of the wadi near its mouth was used during the period under discussion.

Site 15, Raikes' Site 'C' (n.d.; 1980), is a lithic and sherd scatter in association with some poorly defined 'architecture'. Chalcolithic/Early Bronze sherds were the only identifiable ones which the SGNAS collected at the site.

Sites 20 and 10 are actually the west and east sides of Raikes' Site 'E' respectively (n.d.; 1980). Site 20 is located to the southeast of Site 15 and to the southwest of Site 10. Sites 20 and 10 are separated by ca. 500 metres. Between the two sites, but at a lower level, are traces/remnants of an aqueduct, Site 16. Site 20 consists of a cemetery, indications of camping, wall lines, and a heavy lithic and sherd scatter. The wall lines, which could be remnants of domestic structures, were especially noticeably at the south site of the site which is presently cut by erosional gullies. The SGNAS collected a heavy concentration of Chalcolithic/Early Bronze sherds at the site. Site 10 is comprised of what appears to be a domestic structure located on a small mound. There is slag over part of the site. The SGNAS found one quern fragment, along with lithics and sherds, at the site. As for Site 20, the only identifiable sherds, also in heavy concentration, which the SGNAS collected at the site, were Chalcolithic/Early Bronze. Both Sites 20 and 10 could have been used during the period under discussion for watching game moving in the wadi as well as for farming the small terraces along its sides.

Site 30, al-Munbateha/Khirbet Hamr Ifdan, is located to the southeast of the above-discussed sites. It has been visited frequently in the past (Frank 1934; Glueck 1935; Raikes n.d.; 1980; Bachmann and Hauptmann 1984; Hauptmann; Weisgerber; and Knauf 1985; Knauf and Lenzen 1987). It is Raikes' Site 'F' (n.d.; 1980). The people presently living in the area call the site al-Minbateha. However, previous visitors to the site called it Khirbet Hamr Ifdan or Mahamma Ifdan (Frank 1934: 219 and Photo 17). The site has been used as a smelting area in antiquity. It is actually located on what looks like an 'island' on the west side of Wadi Fidan ca. 0.50 km north of 'Ain Fidan. The southeast portion of the site consists of a large slag area with small circles of stones. Slag was located inside these circular structures (hearths ?). Next to the slag is a raised area that looks like a large stone platform. Some of the rock alignments in this area appear to be recent but others appear to be the remains of ancient structures. The northwest portion of the site has an extensive area of slag in and around a visible complex of building foundations which are not unlike the structures in the southeast portion of the site. There are also several circular structures. The area covered by this complex is ca. 50 m square. On the southwest, there is a 'roadway'/'ramp' (?) leading up to the top of the 'island'. It has eroded considerably but there are portions of it still present. What appears to be a retaining wall (?) is located at one segment on the northeast slope of the site. Several periods are represented at the site. The predominant pottery which the SGNAS collected at the site was Chalcolithic/Early Bronze. Several basalt querns were also noted. Only excavations at the site will tell whether or not this site was used as a smelting area as early as the period under discussion.

Table 25 Chalcolithic/Early Bronze Period sites

Site No.	Sample No.	No. of Sherds	Plate No. (if any)
6	12	1	
6	13	10	
9	15	2	
10	17	96	
14	20	9	
14	30	6	
15	31	19	
20	70	119	
29	73	12	
29	74	10	
30	76	75	
30	77	29	
75	116	14	
75	117	6	
76	119	4	
76	228	13	
84	140	57	
86	142	26	
95	146	17	
117	210	58	
137	233	3	
138	234	3	
157	300	1	
169	307	25	
171	308	38	
172	291	7	
181	284	6	
187	330	5	
189	332	13	
208	358	4	
217	374	8	
227	376	10	
233	401	48	

There are also a number of sites, namely, Sites 14; 29; 9; and 117 (?), along the north side of Wadi Fidan from which the SGNAS collected Chalcolithic/Early Bronze sherds. These sites, however, ought not to be viewed in isolation from those along the south side of the wadi.

Site 14, Raikes' Site 'D' (n.d.; 1980), is a cemetery which consists of over 200 graves. Many of the graves are looted. There are still more graves on a second plateau, separated from the first by a small wadi, immediately to the west of the site. Close by and at a lower level are agricultural fields. This site certainly deserves further attention from archaeologists.[1]

Site 29 is a heavy sherd concentration on a steep slope immediately west of the 'Old Road' going north from Wadi Fidan to Wadi al-Ghuweib. What appears to be robbed graves, along with ash and bones, were noted on the slope. The entire site covers an area of ca. 50 x 30 metres.

Site 9 (Raikes n.d.; 1980) is a west-facing cave/rockshelter (Photo 2). It measures ca. 9 x 18 metres. It is one of a series of cave/rock shelters along the east/north side of Wadi Fidan (Photo 3). The floor of the cave/rockshelter is presently covered with animal dung and ash to an unknown depth. There is evidence of ash and charcoal under the overhang. A light scatter of sherds, two of which were Chalcolithic/Early Bronze, were found in small eroded gullies running away from the entrance.

Site 117 is located to the north of Site 14, a distance of ca. 1 kilometre. It does not fit clearly into the description of Chalcolithic/Early Bronze sites along the south and north sides of Wadi Fidan. However, it can be described in association with them. It consists of wall lines, possibly for houses and/or retaining walls spread over an area of ca. 150 (N–S) x 75 (E–W) metres. It could have been a hamlet or farm. There are also signs of graves in the area. However, the wall lines and graves need not be contemporaneous. The only identifiable pottery which the SGNAS collected at the site is dated to the Chalcolithic/Early Bronze Period.

Conclusions

Pottery Neolithic Period sites are confined to the region of Wadis Feifa and Fidan. The discovery of sites from this period in the Feifa region is new.

From the data provided above, there is evidence for more and more sites as one progresses from the Pottery Neolithic through the Chalcolithic/Early Bronze Periods. Moreover, the number of sherds, as expected, increases with time.

With the Chalcolithic/Early Bronze Period there is evidence for human occupation from the northern to the southern extremities of the survey area. During this period all the major wadis surveyed produced evidence of human occupation. The heaviest concentrations were in Wadis Feifa, Umruq, al-Dahal, al-Ghuweib, and Fidan. The most likely location for these sites are the terraces along the wadis. There were undoubtedly many more of them in antiquity. However, erosion and human activity, especially modern development such as irrigation schemes, have partially or completely destroyed them.

The SGNAS surveyed a total of six enclosure sites, namely, Sites 86; 129; 133; 134; 177; and 217, from the periods under discussion. They are spread throughout the survey territory. All appear to be related in some way to the Chalcolithic Period. However, we will treat more of this type of site in association with subsequent, time-stratigraphic units.

Two sites, namely, Sites 10 and 30, from the periods under discussion, which the SGNAS surveyed in Wadi Fidan, had associated slag. There is the possibility, therefore, that these sites at least were in some way involved with the copper smelting activity in the region during the Neolithic Chalcolithic/Early Bronze Periods (Hauptmann 1986: 415–17; Hauptmann and Weisgerber 1987: 421–22; Knauf and Lenzen 1987: 85).

Notes

1   The Wadi Fidan Project, directed by Russell Adams, a member of the SGNAS 1986 team, undertook sampling excavation at this site in the summer of 1989. He assures the writer that the site is indeed a cemetery, but its date was still problematic at the time of the writing of this chapter.

6.   Early–Late Bronze Period Sites

by B. MacDonald

Introduction

This chapter will treat the different Early Bronze Periods, namely, EB I; EB II–III; and EB IV, present in the survey territory. However, many of the Early Bronze sherds collected are undetermined as to just which category they belong. Therefore, there is a section on sites which are called Early Bronze without further specification. It must be kept in mind that some of the sites treated in the previous chapter as Chalcolithic/Early Bronze are probably Early Bronze Period sites. Thus, these sites ought to be considered as well in relation to the Early Bronze Period sites of the survey. Both taken together will give a more complete picture of Early Bronze Age occupation in the Southern Ghors and Northeast 'Arabah. Comments on the lack of Middle and Late Bronze occupation in the area will be made at the end of the chapter.

Early Bronze I and IB Period sites

The SGNAS collected EB I sherds at five sites, namely, Sites 2; 3; 4; 75; and 76 (Table 26) (Figure 11). Moreover, the SGNAS collected EB IB sherds at one of these sites, namely, Site 2, al-Safi (Table 27) (Figure 11). Two of these sites, namely, Sites 2 and 76, are tremendously important for understanding EB I presence in the area.

The SGNAS collected only one EB I sherd at Site 4, Khirbet Sheikh 'Isa, a major Islamic site. The site is in close proximity to Site 2, al-Safi. It will be returned to later.

The mound of al-Safi, Site 2, to the south of Wadi al-Hasa, has been of interest to explorers for decades. It is actually a ridge which at one time jutted further to the west into what is now agricultural fields. Through time, however, it has been cut by the sugar mills, Tawahin al-Sukkar, agricultural fields, and possibly even earlier structures. Today, a Jordan Valley Authority (JVA) townsite is located at the top of the ridge and a military camp is located on its southwestern side.

Table 26: Early Bronze I Period sites

Site No.	Sample No.	No. of Sherds	Plate No.
2	5	1	11 (11)
3	8	15	
4	9	1	
75	117	3	
76	119	34	8 (5)
76	127	64	8 (6;8)

Table 27: Early Bronze IB Period sites

Site No.	Sample No.	No. of Sherds	Plate No.
2	4	8	12 (6;10) 11 (5–6)
2	5	19	12 (5;8;11) 11 (2;5;7–9)
2	6	34	12 (1;9) 11 (10)
2	132	four restorable vessels	13 (2) 12 (2–4;7)
2	217	restorable jar	13 (1;3)

After visiting Tawahin al-Sukkar, Tristram (1866: 345–46) commented about a coarsely-built old chapel or Crusaders' church just above it. Klein (1880: 253) also visited what he calls a Khan at al-Safi which he called Kasr-el-bushirra. This is probably Tawahin al-Sukkar. On a gravely hill he locates the ruin of a hut, El-Mashnaka, 'place of the gallows'. Frank comments about the sugar mills, which he calls Kasr et-Tuba, at al-Safi. He locates it ca. 150 m east southeast of Khirbet Sheikh 'Isa (1934: 205). He was the first to report tombs, measuring ca. 2.00 x 0.50–1.00 m, in the area. He shows pottery and a robbed tomb from al-Safi (1934: 207; Plan 10; and Tafels 21A and 23B). On the basis of Frank's picture, Glueck identified the pottery as belonging 'to the end of the Early Bronze Age and the beginning of the Middle Bronze Age' (1935: 8). Rast and Schaub placed the remains of Early Bronze al-Safi in the area directly behind the ruins of Tawahin al-Sukkar on a flat plateau or more likely farther southeast on the high area where they locate a 'fortress ruins' (1974: 10, Pl. IV). They found robbed tombs to the southeast of Tawahin al-Sukkar which fit the description given by Frank, i.e., cist tombs with walls lined either with slabs or medium-sized smooth stones, and with one end rounded (1974: 10 and Pl. IX, 1). They did not succeed in establishing a definite location for an Early Bronze habitation site at al-Safi. The best they could do was to point to what they called a 'fortress ruins' as its possible location (1974: 10).

Since the visit of Rast and Schaub to al-Safi, the Early Bronze cemetery area has been devastated further. As was mentioned previously, there is a JVA townsite in the cemetery about 300 m southeast of Tawahin al-Sukkar and a military camp on its southwest side. Moreover, there are roads and military trenches cutting through the cemetery. All these

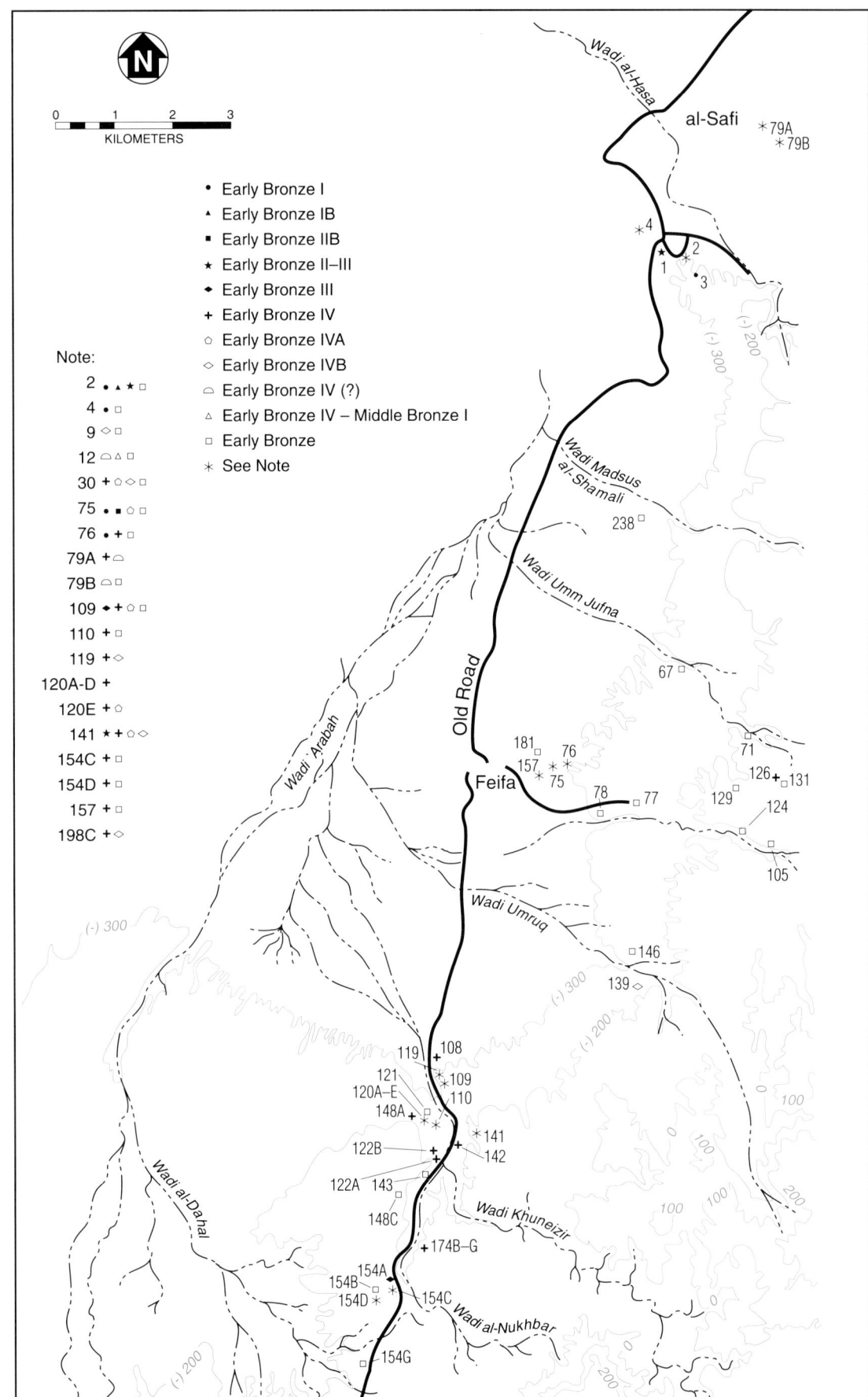

Figure 11 EB I, EB IB, EB IIB, EB II–III, EB III, EBIV, EB IVA, EB IVB, EB IV (?), EB IV–MB I, and Early Bronze settlement pattern map (Northern portion).

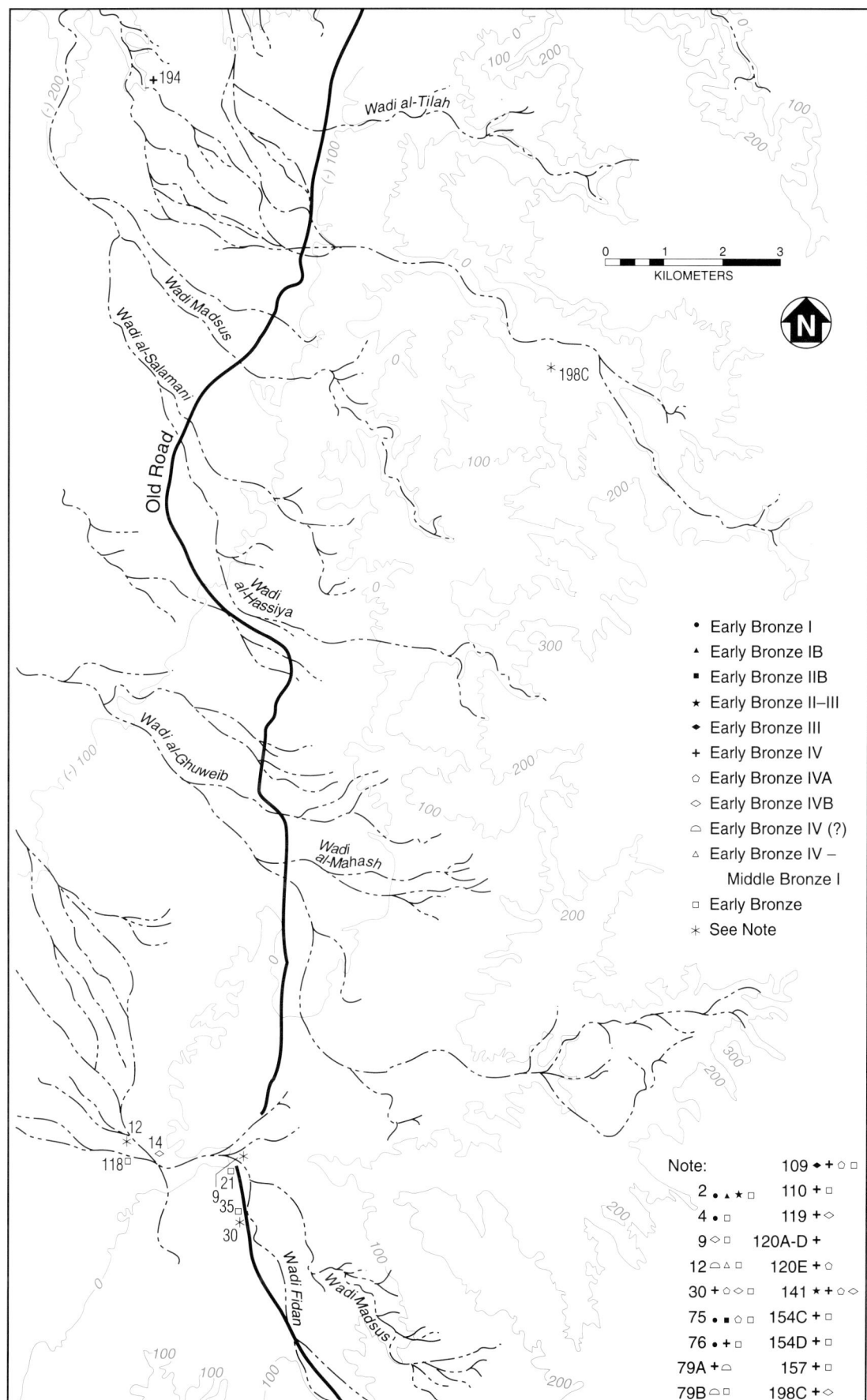

Figure 11 EB I, EB IB, EB IIB, EB II–III, EB III, EBIV, EB IVA, EB IVB, EB IV (?), EB IV–MB I, and Early Bronze settlement pattern map (Southern portion).

building enterprises, as well as erosion, have caused havoc to the Early Bronze cemetery. The JVA townsite appears to occupy the area where Rast and Schuab located 'fortress ruins'. Numerous cist tombs have been exposed by means of construction activity, grave robbing, and erosion.

In 1985, at the time of their visit to al-Safi, Frolich and Lancaster reported the destruction of a small ruin located ca. 75 m southeast of Tawahin al-Sukkar (1985: 10). They saw the ruin as built on top of an old cemetery. They give a sad report of the state of the cemetery. They think that it does not extend much further to the east of the JVA townsite. However, they do report the existence of several exposed, cist tombs ca. 400–500 m south of the JVA townsite (1985: 9 and Figure 6).

The SGNAS' visits to the site in 1985 and 1986 found it pretty much as Frolich and Lancaster had reported. The number of exposed tombs is startling. The pottery associated with these tombs appears to be all EB IB. The pottery collected came, for the most part, from cist tombs which had been either exposed by erosion, military trenching, especially on the south side of the mound, or illicit grave digging. Thus, there is a great deal of restorable pottery associated with these graves. The SGNAS noted a large number of bones as well as several fragments of basalt bowls in association with the pottery and tombs. Transects in agricultural fields to the west of Tawahin al-Sukkar did not result in the collection of many sherds from the EB IB Period.

Aerial photographs, taken in 1977, show the mound at al-Safi as it was before the building of the JVA townsite, the placement of the military camp, and the construction of several roads. These aerial photographs do not show wall lines that would indicate a major structure on the mound. Visible on the photographs are the remnants of two small structures to the southeast of Tawahin al-Sukkar. Could one of these structures be the old chapel or Crusaders' church referred to by Tristram (1866: 345) and/or the ruined hut mentioned by Klein (1880: 253)?

Site 3 is located to the eastsoutheast of the JVA townsite at al-Safi. It consists of one robbed tomb, a line of stones measuring ca. 7 m in length, and a sherd and lithic scatter. There are indications that there may be buried structures and/or tombs at the site.

Site 75 is the western extremity of ancient Feifa (Figure 12) (Photo 4). It must be seen in relation to Site 76, its counterpart, immediately to the east. The two sites occupy a ridge running along the north side of Wadi Feifa. The ridge is being eroded by water action in the wadi (Frolich and Lancaster 1985: 10–11). Frank (1934: 209–11) visited the site in 1932 and it is probable that Glueck (1937: 11) saw it from the air. However, it was the survey of Rast and Schaub of the Southern Ghors which related the site to the Early Bronze culture of the region (1974: 11–12).

Site 75 is located on the western extremity of the ridge where there are two distinct mounds separated by a saddle. The SGNAS collected samples from these three different areas of the site. One mound is located at the western extremity of the ridge where there is now an elevation/surveyor's point. There is a medium scatter of sherds in this area. Sherds can be found on the slope to the west of the elevation point. The survey of Rast and Schaub (1974: 11–12, Pl. V), as well as the 1977 aerial photographs, show a small structure and/or walled area at this point (Figure 12). There are wall lines as well as graves visible in the saddle. What appears to be a ramp leads from the north side of the ridge to this saddle. Rast and Schaub think that this could have been the main entrance to the site at one time (1974: 12, Pl. V). The eastern segment of Site 75 consists of a large enclosure (Rast and Schaub 1974: 11–12, Pl. V) (Figure 12). There is a distinct mound which appears to be a tower within the large enclosure. All this shows up clearly on the aerial photographs. It may have been connected at one time to the structure at the western extremity of the ridge (Rast and Schaub 1974: 11, Pl. V). Site 75, however, may be comprised of structures from several different periods. The pottery collections from the three separate areas of the site are not conclusive. As mentioned previously, the SGNAS collected Chalcolithic/Early Bronze sherds from the site. It, however, also collected sherds from several other periods, besides Early Bronze, at the site. The sherds associated with the larger structure at Site 75 are predominantly from the Iron Age. Thus, this site will be returned to later. It will probably take an excavation at the site to determine the date(s) for its various segments.[1]

Site 76 is the cemetery proper of ancient Feifa. It has been mentioned previously in the discussion of the Neolithic, Neolithic–Chalcolithic, and Chalcolithic /Early Bronze sites of the survey. The cemetery extends over a southern, central, and western ridge system which is dissected by many small wadis. It covers an area of at least 1.00 x 0.50 kilometres. The SGNAS noted many looted tombs at the site. Moreover, military trenching, which shows up clearly on the aerial photographs, has exposed more tombs. The tombs are similar in construction to those at Site 2, al-Safi. They are rectangular, stone-lined cists, with some of the stones being flattened slabs. They measure on the average 1.58 m long by 0.79 m wide (Frolich and Lancaster 1985: 13). Frolich and Lancaster observed that the tombs were constructed in such a way so that a minimum of ca. 40 cm of soil separated the top of the grave from the surface (1985: 12). Thus, continued erosion will expose the tops of the graves and be an advantage to tomb robbers. The burials were apparently disarticulated (Rast and Schaub 1974: 11).[2] On the aerial photos, what appears to be an L-shaped wall (?) is located on the south side of the cemetery, ca. 150 m southeast of the southeast corner of the main structure at Site 75. Moreover, what appears to be a tower is located at the southeastern extremity of the cemetery. This tower (?) is badly eroded by the dirt road which goes from the main Mazra'a–'Aqaba Highway to the JVA's water-collecting system further to the east in Wadi Feifa. It

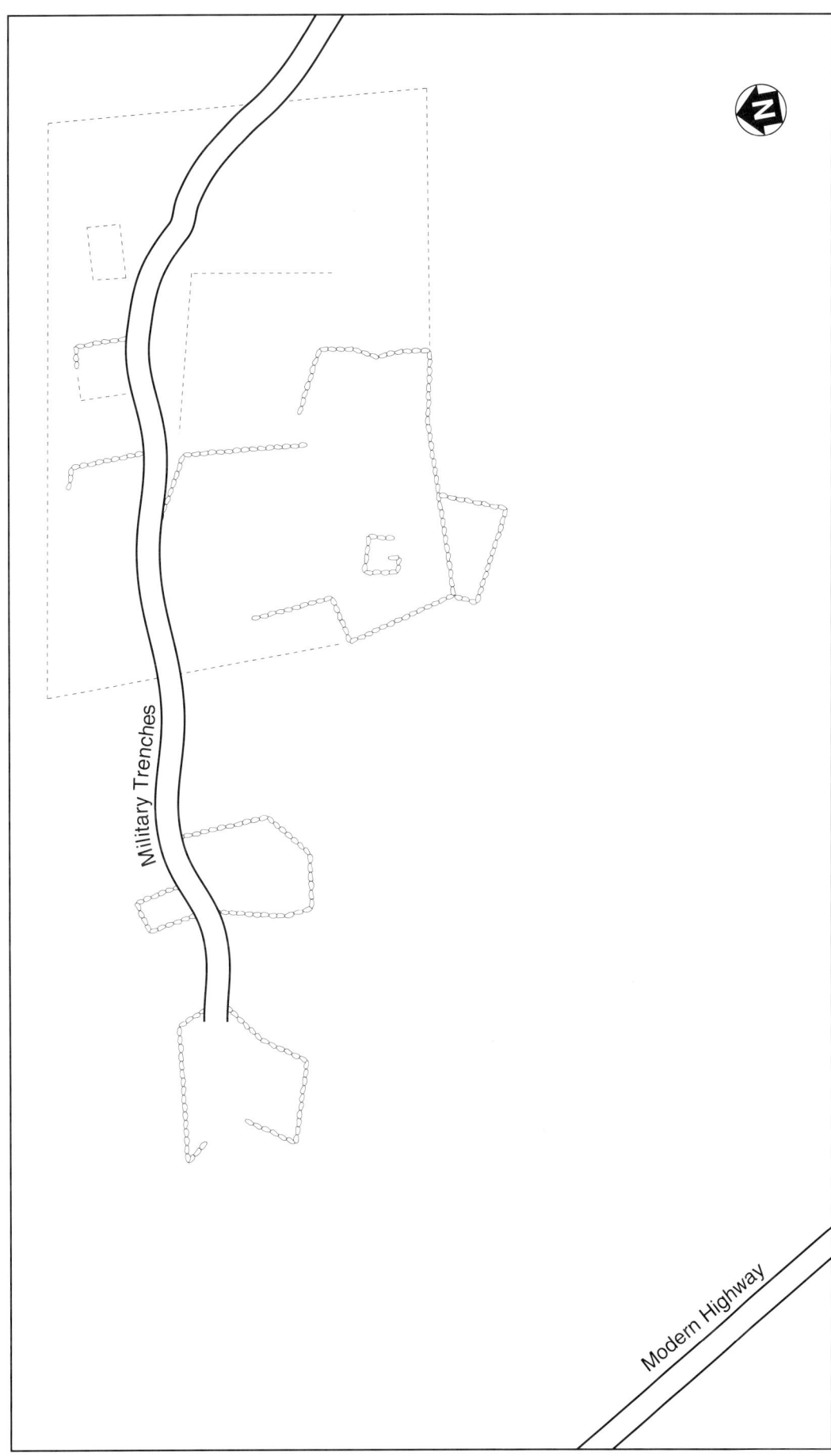

Figure 12 Site 75, ancient Feifa.

could have been associated with the structures which comprise Site 75. However, here again only excavations can determine its function and date.

Early Bronze IIB Period site

The SGNAS collected identifiable EB IIB pottery at only one site, namely Site 75 (Table 28) (Figure 11). The site is described in some detail above.

Table 28 Early Bronze IIB Period sites

Site No.	Sample No.	No. of Sherds	Plate No.
75	117	1	7 (5)

Early Bronze II–III Period sites

The SGNAS collected EB II–III Period pottery at three sites, namely, Sites 1; 2; and 141 (Table 29) (Figure 11). Site 1, Tawahin al-Sukkar, is an Islamic sugar mill and Site 141, Abu Irshareibeh, is a predominantly EB IV site. Thus, they will both be treated later. Site 2, al-Safi, has been described above.

Table 29 Early Bronze II–III Period sites

Site No.	Sample No.	No. of Sherds	Plate No.
1	3	3	
2	4	22	11 (12)
141	281	1	14 (8)

Early Bronze III Period sites

The SGNAS collected EB III sherds at two sites (Table 30) (Figure 11). One of these sites, namely, Site 154A, is an EB IIIA Period site.

Table 30 Early Bronze III Period sites

Site No.	Sample No.	No. of Sherds	Plate No.
109	185	1	10 (4)
154A	252	1	10 (5)

Site 109, located along the north side of Wadi Khuneizir, is associated with Site 108, Rujm Khuneizir, and Site 119. It will, thus, be treated along with them. Site 154 is a predominantly EB IV site. It too will be treated later.

Early Bronze IV Period sites

The SGNAS collected EB IV Period pottery, without further precision, at 18 sites, namely, Sites 30; 76; 79A; 108; 109; 110; 119; 120A–E; 122A–B; 126; 141; 142; 148A; 154C–D; 157; 174B–G; 194; and 198C

(Table 31) (Figure 11); EB IVA at five sites, namely, Sites 30; 75; 109; 120E; and 141 (Table 32) (Figure 11); EB IVB at seven sites, namely, Sites 9; 14; 30; 119; 139; 141; and 198C (Table 33) (Figure 11); EB IV (?) at two sites, namely, Sites 12 and 79A–B (Table 34) (Figure 11); and EB IV–MBI at one site, namely, Site 12 (Table 35) (Figure 11). Several of these sites are spread over large areas. Therefore, the SGNAS collected multiple samples at some of the sites.

EB IV occupation is attested on the plateau to the east of the Southern Ghors (MacDonald *et al.* 1988), at Bab al- Dhra', north of the survey area (Rast 1981: 31–34), as well as to the northwest and west in the Judean Hills and the Central Negev Highlands (Gitin 1975; Cohen and Dever 1978a and b; 1979; 1981;

Table 31 Early Bronze IV Period sites

Site No.	Sample No.	No. of Sherds	Plate No.
30	76	6	15 (4)
30	77	2	15 (6)
30	410	1	
76	118	1	8 (9)
79A	121	1	17 (3)
108	149	8	
109	184	141	15 (2)
109	185	3	
110	186	21	
119	190	37	16 (3)
119	191	24	15 (7;8)
119	192	38	
120A	193	16	16 (1)
120B	194	8	
120C	195	34	15 (1)
120D	196	2	
120E	197	9	
120E	244	22	16 (7)
122A	199	2	
122B	187	12	
126	218	2	
141	237	28	
141	238	13	
141	239	7	
141	240	7	14 (11)
141	241	13	
141	242	2	14 (3)
141	259	24	
141	280	49	14 (6)
141	281	98	14 (10)
142	243	11	
148A	248	1	
154C	253	3	
154D	274	15	
157	300	1	10 (8)
174B	296	5	
174C	297	19	
174D	298	92	
174E	299	21	16 (2)
174F	310	8	
174G	311	9	
194	319	1	
198C	343	6	

approx. 70 m removed from drawing here

Figure 13 Site 141, Abu Irshareibeh.

Table 32   Early Bronze IVA Period sites

Site No.	Sample No.	No. of Sherds	Plate No.
30	410	1	15 (5)
75	116	1	7 (9)
109	184	1	15 (3)
120E	244	1	16 (8)
141	281	4	14 (1;2;4;7)

Table 33   Early Bronze IVB Period sites

Site No.	Sample No.	No. of Sherds	Plate No.
9	15	1	10 (6)
14	30	1	10 (9)
30	76	1	10 (1)
119	190	1	16 (4)
139	235	1	16 (9)
141	280	1	14 (5)
141	281	1	14 (9)
198C	342	1	16 (5)

Table 34   Early Bronze IV (?) Period sites

Site No.	Sample No.	No. of Sherds	Plate No.
12	18	1	10 (7)
79A	121	1	17 (1)
79B	123	1	17 (2)

Table 35   Early Bronze IV–Middle Bronze I Period site

Site No.	Sample No.	No. of Sherds	Plate No.
12	18	1	10 (6)

Dever 1973; 1975; and 1980). However, between Bab al-Dhra' and the area to the west of the Southern Ghors and Northeast 'Arabah it was attested only at Rujm Khuneizir (Rast and Schaub 1974: 18) before 1986. The SGNAS has succeeded in filling up a vacuum in EB IV occupation in the region. Moreover, the number of EB IV sites in the survey territory is surprising. The SGNAS collected EB IV sherds from the northern to the southern extremity of the survey territory, i.e., from Site 79 to al-Minbateha/Khirbet Hamr Ifdan, Site 30. However, the greatest concentration of EB IV sites is in the Wadi Khuneizir-Wadi al-Nukhbar region.

Site 79A–H is a series of tombs spread over a terrace to the north of Wadi al-Hasa and east of modern al-Safi. The SGNAS collected sherds dating to EB IV at 79A, to EB IV (?) at 79A–B, and to Early Bronze, without further specification, at 79B, as well as sherds dating to several other periods at the site.

Site 126 is a heavy sherd concentration located

between Wadi Umm Jufna and Wadi Feifa. A small number (2) of EB IV sherds were among those which the SGNAS collected at the site.

Both sites 75 and 76, ancient Feifa, have been treated above. They yielded one EB IVA and EB IV sherd respectively.

Rujm Khuneizir, Site 108 (Photo 5), has been known for decades through the work of Frank (1934: 212, Tafel 28B), Glueck (1935: 10–11), Rast and Schaub (1974: 12–13, 18), Raikes (n.d.), and Frolich and Lancaster (1985: 13–15). Rast and Schaub were the first to identify it as an Early Bronze site. Moreover, as mentioned previously, they identified EB IV pottery at the site (1974: 18). The site is located on the last alluvial fan before leaving the Southern Ghors and entering the Northeast 'Arabah. The entire area to the north, west, and east within the Southern Ghors can be observed from the site. The site appears to be mainly a tower (?) which still stands 5–6 m high. It is unlikely that it is a townsite. There are walls visible on the northeast side of the site where the slope is not eroded. These walls appear to consist of three levels progressing in a step-like fashion to the summit. Between the first and second 'step' there is about a 1 m distance. It is difficult to find a good corner to the walls. There is a platform area below the summit of the site. The SGNAS collected most of its sherds from this area. There are wall lines here and what appear to be graves. One grave is located ca. 5 m to the north of these wall lines. There is a pile of stones measuring ca. 5–6 m in diameter to the northeast. Rast and Schaub give a plan of what they observed at the site (1974: 180, Pl. VI). The site is presently being destroyed by heavy natural erosion on the eastern banks and by the removal of soil at the northern end for modern construction. The SGNAS collected EB IV sherds from the base and the slopes of the hill on which the above-described structures are located. These sherds appear to be coming from graves which are being eroded or robbed (Photo 6). The graves are cist tombs similar to those reported for al-Safi, Site 2, and Feifa, Site 76. The SGNAS collected no identifiable EB IV sherds from the summit of the site where the tower (?) is located.

Sites 109 and 119 appear to be a cemetery on the east side of Wadi Khuneizir just to the southwest of Rujm Khuneizir, Site 108. The two sites are presently separated by erosional gullies. There is evidence of recent disturbances by bulldozing activity as well as erosion. They are probably one with the area from which the EB IV sherds of Site 108 were collected. The tombs constituting the cemetery are cist tombs similar to those referred to above. Some of the EB IV pottery which the SGNAS collected in association with the graves is restorable. There are many wall lines in the area. These could be associated with a village which will be discussed further in relation to the Nabataean Period sites of the survey. The area of Site 119, which measures ca. 200 (E–W) x 100 (N–S) m, was completely covered by walking transects.

Site 120A–E is an EB IV cemetery located on a terrace on the west side of Wadi Khuneizir. Most of the graves constituting the cemetery appear to be cist tombs not unlike those present at Sites 2, 76, 108, 109, and 119. The SGNAS treated several of the graves as a unit and sampled them separately. Thus, the SGNAS gave them the designation Site 120A, B, etc. (Photo 7).

Site 110 is located immediately to the southeast of Site 120. It consists of a sherd scatter, a stone fence/wall (?), a platform (?), and two stone piles on a terrace on the west side of Wadi Khuneizir. All these elements of the site need not be contemporaneous. The sherd scatter came from a north-facing slope. The fence/wall (?) measures ca. 36 x 2 m and is cut by erosion of Wadi Khuneizir on its southeast end. The platform (?), which measures ca. 5 x 2.5 m, is located to the south a distance of ca. 35 metres. The stone piles are located to the west of these two structures. The only identifiable pottery which the SGNAS collected at the site was EB IV.[3]

Site 122A and B is another site which appears to consist of the type of cist tombs described above. It is also located on the west side of Wadi Khuneizir. Site 122A is located ca. 80 m above the bed of the wadi while Site 122B is located ca. 50 m to the northwest and ca. 30–40 m below Site 122A. Here again, the only identifiable pottery which the SGNAS collected was EB IV. Perhaps the most important EB IV site in the Wadi Khuneizir-Wadi al-Nukhbar region is Site 141, Abu Irshareibeh, a cemetery site (Figure 13).[4] It is located, for the most part, at the base of a high mountain to the east and high above Wadi Khuneizir and to the southeast of Site 108, Rujm Khuneizir. It consists of at least 100 structures spread over an area of ca. 2 kilometres. The structures vary in size from ca. 7–14 m long by 2.5–3.0 m wide (Photos 8 and 9). They do not appear to have any definite orientation. Some of them have been dug into but many of them are still very well preserved with walls still standing two to five courses or 1 m high. The structures are built of unhewn stone. The SGNAS could locate no entrances to the structures. EB IV sherds were predominant throughout the site.

Site 142 is a light sherd scatter, predominantly EB IV, confined to an area measuring ca. 20 x 10 metres. It is on a path going to Site 141.

There is what is almost a continuous but moderate sherd scatter on the plateau immediately south of the Southern Ghors and west of Wadi al-Nukhbar. Site 148 is located at the northern extremity of this plateau and forms the northeastern segment of the sherd scatter. It yielded one EB IV sherd.

Further south, between Wadis Khuneizir and al-Nukhbar, there is another important EB IV site, namely, Site 174. The eight, main structures (A–H) which constitute this site measure anywhere from ca. 8–21 m long by 3–5 m wide. They are similar in appearance to those at Site 141. They, too, are probably EB IV Period tombs. One structure, namely 174C, still stands ca. 1–2 m above ground level. The only identifiable pottery collected in association with these structures was EB IV.

Site 154A–H is located immediately across Wadi al-Nukhbar to the west of Site 174. It is a series of graves/tombs and/or stone piles. However, some of the structures are like those described for Sites 141 and 174. Many of them have associated EB IV pottery similar to that which the SGNAS collected at the above-described sites. They, too, could very well be EB IV tombs.

There are two sites, namely, Sites 194 and 198C, in association with Wadi al-Dahal which yielded small quantities of EB IV sherds. The former is a lithic and sherd scatter among stone piles. It is located far out in the floodplain just east of the main Mazra'a-'Aqaba Highway. The latter is a series of graves, some looted, on the south side of the wadi far to the southeast of Site 194. It yielded pottery which could actually be MB I rather than EB IV.

Site 12 is located on an 'island' at the mouth of Wadi Fidan. It yielded one EB IV (?) and one EB IV–MB I sherd. The site will be treated in more detail below in relation to the Early Bronze Period sites of the survey.

Site 9 and Site 30, al-Munbateha/Khirbet Hamr Ifdan, have both been described previously in relation to the Chalcolithic and Chalcolithic/Early Bronze sites of the survey. They are both located in Wadi Fidan. They both yielded EB IV sherds. At Site 30, the sherds from the period under discussion are found, for the most part, at the northeast segment of the site. A return visit to the site in June 1989 revealed recent illicit digging at the site. Many EB IV sherds, some with a red slip, were noted in the soil from the illicit activity. Since this site is a smelting site, the writer wonders whether or not such activity was carried out at the site during the EB IV Period.

Early Bronze Period sites

The SGNAS collected Early Bronze Period pottery, without further specification, at 29 sites (Table 36) (Figure 11). We have treated many of these sites previously in this chapter. It is not surprising to collect sherds in association with Chalcolithic/Early Bronze, EB I, EB II–III, and/or EB IV Period sites which cannot be identified with any more precision than to label them as Early Bronze. They are actually from one of these periods. Still other of these Early Bronze sites, for example, Sites 4; 77; 78; 157; and 181, are located close by major EB I and EB IV sites and could be associated with them. However, there are other sites at which Early Bronze sherds have been found. These sites will be treated below.

The most northerly located of these sites is Site 79 which we have treated as a site which yielded EB IV sherds. Site 79B, which consists of a complex of ca. 6–10 tombs, yielded Early Bronze Period sherds as well. These sherds may, indeed, be EB IV.

Site 238 is probably a potbust. It covers an area measuring ca. 10 x 10 metres just south of Wadi Madsus al-Shamali. The only pottery which the SGNAS collected at the site was Early Bronze.

Sites 67 and 71 are sherd scatters, probably potbusts, for the most part, along the south side of

Wadi Umm Jufna. The former covers an area measuring ca. 7 x 5 metres. The only pottery which the SGNAS collected was Early Bronze. The latter covers an area of ca. 10 x 6 metres. The sherd scatter, which is predominantly Early Bronze, is comprised, for the most part, of one vessel.

Directly to the south of Site 71 are the remnants of two circular, stone structures, measuring ca. 12 and 8 m in diameter. This site, namely, Site 129, has been discussed in relation to the Chalcolithic Period sites of the survey. It also yielded two Early Bronze sherds.

Site 131 is located immediately to the east of Site 129. It consists of a heavy concentration of very small body sherds and a light lithic scatter in an area measuring ca. 30 x 25 metres. The only sherds which the SGNAS collected at the site were Early Bronze.

Site 124 is located on a large plateau measuring ca. 1.00 (E–W) x 0.50 (N–S) km to the north of Wadi Feifa. A sherd scatter, among which were some Early Bronze sherds, constitutes part of Site 124.

Table 36 Early Bronze Period sites

Site No.	Sample No.	No. of Sherds	Plate No.
2	4	2	11 (4)
2	5	20	
4	9	2	
9	15	1	
12	18	11	
21	71	3	
30	76	1	
35	75	5	
67	58	26	
71	96	1	
75	116	23	
76	119	34	
76	127	1	8 (7)
76	128	39	
76	129	4	
77	130	1	
78	131	5	
79B	123	14	
105	182	2	
109	184	18	
110	186	3	
118	212	1	
121	198	2	
124	211	5	
129	224	2	
129	225	15	
131	227	88	
143	245	71	
146	236	2	
148C	249	8	
154B	252	4	
154C	253	1	
154D	273	6	
154G	278	8	
157	300	31	
181	284	1	
238	405	72	

Site 77 consists of two stone buildings, probably structures associated with milling activities, and an associated aqueduct (Photo 10) along the north side of Wadi Feifa just to the southeast of Sites 75 and 76. It is quite unlikely that the one Early Bronze sherd collected at the site has anything to do with the structures. The site will be returned to later.

Site 79 is a sherd and lithic scatter of low density on a terrace immediately to the southwest of Site 77. Small stone piles may indicate a cemetery in the area. There are also signs of camping on the terrace. The Early Bronze sherds collected at the site could be associated with Sites 75 and 76, ancient Feifa, to the northwest.

Further east in Wadi Feifa and still on its north side is Site 105. It consists of a lithic and sherd scatter. There are no features associated with the site except for what appear to be later graves. Here again the number (2) of Early Bronze Period sherds is very low.

Site 146 is a lithic and sherd scatter located on a plateau north of Wadi Umruq. The area was probably used as a camping site during many different periods. The site yielded two Early Bronze sherds.

Site 121 is a lithic and sherd scatter in an area measuring ca. 200 x 150 m on the west side of Wadi Khuneizir. It is in an area where there are a large number of EB IV graves. The site may be associated with Site 120, an EB IV cemetery which has been discussed above.

There is a tomb and a heavy sherd scatter, Site 143, in an area measuring ca. 10 x 10 m on a spur just to the southwest of where Wadi al-Nukhbar meets Wadi Khuneizir. The site is in an area where there are a number of EB IV sites. The predominant pottery which the SGNAS collected at the site was Early Bronze.

Site 12, Raikes' Site 'A', (Raikes n.d.; 1980) is located on a small 'island' in the mouth of the Wadi Fidan gorge. On the top of the 'island' on the southsouthwest side are the remains of a wall measuring ca. 13 m in length. There are also three or four round-walled structures which measure ca. 2–4 m in diameter in the same area. Other architectural remains were noted throughout the site. The site is a mainly Prepottery Neolithic site. However, the SGNAS collected 11 Early Bronze sherds at the site.[5]

To the southwest of Site 12, a distance of ca. 300 m, is a light lithic and sherd scatter, Site 118. The area is badly disturbed since it has been used as a gravel pit. There are wall lines visible at the site but it is impossible to determine, by surveying alone, whether or not they are ancient or associated with the gravel pit operation. The site also yielded 11 Early Bronze sherds.

Site 35 may have been a farm and/or camp to the northwest of Site 30, al-Munbateha/Khirbet Hamr Ifdan, in Wadi Fidan. There is a stone 'platform' (?) which measures ca. 18 x 5 m at the summit of the hill. (Could this be a tomb?) The SGNAS noted terrace walls and/or fences (?) running up/down the hill (E–W) as well as across its slope (N–S). The SGNAS collected a small number of Early Bronze sherds at the site.

The remainder of the sites listed in Table 36, from which the SGNAS collected Early Bronze pottery, have been treated previously in this or the preceding chapter. They are associated with Chalcolithic/Early Bronze and/or a specific Early Bronze Period.

Middle and Late Bronze Period sites

The SGNAS identified neither Middle nor Late Bronze Period sites in the survey area. The only exception to this is the possibility of MB I sherds at Site 198C in Wadi al-Dahal. This site has been referred to in the treatment of the EB IV sites of the survey. The lack of occupation during the Middle and Late Bronze Periods is in keeping with the findings of the Wadi al-Hasa Archaeological Survey on the plateau to the east (MacDonald *et al.* 1988) as well as with the survey work of Rast and Schaub in the Southern Ghors (1974). Moreover, the traditionally held view is that there was a lack of occupation in Southern Jordan during the periods under discussion (Glueck 1935: 138).

Conclusions

From the above, it is clear that Early Bronze Period sites are found throughout the survey territory. Definite EB I and EB II–III Period sites are confined to the Southern Ghors. They do not extend into the more arid Northeast 'Arabah.

The SGNAS collected EB IV Period pottery throughout the survey territory from north of Wadi al-Hasa at Site 79 to its southern extremity at Site 30. The heaviest concentration of sites from this period are in the Wadi Khuneizir-Wadi al-Nukhbar region. There are several major sites, most of which appear to be cemeteries, in this area. These require more archaeological attention. Wadi al-Dahal, which leads up to the plateau to the east near Buseira, was the only wadi in the Northeast 'Arabah, north of Wadi Fidan, which attested EB IV sites.

On the basis of their work in the Central Negev Highlands, Cohen and Dever postulate that dry-farming and year-round pastoralism on a farily wide scale would have been possible in their area of study during the EB IV–MBI Period (1981; Dever 1980).

Such could also have been the case for the people of EB IV who lived outside the Southern Ghors in the Northeast 'Arabah.

Early Bronze Period pottery, without further precision, is found throughout the survey territory, both in the Southern Ghors and the Northeast 'Arabah. All the above, along with the evidence of the Chalcolithic/Early Bronze Period sites, testifies to a heavy Early Bronze presence in the area especially during the EB I and EB IV Periods. There is less evidence for occupation during the EB II–III Periods.

Site 30, al-Munbateha/Kh. Hamr Ifdan, which yielded Chalcolithic/Early Bronze, EB IV, and Early Bronze Period sherds, is a smelting site. It could have served such a purpose during these periods.

Notes

1 The writer participated in The Southeastern Dead Sea Plain Expedition's excavation at Feifa (SGNAS Sites 75 and 76) and in the Wadi Khuneizir region (at SGNAS Site 141) directed by W. E. Rast and R. T. Schaub in December 1989–January 1990. Preliminary indications from the Feifa excavations are that while there are probably EB I tombs at Site 75, as well as at Site 76, the architecture visible on the surface of the ground probably dates to the Iron II Period.

2 The Southeastern Dead Sea Plain Expedition's excavations of December 1989–January 1990 confirmed the presence of EB I cist tombs at ancient Feifa, SGNAS Site 76.

3 From experience gained excavating at Site 141 with The Southeastern Dead Sea Plain Expedition in December 1989–January 1990, the writer is now inclined to consider these stone fences/walls (?) and platforms (?) as EB IV tombs.

4 The identification of Site 141 as a cemetery rather than a habitation site is a correction to MacDonald *et al.* 1987 and MacDonald, Clark, and Neeley 1988. This correction is based on The Southeastern Dead Sea Plain Expedition's excavations of Site 141 in December 1989–January 1990.

5 The Wadi Fidan Project directed by Russell Adams, a member of the SGNAS 1986 team, excavated this site in the summers of 1989 and 1990. Preliminary indications, according to the excavator, are that PPNB materials are present at the site.

7. Iron Age Period Sites

by B. MacDonald

Introduction

As stated in the previous chapter, there appears to have been, on the basis of the archaeological evidence, an occupational gap in the survey territory during the Middle and Late Bronze Periods. However, there is evidence for renewed occupation at the beginning of the Iron I Period. This chapter will, therefore, treat the Iron I, Iron II, and Iron Age Period sites. As the subsequent discussion will point out, the SGNAS noted the heaviest concentration of Iron I and Iron II Period sherds in the mining and smelting areas of Wadi al-Ghuweib. Once again the presentation will be time-stratigraphical and the sites for each preriod will be presented, for the most part, in a north-to-south order.

Iron IA, IC, and I–II Period sites

The SGNAS collected Iron IA Period pottery at 10 sites, namely, Sites 3; 5; 50; 71; 108; 159; 161; 187; 188; and 191 (Table 37) (Figure 14). It collected Iron IC Period pottery at two sites, namely, Sites 73 and 159 (Table 38) (Figure 14). It collected, moreover, Iron I–Iron II Period pottery at three sites, namely, Sites 28; 75; and 159 (Table 39) (Figure 14).

Sites 3 and 5 are the most northerly located of the Iron I Period sites. Both are located on the ridge immediately south of Wadi al-Hasa and to the east of al-Safi, Site 2. Site 3 has already been discussed as an EB I Period site. Site 5 consists of what appears to be a Bedouin camp, many graves (some of which are looted), and a sherd scatter. There are also signs that the military has used the area recently.

Site 73, Rujm Umm Jufna, yielded one Iron IC Period sherd. It is, however, a predominantly Iron II Period site. It will, therefore, be treated in detail below.

Table 37   Iron IA Period sites

Site No.	Sample No.	No. of Sherds	Plate No.
3	8	4	
5	10	4	
50	93	4	
71	96	19	
108	149	1	
159	287	216	18 (2)
159	288	2	18 (1;3)
159	289	23	
161	301	19	19 (1;5)
161	302	1	19 (2)
187	303	2	
188	331	1	
191	316	5	

Site 71, a sherd scatter along the south side of Wadi Umm Jufna, has been treated previously as an Early Bronze Period site. It also yielded a moderate number (19) of Iron IA Period sherds.

Site 75 (Figure 12), the western segment of ancient Feifa, has generally been associated with the Early Bronze Period (Glueck 1937; Rast and Schaub 1974; Frolich and Lancaster 1985). There are, undoubtedly, Early Bronze remains at this site as well as at its associate, Site 76, immediately to the east.[1] Many of the graves, for example, at Site 76 belong to the Early Bronze Period.[2] Thus, these sites have been treated previously in the discussion of the Early Bronze Period sites of the survey. However, the major structure at Site 75 probably dates to a later period.[3] As mentioned previously, this structure appears to be a large enclosure, possibly a fort. On the 1977 aerial photos, the entire complex appears to be defensive. The predominant pottery associated with this structure dates to the Iron I–II Period. Moreover, the SGNAS collected a moderate number (14) of Iron II sherds at the site.

Site 108, Rujm Khuneizir, have been treated previously as an EB IV Period site. It also yielded one Iron IA Period sherd along with Iron II and Iron Age Period sherds. It will be returned to later.

Sites 187, 188, and 191 are located in Wadi al-Dahal. Sites 187 and 188 are two cemetery sites on the north and south sides of Wadi al-Dahal respectively. The former has been referred to in the discussion of the Chalcolithic/Early Bronze Period sites. The latter consists of more than 20 graves. Both sites yielded a small number, two and one sherds respectivly, of Iron IA Period pottery. Site 191 is far to the east in the same wadi. It consists of a sherd scatter in an area measuring ca. 200 x 60 m where there is evidence of camping and graves. It, too, yielded Iron IA Period sherds. However, because of the nature of these three sites, there is no assurance that the pottery is contemporaneous with the graves.

There are two smelting sites, namely, Sites 159 and 161, in Wadi al-Ghuweib which yielded Iron I Period sherds. Site 159, Khirbet al-Nahas, yielded a large number of Iron IA and a small number of Iron IC Period sherds. Moreover, it also yielded Iron I–II Period sherds. Site 161, Khirbet al-Ghuweib, yielded Iron IA Period sherds. Both sites have been the subject of investigation in the past.

Site 159, Khirbet al-Nahas, is an extensive complex of structures spread over a large area on the south side of Wadi al-Ghuweib (Figure 15). Musil (1907–08: 298), Frank (1934: 218–19 and Plan 16), and Glueck (1935: 26–29 and 166, Plate 4) all visited the site.

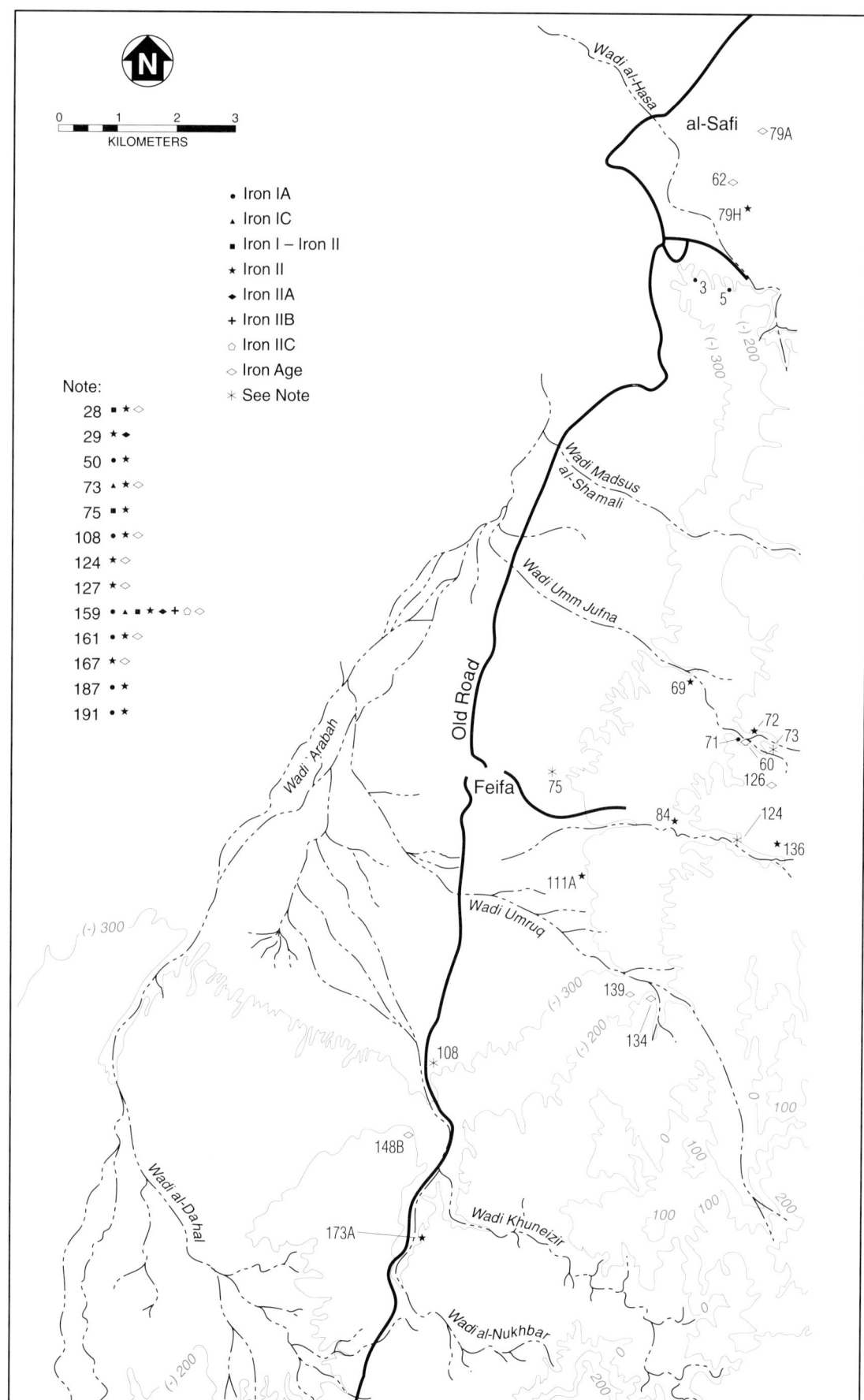

Figure 14 Iron IA, Iron IC, Iron I–II, Iron II, Iron IIA, Iron IIB, Iron IIC, and Iron Age settlement pattern map (Northern portion).

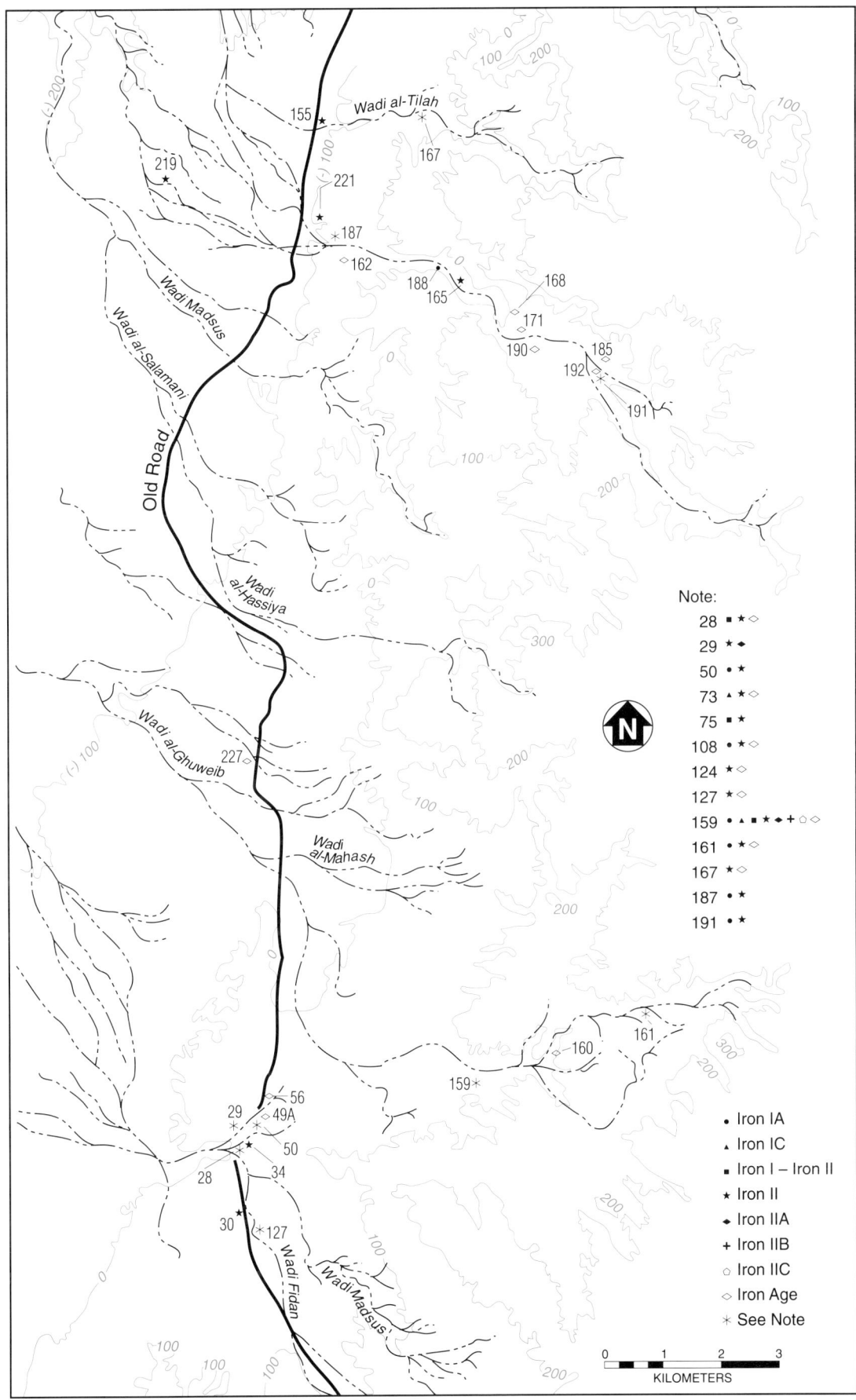

Figure 14 Iron IA, Iron IC, Iron I–II, Iron II, Iron IIA, Iron IIB, Iron IIC, and Iron Age settlement pattern map (Southern portion).

Frank refers to the site as Khirbet al-Samra as well as Khirbet al-Nahas (1934: 216). More recently, the site has come under the archaeometallurgical and mining-archaeological investigations of a team from the German Mining Museum, Bochum, West Germany (Bachmann and Hauptmann 1984; Hauptmann, Weisgerber, and Knauf 1985; Hauptmann 1986; Knauf and Lenzen 1987). Both Glueck and the team from the German Mining Museum date the smelting activity at the site to the Iron I and II Periods. The plans of Frank and Glueck, plus the aerial photographs (Figure 15) show the various segments of the site. There are numerous ruined furnaces and slag heaps. A large enclosure, measuring ca. 76 x 76 m with walls 2 m thick still standing as high as 2–3 m, is situated at the northwest side of the site close to the wadi. Other undetermined strucutres are spread throughout the site.

Site 161, Khirbet al-Ghuweib, is located to the northeast of Khirbet al-Nahas. It is another Iron IA smelthing site. However, it seems to be a village site as well. Glueck seems to have been the first to record the site (1935: 22–23 and 164, Plate 2). It is included in the German Mining Museum archaeometallurgical study of the Feinan region (Hauptmann, Weisgerber, and Knauf 1985; Hauptmann 1986; Knauf and Lenzen 1987). It is located above 'Ain al-Ghuweib on both sides of the wadi. There are ruins of buildings and furnaces and heaps of slag at both segments of the site. There are the ruins of the foundation walls of a building measuring 10 m square in the northern half of the site (Glueck 1935: 22). Graves, some of which are recent, are located throughout the site. A farmer was living at the site at the time of the SGNAS' visit in 1986.

Khirbet al-Jariyeh is another smelting site in the area which dates to the Iron I–II Period (Glueck 1935: 23–25 and 165, Plate 3; Hauptman, Weisgerber, and Knauf 1985; Knauf and Lenzen 1987). The SGNAS did not visit it due to time constraints. Like Khirbet al-Ghuweib, Glueck (1935: 23) was the first to record it. It is located to the northeast of Khirbet al-Nahas, Site

161, and to the west of Khirbet al-Ghuweib, Site 161. According to Glueck, the site lies sprawled over two high, flat areas separated from one another by the Wadi al-Jariyeh. At the time of his visit, 'the two halves of the site were covered with ruins of houses and smelting furnaces and were black with pieces and heaps of copper slag' (1935: 23). He thinks that the two main sections of the site were originally enclosed with strong walls. He describes several furnaces, two of them still fairly intact, at the site (1935: 23–25). Hauptmann and Weisgerber report smelting activity at the site during the Iron I–II Periods (1987: 422).

Site 50 consists of a medium sherd scatter covering an area ca. 20 m square. It is located on a southsouthwest facing drainage slope on the plateau between Wadi al-Ghuweib and Wadi Fidan. It yielded a small number (4) of Iron IA Period sherds.

Site 28 yielded one Iron I–II sherd. It is, however, mainly an Iron II Period site. Therefore, it will be treated below.

Iron II, IIA, IIB, and IIC Period sites

The SGNAS collected Iron II Period pottery, without further specification, at 26 sites, namely, Sites 28; 29; 30; 34; 50; 69; 72; 73; 75; 79H; 84; 108; 111A; 124; 127; 136; 155; 159; 161; 165; 167; 173A; 187; 191; 219; and 221 (Table 40) (Figure 14). It collected Iron IIA sherds at two sites, namely, Sites 29 and 159 (Table 41) (Figure 14). Moreover, it collected one Iron IIB (Table 42) and one Iron IIC (Table 43) sherd at Site 159, Khirbet al-Ghuweib (Figure 14).

Site 79A–H is a series of what appear to be tombs located on a large terrace to the north of Wadi al-Hasa and east of modern al-Safi. The site has been treated previously as one at which the SGNAS collected Early Bronze Period pottery. The SGNAS also collected a small number (2) of Iron II sherds at 79H. In the Wadi Umm Jufna region, the SGNAS collected Iron II pottery at Sites 69, 72, and 73. These three sites are located immediately south of the wadi. Site 69 consists of two graves and a tower/tomb (?) which measures ca. 8 m in diameter. It is the largest feature of the three. The site commands an excellent vantage point from which to view activities to the north, west, and south in particular. Sites 72 and 73 are located to the southeast of Site 69 and are closely associated with one another. The former consists of a tomb, a series of large boulders aligned in an arc which measures ca. 12 m long, and a sherd scatter. The latter, Site 73, Rujm Umm Jufna (Photo 11), is a tower which measures ca. 15 m in diameter and still stands ca. 4–5 m high. Associated with the tower, on its southsouthwest side, are two circular alignments. The site commands a good view of Wadi Umm Jufna as well as the territory in the Southern Ghors. It, like Site 69, would have served as a good place from which to monitor movement in the entire Southern Ghors as well as the area further to the west. The earliest identifiable pottery which the SGNAS collected at the

Table 38 Iron IC Period sites

Site No.	Sample No.	No. of Sherds	Plate No.
73	99	1	18 (11)
159	287	1	18 (5)
159	288	1	18 (7)

Table 39 Iron I–Iron II Period sites

Site No.	Sample No.	No. of Sherds	Plate No.
28	77	1	20 (4)
75	118	36	
159	287	1	18 (6)
159	288	1	18 (4)

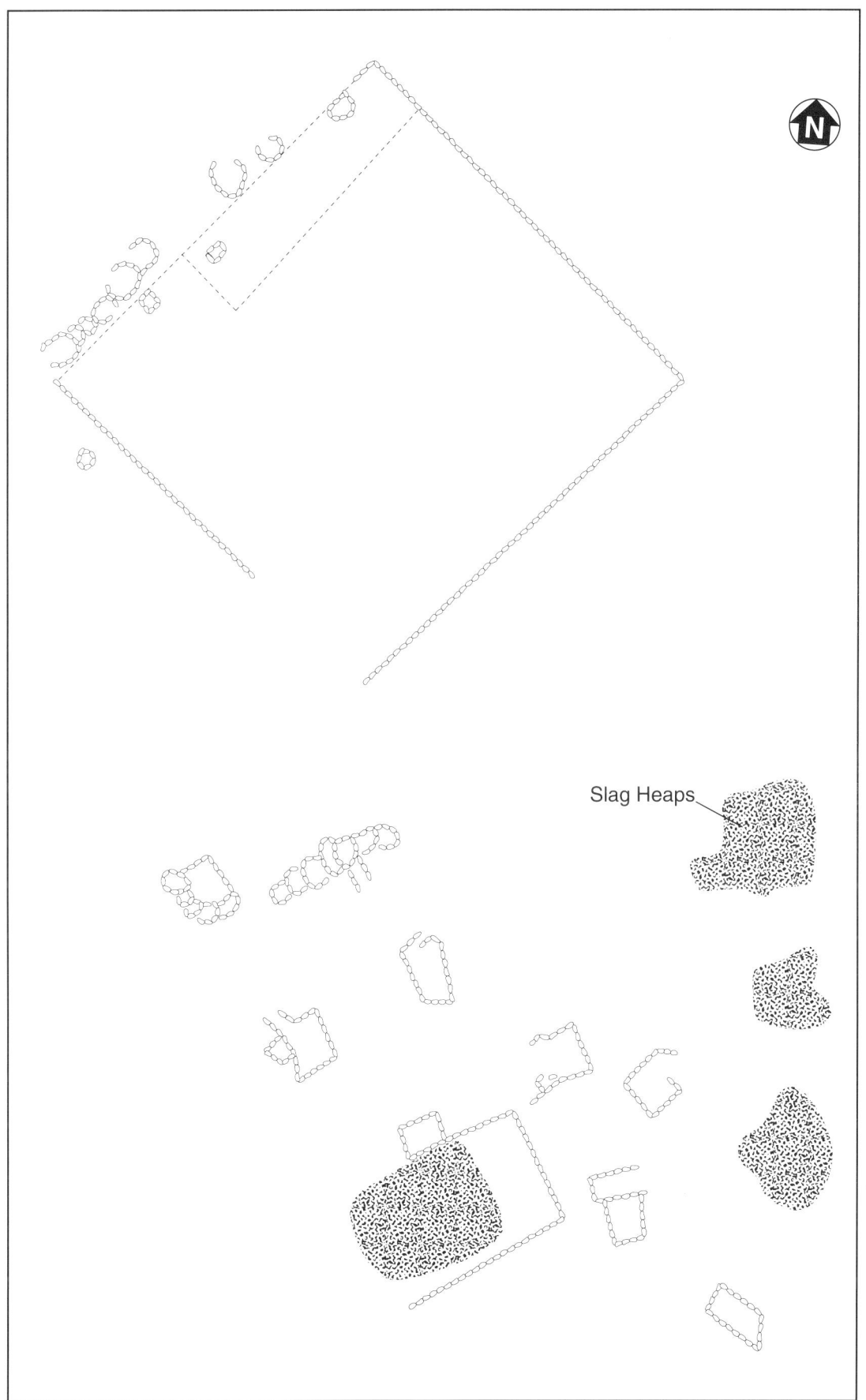

Slag Heaps

Figure 15 Site 159, Khirbet al-Nahas.

site dates to the Iron II period. The site could have been used as a signalling post and/or lookout point during the Iron II as well as subsequent periods.

Site 124, which is located at the western extremity of a large plateau just north of Wadi Feifa, has been treated previously as a site at which the SGNAS collected Early Bronze Period pottery. The outstanding feature of the site is what appears to be a series of 'platforms', possibly graves, each measuring ca. 10 x 3 m, located at the western extremity of the plateau. There are also graves located throughout the plateau. Since the SGNAS collected pottery from several different periods, including Iron II, at the site, it is impossible to determine, on the basis of the available data, to which period(s) the 'platforms' and/or graves belong.

Site 136 is a sherd scatter found on a trail leading away from the plateau on which Site 124 is located. Iron II sherds were the predominant pottery collected at the site.

Site 84 is a lithic and sherd scatter located on the upper terrace on the north side of Wadi Feifa. It has been treated previously as a Chalcolithic and/or Chalcolithic/Early Bronze Period site. The SGNAS collected only one Iron II Period sherd at the site.

Site 75, the western segment of ancient Feifa, has been treated previously as an Iron I–II Period site. As has also been mentioned previously, it yielded Iron II

Table 40   Iron II Period sites

Site No.	Sample No.	No. of Sherds	Plate No.
28	72	18	20 (2)
29	73	19	20 (1;3)
29	74	2	20 (6)
30	77	4	
34	39	15	19 (7–11)
50	93	19	
69	79	16	20 (7–9)
72	97	42	
73	99	44	18 (12)
75	117	2	
75	118	12	
79H	125	2	
84	140	1	
108	148	2	19 (13;12?)
111A	183	1	
124	211	15	
127	221	1	
136	230	35	
155	255	1	
155	256	1	
159	287	2	
161	301	1	19 (4)
161	302	7	19 (6)
165	305	3	
167	279	3	
173A	292	29	
187	330	1	20 (10)
191	316	7	
219	381	1	
221	384	1	

Table 41   Iron IIA Period sites

Site No.	Sample No.	No. of Sherds	Plate No.
29	73	1	20 (5)
159	287	1	18 (9)

Table 42   Iron IIB Period site

Site No.	Sample No.	No. of Sherds	Plate No.
159	288	1	18 (8)

Table 43   Iron IIC Period site

Site No.	Sample No.	No. of Sherds	Plate No.
159	288	1	18 (10)

Period sherds as well.

Site 111A–G is a series of graves on the lower slopes between Wadi Feifa and Wadi Khuneizir. The graves are immediately southeast of the main Mazra'a-'Aqaba Highway. The ones which constitute Site 111A measure ca. 1.5 x 2–2.5 metres. They are spread over an area of ca. 25 x 15 metres. The SGNAS collected only one Iron II Period sherd at the site. It found very little pottery in association with graves A–H. One reason for this may be that the area has been greatly disturbed by road-building activity as well as by the construction of water-control devices.

Rujm Khunzeizir, Site 108, is another site which has generally been associated with the Early Bronze Period (Rast and Schaub 1974; Frolich and Lancaster 1985). As mentioned previously, the cist tombs on the southwest slope of the hill on which the rujm is located appear to date to the EB IV Period. However, the sherds associated with the rujm itself, which still stands ca. 5–6 m high and provides a good vantage point for watching movement in the Southern Ghors to the north and northwest, date, for the most part, to the Iron II Period. Here again, only excavations will determine the date at which the rujm was built (and rebuilt ?). Site 173 is a series of three potbusts on the east side of Wadi al-Nukhbar. The pottery which the SGNAS collected from one of these potbusts, namely, 173A, is Iron II.

Sites 155 and 167 are associated with Wadi al-Tilah. The former, Qasr al-Tilah, is a predominantly Nabataean Period site. As such, it will be treated later. However, it did yield two painted Edomite or Iron II sherds. The latter, located along the south side of the wadi in an area where there are stone piles which may be graves, yielded three sherds from the period under discussion.

The SGNAS collected small quantities (n=1–7) of Iron II pottery at five sites, namely, Sites 165; 187; 191; 219; and 221, in Wadi al-Dahal. The presence of

Iron II pottery in this wadi is expected since it leads up to the important Edomite site of Buseira on the plateau to the east (Bennett 1971; 1973a and b; 1974; 1975; 1976; 1977). This wadi was probably a major travel route among the Edomite settlements on the plateau, the Edomite sites in the Southern Ghors and Northeast 'Arabah, and the Edomite sites in the Negev and the Judaean Hills to the west and northwest respectively (Bartlett 1972; Beit-Arieh and Cresson 1985; Beith-Arieh 1988).

Site 159, Khirbet al-Nahas, Site 161, Khirbet al-Ghuweib, and Khirbet al-Jariyeh have been treated in the discussion of the Iron I Period mining and smelting sites of the Wadi al-Ghuweib region. On the basis of the ceramic evidence, it appears that these three sites were also active during the Iron II Period. Site 159 yielded Iron IIB and IIC sherds as well as Iron II Period sherds, without further precision.

Site 50 is a sherd scatter on the plateau between Wadi al-Ghuweib and Wadi Fidan. It has been treated in the discussion of the Iron I Period sites. It also yielded a moderate number (19) of Iron II sherds.

Site 28, Raikes' Site 'H' (?) (n.d.; 1980), appears to be ancient agricultural fields just to the north of Wadi Fidan. The site is now intersected by the 'Old Road' which goes from Wadi Fidan northward. What appears to be retaining/terrace walls can be seen running east–west for ca. 200 metres. The site yielded a moderate number (18) of Iron II sherds.

There is a heavy sherd concentration, Site 29, on a steep slope, covering an area of ca. 50 (E–W) x 30 (N–S) m, immediately to the south of Site 28. This site has been treated in the discussion of the Chalcolithic/Early Bronze Period sites of the survey. It, like Site 28, yielded a moderate number (21) of Iron II sherds.

Site 34 is a sherd scatter along a tributary drainage on the east side of Wadi Fidan. Iron II was the only identifiable pottery which the SGNAS collected at the site. Two of the sherds collected are the so-called, painted Edomite ware.

Site 30, al-Munbateha/Khirbet Hamr Ifdan, has been treated before in relation to the Chalcolithic/Early Bronze and EB IV Period sites of the survey. It also yielded a small number of Iron II sherds.

There is a looted grave, Site 127, at the southern extremity of the survey territory. It is on the east side of Wadi Fidan. The SGNAS collected only one Iron II sherd at the site.

Iron Age Period sites

What the SGNAS is calling Iron Age Period pottery without further specification was collected at 26 sites, namely, Sites 28; 49A; 56; 60; 62; 73; 79A; 108; 124; 126; 127; 134; 139; 148B; 159; 160; 161; 162; 167; 168; 171; 185; 190; 192; 196; and 227 (Table 44) (Figure 14). Ten of these 26 sites have been treated previously in this chapter as Iron I and/or Iron II sites. Sites 108; 159; and 161 have been treated as both Iron I and Iron II Period sites; Site 126 as an Iron I Period site; and Sites 28; 73; 79; 124; 127; and 167 as Iron II

Table 44 Iron Age Period sites

Site No.	Sample No.	No. of Sherds	Plate No.
28	72	73	
49A	92	3	
56	78	3	
60	112	7	
62	114	6	
73	99	7	
79A	121	28	
108	148	92	
124	211	12	
124	214	35	
126	218	4	
127	221	6	
134	232	12	
139	235	29	
148B	248	1	
159	287	20	
159	288	104	
160	314	6	
161	301	70	
161	302	34	
162	303	14	
167	279	31	
168	306	4	
171	308	47	
185	315	1	
190	336	3	
192	317	2	
196	340	12	
227	375	1	

Period sites. The collection of Iron Age sherds at these 10 sites reinforces the human presence at these sites during the Iron I–II Periods. The remaining 16 sites will be emphasized here.

Site 62 consists of at least six, rock-built tombs in an area measuring ca. 50 x 20 m north of Wadi al-Hasa and east of modern al-Safi. The collection of Iron Age sherds at this site, along with that of Iron II sherds at Site 79H, confirms Iron Age presence in the area.

The SGNAS surveyed Site 196 on the day it made its two transects from the 'Edomite' plateau to the east to the Southern Ghors. The site is associated with the transect between Wadi al-Hasa and Wadi Madsus al-Shamali. It is located on western edge of the so-called 'Edomite' plateau. On a clear day, the site commands an excellent view to the east, west, and south. Wadi al-Hasa blocks the view to the north. The site consists of four graves, possible foundations, and some windbreaks (?), possibly recent. The presence of Iron Age presence in this area is in keeping with the findings of the WHS (MacDonald *et al.* 1988). Further surveying in this area could lead to the discovery of more sites from the period under discussion.

To the west of Site 73, Rujm Umm Jufna, and also along the south side of Wadi Umm Jufna is a light sherd scatter, Site 60, which covers an area of ca. 20 m square. The site is located in a bulldozed area immediately above 'Ain Umm Jufna where there are presently water pipes bringing water from the spring to higher elevations. Site 60, thus, along with Iron Age sherds collected at Sites 126 and 124 to the south, as well as the iron II pottery collected at Sites 69, 72, and 73, confirms Iron Age presence in the Wadi Umm Jufna-Wadi Feifa region.

Sites 134 and 139 are located along the south side of Wadi Umruq. The former has been discussed previously as a Neolithic–Chalcolithic Period site. It also yielded 12 Iron Age body sherds. The latter, a sherd scatter, yielded a moderate number (19) of Iron Age sherds.

Rujm Khuneizir, Site 108 (Photo 5), has been treated previously in this chapter as a site at which the SGNAS collected both Iron I and Iron II sherds. In both cases, however, the number of sherds collected was low. The SGNAS collected a very large number (92) of Iron Age sherds, without further specification, at the site. Moreover, all these sherds were collected at the summit of the site where the tower (?) is located. It would seem that the summit was used at least during the Iron Age Period. As mentioned in the treatment of the site during the discussion of the EB IV sites of the survey, only excavations will determine when the tower was built.

Site 148, which is a segment of a continuous sherd scatter located on the plateau immediately west of Wadi Khuneizir, has been treated as an EB IV and Early Bronze Period site. One identifiable Iron Age sherd was among those which the SGNAS collected at the site.

The collection of Iron Age sherds at Sites 162, 168, 171, 185, 190, and 192 in Wadi al-Dahal confirms the use of this wadi during the periods under discussion. The most westerly located of these six sites is Site 162. It is located along the south bank of the wadi just to east of the 'Old Road'. It is a cemetery plus a lithic and sherd scatter above the south bed of Wadi al-Dahal. The SGNAS collected a moderate number of Iron Age sherds at the site. Site 168 is a cemetery and sherd scatter on a terrace on the north side of the wadi further to the east. Site 171 is a very dense lithic and sherd scatter just to the southeast of Site 168. It has been treated previously as a Chalcolithic/Early Bronze Period site. Site 185 is a domestic cluster and/or camping site located even further east in the wadi. To the south is Site 192, a very large cemetery measuring ca. 500 m square, at the confluence of Wadi al-Dahal and a smaller wadi entering it from the northeast. The graves do not all seem to be from the same period. The SGNAS also noted evidence of camping on the terraces where the graves are located. Site 190 is south of Site 171 across Wadi al-Dahal. It too consists of graves as well as a lithic and sherd scatter. The different elements of all these sites need not, however, be contemporaneous. The only thing that can be said, on the basis of the sherds collected, is that the wadi was an active place during both the Iron I and Iron II Periods.

Site 227 is located at the summit of a hill just to the northeast of Wadi al-Ghuweib and west of the 'Old Road'. It has been treated previously as a Chalcolithic/Early Bronze Period site. It yielded only one Iron Age sherd.

Sites 159, Khirbet al-Nahas, and 161, Khirbet al-Ghuweib, as mentioned previously, are probably Iron I–II smelting sites. Both yielded Iron Age Period sherds as well.

Site 160 is a probable grave and a sherd scatter along Wadi al-Ghuweib. The SGNAS discovered the site on its way to Khirbet al-Ghuweib, Site 161. It collected 16 Iron Age sherds, probably Iron I, at the site.

Site 49 is a series of tombs (?) located on both sides of the 'Old Road' between Wadi al-Ghuweib and Wadi Fidan. Tomb A, which is a circular arrangement of stones measuring ca. 4.5 x 2.3 m, has been disturbed. It yielded a small number (3) of Iron Age sherds.

Site 56 is a lithic and sherd scatter spread over a plateau in the same general area as Site 49.[4] It too yielded a small amount of Iron Age pottery.

Conclusions

The treatment of sites from the Iron I, Iron II, and Iron Age, without further specification, testifies to human presence in the Southern Ghors and Northeast 'Arabah during these periods. The situtation is certainly changed from that of both the Middle and Late Bronze Periods when the area seems to have been largely depopulated.

Iron I Period sherds are found in the area as far north as Wadi al-Hasa and as far south as Wadi al-Ghuweib. However, it is in Wadi al-Ghuweib that the heaviest concentration of Iron I Period sites are present. Only excavations will determine just how extensively the mining and smelting sites in Wadi al-Ghuweib and Wadi al-Jariyeh were used during the period under discussion.

As mentioned previously, the SGNAS also found Iron II Period pottery throughout the survey territory. This evidence is noted at Site 79 at the northern as well as at Site 127 at the southern extremity of the survey territory. Wadis al-Hasa, Umm Jufna, Feifa, Umruq, Khuneizir, al-Dahal, al-Ghuweib, and Fidan were, on the basis of the available evidence, extremely important to the people living in the area during the Iron II Period. The increased number of sites seems to indicate an increase in population during this period. Wadi al-Dahal, which leads up to the plateau near Buseira appears to have been a major route for communication between the plateau to the east and areas of the Southern Ghors, Northeast 'Arabah, and the regions to the west and northwest. It could be that Site 73, Rujm Umm Jufna, was an Iron II watchtower. Moreover, recent excavations at Site 75, the western segment of ancient Feifa, indicates Iron II presence at the site. Excavations also at Site 108, Rujm Khuneizir, are necessary to determine whether or not this site was built and/or rebuilt during the Iron II Period. In the Northeast 'Arabah, the mining and smelting sites of Khirbet al-Nahas, Site 159, Khirbet al-Ghuweib, Site 161, and Khirbet al-Jariyeh were extremely important during the Iron II as well as during the Iron I Period.

The natural resources of the area appear to have been used extensively during the period.

Notes

1   See Chapter 6, notes 1 and 2.
2   See Chapter 6, note 2.
3   See Chapter 6, note 1.
4   Because Site 56 covers such a large area of the plateau between Wadi al-Ghuweib and Wadi Fidan, it cannot be precisely located on Figures 3, 11, and 21. It is in the general area of Site 49A–F.

8. Hellenistic, Nabataean and Roman Period Sites

by B. MacDonald

Introduction

The question of continuity or discontinuity in settlement in Edom east of Wadi 'Arabah between the end of the kingdom of Edom, sometime in the sixth century according to Bartlett (1989: 161), and the beginning of the Nabataean kingdom, is still debated (Bartlett 1979: 53; 1989). Bartlett posits a continuity of settlement in the region with the Nabataean herdsmen moving in as political authority in Edom decayed (1979: 66; 1989: 163–74). Hart, on the other hand, on the basis of his surveys (1986) and excavations (1987) on the Edomite plateau, opts for a contrary position. He states that 'the theory of continuity of settlement between the Edomites and the Nabataeans is becoming a difficult one to maintain' (1987: 47).

The chapter will treat the Classical Period sites of the survey: Hellenistic; Nabataean (=Late Hellenistic–Early Roman); Nabataean (=Early Roman); Nabataean, without further specification; Roman and Late Roman; and Late Roman–Byzantine. The presentation will be chronologically and, for the most part, in a north-to-south direction.

Hellenistic Period sites

The SGNAS collected Hellenistic Period pottery at seven sites, namely, Sites 73; 94; 139; 143; 154A and E; 155; and 237 (Table 45) (Figure 16). However, at two of these sites, namely, Sites 143 and 155, the SGNAS collected only one Hellenistic sherd.

Rujm Umm Jufna, Site 73 (Photo 11), is located along the south side of Wadi Umm Jufna. It is a tower which commands an excellent view of the terrain in the Southern Ghors as well as the territory to the west and the south in the Northeast 'Arabah. It has been treated previously in the discussion of the Iron II and Iron Age sites of the survey. The SGNAS collected 14 identifiable, Hellenistic sherds at the site.

Site 237 is located to the north of Sites 75 and 76, ancient Feifa. It consists of a number of large graves. It yielded a moderate number of Hellenistic sherds.

Rujm Umruq, Site 94, is a tower/tomb located on an isolated 'island' along the north side of Wadi Umruq near its mouth (Raikes n.d.: 38) (Photo 12). The highest point of the site is at least 4–5 m above the sands that surround the 'island'. The tower/tomb is located at the east end of the 'island'. It could have served originally as a tower and only subsequently as a place of burial. The site has been badly disturbed by digging at its highest point. There are bones and pottery sherds scattered about which probably come from this digging. At a lower level on the 'island' and to the west, where there is evidence of more structures

in the form of wall lines, there are further indications of disturbances. There appears to be graves here as well. The site could have served as a monitoring point at the western end of Wadi Umruq to monitor traffic entering and exiting from the wadi. There is a path that goes up along the north side of the wadi. The 1:50,000 scale map shows it continuing to just south of al-Tafila. It is a common practice, even today, to have monitoring points at such locations.

Site 139 is a sherd scatter located at the base of a high mountain to the southeast of Site 94. It has been mentioned previously in relation to the Iron Age sites of the survey. Eight Hellenistic, fish-bowl fragments were among the sherds which the SGNAS collected at the site.

Site 143 consists of a tomb and a sherd scatter on a spur of the plateau just to the west of Wadi Khuneizir. The site has been treated along with the Early Bronze Period sites of the survey. As mentioned previously, the SGNAS collected one Hellenistic sherd at the site.

Site 154A–H is a series of graves/tombs (?), wall lines, and stone piles (?) on the plateau immediately west of Wadi al-Nukhbar. It has been discussed previously in relation to the EB IV Period sites. At two segments of the site, namely, at A and E, the SGNAS collected a large number of Hellenistic sherds. Site 154A consists of a line of stones, measuring ca. 40 m in length and going in a southeast–southwest direction, and a number of stone piles. There is evidence of bulldozing activity in the area and some of the above-mentioned features could be the result of this activity. Site 154E is comprised of a sherd scatter and graves (?). There is no assurance, however, that the Hellenistic sherds collected at these two segments of the site are indeed related to the features described above.

Qasr al-Tilah, Site 155, is a predominantly Roman Period site. Therefore, it will be treated later.

Table 45 Hellenistic Period sites

Site No.	Sample No.	No. of Sherds	Plate No.
73	99	14	21 (4)
94	144	11	21 (1–2; 7–9; 13–14
139	235	8	21 (3;5)
143	245	1	
154A	252	75	21 (12)
154E	276	213	21 (10)
155	256	1	21 (6)
237	404	10	21 (11)

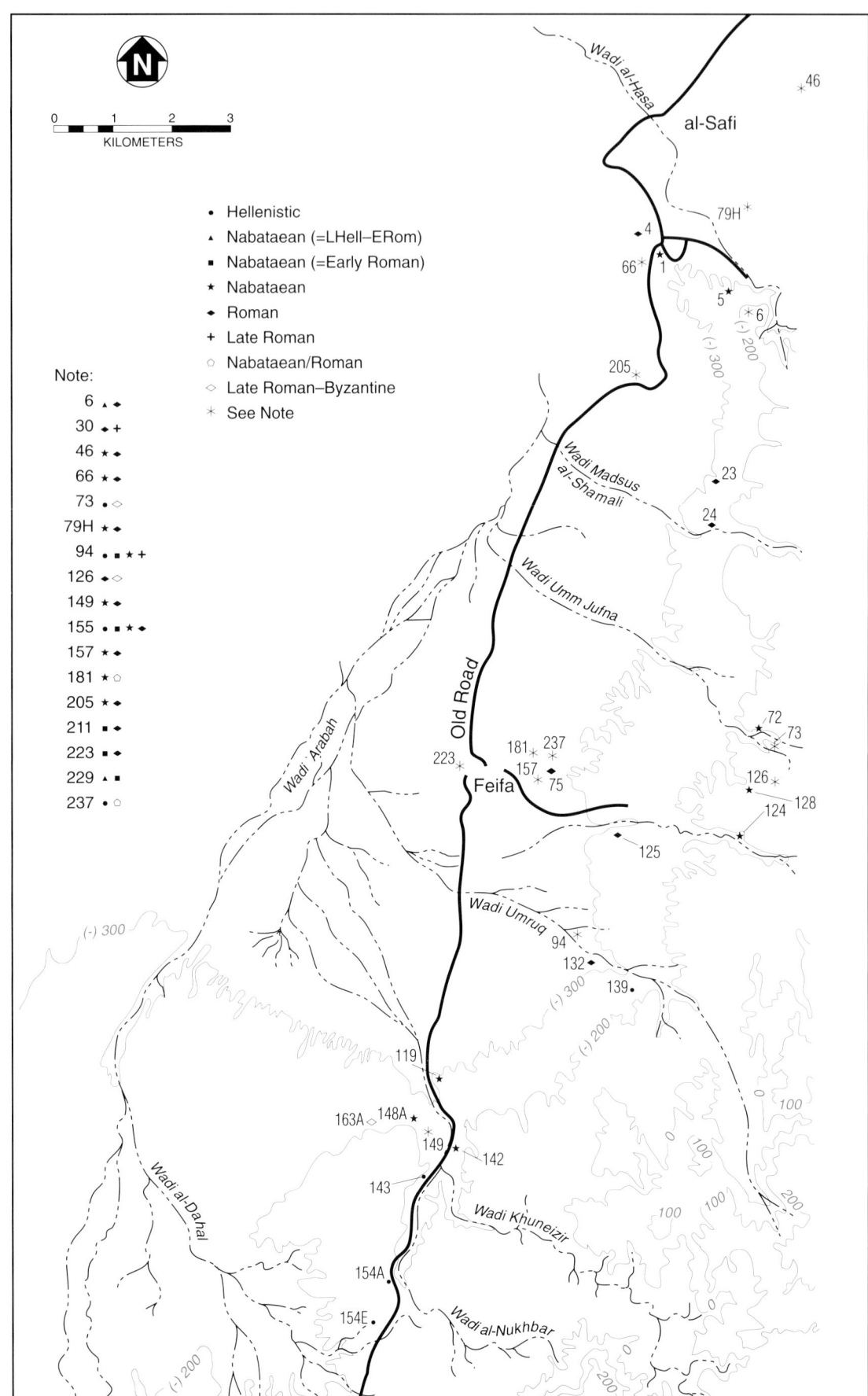

Figure 16 Hellenistic, Nabataean (=LHell–ERom), Nabataean (=ERom), Nabataean, Roman, Late Roman, Nabataean/Roman, Late Roman–Byzantine settlement pattern map (Northern portion).

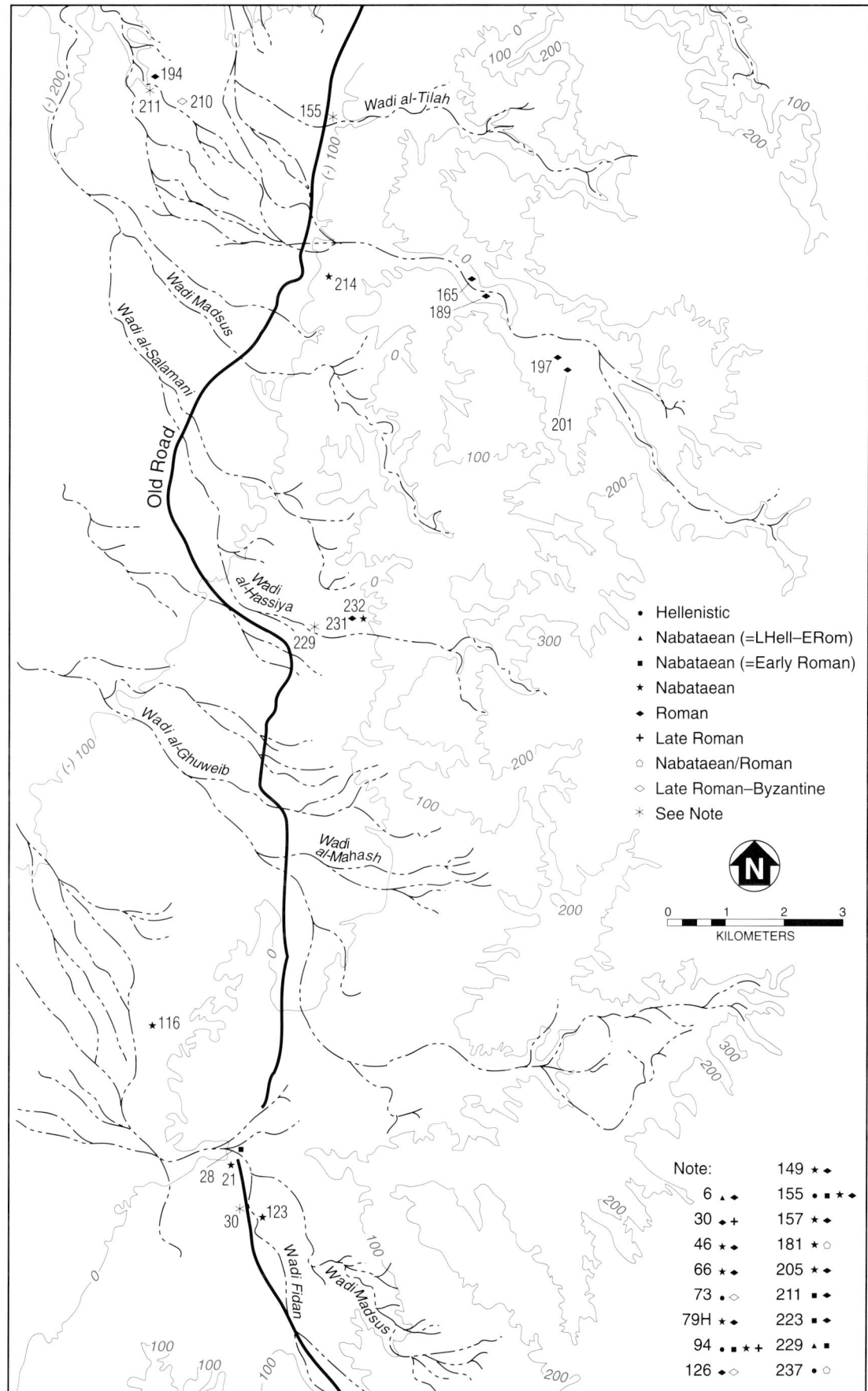

Figure 16 Hellenistic, Nabataean (=LHell–ERom), Nabataean (=ERom), Nabataean, Roman, Late Roman, Nabataean/Roman, Late Roman–Byzantine settlement pattern map (Southern portion).

From the above, it is clear that Hellenistic Period sherds are confined to one segment of the survey territory. They are found between Wadis Umm Jufna and al-Tilah. Thus, they are confined to the central segment of the area, i.e., between the southern segment of the Southern Ghors and the northern segment of the Northeast 'Arabah.

Nabataean (=Late Hellenistic–Early Roman) Period sites

The SGNAS collected Nabataean or Late Hellenistic–Early Roman Period sherds at two sites, namely, Sites 6, and 229 (Table 46) (Figure 16).

Umm al-Tawabin, Site 6, appears to be a very large Nabataean fortress located high above and to the southeast of al-Safi and the Wadi al-Hasa gorge.[1] Hart, who was a member of Kitchener's 1883 expedition to the 'Arabah, discovered the site (1885: 266; Kitchener 1884: 216; Hull 1886: 121; Mallon 1924: 435, 438; Abel 1967: 466–67). The site has also been called Khirbet Labrush/al-Ebrosh (Kitchener 1884: 216; Mallon 1924: 438; Abel 1967: 466). Mallon (1924: 438) cited it as a possible location for the Church of St. Lot of the Madaba map (O'Callaghan 1953; Avi-Yonah 1954; 1977; Gold 1958; Donner and Cüppers 1977). It has been mentioned previously in the discussion of the Chalcolithic/Early Bronze Period sites. It is comprised of two main segments, namely, a lower and upper or 'citadel' area. The lower segment of the site is enclosed by a stone wall, built for the most part on a natural rock ledge. This wall extends for ca. 2.50 km around the site (Figure 17) (Photo 13). It is especially evident on the west, southwest, and southeast segments of the site. On the west and southwest side there are small circular structures both within and outside this wall (Photo 14). For the most part, they measure ca. 2–3 m in diameter with 'entrances' facing northeast (Figure 17). They were probably used as placements for tents for soldiers (Poidebard 1934, Pl. L, 1). On the basis of the available evidence, however, it is not possible to say that they are contemporaneous with all the other segments of the site. The remnants of several larger structures and at least one reservoir (?) are located within the wall in the lower segments of the site, especially along the west and southwest sides. At the southeast extremity of the site there is what appears to be a very large

Table 46 Nabataean (=LHell–ERom) Period sites

Site No.	Sample No.	No. of Sherds	Plate No.
6	11	93	22 (1–2; 5–9;11–18:
6	13	2	
6	14	131	22 (3–4; 10:
229	378	47	23 (4;6–7;12)
229	379	57	23 (5;9–11)

'tower' at the high point of the site in this segment. The 'tower', however, appears to be much more than an ordinary lookout post. This comment is made on the basis of its size. The enclosure wall is particularly evident and large at this point. The upper or 'citadel' portion of the site is located at the northern end of a high ridge within the enclosure wall. There are the remnants of a wall running up the west slope of this ridge and several seemingly human-dug, deep trenches which separate the 'citadel' area from the remainder of the ridge. A deep hole, possibly the remnants of a reservoir, was noted on the 'citadel'. The 'citadel' area provides a sweeping panorama of the entire area to the south and west of the Dead Sea. The site would have provided an excellent vantage point from which to view movements in the Southern Ghors, especially around the south end of the Dead Sea, as well as in the territory further to the west and in the Northeast 'Arabah (Rothenberg 1971). Inhabitants of al-Safi informed the SGNAS that the site was used recently as a military lookout point. The SGNAS collected sherds from several different periods, namely, Chalcolithic/Early Bronze; Nabataean; Roman; Byzantine; and Mamluk, at the site. The SGNAS collected Nabataean pottery from almost all segments of the site and it is the predominant pottery, by far, collected. The best parallels for this Nabataean pottery date to the Late Hellenistic–Early Roman Period, i.e., to the first century B.C. Only excavations at the site will determine when the various segments of the site were built and used.

Khirbet al-Hassiya North, Site 229, is probably a Nabataean caravanserai (Figure 18). Frank was the first to report its existence (1934: 215, Taf. 30 A, Plan 14; Alt 1935: 4). Glueck may have seen it from the air (1937: 21). It is located on the north side of Wadi al-Hassiya and just north of the 'Old Road'. It is comprised of a large rectangular structure measuring ca. 30 x 22 m with rooms on at least the south and west sides. One room on the west side had been robbed by the time of the SGNAS' visit in 1986. There was a great deal of Nabataean pottery lying where the digging had taken place. The walls of the structure are made of unhewn stone and measure ca. 1 m in thickness. Since the structure is located at the base of a hill there is a great deal of silt within it. There is black–brown soil along Wadi al-Hassiya nearby. This could be the location of a midden. The pottery collected at the site is exclusively Nabataean dating to the Late Hellenistic through Early Roman Period. On the basis of the collected ceramics, the site was in operation until the beginning of the second century A.D. It is, thus, later than Site 6, Umm al-Tawabin.[2]

Nabataean (=Early Roman) Period sites

The SGNAS collected Nabataean (=Early Roman) Period pottery at six sites, namely, Sites 28; 94; 155; 211; 223; and 229 (Table 47) (Figure 16). One of

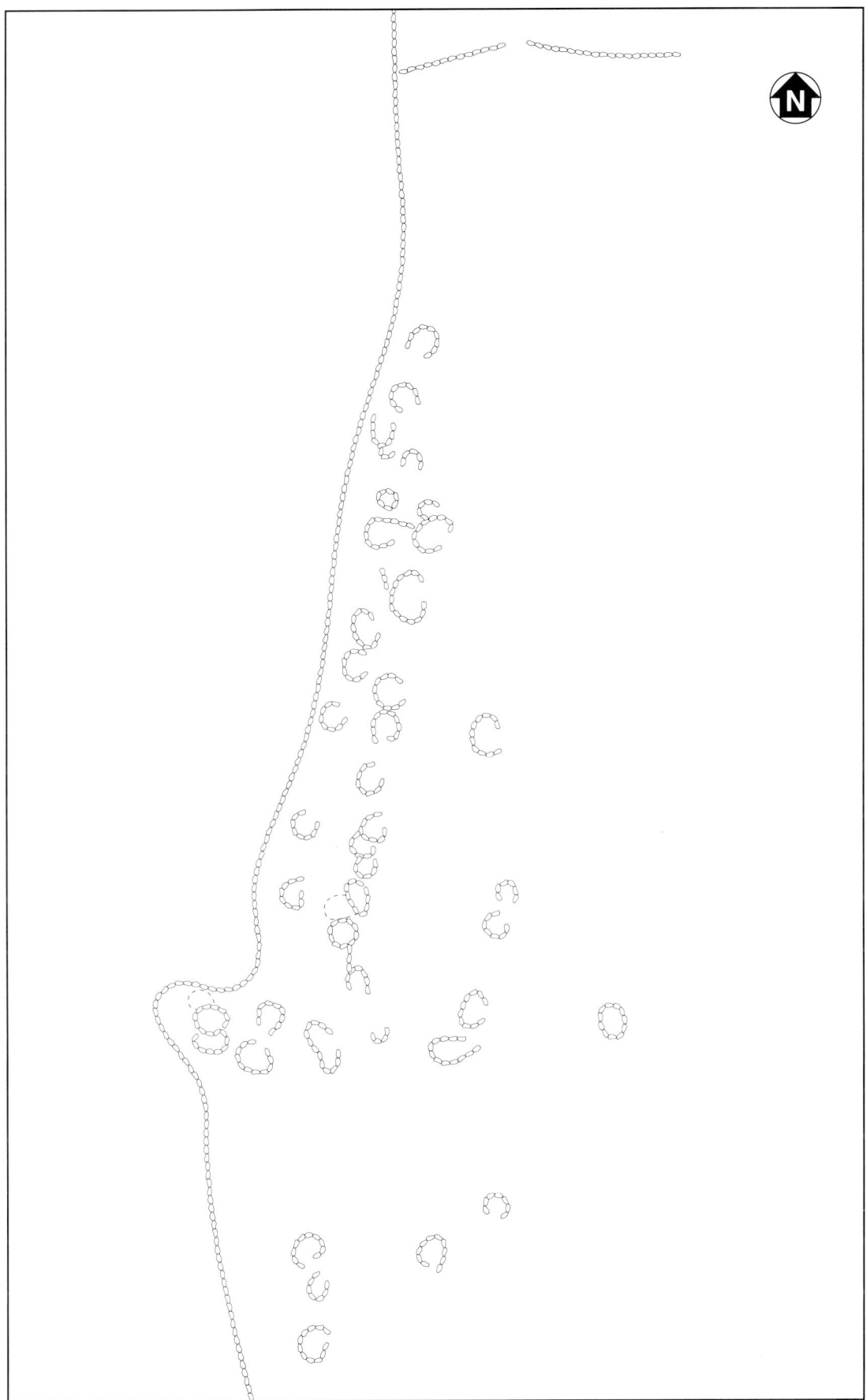

Figure 17 Site 6, Umm al-Tawabin.

Table 47 Nabataean (=Early Roman) Period sites

Site No.	Sample No.	No. of Sherds	Plate No.
28	72	1	24 (6)
94	144	1	24 (1)
155	254	17	23 (3)
211	353	1	25 (5)
223	400	11	24 (2)
223	403	24	23 (2;14)
229	377	65	23 (1;8;13)
229	378	1	23 (4;6–7;12)
229	379	1	23 (5;9–11)

these sites, namely, Site 229, Khirbet al-Hassiya North, has just been treated as a Late Hellenistic–Early Roman site. Two others, namely, Sites 94 and 155, have been treated as Hellenistic Period sites. They will both be referred to later as sites at which the SGNAS collected Nabataean sherds, without further precision.

Site 223 is located in what is now the bed of Wadi Feifa to the southwest of the modern village of Feifa, Site 91. The present course of the wadi is probably different from that of the Classical Period. There is one large stone wall, possibly the foundations of a building, in the area where water is presently running. About 100 m to the northwest, but still in the wadi bed, there are more wall lines and isolated building stones. The soil surrounding the walls is a very dark-coloured, organic-looking soil. The site is probably the remnants of a series of structures. The pottery collected at the site is almost exclusively Nabataean, i.e., Early Roman.

Khirbet al-Dahal, Site 211, is a predominantly Byzantine site. It will, therefore, be discussed in association with other sites from that period. It yielded only one sherd from the period under discussion.

Site 28, located immediatly north of Wadi Fidan, has been treated previously as a site at which the SGNAS collected Iron Age sherds. It also yielded one Nabataean or Early Roman sherd.

Nabataean Period sites

The SGNAS collected Nabataean Period sherds, without further precision, at 22 sites (Table 48) (Figure 16). These sites range from sherd scatters to very large architectural sites. At six of these sites, namely, Sites 1; 21; 79H; 149; 214; and 232, the SGNAS collected only one or two Nabataean sherds. These sites will not be treated in the subsequent discussion.

Deir 'Ain 'Abata, Site 46, is the most northerly located site at which the SGNAS collected Nabataean sherds. However, since this is a predominantly Byzantine site it will be returned to for a full discussion in the chapter on the Byzantine sites of the survey.

Site 5 has been treated previously in relation to both the Early Bronze and Iron Age sites of the survey. It

consists of a series of graves and a Bedouin camp. It yielded 11 Nabataean sherds.

Site 66 is a medium-to-high sherd scatter in an agricultural field immediately to the southwest of Site 1, Tawahin al-Sukkar. The field has been cleared for agricultural purposes. Nabataean, Roman, Late Byzantine–Umayyad, and Abbasid sherds were among those which the SGNAS collected at the site. There is the possibility, on the basis of the number of sherds collected, that there was once an architectural site from the Nabataean–Umayyad Periods in the field. However, all that is left is a sherd scatter. This site will be returned to in the discussion of the Roman and Byzantine Period sites.

Site 205, Sammar, is a midden located in a sandy area just west of the modern Mazra'a–'Aqaba Highway and about midway between Wadi al-Hasa and Wadi Madsus al-Shamali. There is a heavy concentration of Nabataean, Roman, and Byzantine sherds as well as glass at the site. There is much ash present as well. Could this have been the site of a kiln?

Site 72, which is located along the south side of Wadi Umm Jufna, consists of a tomb and a series of large boulders aligned to form an arc. It has been treated as an Iron II Period site. The area could have been reused during the period under discussion.

Sites 128 and 124 are located on the plateau to the north of Wadi Feifa. Both are architectural sites. The former consists of graves, indications of camping, and stone lines (retaining and/or terrace walls [?]). The latter, which consists for the most part of a series of 'platforms', possibly tombs and graves, has been

Table 48 Nabataean Period sites

Site No.	Sample No.	No. of Sherds	Plate No.
1	3	2	
5	10	11	
21	71	2	
46	90	4	
66	111	25	
72	97	4	
72	98	7	
79H	125	1	
94	139	5	
94	144	11	
116	189	10	
119	190	35	
123	213	3	
124	211	29	
128	223	33	
142	243	4	
148A	246	4	
149	247	1	
155	255	1	
155	256	28	
155	257	21	
157	300	5	
181	284	4	
205	354	29	
214	371	1	
232	398	2	

treated previously as an Early Bronze and Iron Age site. The SGNAS collected a moderate number of Nabataean sherds at both sites.

In the vicinity of ancient Feifa, Sites 75 and 76, there are two sites, namely, Sites 157 and 181, at which the SGNAS collected Nabataean sherds. They are sherd scatters which have been treated in the discussion of the Chalcolithic/Early Bronze and Early Bronze sites of the survey.

Rujm Umruq, Site 94 (Photo 12), a tower site at the western entrance to Wadi Umruq, has been discussed previously as a site at which the SGNAS collected Hellenistic sherds. However, it also yielded Nabataean Period pottery.

Site 119 is a sherd scatter on a terrace on the east side of Wadi Khuneizir. It is located just to the southwest of Rujm Khuneizir, Site 108, and has been discussed as a site at which EB IV cist tombs are present. The terrace on which the site is located is now badly disturbed by bulldozing and erosion. The contractor's worshops were situated here during the modern-road construction (Raikes n.d.: 38). There are the remnants of what may have been a terrace wall at the southeast segment of the site. The number of Nabataean sherds at the site indicates presence during the period under discussion. Raikes thinks that there were once Nabataean Period houses at this spot (n.d.: 38).

There is a sherd scatter, Site 142, on the path going to the EB IV site of Abu Irshareibeh, Site 141. The site has been discussed along with the EB IV Period sites of the survey. Four Nabataean sherds were among those which the SGNAS collected at the site.

Site 148 has been treated as a sherd scatter located on the plateau immediately west of Wadi Khuneizir. Along with EB IV, Early Bronze, and Iron Age sherds the SGNAS collected a small number (4) of Nabataean sherds at the site.

Qasr al-Tilah, Site 155, is a well known Nabataean (=Early–Late Roman) fort and caravanserai (Musil 1907: 209–14, fig.214 and figs. 147ff.; Frank 1934: 213–15, Taf. 29A, Plan 13; Alt 1935: 4; Glueck 1935: 12–17; Abel 1967: 181, 486; Rothenberg 1971: 214; Raikes n.d.: 36) (Figure 19). There are extensive agricultural fields associated with the structures (Figure 20). The site is located at the western end of Wadi al-Tilah. Glueck gives the measurements of the reservoir as 34.2 x 33.6 m (1935: 12). The east wall of the structure is flush with the bottom of the slope which rises behind it. The west wall still stands ca. 4.5 m high and like the other walls is 1.3 m thick (Glueck 1935: 12). The entire structure is built of limestone blocks (Figure 19). Remains of plaster can still be seen both on the interior and exterior walls. The steps which lead down into the reservoir are located at the southeast corner. The aqueduct which brought the water from 'Ain al-Tilah to the east can still be seen at places along the north side of the wadi. There are indications that a structure was attached to the southwest corner of the reservoir. A channel leads along the top of the south wall towards this corner. This could have been the location of a flour mill at

one time. Now, however, all that remains are an outline and a stone foundations outside the southwest corner. There are a number of foundation walls immediately to the southwest of the reservoir. The fort is located ca. 50 m to the west of the reservoir (Figure 19). It measures ca. 40 m square and has four, apparently square, corner towers. Two of the towers could still be seen, despite the ruined condition of the structure, on the 1977 aerial photos (Figure 19). The walls measure ca. 2 m thick (Glueck 1935: 13). The fort has been recently damaged by a bulldozer. The likely culprits were road contractors seeking accessible stone. However, some internal partitions are still visible. A looted grave was noted in the middle of the structure. Many of the terracing walls in the agricultural fields to the west and north are clearly visible (Figure 20). They measure ca. 0.50–1.00 m in thickness. In some places these walls have been destroyed by human and/or natural causes. Raikes noted what he called the remnants of a farily large village on the south side of Wadi al-Tilah (n.d.: 36). The SGNAS collected Hellenistic, Nabataean (=Early Roman), Nabataean, Roman, and Byzantine sherds at the site. However, here again, only excavations will clarify the date of the building and use of the various segments of the site.[3]

Site 232 is located just to the northeast of Khirbet al-Hassiya North, Site 229. The SGNAS collected two painted, Nabataean sherds at the site. Since the pottery at the site is predominantly Byzantine, however, the site will be discussed along with other sites from that period.

There are three sites, namely, Sites 21; 116; and 123, in the Wadi Fidan region from which the SGNAS collected Nabataean sherds. Site 21 may be the location of agricultural fields along the south side of the wadi. It has been treated previously as a Neolithic and Early Bronze Period site. Site 116 consists of a cemetery and possible camp north of the Wadi Fidan gorge. Site 123 is a cave measuring ca. 7 x 10 m just above the bed of Wadi Fidan (Photo 3). It has a hole through its southeast end and, thus, it has both a front and back entrance. The SGNAS noted a retaining wall, three courses high, downslope from the mouth of the cave. Within the cave there are storage (?) areas set off by stones. There is evidence of burning both within and outside the cave. There appear to be deposits on the floor of the cave which may warrant further investigations. The cave appears to have been used recently as a place to pen animals. The only identifiable pottery collected at the site dates to the Nabataean Period.

Roman and Late Roman Period sites

The SGNAS collected Roman Period pottery at 24 sites (Table 49) (Figure 16). However, at nine of these sites, namely, Sites 4; 6; 23; 46; 126; 149; 189; 194; and 211, the SGNAS collected only one or two sherds from the period under discussion. Thus, they will not come in for a great deal of consideration as Roman Period sites. Moreover, the SGNAS collected

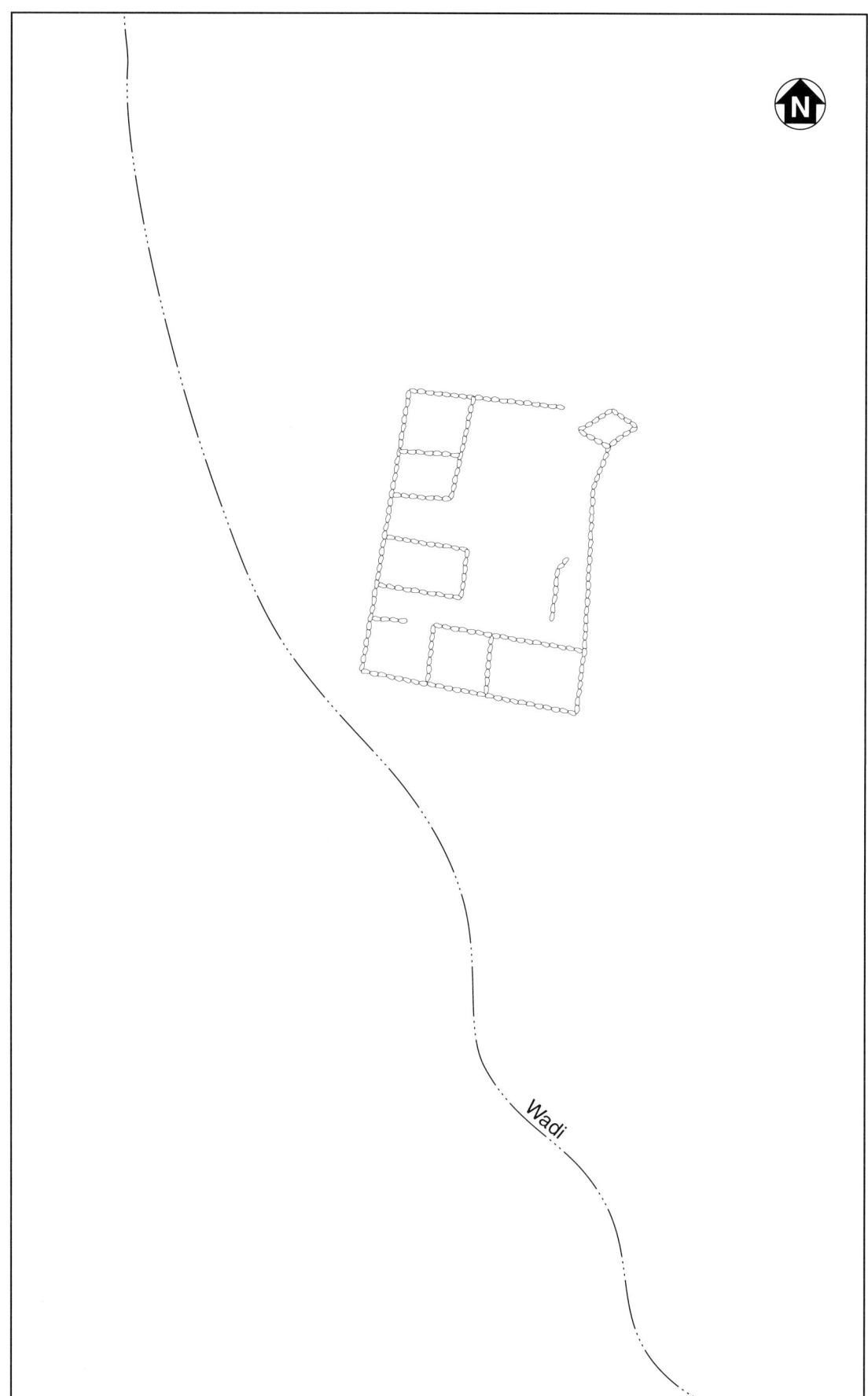

Figure 18 Site 229, Khirbet al-Hassiya North.

Table 49 Roman Period sites

Site No.	Sample No.	No. of Sherds	Plate No.
4	9	1	
6	12	2	
23	34	1	
24	35	5	
30	77	19	
46	90	2	
66	111	3	
75	117	3	
79H	125	4	
125	215	17	
125	216	5	
126	218	2	
132	229	7	
149	247	1	
155	254	9	
155	255	21	
155	257	4	
157	300	5	
165	305	5	
189	332	1	
194	319	2	
197	341	37	
201	347	6	
205	354	3	
211	350	1	
223	400	11	
223	403	14	
231	397	5	

Late Roman Period sherds at two sites, namely, Sites 30 and 94 (Table 50) (Figure 16). Several of these Roman and Late Roman sites, e.g., Sites 6, 94, 155, are major ones which have been treated previously in this chapter. Thus, they will only be alluded to in this segment.

The SGNAS collected small quantities of Roman Period pottery at Site 46, Deir 'Ain 'Abata, and Site 79 north of Wadi al-Hasa. Site 46 is a major, Byzantine site which will be treated in detail in the next chapter. It has been alluded to as a site at which the SGNAS collected a small number (4) of Nabataean sherds. Site 79A–H, a series of gaves spread over a terrace east of modern al-Safi, has been treated previously in the discussion of the Iron II Period sites of the survey. Site 79H is a general surface collection over the entire area.

Umm al-Tawabin, Site 6, is a Late Hellenistic–Early Roman fortress. It is, therefore, not surprising that Roman Period pottery, without further precision, ought to be present at the site.

Site 66, a sherd scatter in an agricultural field immediately to the southwest of Tawahin al-Sukkar, Site 1, has been discussed as a Nabataean (=Late Hellenistic–Early Roman) Period site. The SGNAS collected a small number (3) of Roman sherds at the site.

Site 205, Sammar, between Wadis al-Hasa and Madsus al-Shamali in a sandy area, has been treated along with the Nabataean (=Late Hellenistic–Early

Roman) Period sites of the survey. The SGNAS collected a small number of Roman sherds at the site.

To the southeast and just north of Wadi Madsus al-Shamali, the SGNAS collected Roman sherds at two sites, namely, Sites 23 and 24. The former is a camp and grave site while the latter is probably a potbust.

In the Wadi Feifa region, the SGNAS collected Roman Period sherds at Site 75, ancient Feifa, as well as west, northeast, and southeast of it at Sites 157, 126, 125, and 223. Site 75 has been treated in the discussion of the Neolithic; Chalcolithic/Early Bronze; Early Bronze; Iron I; and Iron II Periods of the survey.[4] Site 157 has been discussed as a Chalcolithic/Early Bronze; Early Bronze; and Nabataean Period site. Site 126 is a sherd scatter which has been treated previously as a site at which the SGNAS collected EB IV and Iron Age sherds. Site 125 is another sherd scatter on a small terrace south of Wadi Feifa. The Roman sherds, which were the predominant identifiable ones in both samples, were in an area which has been distrubed by erosion. Moreover, sherds from the period under discussion were collected in moderate numbers at Site 223 which is located in the present bed of the wadi. This site has also been discussed as a Nabataean (=Early Roman) Period site.

The SGNAS also collected a small number (5) of Late Roman Period sherds, along with Hellenistic and Nabataean ones, at Site 94, Rujm Umruq. The site has been treated previously in relation to the Hellenistic, Nabataean (=Late Hellenistic–Early Roman), and Nabataean (=Early Roman) Period sites. It appears that this tower was of importance during the entire Classical Period.

Site 132 is located immediately to the south of Rujm Umruq. It is a sherd scatter on a terrace on the south side of Wadi Umruq. The terrace has been bulldozed and is dissected by erosional activity. The remnants of an aqueduct cuts through the terrace in several places. Roman sherds in small quantity (7) were among the sherds which the SGNAS collected at the site.

In the Wadi al-Tilah region, the SGNAS collected Roman Period sherds at Site 155, Qasr al-Tilah, as well as at Sites 194 and 211, Khirbet al-Dahal, to the west. Site 155 has been treated extensively above. Site 194 is a lithic and sherd scatter. It has been treated previously as a EB IV Period site. Site 211 is a Byzantine village/hamlet site. It will, thus, be treated along with other sites from this period.

The SGNAS collected Roman sherds from Sites 165, 189, 197, and 201 in Wadi al-Dahal. All these sites consist, for the most part, of graves and a sherd

Table 50 Late Roman Period sites

Site No.	Sample No.	No. of Sherds	Plate No.
30	77	19	24 (5)
30	76	24	
94	144	5	24 (11)

91

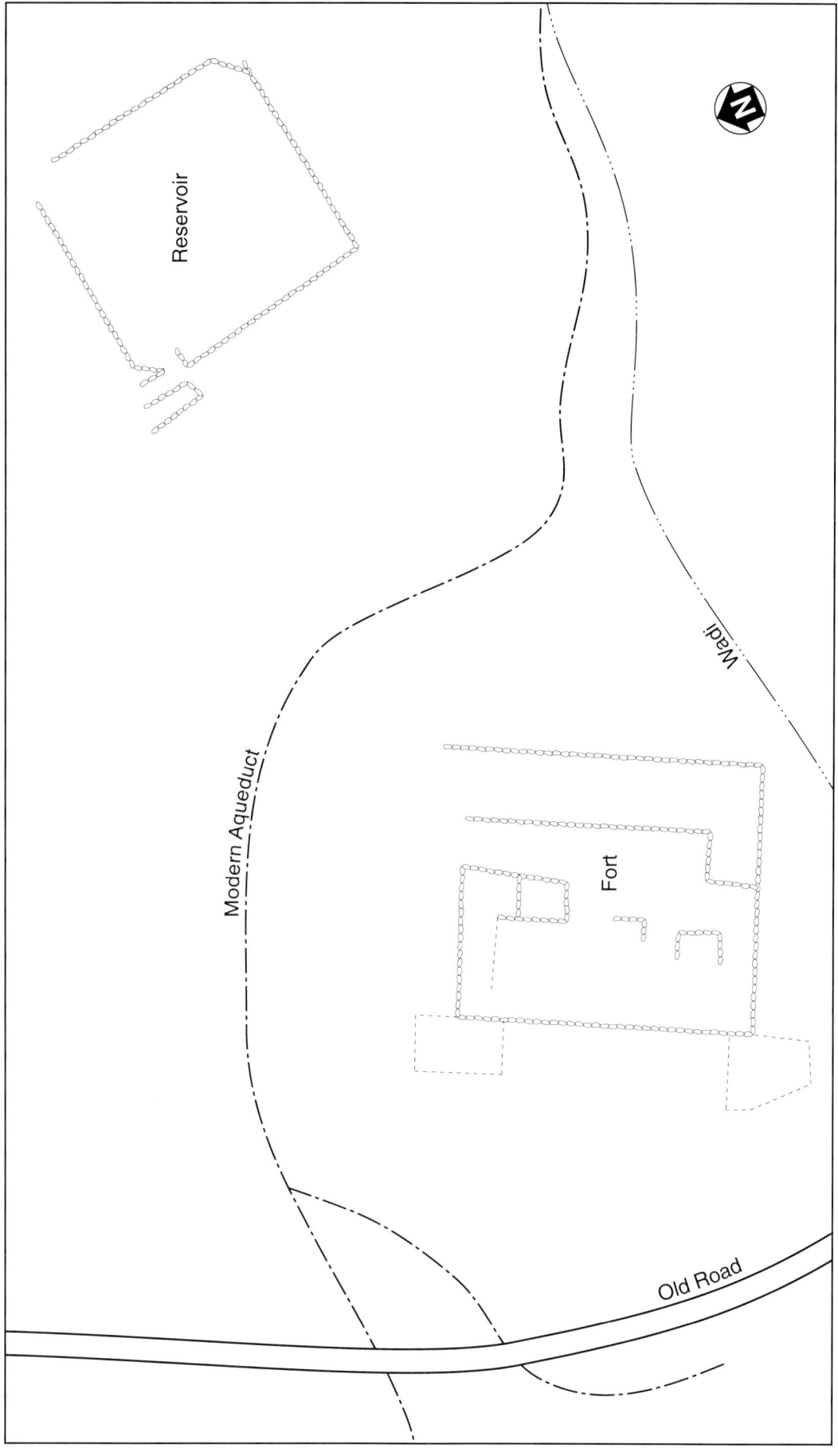

Figure 19 Site 155, Qasr al-Tilah.

Figure 20 Site 155, Qasr al-Tilah and adjoining fields.

scatter and/or potbust. Site 165 has been treated along with the Iron II Period sites of the survey while Site 189 has been discussed in relation to the Chalcolithic/Early Bronze Period sites. The sherds assoicated with Sites 197 and 201 are probably potbusts, for the most part. Immediately north of Wadi al-Hassiya and northeast of Site 229, Khirbet al-Hassiya North, a Nabataean caravanserai, the SGNAS collected Roman sherds in small numbers (5) from Site 231. The site is a cemetery and a sherd scatter. The graves are constructed of unhewn stones. However, the predominant pottery collected at the site is Byzantine. Therefore, it will be returned to later.

Finally, the SGNAS collected Late Roman Period sherds in moderate numbers at Site 30, al-Munbateha/Khirbet Hamr Ifdan, a smelting site on the west side of Wadi Fidan. The site has been described in relation to the Chalcolithic/Early Bronze, EB IV, and Iron II Period sites of the survey. It could have been used for smelting purposes as well during the period under discussion.

Nabataean/Roman Period sites

What the SGNAS is calling Nabataean/Roman sherds were collected at two sites, namely, Sites 181 and 237 (Table 51) (Figure 16). The SGNAS could not decide whether or not these sherds were Nabataean or Roman.

Table 51   Nabataean/Roman Period sites

Site No.	Sample No.	No. of Sherds	Plate No.
181	284	16	
237	404	5	

Site 181 is a sherd scatter in an agricultural field about 700–800 m to the northwest of Wadi Feifa and west of the modern Mazra'a–'Aqaba Highway. The site has already been discussed as one at which the SGNAS collected Chalcolithic/Early Bronze, Early Bronze, and Nabataean (=Late Hellenistic–Early Roman) sherds. Site 237 is located immediately to the east. It consists of a number of large tombs. It has been discussed as an Iron I Period site.

Late Roman–Byzantine Period sites

The SGNAS collected Late Roman–Byzantine Period pottery at four sites, namely, Sites 73; 126; 163A; and 210 (Table 52) (Figure 16).

Site 73, Rujm Umm Jufna, has been treated previously in this chapter as a site at which the SGNAS collected Hellenistic Period sherds. It has also been treated along with the Iron II Period sites of the survey.

Site 126 is a heavy sherd scatter located between Wadi Umm Jufna and Wadi Feifa. It has been treated along with the EB IV, Iron Age, and Roman Period sites of the survey.

Table 52   Late Roman–Byzantine Period sites

Site No.	Sample No.	No. of Sherds	Plate No.
73	99	1	24 (3)
126	126	5	
163A	270	3	
210	370	30	

Site 163A–C, located on the plateau immediately south of the JVA camp just west of Wadi Khuneizir, consists of a number of sherd scatters. Site 163A is in an area measuring ca. 20 m square. It is comprised of a number of potbusts. The SGNAS collected a small number (3) of Late Roman–Byzantine sherds at the site. Site 210 is a lithic and sherd scatter along with evidence of camping on the east side of the main Mazra'a–'Aqaba Highway to the northwest of Wadi al-Tilah. It is located on a small depression caused by erosion. The sherds which the SGNAS collected in the area may not be associated with the camping area.

Conclusions

As stated above, the sites at which Hellenistic Period sherds are found are all located in the central segment of the survey territory. They are located between Wadis Umm Jufna and al-Tilah, i.e., in the area immediatly southeast of the Dead Sea. Two, namely, Sites 73 and 94, of the six sites at which the SGNAS collected Hellenistic sherds are towers. The latter site is important during the entire Classical Period. Could there have been an important transportation route in this area during the Classical Period? Moreover, could these sites have been involved in any way with the mining of bitumen from the Dead Sea? There is no archaeological evidence in the survey territory to substantiate the exploitation of the bitumen of the Dead Sea. Classical writers, however, such as Vitruvius, Diodorus, Pliny, and Strabo wrote about this area as a source of this natural resource (Forbes 1964: 27–29; Hammond 1959). There are also references to the involvement of the Ptolemies of Egypt in the important bitumen fishery. This resulted in their monopoly over the largest source of economical supply of bitumen for export to Egypt. Later still, the Seleucids, the Egyptians again, and the Nabataeans had control of this important industry along the eastern side of the Dead Sea (Forbes 1964: 29–30; Hammond 1959). Thus, during the Classical Period the bitumen industry was of commercial importance.

Site 6, Umm al-Tawabin, and Site 229, Khirbet al-Hassiya North, are major Late Hellenistic–Early Roman Period sites. They were probably related to the farming, trade, and commercial activities of the survey area during the period under discussion. It appears that Qasr al-Tilah, Site 155, played a similar role somewhat later. This evidence must not, however, be seen in isolation. It must be linked with Nabataean presence to the north, for example, at Wadi

Numeira (Glueck 1935: 7) and Wadi 'Isal (Glueck 1935: 6; Jacobs 1983: 267–68); to the south, for example, in the Wadi Feinan region (Glueck 1935: 32–35); to the west (Rothenberg 1971); and to the east (MacDonald *et al.* 1988).

During the period under discussion, just as today, the wadis of the survey area would have been used at least for their water sources. One notable exception is the lack of Classical Period presence in Wadi al-Dahal. This wadi, even though very close to Qasr al-Tilah, Site 155, did not seem to play a major role as a place for camping, farming, and/or communications during the period under discussion.

The area was probably farmed in the past as it is today. Their is evidence of extensive agricultural activity visible at Qasr al-Tilah, Site 155. Glueck dates this activity to the Nabataean Period (1935: 32–35). It is not possible to determine, however, on the basis of the available evidence, just when this activity took place. There is no reason, however, to doubt that during the Classical Period irrigation was practiced extensively not only at Qasr al-Tilah but within the Southern Ghors in the areas of Wadis al-Hasa, Feifa, Umruq, and Khuneizir. The people would have exploited the water and land resources of this area as extensively as they exploited the water and land of Wadi al-Hasa and its tributaries to the east (MacDonald *et al.* 1988). Now, however, due to the extensive development in the Southern Ghors since 1977 (Khouri 1981: 213–27; Khader and Badran 1987: 93–117) most of that evidence has been removed.

Koucky carried out a survey between Bab edh-Dhra' and the Arab Potash Company along the east side of the Dead Sea in conjunction with the 1984 excavations at Numeira (Coogan 1984). He found evidence of Nabataean agricultural activity in the areas immediately west of both Wadi Numeira and Wadi 'Isal (personal communication). Thus, there is evidence for the use of the water and land resources of the area immediately to the north of the survey territory. One can hardly doubt the same type of use of these resources from Wadi al-Hasa southward. The team from the German Mining Museum, Bochum, posit copper mining and smelting during the Roman Period (1st to 4th centuries A.D.) in the immediate vicinity of Feinan which is just southeast of the survey area (Hauptmann, Weisgerber, and Knauf 1985: 172–76; Hauptmann and Weisgerber 1987: 422–23). This activity possibly had an influence in the survey territory during this time.

Notes

1   The SGNAS received the name of the site from D. W. McCreery who carried out a survey of the Ghor al-Safi area for the Jordan Valley Authority in 1979 (1979). McCreery received the name from the people of the area. As stated above, however, an older name for the site is Khirbet Labrush/al-Ebrosh, probably a corruption of el-Bourj (Abel 1967: 466).

2   Abel sees this site, which he calls the 'chateau au W. el-Hasiya', as the site of Classical Hasta (1967: 181).

3   Abel locates Classical Toloha of the *Notitia Dignitatem* at Qasr al-Tilah (1967: 181, 486).

4   Several commentators locate Praesidium of the Madaba Map at SGNAS Site 75 (Abel 1967: 181).

9. Byzantine Period Sites

by B. MacDonald

Introduction

Byzantine Period sites are by far the most common within the survey territory. They are found throughout the area. The SGNAS collected Byzantine Period sherds, without further precision, at 60 sites; Early Byzantine sherds at three sites; Late Byzantine sherds at eight sites; and Late Byzantine–Umayyad sherds at two sites. Two sites, namely, Sites 46 and 66, yielded Byzantine, Early Byzantine, and Late Byzantine Period sherds. Moreover, Site 66 also yielded Late Byzantine–Umayyad Period sherds. Site 79 yielded both Early Byzantine and Late Byzantine sherds. Site 205 yielded both Late Byzantine and Late Byzantine–Umayyad Period pottery. Many of the sites from which the pottery reading is Byzantine, without further precision, are in fact Early Byzantine and/or Late Byzantine Period sites. Many of the Byzantine sites have been described previously in relation to earlier periods. The major Byzantine Period sites, however, will be treated in this chapter in detail. The treatment will be time-stratigraphical and, for the most part, in a north to south direction.

Byzantine Period sites

The SGNAS collected Byzantine Period sherds, without further precision, at 60 sites (Table 53) (Figure 21). Eight of these sites, namely, Sites 56; 91; 94; 97I; 146; 197; 223; and 227, yielded only one or two sherds from the period. Therefore, they will not be considered in any detail in this chapter.

Deir 'Ain 'Abata, Site 46, is the most northerly located of the Byzantine Period sites of the survey. It has been treated previously as a site at which the SGNAS collected Nabataean and Late Roman pottery. It is located at ca. –270 metres. It is, thus, ca. 120 m above the level of the surrounding agricultural fields (Photo 15). It is located on the slope of a high mountain ca. 3–4 km north of the Wadi al-Hasa gorge and just to the northeast of the village of al-Safi. It commands an excellent view of the entire area of the Southern Ghors south of the Dead Sea (Photo 16). The general area in which the site is located is called 'Ain 'Abata ('spring of the abbot'). The SGNAS, on the basis of its study of the buildings and associated artifactual remains at the site, thinks that the site is a church/monastery complex (Photo 17). Therefore, it called the site Deir 'Ain 'Abata (MacDonald and Politis 1988: 291).

What appears to be a main building at the site is on two levels (Figure 22). The top level of this building, which is built up against the side of the mountain, measures ca. 18 (N–S) x 7 (E–W) metres. The remnants of seven arches can be seen within the

building (Photo 18). They project from its western wall. Each arch is spaced ca. 2 m apart (Figure 23). There are pieces of plaster still clinging to the interior of the western wall and to some of the arches. A single arch is still in place against the eastern wall of the building. This arch spans from north-to-south while the previously-described, seven arches span from west-to- east. Some illicit digging has taken place within the structure. This digging reveals the presence of many flat stones and some column drums. The lower level of the building appears to be the main segment. It, too, measures ca. 18 (N–S) x 7 (E–W) metres. There is evidence that it was partitioned at one time. It is now filled with rubble, chiefly in the form of building stone. The northern segment of the western, exterior wall of this segment of the building still stands ca. 3–4 m (16–18 courses) high (Photo 19). There are pieces of wood associated with the rubble of this building. This wood probably served as roofing material. There are the remains of openings at the top of the wall, separating the upper and lower segments of the building. These probably served as windows. Now, however, they are blocked up. The wall separating the two segments of the building measures ca. 1.10 m wide while the exterior wall of the building measures ca. 1 metre. There are the remains of building material around the structure (Photo 20). This consists of wood, previously mentioned; column, base, and capitol fragments; pieces of tile; tesserae; pieces of worked marble; door and/or window frames; and of course, building stones. The building technique is generally crude. The walls, for the most part, are constructed of one row of large stones and then a row of smaller stones. This building technique is usually referred to as 'chinking'. The slopes in front of and down the mountain from this main structure appear to be terraced. These terrace walls run in an east-to-west as well as in a north-to-south direction. Building stones are scattered to the north of the main building for a distance of at least 50 metres. These stones could have been parts of other structures in antiquity. There is a large depression in the slope of the mountain in this area. There are middens to the west and north of the main structure.

The SGNAS collected three pottery samples at Deir 'Ain 'Abata. The pottery in all three sample is predominantly Byzantine. One extremely interesting and fine piece of pottery was the bottom of a ring-base plate (imitation terra sigillata) (Figure 24). The SGNAS discovered it in the northern midden at a place where an animal had dug a hole. The interior base of the plate is stamped with a cross which measures 4.3 x 3.4 centimetres. The depth of the

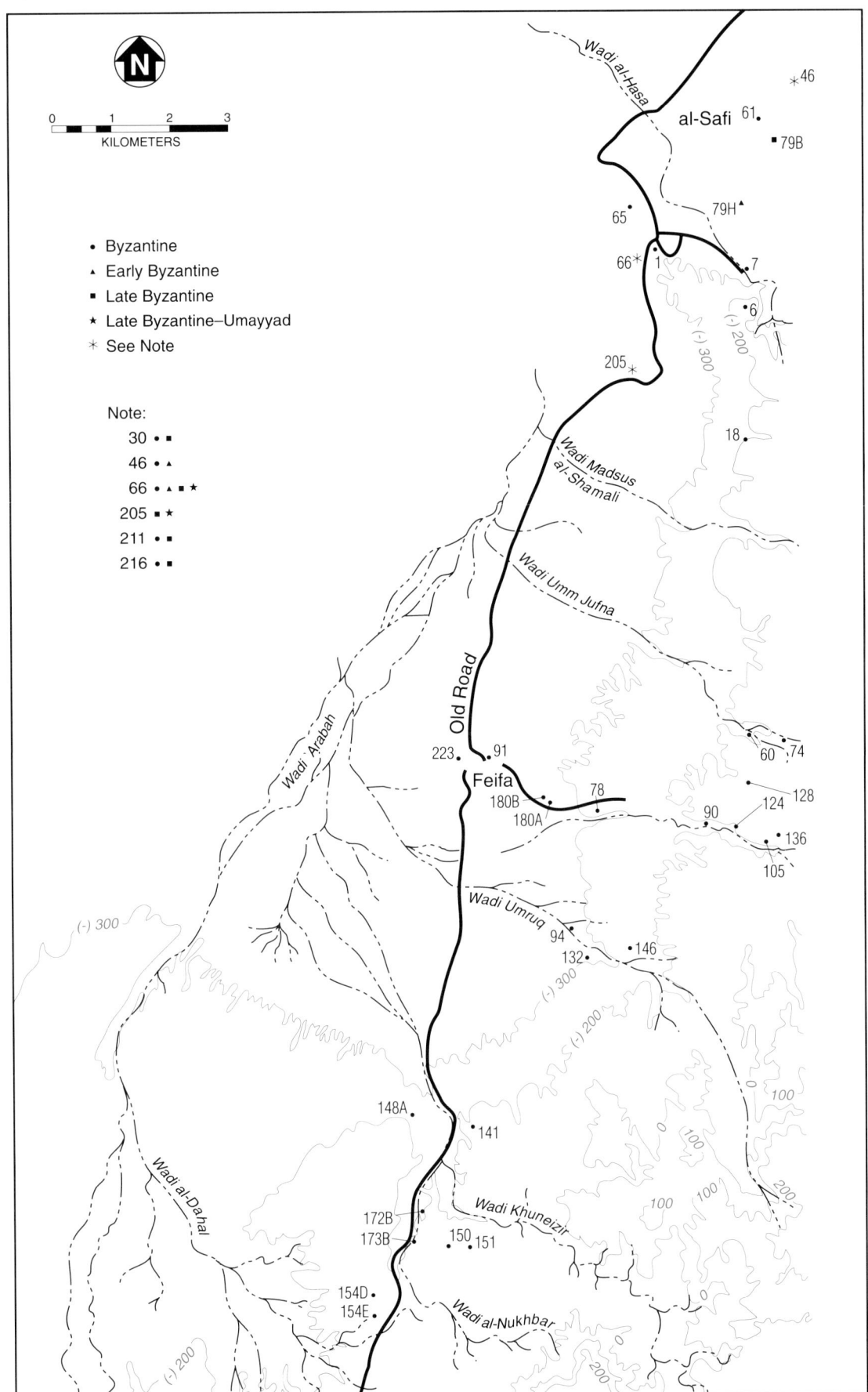

Figure 21 Byzantine, Early Byzantine, Late Byzantine, Late Byzantine–Umayyad settlement pattern map (Northern portion).

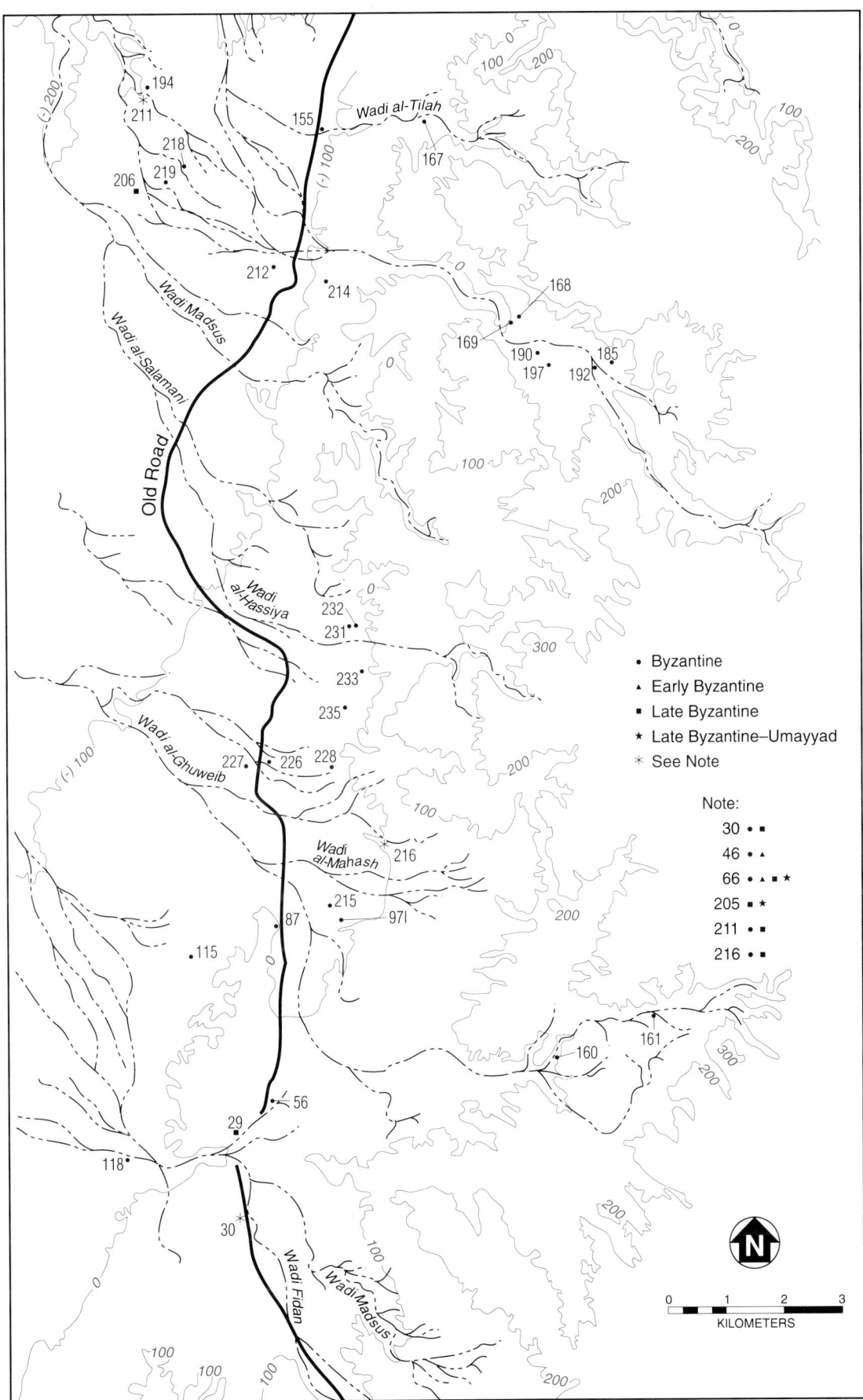

Figure 21 Byzantine, Early Byzantine, Late Byzantine, Late Byzantine–Umayyad settlement pattern map (Southern portion).

99

Table 53 Byzantine Period sites

Site No.	Sample No.	No. of Sherds	Plate No.	Site No.	Sample No.	No. of Sherds	Plate No.
1	3	8		160	314	6	
6	12	8		161	301	8	
6	13	2		167	279	5	
6	14	2		168	306	38	
7	16	24		169	307	21	
18	32	13		172B	291	43	
30	76	1	24 (8)	173B	293	21	
30	77	1	24 (7;10)	173B	294	25	
30	410	2		180A	282	20	
46	90	161	26 (1–3;5–6; 8–10)	180B	283	106	
46	408	25	26 (4;7;13)	185	315	4	
46	409	4	26 (12;14)	190	334	4	
56	78	1		190	335	7	
60	112	4		190	336	4	
61	113	4		192	317	25	
65	110	8		194	319	18	
66	64	1	27 (2)	197	341	1	
66	111	58	27 (1;3;14)	211	339	54	
74	120	5		211	350	74	25 (14)
78	131	34		211	351	72	25 (4)
87	143	14		211	352	39	25 (8;13;15)
90	133	7		211	353	77	25 (3;16)
91	136	2	30 (n)	212	359	3	
94	144	1		214	371	4	
97I	220	2		215	372	86	27 (7;11;13)
105	182	10		215	373	31	
115	188	26		216	390	42	27 (10)
118	212	11		216	391	50	27 (5;9)
124	211	21		216	392	62	27 (4;6;8)
128	219	3		216	393	17	
128	222	24		218	380	9	
128	223	2		219	381	10	
132	229	14		223	403	1	
136	230	15		226	394	30	
141	237	37		227	375	1	
146	236	2		228	396	23	
148A	248	6		228	395	43	
150	250	7		231	397	26	
151	251	6		232	398	23	
154D	273	29		233	399	112	
154E	277	25		233	401	2	
155	256	3		235	389	15	
155	257	1	24 (9)				

stamp impression is very slight, measuring ca. 1 millimetre. The extremity of the right arm of the cross is not closed up. The closest parallels for this style of cross are found in Hayes who characterizes it as a 'cross with a double outline' (1972: 365–67 and fig. 79, #'s 71 and 72). He dates this type of cross to the late 5th to early 6th century with some poorly impressed examples later (1972: 365 and 367). Loffreda reports a similar style of cross from Capernaum (1974: 78, fig. 24, # 7). The Greek letters Alpha and Omega are under the arms of the cross. Canova states that the two Greek letters in this particular style are found in the Karak region of Jordan (1954: Table 2). However, she does not, report them in combination with the style of cross described above. Hayes shows the alpha and omega under the arms of crosses (1972: 364, fig. 78, #'s 65 and 66).

However, the combination of crosses and letters are not exactly the same as on the one under consideration. Moreover, Loffreda does not list this particular stamp in his article on the stamps on terra sigillata of the 4th–6th century in Palestine (1978). This may be the discovery of a new stamp from the Byzantine Period.

On the basis of the analysis of the pottery, the complex appears to date to both the Early and Late Byzantine Periods. Moreover, the stamp on the interior base of the plate agrees with this date. Excavations at the site will pinpoint more precisely this dating.[1]

Identification of the site other than to state, on the basis of the data described above, that is is most probably a church/monastery complex is impossible. Excavations at the site will determine more precisely

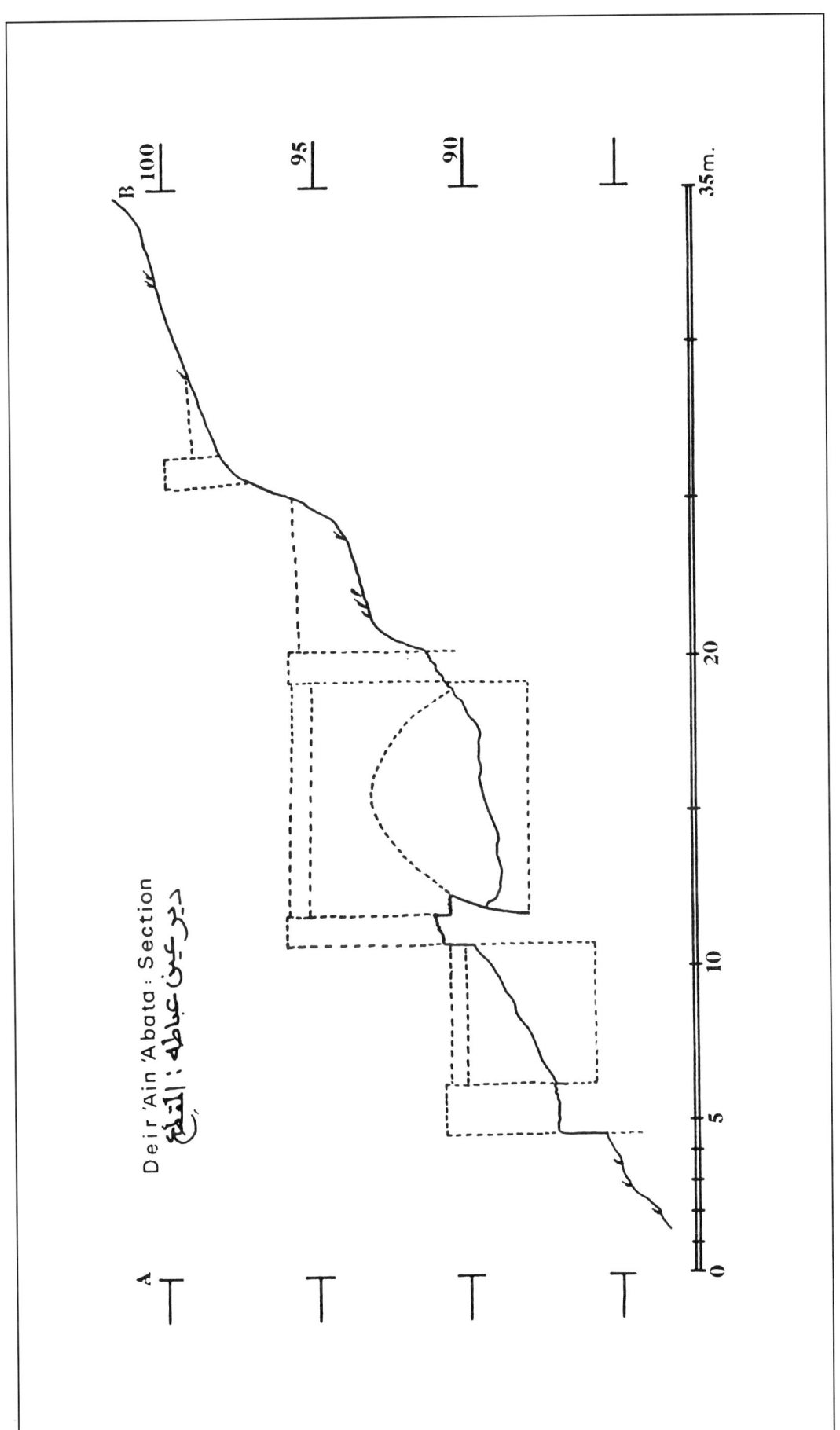

Deir 'Ain 'Abata : Section

دير عين عباطة : القطاع

Figure 22 Site 46, Deir 'Ain 'Abata; section.[2]

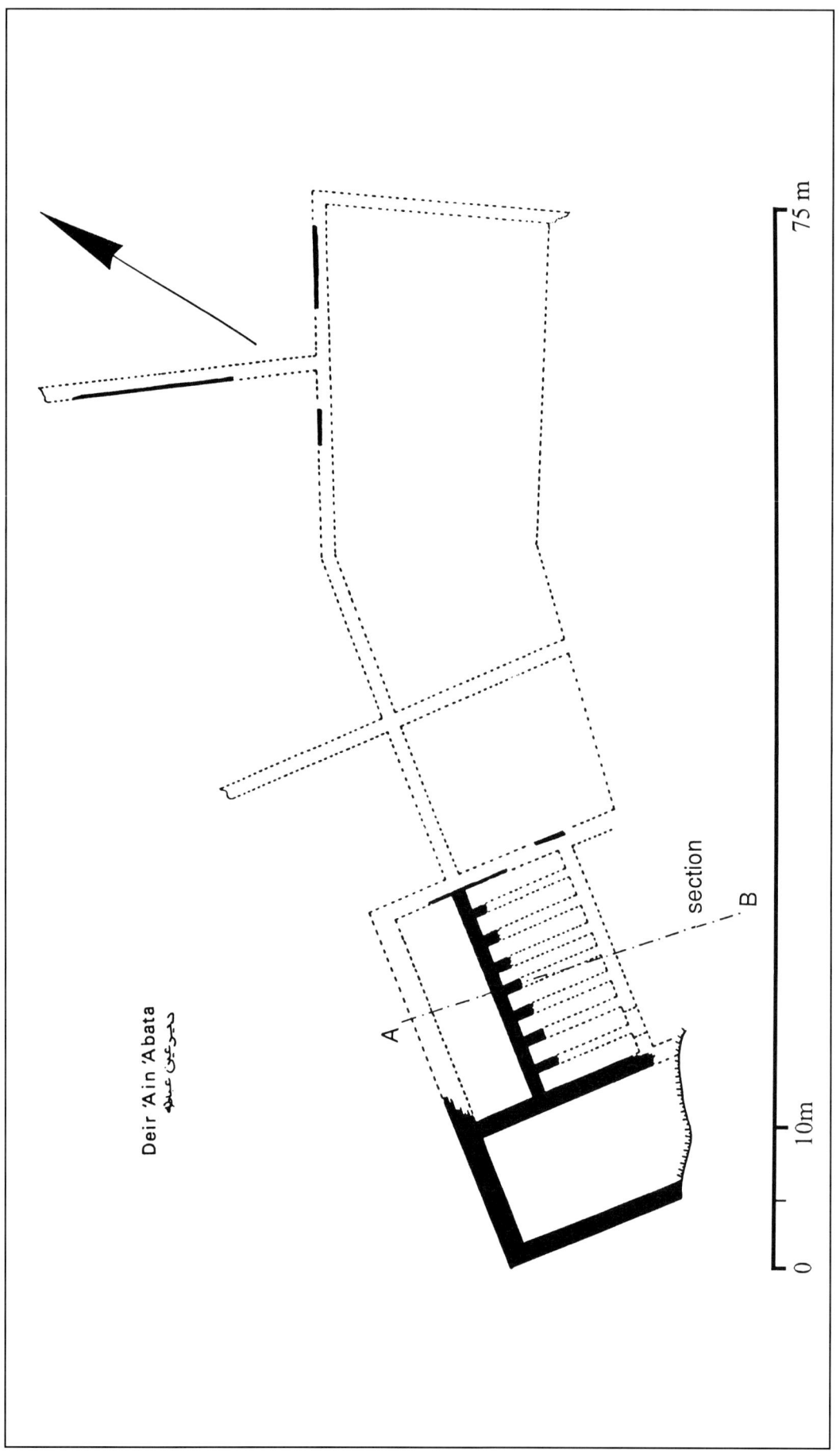

Deir 'Ain 'Abata

دير عين عبطه

Figure 23 Site 46, Deir 'Ain 'Abata; topographic plan.

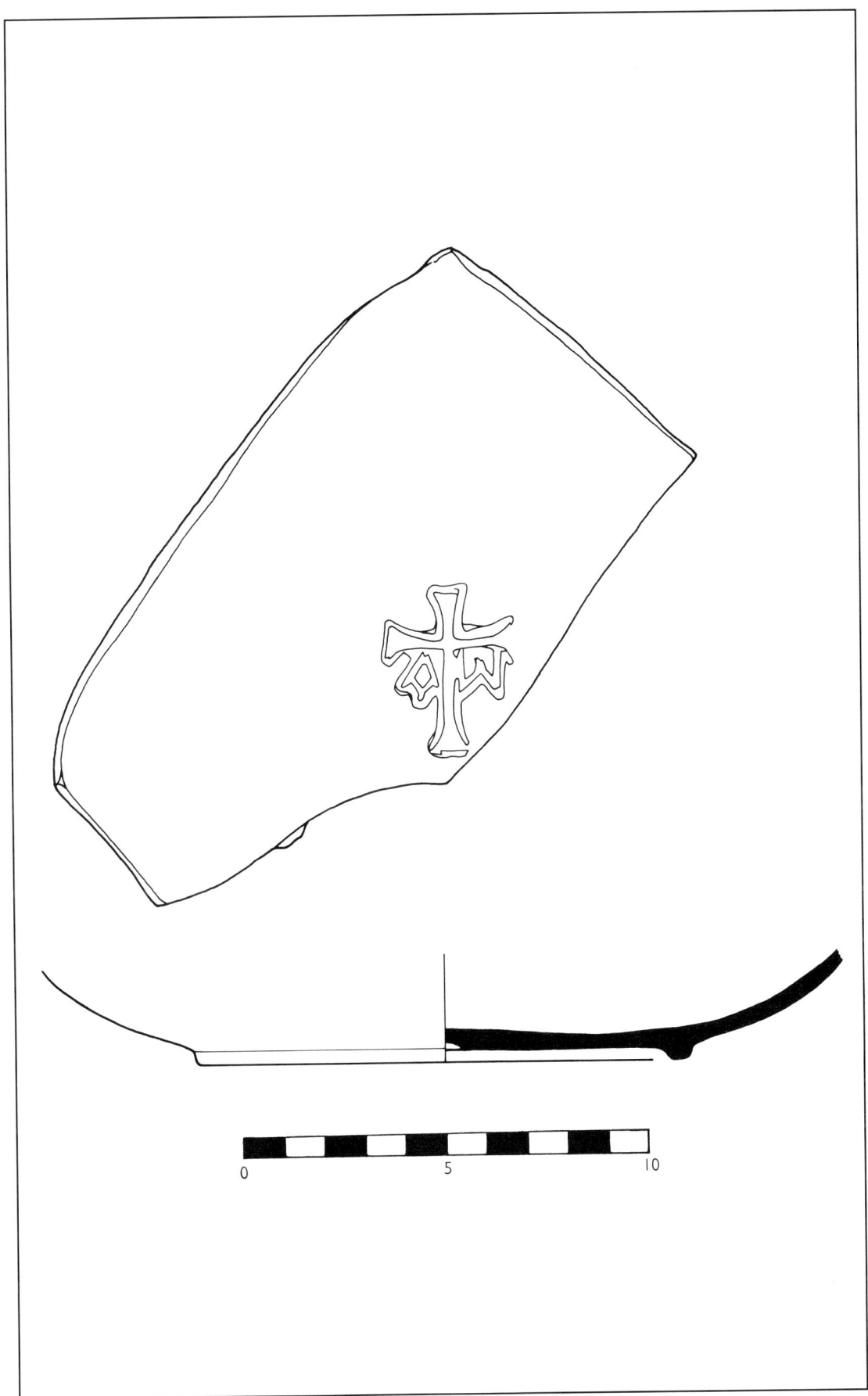

Figure 24 Stamp on ring-base plate from Site 46, Deir 'Ain 'Abata.

its character. However, one question can be asked.

Could Deir 'Ain 'Abata be in fact the 'sanctuary of St. Lot' depicted on the Madaba Map at the southeastern end of the Dead Sea (Saller and Bagatti 1949: 194–95; O'Callaghan 1953; Avi-Yonah 1954; 1977; Gold 1958; Donner and Cüppers 1977). Excavations which uncover an inscription and/or mosaic would help greatly in the identification of the site. Politis thinks that he has found such an inscription which identifies the site as the 'sanctuary of St. Lot' (Politis 1990).[3]

Immediately south of Deir 'Ain 'Abata and still east of modern al-Safi, the SGNAS collected Byzantine pottery in small quantities at Site 61. The site consists of two structures measuring ca. 9 x 5 and 7 x 5 metres. Each structure has an internal partition and a porch (?), on the northeast side, measuring ca. 3 x 1 metres. There are graves in the vicinity. Could the structures which constitute Site 61 be tombs?

Site 7 is a hermitage dating to the Byzantine Period. It is located on the north bank of Wadi al-Hasa just as the wadi opens out into Ghor al-Safi. Frank discovered it in 1932 (1934) and it came in for consideration by Alt and Wickert (1935: 72–73), Canova (1954: 416), MacDonald (1980: 361, note 20), and Donner and Knauf (1985; 1986). It consists of two adjacent, rock-cut chambers and a rock-cut cistern. One chamber, the most westerly located, measures ca. 4 x 5 m while the other measures ca. 1.5 x 4.0 metres. Each chamber is ca. 2 m high and there is a doorway, measuring ca. 55 cm, which permits passage from one to the other. There are two cuts in the rock associated with this passageway which appear to have served the purpose of hanging a door or screen to separate the two chambers. The most westerly located chamber has what appears to be a tomb cut into its floor. However, the tomb has been looted. There is a small niche cut into the right wall of this chamber. The other chamber has remnants of plaster and paint on its ceiling. There is an apse, measuring ca. 1 m wide, cut into the back wall of the chamber. This apse is flanked by a niche, measuring ca. 0.50 x 0.50 m, on either side. An inscription was located on the right side of the doorway/passageway leading into the most westerly located chamber (Alt and Wickert 1935: 72–73; Canova 1954: 416; Donner and Knauf 1986). The cistern is located ca. 5 m southeast of the chambers and ca. 3 m below them. It measures ca. 2.2 x 3.5 m and there is still plaster visible on its interior walls. It has been filled in, however, for the most part, by stone fall. There is a prominent stone wall, a retaining wall (?), southeast of the cistern. Several commentators place the Church of St. Lot of the Madaba Map in this region (Saller and Bagatti 1949: 194–95; O'Callaghan 1953; Avi-Yonah 1954; 1977; Gold 1958; Donner and Cüppers 1977). More precisely, Donner and Knauf see this hermitage as being the location for the church (1985: 430; 1986: 266–67).

The SGNAS collected Byzantine pottery at Site 1, Tawahin al-Sukkar. The number of sherds which the SGNAS collected was small. This is surprising since employees of the Impresit Construction Company informed the SGNAS that there were Byzantine tombs at the highest point of the site. According to our informants, road-building and the construction of the JVA townsite destroyed many of these tombs. Moreover, Site 4, Khirbet Sheikh 'Isa, which is generally identified with Christian Zoara (Klein 1880: 253; De Luynes 1874, I: 247–51; Musil 1907; Mallon 1924: 436–39; Albright 1924: 4; Albright 1926: 57; Frank 1934: 204–5 and Plans 8 and 9A; Glueck 1935: 8; Alt 1935: 4; Abel 1967: 201; MacDonald 1980: 362; Donner and Knauf 1985: 430) of the Madaba Map, is located immediately to the northwest. The SGNAS' sherd collection at Khirbet Sheikh 'Isa was almost exclusively Islamic. King *et al.*, however, report that 'a number of sherds of Byzantine date were also found, although the number of Late Byzantine sherds was small' (1987: 448, 456). The site will be treated in the discussion of the Islamic sites of the survey.

Sites 65 and 66 are sherd scatters immediately to the northwest and southwest respectively of the above-mentioned sites. The SGNAS collected a small number of Byzantine sherds at the former and a large number (59) at the latter. Moreover, the SGNAS also collected both Early and Late Byzantine sherds at the Site 66 which has been treated previously as a Nabataean and Roman Period site. As mentioned previously, the area of this site could have been an important architectural site during several different periods.

Umm al-Tawabin, Site 6, has been discussed extensively as a Nabataean fortress. Byzantine sherds, in small numbers, were present in three of the five samples which the SGNAS collected at the site.

Site 18, a campsite, is located between Wadi al-Hasa and Wadi Madsus al-Shamali. The SGNAS collected a moderate number (13) of Byzantine sherds at the site.

South of Wadi Umm Jufna, the SGNAS collected Byzantine sherds at Sites 60 and 74. These sites are a sherd scatter and a farm (?) respectively. Site 60 has been referred to above as a site at which the SGNAS collected Iron Age Period pottery.

There are a number of sites in the Wadi Feifa region at which the SGNAS collected Byzantine sherds. North of the wadi, the SGNAS collected Byzantine sherds at Sites 105; 124; 128; and 136. These sites are mostly sherd scatters associated with the plateau between Wadis Umm Jufna and Feifa. All of these sites have been treated previously in one of the earlier chapters. Closer to Wadi Feifa, the SGNAS collected Byzantine sherds at Sites 78 and 90. Both of these sites are lithic and sherd scatters.

A high density of Byzantine sherds were present at Site 180A and B which is located in a plowed field to the southwest of Site 75, ancient Feifa, and immediately west of the main Mazra'a–'Aqaba Highway. The number (=126) of Byzantine sherds collected at the site indicates that it was probably much more than just a sherd scatter in antiquity. Now, however, all that remains visible on the surface are the sherds.

Site 91, Qasr al-Feifa, is a predominantly Islamic Period site. It is presently associated with the modern village of Feifa. Therefore, it will be treated in detail later.

Site 223, an architectural site, in the present bed of Wadi Feifa, has been treated previously as a site at which the SGNAS collected Nabataean (=Early Roman) and Roman sherds. The SGNAS also collected one Byzantine sherd at the site.

The SGNAS collected Byzantine sherds in the Wadi Umruq region at Sites 94, 132, and 146. However, except for Site 132, a sherd scatter in a dissected area immediately south of the wadi, the number of sherds from the period under discussion is insignificant. Site 132 has been treated previously as a Roman Period site.

Small numbers of sherds from the period under discussion were collected in the regions of Wadis Khuneizir and al-Nukhbar. Site 148A is a sherd scatter located west of Wadi Khuneizir. It has been discussed previously as an Early Bronze, Iron Age, and Nabataean Period site. Abu Irshareibeh, Site 141, is a predominantly EB IV site. It has been treated extensively as such. The SGNAS collected 37 Byzantine body sherds in one sample at the southwest extremity of the site. Sites 150 and 151 are a sherd scatter and potbust respectively between the two above mentioned wadis. At the two latter sites Byzantine sherds were the only identifiable pottery which the SGNAS collected. Substantial numbers of Byzantine sherd were found in association with Sites 154D and E, 172B, and 173B. Site 154 is a series of tombs (?) on the plateau immediatley west of Wadi al-Nukhbar. It has been discussed previously in relation to the EB IV, Early Bronze, and Hellenistic sites of the survey. Sites 172 and 173 have been mentioned in the treatment of the Chalcolithic/Early Bronze and Iron II sites of the survey respectively. Site 172 is a sherd scatter in association with graves on a terrace on the east side of Wadi al-Nukhbar. Site 173B, in the same area, consists of three potbusts. The pottery which the SGNAS collected at both sites was predominantly Byzantine.

Qasr al-Tilah, Site 155, has been discussed as a major Nabataean (=Early–Late Roman) fort and caravanserai. The SGNAS also collected a small quantity of Byzantine sherds at the site. To the east, on the south side of Wadi al-Tilah, the SGNAS collected five Byzantine sherds at Site 167, a cemetery.

West of Wadis al-Tilah and al-Dahal, the SGNAS found Byzantine pottery at such sites as 194; 211; 212; 218; and 219. Most of these sites are sherd scatters in the floodplains of these two wadis. However, Site 211, Khirbet al-Dahal, is a major, village site. It is located on both sides of Wadi al-Dahal and immediately east of the modern Mazra'a–'Aqaba Highway. The site, which covers an area measuring ca. 200 (N–S) x 150 (E–W) m, consists of several multiroom structures which are probably houses (Figure 25). There are also smaller, one-room structures as well in the complex. All the structures are made from undressed cobbles. Both the exterior and partition walls of the larger structures are two courses wide and still stand one-to-two courses high. The larger, multiroomed structures measure as much as ca. 17–18 x 7–8 metres. The size of their rooms is not uniform. The smaller, single-room structures measure ca. 4.0–3.5 m square. There are other structures which have the appearance of 'platforms'. The SGNAS collected five samples at the site. The pottery in each sample, which may be described as dense, was exclusively Byzantine. A walk in the vicinity of the site reveals many Byzantine sherd scatters. For some reason, major occupation occurred at Site 211, Khirbet al-Dahal, rather than at Site 155, Qasr al-Tilah, during the Byzantine Period.

In Wadi al-Dahal itself, the SGNAS collected Byzantine sherds at seven sites, namely, Sites 168; 169; 185; 190; 192; 197; and 214. Four of these sites, namely, Sites 168; 169; 190; and 192, are cemeteries or at least have a grave or graves associated with the sherd scatter. The remainder appear to be nothing more than sherd scatters which proably indicate campsites. The presence of Byzantine sites within this wadi provides more evidence for its use during several of the ceramic periods represented in the survey.

Further south, in the region of Wadi al-Hassiya, the SGNAS collected Byzantine Period sherds from Sites 231; 232; 233; and 235. Site 231 is a cemetery with an associated sherd scatter while Site 235 is a moderate-density, sherd scatter. The remaining two sites, however, require further elaboration.

Site 232 appears to be a village/hamlet (Figure 26). It is comprised of at least five separate structures, three of which have internal partitions. The walls of the structures are ca. 0.75 m thick and still stand five courses high. Some of the stones used in the buildings appear to be dressed. One of the structures has been 'excavated'. The digging indicates that there is some deposition at the site. The remnants of a sixth structure is located on the north side of a small tributary wadi to the east of the five-main structures. The SGNAS noted a grinding stone at the eastern extremity of the site. Byzantine sherds were predominant at the site. For a seeminly 'domestic' complex, the density of sherds at the site is low.

Khirbet al-Hassiya South, Site 233 (Photo 21), has been mentioned in the treatment of the Chalcolithic/Early Bronze sites of the survey. However, the site is a village/hamlet consisting of many houses and courtyards on the plateau immediately south of Wadi al-Hassiya. The structures which comprise the complex are built of unhewn stone. Some of the walls still stand four–five courses high and some of the interior walls are in good condition. The pottery in the vinicity of the structures is exclusively Byzantine. The Chalcolithic/Early Bronze sherds referred to above were collected downslope from the structures a distance of ca. 40 m in an area measuring ca. 5 m square. Site 233, like Site 232, is one of several, Byzantine period village/hamlet sites along the east side of the 'Old Road' between Wadis al-Hassiya and al-Ghuweib.

Figure 25   Site 211, Khirbet al-Dahal.

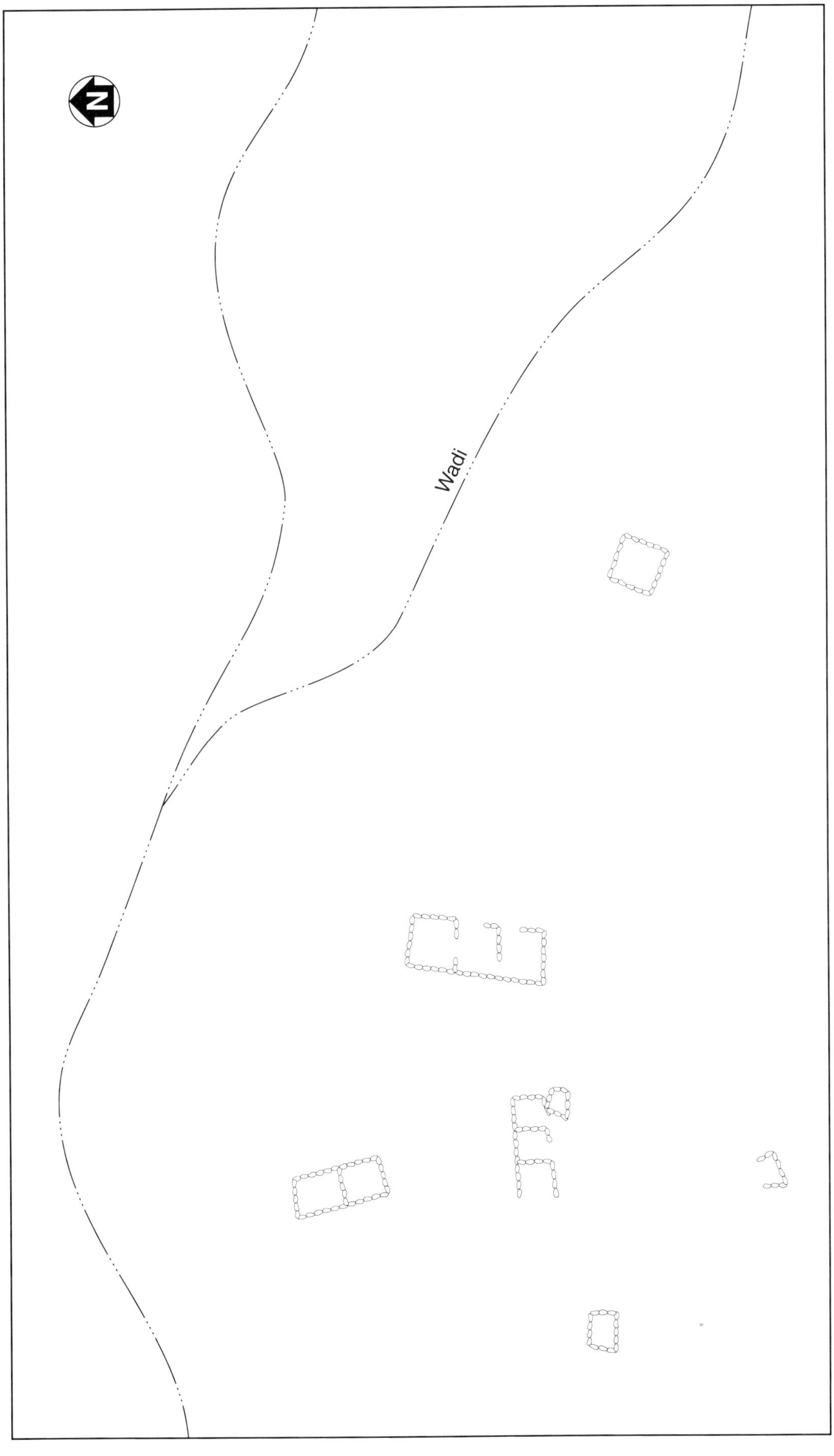

Wadi

Figure 26 Site 232.

A third such site is Site 228 (Photo 22) (Figure 27). It is located to the east of the 'Old Road' between Wadi al-Hassiya and Wadi al-Mahash. It consists of at least seven structures which appear to be domestic dwellings. One of the structures measures ca. 2.5 x 3.5 m interiorly. Its walls are ca. 50 cm thick and still stand three courses high. They are made of undressed stone. The doorway is clearly visible. A second structure is somewhat larger and has a large courtyard, actually larger than the building itself. There is still a larger building to the southeast with an even larger courtyard. The SGNAS noted a very large, basalt, grinding stone at the site. The SGNAS collected glass, as well as sherds, at the site. The sherds were exclusively Byzantine. This site may be the one which Frank identifies as *tell Rabet ed-dschamuse* (1934: 216 and Plan 15).

Site 226 may be related to Site 228. It is a cemetery, which has been badly disturbed by robbing, to the west of Site 228. The tombs which constitute the site are rectangular. They are encirlced by walls which measure ca. 7 x 5 metres. The bottom course of these walls are formed of stones dressed on three sides. The inner-facing side is undressed. Field stones are piled above this foundation course. The SGNAS collected glass fragments, as well as sherds, at the site. Here again, the sherds are exclusively from the Byzantine Period.

Site 216 is a fourth Byzantine, village/hamlet site (Figure 28). It is located ca. 1.5 km east of the 'Old Road' and ca. 0.50 km north of Wadi al-Mahash. It consists of many structures along a dissected ridge. The walls, some of which are built of sandstone cobbles while others are of tabular sandstone, of the structures still stand one-to-four courses high. The SGNAS noted fragments of grinding stones throughout the site. Illicit digging has disturbed some areas of the site. The eastern third of the site is now cut off from the remaining segments by a drainage channel. A large structure, with partitions, is located in this segment of the site. Its walls are constructed of two courses of stones with rubble/small cobbles in between. A doorway is located at the northeast corner of the structure. Several, smaller structures are to the east of this large structure. On a hill, immediately south of the village/hamlet, there is an L-shaped, structure/stone pile. Several metres away is a squared area that is raised ca. 1 m above the ground. The SGNAS sampled this area as part of the main site. All samples collected contained predominantly Byzantine sherds.

Site 215 is a fifth Byzantine village/hamlet site in this area. It is located to the east of the 'Old Road' between Wadi al-Mahash to the north and Wadi al-Ghuweib to the south. This site also gives the impression of being a domestic complex. There are wall lines, stone piles, and what could be graves spread along the terrace between the two, above-mentioned wadis. Some of the walls are two courses wide and are constructed, as for Sites 233; 228; and 216, of undressed cobble stones. At least one of the structures is partitioned. A small, north–south, running

wadi cuts the site. The SGNAS noted a number of grinding stone fragments throughout the site. The SGNAS collected glass fragments as well as sherds at the site. Here again, as for the other Byzantine sites just described, the sherds collected are almost exclusively from the period under discussion. This may be the site which Frank identifies as *rechemat el-bed* (1934: 216).

There are six sites, namely, Sites 56; 87; 97I; 115; 160; and 161, in association with Wadi al-Ghuweib, from which the SGNAS collected Byzantine sherds. Site 87 is an enclosure measuring ca. 19 x 23 metres. The only, identifiable pottery which the SGNAS collected at the site was Byzantine. Site 97I is one grave on a terrace on the east side of the wadi. The SGNAS collected only two Byzantine sherds at the site. Site 115 is a Byzantine sherd scatter located to the south of the wadi. No architecture could be detected in the area. Site 160 and Site 161, Khirbet al-Ghuweib, are farther east in the wadi. The former may be a grave. The latter is a very large smelting and village site which has been described in the treatment of the Iron Age sites of the survey. The SGNAS collected small numbers of Byzantine sherds at both sites. Site 56 is a lithic and sherd scatter located on the plateau between Wadis al-Ghuweib and Fidan. The SGNAS collected only one Byzantine sherd at this site.

Finally, the SGNAS collected Byzantine sherds at Site 118, on the south side of Wadi Fidan, near its mouth, and at Site 30, al-Munbateha/Khirbet Hamr Ifdan, at the southern extremity of the survey area. The former, which appears to have been a gravel pit used for the building of the present Mazra'a–'Aqaba Highway, has been mentioned in the discussion of the Early Bronze Period sites of the survey. The latter has been treated in the discussion of the Chalcolithic/Early Bronze, EB IV, and Roman Period sites.

Early Byzantine Period sites

The SGNAS collected Early Byzantine sherds at three sites, namely, Sites 46; 66; and 79H (Table 54) (Figure 21). As stated above, two of these sites, namely, Sites 46 and 66, also yielded both Byzantine and Late Byzantine Period sherds as well. Moreover, Site 66 also yielded Late Byzantine–Umayyad Period sherds. It must be emphasized, however, that there are Early Byzantine Period sites among those described in the previous segment of this chapter.

Table 54 Early Byzantine Period sites

Site No.	Sample No.	No. of Sherds	Plate No.
46	90	1	26 (11)
66	111	1	
79H	125	1	17 (4)

Site 46, Deir 'Ain 'Abata, and Site 66 have been treated extensively above along with other Byzantine, without further precision, sites of the survey. Pottery

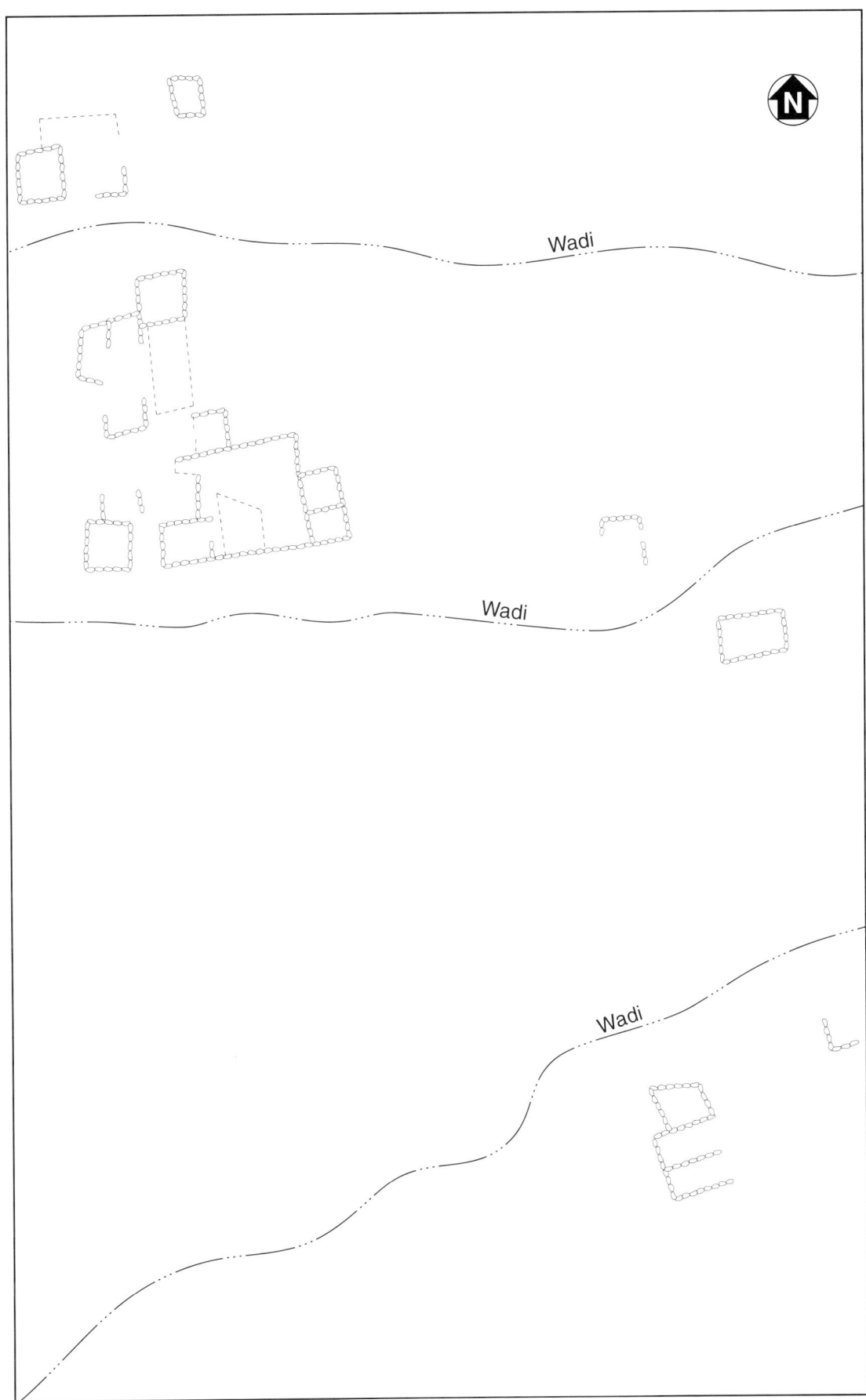

Figure 27 Site 228.

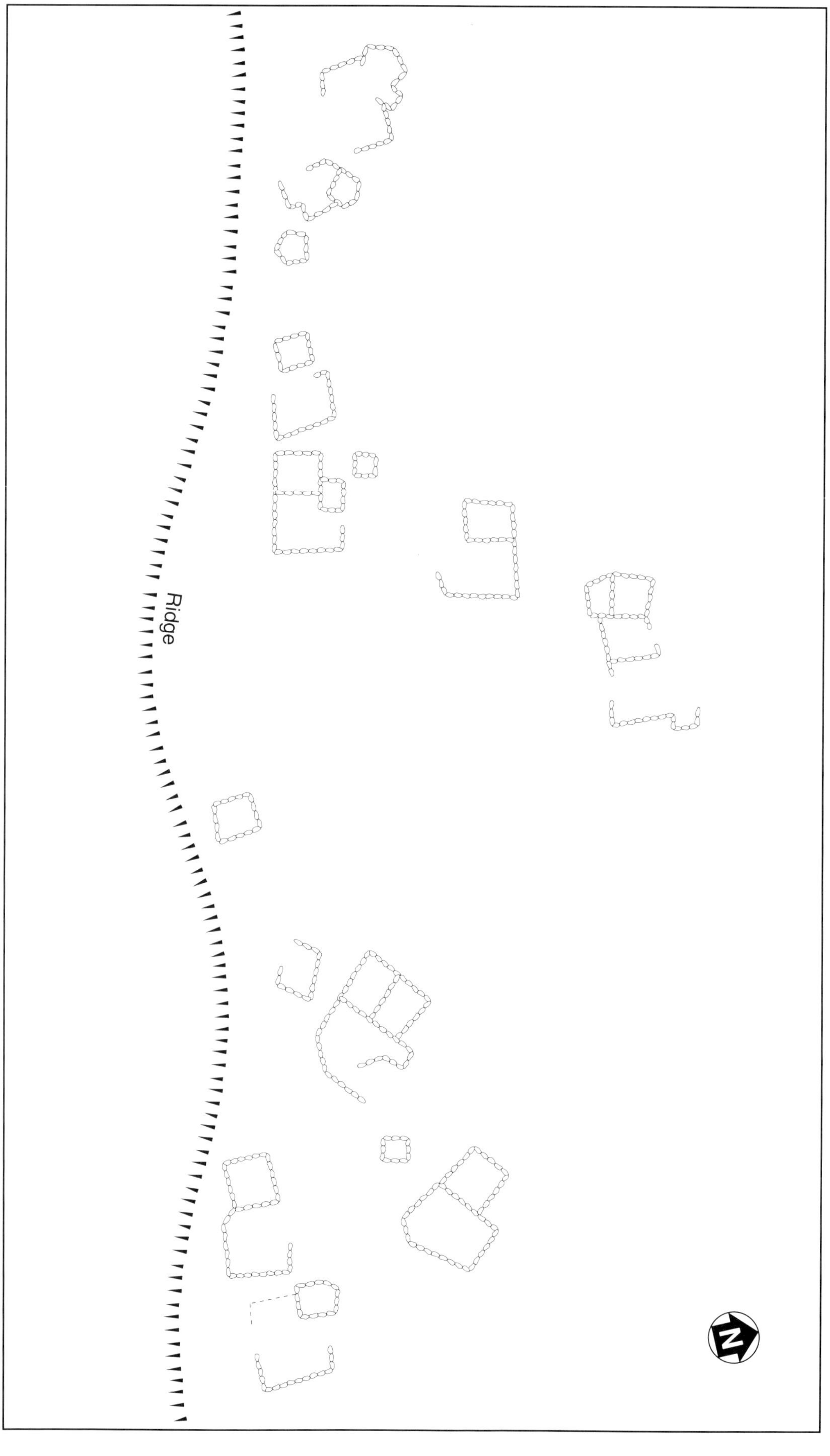

Figure 28 Site 216.

from these sites spans the entire Byzantine Period.

Site 79 appears to be a series of graves. It is located east of modern al-Safi. It has been treated previously in the discussion of the Early Bronze, Iron II, Nabataean, and Roman Period sites of the survey. Site 79 yielded Byzantine, Early Byzantine, and Late Byzantine Period sherds.

Late Byzantine Period sites

The SGNAS collected Late Byzantine Period sherds at eight sites, namely, Sites 29; 30; 66; 79B; 205; 206; 211; and 216 (Table 55) (Figure 21). Sites 30; 46; 66; 211; and 216 have already been treated as Byzantine and/or Early Byzantine Period sites. Once again it must be emphasized that many of the sites which were treated as Byzantine Period sites, without further precision, have in fact a Late Byzantine Period component.

Site 79, as mentioned above, appears to be a series of graves. Aspects of this site have been treated several times previously in this and previous chapters of this report.

Site 205, Sammar, has been referred to as a possible kiln in a sandy area between Wadis al-Hasa and Madsus al-Shamali. It has been treated previously as a site at which the SGNAS collected both Nabataean and Roman Period sherds. However, Byzantine sherds are predominant at the site.

Site 206 is a sherd scatter of low density on the south slope of a small wadi directly east of the old, Dahal Police Post. It covers an area of ca. 20 x 30 metres. The only identifiable pottery which the SGNAS collected at the site dates to the Late Byzantine Period.

Table 55 Late Byzantine Period sites

Site No.	Sample No.	No. of Sherds	Plate No.
29		1	
30	77	1	24 (4)
66	64	1	27 (2)
66	111	1	27 (1)
79B	123	4	17 (5)
205	354	53	28 (2;5;7–11)
205	355	52	28 (1;4;6)
206	356	11	28 (3)
211	351		25 (12)
211	352		25 (9;6)
211	353		25 (2;7)
216	391	1	27 (12)

Table 56 Late Byzantine–Umayyad Period sites

Site No.	Sample No.	No. of Sherds	Plate No.
66	111	1	
205	354	9	

Site 29 is located on a steep slope immediately to the north of Wadi Fidan where the 'Old Road' meets the wadi. The site has been treated previously as an Chalcolithic/Early Bronze and Iron II Period site. It yielded one Late Byzantine Period sherd.

Late Byzantine–Umayyad Period sites

The SGNAS collected Late Byzantine–Umayyad Period sherds at two sites, namely, Sites 66 and 205 (Table 56)(Figure 21). Both sites have been treated previously as Byzantine, Early Byzantine, and/or Late Byzantine Period sites.

Site 66 is a very dense, sherd scatter immediately southwest of Tawahin al-Sukkar, Site 1. Site 205, Sammar, is a possible kiln situated further to the southwest. Both of these sites have been treated as sites at which the SGNAS collected Nabataean, Roman, and Byzantine Period sherds. It is not surprising, therefore, that some sherds which the SGNAS collected at the site are either Late Byzantine and/or Umayyad.

Conclusions

Byzantine Period sites are the most numerous of any period sites in the survey territory. This is not surprising relative to the findings of the Wadi al-Hasa Archaeological Survey (MacDonald *et al.* 1988). These Byzantine Period sites range from very small sherd scatters to village sites.

Dier 'Ain 'Abata, Site 46, could turn out to be a very important site. Excavations will clarify its date, function, and possible identity.

The six Byzantine village/hamlet sites, namely, Sites 211; 232; 233; 228; 216; and 215, in the Northeast 'Arabah and, with the exception of Site 211, east of the 'Old Road' between Wadis al-Hassiya and al-Ghuweib, require further investigation. They are generally similar in construction and are one period, namely, Byzantine Period sites. One is moved to question the existence of so many of these sites from the Byzantine Period in this arid zone. Moreover, Sites 226 and 197 may be cemeteries associated with two of these sites, namely, Sites 228 and 215, from the same period.

It is reasonable to assume that there were also village/hamlet sites, and maybe even towns, from the Byzantine Period in the Southern Ghors. Now, however, as for sites for other periods, they have been destroyed by ancient and/or modern development (Khouri 1981: 213–27). The heavy sherd scatters at such locations as Sites 66 and 180A and B could possibly indicate where some of these sites were situated. Certainly the number of Byzantine sherd scatters in the Southern Ghors indicates dense occupation during the period under discussion.

One surprise of the SGNAS' collection from Khirbet Sheikh 'Isa, Site 4, was the lack of Byzantine sherds since the site is generally identified with Christian

Zoara (De Luynes 1874, I: 247–51; Musil 1907: 210–11; Mallon 1924: 436–39; Albright 1924: 4; Albright 1926: 57; Frank 1934: 204–5; Alt 1935: 4; Glueck 1935: 8; Abel 1967: 201; Donner and Knauf 1985: 30). Some of the above-listed authors report numerous column drums and grave markers with crosses at the site. Albright, for example, reports inscriptions in Greek and Kufic (?), as well as stones with sculptured crosses, and coins, both Byzantine and Kufic (1924: 4) while Mallon shows a picture of a cross on a stone from the area (1924: 435, Figure 17). The SGNAS noted column base fragments in the southeast corner and column drums in the northeast corner of the agriculture field in which the site is now located. These artifacts have been placed there during field clearance. More of these building fragments are now at the entrance to Karak Castle. N. Bega'in of the Department of Antiquities brought them to this place for safekeeping. Moreover, personnel of the Impresit Construction Company, the contractors responsible for laying down the irrigation pipes in the Southern Ghors, told the SGNAS that they uncovered columns about 2 m below the surface of the ground when carrying out their work. This artifactual evidence would tend to confirm the traditional identification of the site with Zoara. Moreover, as stated above, King *et al.* report Byzantine sherds from the site (1987: 448, 456). This site will be returned to in the treatment of the Islamic Period sites of the survey. Once again, as in previously-described periods, the wadis of the survey were extensively used by the Byzantines. There is evidence for such use from the northern to the southern extremity of the survey territory.

Notes

1   K. D. Politis began the excavation of Site 46, Deir 'Ain 'Abata, in November–December 1988 (1988; 1989). He concluded that the main, standing structure at the site 'proved to be a reservoir which included a water catchment and distribution system' (1989: 232). He states that the exact date of the occupation of the main site is yet to be determined. However, 'on the basis of the pottery types found so far, these buildings were constructed and used roughly from the 4th century A.D. to the beginning of the 7th century A.D.' (Politis 1989: 232). He concludes that this was probably the main period of occupation at the site (1988: 462).

Kate Da Costa studied the lamps recovered from Politis' exacavations at Area B of the site. 'She found that they all form part of the standard 5th century A.D. lamp repertoire of southern Jordan, although some of the types identified can be found as early as the 1st century A.D. and as late as the 8th century A.D.' (Politis 1989: 230; see also Da Costa 1989: 3).

2   N. Hagen is responsible for Figures 22 and 23. The figures appeared first in MacDonald and Politis 1988 as Figures 3 and 4. They will be superseded by present and future work at the site.

3   This identification is still tentative.

10. The Islamic Period As Seen From Selected Sites

by D. S. Whitcomb

Introduction

The Southern Ghors represent a remarkable region of Jordan and yet one archaeologically ignored since the 1930's. One important exception has been the survey by Rast and Schaub (1974) and the investigations into the Early Bronze materials which grew out of that research. While this survey indicated some of the Islamic materials to be found in this region, almost a decade elapsed before the first survey for Islamic sites under the direction of King (King *et al.* 1987). The present survey was designed (as may be seen in this volume) to recover broad, long-term patterns of settlement, including the Islamic Periods which were then still unpublished. The same year, 1986, the present author examined a few of the major sites, the results of which are included in this report.[1]

Archaeology and history

Archaeology of the Islamic Periods throughout the Middle East suffers from many misconceptions held both by historians and by archaeologists. For historians, there has yet to be demonstrated the clear value and relevance of information derived from archaeological survey (and often even that from excavation). For archaeologists, there is a continuing prejudice that recent periods are not fully archaeological and thus not pertinent to their research. For both groups, the value of surveys of Islamic Period sites is either ignored or, if such survey has been done, superficial treatment is frequently considered sufficient.

It is apparent, however, that recent surveys in the Southern Ghors, despite the limited nature of each campaign, have proven the tremendous potential importance of archaeological survey and the need to build on these beginnings.

Most archaeologists treating the Islamic archaeology of Jordan divide periods by the chronological dates of the ruling dynasty. This practice introduces numerous problems. Because not one of these dynasties was directly centred in Jordan, the political and cultural influence on this land becomes a very complicated study. Further, the more that is known of regional cultural changes, the clearer one sees that patterns of cultural change are not synchronous with political changes. Thus, a periodization based on neutral archaeological periods is a more useful system for discussing settlement patterns and other cultural manifestations by the archaeologist and cultural historian.

Period designations in arbitrary centuries is less than completely satisfactory and no doubt will be refined with further field work. The Early, Middle, and Late Islamic Periods proposed here entail a descriptive awkwardness (as do archaeological period designations for earlier times, e.g., 'Middle Bronze II'). Thus, dynastic labels are retained but with a chronological caveat that, for instance, 'Umayyad' refers to the period A.D. 600 to 800.

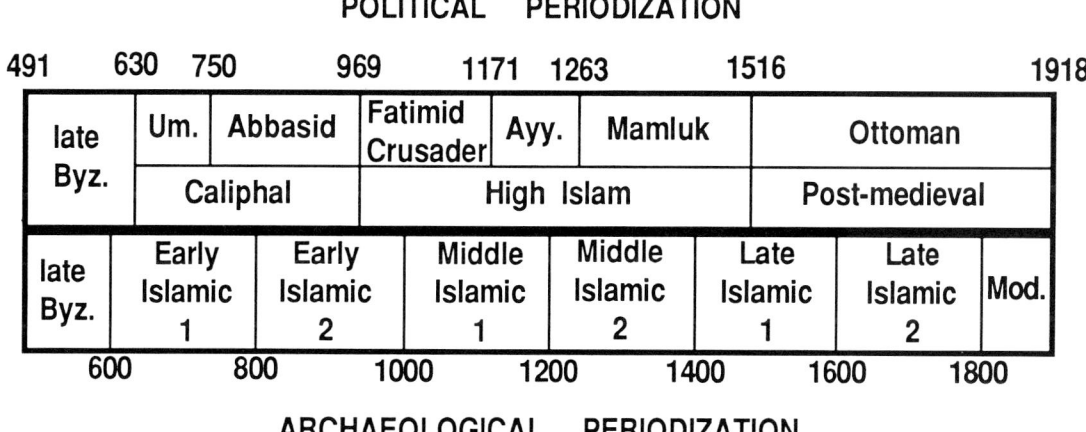

POLITICAL   PERIODIZATION

| 491 | 630 | 750 | | 969 | | 1171 | 1263 | | 1516 | | 1918 |

late Byz.	Um.	Abbasid		Fatimid Crusader	Ayy.		Mamluk		Ottoman		
	Caliphal			High Islam					Post-medieval		
late Byz.	Early Islamic 1	Early Islamic 2	Middle Islamic 1	Middle Islamic 2	Late Islamic 1	Late Islamic 2	Mod.

| 600 | 800 | 1000 | 1200 | 1400 | 1600 | 1800 |

ARCHAEOLOGICAL   PERIODIZATION

Table 57   Political and archaeological periodization during the Islamic Period

113

Surveys and ceramics

The use of archaeological periodization is important in field surveys, especially where chronological diagnostics are not well known or are subject to new revisions. Unfortunately, Islamic ceramics fall into both these categories, especially in the Southern Ghors. Reliable typologies from pertinent excavations are only recently coming to be published and assimilated, for instance, Pella (Walmsley 1986), Karak and other southern castles (Brown 1987), Burj al-Ahmar (Pringle 1986), 'Aqaba (Whitcomb 1987), and many other sites. The results from these excavations indicate that older conceptions of periods (already marred with dynastic designations) must be revised; the corollary to this fact is that the lists provided by 'pottery readers' have little meaning and cannot contribute reliable data (e.g., King *et al.* 1987: 453–59; Whitcomb 1988, n.3). Archaeological diagnostics in the Southern Ghors may begin with extra-regional typologies but ultimately only a careful seriation of site collections within the region will provide a reliable sequence as historical evidence. Drawings of ceramics are the key tool toward establishing testable typologies; Islamic ceramics have appeared in Rast and Schaub (1974, fig. 6, 10–12), from the Wadi 'Isal (Jacobs 1983), and the preliminary report of the SGNAS (MacDonald *et al.* 1987, fig. 6). The following study presents a few of the key Islamic sites with an analysis of the ceramics; this is neither as thorough nor as systematic as would be desirable. Nevertheless, these ceramics produce a general picture of the region, aspects of its settlement and economy, which may serve for hypothesis formation in future research.

Tawahin al-Sukkar

There are a series of sites in the Southern Ghors called Tawahin al-Sukkar (sugar mills); they are easily identified ruins, marked on most maps. The first example is in the Ghor al-Safi (SGNAS Site 1), where Albright made soundings, finding only Byzantine and Arabic materials. He began the archaeological tradition of associating the mill and its medieval sherds with the Byzantine centre of Zoara (1924: 4; 1926: 57; Mallon 1924: 439; Glueck 1935: 7; see Khirbet Sheikh 'Isa, below). Tristram calls the main structure on this site Kasr el Bushariyeh (1873: 63), which may correspond to Qasr Umm al-Shari'ah (Mallon 1924: 438, n.1). A more common name given to the main structure is Qasr al-Tuba (-Tub) or Qasr Safi (Glueck 1935: 7, n.19). The only plan appears to be that of Frank (1934, plan 8) which corresponds to the description in King *et al.* (1987: 446), where they suggest the Qasr and the Tawahin date from different periods.[2]

Ceramics from this site, as reported by King *et al.* (1987: 455–56), are described as Byzantine from the northwest end of the Tawahin (12E) and, from two localities in the Qasr (12B; 12C), Byzantine and Mamluk in 1:4 proportion. Another collection from the Qasr produced only Mamluk sherds, including a number of glazed wares dated to the 12th–13th centuries (12A). All of these diagnostics were body sherds. This last sample would apparently coincide with the ceramics which the SGNAS found in a midden to the north and northeast of the structures (Site 1, Sample 1), within the structures (Site 1, Sample 2), and within a cemetery on the southeast (Site 1, Sample 3; Plate 29j–t). Glazed wares, found on the periphery of the structure, have forms and decorative techniques indicative of the Early Islamic 2 Period (Plate 29n–p). The absence of characteristics more usual in the Middle Islamic 2 Period strongly indicates an earlier, Late Abbasid or Fatimid, deposition.

The identification of this site as one of the Tawahin al-Sukkar, i.e., as a sugar mill, is based in part on the numerous sugar pots and moulds found there. These vessels are often mentioned in archaeological literature but the evidence is rarely presented. The sugar moulds are conical vessels with a wide, thickened, out-turning rim and a rounded base. The base has a single hole for draining the molasses (Plate 31f; other regions have a three hole type). The sugar pot is a tall jar with out-turned rim and, probably, a flat base. The mould was intended to rest on the jar as depicted on similar vessels from Kouklia, Cyprus (von Wartburg 1983, fig. 3). This study of a Lusignan sugar factory presents an early 15th century description by al-Nuwairi:

> The boiled juice is poured into moulds of earthenware, which are narrow below and wide above. In the bottoms are holes, which are plugged with pieces of sugar cane for the first phase of the evaporation process. These moulds are placed on top of other vessels into which in an advanced stage flows the syrup which is separated in fine drops, while after some time the crystallized sugar, formed to a loaf, can be removed from the moulds (von Wartburg 1983: 299).

The large number of vessels necessary for this production explains the common broken sherds and suggests the likelihood of a nearby kiln for vessel production.[3] Both a proximate kiln and the boiling process would explain the dense amounts of ash on this and other sites in the area. The moulds in Cyprus come in three standard sizes, which von Wartburg estimates as producing 1, 4, and 8 liter loaves (types I, II, III; 1983: 310). The moulds at Tawahin al-Sukkar correspond to type II (Plate 29j, k) and type III (Plate 29l, m), which were apparently used for inferior quality crystal sugar (von Wartburg 1983: 310–11).

A second site called Tawahin al-Sukkar may be discussed for comparative purposes. Actually there are two such sites beside the main road passing through the Ghor al-Dhra', about 2 km southeast of Mazra'a. Both are slightly raised areas of dark, grey-brown soil, ca. 200 x 200 m; they were described by Mallon as Islamic (1924: 443) and may be associated with Khirbet al-Resis (Glueck 1935: 5). The western site has remains of stone walls, including walls forming a large rectangle (contra King *et al.* 1987: 443).

Ceramic collections from the western site are described by King *et al.* as Byzantine and Ayyubid/Mamluk (1987: 454–55, 8B, with a 3:1 proportion). The collections from the present author's survey include fine wares and dark red sherds which clearly belong to the Early Islamic 1 Period, i.e., Late Byzantine through Umayyad (Plate 29e–i; especially the fine cups discussed by Gichon 1974, =Plate 29h, i). Glazed bowls have forms and splashed decoration (Plate 29a–d) which belong to the Early Islamic 2 Period, similar to the other Tawahin site. Unfortunately, this brief survey did not collect larger, unglazed sherds and, thus, there is no direct evidence for sugar moulds and pots. Presuming the presence of these industrial diagnostics, one has the remains of two sugar factories associated with pre-Ayyubid/Mamluk ceramics. This archaeological evidence may indicate a beginning of this industry as early as the 10th or early 11th century (see below).

Feifa

Feifa is a small village 10 km south of al-Safi with the rectangular mudbrick walls of a sugar mill (Photo 23). This structure (SGNAS Site 91), called Qasr Feifa, was once about 100 m from the village and a Huweitat cemetery (Mallon 1924: 436). The thick midden of soft grey soil contains scattered stones and a large mill stone in the centre of the building (Glueck 1935: 9–10, fig. 2). Amid the modern trash and graves, particularly on the periphery of the tell, sherds were collected (Site 91, sample 135; sample 136). About 1 km east of Qasr Feifa is an associated site on the west side of an Early Bronze hill-town (Rast and Schaub 1974: 11–12; Frank 1934, 210–11, plans 11 and 12). The 'thick spongy charcoal across much of the site' suggests a refuse area, if not another factory or kilns. This site is called Khirbet al-Feifa by King *et al.* (1987: 450).

Collections from the Qasr indicate the following periods: wares of Byzantine tradition (Plate 30l–n) and cream wares (Plate 30p, q) of the Early Islamic 1; splash glazed wares (Plate 30a, b, e) of the Early Islamic 2; slip-painted glazed wares (Plate 30c, d), geometric painted wares (Plate 30f–h), a glazed cooking pot (Plate 30i), and unglazed forms (Plate 30j, k, n, o) of the Middle Islamic 2. Not depicted here are examples of sugar moulds and pots, which may be associated with the vat rim (Plate 30r); these, with the Early Islamic 2 ceramics, tend to confirm the identification of the Qasr as another sugar factory. The close parallels with Khirbet al-Feifa (Rast and Schaub 1974: fig. 10, 278–91; fig. 11, 292–99) are exclusively with the latest period. The ceramic analysis in King *et al.* (1987: 457) indicates Byzantine and Mamluk/Ottoman Periods in a 1:2 proportion for both sites (but with glazed wares occurring only at the Qasr).

Khirbet Sheikh 'Isa

Khirbet Sheikh 'Isa (SGNAS Site 4, about 150 m northwest of Tawahin al-Sukkar) was described by Tristram:

> on a rising slope are strewn a mass of loose stones, covering several acres, with a few fragments of walls, many solid foundations, and a few portions of round columns. ...[construction of] soft sandstone exclusively. ... not the slightest vestige of any fortification (1873: 62).

Albright made soundings through 3 m of 'Byzantine and early Arabic' deposition to virgin soil (1924: 4; his interest was based, in part, on the tomb stones in Greek and Aramaic dating to the 4th–5th centuries thought to come from excavations by locals here. See also Abel 1931). Frank improves the information on this site with a plan and drawings of architectural elements (1934: 204–5, plan 8, 9A, Taf. 24A). Glueck confines his attention to slag found by Frank (1935: 8–9), and Harding notes the tell, 2 m deep, with a birkeh (reservoir) and fort. This once imposing mound has been severely damaged by agricultural activity and a new road; the tomb of the sheikh who protected the site is now gone. The site is composed of soft grey earth, ca. 200 x 50 m, in which one large stone wall dramatically emerges, possibly an aqueduct. There are plentiful wasters and slag of kilns, as well as sherds.

While the apparent paucity of Byzantine sherds is problematic (King *et al.* 1987: 448, 456; a 1:3 proportion to Mamluk/Ottoman sherds), the numerous column drums would tend to confirm, more than any other artifact, the traditional identification of this site with Byzantine Zoara. An inventory of the ceramic types from Khirbet Sheikh 'Isa may begin with the ubiquitous sugar moulds and pots (Plate 31a–f,v). It would be interesting to know if the kilns on this site were producing these vessels (rather than the glazed wares suggested in King *et al.* 1987: 448). The Early Islamic 1 Period is again evidenced in fine ware (Plate 31n; Plate 32q); Early Islamic 2 has the cream wares (Plate 31m, o, t, u; Plate 32s–v) and splash glazed ware (Plate 32a, b). The Middle Islamic 1 and 2 are represented by a punctate sherd (Plate 31s), geometric painted wares (Plate 31g–l), glazed casseroles (Plate 32m, n), glazed slip painted wares (Plate 32c, h, i) and other slip and sgraffiato wares (Plate 32j–l, o), and underglaze painted frit wares (Plate 32d–g).

Al-Rujoum

The site of al-Rujoum is the largest and most impressive of the Islamic sites in the Southern Ghors (SGNAS Site 45). Located about 1 km southwest of the modern town of al-Safi on the south bank of Wadi al-Hasa (= Wadi Qurahi), the mound measures about 200 x 100 m and is covered, especially on the eastern side, by a modern cemetery (al-Maqbara; King *et al.* 1987: 448). Plentiful sherds and glass fragments are found in the soft grey-brown soil, particularly among the graves. Mallon was the first to discuss this site, known to him as Khirbet Sheikh 'Ali; he identified the tomb and cemetery as the ruins of the late medieval town of al-Safiya (1924: 435).[4]

The large collection of ceramics from this site may begin with sugar pots and moulds (Plate 33a, b), rims of large vats and zir (Plate 33i–k), all of which may suggest that the vessels found other, residential uses. The quantity and variety of glazed wares is impressive compared to other sites in the Southern Ghors; King *et al.* list over 200 glazed sherds, some 40% of their collection (1987: 456–57; one may expect such luxury items to number less the 15% of a scientifically controlled sample). The unglazed forms are characteristic cream wares, a filter neck (Plate 34h), and bowls (Plate 34o, p) of the Early Islamic 2 Period. Splash glazed wares (Plate 35f–h, j) include a sherd from a Fayyumi bowl, an Egyptian type of the 9th century (Plate 35h). Thereafter, the Middle Islamic 1 Period may begin with rolled-rim jars, similar to glazed cooking pots (Plate 33c–e) and associable with the Fatimid style of handle (Plate 33f). A more special import is a Chinese porcelain sherd, probably qingbai ware of the 11th century.

Frit wares include black and blue underglaze painted wares (Plate 35b–e) and a prize piece, a lustre ware bowl (Plate 35a), all of which were imported from Syria and may be dated to the 13th and 14th centuries. Geometric painted wares occur in the form of jars, especially ones with a long narrowing neck (Plate 34a–g, k, l), spouted pots (Plate 34i, j), and bowls (Plate 34m, n, r, s). These and unpainted hand-made wares begin in the Middle Islamic 2 Period and continue into the Late Islamic. The same dating may hold for the slip painted wares (Plate 35l–n), which may be grouped with simple sgraffiato pieces (Plate 35k, o–r). Other glazed wares (Plate 35s–w) would appear to be later, probably Late Islamic 1 or 2, or Ottoman, as may be the heavy lug handles (Plate 33m–o; Crowfoot 1932).

The site of al-Rujoum is apparently the only locality where glass bracelets (Photo 24) have been collected (Plate 36a–h); these may be discussed briefly, as they confirm the chronological pattern of the ceramics.[5] Plain bracelets are extremely difficult to date, the examples here being irregular and flattened in section (Plate 36a, b). Spaer suggests the latter type does not pre-date the Byzantine Period (1988: 54; type A2b). Cobalt blue and turquoise bracelets are common on Late Islamic Period sites in Egypt; figure 8b is paralleled from Quseir al-Qadim from a 14th century context (Whitcomb and Johnson 1980: 59, n, o). Twisted bracelets are likewise unlikely to be pre-Byzantine (Spaer 1988: 59; type C); the examples from al-Rujoum are opaque black, one with a twisted white trail (Plate 36c, d). Again, parallels from Quseir suggest a Mamluk or later date (Whitcomb and Johnson: 1980, 59, p, q). The following two styles are characterized by a light amber or greenish clear bracelet upon which marvered sections (in red, yellow, orange, green) are placed. Twisted bands (black and white, yellow and green) are added around the bracelet (Plate 36e–h). These decorations reflect

glass techniques also used in Mamluk glass vessels (Whitcomb 1983: 106). Bracelets with a semi-circular section appear to belong to the 14th century (Whitcomb and Johnson 1980, 59, r–y), but those with a flat triangular section (Plate 36g, h) are probably later and Ottoman.

Relation between Khirbet Sheikh 'Isa and Al-Rujoum

The ruins at both Khirbet Sheikh 'Isa and al-Rujoum have been suggested as possible remains of the medieval urban centre of Zughar. While further research, especially excavation, will determine the spacial and chronological relationship between these nearby settlements, surface collections suggest the following hypothesis. If Khirbet Sheikh 'Isa was Byzantine Zoara, occupation continued in this Byzantine town after the establishment of Islamic authority. During the Early Islamic 2 Period, the new urban centre of Zughar or Sughar was founded at al-Rujoum. Conditions leading to this innovation in settlement, namely the age of the older town, the need for new suqs (markets) and storage facilities, and a probable psychological readiness for radical change, are likely though difficult to prove. It is clear that Zughar became the commercial focus for an industrial expansion based on indigo and possibly sugar plantations (see below). The explanation of this change and prosperity as a result of the opening of contacts with Egypt (the dominance of Egyptian dynasties) may be too facile, pending more information on the nature of the Abbasid Period in this region. After 500–600 years of occupation, the transfer to Safiya or the modern town of al-Safi may be explained by reasons such as those above and not simply as a mark of decline under the Ottoman rule.

Zughar: an Islamic regional centre

Muqaddasi, a geographer writing in the 10th century, defined Zughar, or Sughar, as the capital of al-Sharat (i.e., Edom). While no other contemporary geographer followed his system of spatial hierarchy, this title was not conferred without reason. His description of this town is worth citing in detail:

> Sughar – the people of the two neighboring districts call the town Saqar (that is, 'Hell'); and a native of Jerusalem was wont to write from here to his friends, addressing 'From the lower Saqar (Hell) unto those in the upper Firdus (Paradise).' And verily this is a country that is deadly to the stranger, for its water is execrable; and he who should find that the Angel of Death delays for him, let him come here, for in all Islam I know not of any place to equal it in evil climate. ...
>
> Its people are black-skinned and thick-set. Its waters are hot, even as though the place stood over Hell-fire. On the other hand, its commercial prosperity makes of it

a little Basra, and its trade is very lucrative. The town stands on the shore of the Overwhelming Lake (the Dead Sea) and is in truth the remnant of the Cities of Lot, being the one that was spared by reason that its inhabitants knew nothing of their abominations. The mountains rise up near by the town.[6]

At least part of Muqaddasi's need to remark on the disagreeable climate, water, and physical character of the inhabitants may stem from the traditional association with Lot; for the moralistic traveler, this was somehow a condemned land and people.[7] At the same time Muqaddasi is rarely entirely negative (or entirely positive) about a town or region. The extensive and profitable trade is unlikely to be hyperbole and the analogy with Basra is worth further consideration. Certainly the port at the head of the Gulf was also characterized by heat, bad water, and dark-skinned inhabitants among the palms, and further, Basra was at the juncture of three regions (Iraq, Iran, and eastern Arabia). It is possible that Muqaddasi saw Zughar as a centre intermediary to the regions of Filastin, Urdunn and al-Sharat.[8]

The prosperity was due to agricultural products of the region, the first of which were special dates (Ist. 24; Ibn Hauq. 184–85, Muq. 178 [who adds 'dibs,' a date honey]; and al-Hamdani 131). A more specifically cash-crop was indigo (al-nil), which Ibn Hauqal praises, 'though the dye does not come up to the standard of Kabul' (124).[9] The growing of indigo needs a very hot climate with little or no rain. The processing of the stalks requires a reliable water source, large vats, and a building for boiling and straining. This last facility is virtually the same as that used in sugar processing. Large-scale indigo plantations and processing facilities have not been considered in archaeological surveys of this region. The reservoir near al-Safi (SGNAS Site 27; birkeh, King *et al.* 1987: 448) might well have served as an indigo vat. Perhaps more intriguing is the possibility that the Tawahin al-Sukkar originally may have been used for indigo manufacture.

The temporal precedence of indigo over sugar may be inferred from the medieval geographers' descriptions of the Jordan Valley and Southern Ghors. The introduction of the latter crop, sugar cane, may be placed in the 10th or 11th centuries (Hamarneh 1977–78; Watson 1983: 28, n.19; and Ashtor 1977: 228). The evidence of glazed ceramics on the Tawahin sites, datable to the Early Islamic 2 or Middle Islamic 1 Periods, indicates either usage for indigo or an introduction of the sugar industry during the late Abbasid/Fatimid Period. The equation of Tawahin sites and an Ayyubid/Mamluk cultural horizon masks a much more complex economic history.

Whatever the industries and their development, in the words of Walmsley, 'the towns of the eastern Wadi 'Arabah experienced a relative economic boom during the later [9–10th] centuries...' (1987: 278). This prosperity seems to have continued at least into the Late Islamic 1 Period. Archaeological and historical

indications of the activity of these markets presumes not only products but commercial movement. One should, thus, consider the broader regional context of the Southern Ghors in the Islamic Periods.

Mercantile relations were no doubt principally with the towns of Filistin, first with Hebron (Habra), Gaza (Ghazza) and Ramla (Plate 36). This latter city, capital of the province, may have been the chief consumer of indigo (Serjeant 1972: 119, on the prominence of the Dar al-Sabbaghin, dyehouse under the Abbasids). On a less specific level, one must remember the long-term exchange patterns between the coast and the transJordanian steppe; relationships between Hebron and Karak would most easily have gone through Zughar (Plate 36). Furthermore, while Gaza was traditionally the principal supplier of foodstuffs to 'Aqaba (Ayla), some of these goods may have originated or been transshipped from the Southern Ghors. This was most important for supplies supporting the passage of the Egyptian pilgrimage (Hajj) through 'Aqaba. Likewise, many of the pilgrims originating in Filistin may have passed through Zughar to Udhruh (Adhruh) (Plate 36) and on into the Hijaz. Zughar was not a crucially central locality; nevertheless, factors of climatic diversity and convenience for long-range movement may begin to explain the prosperity of its markets.

Conclusions

The Southern Ghors would seem to have been something more than Muqaddasi's unpleasant backwater in the Islamic Periods. Where historical documentation has not proven of sufficient detail, archaeological surveys are beginning to fill the lacuna. This archaeological data can hardly present a balanced picture of settlement patterns during the last 1200 years. There is good reason to believe further field research, especially soundings and excavations, will yield an ever more complex and fascinating picture of this unique region.

Notes

1 This was a reconnaissance of only one day, under the guidance of D. W. McCreery. I wish to express my gratitude to him for introducing me to this fascinating region and to Dr. G. Bisheh for permission to use these materials. Finally, I would thank B. MacDonald for rescuing my little 'Ceramic notes on the Southern Ghor' by augmenting these collections with his survey materials; collections by the present author are marked [+], to distinguish them from the SGNAS materials, in the figures. Unfortunately, time has not allowed a complete examination of ceramics from all the SGNAS sites, and, therefore, a general examination of the settlement patterns must await future study.

Place names, it will be noted, have gone through many transliterations; this article follows the usage of MacDonald et al. (1987) with two exceptions, the article is written 'al-', rather than using the spoken form, and diacritics are not used, except where the name is taken as an Arabic word.

2   Rast and Schaub report Byzantine sherds to the southeast, above the Tawahin (1974: 9–11, pl. 4, fig. 6. 150–64), a locality Tristram called El Mushnekk'r and thought to be a Muslim shrine (1873: 64; = al-Mashnaqa). This site was also known as el-Burj, a fort with four towers (var. El-ebrash, Labrush or el-Brosh; Kitchener 1884: 217; Abel 2, 466; and seen as the Chapel of Lot on Madaba Map, Mallon 1924: 438) and may be equivalent to Umm et-Tuwabin, discussed in King et al. (1987: 449) and in Chapter 8 of this report.

3   Further details on this industry may be found in the careful excavation of a sugar factory in southwestern Iran, dated to the late 12th to early 13th century (Boucharlat and Labrousse 1979).

4   Kusur (Qasr) Sheikh 'Ali is noted by Kitchener but apparently confused with Khirbet Sheikh 'Isa (1884: 217). The site is found in Harding's notes as Tell Safi, but with no further details (examined through the courtesy of H. Kurdi, Registration Centre, Department of Antiquities in Amman). This is not to lessen the debt to D. W. McCreery in renewing archaeologists' attention to this important site (King et al. 1987: 448, n.17).

5   While there has been little systematic study of this artifact category, glass bracelets may be expected to become a reliable chronological diagnostic with further research. Citations in archaeological and art historical literature give broad and often meaningless dates. As an example taken at random, Pringle labels a single surface example from Burj al-Ahmar as Byzantine (1986, fig. 52.1); section, colours, and decorative technique suggest a 12–13th century date consistent with primary occupation at that site. A preliminary examination of bracelet dating may be seen in Spaer (1988) and Whitcomb (1983).

6   This translation is from Le Strange (1896: 62–63). The description is strikingly similar to that of Ibn Hauqal, who states that Zughar is a 'city of heat lying in a hot country ... full of good things, ...much indigo.... The trade of the place is considerable, and its markets are greatly frequented' (124). Muqaddasi speaks in similar terms of Jericho (Riha or Ariha) as producing indigo and palms, having excessive heat and 'brown skinned and swarthy' people; at least Sughar was spared the snakes, scorpions and numerous fleas (Le Strange 1896: 55–56).

The description of 'black-skinned people' is reminiscent of travelers' observations. Mallon notes that the people of the Southern Ghors, the 'Ghawarneh, are neither Arabs nor bedouin of Palestine; they are an imported African race in which, it seems, a Nubian element dominates' (1924: 427). The suggestion of slaves working Fatimid plantations in the Southern Ghors is obviously premature; there are no published sherds identifiable as Nubian, from the contemporary Classic Christian Period in Upper Egypt and the Sudan.

7   Zughar has often been derived from Segor, associated with Bala, the Chapel of Lot, seen on the Madaba mosaic. Yaqut sees Sughar as deriving from Zughar, one of the daughters of Lot (Clermont-Ganneau 1886: 19).

8   Ya'qubi alone adds Zughar to the province of Dimashq (114). A similar comparison was drawn between Abbadan (near Basra) and Ayla, medieval Aqaba, which was considered part of Egypt, Syria, and the Hijaz (Muq. 179).

9   The Kabul praised by Ibn Hauqal is a town inland from the port of 'Akka (northeast of Haifa). Apparently the facility for processing indigo was augmented with sugar in the late 10th century; according to Muqaddasi, 'it has fields of cane, and they make there excellent sugar – better than in all the rest of Syria' (Le Strange 1896: 29).

11. Other Islamic Period Sites

by B. MacDonald

Introduction

The previous chapter treated four main sites, namely, Sites 1; 4; 45; and 91, of the SGNAS. These are the most important Islamic sites in the survey territory. However, there are many more sites at which the SGNAS collected Islamic Period pottery. These sites will be treated under the two main categories of the Early and the Late Islamic Periods. Here again, the sites from each period will be treated, for the most part, in a north-to-south order.

Early Islamic Period sites

The SGNAS collected Early Islamic Period pottery, in very small numbers (1 or 2 sherds), at four sites in addition to those treated in the previous chapter. These sites are Sites 66; 73; 75; and 155 (Table 58) (Figure

Table 58 Early Islamic Period sites

Site No.	Sample No.	No. of Sherds	Plate No.
66	111	1	
73	99	1	
75	117	2	7 (8)
155	257	1	

29). All of these sites have been treated in previous chapters. Therefore, they will not be treated extensively in this chapter.

The SGNAS collected one Abbasid Period sherd at Site 66, a sherd scatter to the southwest of Site 1, Tawahin al-Sukkar (Photo 25) (Figure 30), and to the south of Site 4, Khirbet Sheikh 'Isa. This is understandable in the light of the treatment of this site in the previous chapter. The sherd is a Mesopotamian import.

Rujm Umm Jufna, Site 73, has been noted in the discussion of the Iron II, Hellenistic, and Late Roman–Byzantine Period sites of the survey. The SGNAS collected one Umayyad sherd from near the rujm.

Site 75, ancient Feifa, yielded sherds, as has been noted in previous chapters, from several different periods. Among the sherds collected were two which the SGNAS analyzed as Fatimid/Ayyubid.

Finally, the SGNAS collected one Umayyad sherd at Site 155, Qasr al-Tilah. Such is not strange for such a large site which has yielded sherds from the Nabataean–Byzantine Periods as well.

Late Islamic Period sites

The Late Islamic Period can be divided into the Ayyubid/Mamluk and Ottoman Periods. Such, then, is the division of this segment of this chapter.

Mamluk Period sites

The SGNAS collected Mamluk Period pottery at eight sites, namely, Sites 2; 3; 5; 6; 79B; 125; 181; and 216, in addition to those treated in the previous chapter (Table 59) (Figure 29). The majority of these sites have at least been referred to in the discussion of earlier period sites.

Site 2 is located immediately to the east and southeast of Tawahin al-Sukkar, Site 1. It is known especially as the site of an EB I cemetery. Thus, it has been discussed extensively along with the other sites from the Early Bronze Period. The SGNAS collected a total of four Mamluk sherds from two different samples at the site. Because of the proximity of the site to the sugar mill, Site 1, it is understandable that there would be Mamluk sherds in a predominantly, EB I collection.

Site 3 consists of one robbed tomb, a line of stones, and a sherd and lithic scatter to the southeast of Site 2 and the JVA townsite. It has been discussed as a site at which the SGNAS collected Early Bronze, Iron Age, and Byzantine sherds. The SGNAS also collected four Mamluk sherds at the site.

Site 5 is still further to the east and at a higher elevation. It consists of what appears to be a campsite, many graves, and a sherd scatter overlooking Wadi al-Hasa to the north and northwest. The SGNAS collected sherds from several different periods, namely, Iron I; Iron Age; Nabataean; and Mamluk, at the site.

Table 59 Mamluk Period sites

Site No.	Sample No.	No. of Sherds	Plate No.
2	4	1	
2	5	3	
3	8	4	
5	10	10	
6	12	3	
6	13	1	
6	14	2	
79B	123	3	17 (6–8)
125	215	1	
125	216	1	
181	284	1	
216	391	1	

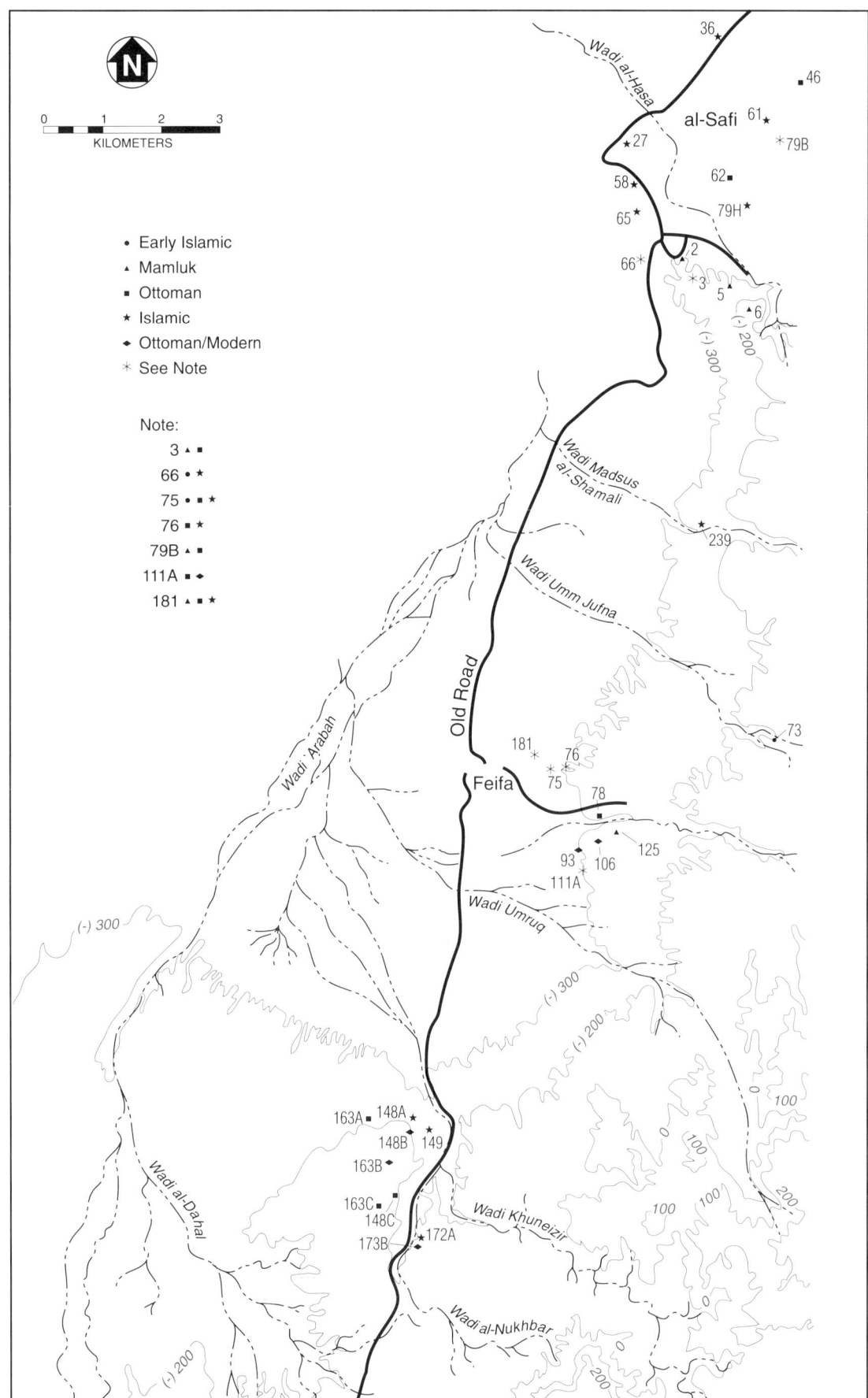

Figure 29 Early Islamic, Mamluk, Ottoman, Islamic settlement pattern map (Northern portion).

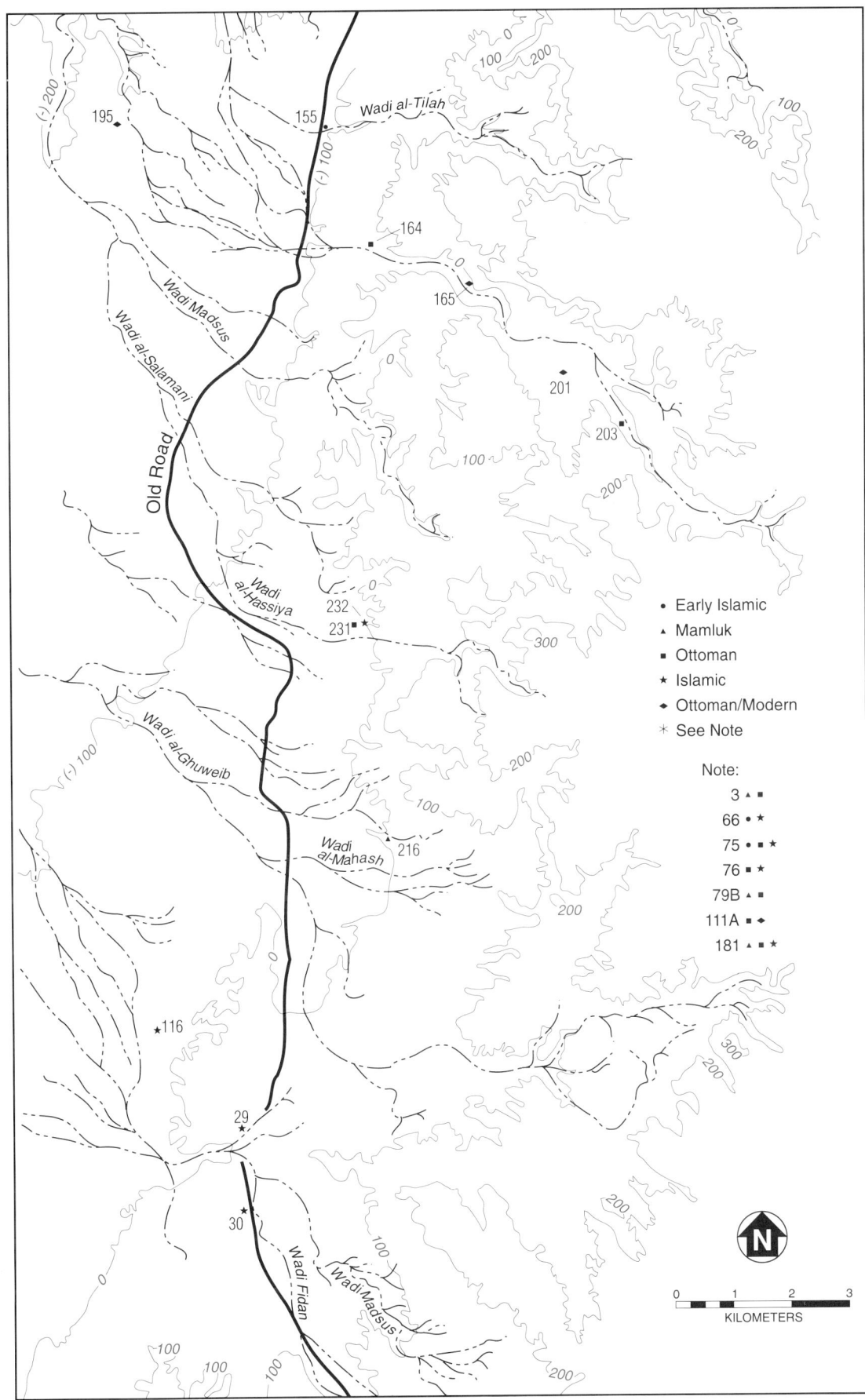

Figure 29 Early Islamic, Mamluk, Ottoman, Islamic settlement pattern map (Southern portion).

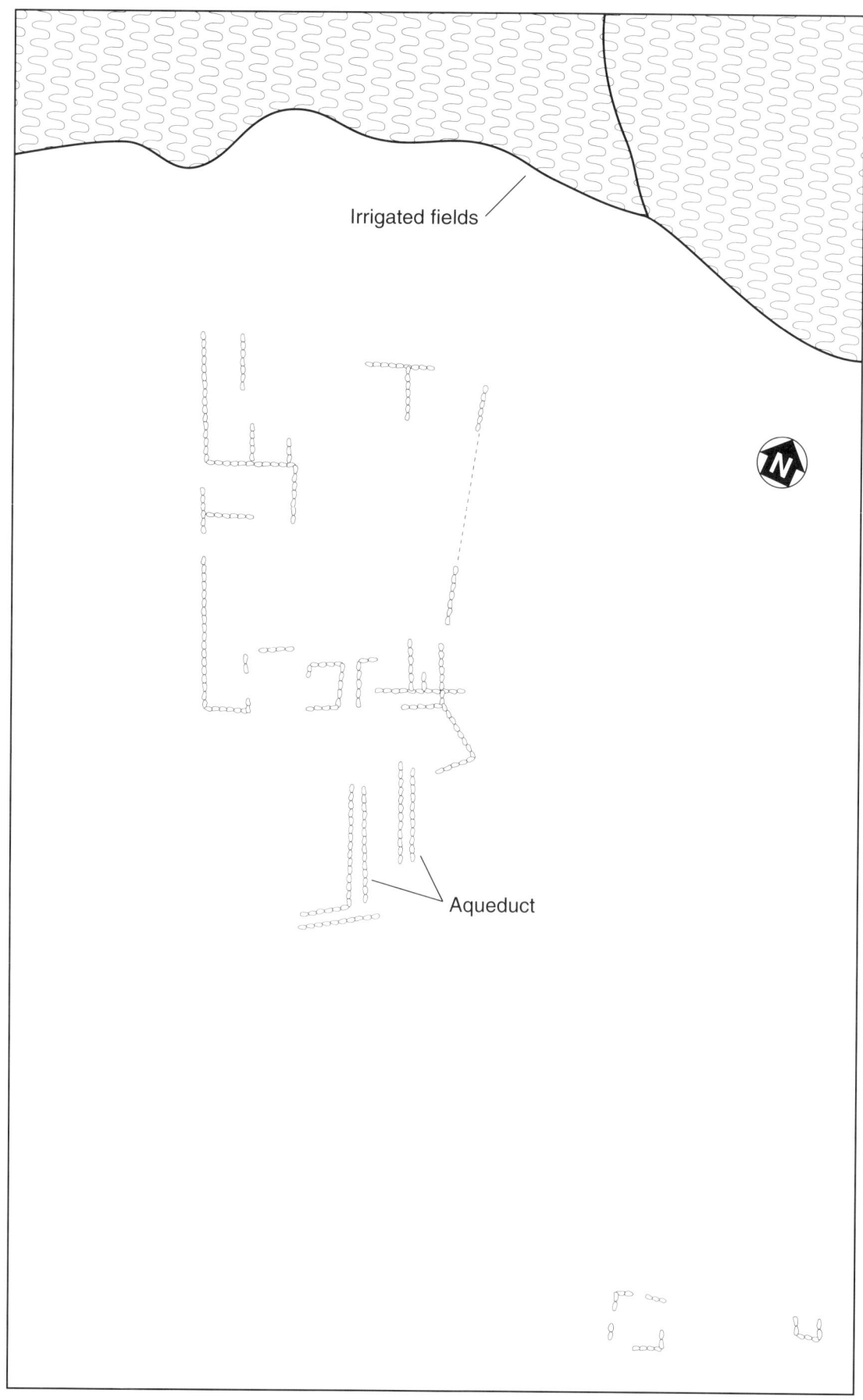

Figure 30 Site 1, Tawahin al-Sukkar.

Umm al-Tawabin, Site 6, is located to the southeast of Site 5 and high in the hills above the Wadi al-Hasa gorge. It has been discussed in detail along with other Nabataean Period sites. The SGNAS collected Mamluk sherds, in low numbers (6), from the site.

The SGNAS collected Mamluk sherds in very low numbers (2) at Site 125, a sherd scatter immediately south of Wadi Feifa. The site has been mentioned in the treatment of the Roman Period sites of the survey.

Site 216 has been treated as a Byzantine village site located just north of Wadi al-Mahash. The SGNAS collected one Mamluk sherd at the site.

Ottoman Period

The SGNAS collected Ottoman Period sherds at 14 sites, namely, Sites 3; 46; 62; 75; 76; 78; 79B; 111A; 148C; 173A and C; 164; 181; 203; and 231 (Table 60) (Figure 29) in addition to Sites 4 and 45 which have been treated in the previous chapter. However, for the most part, the number of sherds which the SGNAS collected at each site was low. For example, at seven or half of these sites, namely, Sites 46; 62; 78; 79B; 111A; 148C; and 164, the SGNAS collected only one or two sherds from the Ottoman Period. Since the majority of these 14 sites have been treated previously they need only be mentioned briefly here.

Site 3 has been treated in the discussion of the Mamluk Period sites. Site 46, Deir 'Ain 'Abata, has been treated extensively as a Byzantine Period site.

The SGNAS collected a relatively large number (29) of Ottoman sherds at Site 75, ancient Feifa. The site has been treated in the discussion of the Early Bronze and Iron Age Period sites of the survey. The majority of the sherds which the SGNAS collected were from the saddle between the mounds that form the western and eastern extremities of the site.

Moreover, the SGNAS collected a small number (5) of sherds from the period under discussion from Site 76, the eastern or cemetery segment of ancient Feifa.

Site 181, a sherd scatter, is located in an agricultural field to the northwest of ancient Feifa. It has been treated previously on several occasions.

Site 163A–C is a series of sherd scatters and/or potbusts on the plateau immediately west of Wadi Khuneizir. The site has been discussed in the treatement of the Late Roman–Byzantine Period.

Site 203 is a campsite and potbust on a terrace along the south side of Wadi al-Dahal. The only identifiable pottery collected at the site was Ottoman. However, the number (6) of sherds collected was low.

There is one Ottoman Period site, namely, Site 231, located north of Wadi al-Hassiya. The site appears to be a cemetery. It has been treated previously as one at which the SGNAS collected Roman and Byzantine Period sherds.

Islamic Period

The SGNAS collected Islamic Period sherds, without further precision, from 18 sites, namely, Sites 27; 29; 30; 36; 58; 61; 65; 66; 75; 76; 79H; 116; 148A; 149; 172A; 181; 232; and 239 (Table 61) (Figure 29). Some of the pottery from these sites falls somewhere in the Islamic Period. However, it is impossible to determine to just where in the period it belongs. The number of Islamic sherds in all cases is low.

Al-Altiahem, Site 36, is the remains of a farm located in agricultural fields to the north of Wadi al-Hasa. The mudbrick farm building which constitutes the site measures ca. 21 x 6 metres. The SGNAS collected five Islamic Period sherds at the site.

Site 61 consists of the remnants of two structures measuring ca. 9 x 5 and 7 x 5 metres. It overlooks modern al-Safi. The site has been treated in the discussion of the Byzantine Period sites. A small number of sherds, one of which was Islamic, was collected at the site. Immediately to the south is Site

Table 60   Ottoman Period sites

Site No.	Sample No.	No. of Sherds	Plate No.
3	8	2	
46	408	1	
62	114	1	
75	116	5	
75	117	24	
76	129	4	
76	228	1	
78	131	1	
79B	123	1	
111A	183	1	
148C	249	2	
163A	270	1	
163C	272	14	
164	304	2	
181	284	6	
203	349	6	
231	397	3	

Table 61   Islamic Period sites

Site No.	Sample No.	No. of Sherds	Plate No.
27	38	8	
29	74	1	
30	76	3	
36	51	5	
58	55	5	
61	113	1	
65	110	1	
66	111	2	
75	116	3	
75	117	7	
76	119	1	
76	228	1	
79H	125	1	
116	189	3	
148A	246	3	
149	247	1	
172A	290	2	
181	284	4	
232	398	3	
239	406	1	

79A–H, a series of tombs. Site 79H is a general surface collection from the area. There is one Islamic, green-glazed, body sherd in the collection.

Al-Jor, Site 27 (Photo 26), is the remnant of what was at one time a reservoir (Kitchener 1884: 217; Albright 1924: 4). It is located in the midst of agricultural fields to the south of Al-Rujoum, Site 45, to which it could have been associated. The north and south walls of the structure are partially preserved. The interior, however, of the reservoir is now used as an agricultural field. There is a mound located to the northwest of the structure. The SGNAS noted some burials, both of children and adults, in the mound. It collected only 12 sherds at the site. Eight of these sherds are Islamic, possibly Mamluk, body sherds[1].

Site 58 consists of a sherd scatter in agricultural fields immediately south of Wadi al-Hasa. The SGNAS collected five Islamic body sherds at the site. Two of the sherds are glazed.

Sites 65 and 66 are located in agricultural fields to the south of Site 58. Both sites have been discussed previously. Among the sherds which the SGNAS collected at the sites are a very small number of Islamic Period pieces.

A rectangular enclosure, measuring ca. 10 x 15 metres, constitutes Site 239. The SGNAS noted many graves nearby. The only identifiable pottery which the SGNAS collected at the site dates to somewhere in the Islamic Period.

Site 181 is a sherd scatter in an agricultural field to the northwest of Wadi Feifa. The site has been discussed in relation to several earlier periods. The SGNAS collected four Islamic Period body sherds at the site. Sites 75 and 76, ancient Feifa, are located immediately to the southeast. Both sites have been treated extensively especially in the discussion of the Early Bronze and Iron II Period sites. They both yielded what the SGNAS is calling Islamic sherds, without further qualification.

Sites 148A and 149 are located in the same general area, i.e., on the plateau immediately west of Wadi Khuneizir. Both sites have been discussed previously. Both yielded a small number of Islamic Period sherds.

Site 172A is located on a terrace within Wadi al-Nukhbar. It consists of a sherd scatter and two graves. Islamic body sherds were the only identifiable pottery which the SGNAS collected at the site. Site 232 has been discussed as a Byzantine hamlet/village. It is located north of Wadi al-Hassiya. The SGNAS collected three Islamic body sherds at the site.

Site 116 is a cemetery and possible camp located north of the Wadi Fidan gorge. The predominant, identifiable pottery which the SGNAS collected at the site dates to the Nabataean Period. The SGNAS also collected three Islamic sherds, probably late, at the site.

Site 29 has been referred to in the discussion of the Chalcolithic/Early Bronze and Iron II Period sites. It also yielded one Islamic sherd. To the south is Site 30, al-Munbateha/Khirbet Hamr Ifdan, a smelting site. It, too, has been treated on several occasions previously. Among the sherds which the SGNAS collected at the

site were three from somewhere in the Islamic Period.

Ottoman/Modern Period

The SGNAS collected Ottoman/Modern Period pottery at nine sites, namely, Sites 93; 106; 111A; 148B; 163B; 165; 173B; 195; and 201 (Table 62) (Figure 29).

Site 106 consists of a sherd scatter and a possible campsite immediately south of Wadi Feifa. Site 93 is located to the southwest. It is a possible cemetery and a sherd scatter along with a stone 'platform' (?) structure at the top of a small hill ca. 0.50 km south of the wadi and just east of the main Mazra'a-'Aqaba Highway. The only identifiable pottery which the SGNAS collected at both sites was Ottoman/Modern. Further south still, but in the same environmental zone, is Site 111A–G. The site consists of a number of graves (?) with very little associated pottery. Site 111A consists of a number of oval and rectangular graves outlined with small piles of stone. Each grave measures ca. 1.5 x 2–2.5 metres. Along with Iron II, Byzantine, and Ottoman sherds, the SGNAS collected five Ottoman/Modern sherds at the site.

Site 148A–C, which is a sherd scatter on the plateau immediately west of Wadi Khuneizir, has been referred to in the treatments of the EB IV; Early Bronze; Iron Age; Nabataean; Byzantine; and Islamic Period sites. Site 148B yielded one Ottoman/Modern sherd. Site 163A–C, is another sherd scatter in the same general area. Site 163B consists, for the most part, of a very concentrated sherd scatter which is comprised of at least two potbusts. Ottoman/Modern were the only identifiable sherds which the SGNAS collected at the site.

Site 173A and B consist of potbusts for the most part. The site is located on a terrace on the east side of Wadi al-Nukhbar. Site 173B has been discussed previously as a site at which the SGNAS collected Byzantine sherds. The only other pottery at the site was Ottoman/Modern.

There are three sites in association with Wadi al-Dahal from which the SGNAS collected Ottoman/Modern sherds. Site 195 is located in the wadi's flood plain immediately to the west of the main Mazra'a-'Aqaba Highway. The area is badly eroded. Ottoman/Modern was the only identifiable pottery

Table 62 Ottoman/Modern Period sites

Site No.	Sample No.	No. of Sherds	Plate No.
93	138	10	
106	147	22	
111A	183	5	
148B	248	1	
163B	271	142	
165	305	53	
173B	293	6	
195	338	9	
201	347	18	

which the SGNAS collected at the site. Further east is Site 165, a cemetery and a sherd scatter on a terrace on the north side of the wadi. The SGNAS collected a large number (43) of Ottoman/Modern sherds at the site. To the southeast is Site 201. It is another sherd scatter. This site has been discussed already in relation to the Roman Period sites of the survey. The SGNAS collected a moderate number (18) of sherds from the period under discussion at the site.

Conclusions

As stated in the previous chapter, the Early Islamic Period is well represented in the survey territory at such major sites as al-Rujoum, Site 45; Khirbet Sheikh 'Isa, Site 4; Tawahin al-Sukkar, Site 1; and Qasr al-Feifa, Site 91. At all of these sites, settlement continues at least into the beginning of the Late Islamic Period.

Following the Mamluk Period there appears to be a decrease in population in the survey territory. The Ottoman Period presence is confined to sherd scatters which represent potbusts and possibly camps. Nowhere in the survey territory is there evidence for a substantial, Ottoman presence. The exception, however, is set forth in the previous chapter. This is confirmed by the eye-witness accounts of the explorers in the area during the 19th century who speak of a village in the neighbourhood of Wadi al-Hasa (Burckhardt 1822; Kitchener 1884).

What is either Ottoman and/or Modern pottery is confined to three areas, namely, south of Wadi Feifa; in the Wadi Khuneizir-Wadi al-Nukhbar region; and in association with Wadi al-Dahal. All the sites from which the SGNAS collected this pottery are either sherd scatters and/or potbusts. There are sometimes associated graves. This would be the type of sites associated with people living a semi-nomadic life and crossing from east-to-west and vice-versa in the Wadi 'Arabah region. Once again, Wadi al-Dahal shows evidence of having been used as a main travelling route during the Ottoman/Modern Period.

Notes

1   On the possibility of this site as an indigo vat see the previous chapter.

12. Glass From The 1986 Season

by C. Meyer

Introduction

The glass sherds from the SGNAS are valuable in its own right as an archaeologically collected sample with known site provenences. Also of great interest, however, is the opportunity to test a glass corpus as an independent means of dating, possibly the first opportunity. With a few notable exceptions such as the Karanis material, glass finds from Near Eastern sites have, until quite recently, been poorly sampled and spottily published, and without stratified, dated, material it is impossible to date a surface collection. Now, however, large, dated, published glass corpora are becoming available at an accelerating rate from sites such as Karanis (1936), Corinth (1952), Hama (1957, though with problems in dating), Mezad Tamar (1977), Debira West (1978), Sardis (1980), Queseir al-Qadim (1979, 1981), Carthage (1984), and Jerash (1987), as well as from numerous smaller corpora – with promise of much more information from sites still under study such as 'Aqaba, Lejjun, and the Serçe Limani shipwreck. Largely because of the lack of interest in 'late' periods in Near Eastern archaeology and the consequent sparseness of archaeological studies, glass finds, which may be very numerous if not bulky, have been seriously underutilized for dating and other questions. Harden (in Shinnie and Harden 1955) did use the Soba glass as the main dating criterion for the site, but at that time there were no pottery or other dates available as a check or test. In the present case, the SGNAS glass may be dated by comparison to other sites and then checked against the pottery, inscriptional, and other dating evidence already available from the SGNAS. The glass and other dating criteria should support each other, and if not, why not.

Methodology

Without knowing the exact collecting strategy but judging from the small size of sherds and beads gathered, it would appear that everything within the designated collection zone was taken. The labeled samples were mechanically cleaned and tabulated (167 items). Being surface finds rather than excavated material, much of the decomposition layers had worn off, but where present they were noted. This and the colour and decoration of the glass are, as for pottery, clues to dating. The glass fabric may also provide information as to the chemical composition and hence the place or region of manufacture, but these are problems that cannot be addressed at this time. Sixty-one diagnostic sherds (37% of the collection) were drawn with reconstructed diameters and profiles where possible; few categories of artifacts gain more

by being drawn than glass. Sherds representing less than one-fourth the circumference of the vessel were drawn in; conversely, if there is no sherd outline on the drawing then at least a quarter of the circumference was preserved. All but three virtually duplicate drawings (noted in the site discussions) are shown on Plates 37 and 38, with the important exception of the glass bracelets which are discussed by Whitcomb (Chapter 10).

The inked, and for study purposes coloured, drawings could then be compared to excavated glass from other sites, a process similar to dating pottery. For this study, comparisons are made almost exclusively with excavated rather than purchased glass corpora. Given that glass dating is still being worked out for many regions of the Near East, citations of site and date are given rather than simply 'Umayyad' or 'Late Byzantine,' or whatever may be. In the cases of third season Queseir al-Qadim and 'Aqaba, which is still being excavated, study of the glass is still in progress and not yet published. It is relatively easy to separate Roman fabrics and forms from Byzantine/Umayyad, from Abbasid and Mamluk, and sometimes, within these broad groupings, to narrow the dates further. A frequency distribution is even available for the Byzantine and Umayyad glass from Jerash (Meyer 1984), with the proviso that it pertains to a sample from an urban site in north Jordan rather than the south Jordan area. The dates used are taken from the Queseir al-Qadim, Jerash, and 'Aqaba studies: Roman, 1st and 2nd century A.D.; Late Roman, 3rd century to 324; Early Byzantine, 324 to 491; Late Byzantine, 491 to 636; Umayyad, 661 to 750; Abbasid, 750 to 1250; and Mamluk, 1250 to 1516, with the note that Late Byzantine and Early Umayyad material is virtually impossible to distinguish and that Late Byzantine/Umayyad, therefore, covers approximately 630 to 670 A.D. The broad Abbasid period might be subdivided by the periods of Egyptian intervention, perhaps 9th century Tulunid and probably late 10th to late 12th century Fatimid, but in terms of glass studies this is still a question to be asked, not an established position. The date markers are obviously historical pegs that more or less conveniently bracket building episodes or artifact styles rather than determining, suddenly, Abbasid versus Umayyad glass styles.

Once the probable date(s) for the glass sherds from a site are determined, then they may be checked against the pottery dates and other information already available for the survey sites. Sites 10, 148A, 161, 180, and 232 have no or poorly diagnostic glass sherds; 59 and 214 are modern. For the sites with diagnostic sherds the fit with the pottery dates is generally fairly good, with the partial exception of the Medieval Islamic material, perhaps due to the paucity of archaeological research until recently. The discrepancies are discussed below as the cases arise. By and large, the dates assigned are very broad indeed, several centuries or so, and much as one might like to narrow this the question does arise as to whether a first-time surface survey can do much more.

Sites

The sites that yielded diagnostic glass are listed and illustrated on Plate 37 in numerical order, with the exception of Site 45 which had enough glass to be shown separately on Plate 38. Comparanda for individual items are given with the excavators' dates unless there is some reason to challenge them. Comments on a vessel's original form and function and possible region of manufacture are noted where possible and finally the date(s) for all the glass is compared to the pottery dates.

Site 4, Khirbet Sheik 'Isa (Plate 37a – f)

Plate 37a is a large bowl or dish of clear glass with a turquoise coil partly marvered in. There are a number of bowls with similar decoration from 'Aqaba (nyp), which would indicate an Abbasid date. The 'Aqaba bowls are smaller, ranging from ca. 17 to 12 cm, and some smaller beaker (?) rims have similar decoration, but the Site 4 bowl is reconstructed from a little sherd and could conceivably have broken off a smaller, irregular vessel.

Plate 37b is a simple rim fragment of a common light blue-green glass that weathers white with an opalescent sheen, a fabric prevalent in Byzantine and Late Byzantine/Umayyad times, although it does occur later. The rim could be a piece of a stemmed goblet, a standard Late Byzantine to Umayyad type (Meyer 1984; 1987), or a fragment of a large-mouth jar as known from 'Aqaba (Abbasid) and Hama, possibly 9th to 10th century (Riis and Poulsen 1957: 36–37). The rim form, however, is so unspecialized that even later Mamluk parallels may be mentioned from Aidhab on the Red Sea, probably 11th to 14th century (Shinnie and Harden 1955: 73–74) and from Jerash (unpub).

Plate 37c. The thickened rim of this bowl is similar to rim forms at 'Aqaba, but the colour, a rich dark purple, makes it likely that the sherd is post-Abbasid, probably Mamluk (cf. Hama; Riis; and Poulsen 1957).

Plate 37d shows a handsome dark olive green bowl with a marvered and dragged herringbone design characteristic of Mamluk decoration. Green and white marvered decoration is reported at Quseir al-Qadim, generally on small bottles or vials (Roth 1979: 179; Whitcomb 1981: 234–35), and a flask or jug from Debira West (mainly 10th to 11th century) has a marvered and dragged decoration in white and light blue on a clear brown base (Harden 1978: 86, 91). The best parallels for the vessel form and decoration,

however, are some white on purple marvered and dragged bowls from Hama, probably Mamluk (Riis and Poulsen 1957: 64–66).

Plate 37e is a very long-lived type of base made by pushing the base outwards and then kicking it up at the area of the pontil wad until it forms a loop, as seen in cross section. Looped bases are known from a series of Early Byzantine beakers (Tatton-Brown 1984: 197, fig. 65; Meyer 1987: fig. 5u, v) though the sides tend to be straighter. Similar bases may be noted on a 5th century flask from Kish (Harden 1934: 134–35), some high looped bases from 'Aqaba (nyp), 11th to mid-12th century vessels from Corinth (Davidson 1952: 108, 111), and on a blue and white marvered and dragged vessel from Hama (Riis and Poulsen 1957: 62–63).

Plate 37f is the base of a hollow-stem lamp shaped something like the shallow variety of champagne glass without a foot. Such lamps sat in a polycandilon, a metal disk pierced with two to eleven or more holes and suspended by chains. The hollow-stem lamps seem to have developed from an Early Byzantine conical type such as examples from Karanis and Kish (Harden 1934: 132, 135) and Cyprus (Vessberg 1952: 151, pl. X). The characteristic narrow-stemmed and broad-mouth type appears to have become widespread and common by the 8th century, as represented at Jerash (Baur 1938: 520–24; Kehrberg 1986: 368, 383; Meyer 1987: 203); Magen, from a Byzantine church (Feig 1985: 38); Pelusium in Egypt (Fontaine 1952: 78, pl. 3); and Carthage (Tatton-Brown 1984: 202, fig. 66). Later, Mamluk examples are known from Aidhab (Harden 1955: 73, 75) and Quseir al-Qadim (unpub) on the Red Sea; other kinds of hollow-stem lamps seem to be thicker, differently shaped, or knobbed at the end. The colour of the Site 4 lamp is an unusual light grey, possibly a discoloration of an originally clear fabric, though two of the bases from Site 45 (Plate 38n and o) are also light grey.

Judging from the glass sherds, then, Site 4 has a Mamluk component (37c and d), Abbasid (37a), and probably Late Byzantine/Umayyad (37f); the rim 37b and looped-up base 37e do not contradict these dates. The periods represented according to the pottery typology are Early Bronze, Roman, Byzantine, Mamluk, Ottoman, and undetermined, the possible discrepancy being the Abbasid sherd 37a.

Site 27, Al-Jor (Plate 37g)

Plate 37g. Looped-out rims, like looped-up bases are a fairly common means of finishing a vessel. A series of relatively shallow bowls with looped-out rims and two or three handles is reported from Umayyad contexts at Jerash (Baur 1938: 528, 530; Gawlikowski and Musa 1986: 151, 153; Meyer 1987: 210, 212) and a little earlier at Sardis (von Saldern 1980: 45). Tumbler lamps, especially prominent in Late Byzantine and Umayyad periods (Meyer 1984), had looped-out rims as well but tended to have straighter sides. Looped-out rims are attested at least as early as the Byzantine period (Delougaz and Haines 1960: pl. 60; Meyer 1984), and as late as Mamluk (Roth 1979: 161). The round, bull's-eye or crown window panes were strengthened with folded out rims from at least mid-6th century onwards (Harden 1978: 88, 89, 93; Meyer 1989), though window pane diameters tend to be greater than the 12 cm of Plate 37g. The light blue-green colour would support a Byzantine to Umayyad date.

The pottery dates include 'Islamic' and 'probable Mamluk.' The single rim Plate 37g is by no means conclusively Umayyad.

Site 45, Al-Rujoum (Plate 38)

Plate 38a is a small fragment of a fairly thick ribbed vessel. The most likely case is that the sherd came from one of the Roman ribbed, mold-formed bowls common in the last half of the first century B.C. and the first century A.D. (Isings 1957: 17–21; Weinberg 1973; Grose 1977, 1979: 54, 56, 61; 1984: 28) and distributed from Europe and the Near East as far as the Crimea (Harden 1936: 99–100), Afghanistan (Hackin 1939: pl. IX), and even eastern India (Wheeler 1946: 102). Thinner mold-blown ribbed vessels are also known from Roman times, and in the 8th century and later mold-blown vessels became once again reasonably abundant (Meyer 1987: 213–16). Many of the Islamic vessels seem to be ribbed jars or bottles rather than bowls, and the thick shoulders thin rapidly to the sides ('Aqaba nyp).

Plate 38b may be a rim fragment of a slightly flaring cylindrical cup, a type well attested at 'Aqaba. Other possible dated parallels for the form are reported from Aidhab, 11th to 14th century (Harden 1955: 73–74); the Serçe Limani shipwreck, ca. 1025 (Bass 1984: 68–69, fig. 5); Corinth, 11th to mid-12th century (Davidson 1952: 107–8); and Susa, A.D. 810 to 950/1000 (Kervran 1984: 214, 220–21).

Plate 38c would be the same sort of cylindrical cup but with a slight ridge below the rim, a variant common at 'Aqaba.

Plate 38d may have come from the mouth of a bottle with a flaring mouth. There are some parallels for the form at Quseir al-Qadim, Mamluk loci (Roth 1979: 161, 173). The colour of the 45 sherd, light purple but probably originally clear, is compatible with the Quseir fabrics, clear or clear with a pink tint.

Plate 38e and f are both bowls of dark purple glass with white or light blue lines trailed on and marvered in; 38f is made of surprisingly crude glass with many impurities and 'stone.' There are close parallels for both the larger and smaller bowls at Quseir al-Qadim, Mamluk loci (Whitcomb 1981: 234, pl. 58) and at Hama (Riis and Poulsen 1957: 63–64), presumably before the 14th century.

Plate 38g shows the rim of a light blue-green bottle with an unevenly finished rim. There is a series of rather baggy, crude bottles from 'Aqaba in clear, blue, and blue-green glass, and a green bottle with out-turned lip like 38g from Hama, thought to be 8th–9th century on the basis of parallels elsewhere (Riis and Poulsen 1957: 41). An opaque grey rim from Susa is dated to A.D. 810 to 950/1000 (Kervran 1984: 216–17). Mamluk loci at Quseir al-Qadim have

yielded a tall, almost cylindrical bottle with a flaring mouth (Whitcomb 1981: 234, pl. 58) and a series of 'bubble-neck bottles' with a broad bulge or bubble below the mouth (Roth 1979: 167, 173; Whitcomb 1981: 234, pl. 58). Thus, it is difficult to claim more than a broad 'Islamic' date for the 38g rim sherd.

Plate 38h. Small bottles, unguentaria, or vials with folded-in rims are known from Roman times onwards, but the deep purple colour, as for the 38e and f bowls, suggests a Mamluk date. Somewhat earlier 'toilet bottles' with similar rims are known from Debira West, probably 10th–11th century (Harden 1978: 85, 91) and 'Aqaba (nyp) in amber and green shades.

Plate 38i is probably the flaring rim of a large jar or bottle reminiscent of a green jar rim from Hama (Riis and Poulsen 1957: 40). The light purple shade is similar to the colour of the bottle rim 38d.

Plate 38j. The thickened rim of this jar is similar to a series from 'Aqaba, at least one of which is also of clear glass, the others being a common light blue or blue-green. An Abbasid date, then, is possible or probable.

Plate 38k is the neck of a tall bottle with a coiled-on decoration. A tall, almost cylindrical bottle from Quseir al-Qadim, Mamluk period, is illustrated by Whitcomb (1981, fig. 58: hh) and another bottle neck with thin coiled threads was recovered during the 1982 season (nyp). However, this is either a long-lived type or hard to date. Davidson (1952: 118–19) reported a pale olive green bottle with blue coils around the neck from Corinth, late 12th century or later. A flask with spiral decoration on the neck from Carthage, found in a 6th century context, is thought to be intrusive, possibly 8th–10th century (Tatton-Brown 1984: 205, fig. 67). An olive green bottle neck with self coil from Wadi al-Daliyeh, Cave II, is thought to be Roman or Late Roman (Weinberg and Barag 1974: 105, pl. 39), but a ewer from Beth Shan from 'Arab and Byzantine levels' (Fitzgerald 1931: 42, pl. 39) has no assigned date. A transparent pink, tall bottle neck from Hama with a coiled decoration (Riis and Poulsen 1957: 60–61) is probably Islamic, and a series of bottles from Iran (Lamm 1935: 14, pl. 41) and reputedly from Syria (Lamm 1929: pl. 27) are said to be 13th–14th century. The only well-dated examples of this kind of bottle, then, appear to be Mamluk, though an earlier date seems possible.

Plate 38l may be the base of a hollow-stem lamp (see the discussion of the one from Site 4, Plate 37f). The colour of the 38l lamp, dark blue, is most unusual, assuming that a lamp should be translucent to let the light shine through. The sherd might also be a vial base, though they tend to be flat enough to stand up and square or polygonal. There is, however, a black vial base from Quseir al-Qadim, Mamluk, that is similar in shape (nyp). Plate 38m. Flat bases such as this example are known from Roman times onwards, but the colour, light blue-green, suggests a Byzantine or later date. The vessel seems to have been mold-blown, which suggests an Umayyad or later date; the pontil wad was attached off centre. For pontil scars that project below the flat base of a vessel, there are examples from Serçe Limani, ca. 1025 (Bass 1984: 68–69, fig. 5); Jerash, in post-Mamluk context (Meyer 1987: 214); and Qaraw in the Aden vicinity (Gus Van Beek, personal communication).

Plate 38n is a looped base for a flat or shallow dish or bowl. The form has a parallel in a heavy, clear looped base from 'Aqaba, probably Abbasid (nyp), but as indicated earlier, looped bases were a common means of finishing vessels from Early Byzantine times on.

Plate 38o shows a more arched looped base, also light grey. The form has parallels ranging in date from 2nd century Corinth (Davidson 1952: 80, 99–100); 5th century Kish (Harden 1934: 135); 9th century Susa (Kervran 1984: 222–23); 'Aqaba, probably Abbasid (nyp); and Mamluk Quseir al-Qadim (Roth 1979: 181).

Plate 38p, a base with a high kick, is perhaps a slightly better diagnostic shape. Similar forms are known from 4th–5th and 7th century contexts at Jerash (Meyer 1987: 192, 208); 5th–6th century at Shavei Zion (Barag 1967: fig. 16); and Khirbat al-Karak, Late Byzantine/Umayyad (Delougaz and Haines 1960: pl. 59) (see the discussion of the smaller, high-kick base from Site 4 on Plate 37e). The dark purple colour, however, would suggest that this particular base is Mamluk.

Plate 38q is the waist of a vessel shaped something like a fruitstand; the upper wall probably flared out more nearly horizontal than indicated on the reconstruction here. The base ring was separated from the bowl by the unusual method of kicking the walls in deeply at the waist until the centre hole was closed or was so small that a plug of glass could fill it. A light grey Mamluk bowl of this sort was recovered at Quseir al-Qadim (Roth 1979: 181) and at least three more from Hama (Riis and Poulsen 1957: 40, 47–48, 53–55). Plate 38r is a sherd with mold-blown lozenge decoration. Mold-blown decoration began as early as the 1st century A.D., but the best parallels seem to be later, from Sassanian (Qasr-i Abu Nasr; Whitcomb 1985: 155, 159) and Umayyad vessels (Jerash; Meyer 1987: 210) to Abbasid cylindrical bowls and bottles from 'Aqaba (nyp) and Soba (Harden 1955: 64, fig. 37).

The periods represented in the glass corpus are Mamluk (38d, e, f, q, and perhaps i and p); Mamluk or earlier (38k); early Mamluk or late Abbasid (38h); Abbasid (38b, c, and j); unspecified Islamic (38g, l, m, and r); possible Roman (38a); and non-diagnostic (38n and o). With the exception of the very small possibly Roman fragment, this agrees well with the pottery reading of Abbasid to Mamluk.

The beads, Plate 38s–gg, are presented with some diffidence as comparanda and hence dates are almost non-existent. Many or all of the beads may be modern as a cemetery is mentioned to the east of the mound. They are treated in more detail in the report by Broeder and Skinner (Chapter 13). However, if all investigators fail to report beads because of lack of other bead corpora, then no one will ever get anything out of an ubiquitous and generally popular item of personal adornment. These beads are therefore presented more for future than for present information.

A few comments are possible, however. Beads 38t and z appear to have been made by coiling a thread of glass around some removable core, a technique noted at Debira West for a yellow bead, probably 10th–12th century in date. Bead 38u may be collared, i.e., broken from a short string of segmented beads, a process also attested at Debira West, probably 10th–12th century but possibly earlier (Shinnie and Shinnie 1978: 82, fig. 114). Hexagonal or pentagonal beads such as 38cc are found at Corinth, 11th–12th century (Davidson 1940: 322–23) and at Quseir al-Qadim, Mamluk (Whitcomb 1981: pl. 59). The facetted bead 38ff, possibly an imitation of a type of stone bead, is also reported from Soba, 9th–12th century (Shinnie and Harden 1955: 52, 54–55) and Debira West, probably 10th–12th century or later (Shinnie and Shinnie 1978: 82, fig. 114).

Site 46, Deir 'Ain 'Abata (Plate 37h–j)

Plate 37h is a 'blob handle' made by attaching a blob of hot glass to the side of a vessel and swinging it up, usually to a point at or near the rim. A second handle fragment, with a bit of a looped-out rim preserved, was also recovered from Site 46 but as it is virtually identical to the handle from Site 75 (Plate 37k); it is not illustrated here. Blob handles were in use as early as the Early Byzantine period (Meyer 1987: 190) or earlier (Dussart 1986: 75) but were more common in Late Byzantine and Umayyad times (Meyer 1984). Many of them must have come from the three handled tumbler lamps. In later periods, at least some blob handles, as at 'Aqaba, probably Abbasid (nyp), and three handled vessels, as at Corinth, 11th–12th centuries (Davidson 1952: 112–13), were still used.

Plate 37i is the rim of a fairly large but thin bowl of a common light blue-green fabric. Perhaps the best parallel is a series of vessels from Mezad Tamar, some decorated with thin trailed-on threads, datable to the late 3rd to early 7th centuries (Erdmann 1977: 130, 132, pls. 5, 6). A later series of large cups or small bowls with thin, flaring sides comes from Corinth, some of which are late 11th–12th century (Davidson 1952: 89, 112–13), and there is at least one possible Abbasid parallel from 'Aqaba (nyp). A less likely comparison would be the smaller, thin walled beakers or goblets from 'Araq el-Emir (Lapp 1983: 52, fig. 22) and Jerash (Kehrberg 1986: 368, 381; Meyer 1987: 208).

Plate 37j is clearly Abbasid, however. The oval pattern was made by pincering the hot glass with specially designed pincers that leave a squeezed profile in the body of the glass. The technique is usually considered 10th–12th century, and both the oval design and pincering are well attested in the 'Aqaba corpus. Some at least of the pincered vessels are known to have been manufactured in Egypt.

Site 46, thus, gives us one definitely Abbasid sherd and three that could have the same date but could also be Byzantine or Umayyad. Judging from other indicators, the periods represented at the site are: Nabataean; Late Roman; Byzantine (predominant); Ottoman; and undetermined. The site seems to have been a church or monastery, and if the two blob handles did come from tumbler lamps this would be consistent with the early and extensive use of glass lamps in churches (Gawlikowski and Musa 1986; Meyer 1987: 219). Again, the odd Abbasid sherd seems to be the stranger.

Site 66 (not illustrated)

A fairly large, blue-green, blob handle (cf. Plate 37h) was recovered, probably Byzantine or Umayyad in date, which agrees with the list of periods represented: Nabataean; Parthian; Roman; Late Byzantine; Umayyad; Islamic; Modern; and undetermined.

Site 75, Ancient Feifa, Western Segment (Plate 37k)

The blob handle on Plate 37k is the only diagnostic glass sherd from the site. What was said about the two examples from Site 46 pertains to this one; only here a remnant of the looped-out rim may be seen as well as a little of the body of the vessel. The dates, as before, would probably be Late Byzantine or Umayyad, but possibly as late as Abbasid.

The wide range of periods represented at Site 75 includes Roman, Islamic, Mamluk(?), Ottoman, and undetermined.

Site 91, Feifa Village (Plate 37l and m)

Plate 37l shows the neck of a very dark purple bottle ornamented with opaque white threads and coils. There is a similar bottle neck from Hama of purple glass with an opaque white spiral, found below the 'couche superficielle' (Riis and Poulsen 1957: 60–61), which seems to mean before 1400.

Plate 37m has both a marvered design and a slightly ribbed surface. This too has close parallels in some brown and white and purple and white cups at Hama (Riis and Poulsen 1957: 63–65).

The pottery dates given are Islamic, Mamluk, and undetermined. The two glass sherds would confirm the Mamluk dating.

Site 155, Qasr al-Tilah (Plate 37n)

Plate 37n is the rim of a cup or perhaps a hollow stem lamp with very thin walls and a thickened everted rim. The closest parallels seem to be some rims from 'Araq el-Emir, estimated as dating ca. 335 to 500 or later (Lapp 1983: 58, fig. 24); Wadi al-Daliyeh, Cave II (Weinberg and Barag 1974: 104, pl. 39); and Jerash, Late Byzantine (Meyer 1987: 196, 198). Rims of some hollow stem lamps from Samaria (Crowfoot 1957: 414–15) and Cyprus (Vessberg 1952: 151–52, pl. X) are also quite similar, though unfortunately none of the lamps are well dated. Some everted but thicker rims have been published from Mezad Tamar, late 3rd to early 7th century (Erdmann 1977: 137–38, pl. 7); Qasr-i Abu Nasr, Sassanian (Whitcomb 1985: 159);

Jerash, 7th century (Baur 1938: 526, 529; Meyer 1987: 206, 208); 'Aqaba, probably Abbasid (nyp); and Quseir al-Qadim, Mamluk (Roth 1979: 161).

The periods represented at Site 155 include Nabataean, Roman, Byzantine, Umayyad, Modern, and undetermined. This makes the suggested Byzantine date for the glass sherd even more likely.

Site 205, Sammar (not illustrated)

A base angle of a vessel with a thin body and relatively thin base but very thick at the angle itself may be Abbasid. The periods noted at the site, however, are Nabataean, Roman, Byzantine, Late Byzantine–Umayyad, and undetermined.

Site 211, Khirbet al-Dahal (Plate 37o)

The single glass sherd illustrated from Site 211 is clearly the rim of a Roman unguentarium with a broad flat mouth made by folding the rim out and back in, leaving a characteristic ridge inside. The relatively poor quality green glass with bubbles and impurities is also typical of the Roman unguentaria. The 37o sherd seems to be Hayes' type D, disk rims, pale green or blue-green fabric, and a small body capacity, datable to the 2nd century A.D. (Hayes 1975: 42–45).

A body sherd, not shown, with thin trailed thread decoration is probably Byzantine or Umayyad.

The pottery readings for the site include Late Roman, Byzantine, Modern, and undetermined.

Site 215 (not illustrated)

A light-blue body sherd, with turquoise thread decoration (cf. Plate 37s), would probably be Byzantine or Umayyad. Periods noted at the site are in fact Nabataean (?), Byzantine, and undetermined.

Site 216 (Plate 37p–w)

Plate 37p shows a bowl with an unusual incurved rim and an uncommon colour, namely, amber. There are a few incurved rims at Jerash, Umayyad loci (Meyer 1987: 213–14) and from 'Aqaba (nyp). A general 'Islamic' date is perhaps all that can be assigned.

Plate 37q is a rim of a shallow bowl with a looped-out rim. Much of what was said about the looped-out rim from Site 27 pertains to 37q, except that the latter is larger and some further comparanda may be noted. A wide Byzantine bowl from Dibon seems to have an angled body reminiscent of 37q (Tushingham 1972: 157, fig. 13). At least two broad bowls with looped-out rims and angled bodies are known from Jerash, Mamluk locus, but possibly Late Byzantine/Umayyad manufacture (Meyer 1987: 214, 216).

Plate 37r is a thin, rolled-in rim with the top of a handle still attached. If there were originally two handles this could be a kohl flask of a well-known Late Byzantine/Umayyad type. Datable pieces are reported from a tomb cave near Netiv Ha-Lamed He, complete with a kohl stick, mid 5th to early 7th century (Barag 1974: 13, 83); Mezad Tamar, late 3rd to early 7th century (Erdmann 1977: 119, pl. 3); and

Jerash, 7th century (Meyer 1987: 200, 202, 204, 207). If, however, the vessel had only one handle originally it could be a small ewer, an uncommon type of vessel for which rim and handle forms vary widely. Two of the most plausible parallels seem to be a jug from Kish, from the Sassanian buildings (Harden 1934: 135–36) and 5th–7th century jug from Nessana (Harden 1962: 76, 89, pl. 20), a similar date even if the identification of the original form of 37r remains unsatisfactory.

Plate 37s is part of a tall bottle neck decorated with thin trailed-on threads and a thicker coil. This kind of thread decoration is most common in the Late Byzantine and Umayyad periods, and the very tall bottles are characteristic of the Syro-Palestinian region. Numerous comparable pieces have been reported from north Jordan (Harden 1971: 79); Jerash (Baur 1938: 530–35, 545; Kehrberg 1986: 368, 381, 383; Meyer 1984; 1987: 204, 207); Mount Nebo (Saller 1941: 320–21, pl. 142); 'Aqaba (nyp); Beth Shan (Fitzgerald 1931: 42, pl. 39); Khirbat al-Karak (Delougaz and Haines 1960: pls. 59, 60); Shavei Zion (Barag 1967: fig. 16), and Mezad Tamar (Erdmann 1977: 110, 112, 143, pls. 1, 8), as well as a few from Sardis (von Saldern 1980: 82–84, pl. 27); Alexandria (Rodziewicz 1984: pl. 74); and Carthage (Tatton-Brown 1984: 204–5, fig. 67).

Plate 37t. This small bottle neck and mouth are much harder to date. A possible comparison for the rim form comes from Quseir al-Qadim, Mamluk context (Roth 1979: 167).

Plate 37u is a handle rather different from the 'blob handles' in making a rounder loop. A lamp handle from Carthage (6th–7th century) is nearly as round (Tatton-Brown 1984: 202, fig. 66) and one from Mezad Tamar (late 3rd to early 7th century) makes a complete loop (Erdmann 1977: 121, pl. 4). Another possibility might be the handles of a type of cup found by the score at Carthage in 11th to 12th century contexts (Davidson 1952: 108, 111). The two-colour decoration, i.e., amber on light blue, is also noted at 'Aqaba (nyp) (see the glass sherd 37y from Site 228, below).

Plate 37v is probably the flaring mouth of a large, heavy bottle with a thick coil under the rim. Several such flasks are reported from Carthage, 6th–7th century loci (Tatton-Brown 1984: 204, fig. 67); Mezad Tamar, late 3rd to early 7th century (Erdmann 1977: 130, pl. 5); and Sardis, ca. 400–616 (von Saldern 1980: pl. 27). However, there are other, later rims with heavy coils from 'Aqaba, probably Abbasid (nyp) and from Corinth, after the 12th century (Davidson 1952: 120, 122).

Plate 37w, a fragment of ruffle decoration, is as distinctive as the bottle neck with trailed threads, and dates to the same time range, Late Byzantine to Umayyad. The 37w sherd is gently curved enough that it seems to have broken off a bottle body rather than a neck, perhaps the most common place for ruffles. Such decoration is attested as early as the Late Byzantine period but is more common in Late Byzantine/Umayyad and later periods (Meyer 1984).

Ruffle decoration is noted at Mount Nebo (Saller 1941: 320, pl. 141); Jerash (Baur 1938: 534–35, 538, 543; Meyer 1987: 206–7); Samaria (Crowfoot 1957: 418); Khirbat al-Karak (Delougaz and Haines 1960: pl. 59); and Egypt (Harden 1936: 198; Fontaine 1952: 79, pl. 4).

Not illustrated is a looped-out rim almost identical to Plate 37g. It is of a similar blue-green colour. Likewise, it may be dated to Byzantine or Umayyad periods, or possibly even later.

In sum, Site 216 appears to have one Late Byzantine sherd (37r), two Late Byzantine or Umayyad (37s and w), four probably Late Byzantine to Umayyad but possibly later (37q, u, v and one not illustrated), and one general 'Islamic' sherd. This agrees very well with the other dating evidence, namely, the pottery, for Byzantine and Mamluk components.

Site 228 (Plate 37x and y)

Plate 37x may be a fragment of a cylindrical cup, a type well attested at 'Aqaba (nyp), many of which have slightly incurved rims. Some similar cups from Susa are dated somewhat earlier, ca. A.D. 750–810 (Kervran 1984: 220–21). Other possible parallels are some incurved rim vessels from Jerash, Umayyad period (Meyer 1987: 214); Mezad Tamar, late 3rd to early 7th century (Erdmann 1977: 139, pl. 7); and Khirbat al-Karak (Delougaz and Haines 1960: pl. 59). The most reasonable dating, then, would be 'Islamic.'

A nearly identical light blue-green rim sherd with a slightly smaller rim diameter is not illustrated but would have the same general Islamic date.

Plate 37y is a small sherd with trailed-on, yellow-green decoration on a light blue-green body. It is probably Abbasid as an apparently random or free style, trailed-on decoration has been found at 'Aqaba (nyp) and also at Hama (Riis and Poulsen 1957: 53–55). Two-colour decoration is attested at 'Aqaba, if not abundantly, including blue on yellow-green, olive on light blue, amber on light yellow-green, and light yellow-green on light blue like the 37y sherd. Note also the two-colour handle from Site 216, Plate 37u.

The glass sherds seem to be Islamic and/or Abbasid. However, the pottery reading for Site 228 is Byzantine and undetermined.

Conclusions

How well, then, does the glass dating compare with the pottery and other dating for the survey sites? Does it conflict or add any new information? Perhaps this may be seen most clearly in tabular form (Table 63). Particular problems are highlighted.

All of the periods attested by the pottery and other dating evidence are also represented in the datable glass corpus at Sites 4, 66, 91, 155, and 211. There is little discrepancy between the ceramics and glass readings for Sites 215 and 216. The Byzantine to Umayyad glass from Sites 27 and 75 suggest a refinement of the broad 'Islamic' or undetermined categories. Site 45 seems to pick up a period, Roman,

Table 63 Glass and pottery dating compared

Site No.	Glass Dating	Pottery Dating
4	LByz/Um; Abb;Mam	EB I; EB; Rom; Byz; LByz–Um; Abb; Fat; Ayy–Mam; Ud
27	Byz–Um	Isl; Mod; Ud
45	Rom?; Abb; Mam	Abb; Fat; Ayy–Mam; Mam and/or Ott
46	Byz?; Um?; Abb	Nab; Rom; Byz (E and L);Ott; Ud
66	Byz–Um	Nab; Rom; Byz (E and L); LByz–Um; Abb; Isl; Mod; Ud
75	LByz–Um	PNL; PNL–Chal; Chal; Chal/EB; EB I; EB IIB; EB IVA; EB; Iron I–II; Iron II; Rom; Fat/Ayy; Isl; Ott; Ud
91	Mam	Byz; Um; Abb–Fat; Mam;Isl;Ud
155	Byz	Iron II; Hell;Nab; Nab (=ERom); Rom; Byz; Um; Mod; Ud
205	Abb?	Nab; Nab (?); Rom; LByz; LByz–Um; Ud
211	Rom	Nab (=ERom); Rom; LRom; Byz; LByz; Um; Mod; Ud
215	Byz–Um	Nab (?); Byz;Ud
216	LByz; LByz/Um;later?	Byz; LByz; Mam; Ud
228	Abb; Islamic	Byz; Ud

not identified in the pottery corpus. Unfortunately, the possible Roman glass sherd is so small it cannot be considered conclusive.

The main discrepancy between the glass and other dating seems to lie in the Abbasid material, which may not be too surprising given the small amount of attention directed to Medieval Islamic archaeology until recently. Based largely on comparisons with the newly excavated finds from 'Aqaba, an Abbasid component is definitely attested at Sites 46, 228, and perhaps 205. Conceivably, some of the undetermined potsherds might pertain to this period.

Glass dating is not going to replace pottery dating. It may, however, serve to complement or refine it in some respects, as seen above. Moreover, more information may be gleaned from glass sherds than might seem possible at first glance. In terms of function, the glass vessels may also prove informative. For instance, the number of probable lamp handles from Site 46, two out of four diagnostic sherds, does support the identification of the site as a church or monastery. Given the difficulty of dating ancient sites from surface collections in which epigraphic and numismatic data are generally lacking, no reasonable source of information should be overlooked. Rather, the pottery, architectural remains, glass, worked stone, and other clues should all be used together, possibly serving as a check on each other, and ideally all should reinforce each other. The continual readjustments in understanding the pottery or glass or flint corpora should help refine the other corpora. Rather than circular reasoning, this should be seen as improving and reinforcing the scaffolding around our understanding or image of the use of ancient artifacts over time, their distribution over the countryside, and who dropped what where and why.

13. Beads From The 1986 Season

by N. H. Broeder and H. C. W. Skinner

Introduction

One of the primary objectives of archaeological surveys is 'to select sites whose excavation will lead to at least partial answers for specific problems or will help to test previously formulated hypotheses' (Hester, Heizer, and Graham 1975: 36). The jewellery, which we describe herein, makes an important contribution. Several samples support the early age of one of the sites surveyed by the SGNAS during 1986 season (see Figure 31). In addition, the source of these ancient samples is located toward the south. The site, namely, Site 120E, from which these important samples were collected, is located near Wadi Khuneizir, which has been identified as a primary EB IV area (Rast personal communication). Other sites, with samples in different compositions, were modern. Both ancient and modern compositions indicate a lifestyle not much different than that observed in the region today.

MacDonald, the director of the SGNAS, made only a portion of the surface-collected bead samples available to us (Photo 27). Whitcomb discusses the remainder of the jewellery from the area (Chapter 10). Each sample we studied is individually listed in the accompanying appendix which is a compilation of all the data we obtained on the artifacts during examination at Yale University. Since the registration numbers of the artifacts were assigned serially in the field, the sample numbers are not sequential, but are presented in numerical order. The SGNAS found a total of 241 beads or fragments of beads at five sites during the 1986 season:

Site 120E	208 samples
Site 45	30 samples
Site 149	1 sample
Site 211	1 sample
Site 232	1 sample

The beads date to both ancient and modern time periods. The ancient beads are composed of both mineral and shell; the modern ones are of glass and quartz. The ancient beads of aragonite may be made from shell or from sedimentary deposits. Figure 32 presents the distribution of the different shapes represented by these samples, following the classification of Beck (1928), and delineates the compositional data.

Samples are discussed by site in the order listed above, i.e., the site with the largest number of beads first. For each site, the date of the surface potsherds and a brief description of the site is presented (see Appendix 1 for a complete site description). For each bead, the composition, determined by mineralogical testing, is given and the shape described. The samples are then compared to similar composition and shape material found at other excavations. Using the comparisons, we make some suggestions and draw a few conclusions on the significance of these samples.

Methodology

Scholars in the past have bemoaned the fact that:

> '...no accurate analyses of many ancient materials ... have been recorded. Without fuller and more accurate data, it is idle to speculate on the nature of ancient technical processes, the trade routes by which they were disseminated and the cultural contacts that they show'
>
> (Aldred 1978: 45)

And more pertinent to beads:

> 'Archaeologists have paid them only scant attention and so our attempts to make detailed comparisons with other sites have been largely unsuccessful'
>
> (Bar-Yosef *et al.* 1977: 73)

Much of the information written on beads from other excavations relies on general description derived from visual examination only. In contrast, we provide, in addition to visual examination results, x-ray diffraction and other tests on the SGNAS bead materials to confirm their identification.

We define 'bead' as an essentially spherical object, with or without facets, distinguished by a hole usually drilled through the center. Bead shapes, described below, follow the terminology presented by Beck (1928). When comparing our material with other sites where his terminology is not used, we have substituted his terms, thus facilitating comparison of like objects. For example, Beck defines a 'standard' or 'equant' bead as having a length between 0.9 times 1.1 times the diameter; 'long' beads have a length more than 1.1 times the diameter; 'short' beads have lengths between 0.33 and 0.9 times the diameter.

The Munsell Soil Color Charts (Munsell 1975) and A Color Notation (Munsell 1981), with accompanying colour chips, were used for the designation of colour. When assigning colours to mottled or variegated samples, only the dominant colour is stated.

Hardness was determined using a Mohs' hardness kit (GEM Instruments Corporation, Santa Monica, CA), and specific gravity was obtained using the liquids with densities 2.67 and 3.32.

Samples were examined using a binocular microscope with magnifications up to 50x. On selected samples, x-ray diffraction results were obtained employing a Guinier-de Wolff multiple

135

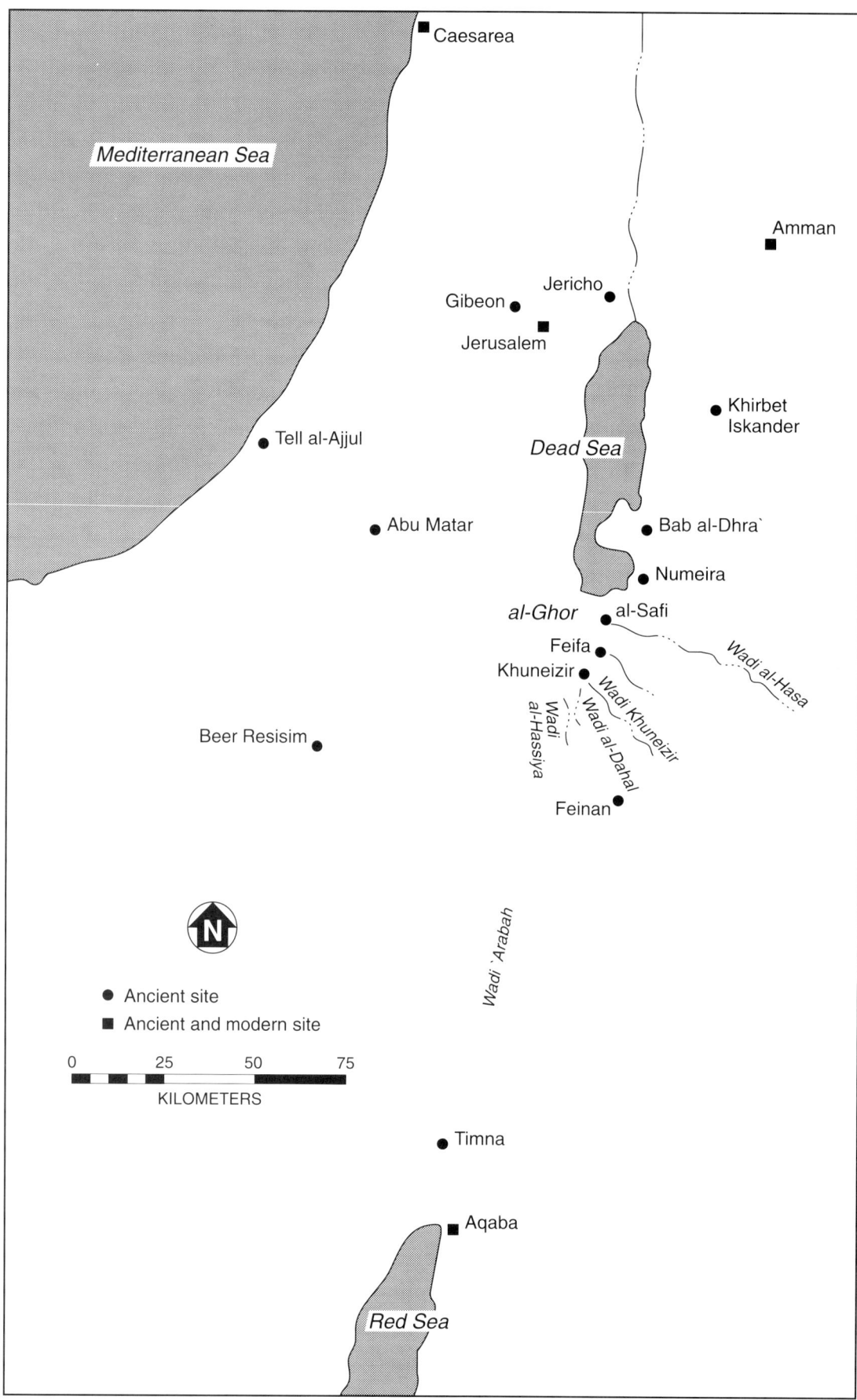

Figure 31 Modern and ancient sitees in the Eastern Mediterranean.

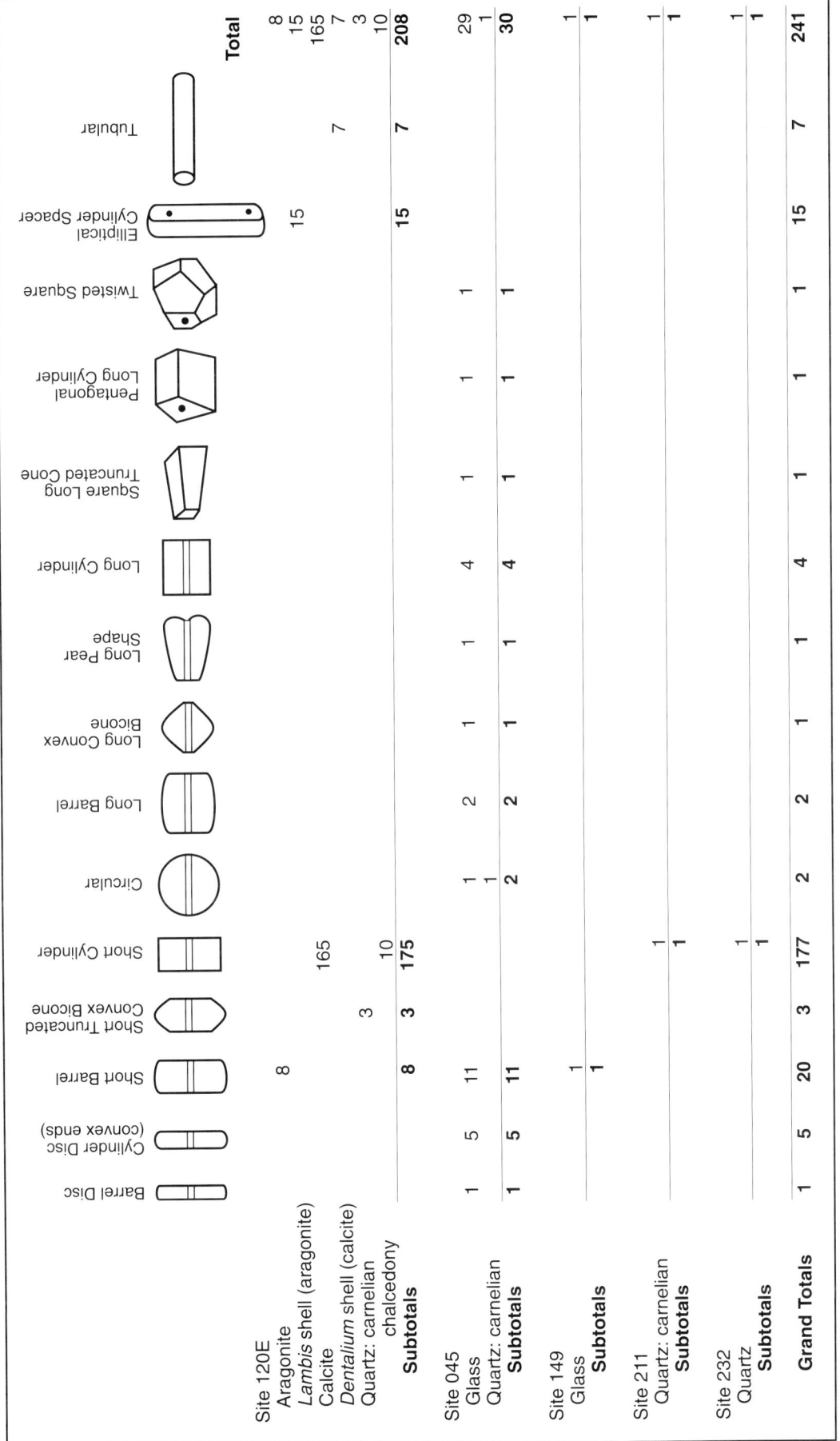

	Barrel Disc	Cylinder Disc (convex ends)	Short Barrel	Short Truncated Convex Bicone	Short Cylinder	Circular	Long Barrel	Long Convex Bicone	Long Pear Shape	Long Cylinder	Square Long Truncated Cone	Pentagonal Long Cylinder	Twisted Square	Elliptical Cylinder Spacer	Tubular	Total
Site 120E																
Aragonite			8													8
Lambis shell (aragonite)														15		15
Calcite					165											165
Dentalium shell (calcite)															7	7
Quartz: carnelian				3												3
chalcedony					10											10
Subtotals			**8**	**3**	**175**									**15**	**7**	**208**
Site 045																
Glass	1	5	11			1	2	1	1	4	1	1	1			29
Quartz: carnelian						1										1
Subtotals	**1**	**5**	**11**			**2**	**2**	**1**	**1**	**4**	**1**	**1**	**1**			**30**
Site 149																
Glass			1													1
Subtotals			**1**													**1**
Site 211																
Quartz: carnelian					1											1
Subtotals					**1**											**1**
Site 232																
Quartz					1											1
Subtotals					**1**											**1**
Grand Totals	1	5	20	3	177	2	2	1	1	4	1	1	1	15	7	241

Figure 32 Bead materials and shapes (Classification System after Beck 1928).

137

sample camera, using Cu/Ni radiation. All techniques are summarized in the Appendix.

The Appendix summarizes both the visual and the several tests or properties performed on each sample. When identification was straightforward and unambiguous, tests were not performed. Where tests were performed, the details are included. For example, hardness, if listed, means that the material was tested. Where x-ray diffraction was employed, the ASTM (American Society for Testing Materials) Card Number is entered. Dana and Ford (1932) and Fleischer (1987) were consulted in the identification of the materials.

Although it is not part of the mineralogical methodology outlined above, relative dating affects the soundness of our conclusions. The dating of sites we use for comparison follows the chronologies for Egypt, Palestine, and Mesopotamia set forth in Edwards, Gadd, and Hammond (1970).

Results

Site 120E

Site 120E is a cemetery located on a terrace on the west side of Wadi Khuneizir (Figure 31). There are at least eight graves at this site, most of which appear to be EB IV cist tombs, stone-lined shallow graves. The samples we examined are from the surface of two nonadjacent graves, designated 'E'. Both graves have been disturbed. Unfortunately, since the beads were gathered into one packet in the field, it is impossible to assign particular beads to a specific grave. The SGNAS identified the sherds collected as EB IV.

Site 120E provided the largest quantity of beads in the survey collection, 208 out of 241 samples (86 percent) (Photos 28–29). All the bead samples are in excellent condition. There are, in addition, a few fragments. Figure 33 illustrates nine bead forms, six of which were from Site 120E. The following list gives the total number of samples from the site: A) one hundred sixty-five white, pinkish-white, and greyish-brown, short cylinder beads composed of calcite; B) ten short cylinder beads of opaque quartz, coloured an intimate mixture of reddish-yellow, pink, and brown; C) eight white, short barrel beads of aragonite; D) seven white beads identified as the calcitic exoskeletons of thin-shelled mollusc *Dentalium*, naturally tubular in form; E) six white, elliptical cylinder beads and nine fragments of beads identified as aragonite and thought to derive from thick-shelled mollusc (beads of this shape are termed 'spacer beads' by Beck (1928); and F) three convex truncated bicone disc beads of translucent red quartz, variety carnelian.

The designation of these artifacts as beads or spacer beads encompasses the range in size and disposition of the drilled holes. The several colours, as well as the type of material, would impart an esthetic attraction to these materials as adornments.

It is our opinion that all these samples are decorative objects worn by women, probably threaded on necklaces or arm bands, and that the graves which were disturbed were of female interments, a bias that is coloured by the observations and writings of Brunton (1927). He reviewed samples from the Fourth to Eleventh Dynasties (ca. 2600–2100 B.C.) in Egypt. Of the 229 buttons and scarabs he described, 'only 5 buttons, 1 animal (artifact), 4 scarabs, and 1 plaque are found on male bodies." Although it was clear that he expected the adornments to be worn by males and that he wondered whether there was an error in the sexing of the skeletons, his final remarks were: 'It seems fair to say, therefore, that they were extremely rarely worn by men, and then only in the early time of their general use among the middle and lower classes' (Brunton 1927: 58).

It is possible that some or all of the two-holed samples found in this collection served as the ornaments for clothing or dagger pommels (Kenyon and Holland 1983: 558, fig. 226; Guy 1938: 165, fig. 171; Starkey and Harding 1932: pls. 42, 43). The SGNAS two-hole beads have been drilled through the width of the bead rather than through the length. Dagger-pommel holes, as pictured by Starkey and Harding (1932: pl. 42), are drilled central to the ornament. All the SGNAS beads and fragments have holes near the end of the length of the beads (Figure 33, A). Since there are two holes and horizontal alignment of holes in our samples, we have called the beads elliptical cylinder spacer beads following Beck (1928): fig. 15) and Dubin (1987: 43, 187). We shall, hereafter, refer to these SGNAS samples as spacer beads.

A more detailed discussion of these six classes of beads from Site 120E (Figure 33, A–F) follows.

Calcite cylinders (Figure 33, A)

Of the 165 cylindrical samples, we selected for x-ray analysis Bead Nos. 67.002 and 73.006. We confirmed them to be composed of calcite. The precise measurements and colours of these beads are as follows:

SGNAS Reg. No.

67.002:	D: 0.5 cm; L: 0.3 cm; pinkish-white, 7.5YR 8/2;
73.006:	D: 0.2 cm; L: 0.1 cm; white, 10YR 8/1

The remaining 163 short cylinders (Reg. No. 73.009) were identical in colour, 10YR 8/1, white, and size, D: 0.2 cm; L: 0.1 cm, to Reg. No. 73.006 and were identified as calcite by visual examination and testing with dilute hydrochloric acid. We are confident that these beads are mineral calcite as opposed to calcite from shell origin because we do not see any of the internal structure usual in shell material.

Brunton (1928: pl. 102) found calcite cylinder beads at the Qau-Badari area (ca. 600 km from the Southern Ghors) in Egypt. A calcite, short, cylinder bead, Type 86 L24, excavated from Tomb 1045, which dates to the Ninth–Tenth Dynasties (late First Intermediate

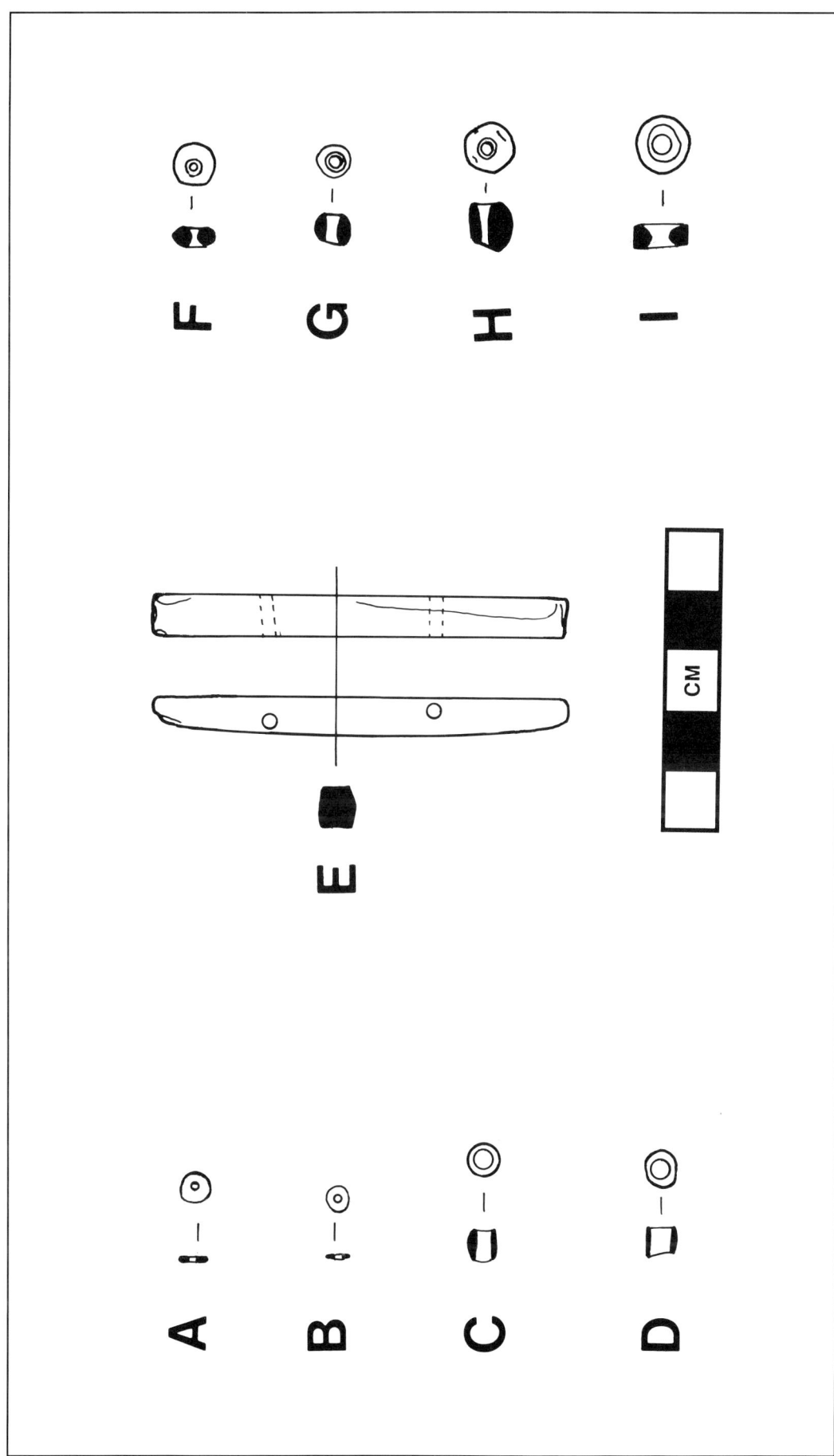

Figure 33 Beads from Sites 120E (A–F), 45 (G–H), and 211 (I); Scale 1:1.

Period – ca. 2100 B.C.), was identical with the results of our examination. Brunton's bead was found on the left wrist of a skeleton along with beads of carnelian, white limestone, black paste, and talc.

Kenyon and Holland (1983: 799) list at Jericho 111 calcite beads whose age was designated Early Bronze–Middle Bronze (Kenyon's Intermediate Early Bronze–Middle Bronze period which is commonly called EB IV). They were found in Tomb A113 (Dagger Type tomb). Five of these beads are called long cylinders with the length ranging from 0.7 to 1.0 centimetres. The remaining 106 are termed cylindrical, probably qualifying as Kenyon and Holland's 'small cylinders' because the length ranges from 0.1 to 0.3 cm, making them identical in length to some of the SGNAS samples. The size of the diameters of the 106 small cylinders are said to be the same as that of the five long cylinders, but measurements were not presented.

In addition, the site at Jericho has provided many beads labeled 'stone.' Some of these samples may also be composed of the common mineral calcite.

Thirty-five kilometres from Wadi Khuneizir at the neighboring site of Bab al-Dhra' (BD), two out of 15 bead samples of calcite (personal observation) from late EB III/IV contexts have been identified as similar in colour and shape to the SGNAS beads:

BD Reg. No.

2877.001:	D: 0.5 cm; L: 0.2 cm; white, 5Y 8/1
2854.001:	D: 1.1 cm; L: 0.7 cm; white, 10YR 8/2

The Bab al-Dhra' short cylinder, which is white, 10YR 8/2, is similar in hue and value to the white SGNAS short cylinder, 73.006, designated 10YR 8/1, but differs in chroma. The same BD white, short cylinder (2854.001) and the pinkish-white, SGNAS, short cylinder (67.002) are both yellow-red in hue, but the BD bead is more yellow and less red. However, it should be noted that colour difference may result from changes due to burial or exposure as well as slightly different original starting material.

Calcite is a common mineral in the sedimentary horizons in the Near East. Ease of working, because of softness and colour, may have contributed to its use as bead material.

Quartz (variety chalcedony) cylinders (Figure 33, B)

Ten short cylinders of opaque quartz were found in the Site 120E graves. Each of these tiny beads (Reg. No. 73.008), ranging from a diameter of 0.2 to 0.4 cm with a length of only 0.1 cm, is an intimate mixture of reddish-yellow, 7.5YR 6/6; pink, 7.5YR 7/4; and brown, 7.5YR 5/2.

Quartz, a much harder mineral than aragonite and calcite, measures 7 on the Mohs' hardness scale in comparison to the 3 of calcite or aragonite (Hurlbut and Switzer 1979) and occurs in a number of varieties. Transparent quartz varieties are rock crystal (clear), amethyst, citrine, smoky quartz, or rose quartz. Other varieties are milky quartz, and the microcrystalline fibrous varieties, such as chalcedony, with subvarieties given special names reflecting colour variations. The SGNAS opaque beads of quartz show a range of colours and have been designated chalcedony.

Lucas (1934: 67) states that the hardest rock worked in ancient Egypt was quartz. Shells of aragonite or calcite were popular bead materials during the Neolithic Period. Harder materials, such as quartz, gained popularity during the Early Bronze Age (Dubin 1987: 328). Quartz is plentiful in the Eastern Desert near Aswan, and pebbles of chalcedony can be easily gathered today from the wadis of the Southern Ghors (Broeder personal observation).

At Jericho, large numbers of stones are called 'chalcedony' in the registry (Kenyon and Holland 1983). It is assumed that the material is not carnelian, since that is identified separately. Of the 327 beads recorded as chalcedony, all appear to be virtually identical in length and shape to those found and described above from the SGNAS. An additional four beads are similar but larger in diameter.

Kenyon and Holland's (1983: 799) Tomb A113 (Early Bronze–Middle Bronze Dagger Type) contains:

> 288 cylindrical chalcedony beads, all of which range in length (?) 0.1–0.2 cm; 1 short cylinder chalcedony bead with no length given, but a D: 0.6 cm; and 3 short cylinder milky quartz, also no length given, but a D: 0.6 cm
>
> Tomb K27 (Early Bronze–Middle Bronze Bead Type)[1], contains 39 cylindrical chalcedony beads, also ranging 0.1–0.2 cm (in length?).

Since we do not have complete measurements of the beads from Jericho, we cannot definitely show how they compare with the beads from the SGNAS. However, four of the Jericho beads are greater in diameter (0.6 cm) than those of the SGNAS (0.2 to 0.4 cm). The beads from Tomb K27 may have been on clothing.[2] As early as Upper Paleolithic, persons were buried with beads adorning their costumes (Clark 1986: fig. 1). We cannot determine whether or not the SGNAS beads were originally attached to clothing.

No definitive colours were given for the Jericho chalcedony beads. Three other beads, however, are described as milky quartz. Since the SGNAS beads are a mixture of reddish-yellow, pink, and brown chalcedony, and this is a common mineral used in ornament making, all these samples with small variations in colour are well within the ranges expected for this material no matter when or where it is found.

Chalcedony was found at the Bab al-Dhra' town site in the sanctuary area, Field XVI, Square 2 (Broeder personal observation). One pale brown, 10YR 7/3, convex bicone disc, registered as Bab al-Dhra' No. 1634.001, has measurements of D: 1.7 cm; L: 0.8 centimetres. This object has no hole. However, a centrally-located, unpolished, minute depression on both sides may indicate the beginnings of a hole. This sample is considerably larger in length (0.8 cm) and diameter than those from the SGNAS (0.2 to 0.4 cm).

Aragonite barrels (Figure 33, C)

There are eight short, barrel beads (Reg. No. 73.010) from the SGNAS. Composed of aragonite, they measure from a maximum size of D: 0.5 cm by L: 0.2 cm to D: 0.4 cm by L: 0.3 centimetres. All are white, 10YR 8/2. Since beads were often fashioned from shell material (Hurlbut and Switzer 1979: 171), we believe these aragonite barrel beads were probably made from *Lambis* shell (see E below).

While the SGNAS samples could have been made from the shell debris of a *Lambis* shell workshop, such as the one excavated at Beer Resisim (Cohen and Dever 1979c: 51, 52), they also could have been fashioned from sedimentary aragonite, which could have been locally obtained.

Only one bead from the adjacent site of Bab al-Dhra' can be used for comparison. A standard barrel, shell bead was found in Locus 2 of Field XVI, Square 2 (Reese, personal communication). The bead measures 0.4 cm in diameter and 0.4 cm long, only 0.1 cm longer than one of the Site 120E aragonite beads (0.4 cm in diameter by 0.3 cm long). Unfortunately for us, the identification of the Bab al-Dhra' sample as shell does not define the material as aragonite, and molluscs may be either calcitic or aragonitic (and see next section).

Mollusc tubes (Figure 33, D)

Seven beads, registered as No. 73.005, have been identified as composed of calcite by visual examination and testing with dilute hydrochloric acid. Ranging in length from 0.3 cm to 0.5 cm, these white, 10YR 8/2, samples are 'ready-made' beads: water-worn *Dentalium* shells. It is possible that they may have been additionally fashioned for stringing, responding to the already widely known use of 'calcareous armour of shellfish for personal decoration' (Webster 1983: 567).

The genus *Dentalium* is represented by thin-shelled molluscs resembling elephant tusks, ranging from 1 to 5 inches in length and open at both ends (Wagner and Abbott 1967: 10). The calcium carbonate in *Dentalium* is present as calcite. According to Reese (personal communication), these molluscs could come from the Mediterranean or the Red Sea ca. 110 km and 190 km respectively from the Southern Ghors. Examples can be obtained from either site today.

Dentalium appears to have been used as beads since the Natufian (ca. 10,000 to 3000 B.C.) cultural assemblage (Dubin 1987: 338). According to Reese (1986), use of *Dentalium* is the 'hallmark of the Epipaleolithic of the Near East and the Neolithic and Chalcolithic of Cyprus'. It is possible that the beads we describe were fashioned earlier than EB IV, the date we are proposing for this SGNAS site, and reused because they are such an ideal shape.

Jewellery made from *Dentalium* was found during the excavation into the Natufian Level B (ca. 8,000 B.C.) at Magharet al-Wad in Palestine (Reese 1982; Redman 1978: fig. 3–14; Dubin 1987: fig. 8).

No *Dentalium* beads have been excavated from EB IV contexts at the town site of Bab al-Dhra'. However, nine *Dentalium* beads ranging in length from 0.3 cm to 0.9 cm were found in the adjacent cemetery in an EB II/III charnel house (Broeder personal observation). The species identifications have been verified by Reese (personal communication). One of the Bab al-Dhra' samples is longer than the SGNAS beads by as much as 0.4 centimetres. Yet, another agrees precisely with the one in the SGNAS collection having a length of 0.3 centimetres.

The shell material recorded from Jericho is contradictory. First, no *Dentalium* beads are recorded for EB IV contexts. Kenyon and Holland (1983: 798) state that no shells of any species were found in the Early Bronze–Middle Bronze Jericho tombs, but earlier two shells were cited as from Early Bronze–Middle Bronze Tomb N4 (Kenyon 1965: 60). Whether or not shell beads were found in the Early Bronze– Middle Bronze levels could affect the hypothesis that new groups of Early Bronze–Middle Bronze peoples entered Palestine by way of water, not by land. Evidence of shell beads in the tomb supports, at least, trade, if not entrance, by way of the shoreline. Kenyon and Holland (1983: 794) apologize for inaccurate recording, explaining that some beads crumbled and that beads were dispersed to all parts of the world. Since many of these Jericho samples remain to be tested, it is possible that some of the untested samples may be shell material. We are making plans to locate and test beads from Jericho which are in museum collections.

E) Mollusc spacers (Figure 33, E)

The six elliptical cylinder beads (spacer beads) and nine large fragments of spacers from Site 120E had been tentatively field identified as 'ivory.' We have determined, and confirmed by x-ray diffraction, that the material is actually aragonite, $CaCO_3$, calcium carbonate. On optical examination, internal cross-lamellar structure is obvious, which leads us to propose that the source of the material was mollusc shell.

Cross-lamellar structure is distinctive for mollusc shell (Rhoads and Lutz 1980; Wilbur and Saleuddin 1983: 257). The mineral of the shell is deposited in sequential lamellae. The primary lamellae are at a 45-degree angle to secondary lamellae that are made up in turn of tertiary, rod-like crystals fused together (Feinberg 1979: 40; Wilbur and Saleuddin 1983: 257, fig. 6). Since the orientation runs in different directions in adjacent layers alternating throughout the external shell of the mollusc, the result is a resiliant and tough structure. Toughness is not necessarily related to mineral hardness, as pure aragonite is soft – measuring 3 1/2 to 4 on the Mohs' scale. It is apparent that the person who fashioned the spacer beads took advantage of the sturdy molluscan architecture which included a mineral soft enough to be easily worked.

We are calling these samples spacer beads because they are elongated and have two holes pierced horizontally near their ends. The holes were fashioned by drilling from both sides, a technique which prevents breakage. Spacer beads, which are employed to keep many-layered pectorals and necklaces lined up properly, were common during the period 2133–1786 B.C. (Dubin 1987: 39).

According to Wilbur and Saleuddin:

> ...calcium carbonate crystals of molluscan shell occur as aragonite in some species, calcite in others, and still others have aragonite in one layer and calcite in another. Vaterite, a third polymorph, is not commonly present. The mechanism of control of crystal type in molluscan shell is not well understood (1983: 273).

We have not found many references denoting the mineral species of particular molluscs, apparently because x-ray diffraction testing, which would give positive identification of the mineral, has only recently come into common usage in malacology (Saleuddin and Wilbur 1983: 272).

Three families of mollusc, which could be aragonitic or calcitic, offer themselves as candidates for the source of the spacer material: 1) Strombidae; 2) Cassidae; and 3) Tridacnidae. Although there are arguments in favor of identifying the beads of Cassidae (Reese 1989) or Tridacnidae (Reese 1983: 224–266; 1984: 13), we believe the beads were most likely made from a member of the Family Strombidae, genus *Lambis*, which is the Red Sea Spider Conch or Scorpion shell, and we have conclusively identified the material as aragonite. Our conclusion is further based on the finding of identical beads at a Negev site associated with worked *Lambis* shells. Worked shell bars, identical in size and shape, have been excavated at Beer Resisim in the Central Negev Highlands (Cohen and Dever 1979: fig. 12). They have been identified as *Lambis truncata sebae* (Kiener, 1834) by Reese (personal communication). *Lambis* presently lives in the Red Sea 'limited to the shallow waters of the Indo-Pacific' (Wagner and Abbot 1967: 41). The mollusc does not live in the Mediterranean Sea.

Also identified as being made from *Lambis truncata sebae* are mollusc bracelets from the *nawamis*[3] at 'Ein Huderah in the Sinai, near copper deposits (Bar-Yosef *et al.* 1977: 76, pl. 11: C), and from Bab al-Dhra' Tomb A76E (Rast and Schaub in press) near Numeira, a site where evidence of secondary copper refining was found (Coogan 1984: 77).

The length of the spacers from Site 120E at Wadi Khuneizir ranges from 6.2 to 7.5 centimetres. The bead measuring ca. 5 cm long (Cohen and Dever 1979: fig. 12) excavated from Building 4 at Beer Resisim is obviously similar to those from Site 120E, although no colour is given for the Beer Resisim beads. The Site 120E beads range from white, 10YR 8/1, to pinkish-grey, 7.5YR 6/1. It is possible that all the Site 120E mollusc beads and fragments came from one *Lambis* shell, one adult *Lambis truncata* being about 30 cm in length (Abbott 1979: 158).

In view of the fact that EB IV potsherds were found at Wadi Khuneizir (MacDonald *et al.* 1987: 406; Rast

and Schaub 1974: 18) and that identical mollusc beads were excavated at EB IV–MBI Beer Resisim, we suggest that these mollusc spacer beads are EB IV in date. We cannot eliminate the possibility that the Site 120E spacers represent shell material reused at a later date. However, the following comparisons support our conjectured date of EB IV by highlighting the rarity of large molluscs, and showing agreement with Reese, Mienis, and Woodward (1986: 83) that shell material often served as offerings in graves and sanctuaries during early periods.

At Tel Masos in Palestine (50 km from the Southern Ghors), Reese (1983) has identified both *Tridacna* and cassid fragments in an Iron Age I settlement context. This site is 60 km from the Mediterranean and 200 km from the Red Sea. Reese observes that although *Tridacna* is edible, 'the distance from the seas and the rarity of the shells suggests that they were probably used as ornaments' (1983: 226). If this is true, and we have no reason to doubt the reasoning, the contributions jewellery makes to archaeology can be illustrated. For example, all species of the giant clam genus *Tridacna* are limited to the Indo-Pacific area and, therefore, would not be found in the Mediterranean (Wagner and Abbott 1967: 219). Cassid shells, on the other hand, inhabit the warm waters all over the world (Wagner and Abbott 1967: 81) so that cassid shells could be found in the Red Sea or the Mediterranean Sea. The occurrence of the *Tridacna* material in such an early age settlement begs the question of mode of transport of this special shell material so far from its source.

Reese (1989: 34) cites the EB III–IV Tomb L I at Tell Hadidi, Syria, as yielding cassid material in the form of 'five water-worn lips ranging in length from 2.8 to 4.3 cm (fig. 3).' 'Lips' refer to the edge segment of the shell aperture, a naturally useful portion of the shell for jewellery.

A very water-worn cassid lip was found in the Jordan Valley at Tiwal esh-Sharqi, Grave SE14. It measures ca. 4.5 cm long (Reese 1989: 35).

Finally, at Ghassul and Al-Gedi, two sites only 75 km away from the Southern Ghors, Reese identified cassid lip material which clearly was conserved and revered, but misidentified:

> Chalcolithic Teleilat Ghassul in Jordan (95 km) produced one water-worn lip, holed at both ends, from Level IVA; it originally was identified as bone (Koeppel 1940: 85, pl. 97: 2; Bodenheimer 1972: fig. 24: 13). The altar of the contemporary shrine at En-Gedi in Israel (80 km) produced a lip holed at both ends and said to be carved bone (Ussishkin 1980: 25, fig. 10: 21, pl. 14: 12) (Reese 1989: 33–34).

It is interesting that cassid shell material is not only prevalent elsewhere but has been misidentified. However, cassid and *Tridacna* fragments are not the only shell material found as jewellery in this area.

During the second season of the Central Negev Highlands Project at the EB IV–MB I site of Beer

Resisim (80 km from the Southern Ghors), evidence of shell working activity was discovered in Building 4 and outside of Building 8 in area 8A (Cohen and Dever 1979: 51, 52; fig. 12). Reese (personal communication) identified the mollusc material as *Lambis truncata sebae* (Kiener, 1834). He recognized the species as the Giant Spider Conch or Scorpion shell, which presently lives in the Red Sea (Wagner and Abbott 1967: 41) from a photograph of a nearly whole shell specimen found in the shell workshop (Cohen and Dever 1979: fig. 12). The beads at Beer Resisim were found in association with worked pieces of *Lambis truncata*. Beads from Site 120E are identical, and it is tempting to suggest a date of EB IV for the Site 120E graves. It is virtually impossible to discern the species of the shell from which a bead has been carved by looking at the finished bead. Only when a bead is found in association with a large fragment of worked shell can logical assertions with that particular species be made. Alternatively, a detailed look at the trace element composition might be effectively used.

From the Early Bronze–Middle Bronze or EB IV period, at Jericho, Kenyon and Holland (1983: 816: fig. 368: 7, 8) identified two miscellaneous objects from the tell as possible whetstones. These Jericho samples greatly resemble in size and shape the mollusc spacers from Site 120E. Since the identification for these Jericho samples is based on observation alone, it is possible that these samples may be of mollusc material, even though the term 'whetstone' invokes a hard material, certainly harder than aragonitic shell material. To adequately compare these samples from Jericho, they should be subjected to laboratory tests.

Kenyon and Holland (1983: fig. 226: 17, 18) identified in the field two objects from the Middle Bronze Period at Jericho as spacer beads of 'ivory' (calcium phosphate composition). These samples are identical in shape to the SGNAS spacers. The measurements are similar as well:

SGNAS: L: 6.2–7.5 cm
W: 0.6–0.7 cm
TH: 0.5 cm
D of holes: 0.2 cm;

Jericho: L: 6.0–8.0 cm
W: 0.7 cm
TH: 0.6 cm
D of holes: 0.2 cm.

It is possible that the Jericho objects may also be composed of mollusc shell.

In reviewing sites where the mollusc species *Lambis* was identified during EB IV, there appears to be a connection between *Lambis* shell and copper working areas. According to Cohen and Dever (1981: 74), access to copper sources was important to the EB IV copper-working community at Beer Resisim. This connection was true during the EB I period as well. *Lambis* bracelets appear to have been used by the copper-working community at 'Ein Huderah in Sinai where shell bangles were found to be *Lambis truncata sebae* (Bar-Yosef *et al.* 1977: 76). Furthermore, points

of almost pure copper were found in the stone structures called by the Bedouin *nawamis*. Builders of the *nawamis* seem to have been the local Sinai inhabitants who were involved in copper mining (Bar-Yosef *et al.* 1977: 87). Unlike most Chal–EB I sites, at 'Ein Huderah beads were the most common artifact! The dating of the stone structures at 'Ein Huderah as Late Chalcolithic and EB I periods by Bar-Yosef *et al.* (1977: 88) is based on the fact that the *Lambis* shell bangles go out of use in Egypt during Dynasty II (ca. 2900 B.C.). Bar-Yosef *et al.* (1977: 76) state that the bracelets described as ivory from Beer Abu Matar seem to be made of mollusc (carbonate). Beer Abu Matar is one of the copper-working sites in the Beersheba Valley which has been assigned a date in the Chalcolithic Period, ca. 4000–3200 B.C. (Perrot 1955: 185).

We have performed laboratory tests to obtain positive identification of 497 beads and personal ornaments collected during the season of 1977 by Rast and Schaub from the EB IA cemetery at Bab al-Dhra'. In the northwest chamber of EB IA Tomb A89, ten beads were found which we determined were a mineral from the secondary enrichment zone of the copper mine. Two mollusc shell bangle bracelets were found in nearby Tomb A92. One mollusc bracelet, dating also to EB IA, was found during the 1965–1967 excavations by Lapp in Tomb A76E in the same cemetery. Reese (Rast and Schaub 1989) has identified all the bangle bracelets as sawn from *Lambis truncata sebae*. These findings seem to indicate a connection between *Lambis* and copper working.

Further sites, ranging in date from the Chalcolithic Period through EB II (ca. 4000–2700 B.C.), at which mollusc ornaments have been identified (Rast and Schaub 1989) include the following:

Palestine
Tell al-Far'ah (North) Tombs 5, 8, and 14;
Bethlehem; Teleilat Ghassul; and
Jericho Tomb A 94.

Egypt
Tarkhan Grave 269;
Mahasna Grave H128;
Armant Grave 1579;
Diospolis Parva Tombs U256 and U278;
Aniba; and
Gebel Tarif.

With the mollusc material we have identified from Site 120E at Wadi Khuneizir, there is additional evidence suggesting that during EB IV people continued to use shell material and perhaps again traveled to the Red Sea to obtain *Lambis*. A likely option is that they passed them along one to another along the copper trade routes!

Field identification for two rod-shaped samples from the EB II/III walled-town, period sanctuary (Field XII) at Bab al-Dhra' (BD) was ivory. These samples, BD Registration Nos. 774.001 and 759.001, have been identified by us, using x-ray diffraction testing, as aragonite. The samples also exhibited cross-lamellar structure, which we infer means the source is thick-shelled mollusc, identical to the Site 120E samples. Not only do they agree in natural structure, but some samples agree in colour. SGNAS Reg. No. 73.002 matches BD Reg. No. 759.001 as Munsell colour 10YR 8/2, white. Above, we have cited the use of mollusc ornaments in Chalcolithic–EB I and EB IV. The EB II/III samples offer evidence that mollusc was employed continually as a source of decorative material in Southwest Asia throughout the Early Bronze Age!

Although much later, mollusc samples were among the artifacts gathered from the 7th century B.C. Temple of Hera on the Island of Samos in the Aegean (Reese 1984: 13). Reese has identified 'both unworked and hand-carved *Tridacna* or giant clam shells which must have been imported from the Red Sea, four unworked hippopotamus lower canines, and ostrich eggshells, the latter two creatures being native to the Levant or North Africa' (1984: 13).

Teeth and ostrich eggshell artifacts are not confined to the Aegean nor to later periods. The Chalcolithic Period is well-known for its worked, hippopotamus ivory from Nahal Mishmar (Bar Adon 1962: pl. 39b). A sample from the EB IV sanctuary area at Bab al-Dhra' (Field XVI; Reg. No. 3112.001) has been identified by us as animal ivory, probably hippopotamus because 'lines of Retzius,' the striae which identify elephant ivory (Webster 1983: 590), are not discernible. The hippopotamus lived in the coastal swamps of Palestine until the end of the Iron Age around 540 B.C. (Perrot 1955: 172).

Further, 36 ostrich eggshell beads have been retrieved from the megalith area (K1) at Bab al-Dhra' (personal observation). Megaliths (or menhirs) have been found in what appear to be cultic areas (Dever 1976: 438), possibly to mark tribal ceremony sites. One ostrich eggshell fragment has also been identified at a SGNAS site (Chapter 14).

Thus, for over 2000 years, large, mollusc-shell material, hippopotamus ivory, and ostrich eggshell beads, were associated with sanctuaries or areas of special significance, perhaps as royal burial offerings, as so frequently mentioned by Woolley (1934: 262–83, pls. 100–02). The occurrence of large mollusc material in the burials at Site 120E might, therefore, indicate burials of persons of prominence.

F) Carnelian bicones (Figure 33, F)

Three poorly fashioned beads of red, 10R 4/6, carnelian variety of quartz were found at Site 120E. All three samples (Reg. No. 73.004) were shaped into short convex truncated bicones with the following dimensions:

a)   D: 0.7 cm; L: 0.3 cm;
b)   D: 0.6 cm; L: 0.3 cm; and
c)   D: 0.5 cm; L: 0.2 cm (internally exhibits 2 small dark areas).

Hoffman (1979: 189) writes that 'it is absolutely essential that we understand the social and economic context of goods like beads – goods that point toward social exchange and the whole body of ideas,

relationships, and even myths that often accompany exchange.' The presence of carnelian beads in the Southern Ghors should be considered important not because carnelian is an exotic material, but because of the lore and the significance of social relationships associated with the exchange of carnelian.

Carnelian, a variety of the mineral quartz, is 'abundant in the Eastern Desert' of Egypt (Lucas 1934: 341). A semitransparent to translucent orange-red to brownish-red or brownish-orange chalcedony, carnelian was cherished for its alleged therapeutic effects. Reddish stones were thought to be remedies for hemorrhages (Kunz 1971: 370), on the principle that 'like cures like.'

Two tombs at the Khirbet Iskander EB IV cemetery (ca. 100 km from the Southern Ghors) produced several carnelian beads (Richard personal communication). The following samples are carnelian:

Tomb Area D.9:

Reg No.: A:355   D: 0.5 cm; L: 0.5 cm.

Tomb Area D.10:

Reg No.: A:354   D: 0.5 cm; L: 0.2 cm;
Reg No.: A:408   D: 0.5 cm; L: 0.2 cm; and
Reg No.: A:409   D: 0.5 cm; L: 0.5 cm.

These beads have not been subjected to laboratory examination; the measurements were taken in the field. However, it is clear that one of the SGNAS (Reg. No. 73.004) carnelian beads (above) is identical in diameter and length to two of the Khirbet Iskander samples (A:354 and A:408). We plan to examine the Khirbet Iskander beads at the Madaba Museum, Jordan, to see whether they also agree in colour and fashioning.

One highly polished carnelian bead fragment was broken, although its original cylindrical shape was obvious. It was found at the EB IV sanctuary at Bab al-Dhra', Field XVI (personal observation). Registered as No. 1961.001, this bead measures D: 0.9 cm; L: 1.8 cm, and would have qualified as a long cylinder had it been whole. Long cylinders were 'more usual' in the Old Kingdom (Brunton 1928: 17) as evidence of the desirability of that form. Larger pieces of raw material must have been available for fashioning the longer beads. The colour of this sample is red, 10R 4/8, which is closely related to that of the three SGNAS samples (No. 73.004) of red, 10R 4/6. The beads agree in hue and value, differing only in chroma.

Once beautifully cut and polished, this longitudinal half of a long cylinder may represent a reused bead from an earlier time period when a greater percentage of finer work was done. At Qau-Badari, a Dynasty VII–VIII (ca. 2300 B.C.) trinket box contained Predynastic (ca. 3200 B.C.) beads (Brunton 1928: 22), representing reuse 900 years later!

According to Petrie (1931: 3), carnelian beads have been found associated with an ovate jar at Tell al-Ajjul (115 km from the Southern Ghors). The 63 samples of carnelian in the drawings of these beads illustrate the following variety of shapes: long convex bicones; long cylinders; short barrels; and barrel discs.

Petrie claims (1931: 3) that the EB IV (his Copper Age) carnelian is 'not so finely formed or so translucent' as Dynasty V carnelian, yet the Dynasty V samples are 'much better than' those from the close of Dynasty VI. It is clear that the technology of working harder material, and in especially carnelian, varied during the Egyptian dynasties. The SGNAS carnelian samples from Wadi Khuneizir are crudely formed, which leads us to suggest they date to EB IV (Dynasties VII–X) in line with Petrie's observations.

Twelve carnelian beads from two tombs of the EB IV period are listed from Gibeon (107 km from the Southern Ghors). By taking measurements from Pritchard's (1963) drawings, we record the following.

Tomb 32 (fig. 72: 9) contained three carnelian beads: one 'long cylinder,' a standard truncated bicone, D: 0.9 cm; L: 1.0 centimetres. This sample is overall larger than any of the SGNAS samples.

Two 'short cylinders': one measures D: 0.8 cm; L: 0.4 cm, a somewhat different shape than the SGNAS beads. The other is a short convex truncated bicone D: 0.9 cm; L: 0.6 cm, longer in diameter and length than the SGNAS beads.

Tomb 32 (fig. 72: 10) contained eight carnelian beads, illustrated by two drawings of Pritchard's 'long cylinders'   D: 0.8 cm; L: 1.7 cm (long cylinder) D: 0.6 cm; L: 1.0 cm (long truncated bicone).

Pritchard notes that the 'cylinders' range from 0.7 cm to 1.7 cm in length. All eight beads are longer than the SGNAS samples.

Tomb 54 (fig. 72: 22) contained one long barrel, D: 0.8 cm; L: 1.7 centimetres. Again the bead is considerably longer than the SGNAS beads. The diameter is only 0.1 cm larger than one described at SGNAS.

In these comparisons, the shapes of the SGNAS artifacts differ from Pritchard's beads. Some of his seem to be convex truncated bicones. Fine differences are not always clear in drawings, so we cannot be too precise in this comparison. We cannot compare the colours, as Prtichard has not noted the colour of his samples.

From the Jericho tell, there is one bead dating to EB IV (Kenyon and Holland 1983: 793). This sample (fig. 364) resembles the three SGNAS samples. It is a short truncated convex bicone with D: 0.85 cm; L: 0.35 centimetres. The lengths are almost identical, but the diameter of the Jericho bead is 0.15 cm longer than the SGNAS bead.

One hundred thirty-six other carnelian beads have been described at the many EB IV tombs at Jericho by Kenyon (1960 and 1965) and Kenyon and Holland (1983). 'Annular' is the term used by these authors for beads whose sides are mainly flat. In order for us to compare like beads, we have reworked the list to follow Beck's classifications. Eighty beads had to be eliminated, as they lacked descriptions. The following 56 forms of carnelian beads are noted:

4	barrel discs;
2	cylinder discs;
23	short barrels;
1	short truncated convex bicone;
2	short cylinders;
2	standard barrels;
20	long barrels;
1	long convex bicone;
1	long cylinder.

This list of Jericho tomb beads shows an emphasis on barrels and cylinders – the type of the beads typical of the Sixth Dynasty Qau and Badari area in Egypt (Brunton 1928: 17, 18). Why some bead shapes are typical of a specific time, we do not know. Perhaps fashion operated in ancient as well as modern times.

Kenyon and Holland (1983: 797) have found that at Jericho relatively fewer carnelian beads have been excavated from loci dating to the urban phases of Early Bronze Age than those dating to the semisedentary periods of EB IA (Kenyon's Proto-Urban A) and EB IV. This lack of carnelian in the urban phases of Jericho is reflected in the findings at Bab al-Dhra', where out of 822 beads from the EB III urban period cemetery, only 23 beads (or 3 percent) are carnelian or carnelian agate (personal analysis). Out of 501 beads from the EB IA semisedentary population cemetery, 95 (or 19 percent) are carnelian (personal observation). Was carnelian actually out of fashion in some parts of Palestine during EB III, or was the material in short supply? The similar patterns at Jericho and Bab al-Dhra' probably indicate some consistent factor. The ample Jericho collection of EB IV carnelian indicates the respect the local, nonurban population had for its healing or magical powers. Availability of raw material in local watercourses also probably played a part. Although some bead experts such as Francis (1982: 33) and Dubin (1987: 186, 187) emphasize the importance of carnelian workshops during the Chalcolithic Period in India, and trade therefrom, it is our opinion that the local population in Palestine was probably responsible for making the beads found in the Southern Ghors and Northern 'Arabah.

A necklace of 51 beads was found at the EB IV levels at Hama in Syria. The majority of the beads were carnelian (Ingholt 1940). The other beads were made of materials that included jade, a relatively rare mineral. Jade, however, was obtainable near Syria in the Taurus Mountains of Southern Anatolia (Moore personal communication). The mining of jade in the Taurus suggests that we should expect it to be more readily found at the northern sites in the Levant.

At Byblos, Montet discovered a significant bead collection in a closed deposit which covered a third millennium shrine. The find was the so-called Montet Jar, which contained over 600 beads, 158 of which are carnelian. The jar also contained scarabs, figurines, metal artifacts, and so on, that Tufnell used to date the contents to ca. 2130–2040 B.C. (Tufnell and Ward 1966: 205). This date is supported by Richard (personal communication), the principal investigator at the site of Khirbet Iskander which exhibits EB IV occupation. Contact with Palestine is suggested by the similarity of the Tell al-Ajjul long, barrel, carnelian beads (see above) with two long barrels found in this Byblos jar. The most popular shapes appear to agree with the forms recorded for Egyptian Dynasties IV–XI by Brunton (Tufnell and Ward 1966: 200). In spite of their being 158 carnelian beads in the jar, there are no beads similar to the carnelian short convex truncated bicones of Site 120E.

Finally, a Dynasty VIII carnelian bead from Tomb 1977 at the Qau-Badari area in Egypt is called a 'ring' bead by Brunton (1928) and labeled Type 86F6 on his Plate 102. This bead measures D: 0.7 cm; L: 0.3 cm, and is identical in size and shape to the largest of the SGNAS carnelian beads, which measures also D: 0.7 cm and L: 0.3 centimetres.

It would appear that carnelian artifacts were popular and conserved throughout the greater area surrounding Site 120E. The small variations in size and colour of the comparison samples delineated above does not detract from the consistency of the use. In fact, if anything, it may reinforce the success of locating the source of this material, its durability, and most important, the fact that it was preferentially employed for ornamentation, or at least, consistently deposited in tombs or sanctuary areas, possibly because of special powers associated with its colour.

Site 45

Out of the 241 samples in the survey we describe herein, the second largest collection of beads in the survey, 12% of the total, 29 glass samples and 1 carnelian bead, comes from Site 45. These are probably modern beads. They have been found in a cemetery area which seems to be located on the eastern segment of an ancient site (see Chapter 10). Since the beads have been found in a mixed context, we cannot rule out the possibility of their being ancient.

Site 45, Al Rujoum, is located immediately south of the Wadi al-Hasa and about 7.5 km north of Wadi Khuneizir (Figure 31). Both a cemetery, with a considerable amount of sherd scatter, and a mound constitute the site. Sherds found at this site were identified as Abbasid-Mamluk ware; Syrian imports; and modern. Glass beads from the cemetery will be discussed first because they outnumber the carnelian.

A) Glass beads

In Chapter 12 Meyer presents 15 drawings of glass beads. Our glass samples are correlated to Meyer's Plate 38 except for No. 51.001, and we use Munsell colour chart designations. The discussion below focuses on the beads as jewellery, and therefore, we discuss it in this chapter.

Glass, a complicated substance made from silica, and alkali, a stabilizer and (usually) a coloring agent, is molten when raised to a high temperature, and becomes solid at room temperature. Two principal methods of manufacture are: (1) by drawing out a bubble of molten or viscid glass into a long, slender tube, and (2) by winding threads of molten glass around a wire which is later withdrawn. A third method, probably used in conjunction with each of

the above, is by molding the beads in two-part molds while the glass is still viscid (Kidd and Kidd 1983: 221).

Examples of 'drawn,' 'wound,' and 'molded' glass beads have been recovered from Site 45. Pfeiffer writes that wound glass beads are the 'oldest and simplest kind' (1982: 23).

Although Brill (1963: 120) states that the earliest manufactured glass appeared about 3500 years ago, he does not state the location of such an important technological advance, nor does he say in what form it appeared. Morey (1954: 5) writes that glass beads, whose dating is not doubted, come from Deir al Bahri, Egypt, from the coffin of a child queen of King Mentuhotpe (2196–2172 B.C.).

In early times, glass was highly prized because of its rarity (Morey 1954: 8). More recently, glass beads of a variety of colours, which were easily manufactured, became ubiquitous and were used to emulate the more valuable natural minerals.

The beads at Site 45 are similar to beads found at Caesarea Maritima in Palestine. Pfeiffer studied burials, dating to A.D. 1700–1900, at Caesarea. She kindly offered comments regarding the Site 45 glass bead corpus.

Bead No. 46.001 (Plate 38s) appears to have been wound around a rod when manufactured. Red in colour, in imitation of coral, 5.0R 4/8, the short, barrel bead measures D: 0.8 cm; L: 0.7 centimetres. Similar beads are often found in shops in North Africa today.

The standard circular white bead, No. 46.002 (Plate 38t), also a wound glass bead, measures 1.2 cm in diameter. This is a white, 10YR 8/2, opaque bead whose surface appears to be devitrifying. Pfeiffer (1983: 209) states that beads identical to this SGNAS sample were found in a cist burial at Caesarea Maritima in the grave of an adult female, whose age was approximately 30–35 years. The burial, which is roughly dated to the period A.D. 1500–1899, had a coin from the nineteenth century associated with it. Thus, the date of the burial would be in that century. Beads similar to the Site 45 white bead were excavated at a site in Amsterdam dating to the 17th and early 18th century A.D. (Karklins 1983: 126, fig. 2).

Reg. No. 46.003 (Plate8u), a long convex bicone bead of green, 5.0G 4/4, appears to be a wound, glass bead. Pfeiffer knows of no similar bead.

Pfeiffer was unable to tell whether the three bead halves of blue, 5.0B: 6/6, 5/6, and 5/10, Reg. No. 46.004 (Plate 38v) are wound or drawn. The samples seem to be 17th–18th century, but perhaps as late as the 19th century. These short barrel translucent fragments are worn and do not fit together. They measure D: 0.9 cm; L: 0.8 cm; D of projected hole: 0.3 centimetres. This type of bead was commonly used for trade with the Indians, and they are regularly on display in North American museum showcases.

The six whole beads, Reg. No. 46.005 (Plate 38w) with red-purple, 5.0RP 4/6, exterior and white, 5YR 8/1, interior are commonly called 'ox-eye' beads (Pfeiffer personal communication). These too are trade beads. Opaque, with a dull surface, the largest of these drawn beads measures D: 0.7 cm; L: 0.6 cm, and the smallest, D: 0.5 cm; L: 0.5 centimetres. They were apparently used in Africa in the slave trade.

The three red, 5.0R: 5/8, 5/8, 4/6, beads, Reg. No. 46.006, (Plate 38x) are trade beads, according to Pfeiffer. Typically, they were made as long tubes and then broken into smaller lengths. The ends were then ground down to achieve rounded beads. The Site 45 specimens may have been finished beads, or they may have been intended to be ground into smaller beads like those discussed above (No. 46.005). The largest bead measures D: 0.5 cm; L: 1.5 centimetres. The smallest one is D: 0.4 cm; L: 0.4 centimetres. No comparisons have been found.

Pfeiffer suggests that a yellow, 5.0Y 8/6, long barrel bead, Reg. No. 46.007 (Plate 38y), is a wound glass type dated to the 19th century. A semitranslucent bead, it measures D: 1.1 cm; L: 1.3 centimetres. This bead is similar to a sample measuring D: 1.0 cm and L: 1.6 cm from the Boeren-Wetering site in Amsterdam (Karklins 1983: 126).

The SGNAS green, 5.0G 7/4, long barrel bead, Reg. No. 46.008 (Plate 38z), is another wound glass sample which Pfeiffer suggests dates to the 19th century. The green, worn, opaque bead measures D: 0.6 cm; L: 1.3 centimetres. Comparisons could not be found.

The yellow, 5.0Y 8/4, long pear-shaped bead, Reg. No. 46.009 (Plate 38aa), may be compared to those in the cist burial from Caesarea Maritima discussed above (No. 46.002). The measurements of this semitranslucent bead are D: 1.1 cm; L: 2.2 centimetres. It, too, dates from the 19th century.

The green, 5.0G 5/8, semitranslucent, truncated cone bead, Reg. No. 46.010 (Plate 38bb), appears to be a wound bead which has been pressed into shape. Pfeiffer (1982: 24) notes that half-molten beads can be pressed into hexagonal, square, biconical, or barrel shapes. The diameter of the cone is 0.5 cm; the length is 1.5 centimetres. No comparisons were found.

The purple-blue, 5.0PB 3/2, pentagonal cylinder, Reg. No. 46.011 (Plate 38cc), may have originally been intended to be cut into shorter lengths or drawn into a hexagonal bead (Pfeiffer personal communication). Worn and bubbly in appearance, this bead measures D: 0.6 cm; L: 2.2 centimetres. Two of the graves at Caesarea Maritima had short, blue, hexagonal beads which may be similar.

The long cylinder opaque bead, Reg. No. 46.012 (Plate 38dd), whose colour is blue-green, 5.0BG 3/4, is a drawn bead, according to Pfeiffer (personal communication). It measures D: 0.2 cm; L: 2.6; D of hole: 0.05 centimetres. Pfeiffer cannot recall any similar beads.

The yellow-red, 5.0YR 5/4, barrel disc bead, No. 46.013 (Plate 38ee), is a wound bead. Having an extra large hole, this bead measures D: 1.3 cm; L: 0.4 centimetres. The diameter of the hole is 0.8 centimetres.

The blue-green, 5.0BG 4/6, bead, Reg. No. 46.014 (Plate 38ff), showing opalescence, fits Beck's (1928) description of cornerless cubes: 'these beads are cubes or rectangles which have had all their corners cut off." The particular variety found at Site 45 agrees in shape with Beck's 'twisted square' (crystallographic name is a truncated tetragonal tapezohedron). It measures D: 1.1 cm; L: 1.3 cm and has a counterpart from Amsterdam (Karklins 1983: 126).

Schienerl (1985: 8) describes the use of a green, cornerless cube bead (which he thinks may be agate) as an amulet against the 'Evil Eye.' To protect her baby, a Bedouin woman living in the Fayyum Oasis in 1973 fastened the bead to her child's head covering. According to Schienerl (1985: 9), 'similar traditions are still alive in Jordan'. Dale (1986: 6) objects to Schienerl's assertion that 'no other material [except for agate?] seems to have been used for cornerless cube beads.' Dale has in her collection cornerless cubes of rock crystal, carnelian, amber, and jet. She states that the cornerless, cube shape was copied in glass as early as 900 B.C. (1986: 6). There is a carnelian example on a Hellenistic, gold chain in the Nicosia Museum on the island of Cyprus.

Not only is there no consensus on the ancient dating of the cornerless cubes, there is no agreement on where the A.D. 17th–19th century beads were manufactured. Possible candidates for factory locations are Holland, Indonesia, Venice, or 'some other [European ?] center' (Francis 1987: 10).

Four and one-half beads of red, 5.0R 5/10, glass, Reg. No. 46.015 (Plate 38gg), molded to imitate coral (Pfeiffer personal communication), may have served as spacers, since they are pierced horizontally. A date for these beads has not been suggested. The largest sample measures D: 1.8 cm; L: 0.4 centimetres. The smallest is D: 1.8 cm; L: 0.375 centimetres. They are shaped as cylinder discs with two convex ends, like capsules.

Because of the extreme pitting of the surface of the blue-green, 5.0BG 4/4, glass bead, Reg. No. 51.001 (Figure 33, G), Pfeiffer is unable to say for certain whether this bead is wound. This short barrel bead measures D: 0.5 cm; L: 0.4 centimetres.

B) Carnelian bead

Carnelian, as a personal ornament, has been discussed above. The suggestion that carnelian protects from evil carried through to the present times. Eastern peoples believe that those who envy you can do you no harm with their envy if you wear carnelian (Kunz 1913: 63). In spite of the continuing popularity of carnelian, no circular beads could be found listed as excavated at a modern site, although a circular, carnelian bead from the Roman Period is numbered 36ld on Dubin's (1987) bead chart. The SGNAS bead (Figure 33, H), 0.8 cm in diameter, could be an example of an older bead reused, a common happenstance. Its colour ranges from red, 2.5YR 4/8, to light reddish-brown, 2.5YR 6/4.

All these samples appear to be modern. Therefore, we do not discuss any conclusions pertinent to archaeological arguments.

Site 149

Site 149 is represented by a single bead. In fact, it is 1/2 of a short barrel-shaped, purple-blue, 5.0PB 4/10, bead that is made of glass. The dimensions of the 1/2 bead, Reg. No. 72.001, are D: 0.35 cm; L: 0.25 centimetres.

This site is a tower/tomb complex overlooking Wadi Khuneizir (Figure 31) to the northeast and offers a view of Rujm Khuneizir, Site 108, from a well-built 6 x 6 m platform. This platform may have been the support for a tower. The area seems also to have been used as a burial place. Sherds picked up on the site are Nabatean-painted, Late Roman, and Islamic pottery.

Site 211

One yellow-red, 5YR 4/6, cylinder disc bead, Reg. No. 84.001 (fig. 33I), collected at Site 211 is made of translucent carnelian. Numerous conchoidal fractures are visible on the surface of this D: 0.9 cm by L: 0.5 cm bead.

Site 211, Khirbet al-Dahal, is located along both sides of Wadi al-Dahal (Figure 31) to the east of the Mazra–'Aqabah highway. It consists of several multiroom structures. All the structures are made from undressed cobbles. Pottery sherds from the Byzantine Period were found at the site. However, Late Roman, Umayyad, and Modern Period sherds are also present at the site.

The type of skill exhibited on the carnelian bead from Site 211 may indicate it was an unfinished bead. Descriptions of similar Byzantine, Roman, or Modern carnelian samples were not found. Therefore, we cannot make any comparisons.

Dubin's (1987: 66) map shows carnelian beads being transported from Yemen and India to Constantinople from A.D. 330 to 1400 (the Byzantine through Mamluk Period).

Site 232

The SGNAS collected one bead at Site 232. It is a short cylinder bead of blue-green, 5.0BG 6/4, quartz, Reg. No. 101.001, measuring D: 0.5 cm; L: 0.2 centimetres. No description of beads similar to this quartz, short cylinder have been found in the literature.

Site 232 is located to the north of Wadi al-Hassiya (Figure 31). The SGNAS collected very few sherds in association with the five buildings which constitute the site. This fact makes one question the function of the structures. To the north and east of the structures are many graves. This site is associated with remains of Nabatean-painted, Roman, Byzantine, Islamic, and Modern pottery samples.

For these last three samples, we are presenting this data as useful for other researchers. As stated above, we cannot make appropriate and meaningful comparisons. These are unique descriptions.

Summary and discussion

We submitted bead samples collected from five sites in the Southern Ghors and Northeastern 'Arabah to laboratory testing for accurate identification of the materials in addition to the usual description of the shapes of the beads. The results are summarized in Figure 32 and the Appendix. Eighty-six percent of the total of 241 beads come from Site 120E gravesites, which we believe dates to EB IV. Twelve percent are glass beads from what appears to be a Modern Period cemetery component of Site 45. Periods represented at Site 45 are Abbasid-Mamluk, Syrian imports, and Modern (see Chapter 10). At the three other sites, namely, Sites 149, 211, and 232, the SGNAS found only one bead at each: at Site 149, a glass bead coloured purple-blue; at Site 211, a carnelian bead; and at Site 232, a bead of blue-green quartz. The latter two may well be old beads, but we have not found similar material described in the literature. Quartz and glass are common materials for the periods represented by the potsherds collected from these three sites. The several beads from ancient Site 120E and the apparently modern, eastern component of Site 45, the two areas with significant numbers of beads, are summarized as follows.

Site 120E

This site yielded a total of 208 beads identified as follows:

A) one hundred sixty-five white, pinkish-white, and greyish-brown, short cylinder beads composed of calcite;

B) ten short cylinder beads of opaque quartz, coloured an intimate mixture of reddish-yellow, pink, and brown;

C) eight white, short barrel beads of aragonite;

D) seven white beads identified as the calcitic exoskeletons of thin-shelled mollusc *Dentalium* in natural tubular form;

E) six white, elliptical cylinder beads and nine fragments of beads identified as aragonite and thought to derive from a thick-shelled mollusc, *Lambis*; and

F) three convex truncated bicone disc beads of translucent red quartz, variety carnelian.

We showed that six beads which had been previously field identified as ivory (calcium phosphate composition) were calcium carbonate as aragonite. The most probable source for this material was thick-shelled mollusc, *Lambis truncata sebae* (Kiener, 1834). Identical spacer beads from a shell workshop at the EB IV–MB I Period site of Beer Resisim in the Central Negev Highlands permitted accurate identification of the species of mollusc. Thus, we suggest the time period for Site 120E is EB IV.

Lambis or Giant Spider conch (Scorpion shell), is found in the Red Sea but not in the Mediterranean. Therefore, we surmise that the people from Site 120E were oriented (or their jewellers were oriented) to the south for the source of materials.

Ease of working and access to raw material

probably explains the preponderance of calcite, aragonite, and shell material at ancient sites.

The SGNAS collected only three bicones of carnelian at Site 120E. Carnelian, which was revered because of the lore associated with it, is harder material and more difficult to fashion than calcite and shell. The SGNAS EB IV carnelian beads are not as evenly shaped and highly polished as beads described from other sites in the Near East which date to earlier time periods.

Our tabulations regarding excavations (rather than surveys) at Near Eastern sites show that, overall, fewer carnelian beads have been found at levels dating to the EB III urban period in Palestine than those of the EV IV period, which is thought to be characterized primarily by nomadism. Although this evidence points to more carnelian during EB IV, our study shows that the SGNAS collected few carnelian beads from the EB IV gravesites. Is this small number of beads just a reflection of survey collecting methodology? Will more carnelian be found beneath the surface, thereby, validating the presently observed popularity of carnelian during EB IV?

Significant numbers of carnelian beads were excavated at sites dating to EB IV located to the north and west. To the north at Byblos, the Montet jar contained 158 carnelian samples. At Jericho, also to the north, 136 carnelian beads were excavated from the EB IV tombs. At coastal Tell al-Ajjul, to the west, at least 63 carnelian beads were found.

Contrarily, toward the south at Bab al-Dhra' only one carnelian bead dated to EB IV. It was found in the sanctuary area. Why was there only one carnelian bead found at Bab al-Dhra' at a time when carnelian beads seem exceedingly popular in the regions to the north and near the Mediterranean coast? Does the small number of carnelian beads found during the survey reflect the smaller numbers of beads in general during EB IV? Are there fewer EB IV tombs in the south in which to find beads? Has tomb robbing eliminated evidence of carnelian? Was carnelian more readily available in the north, or more prized? These questions await further archaeological investigation for answers.

The predominant shapes assigned to the EB IV period are short cylinders and elliptical spacers (Figure 32). Other shapes determined to be EB IV are short barrel, short truncated convex bicone, cylinder, and natural tubular.

Current anthropological discussions have centered on similarities and differences of the economies of the sedentary and the nonsedentary peoples during the enigmatic EB IV–MB I interlude between two major urban periods (Cohen and Dever 1981: 75). Written documentation during EB IV is not available from the Ghors; therefore, archaeological clues must be sought for answers to questions such as: Were the economies at this time primarily pastoral and agricultural? How large a role did mining activities play? We have shown that *Lambis* shell was associated with mining communities. Was the area of the Southern Ghors and Northeastern 'Arabah the industrial center? Were

population movements oriented toward the Red Sea because of the mines in the south?

The jewellery specimens from Site 120E are perceived to be exceptional 'symbols of excellence,' a term coined by Clark (1986), and, therefore, it is essential to incorporate an archaeological investigation of Site 120E into the research design for the Southern Ghors. Rast (personal communication) surmises the mollusc spacers are the indicators of population movement between the Southern Ghors and the Negev. This hypothesis should be tested by stratigraphical excavation.

Eastern component of Site 45

The materials provided us for analysis included beads from what appears to be a Modern Period cemetery which may overlay the eastern segment of an ancient site (see Chapter 10). Comparison with modern sites in Caesarea Maritima and Amsterdam are responsible for our dating the surficial remains of the eastern component of Site 45 to the period A.D. 1700–1900. Twenty-nine glass beads of nine different colours and one carnelian bead occur at this location. The samples show eleven different shapes! The glass beads exhibit all three basic techniques for glassmaking: drawing, winding, and molding. They are assumed to be trade beads because of the great variety of shapes.

Included in the collection were barrel disc; cylinder disc with two convex ends; short barrel; circular; long barrel; long convex bicone; long pear-shape; square long truncated cone; pentagonal long cylinder; and twisted square, all of which can be assumed to date from A.D. 1700–1900. Shapes for which dates are undetermined include short barrel and short cylinder.

The materials we have analyzed do not appear to be particularly distinctive or unique to the SGNAS locality.

Varia

We look forward to examining the personal ornaments from future proposed excavations in the Southern Ghors and Northeastern 'Arabah. The results of our investigations add a new dimension to the lifeways of the ancient inhabitants relative to those in the region today. It is instructive to review the historical perspective, especially with our modern concerns regarding the connections between industrialization and ecology!

Acknowledgments

We are especially grateful for the opinions and comments from Reese of the Field Museum in Chicago, who is an authority on archaeological shells, and from Pfeiffer, who is a specialist on modern glass beads.

The drawings in Figure 33 were furnished by Barbro Evans, Pittsburgh, PA. We appreciate her skillful contribution.

Appendix

Beads or fragments of beads included in this appendix are listed by registration numbers assigned serially in the field. Hence, the sample numbers of beads are scattered throughout the listing.

An extension number (.XXX) has been added to the field registration numbers in order to separate the several objects excavated from the same site. Objects from the same site which agree in colour, shape, and material are included in one extension number. Registration numbers are in numerical order.

Appendix Format

Registration Number
Sample Number
Site Number: time periods determined by pottery and glass

Description from Visual Observation

Material Characteristics:
  Shape (following Beck 1928)
  Degree of transparency
  Ornamental nature (bead, pendant,
    necklace, earring, object)
Number of pieces
Size of largest piece and smallest piece, if more than
  one (in order to give range): diameter (D)
  measured at widest point; length (L); and
  width (W).
Colour (following Munsell's *Soil Color Charts* and *A
  Color Notation*) (Luster, if distinctive)

Tests

Hardness (H), using Mohs' hardness kit (Streak, if
  distinctive)
Density: Specific Gravity (SG) using Gem Mini-lab liquids
  with densities 2.67 and 3.32 (Gem Instruments
  Corporation, Santa Monica, CA) and alpha-
  bromo-napthalene with a density of 1.6347
Chemical tests (described for each sample, i.e., acid
  reactions)
X-ray diffraction (using Guinier-de Wolff camera, Cu/Ni
  radiation)
Optical characteristics (i.e., Refractive Index (RI),
  pleochroism

Other Properties

Other physical or chemical properties determined by thin section or other analysis techniques (i.e., magnetic, metallic; or growth phenomena, such as twinning, colour zoning, or swirl marks).

Identification of sample(s)

Reg. No.: 46.001
Sample No.: 053
Site 45: Rom (?); Abb; Fat; Ayy-Mam; Mam and/or Ott
MC: short barrel
  opaque
  bead
Pieces:1
Size: D: 0.8 cm; L: 0.7 cm; D of hole: 0.1 cm
Colour: 5.0R 4/8, red
ID: glass

Reg. No. 46.002
Sample No. 053
Site 45: Rom (?); Abb; Fat; Ayy-Mam; Mam and/or Ott
mc: standard circular opaque, surface thick with decomposition
  bead
Number: 1
Size: D: 1.2 cm; L: 1.2 cm; D of hole: 0.3 cm
Colour: 10YR 8/2, white
ID: glass

Reg. No.: 46.003
Sample No.: 053
Site 45: Rom (?); Abb; Fat; Ayy-Mam; Mam and/or Ott
MC: long convex bicone
  opaque
  bead
Number: 1
Size: D: 0.4 cm; L: 0.6 cm; D of hole: 0.1 cm
Colour: 5.0G 4/4, green
ID: glass

Reg. No.: 46.004
Sample No.: 053
Site 45: Rom (?); Abb; Fat; Ayy-Mam; Mam and/or Ott
MC: short barrel
  translucent, worn
  bead
Number: 3 samples: 3 halves
Size: D: 0.9 cm; L: 0.8 cm; D of projected hole: 0.3 cm
Colours: 5.0B 6/6, blue
  5.0B 5/6, blue
  5.0PB 5/10, purple-blue
ID: glass

Reg. No.: 46.005
Sample No.: 053
Site 45: Rom (?); Abb; Fat; Ayy-Mam; Mam and/or Ott
MC: short barrel
  opaque, dull surface
  beads
Number: 6
Size: largest: D: 0.7 cm; L: 0.6 cm; D of hole: 0.3 cm
  smallest: D: 0.5 cm; L: 0.5 cm; D of hole: 0.2 cm
Colour: exterior 5.0RP 4/6, red purple
  interior 5YR 8/1, white
ID: glass

Reg. No.: 46.006
Sample No.: 053
Site 45: Rom (?); Abb; Fat; Ayy-Mam; Mam and/or Ott
MC: long cylinder
  opaque, dull surface
  beads
Number: 3
Size: largest: D: 0.5 cm; L: 1.5 cm; D of hole: 0.2 cm
  smallest: D: 0.4 cm; L: 1.4 cm; D of hole: 0.1 cm
Colour: 2 beads 5.0R 5/8, red
  1 bead 5.0R 4/6, red

ID: glass

Reg. No.:   46.007
Sample No.: 053
Site 45:   Rom (?); Abb; Fat; Ayy-Mam; Mam and/or Ott
MC: long barrel
             semitranslucent
             bead
Number: 1
Size: D: 1.1 cm; L: 1.3 cm; D of hole: 0.4 cm
Colour: 5.0Y 8/6, yellow
ID: glass

Reg. No.:   46.008
Sample No.: 053
Site 45:   Rom (?); Abb; Fat; Ayy-Mam; Mam and/or Ott
MC: long barrel
             opaque, worn
             bead
Number: 1
Size: D: 0.6 cm; L: 1.3 cm; D of hole: 0.2 cm
Colour: 5.0G 7/4, green
ID: glass

Reg. No.:   46.009
Sample No.: 053
Site 45:   Rom (?); Abb; Fat; Ayy-Mam; Mam and/or Ott
MC: long pear-shape
             semitranslucent
             bead
Number: 1
Size: D: 1.1 cm; L: 2.2 cm; D of hole: 0.3 cm
Colour: 5.0Y 8/4, yellow
ID: glass

Reg. No.:   46.010
Sample No.: 053
Site 45:   Rom (?); Abb; Fat; Ayy-Mam; Mam and/or Ott
MC: square long truncated cone
             semitranslucent
             bead
Number: 1
Size: D: 0.5 cm; L: 1.5 cm; D of hole: 0.2 cm
Colour: 5.0G 5/8, green
ID: glass

Reg. No.:   46.011
Sample No.: 053
Site 45:   Rom (?); Abb; Fat; Ayy-Mam; Mam and/or Ott
MC: pentagonal long cylinder
             opaque, worn, bubbly
             bead
Number: 1
Size: D: 0.6 cm; L: 2.2 cm; D of hole: 0.2 cm
Colour: 5.0PB 3/2, purple-blue
ID: glass

Reg. No.:   46.012
Sample No.: 053
Site 45:   Rom (?); Abb; Fat; Ayy-Mam; Mam and/or Ott
MC: long cylinder
             semitranslucent
             bead
Number: 1
Size: D: 0.2 cm; L: 2.6 cm; D of hole: 0.05 cm
Colour: 5.0BG 3/4, blue-green
ID: glass

Reg. No.:   46.013
Sample No.: 053
Site 45:   Rom (?); Abb; Fat; Ayy-Mam; Mam and/or Ott
MC: barrel disc with an extra large perforation
             semitranslucent, worn
             bead
Number: 1
Size: D: 1.3 cm; L: 0.4 cm; D of hole: 0.8 cm
Colour: 5.0YR 5/4, yellow-red
ID: glass

Reg. No.:   46.014
Sample No.: 053
Site 45:   Rom (?); Abb; Fat; Ayy-Mam; Mam and/or Ott
MC: polygonal
             opaque, some opalescence, worn
             bead
Number: 1
Size: D: 1.1 cm; L: 1.3 cm; D of hole: 0.2 cm
Colour: 5.0BG 4/6, blue-green
ID: glass

Reg. No.:   46.015
Sample No.: 053
Site 45:   Rom (?); Abb; Fat; Ayy-Mam; Mam and/or Ott
MC: cylinder disc with two convex ends,
             horizontal piercing
             opaque, dull, moulded
             bead
Number   4.5
Size: largest: D: 1.8 cm; L: 0.4 cm; D of hole: 0.1 cm
             smallest whole bead: D: 1.8 cm; L: 0.375; D of hole: 0.1 cm Munsell colour 5.0R 5/10, red
ID: glass

Reg. No.:   46.016
Sample No.: 053
Site 45:   Rom (?); Abb; Fat; Ayy-Mam; Mam and/or Ott
MC: circular
             semitranslucent, with dark spot near perforation
             bead
Number: 1
Size: D: 0.8 cm; L: 0.8 cm; D of hole: 0.2 cm
Colour: 2.5YR 4/8, red to 2.5YR 6/4, light reddish brown
ID: quartz (carnelian)

Reg. No.:   51.001
Sample No.: 054
Site 45:   Rom (?); Abb; Fat; Ayy-Mam; Mam and/or Ott
MC: short barrel
             semitranslucent
             bead
Number: 1
Size: D: 0.5 cm; L: 0.4 cm; D of hole: 0.2 cm

Colour:	5.0BG 4/4, blue-green
ID:	glass

Reg. No.:	67.001
Sample No.:	197
Site 120E:	EB IV; EB IVA; Ud
MC:	elliptical cylinder spacer
	opaque
	beads
Number:	5
Size:	largest;　　L: 7.5 cm; W: 0.7 cm; TH: 0.5 cm; D of each of 2 holes: 0.2 cm
	smallest;　　L: 6.2 cm; W: 0.7 cm; TH: 0.5 cm; D of each of 2 holes: 0.2 cm
Colour:	each bead an intimate mixture of white and grey;
	lightest; 10YR 8/1, white;
	darkest; 7.5YR 6/1, pinkish grey
Optical:	25x binocular microscope: cross-lamellar structure
Acid:	effervesces
X-ray Dif.:	aragonite, CaCO3 calcium carbonate, ASTM Card No. 5-0453
ID:	aragonite = thick-shelled, cross-lamellar structure mollusc

---

Reg. No.:	67.002
Sample No.:	197
Site 120E:	EB IV; EB IVA; Ud
MC:	short cylinder
	opaque
	bead
Number:	1
Size:	D: 0.5 cm; L: 0.3 cm; D of hole: 0.1 cm
Colour:	7.5YR 8/2, pinkish white -
Acid:	effervesces
X-ray dif.:	calcite, CaCO3 calcium carbonate, ASTM Card No. 5-0586
ID:	calcite

Reg. No.:	67.003
Sample No.:	197
Site 120E:	EB IV; EB IVA; Ud
MC:	elliptical cylinder spacer
	opaque
	fragments of beads
Number:	6
Size:	largest; L: 2.2 cm; W: 0.8 cm; TH: 0.5 cm;
	smallest; L: 0.6 cm; W: 0.5 cm; TH: 0.3 cm;
Colour:	each bead an intimate mixture of colours;
	lightest: 10YR 8/1, white
	darkest; 7.5YR 6/1, pinkish grey
Optical:	25x binocular microscope: cross-lamellar structure
Acid:	effervesces
ID:	aragonite (est.) = thick-shelled, cross-lamellar structure mollusc

---

Reg. No.:	72.001
Sample No.:	247
Site 149::	Nab-painted; Rom; Isl; Ud
MC:	short barrel
	semitranslucent
Number:	.5
Size:	D: 0.35 cm; L: 0.25 cm; D of projected hole: 0.3 cm
Colour:	5.0PB 4/10, purple-blue
Optical:	25x binocular microscope: conchoidal fracture; bubbles visible

ID:	glass (est.)

Reg. No.:	73.001
Sample No.:	-0-
Site 120E:	(sifted) EB IV, EB IVA; Ud
MC:	short cylinder
	opaque
	bead
Number:	1
Size:	D: 0.2 cm; L: 0.1 cm; D of hole: 0.1 cm
Colour:	intimate mixture of colours;
	7.5YR 6/6, reddish yellow
	7.5YR 7/4, pink
	7.5YR 5/2, brown
X-ray Dif.:	quartz, SiO2
	silicon dioxide, ASTM Card No. 5-0490
ID:	quartz

Reg. No.:	73.002
Sample No.:	-0-
Site 120E:	(sifted) EB IV; EB IVA; Ud
MC:	elliptical cylinder spacer
	opaque
	bead
Number:	1
Size:	L: 6.9 cm; W: 0.6 cm; TH: 0.5 cm; D of each of 2 holes: 0.2 cm
Colour:	10YR 8/2, white
Optical:	25x binocular microscope: cross-lamellar structure
Acid:	effervesces
ID:	aragonite (est.) = thick-shelled, cross-lamellar structure mollusc

---

Reg. No.:	73.003
Sample No.:	-0-
Site 120E:	(sifted) EB IV; EB IVA; Ud
MC:	elliptical cylinder spacer
	opaque
	fragments of beads
Number:	3
Size:	largest; L: 2.4 cm; W: 0.7 cm; TH: 0.3 cm
	smallest; L: 2.0 cm; W: 0.3 cm; TH: 0.3 cm
Colour:	each fragment an intimate mixture of white and grey;
	lightest; 10YR 8/1, white
	darkest; 7.5YR 6/1, pinkish grey
Optical:	25x binocular microscope: cross-lamellar structure
Acid:	effervesces
ID:	aragonite (est.) = thick-shelled, cross-lamellar structure mollusc

---

Reg. No.:	73.004
Sample No.:	-0-
Site 120E:	(sifted) B IV; EB IVA; Ud - convex truncated bicone disc
MC:	translucent
	beads
Number:	3
Size:	largest; D: 0.7 cm; L: 0.3 cm; D of hole: 0.1 cm
	smallest; D: 0.6 cm; L: 0.3 cm; D of hole: 0.1 cm
Colour:	10R 4/6, red
H:	>5
ID:	quartz variety carnelian (est.)

Reg. No.:	73.005

Sample No.: -0-
Site 120E: (sifted) EB IV; EB IVA; Ud
MC: tubular
opaque
beads
Number: 7
Size: largest; D: 0.5 cm; L: 0.5 cm; D of hole: 0.3 cm
smallest; D: 0.4 cm; L: 0.3 cm; D of hole: 0.2 cm
Colour: 10YR 8/2, white
Optical: 25x binocular microscope: ridges on surface
Acid: effervesces
ID: *Dentalium* shell fragments (est.)

Reg. No.: 73.006
Sample No.: -0-
Site 120E: (sifted) EB IV; EB IVA; Ud
MC: short cylinder
opaque
bead
Number: 1
Size: D: 0.2 cm; L: 0.1 cm; D of hole: 0.1 cm
Colour: 10YR 8/1, white
Acid: effervesces
X-ray Dif.: calcite, CaCO3 calcium carbonate, ASTM Card No. 5- 0586
ID: calcite

Reg. No.: 73.007
Sample No.: -0-
Site 120E: (sifted) EB IV; EB IVA; Ud
MC: short barrel
opaque
bead
Number: 1
Size: D: 0.4 cm; L: 0.3 cm; D of hole: 0.25 cm
Colour: 10YR 8/2, white
Acid: effervesces
X-ray Dif.: aragonite, CaCO3 calcium carbonate, ASTM Card No. 5- 0453
ID: aragonite

Reg. No.: 73.008
Sample No.: -0-
Site 120E: (sifted) EB IV; EB IVA; Ud
MC: short cylinder
opaque
beads
Number: 9
Size: largest; D: 0.4 cm; TH: 0.1 cm; D of hole: 0.1 cm
smallest; D: 0.2 cm; TH: 0.1 cm; D of hole: 0.05 cm
Colour: each bead an intimate mixture of colours;
7.5YR 6/6, reddish yellow
7.5YR 7/4, pink
7.5YR 5/2, brown
Optical: 25x binocular microscope: characteristics similar to 73.001 -
ID: quartz (est.)

Reg. No.: 73.009
Sample No.: -0-
Site 120E: (sifted) EB IV; EB IVA; Ud
MC: short cylinder
opaque
beads
No. of Pices: 163

Size: largest; D: 0.5 cm; L: 0.15 cm; D of hole: 0.1 cm (disc bead)
smallest; D: 0.2 cm; L: 0.1 cm; D of hole: 0.05 cm (short bead)
Colour: lightest; 10YR 8/1, white
darkest; 10YR 5/2, greyish brown
Optical: 25x binocular microscope: characteristics similar to 73.006
Acid: effervesces
ID: calcite (est.)

Reg. No.: 73.010
Sample No.: -0-
Site 120E: (sifted) EB IV; EB IVA; Ud
MC: short barrel
opaque
beads
Number: 7
Size: largest; D: 0.5 cm; L: 0.2 cm; D of hole: 0.35 cm
smallest; D: 0.4 cm; L: 0.3 cm; D of hole: 0.25 cm
Colour: 10YR 8/2, white
Acid: effervesces
ID: aragonite (est.)

Reg. No.: 84.001
Sample No.: 351
Site 211: Nab (=ERom); Rom; LRom; Byz; LByz; Um; Mod; Ud
MC: cylinder disc
translucent
bead
Number: 1
Size: D: 0.9 cm; L: 0.5 cm; D of hole: 0.3 cm
Colour: 5YR 4/6, yellowish red
Optical: 25x binocular microscope: conchoidal fractures
H: >5
ID: quartz variety carnelian (est.)

Reg. No.: 101.001
Sample No.: 398
Site 232:: Nab-painted; Rom; Byz; Isl; Mod; Ud
MC: short cylinder
opaque
bead
Number: 1
Size: D: 0.5 cm; L: 0.2 cm; D of hole: 0.2 cm
Colour: 5.0BG 6/4, blue-green
X-ray Dif.: quartz, SiO2 silicon dioxide, ASTM Card No. 5-0490
ID: quartz

TOTAL: 241 samples

Notes

1 Differing inventory lists have been printed in *Jericho* Vols. II and V (p. 800). A carnelian bead is included in both lists; however, Vol. V lists the shape as a barrel.

2 Refer to Woolley (1934: 238–248) regarding locations of bead on persons or clothing during the Early Bronze Age.

3 In the 19th century circular structures of stone in Southern Sinai were called *nawamis* by the Bedouin. The term now applies to all single structures (Bar-Yosef *et al.* 1977: 65).

14. Shells From the 1986 Season

by D. S. Reese

Eleven of the SGNAS sites surveyed in the 1986 season produced marine or fresh-water shell remains. Moreover, one site produced an ostrich eggshell fragment. Table 64 describes each shell or eggshell found. The general types of shells found and the relevant comparanda are discussed below.

Cowries, frequently with ground-down dorsi, e.g., the samples from Site 45, al-Rujoum, are known from numerous Near Eastern sites (Reese 1986: 328–30, 332, fig. 104: 2, 5, Pl. 39: b left, d). In Jordan, they are known from Bab al-Dhra', Ghrareh, Buseirah, Umm al-Biyara, Tell Hesban, Mount Nebo, Dhuweila, Tell al-Mazar, Deir 'Alla, Tell al-Sa'idiyeh, and the Baq'ah Valley tombs.

Glycymeris holed at the umbo, e.g., the sample from Site 1, Tawahin al-Sukkar, are known from a number of Jordanian sites. These sites include Ghrareh, Buseirah, Tawilan, Umm al-Biyara, and Dhuweila.

Holed *Nerita*, e.g., the sample from Site 75, ancient Feifa, are known from numerous Near Eastern sites (Reese 1986: 327, 331, fig. 104: 3, Pl. 39: b right). In Jordan, they are known from Bab al-Dhra', Ghrareh, Buseirah, Petra, Beidha, Tawilan, Dhuweila, Jebel al-Jill 14, Wadi Jubayid J2, Tell al-Sa'idiyeh, Teleilat al-Ghassul, 'Ain Ghazal, and the Baq'ah Valley tombs.

The shell 'spacer beads' from Site 120E, an EB IV tomb, are a worked shell type not previously reported from Jordan (fig. 33E) (Photo 28). However, very similar examples, along with the debris from their manufacture, have been found at Beer Resisim in the Central Negev Highlands (Cohen and Dever 1978a and b; 1979; 1981). Beer Resisim is located, on a straight line, about 85 km to the southwest of Site 120E and about 140 km northwest of the Red Sea (fig. 31).

The shell spacers at Beer Resisim were found in the EB IV–MB I Building 4 (Cohen and Dever 1979: 51, fig. 12) and are said to be 80–100 mm long. The debris from the shell manufacture allows us to identify the shell used as *Lambis truncata sebae* (Kiener, 1843), the Spider conch or Scorpion shell. Such an identification would not be possible based solely on the finished examples from Site 120E.

The ostrich eggshell from Site 2, al-Safi, is most likely to come from an Early Bronze tomb. Ostrich eggshells are known from numerous Near Eastern and Mediterranean sites. Live ostriches were still found in Jordan into the 1950's (Reese 1985: 374–78).

Early Bronze Bab al-Dhra' produced at least two holed eggshells: one with a central hole and two additional holes; and another with a central hole and four additional holes. The additional holes were probably for the attachment of a spout. These ostrich eggshells are on display in the Karak Museum, Jordan.

An EB I (Dunand 1945: Pl. IIb, d) or 'Enéolithique Recent' (Dunand 1973: Pl. CLIX (T. 272), 18553) tomb at Byblos produced a complete ostrich eggshell with a large hole for a spout and about 10 smaller holes around it. These additional holes were probably for the attachment of a spout.

Table 64 Shells from the 1986 Season of the SGNAS (unless otherwise noted, distances given are by road to 'Aqaba; measurements are in millimeters.)

Site 1 Tawahin al-Sukkar (Sugar Mill), from around upper structure; ca. 120 km from the Mediterranean Sea;
Pottery reading: EB II–III; Nab; Byz; LByz–Um; LAbb/Fat; Mam; Mod; Ud;
Sample #3, object #58: 1 *Glycymeris* (Dog-cockle) – water-worn, 32 x 31.75 mm, large hole at umbo 9 x 5.5 mm.

Site 2 al-Safi (mainly an Early Bronze cemetery);
Pottery reading: EB I; EB IB; EB II–III; EB; Mam; Mod;
Sample #6, object #16: 1 ostrich eggshell fragment.

Site 12 Raikes' Site 'A' (some shell is from the southwest side of the summit area and is associated with bone); ca. 150 km from the Red Sea;
Pottery reading: EB; EB IV (?); EB IVB–MB I (?); Ud;
Sample #24, object #28:
fragments of 9 small *Conus* (Cone shell) – holed at the apex.

Site 27 al-Jor (reservoir);
191 km from the Red Sea;
Pottery reading: Byz–Um; Isl, poss Mam; Mod; Ud;
Sample #38, object #34:
1 gastropod – fragment.

Site 45 al-Rujoum (ancient town-site and modern cemetery);
192 km from the Red Sea;
Pottery reading: Rom (?); Abb; Fat; Ayy–Mam; Mam and/or Ott;
Sample #53, object #44:
3 *Cypraea moneta* (Linnaeus, 1758) (Money cowrie) – all with a ground-down dorsum: 17.25 x 12, ht 6.25, open dorsum 11.5 x 7.5; 15 x 12, ht 5.5, open dorsum 9 x 6.25; 15 x 10.25, ht 5, open dorsum 8.5 x 5;
6 gastropods – 16, 14 (burnt), 13.25.

Site 46 Deir 'Ain 'Abata (monastery/church complex);
193 km from the Red Sea;
Pottery reading: Nab; Rom; Byz (E and L) (predominant); Byz (?); Um (?); Abb; Ott; Ud;
Sample #90, object #41:
1 *Turbo radiatus* (Gmelin, 1791) (Turban shell) – 47 x 47.

Site 64 (campsite);
ca. 190 km from the Red Sea;
Pottery reading: Ud;
Sample #100, object #65:
1 *Cypraea annulus* (Linnaeus, 1758) (Money cowrie, Gold-ringer) – unmodified, 16.75 x 12.25, ht 8.

Site 66 (sherd scatter);
Pottery reading: Nab; Rom; Byz (E and L); LByz–Um;
Abb–import from Mesopotamia; Isl; Mod; Ud;
Sample #111; object #54:
1 *Melanopsis praemorsa* (Linnaeus, 1758) (freshwater gastropod) – unmodified.

Site 75 ancient Feifa, western segment, saddle between east and west mounds (ancient town, village and/or fort (?) and cemetery);
ca. 180 km from the Red Sea;
Pottery reading: PN; PN–Chal; Chal; Chal/EB; EB I; EB IIB; EB IVA; EB; Iron I–II; Iron II; Iron Age – Edomite; Rom; LByz–Um; Fat/Ayy; Isl; Ott; Ud;
Sample #117; object #64:
1 *Nerita albicilla* (Linnaeus, 1758) (Nerite) – 18 x 13.25, ground-down hole on body with ground-down area 10 x 7.5 and hole 3.25.

Site 120E (tomb in EB IV cemetery);
ca. 170 km from the Red Sea;
Pottery reading: EB IV; EB IVA; Ud;
Sample #197; object #67:
6 complete and 9 fragments of worked *Lambis* 'spacer beads' (fig. 13.3E). Measurements of some of these are given here:

length width	*max. diameter*	*hole*
75	7.25	2–2.75
67.75	7	2–2.25
67	7	2–2.25
63.25	7	2–2.25
61.25	7	2–2.25
23+	7.25	2
19+	7	2.25
18.75+	6.75	2

Sample #197; object #73:
1 complete and 1 fragment worked *Lambis* spacers:

70	6.25	2–2.25
7	2	

7 *Dentalium* sp. shell beads, 3–5 long.

Site 174D (tomb in EB IV cemetery or village site [?]);
167 km for the Red Sea;
Pottery reading: EB IV; Ud;
Sample #298; object #75:
1 *Trachycardium 'flavum'* (Linnaeus, 1758) (Golden cockle) – broken, W 43.

Site 211 Khirbet al-Dahal (village site);
162 km from the Red Sea;
Pottery reading: Nab (=ERom); Rom; LRom; Byz (predominant); LByz; Um; Mod; Ud;
Sample #353; object #89:
large gastropod (possibly *Lambis*) columella fragment – preserved L 37.5, preserved W 20.

15. Summary and Conclusions

by B. MacDonald

Introduction

A comparison of the results of the SGNAS with those of the WHS (MacDonald *et al.* 1988) is informative. This comparison leads to a knowledge of the archaeological similarities and differences between the two areas. Moreover, it will give a preliminary archaeological history of an area of Southern Jordan which is greater than that of either the WHS or the SGNAS taken individually.

The WHS settlement patterns

The WHS reported evidence of human presence in the area beginning with the Lower Paleolithic Period. It collected lithic materials spanning the Lower Paleolithic to the end of the Early Bronze Period (ca. 500,000–2000 B.C.). It organized the Paleolithic materials into seven, time – stratigraphic, analytical units, namely, the Lower/Middle Paleolithic (undifferentiated); the Middle Paleolithic; the Middle/Upper Paleolithic (combined); the Upper Paleolithic; the Upper/Epipaleolithic (combined); the Epipaleolithic/Prepottery Neolithic (combined); and the Prepottery Neolithic.

The WHS found little evidence of Pottery Neolithic presence in the area with the exception of three sites in the western universe. The number of Chalcolithic sites seems to indicate an increase in population at this time. This trend towards increased population continues into the EB I Period, however, it does not continue into EB II–IV. There are, however, sites from all these periods in the WHS territory.

The Middle Bronze Period seems to be one in which virtually nothing was taking place, as far as human presence is concerned, in the WHS territory. The Late Bronze is also poorly represented in the area. However, there is evidence for the resumption of settlement at the very end of this period.

There are further indications of population increase during the Iron I Period. There does appear to be permanent, albeit small, settlements along the south bank of Wadi al-Hasa by the 12th century B.C. but only in the western universe. The population increase seems to accelerate during the Iron II Period. However, even during this period, Wadi al-'Ali seems to be the eastern frontier for sedentary and pastoral occupation.

On the basis of the present archaeological data, it is impossible to determine whether or not there was continuity in the territory between the end of the Iron II Period and the Hellenistic Period. The latter period shows evidence of only a slight population.

Nabataean Period sites are more numerous than those from any other period in the WHS territory. The WHS found sites from this period throughout the area and especially in the wadis. This is especially true in the western and central universes. However, even in the eastern universe there are important Nabataean forts and/or caravanserais. Roman Period sites are also found throughout the territory. Parts of the *Via Nova Trajana* (WHS Site 429) are well preserved in the central universe.

Next to the Nabataean Period, the Byzantine Period seems to be, on the basis of the number of sites, the one of greatest population in the area. However, the settlement pattern is changed from the previous one. Byzantine presence is best documented in the western universe, especially on the plateau. The Byzantines do not appear to have made as much use of the wadis as did the Nabataeans. The WHS found very little evidence of Byzantine presence in the central universe while in the eastern universe it is generally associated with Nabataean–Roman sites.

Early Islamic evidence is almost completely absent from the WHS study area. There are, however, several major Ayyubid/Mamluk sites in the western universe of the WHS territory at the beginning of the Late Islamic Period. Ottoman–Modern period sites, especially in the form of sherd scatters, are found throughout the area. Moreover, major village sites from the period are found in the western universe and in the eastern universe there are Ottoman Period village sites associated, most probably, with the pilgrimage route to Mecca.

The SGNAS settlement patterns

The earliest occupational evidence in the SGNAS territory is attributed to the Lower/Middle Paleolithic Period. This period is represented by only one site and that is in the southern-most portion of the survey area, that is, in the Wadi Fidan region. Middle Paleolithic sites are also few in number and are limited in space. These sites, too, are restricted to the southern segment of the territory. The explanation for the absence of sites further north in the survey territory probably lies in the levels of Lake Lisan during the Paleolithic Periods. Sites of an Upper Paleolithic or Epi-Paleolithic character are absent from the entire survey region. There is, thus, little evidence of early Paleolithic presence in the territory. The Prepottery Neolithic is represented by eight sites in the SGNAS region. It is during this period that there is evidence for occupation in the area north of the Wadi Fidan region. Besides Wadi Fidan, the SGNAS collected Prepottery Neolithic artifacts in Wadi Feifa and Wadi Madsus al-Shamali. However, in the latter area, the

Prepottery Neolithic is represented by a single point fragment. Pottery Neolithic Period sites are confined to the same regions, i.e., to Wadis Fidan and Feifa. The Neolithic sites in Wadi Feifa are the first sites located in areas considerably below sea level, ca. Minus 295 metres.

Chalcolithic Period lithic sites are concentrated in three areas, namely, in Wadis Feifa, al-Dahal, and Fidan. The SGNAS collected ceramic material from this period in these three areas as well as throughout the survey territory. In other words, the SGNAS collected Chalcolithic sherds from the northern to southern extremity of the survey territory.

Occupation in the survey area appears to intensify during the Chalcolithic/Early Bronze Period. The SGNAS found evidence of Chalcolithic/Early Bronze presence, in the form of both lithics and sherds, from Wadi al-Hasa in the north to Wadi Fidan in the south. The heaviest concentration is in Wadis Feifa, Umruq, al-Dahal, al-Ghuweib, and Fidan. Chalcolithic/Early Bronze presence is particularly abundant in the latter wadi. Not only is there occupation throughout the territory, but the number of sites increases as well. Many of the stone enclosures, e.g., Sites 236 (Photo 30) and 240 (Photo 31), which the SGNAS surveyed may date to the Chalcolithic/Early Bronze Periods. It is also during this period that slag is associated for the first time with lithics and sherds. This evidence comes from Wadi Fidan. There is the possibility, therefore, that copper mining and smelting activity began in this and neighbouring regions during the periods under discussion.

The Early Bronze, too, is represented by both lithic and ceramic sites. Here again, as for the previous period, evidence of human presence spans the region from Wadi al-Hasa to Wadi Fidan. The EB I-III presence is confined, on the basis of the available evidence, to the Southern Ghors. Although there is evidence to the north, e.g., at Bab al-Dhra' and Numeira, for settlement during the EB I–III Periods, there is not sufficient data from the work of the SGNAS to conclude to the presence of habitation sites in the territory under discussion. There is, nevertheless, evidence for large cemeteries in the region. For example, EB I is represented by cemeteries at both al-Safi, Site 2, and ancient Feifa, Sites 75 and 76. Moreover, there is abundant evidence throughout the territory for burials dating from the EB IV Period. This is especially true for the Wadi Khuneizir-Wadi al-Nukhbar region. This EB IV presence was one of the major surprises of the SGNAS. During this period, as in the previous one, there may have been mining and smelting activity in the SGNAS territory as well.

The SGNAS identified neither Middle or Late Bronze Period sites in the survey area. The only exception to this is the possibility of MB I sherds at one site in Wadi al-Dahal. Thus, the area seems to have been largely depopulated during these periods.

The situation changes at the beginning of the Iron Age. The SGNAS found Iron I Period sherds in the area as far north as Wadi al-Hasa and as far south as Wadi al-Ghuweib. However, it is in the latter wadi that the SGNAS surveyed the highest concentration of Iron I sites. Iron I Period presence appears to be associated in this wadi with mining and smelting activities. On the basis of the available evidence, it appears that such wadis as al-Hasa, Umm Jufna, Feifa, Umruq, Khuneizir, al-Dahal, al-Ghuweib, and Fidan were extremely important to the people living in the area during the Iron II Period. Wadi al-Dahal, which leads up to the plateau near Buseira, seems to have been a major route for communication between the plateau to the east and areas of the Southern Ghors, Northeast 'Arabah, and the regions to the west and northwest during the periods under discussion. There is the possibility that there were a number of fortresses and/or watchtowers in the Southern Ghors during the Iron II Period. Moreover, there are indications of increased activity at the mining and smelting sites in the survey territory during this period. Natural resources, e.g., copper-manganese ores, were probably extensively exploited during the entire Iron Age Period.

The sites at which the SGNAS found Hellenistic Period pottery are all located in the central segment of the survey territory, i.e., in the area between Wadis Umm Jufna and al-Tilah or immediately southeast of the Dead Sea. The question can justifiably be asked as to whether or not these sites were in some way involved in the mining of bitumen from the Dead Sea? There are major Late Hellenistic-Early Roman Period sites in the survey territory. The Nabataeans probably carried out agriculture, trade, and the mining of bitumen in the area. It is hard to believe that the Nabataeans would not have made use of the water of such wadis as al-Hasa, Feifa, Khuneizir, al-Tilah, and Fidan for irrigation purposes. The evidence for such activity within the Southern Ghors and Northeast 'Arabah in which the SGNAS worked is strengthened by evidence from areas to the north in the Dead Sea Valley as well as in the areas to the east and west. Moreover, there is evidence of copper mining and smelting during the 1st to the 4th centuries A.D. in the Wadi Feinan region immediately to the south of the survey territory.

Byzantine Period sites are the most numerous of any period sites in the survey territory. These sites range from very small sherd scatters to village and/or town sites. These sites are found in both the Southern Ghors and in the Northeast 'Arabah. Once again, during this period, the wadis were extensively used by the Byzantines. Excavations of the major Byzantine sites in the Southern Ghors as well as the Byzantine hamlet/village sites in the Northeast 'Arabah will greatly increase our knowledge of the function of these sites, why so many of them appear to be one period sites, and why the ones in the Northeast 'Arabah are located in such an arid zone.

Whitcomb's study of four major Islamic sites in the Southern Ghors indicates that the area was not an unpleasant backwater in the Islamic Periods. The ceramics which Whitcomb studied from Tawahin al-Sukkar, Site 1, indicates that it was a sugar mill in use during the Early Islamic 2 or Late Abbasid or Fatimid Periods. As for Khirbet Sheikh 'Isa and al-Rujoum, Sites 4 and 45 respectively, there was a settlement at the former site during the Early Islamic 1 Period. However, during the Early Islamic 2 Period, the new urban centre of Zughar was founded at al-Rujoum. After 500–600 years of occupation, according to Whitcomb, the settlement was transferred to the modern town of al-Safi. Further south, there are ceramic wares of the Early Islamic 1 and 2 and Middle Islamic 2 Periods at Qasr Feifa, Site 91. The entire area of the Southern Ghors appears to have been a fertile region for the growing and processing of sugar cane and indigo during at least the periods discussed above. There is ceramic evidence for human presence in the survey territory during the Ottoman Period. This presence is supported by the eye-witness accounts of the explorers in the area during the 19th century who speak of a village in the neighbourhood of Wadi al-Hasa.

A study of the glass which the SGNAS collected complements the dating provided by the analysis of the ceramics. Moreover, the study of the glass sherds often provides an indication of the function of a particular site.

An analysis of the jewellery which the SGNAS collected makes an important contribution to the understanding of the people who lived in the survey area. Several samples support the early age of one of the sites. A more indepth study of the materials led to a correction of a field identification, namely, from ivory to shell for the spacer beads. Moreover, this study, along with the study of the shells, gives some indications of the minerals which the people living and/or buried in or passing through the area had at their disposal. It also indicates the areas outside the region with which the people had contact.

Comparison of the two surveys

It must be noted that the WHS and SGNAS differ in several respects. Both include several different environmental zones. The WHS territory is much larger in area than that of the SGNAS. With the exception of its southern extremity, the SGNAS territory is below sea level. The WHS territory, on the other hand, is at some points over 1200 m above sea level. The WHS territory depends much more on rainfall than irrigation for the growing/growth of food for human and animal consumption. The SGNAS depends almost entirely on irrigation for the growing of crops. Such was probably true for the past several millennia. The climate in both areas also differs sharply. A comparison of winter and summer temperatures in the two areas shows a marked contrast.

One further difference between the two surveys is the length of the infield seasons. The WHS was in the field almost twice as long as was the SGNAS, namely, four versus two infield seasons.

As regards the SGNAS area, lithic materials, with the exception of the later lithic periods, i.e., the

Neolithic–Early Bronze Periods, are confined to the Northeast 'Arabah in the SGNAS territory. This is the area which is at or just above sea level. Earlier lithic materials are not found in the Southern Ghors. As has been pointed out previously, the probable explanation for this is the various levels of Lake Lisan during the Paleolithic Period. The WHS shows evidence of human occupation during almost the entire Paleolithic Period. This occupation is especially impressive during the Middle Paleolithic Period. This is a major contrast between the findings of the two surveys. On the other hand, the Pottery Neolithic and Chalcolithic Periods are well attested in both the WHS and SGNAS territories.

The EB I is evidenced in both territories. However, the SGNAS territory is characterized by at least two major cemeteries, namely, at al-Safi, Site 2, and ancient Feifa, Sites 75 and 76, from the EB I Period. Such is not the case in the WHS territory. However, further investigation, especially in the form of excavations, could lead to a change in this information. The EB II–III Periods are only slightly attested in both areas. Such is not the case for the EB IV Period. There is very little evidence of EB IV presence in the WHS territory. However, the EV IV presence in the SGNAS territory is amply documented, especially in the form of cemeteries and/or burials. There is no firm evidence of settlement sites in the SGNAS area during the EB IV Period. The contrast between EB IV presence in both surveys is another major contrast between the WHS and SGNAS.

Both the WHS and SGNAS turned up little to nothing of Middle Bronze–Late Bronze presence. This finding is generally in keeping with pre-1980 archaeological evidence for Southern Jordan.

The Iron Age is attested in both areas. The Iron I and II presence in the WHS territory appears to be tied to both sedentary and pastoral activities. The habitation sites are located in the western universe only. The SGNAS, on the other hand, shows the strongest evidence of Iron I–II presence in association with the smelting sites of Wadi al-Ghuweib. However, there is strong evidence of Iron II presence associated with architectural sites, especially possible watchtowers, in the Southern Ghors.

The Classical Period is well represented in both areas. All periods indicate such activities as farming, nomadic existence, and trade. Moreover, the smelting of copper from the Northeast 'Arabah and the mining of bitumen from the Dead Sea in the Southern Ghors are attested if not in the archaeological then in the literary record. A segment of the *Via Nova Triana* passes through the WHS territory. There were undoubtedly major routes of communication going in north–south and east–west directions in the SGNAS territory during the Classical Period.

The Byzantine Period is very well documented in both areas. It appears on the basis of the presence of hamlet/village and/or town sites that agriculture was a main activity of the Byzantine inhabitants of both areas. Moreover, both areas attest the ecclesiastical character of Byzantine society.

Early Islamic presence, especially during the Umayyad–Fatimid Periods (Early Islamic 1–Middle Islamic 1) is virtually absent from the WHS territory. However, such is not the case in the Southern Ghors where these periods are represented especially at sites associated with the growing and processing of sugar cane and indigo. This activity continues into the succeeding period, i.e., the Ayyubid–Mamluk Period (Middle Islamic 2–Late Islamic 1). Evidence for Ottoman presence in the two territories is also attested.

It is not unlikely that transhumance between the areas covered by the WHS and SGNAS took place throughout the millennia. In the area of the Southern Ghors, the easiest access to the highlands to the east is by way of Wadis Feifa and Umruq. Further south, there appears to have been access by means of Wadi al-Dahal in particular. Access by means of other wadis of the SGNAS would have been possible although not easy. The most probable scenario would be for pastoralists to spend the late spring, summer, and early fall months on the plateau to the east and to come down into the Southern Ghors and Northeast 'Arabah for the winter months when the temperature is cold on the plateau but almost ideal in the Southern Ghors and Northeast 'Arabah. The wadis which the SGNAS surveyed give evidence of use during most of the periods of human occupation documented by both surveys. Moreover, this transhumance would not have been limited to the plateau to the east and the area of the Dead Sea Rift. A comparison of archaeological evidence from the SGNAS with that from Southern Judea and the Negev shows that there was transhumance to the west as well. This evidence is abundantly clear for such periods as EB IV, Iron II, the Classical, and the Byzantine Periods in particular.

The SGNAS's findings at Khirbet Sheikh 'Isa, Site 4, did not turn up either Iron Age or Byzantine sherds. Thus, the SGNAS found no evidence that the site is either biblical or Byzantine Zoara. However, King *et al.* report finding Byzantine but no Iron Age sherds at the site (1987: 448, 456). Whitcomb thinks that the numerous column drums would tend to confirm, more than any other artifact, the traditional identification of this site with Byzantine Zoara.

The ceramic evidence from al-Safi, Feifa, and Qasr al-Tilah are not sufficient evidence for locating Roman Zoara, Praesidium, and Toloah respectively at these sites (Abel 1967). However, the evidence which the SGNAS collected at these sites is not a rejection of such locations for these sites.

The Church of St. Lot of the Madaba Map is not, at this writing, definitely located. However, the excavations of Politis (1988; 1989; 1990) at SGNAS Site 46, Deir 'Ain 'Abata, are helping in the location of this important Byzantine Period site.

Although these are very different environmental zones, there was surely contact throughout the centuries. There would have been contact in the past just as there is today. And, as Harlan has pointed out, the water resources of the Southern Ghors and the

Northeast 'Arabah are dependent on rainfall in the highlands to the east. And so much in the SGNAS territory is dependent on rainfall.

In concluding this section, it can be stated that there are many similarities and some differences, archaeologically speaking, between the territories covered by the WHS and the SGNAS. Excavations will lead to greater precision in the archaeological histories of both areas.

Undetermined ceramics and sites

There are always lithics, sherds, and glass in any survey collection with are undetermined. This means that the individuals who studied these sherds were unable to identify them. However, there is the possibility that other individuals would be able to assign them a definite or probable date. For this reason, all the lithics, sherds, and glass of the SGNAS are in storage for future study by interested individuals. As has been noted in the introduction to this report, the lithics are at Arizona State University, the sherds at the Department of Antiquities Museum in Karak, and the glass at the Oriental Institute, University of Chicago.

Moreover, there are always sites to which a survey team cannot assign, on the basis of the available data, a period(s) or function(s). For example, many of the stone enclosures in the SGNAS territory yielded artifacts, especially lithics and sherds, from several different periods. Thus, it would seem that the architectural remains at these sites could date to one, several, or more of the periods represented by the lithics and sherds which the SGNAS collected. On the other hand, they could date to none. Sites 236 (Photo 30) and 240 (Photo 31) are good examples. The ceramic reading for the former is 'Byzantine, probable' while the reading for the latter is 'Iron II (?), Nabataean (?), and Undetermined.' But it is possible that the enclosures date to none of the periods represented by the ceramic evidence. They could, indeed, even date to a period prior to the introduction of pottery into this part of Jordan. Again, the ceramic evidence from Sites 77 (Photo 10) and 112 (Photo 32), aqueducts in Wadis Feifa and Khuneizir respectively, is not conclusive. The ceramic readings for the former is 'Early Bronze, Islamic (?), and Undetermined.' The SGNAS found no ceramics associated with the latter. Excavations could help greatly in the identification of the periods in which these structures were built and used.

Continuing the work of archaeological surveying

Once the work of archaeological surveying has ended and the process of publication of the results has begun to be circulated, then the further work of excavation begins. As in the case of the WHS (MacDonald *et al.* 1988), so in the case of the SGNAS (MacDonald, *et al.* 1987; MacDonald, Clark, and Neeley 1988;

MacDonald and Politis 1988), the dissemination of the findings has already led to excavations in the survey area. Excavations currently in progress at such sites as Site 46, Deir 'Ain 'Abata (Politis 1988, 1989, 1990); Sites 75, 76, ancient Feifa, and Site 141, Abu Irshareibeh (by The Southeastern Dead Sea Plain Expedition), and Sites 12 and 14 (Adams 1991) is already adding greatly to the information contained in this report on the archaeological history of the Southern Ghors and Northeast 'Arabah of Jordan. Moreover, it is the hope that the publication of this report will lead to further excavation of sites in the

SGNAS territory as well as more indepth survey of the areas covered by the survey, especially those areas which the SGNAS covered only superficially. One such area, as pointed out in Chapter 1, is the area in the hills to the east of the survey territory or the area between that covered by the SGNAS and the WHS.

The publication of this report will lead to greater interest in the area which the SGNAS surveyed. This interest will undoubtedly lead to more surveying and excavations in the area as well as in neighbouring areas.

Photographs

Photograph 1   JVA camp at Mazra'a; looking west.

Photograph 3   Site 123, rockshelter, on east side of Wadi Fidan.

163

Photograph 4   Site 75, ancient Feifa; looking northwest.

Photograph 5   Site 108, Rujm Khuneizir; looking northeast.

Photograph 6   Robbed, cist tomb at Site 108, Rujm Khuneizir.

Photograph 7   Site 120E, robbed tomb; looking northwest.

Photograph 8   One of many structures at Site 141, Abu Irshareibeh; looking west.

Photograph 2   Site 9, rockshelter, on east side of Wadi Fidan.

Photograph 9   One of many structures at Site 141, Abu Irshareibeh; looking southwest.

Photograph 10   Site 77, aqueduct and milling structures (?) on north side of Wadi Feifa.

Photograph 11   Site 73, Rujm Umm Jufna; looking northeast.

Photograph 12   Site 94, Rujm Umruq; looking southeast.

Photograph 13   Site 6, Umm al-Tawabin; looking northeast.

Photograph 14   Circular structures within enclosure wall; west side of Site 6, Umm al-Tawabin; looking west.

Photograph 15   Agricultural fields and Impresit Construction Company camp; looking northwest from Site 46.

Photograph 16   Agricultural fields and Impresit Construction Company; looking west from Site 46.

Photograph 17   SGNAS team members at Site 46, Deir 'Ain 'Abata.

Photograph 18   Remnants of arches at Site 46, Deir 'Ain 'Abata; looking west.

Photograph 19   West exterior wall at Site 46, Deir 'Ain 'Abata; looking northeast.

Photograph 20   Architectural fragments at Site 46, Deir 'Ain 'Abata.

Photograph 21   Rectangular structure at east end of Site 233, Khirbet al-Hassiya South; looking west.

Photograph 22   Site 228; looking north.

Photograph 23   Milling stone at Site 91, Feifa village.

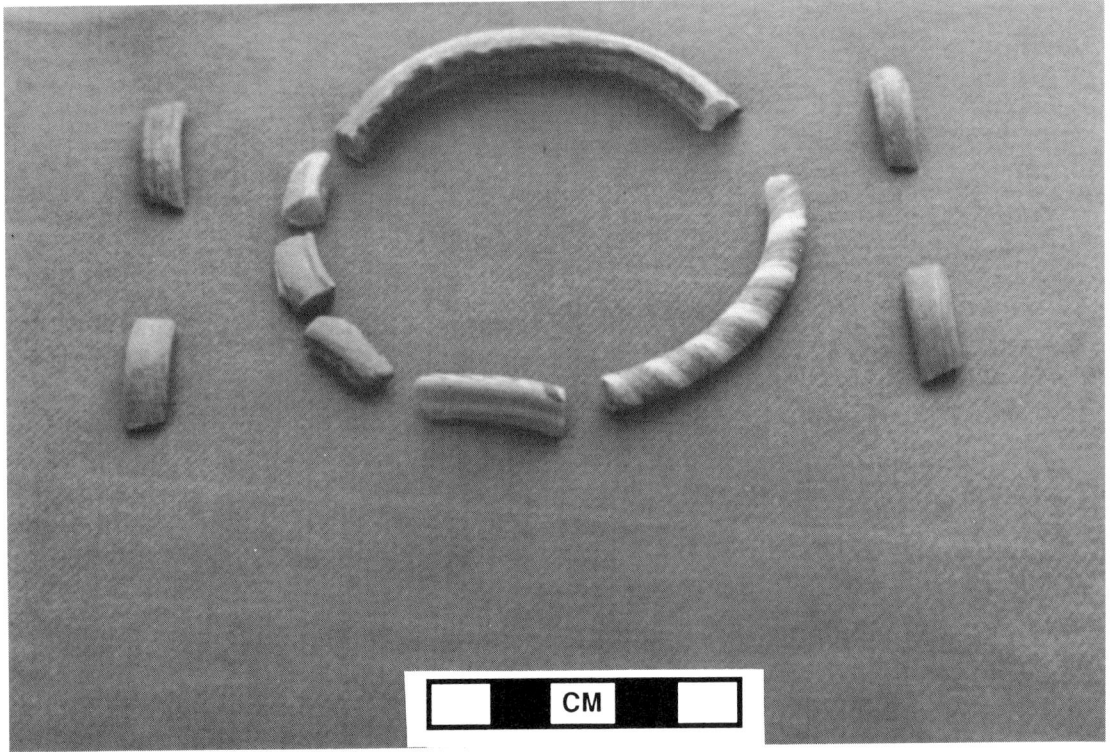

Photograph 24   Bracelet fragments from Site 45, al-Rujoum.

Photograph 25   Site 1, Tawahin al-Sukkar; looking southwest.

Photograph 26   Site 27, al-Jor, remnant of reservoir; looking north.

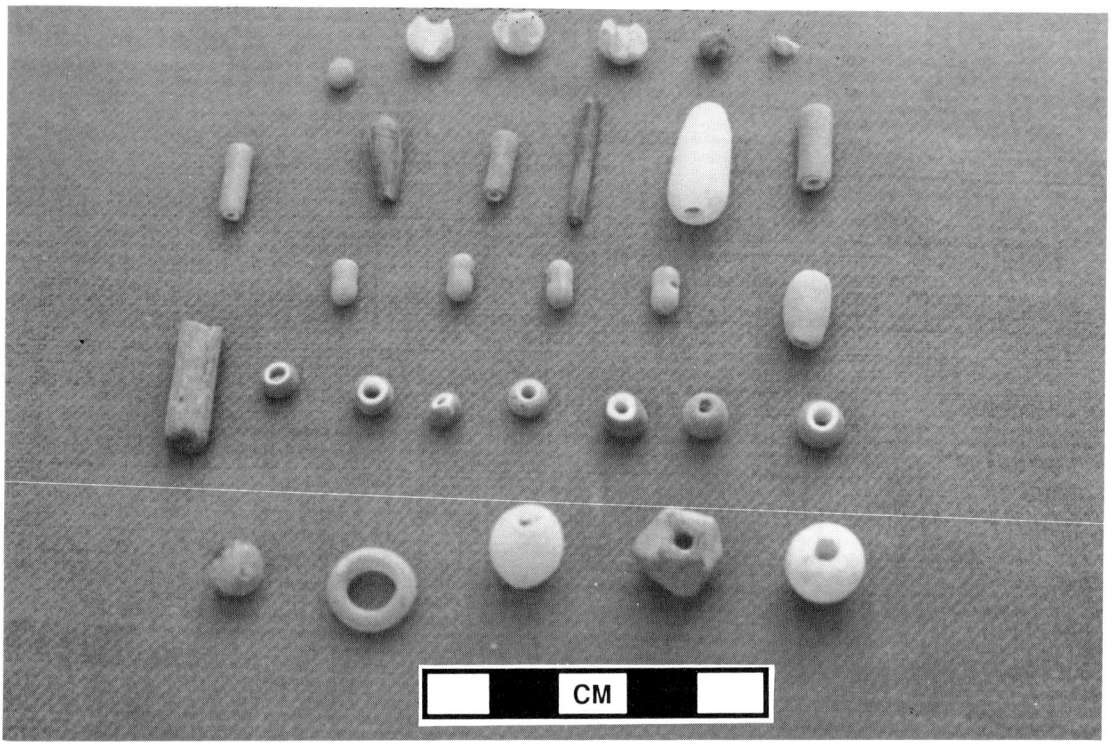

Photograph 27   Beads from various sites.

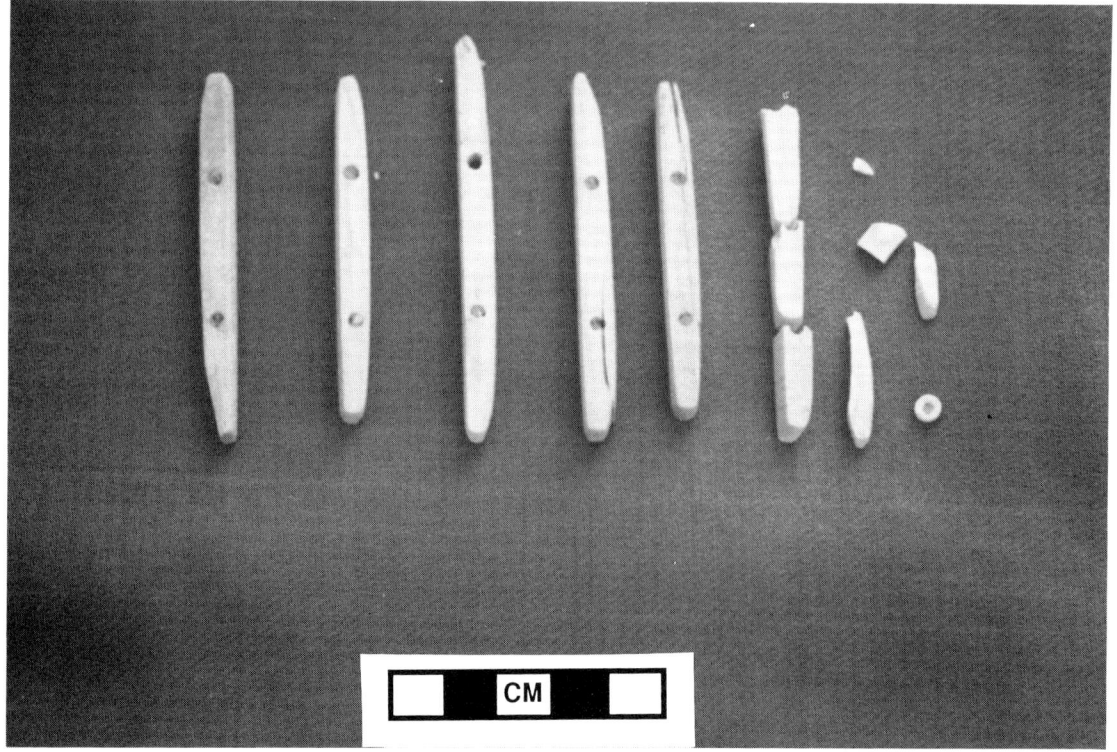

Photograph 28   Spacer beads from Site 120E.

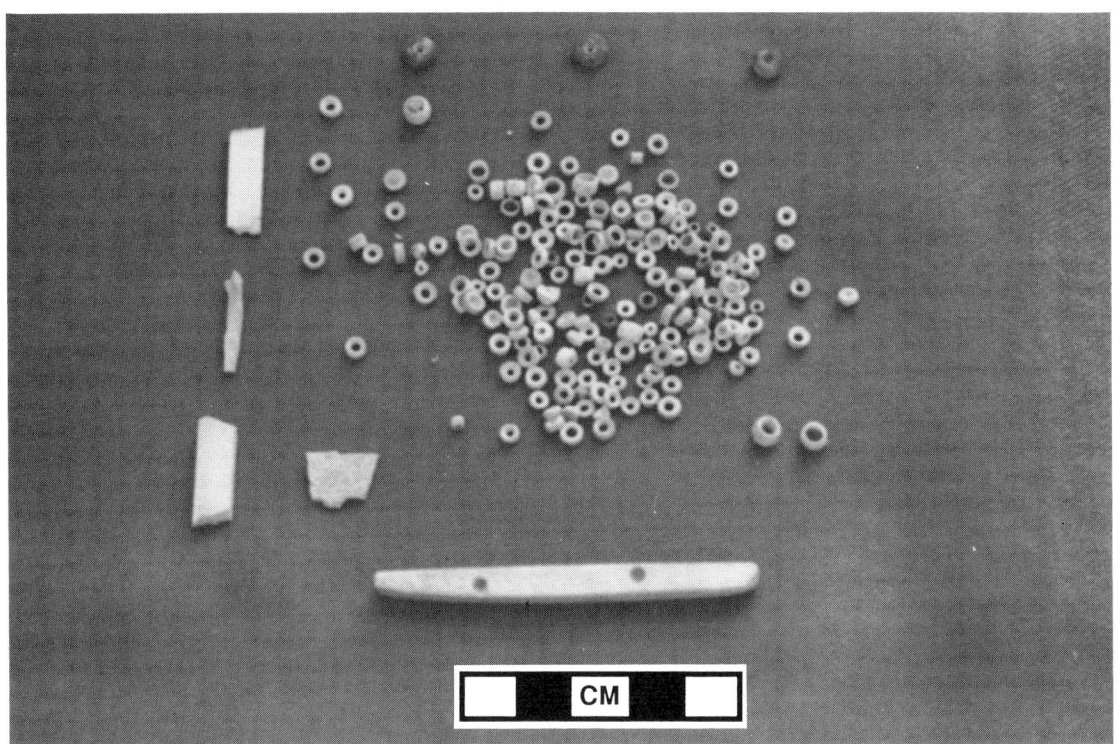

Photograph 29   Spacer beads (mostly fragments) and small beads from Site 120E.

Photograph 30   Site 236, stone enclosure; looking north.

Photograph 31   Site 240, stone enclosure; looking west.

Photograph 32   Site 112, aqueduct on east side of Wadi Khuneizir.

Plates 1–38*

* The pottery reading given in parenthesis in the notes on Plates 6–28 is from the author(s) cited in the notes, e.g., Plate 6, No. 1, Site 29, Sample 73 is read as PNB by Kenyon and Holland 1982: fig. 32.18. The pottery reading given in square brackets in the notes on the plates is from 'Amr, e.g., Plate 6, No. 2, Site 29, Sample 73 is read as Chal by 'Amr.

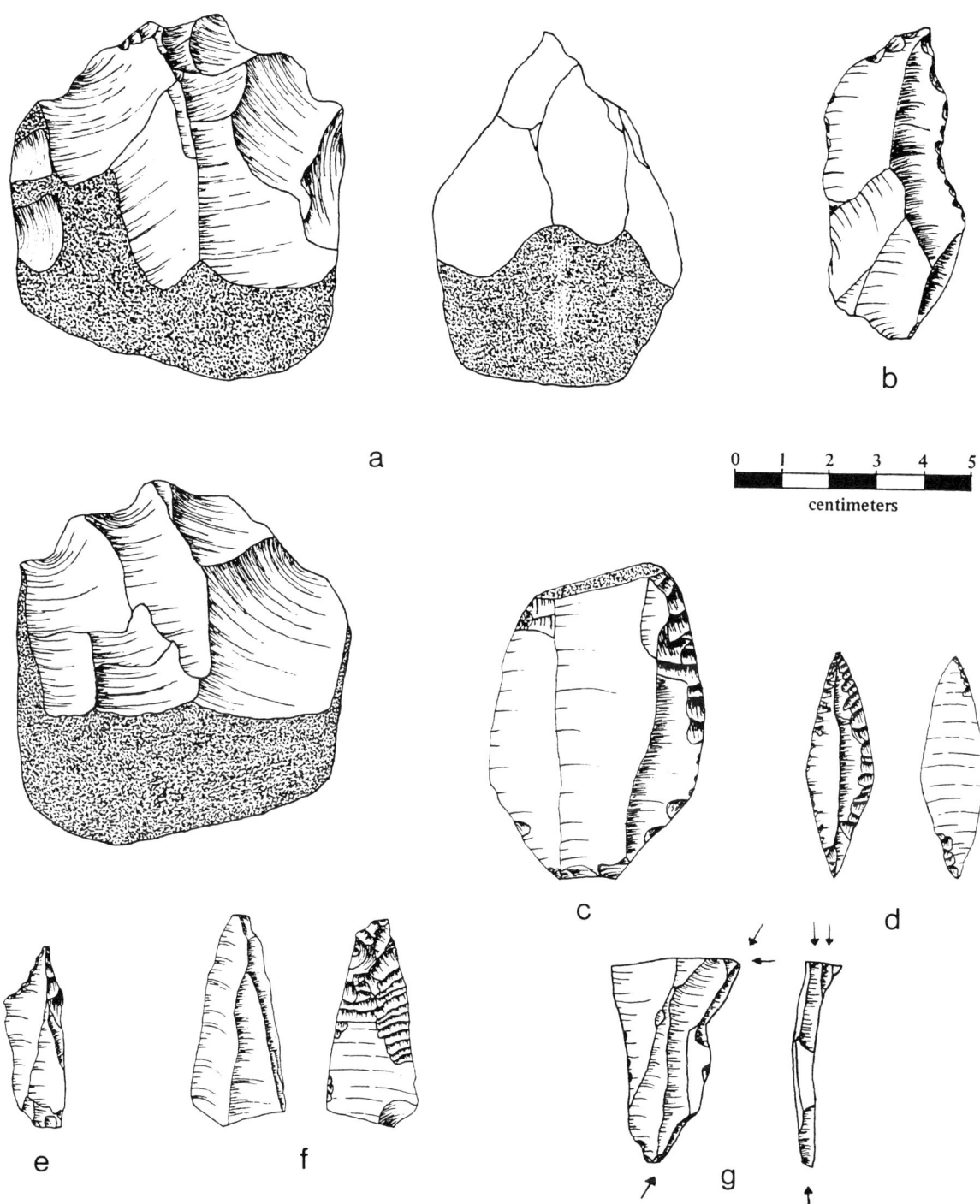

centimeters

Plate 1   Lower/Middle Palaeolithic and Neolithic Flints

a   Site 32 chopper.
b   Site 33 retouched blade.
c   Site 33 sidescraper.
d   Site 44 projectile point.
e   Site 44 drill/borer.
f   Site 44 invasive retouched piece.
g   Site 15 multiple dihedral burin.

179

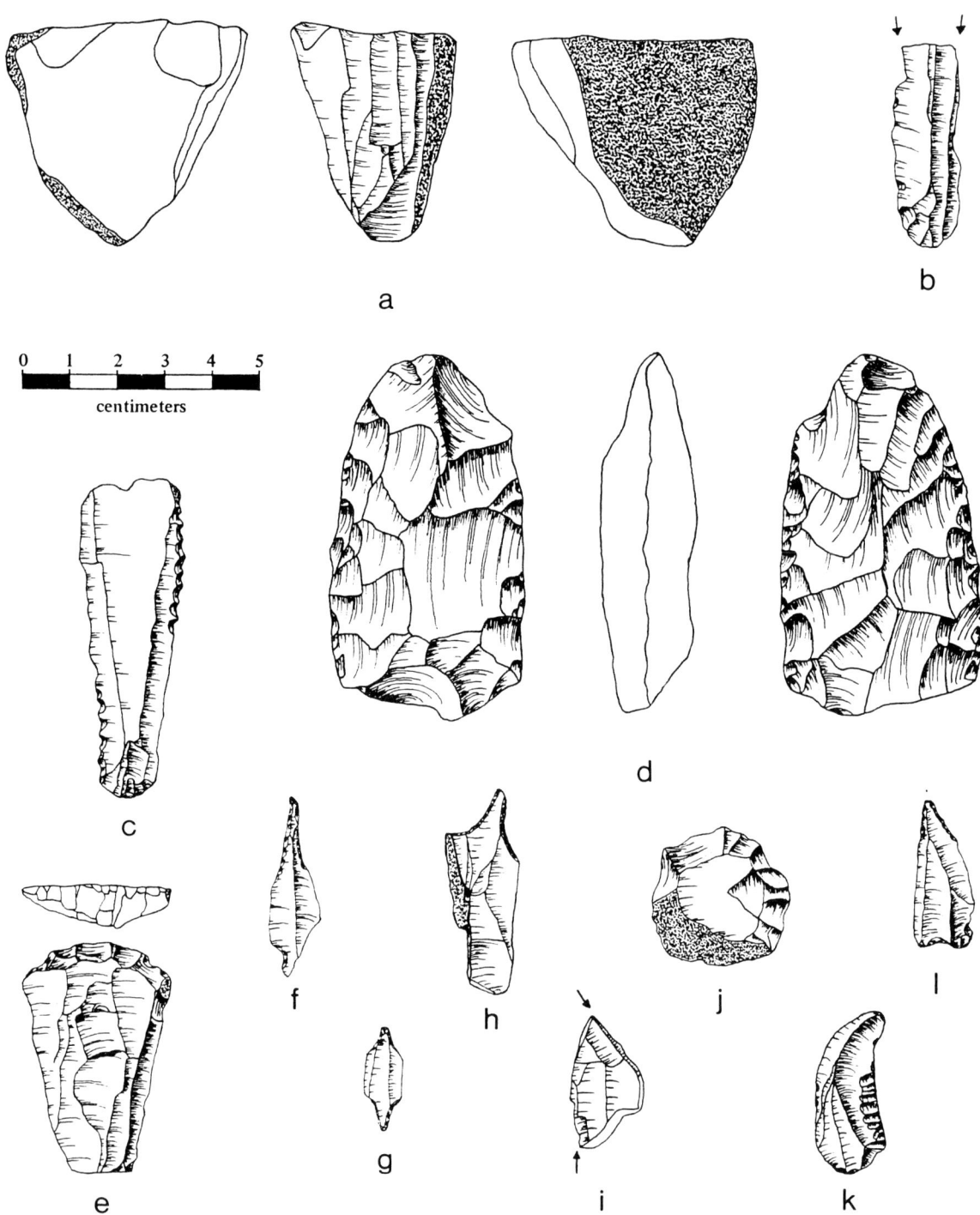

Plate 2   Neolithic Flints

a   'Dhra single platform core.
b   'Dhra double burin.
c   'Dhra denticulate.
d   Site 15 broken biface.
e   'Dhra endscraper.
f   'Dhra drill/borer.
g   Site 15 drill/borer.
h   Site 15 drill/borer.
i   Site 12 multiple burin.
j   Site 44 core scraper.
k   Site 15 retouched bladelet.
l   'Dhra drill/borer.

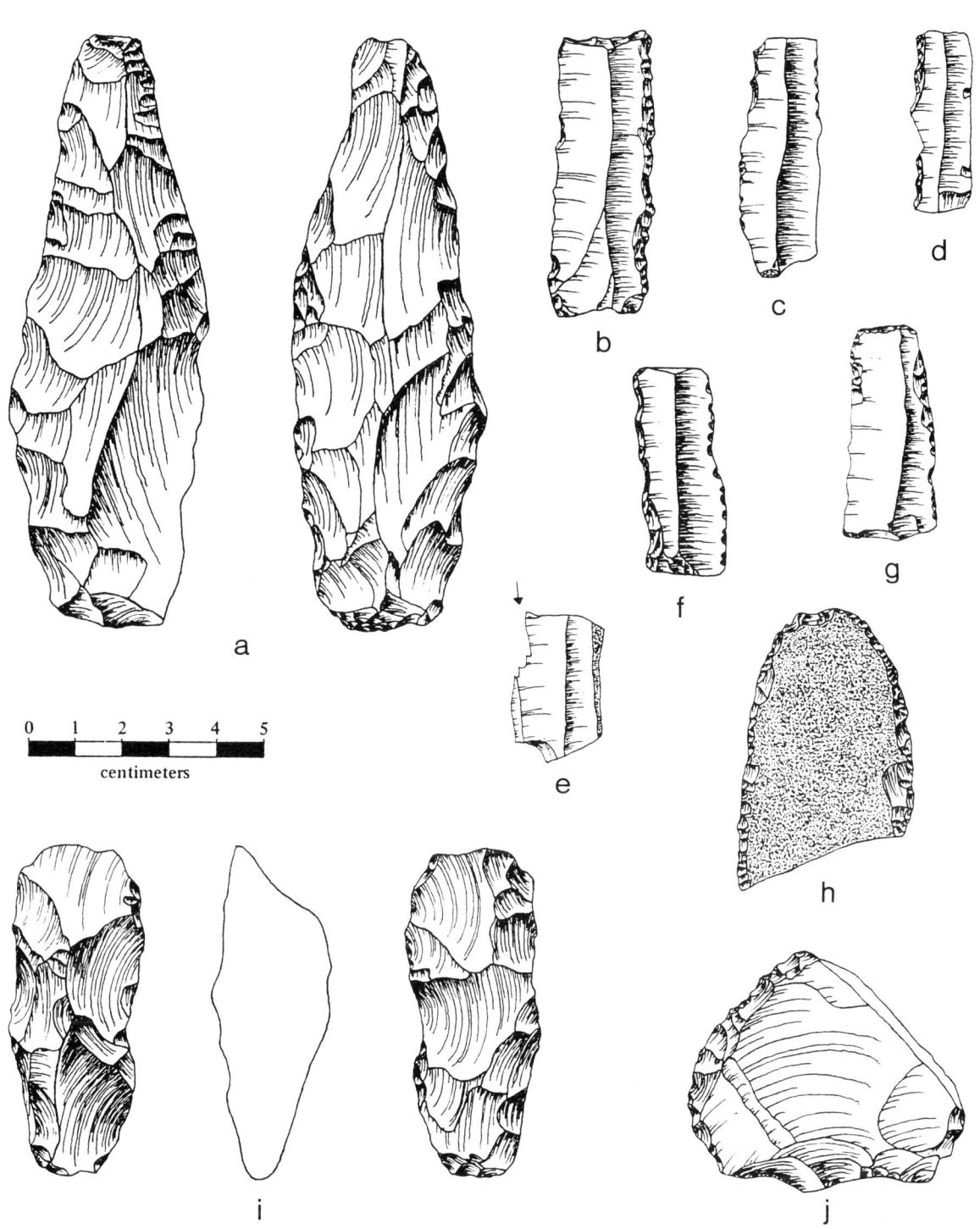

Plate 3   Chalcolithic and Chalcolithic/Early Bronze Flints

a	Site 185 pick/chisel.
b	Site 30 sickle blade.
c	Site 20 sickle segment.
d	Site 30 sickle segment.
e	Site 14 burin.
f	Site 20 sickle segment.
g	Site 14 sickle segment.
h	Site 20 tabular scraper.
i	Site 86 adze/biface.
j	Site 20 sidescraper.

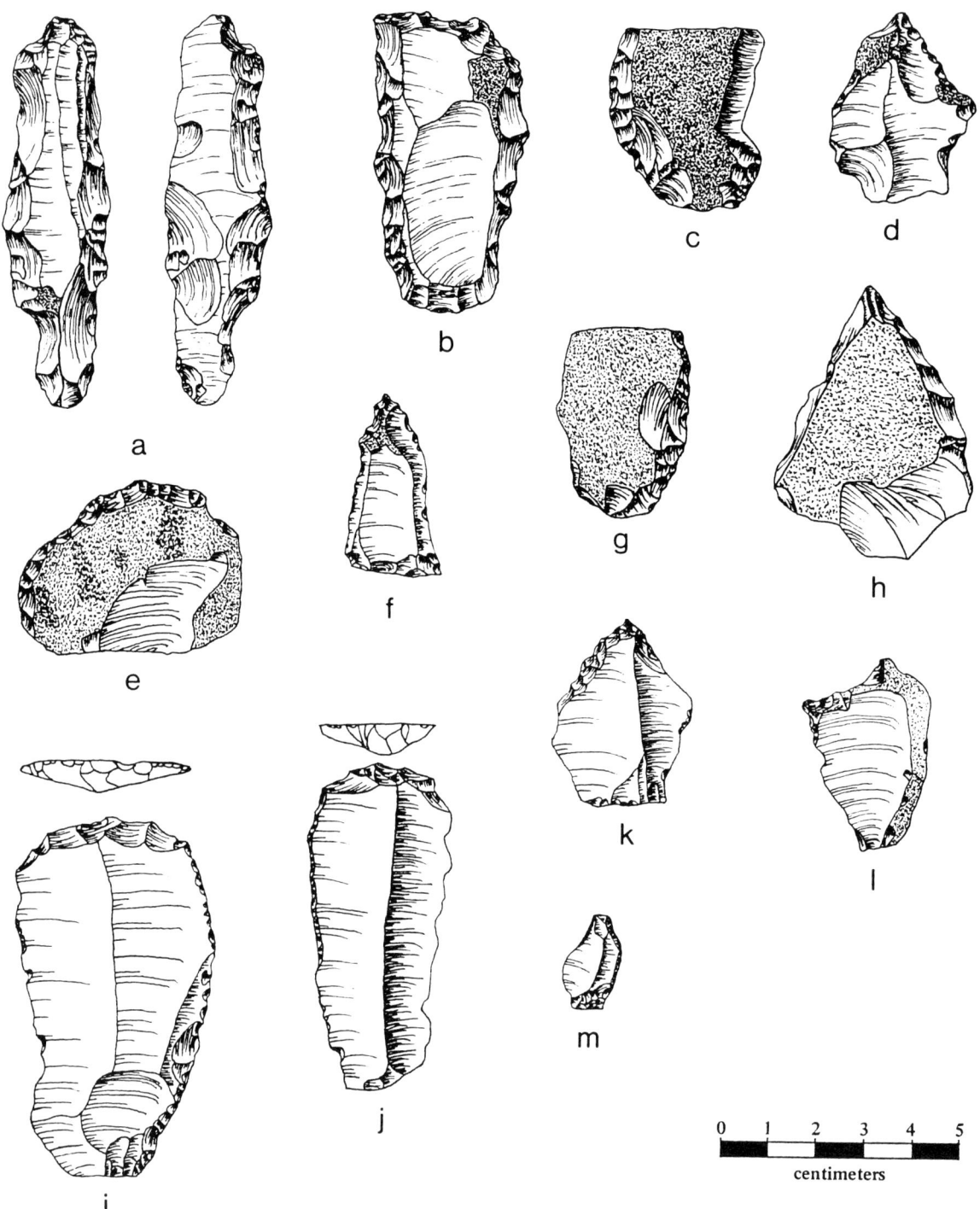

Plate 4   Chalcolithic and Early Bronze Flints

a   Site 105 borer/chisel.
b   Site 194 scraper/denticulate.
c   Site 224 tabular scraper.
d   Site 105 drill/borer.
e   Site 86 tabular scraper.
f   Site 186 drill/borer.
g   Site 86 tabular scaper.
h   Site 95 tabular scraper.
i   Site 20 endscraper.
j   Site 20 endscraper.
k   Site 171 drill/borer.
l   Site 185 drill/borer.
m   Site 14 retouched bladelet.

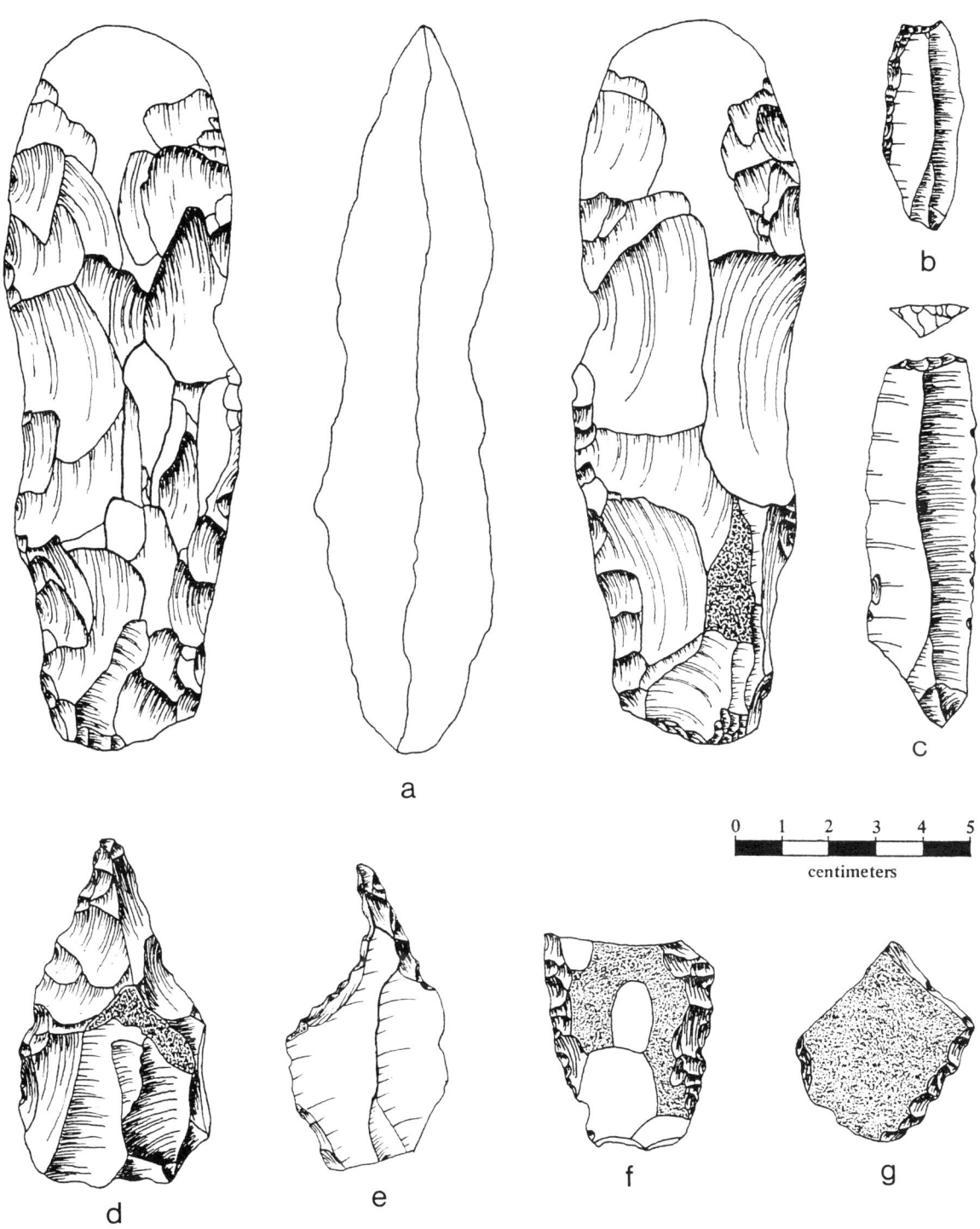

a

b

c

d

e

f

g

Plate 5   Chalcolithic/Early Bronze Flints

a   Site 3 axe.
b   Site 117 retouched blade.
c   Site 20 endscraper.
d   Site 83 pick.
e   Site 10 borer.
f   Site 86 tabular scraper.
g   Site 86 tabular scraper.

Plate 6   Late Neolithic–Chalcolithic: Sites 10 and 29 (all hand-made)

No	1
Site	29
Sample	73
Ware/Core	Crude; 2.5YR 6/7 lt red;core 10YR 6/1.5 lt grey/grey/lt brownish grey; many small–large white (lime), black (basalt) and some brown mineral grits; some mica flecks; some chaff impressions; some spalling, blistering and cracking on surfaces; some small–large oval and semi-angular voids showing surfaces
Exterior	Secondary burning plus somewhat heavy ash encrustation; 2.5YR 6/7 lt red – 10YR 6.5/4 v pale brown/lt yellowish brown – 5Y 8/1.5 white (under base)
Interior	Some ash encrustation, as ware
Notes	Kenyon and Holland 1982: fig. 32.18 (PNB)

No	2
Site	29
Sample	73
Ware/Core	Crude and rough; 10YR 5/1 grey – 8.2YR 6/4 lt brown/lt yellowish brown – 8.2YR 7/6 reddish yellow/yellow; core 10YR 5/1 grey; many large angular black (basalt) and v large white (lime) grits turning powdery, some quartz and mica; many reed impressions; some medium to v large voids showing surfaces
Exterior	Finger marks in varying directions; 10YR 5/1 grey – 8.2YR 6/4 lt brown/lt yellowish brown
Interior	Vertical and diagonal finger marks; 8.2YR 7/6 reddish yellow – 2.5Y 7/3 lt grey/pale yellow
Notes	[Chal]

No	3
Site	10
Sample	17
Ware/Core	10R 5.5/8 lt red/red; core 5YR 4/1 dk grey; many small–large angular white (lime + quartz), grey (chert) and brownish red (grog) grits; few chaff impressions; some small–large semiangular voids showing surfaces
Exterior	Patch of secondary burning; thick matt slip 10YR 7.5/3 v pale brown
Interior	Vertical finger marks; as ware
Notes	De Contenson 1956: fig. 1.3 (Chal)

No	4
Site	29
Sample	74
Ware/Core	N 5.5/0 grey – 10YR 5/1.5 grey/greyish brown; many small–large white (lime), grey and red grits; some chaff impressions; some spalling surfaces; join of knob handle not smoothed at underside
Exterior	As ware
Interior	As ware
Notes	[NL–Chal]

No	5
Site	29
Sample	23
Ware/Core	Extensively burnt; crude; 7.5YR 5/4 brown – 10YR 5.5/1 grey; many small–large angular white (lime), grey, black and red (grog + mineral) grits; some chaff impressions; some spalling int; some medium–large oval and angular voids showing surfaces
Exterior	Patch of 7.5YR 5/4 brown – N 2.5/0 v dk grey/black
Interior	Vertical smoothing marks body; horizontal smoothing marks rim; N 2.5/9 v dk grey/black
Notes	De Contenson 1956: fig. 6.20 (Chal)

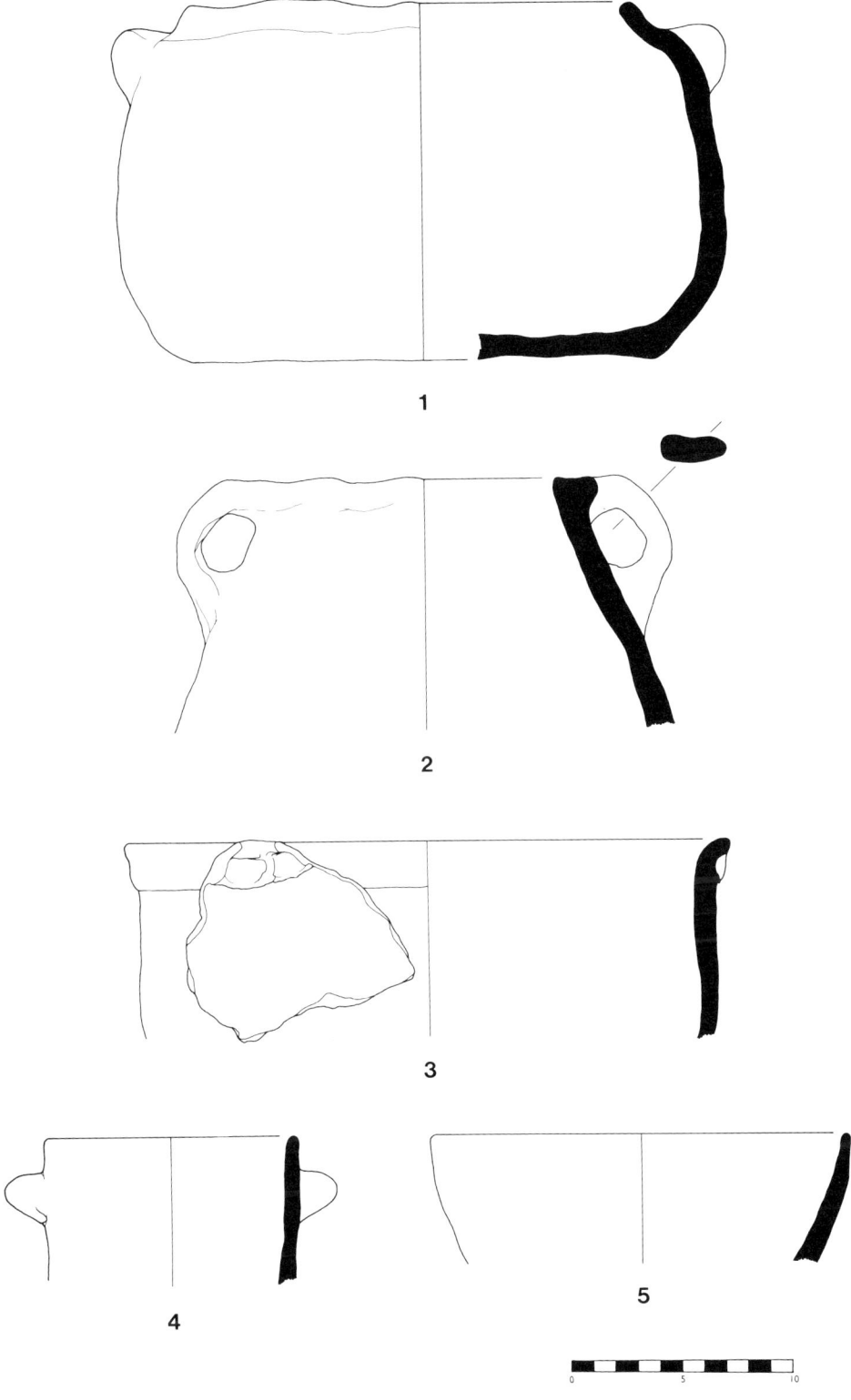

Plate 6   Late Neolithic–Chalcolithic: Sites 10 and 29 (all hand-made)

Plate 7   NL, Chal, EB, and Fat: Site 75

No	1
Site	75
Sample	117
Ware/Core	Hand-made; 2.5YR 6/7 lt red; core 10 YR 5/5 v pale brown/yellow; many small–medium white (lime), grey, black (basalt) and rare red grits; many chaff impressions
Exterior	Thin matt slip (?) 7.5YR 8/3 pinkish white/pink; paint faded to varying degrees, 10R 4.5/6 red where thickest
Interior	Thin matt slip (?) 5YR 7/5 pink/reddish yellow; paint as ext
Notes	Paint: Kafafi 1982: pls. 29.30; 37.18 (LNL 2)

No	2
Site	75
Sample	117
Ware/Core	Hand-made, thickness 0.55–0.66 cm; 2.5YR 6/7 lt red; core N 4/0 dk grey; many small–medium white (lime) and grey grits; many chaff impressions
Exterior	Medium thick matt slip 7.5YR 7/3 pinkish grey/pink; paint 10R
Interior	5YR 6/5 lt reddish brown/reddish yellow
Notes	[PNB]

No	3
Site	75
Sample	117
Ware/Core	Hand-made; 10YR 8/3.5 v pale brown; core N 5/0 grey; many small–large (up to 0.3 cm), semiangular white (lime), grey (chert), red and brown (grog) grits; many reed impressions giving 'textured' surfaces
Exterior	5YR 7/7 reddish yellow – 5YR 7/5 pink/reddish yellow patches of 10YR 8/3.5 v pale brown and patch of N 5/0 grey
Interior	5YR 7/5 pink/reddish-yellow
Notes	Sherd has the feel of being a lid rather than a small bowl; no NL pottery lids were found in literature [NL]

No	4
Site	75
Sample	116
Ware/Core	Hand-made; 5YR 7/5 pink/reddish yellow – 10YR 8/3.5 v pale brown; many small–large white (lime), grey, red and brown grits; many reed impressions
Exterior	As ware
Interior	As ware
Notes	Kafafi 1982: pl. 9:3 (LNL1–EChal)

No	5
Site	75
Sample	117
Ware/Core	Hand-made; 7.5YR 7/5 pink/reddish yellow; core

	N 3.5/0 dk grey/v dk grey; many small–medium white (lime), grey and brown grits; many chaff impressions
Exterior	As ware
Interior	As ware
Notes	Callaway 1972: fig. 46. 11, 'Ai Phase V (2860–2720=EB IIB)

No	6
Site	75
Sample	117
Ware/Core	Hand-made; 2.5YR 6/7 lt red; core 6/0 lt grey/grey; many small–large angular white, grey (chert), dk grey and red grits protruding surfaces; some chaff impressions many small–large frequently deep, voids showing surfaces
Exterior	Medium thick matt slip 10YR 7/4 v pale brown; cracked
Interior	As ware; slip on ext extending over rim
Notes	De Contenson 1956: fig. 2 10–12 (Chal)

No	7
Site	75
Sample	116
Ware/Core	Wheel-made; 2.5YR 6/7 lt red; patchy core N 3.5/0 dk grey/v dk grey; many small–large white (lime) and grey grits; rare chaff impressions
Exterior	Knife cut base; thin matt slip (?) 10R 5/5 weak red/red
Interior	As ext
Notes	Cleveland 1960 pl. 22(B).5, Ader Phase C [EB IVB]

No	8
Site	75
Sample	117
Ware/Core	Wheel-made; 2.5YR 4/5 reddish brown/red; some small–medium white and grey grits; few reed impressions
Exterior	Secondary burning; colour as ware; few small spots of deep reddish brown glaze
Interior	As ext
Notes	Tushingham 1972: figs. 7. 26, 27, (probably Ayyubid/Mamluk); Brosh 1986: 4.2,3 (Crusader 1099–1921); [Fat]

No	9
Site	75
Sample	116
Ware/Core	Hand-made; 6.2YR 7/7 reddish yellow – 3.2YR 6.5/6 lt red/reddish yellow; many small–large angular white (lime), grey (chert), red and brown grits; rare chaff impressions
Exterior	As ware
Interior	As ware; vertical finger smoothing marks
Notes	Cleveland 1960: pl. 24(A).2, Ader Phase B [EB IVA]

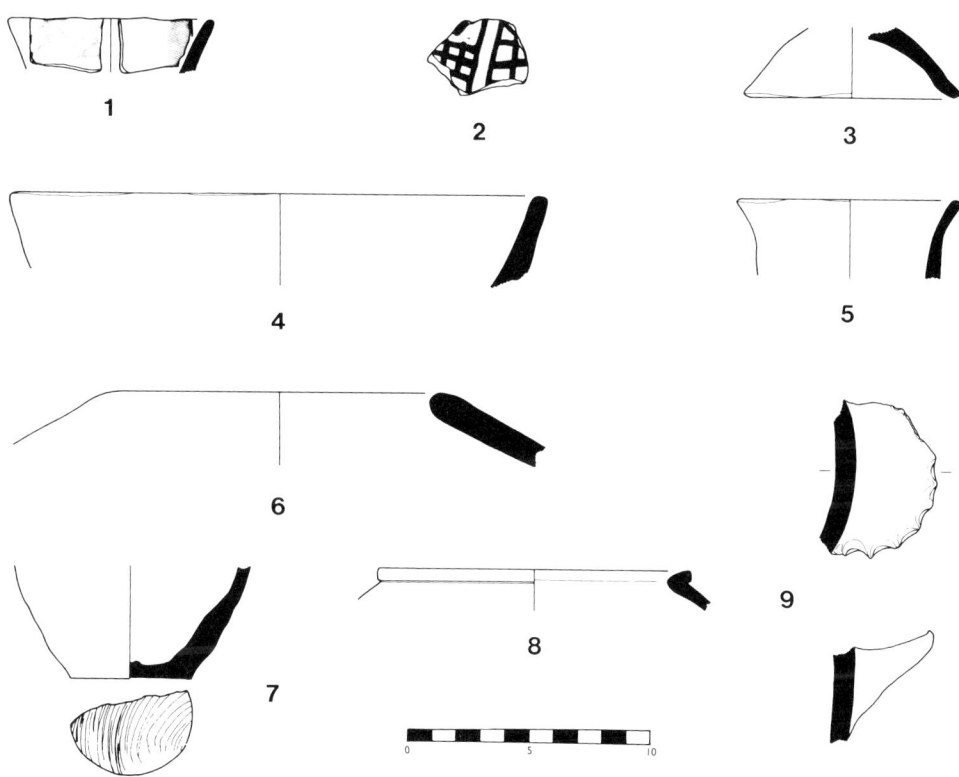

Plate 7   NL, Chal, EB, and Fat: Site 75

Plate 8   Neolithic–Early Bronze: Sites 75 and 76 (all hand-made)

No	1
Site	76
Sample	119
Ware/Core	7.5YR 6.5/6 reddish yellow; many medium–large white (lime) and grey grits; some blistering and cracking
Exterior	8.2YR 7/6 reddish yellow/yellow; paint 5YR 3.5/3 reddish brown/dk reddish brown; overall burnish
Interior	Slight lime encrustation; uneven paint as ext where thickest
Notes	[NL]

No	2
Site	76
Sample	119
Ware/Core	Asymmetrical; 5YR 6.5/6 reddish yellow – 8.2YR 8/3.5 pinkish white/pink/v pale brown; very abundant large white (lime), grey (chert), black (basalt) and pink (quartz) grits protruding surfaces giving multi-coloured spotted appearance; cracked int; voids mainly due to loss of inclusions (inclusion casts)
Exterior	As ware
Interior	As ware
Notes	Kafafi 1982: pl. 20.21 (LNL–Chal)

No	3
Site	76
Sample	119
Ware/Core	2.5Y 5.5/2 lt brownish grey/greyish brown; many small–large angular light grey (lime), grey (chert) and pale pinkish white (quartz) grits; some mica flecks; many chaff impressions
Exterior	10YR 7/3.5 v pale brown; longitudinal patch at rim 5YR 7/4 pink, may indicate a strip of red paint at rim (?)
Interior	Badly abraded giving (smoothly) pitted surface; 10YR 7/3.5 v pale brown
Notes	Kafafi 1982: pl. 45.12 (LNL 2–beg Chal)

No	4
Site	76
Sample	128
Ware/Core	5YR 6/5 lt reddish brown/reddish yellow; many medium–large angular white (lime), grey (chert) and red (grog) grits
Exterior	10YR 6.5/4 v pale brown/lt yellowish brown; slightly burnished
Interior	as ware
Notes	Kenyon and Holland 1982: fig. 14.4 (PNA)

No	5
Site	76
Sample	119
Ware/Core	10R 5.5/8 lt red/red at 0.1–0.2 cm from ext – 5YR

	7/7 reddish yellow; patches of thin core 10YR 6/2.5 lt brownish grey/pale brown and 10YR 5/1 grey; many small–large angular white and red (grog), few grey grits protruding surfaces; some reed impressions
Exterior	Diagonal finger smoothing 'grooves' (marks); thin matt slip 5YR 7/3.5 pink – 10YR 7.5/3 v pale brown
Interior	2.5YR 6/5 lt reddish brown/lt red
Notes	[EB I]

No	6
Site	76
Sample	127
Ware/Core	2.5YR 6/7 lt red; core N 5/0 grey; many small–medium angular white (lime) and grey grits
Exterior	Impressed decoration; thin matt slip 10YR 7.5/3 v pale brown
Interior	As ware; slip as exterior extending onto flaring rim
Notes	[EBI]

No	7
Site	76
Sample	127
Ware/Core	5YR 7/5 pink/reddish yellow; many small–medium angular white, grey and pink grits; some mica flecks
Exterior	5YR 6.5/3 pink/lt reddish brown; traces of thick matt slip 5YR 6.5/6 reddish yellow
Interior	As ware
Notes	Kenyon and Holland 1982: fig. 63.25 (white wash ext), (EB)

No	8
Site	76
Sample	127
Ware/Core	2.5YR 6/4 lt reddish brown; many small–medium white (lime) and brown (grog) grits; some cracking int
Exterior	Wet-smoothed; 10YR 7/5 v pale brown/yellow
Interior	7.5YR 7/5 pink/reddish yellow
Notes	[EB I]

No	9
Site	75
Sample	118
Ware/Core	2.5YR 6/4 lt reddish brown; core 5YR 7/1.5 lt grey/pinkish grey; many small–medium white (lime), grey, red (grog) and some quartz grits; many reed impressions
Exterior	2.5YR 6/6 lt red – 8.2YR 7/8 reddish yellow/yellow; traces of slip 2.5Y 8/4 pale yellow
Interior	5YR 7/5 pink/reddish yellow
Notes	[EB I]

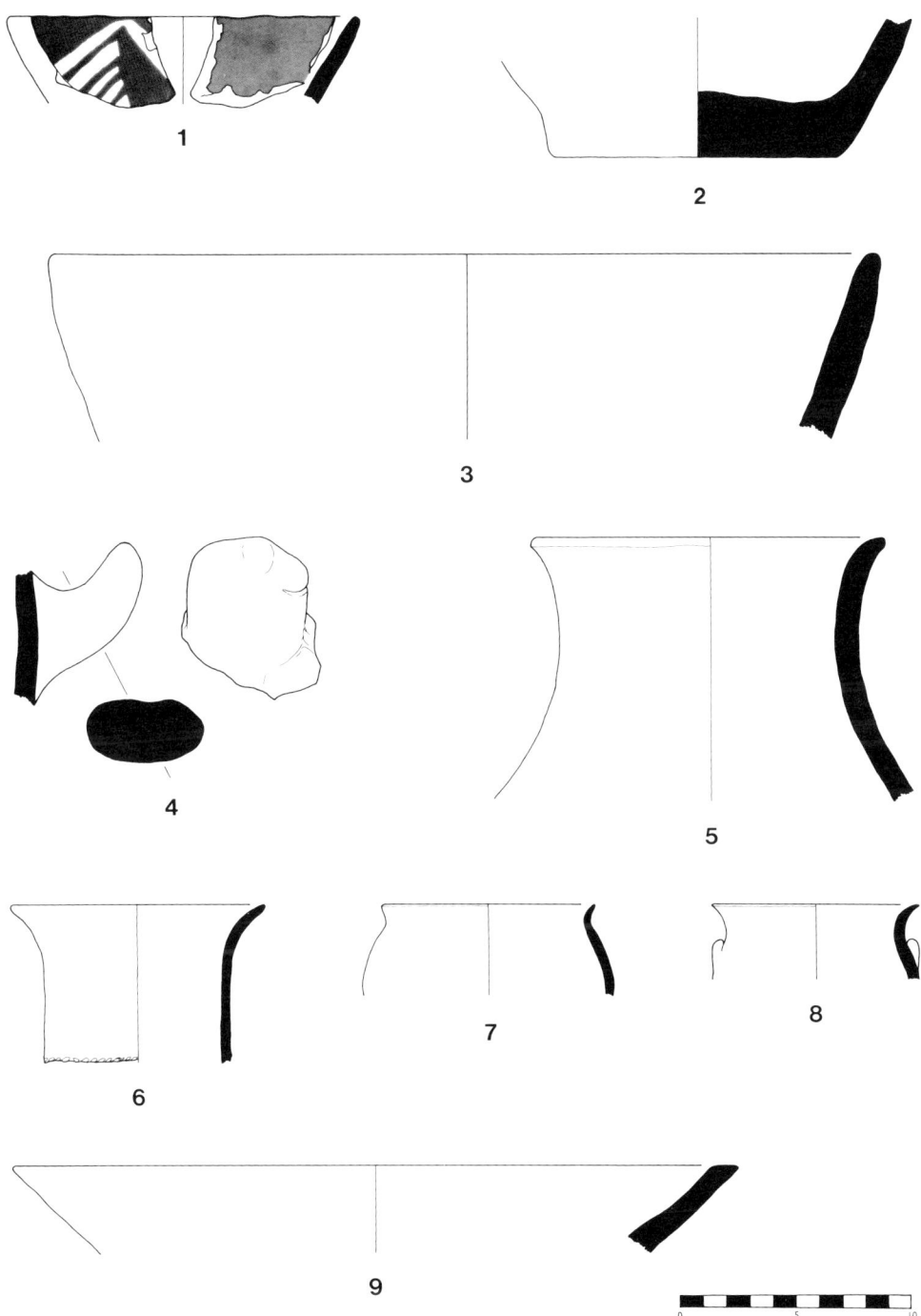

Plate 8   Neolithic–Early Bronze: Sites 75 and 76 (all hand-made)

Plate 9   Neolithic–Chalcolithic: Sites 20, 92, and 133 (all hand-made)

No	1
Site	92
Sample	137
Ware/Core	6.2YR 5/6 yellowish red/strong brown; core 10YR 4.5/2 greyish brown/dk greyish brown – 10YR 5.5/3 pale brown/brown; many small–large white (lime), grey and brown (grog) grits; many reed impressions
Exterior	5YR 6/5 lt reddish brown/reddish yellow; – 7.5YR 6/7 reddish yellow; traces of wash under knob handle 7.5YR 7.5/4 pink
Interior	Thin matt wash 7.5YR 7.5/4 pink
Notes	Kenyon and Holland 1982: fig. 3.5 (PNA)

No	2
Site	92
Sample	137
Ware/Core	2.5YR 5.5/6 lt red/red; core 5YR 7/3 pink – 5YR 6.5/1 lt grey; many small–medium white (lime), grey, red (grog) and quartz grits; many reed impressions; some cracking int
Exterior	As ware; strip of (faded) paint at rim 2.5YR 5.56/6 lt red/red
Interior	As ware
Notes	De Contenson 1956: fig. 7.8 (Chal) Hennessy fig. 6.2 Teleilat Ghassul Phase B (Chal)

No	3
Site	92
Sample	137
Ware/Core	2.5YR 6/7 lt red; core 7.5YR 6.5/2 pinkish grey; many small–medium white (lime) and grey (quartz) grits; many reed impressions, giving uneven int
Exterior	As ware, patch of 7.5YR 7/4 pink
Interior	As ware
Notes	[NL–Chal]

No	4
Site	20
Sample	70
Ware/Core	10R 4.5/8 red; rough; core 5YR 5.5/2.5 (mostly lt reddish brown); many medium–large white (quartz) grits; some cracking at surfaces
Exterior	As ware
Interior	2.5YR 5.5/7 lt red/red
Notes	[Chal]

No	5
Site	133
Sample	731
Ware/Core	2.5YR 5.5/8 lt red/red; core 5YR 6/1.5 grey/pinkish grey; many small–large white (lime), grey (chert), and black (basalt) grits; rare chaff impressions; some cracking and spalling at surfaces

Exterior	Much discoloured, may be 5YR 6/6 reddish yellow
Interior	5YR 5.5/5 (mostly lt reddish brown)
Notes	De Contenson 1956: fig. 3.1,3 (Chal); Hennessy 1969: fig. 5.7 Teleilat Ghassul Phase A (Chal)

No	6
Site	20
Sample	70
Ware/core	Unevenly fired, 2.5YR 5.5/7 lt red/red – 5YR 5/3 reddish brown – 10YR 4.5/6 red – 10R 4.5/4 weak red; core 5YR 4.5/1 grey/dk grey; rough and crude, very uneven cracked surfaces; many small–large, angular white, grey and red (grog) grits; many chaff impressions
Exterior	2.5YR 5.5/7 lt red/red – 10R 4.5/6 red; finger impresed handle
Interior	Heavily lime encrusted; 5YR 5/3 reddish brown – 10R 4.5/4 weak red
Notes	[Chal]

No	7
Site	92
Sample	137
Ware/Core	7.5YR 6.5/6 reddish/yellow; core 10YR 5/1.5 grey/greyish brown; coarse and rough; many medium–large angular white (lime) and brown (grog) grits; many reed impressions
Exterior	Much abraded, down to core at body; colour as ware; mat impressed
Interior	As ware
Notes	Kafafi 1982: pl. 32.5 (LNL 2–Chal)

No	8
Site	92
Sample	137
Ware/core	1.2YR 6/5 pale red/lt red/lt reddish brown; many small white and grey grits; many reed impressions giving very uneven ext
Exterior	As ware
Interior	As ware
Notes	Kenyon and Holland 1982: fig. 13.16 (PNA); Kafafi 1982: pls. 42.35; 53.23 (LNL 2–beg Chal)

No	9
Site	92
Sample	137
Ware/core	Mostly 10R 5.5/8 lt red/red (also ext and int colours); core 10YR 4/1.5 dk grey/dk brownish grey; many small–medium white, grey and quartz grits, giving a sandy texture; many chaff impressions
Exterior	Redder than 10R 5/6 – 10R 5.58 lt red/red; traces of thick matt slip 10YR 8/2.5 white/v pale brown
Interior	Paler than 1.2YR 6/4 pale red
Notes	[Chal]

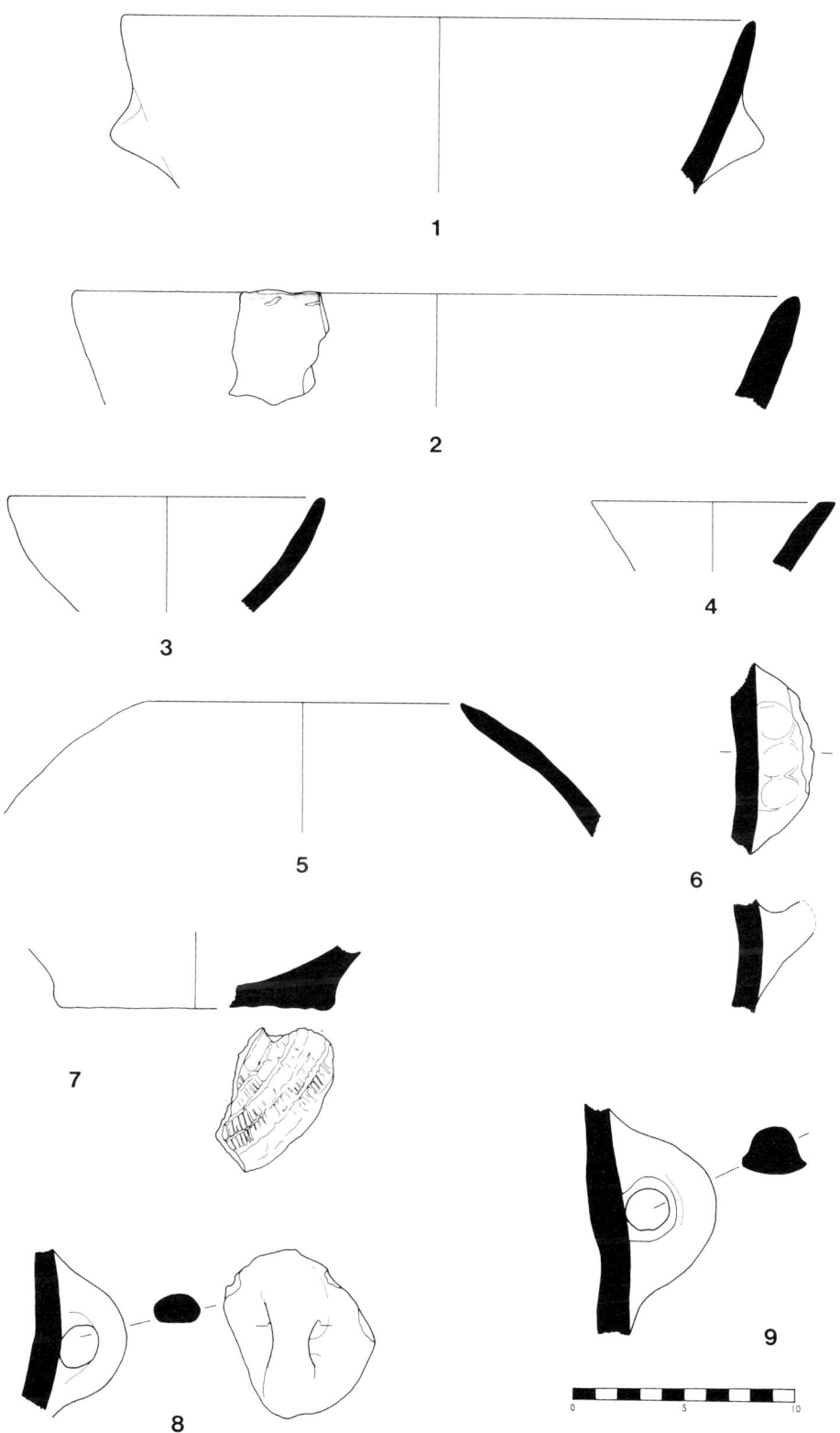

Plate 9   Neolithic–Chalcolithic: Sites 20, 92, and 133 (all hand-made)

Plate 10   Chal–EB: Sites 12, 14, 30, 108, 109, 154, 157 and 177

No	1
Site	30
Sample	76
Ware/Core	Hand-made; 2.5YR 5.58 lt red/red; core 2.5YR 4.5/4 reddish brown; many small–medium and some large white (lime + quartz) and grey grits; few chaff impressions; rare spalling
Exterior	Slight secondary burning; thick matt slip 2.5Y 7.5/3 white/lt grey/pale yellow – 5Y 7.5/3 pale yellow near rim
Interior	Thick matt slip; 10YR 7/5 v pale brown/yellow
Notes	Olavarri 1969: fig. 5. 10 (no slip), 'Aro'er Level VIa, (2050–1900B.C.)

No	2
Site	177
Sample	309
Ware/Core	Hand-made; 7.5YR 6/5 lt brown/reddish yellow; core 2.5YR 6/7 lt red; many small–large angular greyish white (chert), brown (grog) and few medium black (basalt) grits protruding surfaces; some small–large round and oval voids showing surfaces
Exterior	As ware
Interior	As ware
Notes	[Chal]

No	3
Site	108
Sample	148
Ware/Core	Hand-made; unevenly fired N 3.5/0 dk grey/v dk grey – 5YR 7/7 reddish yellow; many small–large angular white (lime), grey and black grits; rare blistering ext; some small–medium round and semiangular voids showing surfaces
Exterior	5Y 5.5/2 lt olive grey/olive grey – N 3.5/0 dk grey/v dk grey – 5YR 7/7 reddish yellow at rim
Interior	10YR 6/4 lt yellowish brown – 5YR 7/7 reddish yellow
Notes	Hennessy 1969: fig. 7a.10 Teleilat Ghassul Phase B (Chal)

No	4
Site	109
Sample	185
Ware/Core	Hand-made; 2.5YR 6/7 lt red to ~0.3 cm from ext, 5YR 8/3.5 towards int; many small–medium, some large white (lime + quartz) and grey grits; some small–large, somewhat deep, round angular voids showing surfaces
Exterior	Thick slip with (matt) wide horizontal burnish bands 10R 4.5/6 red; cracked
Interior	Very badly worn giving rough uneven surface; 5YR 8/3.5 pink
Notes	[EB III]

No	5
Site	154A
Sample	252
Ware/Core	Hand-made; 2.5YR 6/6 lt red – 7.5YR 7/5 pink/reddish yellow; many small–medium white (lime), grey, red (grog) and quartz grits
Exterior	Silica encrusted; as ware; traces of thick slip with wide horizontal burnish band(s) 10R 4/5 weak red/red
Interior	As ware
Notes	Callaway 1972: fig. 59.17, 'Ai Phase VI (2700–2550 B.C. =EB IIIA)

No	6
Site	12
Sample	18
Ware/Core	Slow-wheel (?); 5YR 7/7 reddish yellow – 2.5YR 6/7 lt red; many small–medium white (lime), grey (chert), reddish brown and quartz grits; sandy texture; some small–medium, few deep large semiangular voids showing surfaces
Exterior	Lime encrusted, wet smoothed (?); colours as ware
Interior	Secondary burning; traces of medium thick matt slip 10YR 8/3 v pale brown; colours as ware
Notes	Schaub 1973: figs. 6.11, 15 (no slip); 7.16 (red slip ext); 8.22 (red slip ext); (EB2, EBIV–MB I)

No	7
Site	12
Sample	18
Ware/Core	Slow-wheel (?); 2.5YR 6/7 lt red; core N 6/0 grey; many small–medium white (lime), grey and red grits
Exterior	As ware; traces of matt reddish yellow slip
Interior	As ware
Notes	[EB IV (?)]

No	8
Site	157
Sample	300
Ware/Core	Hand-made; 3.2YR 6/4 lt reddish brown/pink; many small–medium white (lime), grey (basalt) and quartz grits
Exterior	5YR 7/5 pink/reddish yellow
Interior	
Notes	[EB IV]

No	9
Site	14
Sample	30
Ware/Core	Hand-made; 5YR 6/5 lt reddish brown/reddish yellow; many small–medium white, grey, red and quartz, few large angular white (lime) grits
Exterior	7.5YR 6/4 lt brown; vertical wet-smoothing marks on body; traces of very pale brown (cream) slip on top of handle
Interior	Discoloured; as ware
Notes	Prag 1971: figs. 22.6, 29.6 (both Iktanu Phase 2); 40.16; 49.12 (EB–MB)

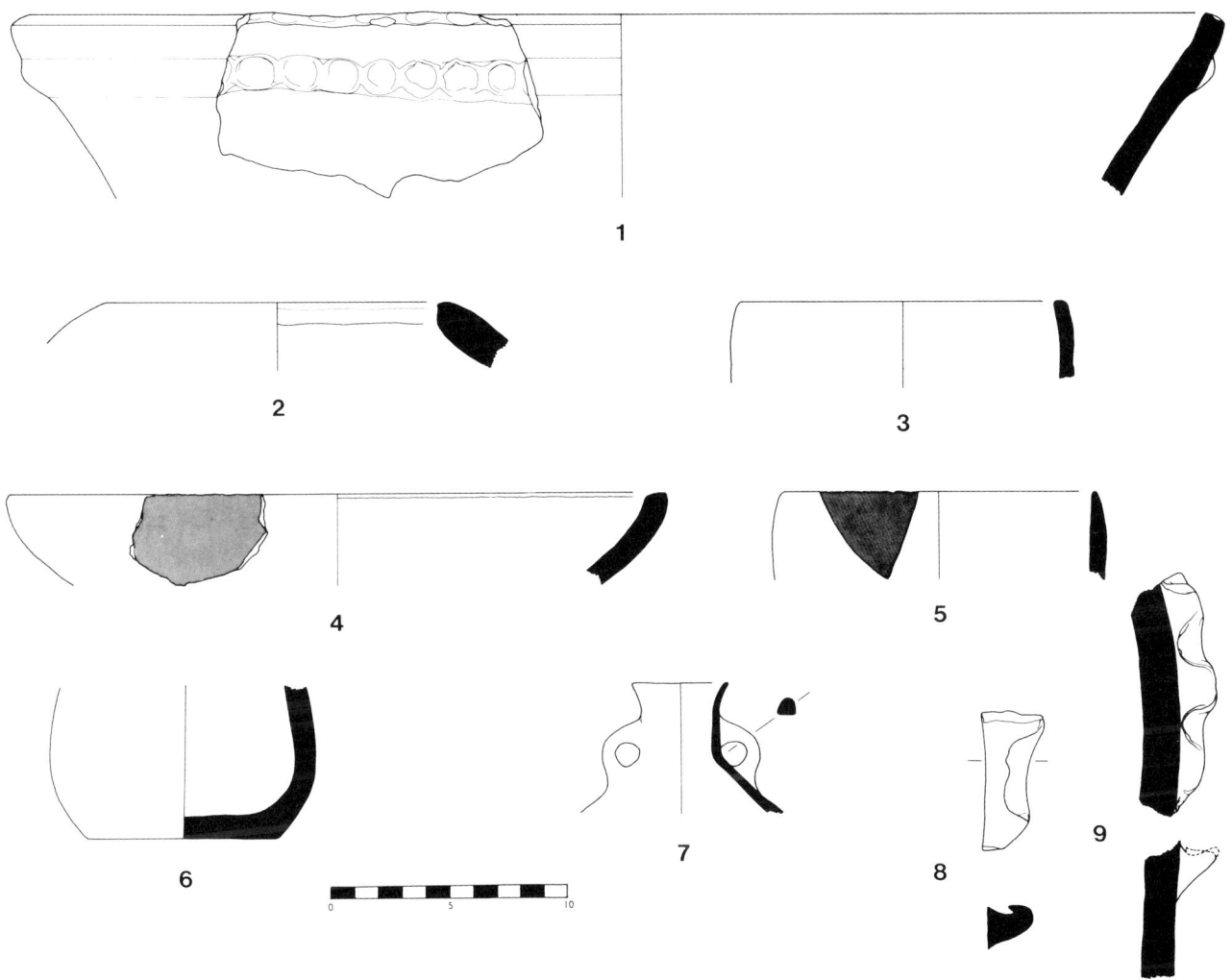

Plate 10 Chal–EB: Sites 12, 14, 30, 108, 109, 154, 157 and 177

Plate 11   EB IB and EB II–III: Site 2 (all hand-made)

No	1
Site	2
Sample	5
Ware/Core	8.2YR 5.5/4 (mainly lt brown); many small–medium white (lime), grey and brown (grog) grits; some reed impressions
Exterior	Thick matt slip 10YR 7/3.5 v pale brown, extending over top of rim and maybe int rim (?)
Interior	As ware
Notes	[EB II–III (?)]

No	2
Site	2
Sample	5
Ware/Core	7.5Yr 6.5/4 pink/lt brown; core 7.5YR 5/3 brown; many small–medium white (lime), grey and red-brown grits
Exterior	Medium thick matt slip 3.2Y 8/3 white/pale yellow, extending over int rim
Interior	As ware; slip over rim as ext
Notes	Callaway 1972: fig. 17.10 'Ai Phase II (3100–3000 B.C.)

No	3
Site	2
Sample	5
Ware/Core	7.5YR 6.5/6 reddish yellow; core 7.5YR 5.5/2 pinkish grey/brown; many small–large white (lime), grey (chert), black basalt, red-brown (grog) grits; few reed impressions
Exterior	Ash and silica encrustations; 7.5YR 6.5/6 reddish yellow – 7.5YR 6.5/4 pink/lt brown; diagonal finger smoothing marks at body
Interior	Lime encrustations; colour as ware; thin shallow horizontal tool marks at body
Notes	Kenyon and Holland 1982: fig. 58.27 (EB) tool

No	4
Site	2
Sample	4
Ware/Core	5YR 6.5/8 reddish yellow; many small–large white (lime), grey (chert) and brown (grog) grits; some chaff impressions
Exterior	Thin matt slip 10YR 8/2.5 white/v pale brown
Interior	As ware
Notes	Kenyon and Holland 1982: fig. 61.1 (EB)

No	5
Site	2
Sample	4
Ware/Core	7.5YR 6.5/4 pink/lt brown; many small–large white (lime + quartz), grey (chert), dk grey, pink (quartz), red (grog) grits; some mica flecks; rare chaff impressions; some hair-line cracking at surfaces
Exterior	7.5YR 6.5/4 pink/lt brown – 3.2YR 6.5/6 lt red/reddish yellow
Interior	3.2YR 6.5/6 lt red/reddish yellow
Notes	Schaub 1981: fig. 5.2 (EB IB)

No	6
Site	2
Sample	4
Ware/Core	5YR 6.5/6 reddish yellow; core 5YR 6/3.5 lt reddish brown; many small–large white (lime), grey (chert), dk grey, reddish brown (grog) and red (mineral) grits; rare mica flecks; rare chaff impressions
Exterior	5YR 7/5 pink/reddish yellow; diagonal finger smoothing marks
Interior	As ware
Notes	Callaway 1972: fig. 15.4 'Ai Phase I (3100–3000 B.C.)

No	7
Site	2
Sample	5
Ware/Core	3.2YR 6/6 lt red/reddish yellow; core N 5.5/0 grey; many small–large angular white (lime), grey (chert), black (basalt) red-brown (grog) grits
Exterior	Medium thick matt slip 10YR 8/2.5 white/v pale brown extendng in patches over top of rim
Interior	7.5YR 7/5 pink/reddish yellow – 5YR 6/6 reddish yellow
Notes	[EB IB]

No	8
Site	2
Sample	5
Ware/Core	Mostly 2.5YR 6/6 lt red; core N5.5/0 grey; many small–large white (lime), grey (chert), black (basalt, predominant) and red-brown (grog) grits
Exterior	Uneven matt slip: 7.5YR 7.5/5 pink/lt brown/reddish yellow where thin – 10YR 7.5/4 v pale brown where thicker + patch of 2.5YR 6/6 lt red; horizontal tool smoothing marks
Interior	Thick slip top of rim 8.2YR 7/5 pink/v pale brown, thinning to 8.2YR 7/5 (mostly v pale brown) – 6.2YR 7/6 reddish yellow – 5YR 6.5/6 reddish yellow
Notes	Callaway 1972: fig. 17. 17 'Ai Phase II (3100–3000 B.C.)

No	9
Site	2
Sample	5
Ware/Core	3.2YR 5.5/6 lt red/reddish yellow; core 5YR 6/2.3 pinkish grey/lt reddish brown; many small–large white, light and dk grey (chert), black (basalt) and brown (grog) grits
Exterior	3.2YR 5.5/6 lt red/reddish yellow – 10YR 7.5/4 v pale brown (matt slip?)
Interior	As ware
Notes	[EB IB]

No	10
Site	2
Sample	6
Ware/Core	10R 6/7 lt red; core N 6/0 – N 5/0 grey; many small–medium white (lime), grey and brownish red (grog) grits; some reed impressions, somewhat crude; base made as cut disc joined roughly to body ext, join well smoothed int
Exterior	Unevenly fired, uneven matt slip: 7.5YR 6.5/4 pink/lt brown – 7.5Y 7.5/2 white/lt grey – 10YR 7/3 v pale brown – 5YR 5.5/1 grey; rare spalling
Interior	As ware; some cracking
Notes	[EB IB]

No	11
Site	2
Sample	5
Ware/Core	1.2YR 5/8 red; core 5YR 5.5/1 grey; many small–large white (lime), grey (chert) and red (grog) grits; some reed impressions
Exterior	3.2YR 6.5/6 lt red/reddish yellow – 1.2YR 5/8 red; traces of thick matt slip 10YR 7.5/2.5 white/lt grey/v pale brown
Interior	2.5YR 6/7 lt red
Notes	[EB I]

No	12
Site	2
Sample	4
Ware/Core	5YR 6/7 reddish yellow; many small–large white (lime), grey (chert), black and red (grog) grits; some mica flecks; some reed impressions
Exterior	5YR 6.5/4 pink/lt reddish brown – 3.2YR 6/6 lt red/reddish yellow; traces of thick slip 10R 7.5/7 red; incised potter's mark bottom of base
Interior	As ware
Notes	[EB II–III]

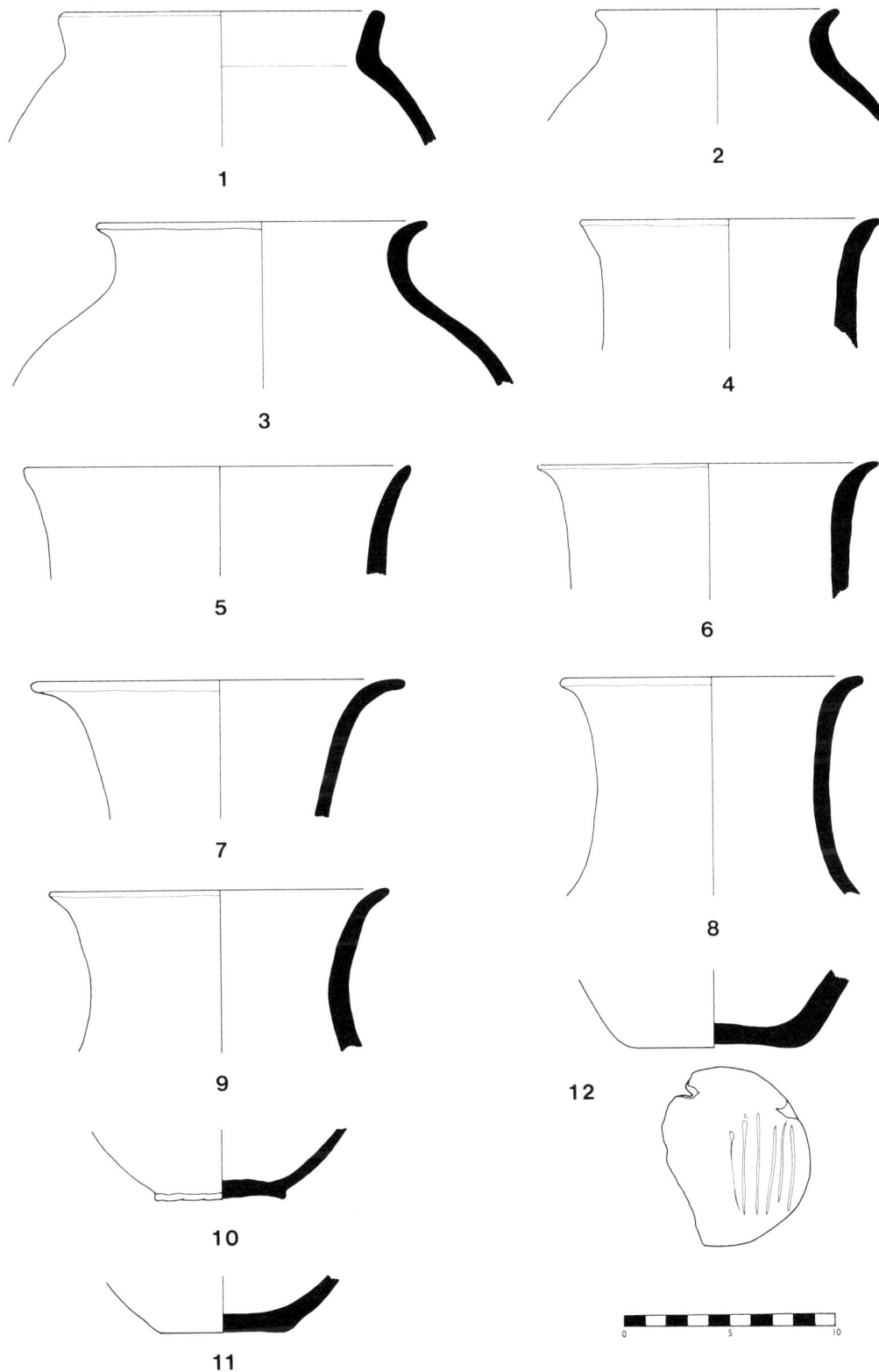

Plate 11 EB IB and EB II–III: Site 2 (all hand-made)

Plate 12   EB IB: Site 2 (all hand-made)

No	1
Site	2
Sample	6
Ware/Core	3.2YR 5.5/7 lt red/red/reddish yellow; core 5YR 6/1.5 lt grey/pinkish grey; many small–medium white (lime + quartz), grey (chert) and brown grits; some mica flecks; rare chaff impressions; some shallow cracks at surfaces
Exterior	Traces of burnished slip at rim, may be 10R 5.5/8 lt red/red
Interior	Traces burnished slip 10R 5.5/8 lt red/red
Notes	Callaway 1972: fig. 16. 29 'Ai Phase I (3100–3000 B.C.); Schaub 1981: fig. 20.1 Bab edh-Dhra' Tomb A56 (beg. of EB II); Kenyon and Holland 1982: fig. 49.24 (EB)

No	2
Site	2
Sample	132
Ware/Core	Unevenly but well fired, mostly 5YR 6/4 lt reddish brown; many small–medium white (lime + quartz), grey and reddish brown grits; many mica flecks; rare chaff impressions
Exterior	Salt encrusted; 7.5YR 6/4 lt brown – 8.2YR 6.5/4 (mainly pink) – 2.5YR 6/6 lt red
Interior	Lime (?) encrusted; 7.5YR 6.5/6 reddish yellow – 2.5YR 6/6 lt red
Notes	Handle partly reconstructed from a complete handle collected in the same bag belonging to another less complete vessel of the same form and ware; pll for handle: Schaub 1981: fig. 6.11

No	3
Site	2
Sample	132
Ware/Core	5YR 6/3.5 lt reddish brown to within 0.35 cm from ext at base, rest as int; many small–medium white (lime + quartz), grey (chert), dk grey (basalt) and reddish brown grits; many mica flecks; rare chaff impressions
Exterior	Unevenly fired 7.5YR 6.5/2 pinkish grey – 8.2YR 6.5/4 (mainly v pale brown) – 2.5YR 6/6 lt red
Notes	Mostly 2.5YR 6/6 lt red

No	4
Site	2
Sample	132
Ware/Core	Mostly 5YR 6/3.5 lt reddish brown; many small–medium white (lime + quartz), grey and red grits; many mica fleaks; rare chaff impressions
Exterior	Unevenly fired 7.5YR 6.5/3 pinkish grey/pink/lt brown – 8.2YR 6.5/4 (mainly v pale brown) – 3.2YR 6.5/6 lt red/reddish yellow
Interior	Unevenly fired 7.5YR 6.5/6 reddish yellow – 2.5YR 6/6 lt red – 1.2Y 8/6 yellow

No	5
Site	2
Sample	5
Ware/Core	7.5YR 6/3 pinkish grey/lt brown; some small, rare medium white (lime), grey (chert) and dk grey grits; many mica flecks
Exterior	As ware
Interior	As ware
Notes	Kenyon and Holland 1982: fig. 63.29 (EB)

No	6
Site	2
Sample	4
Ware/Core	2.5YR 5.5/5 (mainly reddish brown); many small–large white (lime) and red-brown (grog)

	grits
Exterior	5YR 5.5/6 reddish yellow/yellowish red; wet smoothed
Interior	Colour as ext
Notes	Schaub 1981: fig. 11.4

No	7
Site	2
Sample	132
Ware/Core	Mostly 3.2YR 6/6 lt red/reddish yellow; core lower body only towards ext and showing in patches ext N 6/0 grey; many small–medium white (lime), dk grey and reddish brown grits; rare mica flecks; some chaff impressions
Exterior	Unevenly fired, 8.2YR 7.5/4 pink/v pale brown – 2.5YR 6/7 lt red – N 6/0 grey; deep red paint (colour not comparable to Munsell Soil Color Charts)
Interior	Unevenly fired 3.2YR 6/6 lt red/reddish yellow – 5YR 7/5 pink/reddish yellow
Notes	Schaub 1981: fig. 10.7,10; Kenyon and Holland 1982: fig. 42.1 (EB)

No	8
Site	2
Sample	5
Ware/Core	3.2YR 6/7 lt red; core N 5.5/0 grey; many small–large white (lime), grey and red (grog) grits; few reed impressions
Exterior	Thick matt slip 1.2Y 8/3 v pale brown/white/pale yellow marks
Interior	As ext, slip thinning towards body; finger smoothing marks

No	9
Site	2
Sample	6
Ware/Core	As corresponding surface colours; core N 6/0 lt grey/grey some small–large angular white (lime), grey, black and red (grog) grits, causing blistering and spalling
Exterior	Mostly 3.2YR 6/8 lt red/reddish yellow; partially covered with thin matt slip 7.5YR 8/4 pink
Interior	Approx. top 3.5 cm as ext – 10R 6/3.5 pale red; salt encrusted, finger smoothing marks (uneven)

No	10
Site	2
Sample	4
Ware/Core	5YR 6/6 reddish yellow; core 10YR 6.5/2 grey/lt brownish grey; many small–medium white (lime), grey and reddish brown (grog) grits; few reed impressions
Exterior	Thin uneven matt slip, 2.5Y 8/3 white/pale yellow where thickest – 6.2YR 7/6 reddish yellow where thin; spilling inside
Interior	5YR 6.5/6 reddish yellow, patch of slip as ext; shallow crack joint marks, finger smoothing marks at body

No	11
Site	2
Sample	5
Ware/Core	5YR 7/7 reddish yellow; core 10YR 6/1.5 lt grey/grey/lt brownish grey; many small–large white (lime), grey, dk grey, and reddish brown (grog) grits; some reed impressions
Exterior	Thin uneven matt slip 10YR 8/3.5 v pale brown where thickest – 5YR 6.5/6 reddish yellow where thin; extending over flaring rim
Interior	As ware; deep finger smoothing marks at body

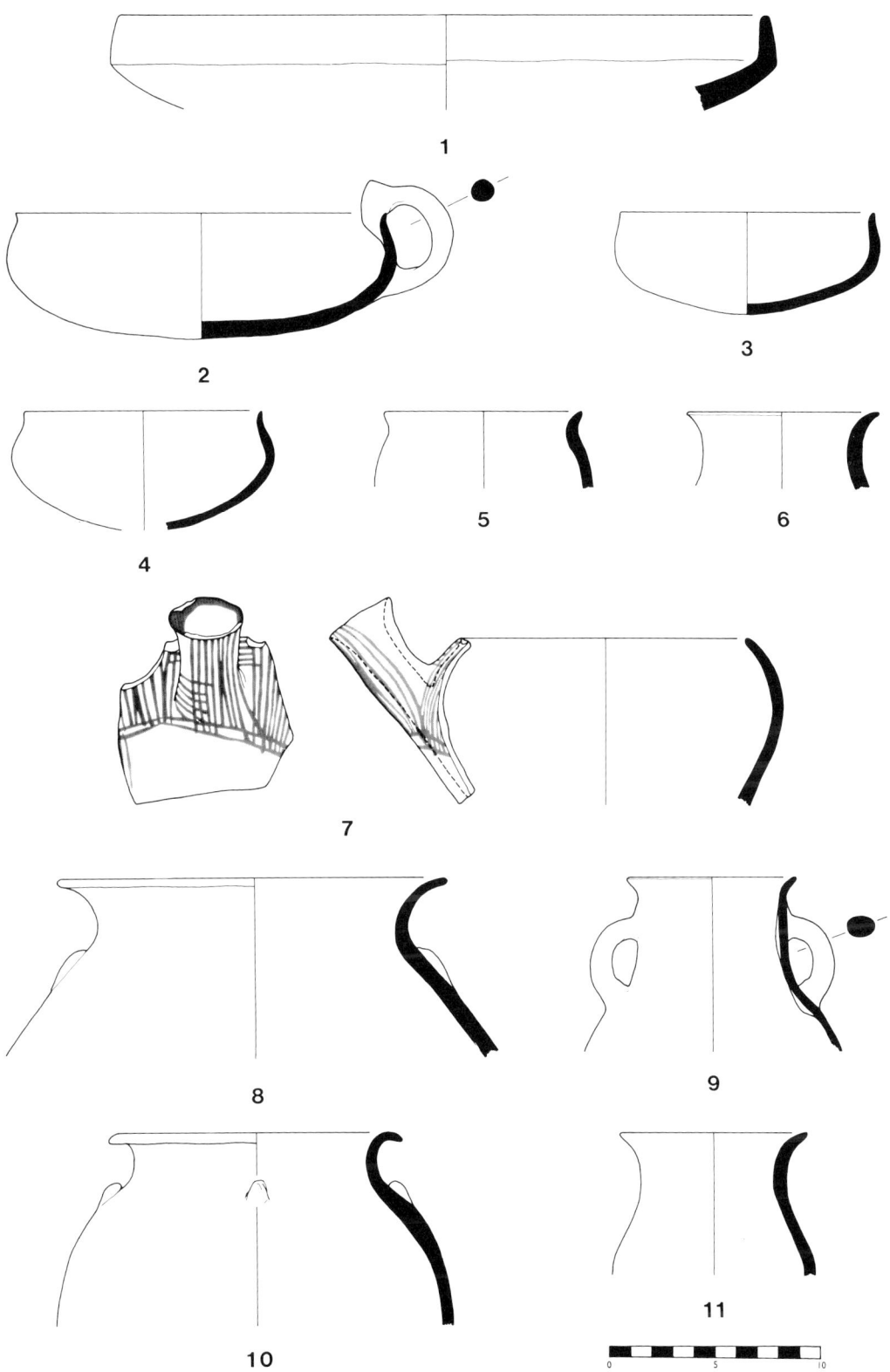

Plate 12   EB IB: Site 2 (all hand-made)

Plate 13   EB IB: Site 2 (all hand-made)

No	1
Site	2
Sample	217
Ware/Core	2.5YR 6/6 lt red; core N 5.5/0 grey; many small–large white (lime), grey and red-brown (grog) grits; some chaff impressions
Exterior	Thin matt slip; 8.2YR 6/4 lt brown/lt yellowish brown – 10YR 6/3.5 pale brown/lt yellowish brown – 10YR 7/3.5 v pale brown
Interior	Mostly 5YR 6/5 lt reddish brown/reddish yellow
Notes	Rim pll Callaway 1972: fig. 17.8, 'Ai Phase II (3100–3000 B.C.)

No	2
Site	2
Sample	132
Ware/Core	10R 5.5/5 weak red/red; small patch near base due to uneven firing 5YR 6.5/ 1.5 lt grey/pinkish grey; many small–medium white (lime), red (grog), few grey grits
Exterior	Somewhat lime encrusted; matt medium thick white slip covering base, deep red paint; (colours not comparable to Munsell Soil Color Charts)
Interior	Lime encrusted; 5YR 7/8 reddish yellow; well smoothed diagonal finger marks

No	3
Site	2
Sample	217
Ware/Core	2.5YR 6/6 lt red; patchy core at handle join 5YR 6.5/1 lt grey; many small–large white (lime), red-brown (grog) grits; reed impressions
Exterior	Thick matt white slip, deep dark red paint (colours not comparable to Munsell Soil Color Charts)
Interior	5YR 6.5/6 reddish yellow; well smoothed diagonal and vertical finger marks
Notes	Kenyon and Holland 1982: fig. 41.13

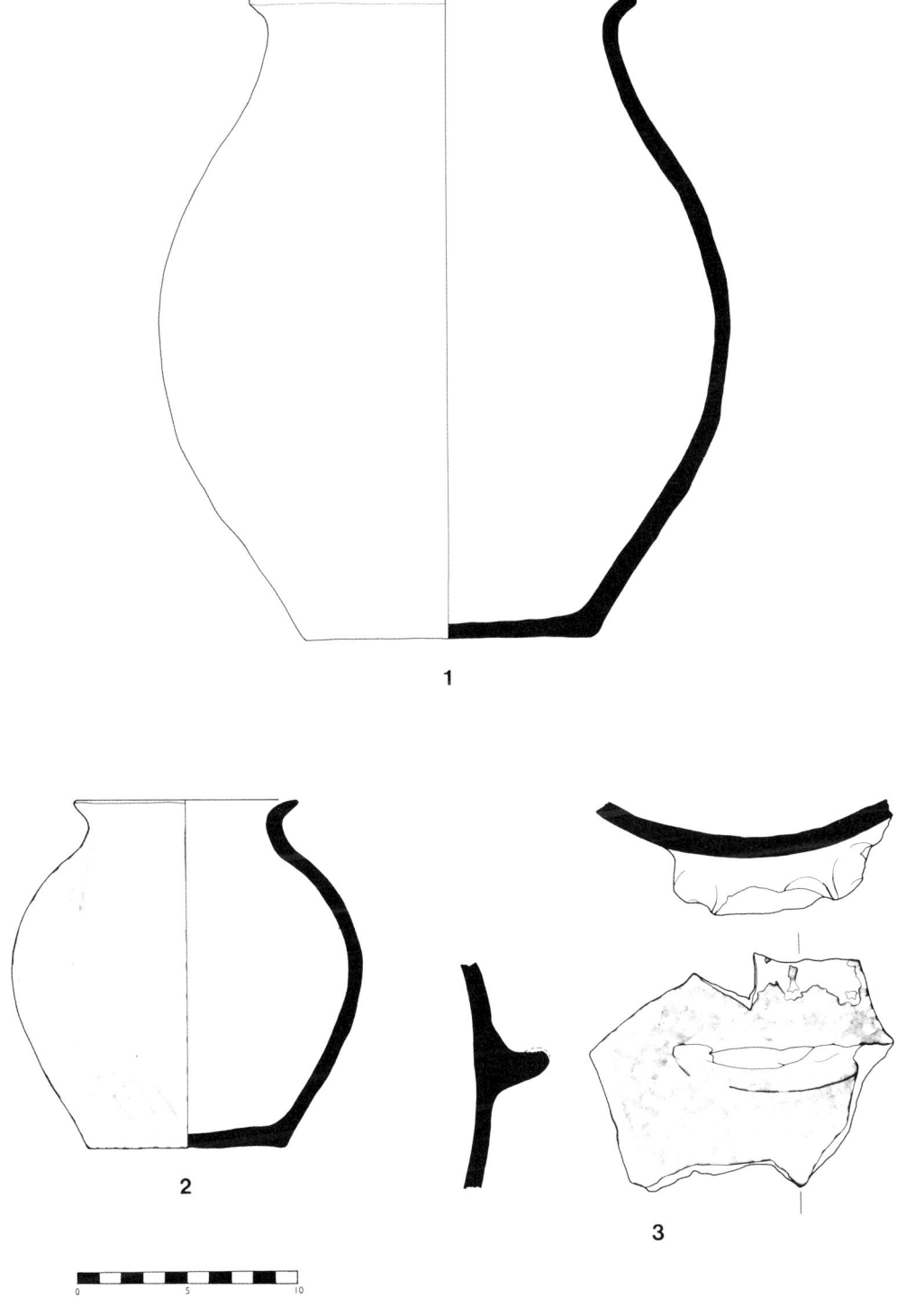

Plate 13 EB IB: Site 2 (all hand-made)

Plate 14   EB IV: Site 141

No	1
Site	141
Sample	281
Ware/Core	Hand-built (?), rim turned to 4 cm from top; 1.2YR 6/8 lt red; core 10R 6/3.5 pale brown/lt yellowish brown; many small–medium white (quartz, few lime), grey and red (grog) grits
Exterior	5Y 8/2.5 white/pale yellow
Interior	As ext
Notes	Olavari 1969: fig. 1.18 has burnished red slip 'Aro'er Level VIb (2250–2050B.C.)
No.	2
Site	141
Sample	281
Ware/Core	Hand-built, shallow join lines int; ext rim turned; 2.5YR 5/8 red; core 7.5YR 7/7 reddish yellow; many small–medium white (quartz), grey and brown grits; rare chaff impressions
Exterior	2.5Y 7.5/4 pale Yellow near rim – 7.5YR6/6 reddish yellow towards body
Interior	2.5Y 8/5 pale yellow/yellow at rim – 5YR 6/6 reddish yellow at body
Notes	Kenyon 1956: fig. 7.1; Olavarri 1969: fig 2.10 (burnished) 'Aro'er Level VIb (2250–2050 B.C.); Schaub 1973: fig. 6.13 (has red slip)
No	3
Site	141
Sample	242
Ware/Core	Hand-built (?), rim turned; 3.2YR 6.5/6 lt red/reddish yellow; patchy core 10YR 7/2.5 lt grey/v pale brown; many small–medium white (quartz, few lime), grey and red grits
Exterior	5Y 8/1.5 white
Interior	As ext
No	4
Site	141
Sample	281
Ware/Core	Hand-built, wheel-finished (?); 2.5YR 6/7 lt red; core 2.5Y 7.5/2 white/lt grey; many small–medium white (quartz), grey and red grits
Exterior	Roughly abraded; 5Y 8/3.5 pale yellow
Interior	Colour as ext
Notes	Olavari 1969: fig. 1:12 (has red slip); 'Aro'er Level VIb (2250–2050 B.C.)
No	5
Site	141
Sample	280
Ware/Core	Hand-built, rim turned; 5YR 6.5/8 reddish yellow; many small–medium white (quartz, few lime), grey and red grits
Exterior	5Y 8/3.5 pale yellow (extending up to 0.2 cm into body section)
Interior	Colour as ext
Notes	Olavarri 1969: fig. 4.16 (has burnished red slip) 'Aro'er Level VIa (2050–1900 B.C.)
No	6
Site	141
Sample	280
Ware/Core	Wheel-finished; 2.5YR 6/7 lt red; many small–medium white (quartz), grey and red grits
Exterior	2.5Y 7.5/4 pale yellow near rim – 7.5YR 6/5 lt brown/reddish yellow
Interior	2.5Y 8/4 pale yellow
No	7

Site	141
Sample	281
Ware/Core	Wheel-finished; 7.5YR 7/6 reddish yellow; some small–medium white (quartz), grey (chert) and brown grits, rare large angular lime; rare chaff impressions
Exterior	Much discoloured; thick horizontal burnished slip also covering int rim 5YR 6/8 reddish yellow
Interior	Much discoloured, may be same as ware
Notes	Olavari 1969: fig. 1.2 'Aro'er Level VIb 2250–2050 B.C.); Prag 1971: fig. 30.3 (has buff slip)
No	8
Site	141
Sample	281
Ware/Core	Manufacturing technique difficult to determine by eye; 5YR 6.5/8 reddish yellow; many small–large angular white (lime + quartz) grits, many small grey and brown grits, rare mica
Exterior	Remains of thick (burnished?) slip 10R 4.5/4 weak red
Interior	As ext
Notes	[Form and slip close to EB II–III types, i.e. LEB II–EEB III]
No	9
Site	141
Sample	281
Ware/Core	Hand-built, rim turned; 10YR 6/2.5 lt brownish grey/pale brown; core 2.5YR 6/7 lt red; many small–medium white (lime + quartz), grey and red grits; rare chaff impressions
Exterior	5Y 8/2.5 white/pale yellow; combed decoration
Interior	Colour as ext
Notes	Decoration similar to Olavarri 1969: pl. III.16, 'Aro'er Phase VIa (2050–1900 B.C.); Prag 1971: fig. 31.5
No	10
Site	141
Sample	281
Ware/Core	Hand-built; 5YR 6.5/8 reddish yellow, secondary burning at part of rim turning colour to 1.2YR 5/6 red; many small–large angular white (lime + quartz), pink (mineral), grey (chert), green (schist?), red and brown grits; rare chaff impressions; rare cracking int
Exterior	Extensively lime-encrusted; may be as ware – 2.5Y 7/5 pale yellow/yellow
Interior	As ware
Notes	Prag 1971: fig. 33.1 (has red burnished slip)
No	11
Site	141
Sample	240
Ware/Core	Int base has wheel-marks, finger marks int where base is joined to hand-built body; 10YR 6/4 lt yellowish brown; core 2.5YR 6/7 lt red; many small–medium white (quartz), grey and red grits; few chaff impressions; rare spalling int
Exterior	3.2Y 8/3 white/pale yellow
Interior	Much discoloured, may be 2.5YR 6/7 lt red (as core) at base – 3.2Y 8/3 white/pale yellow as ext) at body
Notes	Kenyon and Holland 1982: fig. 95.15 (EB–MB)

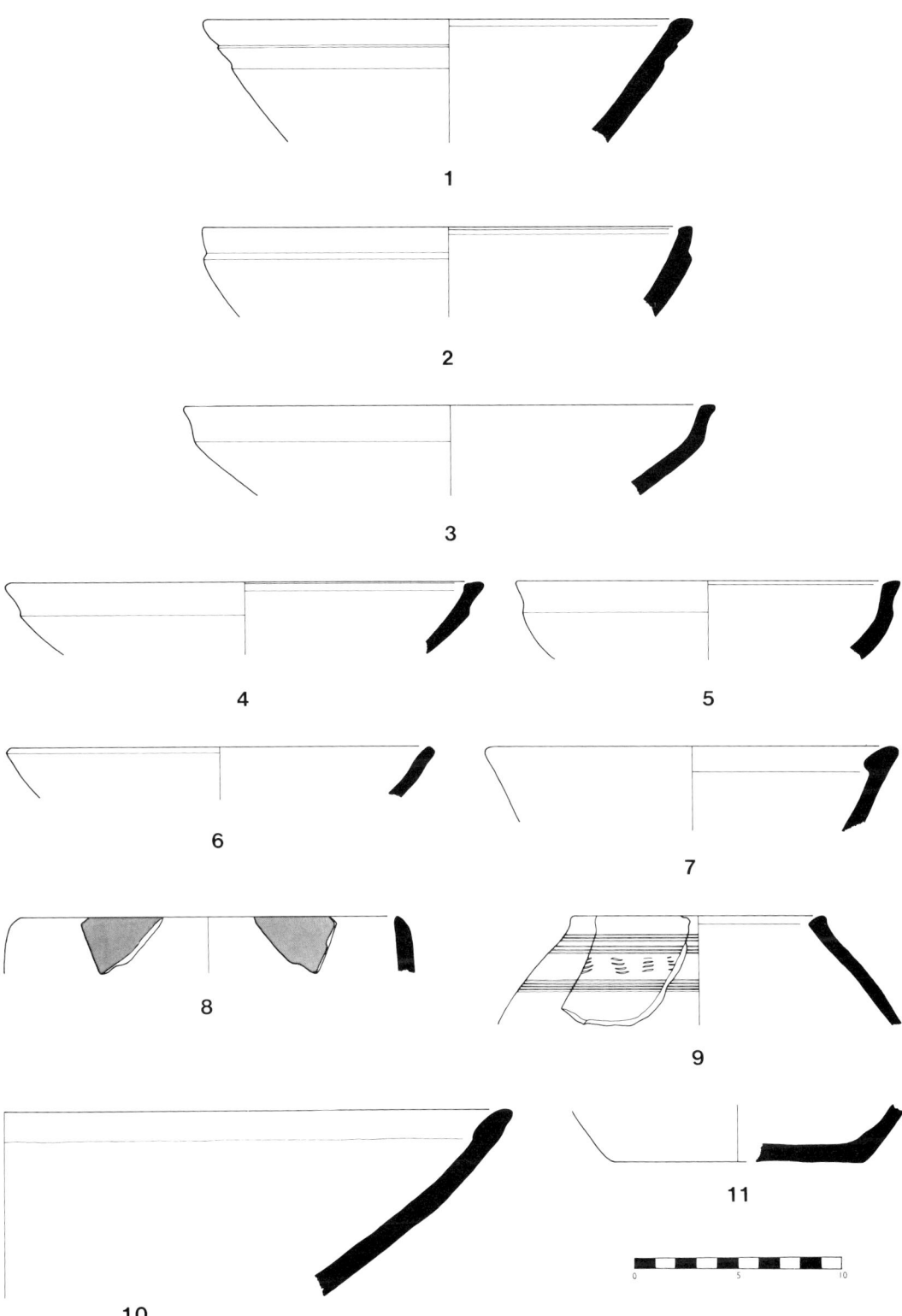

Plate 14   EB IV: Site 141

Plate 15   EB IV: Sites 30, 109, 119, and 120

No   1
Site   120C
Sample   195
Ware/Core   Slow-wheel; 3.2YR 6/6 lt red/reddish yellow;
              many small–medium white, grey and reddish
              brown grits
Exterior   Some secondary burning; 5YR 6/7 reddish yellow
Interior   Some lime encrustation; as ext
Notes   Prag 1971: fig. 31.13; Kenyon and Holland 1982:
              fig. 95.12 (EB–MB)

No   2
Site   109
Sample   184
Ware/Core   Hand-made, wheel finished rim and combing;
              1.2YR 6/6 lt red; core 7.5YR 5.5/2 pinkish
              grey/brown; many small–large white (lime), grey,
              deep red and quartz grits; some cracking and
              spalling at surfaces
Exterior   Thick uneven matt slip 5Y 8/3 pale yellow –
              10YR 7.5/4 v pale brown
Interior   As ext

No   3
Site   109
Sample   184
Ware/Core   Slow-wheel; 2.5YR 6/7 lt red; core 10YR 6/2.5 lt
              brownish grey/pale brown; many small–medium
              white (quartz ?), grey and red grits
Exterior   Thick matt slip 2.5Y 8/3 white/pale yellow white
Interior   Thick matt slip, paler than 5Y 8/1 white
Notes   Cleveland 1960: fig. 15.9, (burnished red slip),
              Ader Phase A/B; Olavarri 1969: fig. 1.19
              (burnished red slip) 'Aro'er Level VIb (2250–2050
              B.C. MB I); Prag 1971: fig. 33.3 (burnished red
              slip); Kenyon and Holland 1982: fig. 95.13
              (EB–MB)

No   4
Site   30
Sample   76
Ware/Core   Wheel-made; 10R 5/8 red; core N 4.5/0 grey/dk
              grey; many small–medium white, dk grey and
              quartz grits
Exterior   2.5YR 4.5/6 red; traces of matt slip 2.5Y 6.5/2 lt
              grey/lt brownish grey

Interior   Thick matt slip 2.5Y 6.5/2 lt grey/lt brownish grey

No   5
Site   30
Sample   410
Ware/Core   Hand-made, rim turned; 10R 5/7 red; core N 4.5/0
              grey/dk grey; many small–large white, grey and
              brown and red (grog) grits; rare mica flecks few
              chaff impressions
Exterior   Thin matt slip 2.5YR 5/5 reddish brown/red
Interior   Thick matt slip 10YR 7/3 v pale brown
Notes   Cleveland 1960: fig. 14.5 (burnished red slip),
              Ader Phase B (21st c B.C.); Prag 1971: fig. 31.15
              (matt red slip)

No   6
Site   30
Sample   77
Ware/Core   Hand-made, rim turned; 10R 5/7 red; core N 4.5/0
              grey/dk grey towards and showing in patch ext;
              many small–medium white and grey grits
Exterior   As ware
Interior   As ware

No   7
Site   119
Sample   191
Ware/Core   Hand-made, rim turned; 2.5YR 6/7 lt red;
              mending hole (?); many small–medium,
              semiangular white, grey and red mineral grit
Exterior   Thick matt slip 5Y 8/2.5 white/pale yellow
Interior   As ext
Notes   Stance doubtful, due to small size of sherd and
              abraded rim

No   8
Site   119
Sample   191
Ware/Core   Hand-made or slow-wheel; 5YR 7/7 reddish
              yellow – 3.2YR 6/8 lt red/reddish yellow; many
              small–medium white (lime + quartz), greyish
              brown, black (basalt) and mineral red grits; rare
              chaff impressions
Exterior   As ware
Interior   As ware

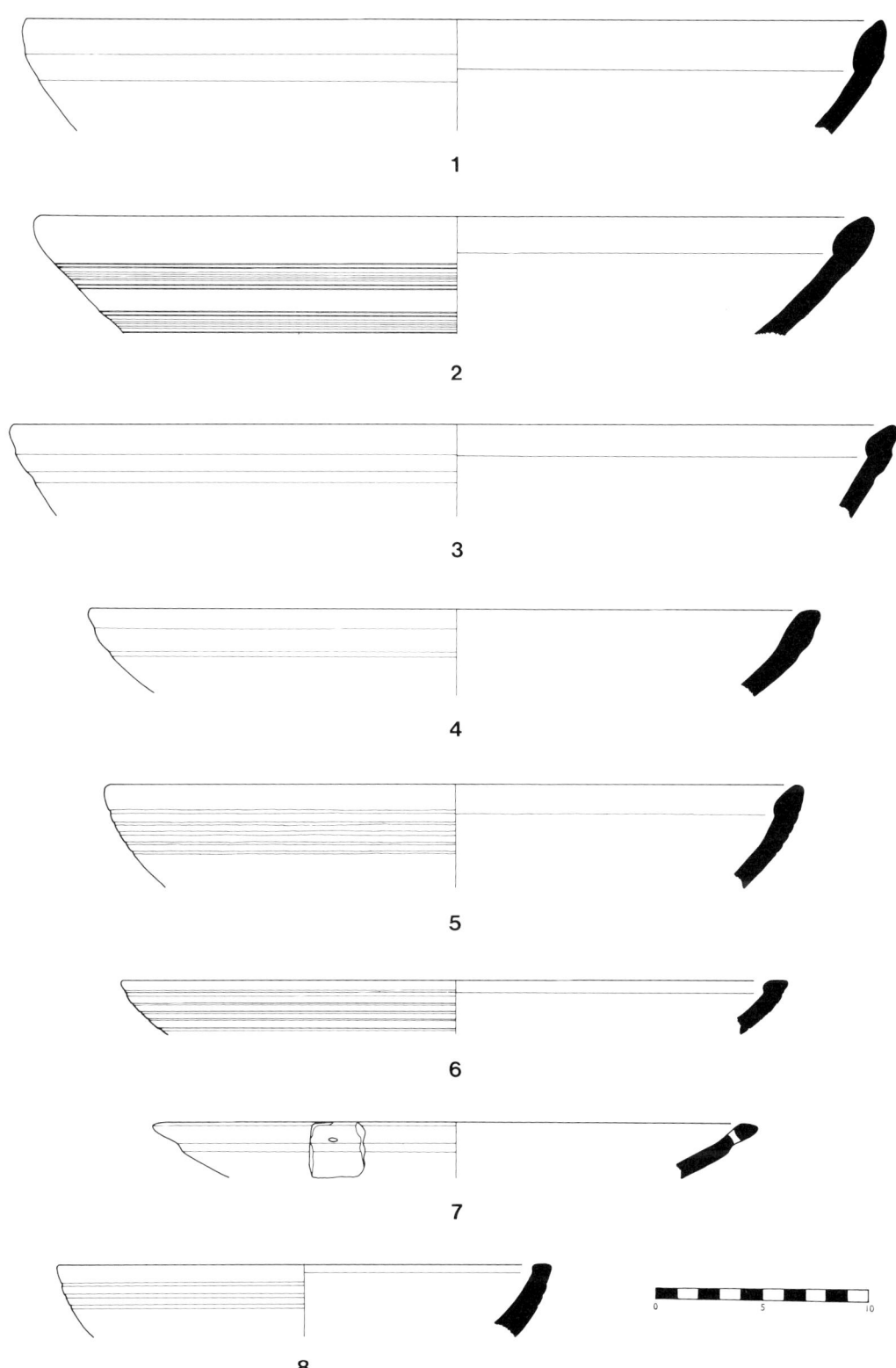

Plate 15   EB IV: Sites 30, 109, 119, and 120

Plate 16   EB IV: Sites 9, 119, 120, 139, 174, and 198

No	1
Site	120A
Sample	193
Ware/Core	Hand-made; 7.5YR 7/4 pink; many small white, grey and quartz grits; some chaff impressions
Exterior	Wet-smoothed surface; 6.2YR 8/4 pink
Interior	Wet-smoothed, slightly burnished surface; 5YR 7/5 pink/reddish yellow
Notes	Johnston and Schaub 1978: fig. 4.40 (LEB III–EEB IV); Kenyon and Holland 1982: fig. 94.24 (EB–MB)

No	2
Site	174E
Sample	299
Ware/Core	Hand-made, rim and body turned near carination; 2.5YR 5/7 red; many small–medium white, grey, mineral brown and quartz grits
Exterior	Shallow combing 5YR 6.5/8 reddish yellow; traces of thick slightly burnished slip 5Y 7.5/2 white/lt grey
Interior	Colour and slip as ext

No	3
Site	119
Sample	190
Ware/Core	Slow-wheel; 2.5YR 6/7 lt red; core N 4.5/0 grey/dk grey; many small–medium white (lime), grey, red (grog) and brown grits; many small–medium voids giving finely poked appearance
Exterior	Shallow combing and punctate decoration; thin matt slip 7.5YR 7/7 reddish yellow – 10YR7.5/4 v pale brown
Interior	Lime encrusted; 6.2YR 6.5/6 pink/lt reddish brown/reddish yellow

No	4
Site	119
Sample	190
Ware/Core	Hand-made, rim turned; 5YR 6.5/6 reddish yellow; many small white, grey, red and quartz grits, giving sandy finely mottled texture
Exterior	Shallow combing; as ware; small patch of badly worn slip 2.5YR 5/7 red
Interior	Lime encrusted; as ware
Notes	Olavarri 1969: fig. 4.13, 'Aro'er Level VIa (2050–1900 B.C.)

No	5
Site	198C
Sample	342
Ware/Core	Slow-wheel (?) made; 10YR 6.5/3 v pale brown/pale brown; many small–large white (lime), grey (basalt?) and red (grog) grits; some spalling; few chaff impressions
Exterior	Shallow combing; medium thick matt slip 2.5Y 7.5/2 white/lt grey

Interior	Much abraded; as ware
Notes	Prag 1971: fig. 26.3 (Iktanu Phase 2)

No	6
Site	9
Sample	15
Ware/Core	Hand-made; rim turned; 8.2YR 3.5/2 dk brown/dk greyish brown/v dk greyish brown; core N 3/0 v dk grey; many small–medium white (lime + quartz), grey and red (mineral + grog) grits; some spalling int
Exterior	Shallow combing, impressed decoration; 6.2YR 6/3 lt reddish brown/pinkish grey/lt brown
Interior	N 3.5/0 dk grey/v dk grey
Notes	Ware and neck (smaller diameter) similar to Olavarri 1969: fig. 5.8 'Aro'er Level VIa (2050–1900 B.C.)

No	7
Site	120E
Sample	244
Ware/Core	Hand-made, rim turned; extensive damage due to salt recrystalisation in fabric; 7.5YR 7/7 reddish yellow; many small–medium white (lime), grey, black (basalt?), pale brown and red (mineral) grits
Exterior	Shallow combing; thick matt slip 5Y 8/2.5 white/pale yellow
Interior	As ware; slip as ext extending onto rim and neck
Notes	Kenyon and Holland 1982: fig. 97.26

No	8
Site	120E
Sample	244
Ware/Core	Hand-made, rim turned down to combed decoration level; cracks at coil joins interior body; 5Y 7.5/2 white/lt grey; many small white grey, red (grog) and quartz grits
Exterior	Medium deep combing; uneven thin matt slip 8.2YR 7/6 reddish yellow/yellow – 2.5Y 7.5/2 white/lt grey
Interior	As ware
Notes	Olavarri 1969: fig. 2.2 (has pink ware, no knob handle) 'Aro'er Level VIb (2250–2050 B.C.)

No	9
Site	139
Sample	235
Ware/Core	Hand-made; 2.5YR 6/7 reddish yellow; core 10YR 6/1.5 grey/lt brownish grey; many small–medium white (lime), black (basalt), brown (grog) and some pyrite (?) grits
Exterior	Shallow wide combing; wet-smoothed; slight over-all burnishing body; 7.5YR 6.5/6 reddish yellow
Interior	5YR 6.5/6 reddish yellow
Notes	Olavarri 1969: fig. 5.14 (greyish ware); pl. IV.3, both 'Aro'er Level VIa (2050–1900 B.C.); Prag 1971: fig. 41.11

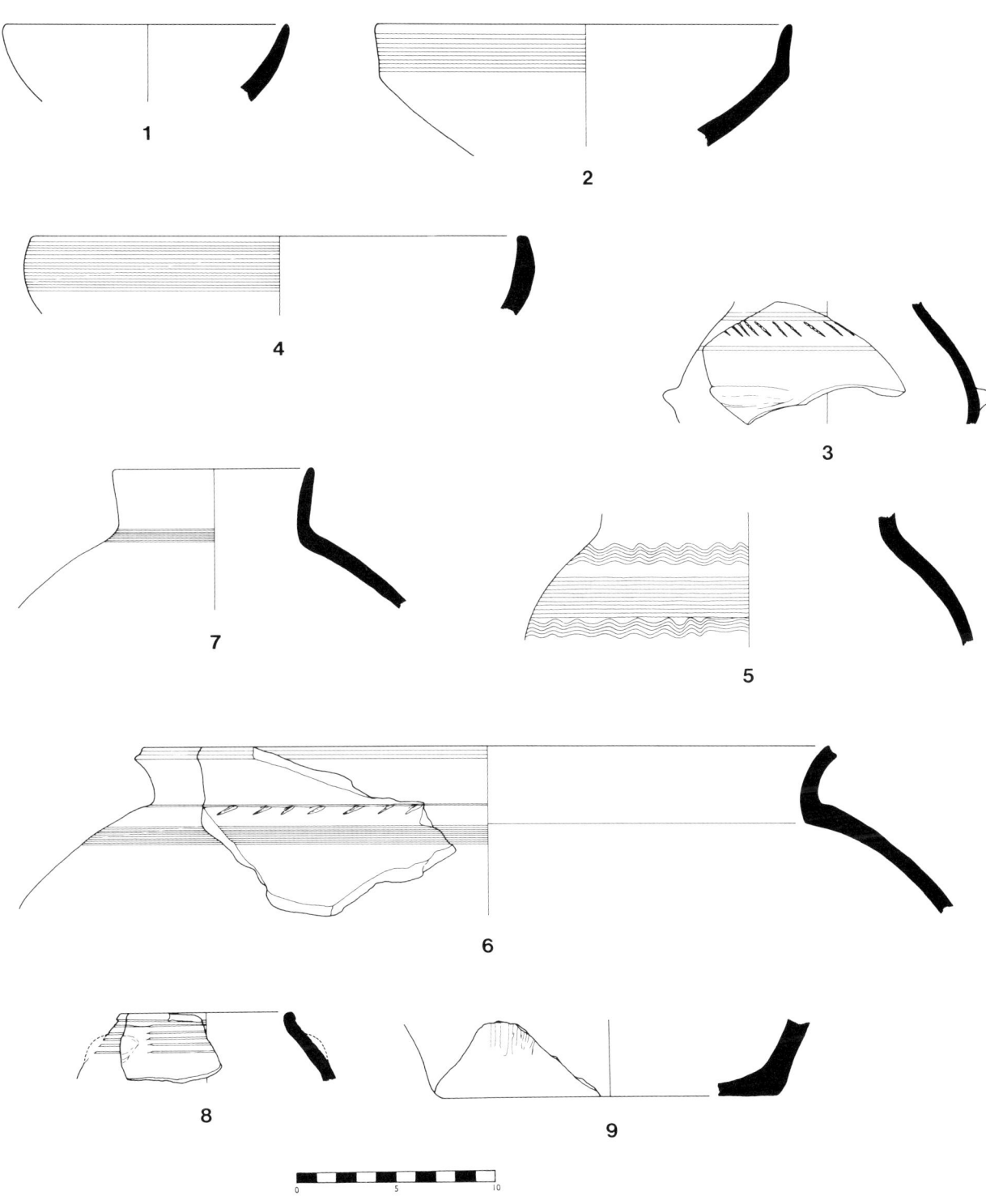

Plate 16 EB IV: Sites 9, 119, 120, 139, 174, and 198

Plate 17   Early Bronze, Byzantine, and Late Islamic: Site 79

No	1
Site	79A
Sample	121
Ware/Core	Hand-made; 8.2YR 7/3 pinkish grey/pink/v pale brown towards ext – 5Y 7/5 pale yellow/yellow – 10YR 6/3.5 pale brown/lt yellowish brown towards int; many small–large white, grey, black, pink and brown grits protruding int
Exterior	8.2YR 7/3 pinkish grey/pink/v pale brown
Interior	5Y 7/5 pale yellow/yellow at rim – 10YR 6/3.5 pale brown/lt yellowish brown at body
Notes	[EB IV (?)]

No	2
Site	79B
Sample	123
Ware/Core	Hand-made; 7.5YR 5.5/4 lt brown/brown; many small–medium white, grey (chert) and some brown grits; some mica flecks
Exterior	Thumb impressed (protruding) decoration; 8.2YR 7/4 pink/v pale brown
Interior	8.2YR 6.5/6 reddish yellow/yellow/brownish yellow
Notes	[EB IV (?)]

No	3
Site	79A
Sample	121
Ware/Core	Hand-made, wheel-finished ext; 2.5YR 6/6 lt red; core 10YR 6/5 lt brownish yellow/yellowish brown; many small–large white (lime), grey (basalt), some red, brown and quartz grits; some chaff impressions; rare mica flecks
Exterior	Much abraded; thick matt slip 2.5Y 7.5/4 pale yellow
Interior	Somwehat abraded; slip as ext
Notes	Kenyon 1956: fig. 7.2 (EB–MB)

No	4
Site	79H
Sample	125
Ware/Core	Wheel-made; 2.5YR 6/7 lt red; few small white (lime), rare small red and grey grits
Exterior	Heavily lime encrusted; thin matt slip 1.2YR 5.5/8 lt red/red
Interior	As ware; slip as ext to within 0.5 cm inside rim
Notes	[EByz]

No	5
Site	79B
Sample	123
Ware/Core	Wheel-made; 10R 5/7 red; many small white (lime), brown and quartz grits
Exterior	Thick matt slip 10YR 6/1.5 lt grey/grey/lt brownish grey
Interior	Thin matt slip 2.5YR 5/3 weak red/reddish brown
Notes	[LByz]

No	6
Site	79B
Sample	123
Ware/Core	Hand-made; 5YR 6.5/8 reddish yellow; many small–large white (lime), grey and brown grits; few mica flecks
Exterior	5YR 7/5 pink/reddish yellow; thin slightly burnished slip (horizontally) 10R 6/7 lt red
Interior	Colour as ext; traces of slip similar to ext
Notes	[LIsl, Mam?] looks similar to No. 8

No	7
Site	79B
Sample	123
Ware/Core	Wheel-made; 10YR 7.5/3 v pale brown towards ext – 6.2YR 7.5/4 pink towards int; many small–medium, angular white (lime), grey (chert + basalt), brown, quartz, one large (0.4 cm) and one medium (0.1 cm) schist and one large (1.2 cm) pink chert grits; some mica flecks; some chaff impressions
Exterior	Surface totally abraded; 10YR 7.5/3 v pale brown
Interior	Surface abraded near rim; 6.2YR 7.5/4 pink
Notes	[Mam]

No	8
Site	79B
Sample	123
Ware/Core	Hand-made; 5YR 7/7 reddish yellow; patchy core 10YR 6/1.5 lt grey/grey/lt brownish grey; many small–large white (lime), grey and brown grits; rare mica flecks; rare spalling and cracking int
Exterior	As ware; thin, slightly burnished slip 2.5YR 5/6 red, worn under handle
Interior	Slip as ext
Notes	Tushingham 1972: fig. 8.4 (pierced handle, no paint, Turkish); [Mam?] looks similar to No 6

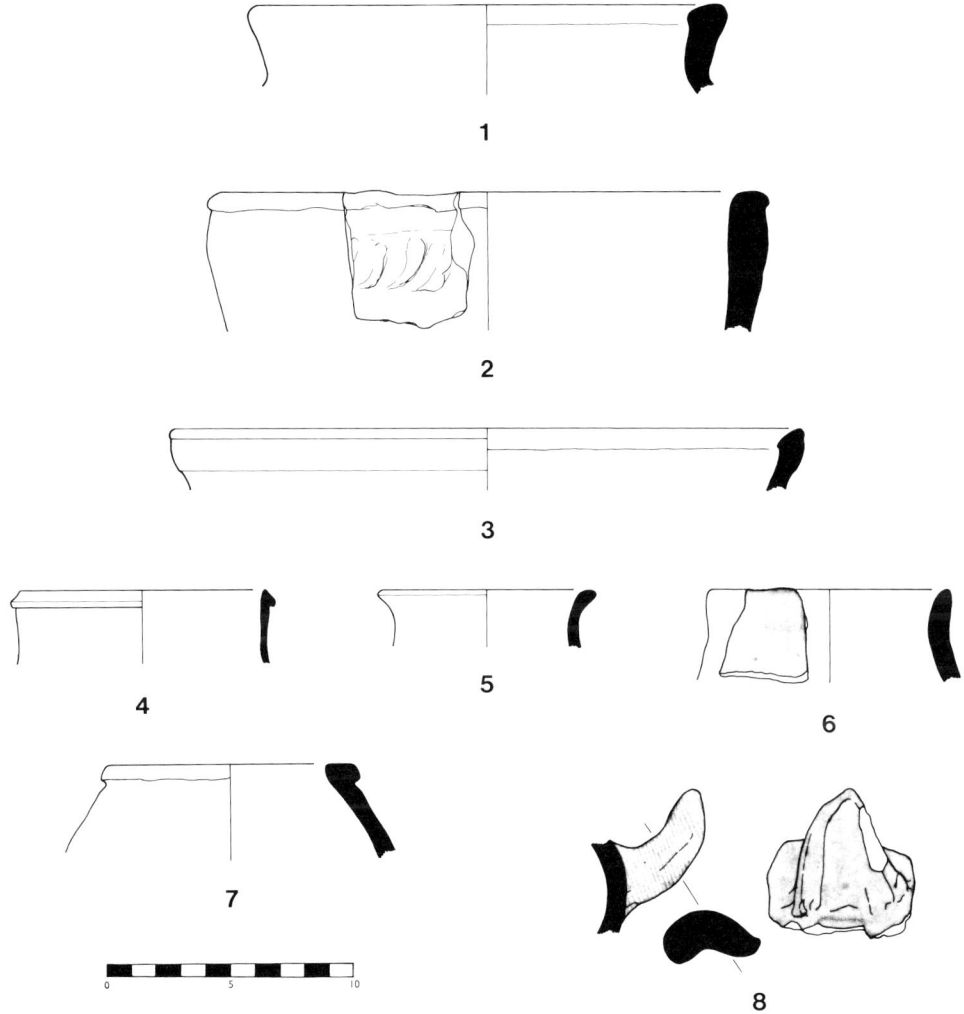

Plate 17   Early Bronze, Byzantine, and Late Islamic: Site 79

Plate 18   Iron I and II: Sites 73 and 159 (all wheel-made)

No	1
Site	159
Sample	288
Ware/Core	2.5YR 5.5/8 lt red/red; core 5YR 5/1 grey; many small–large white (lime), grey and red grits; some mica flecks; many small–large deep voids giving poked appearance
Exterior	Discoloured; 7.5YR 5.5/4 lt brown/brown
Interior	Discoloured; 5YR 5.5/5 reddish brown/yellowish red
Notes	Harding 1953: fig. 14.59 (lighter colours) 1250–1150 B.C.=EIron I)

No	2
Site	159
Sample	287
Ware/Core	2.5YR 5/6 red; core 5YR 4.5/2 reddish grey/dk reddish grey – 5YR 3/1 v dk grey; many small–large white (lime) and black (basalt) grits; many small–large deep voids giving pocked appearance
Exterior	Discoloured; slipped (?) 7.5 YR 5.5/2 pinkish grey/brown – 7.5YR 4.5/1 grey/dk grey/brown
Interior	Discoloured; 5YR 4.5/1.5 mostly dk reddish grey
Notes	[Iron I]

No	3
Site	159
Sample	288
Ware/Core	2.5YR 5/5 reddish brown/red; core 5YR 4/1 dk grey; many small–large white (lime), grey and black (basalt) grits
Exterior	Discoloured; 5YR 5/3.5 mainly reddish brown – 5YR 4/1 dk grey
Interior	Discoloured; 5YR 4.5/2 reddish grey/dk reddish grey – 5YR 4/1 dk grey
Notes	Rast 1978: fig. 1.1 Taanach Period IA (1200–1150 B.C.=Iron IA)

No	4
Site	159
Sample	288
Ware/Core	Crude, may be hand or slow-wheel made; core completely filling section and showing surfaces 10YR 3/1.5 v dk grey/v dk greyish brown; many small–large white, light reddish yellow (lime), light grey, dk grey and brown grits; rare chaff impressions; many small–large deep voids giving pocked appearance
Exterior	Discoloured; 5YR 5/3.5 reddish brown – 10YR 3/1.5 v dk grey/v dk greyish brown
Interior	Somewhat discoloured; 5YR 5/3.5 reddish brown to within 0.7 cm from rim; body 2.5YR 5/5 reddish brown/red with striations of 10YR 3/1.5 v dk grey/v dk greyish brown
Notes	[Iron I–EII]

No	5
Site	159
Sample	287
Ware/Core	2.5YR 5.5/6 lt red/red; core 5YR 4.5/1.5 mainly dk reddish grey; many small–large angular white (lime), black (basalt) and brown grits; many small–large deep voids giving pocked appearance
Exterior	Discoloured; thick matt slip 8.2YR 6/2 pinkish grey/lt brownish grey
Interior	As ext
Notes	Rast 1978: fig. 33.1 Taanach Period IIB (960–918 B.C.= Iron IC); Kenyon and Holland 1982: fig. 209.17

No	6
Site	159
Sample	287
Ware/Core	10R 4.5/8 red; core 2.5YR 4/1 dk grey/weak red; many small–large angular white (lime), black (basalt) and red grits; rare mica flecks; rare chaff

impressions; many small–large deep voids giving pocked appearance

Exterior	Discoloured; 5YR 4.5/3.5 reddish brown
Interior	Discoloured; 10YR 5.5/3 pale brown/brown
Notes	[Iron I–EII]

No	7
Site	159
Sample	288
Ware/Core	3.2YR 4.5/6 red; core 5YR 4.5/1 grey/dk grey; many small–large white (lime + quartz?), black (basalt) and brown grits
Exterior	Slightly discoloured; 5YR 5/4 reddish brown
Interior	As ext
Notes	Rast 1978: fig. 65.2 Taanach Period IIB (960–918 B.C.=Iron IC)

No	8
Site	159
Sample	288
Ware/Core	3.2YR 5/7 red; core 5YR 5/2 reddish grey – 5YR 3/0.5 v dk grey towards ext; many small–large white (lime), black (basalt) and brown grits; many small–large deep voids giving irregular pocked appearances
Exterior	Discoloured; as ware
Interior	Much discoloured; may be as ware
Notes	Pritchard 1985: fig. 16.8 (brown) Tell es-Sa'idiyeh Stratum IV (730?–600 B.C.=Iron IIB)

No	9
Site	159
Sample	287
Ware/Core	2.5YR 5/4 reddish brown; core patchy at body, filling handle section N 4/0 dk grey; some small–large white (lime) and brown grits; many small–large deep voids giving pocked appearance
Exterior	As ware
Interior	As ware
Notes	Pritchard 1985: fig. 3.26 Tell es-Sa'idiyeh Stratum VII (825–790 B.C.=Iron IIA)

No	10
Site	159
Sample	288
Ware/Core	2.5YR 5/4 reddish brown; core N 3/0 v dk grey; many small–medium white (lime), black (basalt) and brown grits; rare chaff impressions
Exterior	Discoloured; 3.2YR 4/2 weak red/dk reddish grey – 2.5YR 4.5/4 reddish brown
Interior	As ext
Notes	Yassine 1984: fig. 4.1 (Iron IIC/Persian)

No	11
Site	73
Sample	99
Ware/Core	6.2YR 7/8 reddish yellow; core 6.2YR 6/1.5 grey/pinkish grey; many small–medium grey (chert), red (grog) and quartz grits
Exterior	As ware
Interior	As ware
Notes	Rast 1978: fig. 58:3 Taanach Period IIB (960–918 B.C.=Iron IC)

No	12
Site	73
Sample	99
Ware/Core	Core completely filling section N 4/0 dk grey; many small–medium white (lime), brown (grog) and few grey grits; rare mica flecks
Exterior	5YR 4/1 grey at body; 5YR 4.5/3 reddish brown top of rim
Interior	6.2YR pink
Notes	McNicoll, Smith and Hennessy 1982: pl. 126.9 (lighter colours) 8th–7th, perhaps also 6th c B.C.=Iron IIC

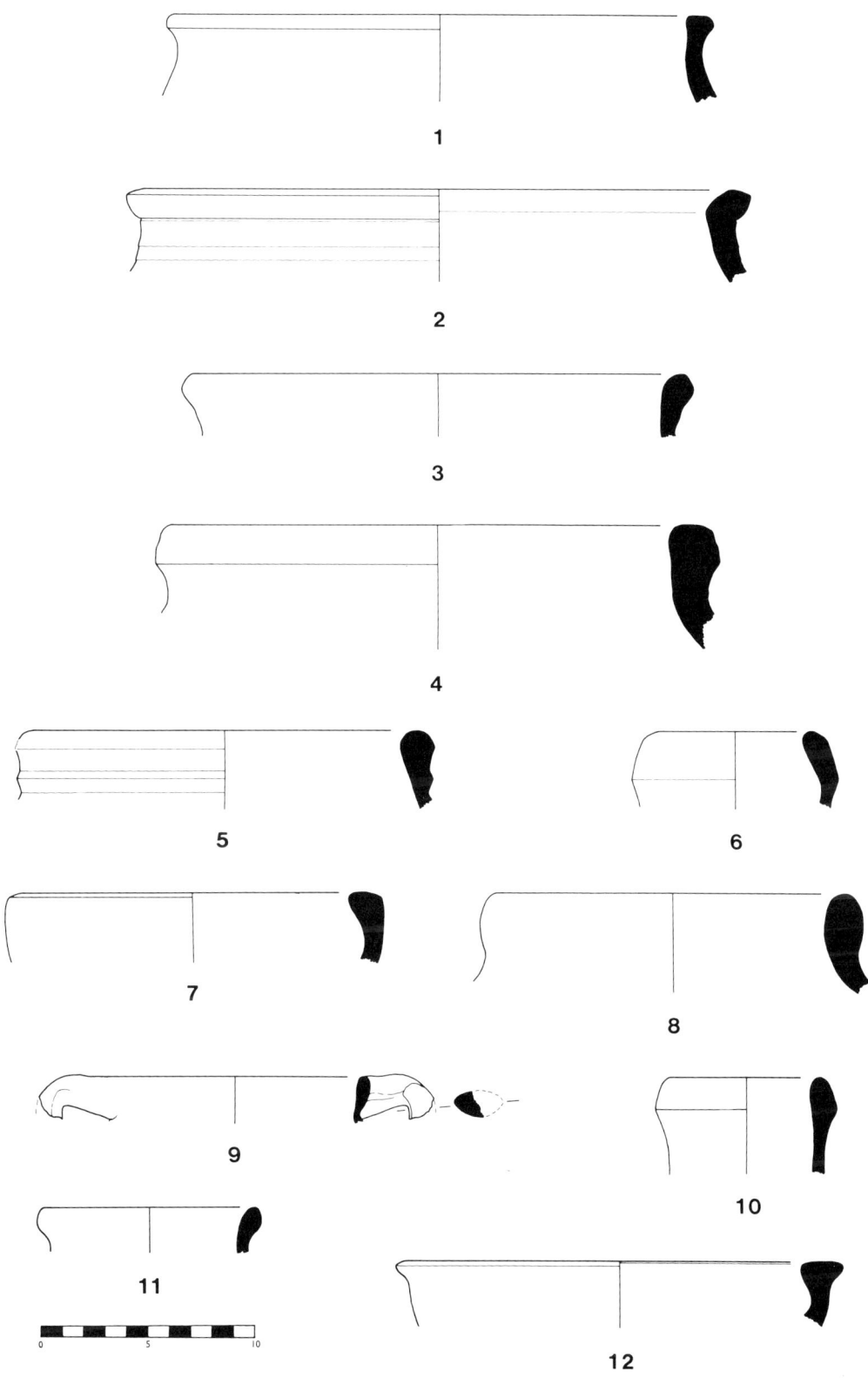

Plate 18   Iron I and II: Sites 73 and 159 (all wheel-made)

Plate 19   Iron I and II: Sites 34, 108, and 161 (all wheel-made)

No   1
Site   161
Sample   301
Ware/Core   5YR 4.5/4 reddish brown; core 5YR 5/1.5 grey/reddish grey; many small–large white (lime), grey and reddish brown (grog) grits
Exterior   5YR 5.5/4 lt reddish brown/reddish brown
Interior   5YR 5/5 reddish brown/yellowish red
Notes   [Iron I]

No   2
Site   161
Sample   302
Ware/Core   Core completely filling section 5YR 4/1 dk grey; many small–medium white (lime + quartz), grey and brown grits; few mica flecks
Exterior   7.5YR 6.5/4 pink/lt brown
Interior   7.5YR 5.5/2 pinkish grey/brown at body – 7.5YR 6/4 lt brown at rim
Notes   Franken 1969: fig. 65. 38 Deir 'Alla Phase G (1150–1050 B.C.)

No   3
Site   161
Sample   302
Ware/Core   5YR 5/2 reddish grey; core 5YR 3.5/1 dk grey/v dk grey; many small–medium white (lime + chert), grey (chert) and dk grey grits
Exterior   3.2YR 5/4 reddish brown – 2.5YR 4.5/6 red
Interior   2.5YR 4.5/6 red at rim – 5YR 5.5/4 lt reddish brown/reddish brown at body
Notes   [Iron I]

No   4
Site   161
Sample   301
Ware/Core   5YR 6/4 lt reddish brown; core 5YR 5.5/1 grey; many small–medium white (lime), grey and red-brown (grog) grits; some chaff impressions; rare mica flecks
Exterior   5YR 6.5/6 reddish yellow
Interior   As ware
Notes   Crowfoot, Crowfoot and Kenyon 1957: fig. 21.4, Samaria Period V–VI (EIron II, pre-7th c B.C.)

No   5
Site   161
Sample   301
Ware/Core   2.5YR 5/6 red; core 10YR 5/2 greyish brown; many small–medium, white and dk grey grits
Exterior   As ware
Interior   As ware
Notes   Franken 1969: fig. 75. 14, Deir Alla Phase L (last quarter of 11th c B.C.)

No   6
Site   161
Sample   302
Ware/Core   2.5YR 6/7 lt red; core 10YR 4.5/1 grey/dk grey; many small–large white (lime), dk grey and red (grog) grits; rare chaff impressions many small–large deep voids giving somewhat pocked appearance
Exterior   As ware
Interior   As ware
Notes   Crowfoot, Crowfoot and Kenyon 1957: fig. 30.8, Samaria Period V–VI (EIron II, pre-7th c B.C.)

No   7
Site   34
Sample   39
Ware/Core   7.5YR 5.5/2 pinkish grey/brown; many small–large white (lime), dk grey (basalt?) and few red-brown grits, some protruding surfaces; rare chaff impressions; some cracking int
Exterior   Thin matt slip 2.5Y 7.5/2 white/lt grey; base of handle mended with lighter coloured clay
Interior   7.5YR 6.5/2 pinkish grey; mending in area opposite base of handle with clay similar to that

used ext
Notes   Crowfoot, Crowfoot and Kenyon 1957: fig. 22.6, Samaria Period V–VI (EIron II, pre- 7th c B.C.); Oakeshott 1978: pl. 36.32 (Iron II)

No   8
Site   34
Sample   39
Ware/Core   2.5Y 6/3 lt brownish grey/lt yellowish brown; many small–large white, dk grey (basalt) and pink (quartz) grits; rare mica flecks
Exterior   As ware
Interior   As ware
Notes   Oakeshott 1978: pl. 37.6 (Iron II)

No   9
Site   34
Sample   39
Ware/Core   N 5/0 grey; core 2.5YR 5/7 red; many small white and quartz grits giving sandy texture
Exterior   7.5YR 4.5/2 brown – 5YR 7/7 reddish yellow over ledge to rim
Interior   As ware
Notes   Oakeshott 1978: pl. 29.24, ware more similar to 29.25 (same type of jar) (Iron II)

No   10
Site   34
Sample   39
Ware/Core   5Y 6.5/3 pale yellow/pale olive; few small–medium white (lime), red and many small–large black (vitrified porous) grits protruding surfaces
Exterior   As ware; rim area N 7.5/0 white/lt grey
Interior   As ext
Notes   Oakeshott 1978: pl. 37.7; pl. 50.4 (Iron II)

No   11
Site   34
Sample   39
Ware/Core   7.5YR 5.5/4 brown/lt brown; core 10YR 5/1 grey; many small–medium white (lime), black (basalt) and red (grog) grits; rare mica flecks
Exterior   Horizontal tool trimming marks bottom body; medium thick matt slip 6.2YR 8/4 pale brown/pale yellow extending over rim; paint: band near rim 5YR 5/5 reddish brown/yellowish red; stripes top of rim 7.5YR 4/2 dk brown
Interior   7.5YR 6/4 lt paint: band near rim as ext, lower bands 7.5YR 4/2 dk brown – 7.5YR 6/2 pinkish grey (faded)
Notes   Many parallels to paint in Oakeshott 1978; parallels to form (all not painted): Crowfoot, Crowfoot and Kenyon 1957: fig. 13.16, Samaria Period IV, (EIron II, pre-7th c B.C.); Oakeshott 1978: pls. 13.5; 14.3 (Iron II); 'Edomite painted' tradition

No   12
Site   108
Sample   148
Ware/Core   2.5YR 6/6 lt red; many small–large white (lime), grey and brown (grog) grits
Exterior   Traces of thick (slightly burnished?) slip 10YR 7.5/4 v pale brown
Interior   As ware
Notes   Rast 1978: fig. 85.1 (no slip, dark core), Taanach Period VIB (425–400 B.C., Iron II/Persian?)

No   13
Site   108
Sample   148
Ware/Core   10R 5.5/ lt red/red; patchy core slightly greyer than ware; many small–medium white, grey and deep red grits
Exterior   As ware; faint traces of pale brown (=cream) slip
Interior   As ware
Notes   [Iron II]

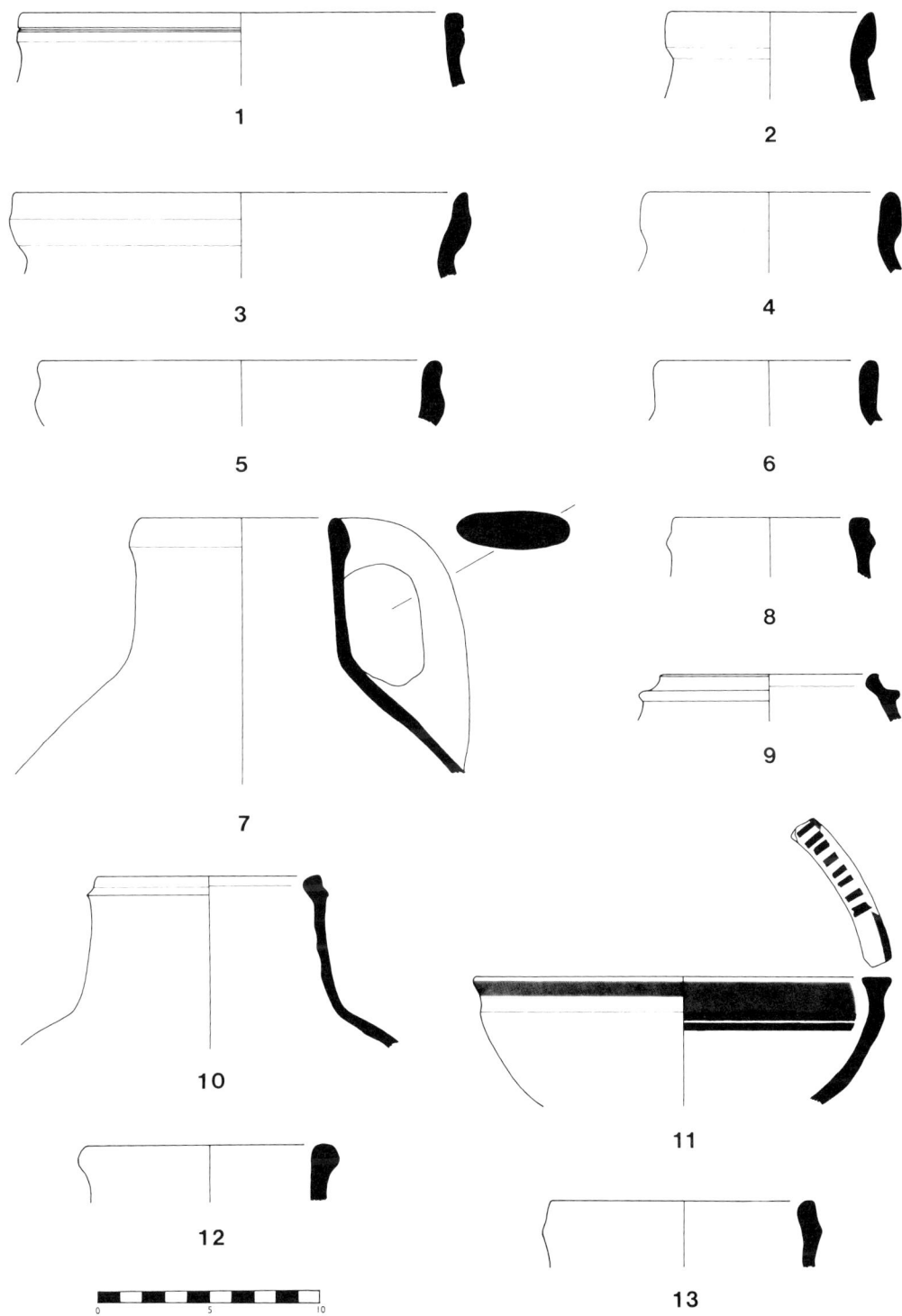

Plate 19   Iron I and II: Sites 34, 108, and 161 (all wheel-made)

Plate 20 Iron II: Sites 28, 29, 69, and 187 (all wheel-made)

No	1
Site	29
Sample	73
Ware/Core	2.5YR 6/7 lt red; many small–large white (lime), grey and brown (grog) grits; some mica flecks
Exterior	Thick matt slip 10YR 7.5/2 white/lt grey
Interior	As ware; slip as ext to within 0.7 cm from rim
Notes	[EIron II]

No	2
Site	28
Sample	72
Ware/Core	Body may be hand-built; 2.5YR 5.5/6 lt red/red; core 10YR 4/1.5 dk grey/dk greyish brown; many small–large white (lime), grey and red grits; some mica flecks
Exterior	Badly worn, areas flaked off; somewhat deep horizontal trimming tool marks 2.5YR 5.5/6 lt red/red–large patch 7.5YR 6.5/2 pinkish grey
Interior	Slight lime encrustation; colour as ware
Notes	Oakeshott 1978: pl. 30.14

No	3
Site	29
Sample	73
Ware/Core	Core completely filling section N 5.5/0 grey; many small–large white (lime + quartz), grey and deep red (grog) grits; few chaff impressions; rare mica flecks
Exterior	5YR 5/1.5 grey/reddish grey
Interior	As ext at body; 5YR 6/4 lt reddish brown at rim
Notes	Oakeshott 1978: pl. 30.15

No	4
Site	28
Sample	77
Ware/Core	2.5YR 6/6 lt red; core 10YR 5/1 grey; many small–large white (lime), grey (chert) and brown (grog) grits; rare mica flecks
Exterior	7.5YR 6.5/4 pink/lt brown; traces of matt slip top of rim 10YR 7.5/3 v pale brown
Interior	7.5YR 6/4 lt brown
Notes	Kenyon and Holland 1982: fig. 196.16 (Iron); Yassine 1988: 123, fig. 3.4 (2nd half of 10th c B.C.=LIron I–EIron II)

No	5
Site	29
Sample	73
Ware/Core	5YR 7/7 reddish yellow; core 8.2YR 6/3.5 pinkish grey/lt brown/pale brown; many small–large white (lime), black (basalt) and brown (grog) grits; rare mica flecks
Exterior	Some lime encrustation; secondary burning under handle stub where ware colour is showing; uneven matt slip 10YR 7.5/4 v pale brown where thick – 5YR 7/7 reddish yellow where thin
Interior	Lime encrusted 7.5YR 6/3 pinkish grey/lt brown
Notes	Pritchard 1985: fig. 4.33, Tell es-Sa'idiyeh Stratum VII (825–790 B.C.)

No	6
Site	29
Sample	74
Ware/Core	2.5YR 5/7 red; core 10YR 5.5/1 grey; many small–medium white (lime) and deep red-brown (grog) grits; some small–medium voids, many showing interior as flaking where inclusions are close to the surface, giving somewhat pocked appearance
Exterior	Heavily lime encrusted; may be slightly lighter than ware
Interior	Horizontal tool trimming bands upper flange; colour as ware
Notes	Tushingham 1972: fig. 15.11 (lamp body flange)

No	7
Site	69
Sample	79
Ware/Core	8.2YR 6/5 (mainly lt yellowish brown); core 5YR 5/1 grey; many small–large white, grey and dk grey grits; many small–large deep voids giving somewhat pocked appearance
Exterior	Medium thick matt slip 7.5YR 6/5 lt yellowish brown
Interior	As ext

No	8
Site	69
Sample	79
Ware/Core	5YR 7/7 reddish yellow; patchy core 5YR 6/1.5 grey/pinkish grey; many small–large yellow (lime), dk grey (basalt) and brown grits rare cracking int; many small–large deep voids giving somewhat pocked appearance
Exterior	Wet-smoothed; 5YR 6/5 reddish yellow
Interior	As ware

No	9
Site	69
Sample	79
Ware/Core	10R 5/8 red; few medium white (lime), brown (grog) and many small quartz grits giving sandy texture
Exterior	2.5YR 6/7 lt red – 10R 5/8 red below ledge
Interior	Heavily lime encrusted; colour as ware
Notes	Form similar to cooking pots but ware completely different, more like some jars of Iron II

No	10
Site	187
Sample	330
Ware/Core	5YR 5.5/6 reddish yellow/yellowish red; core 5YR 5.5/1 grey; many small–large white (lime), black (basalt) and red (grog) grits; many small–large voids giving pocked appearance
Exterior	As ware; traces of matt slip 10YR 7.5/3 v pale brown
Interior	5YR 5.54 lt reddish brown/reddish brown
Notes	Oakeshott 1978: pl. 29.9 (no slip)

212

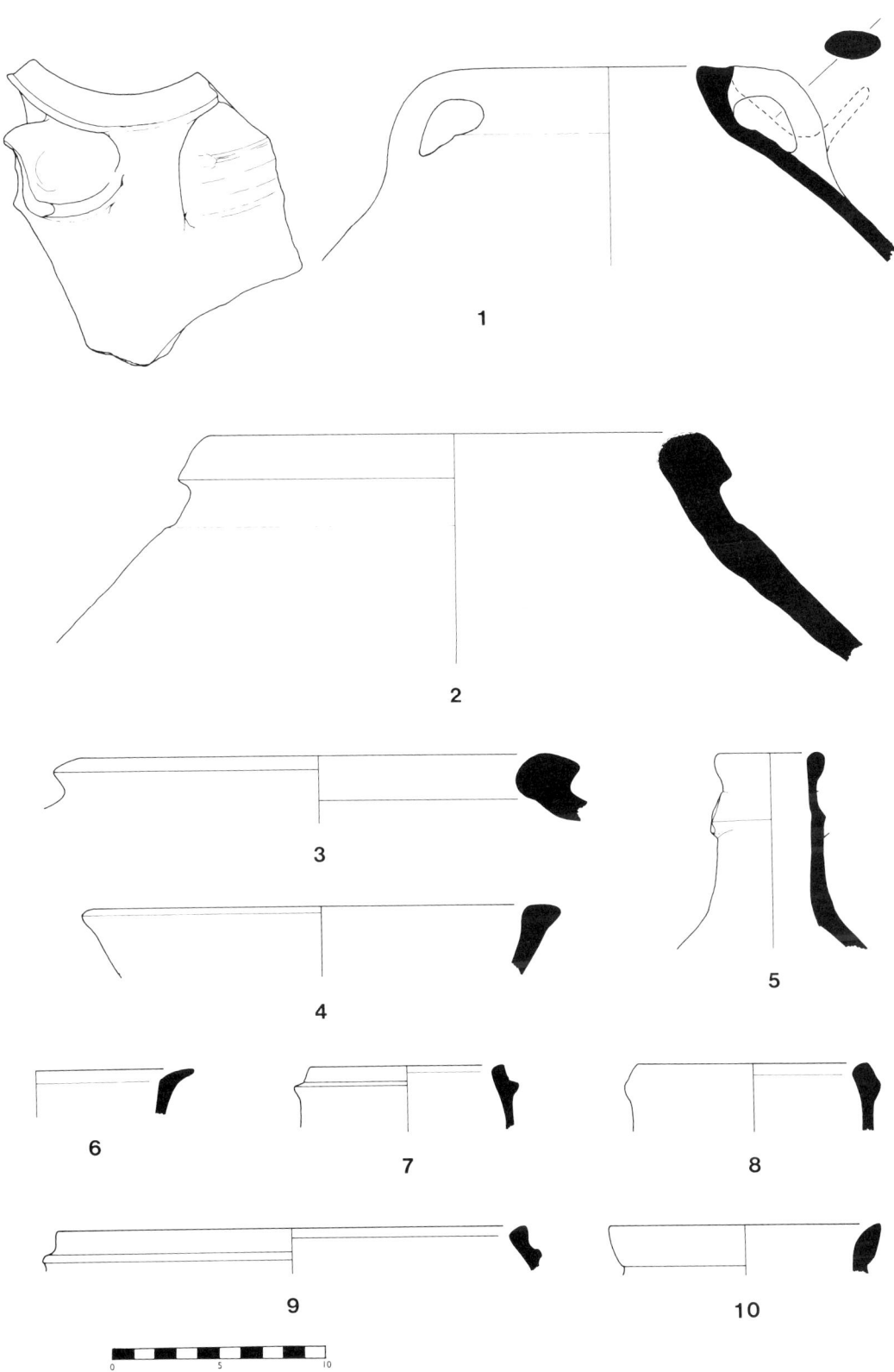

Plate 20 Iron II: Sites 28, 29, 69, and 187 (all wheel-made)

Plate 21   Hellenistic: Sites 73, 94, 139, 154, 155, and 237 (all wheel-made)

No	1
Site	94
Sample	144
Ware/Core	2.5YR 6/7 lt red; few small white (lime) and some small–medium quartz grits; rare mica flecks
Exterior	6.2YR 7/6 reddish yellow; traces of medium thick matt slip 5YR 4.5/3 reddish brown
Interior	As ext

No	2
Site	94
Sample	144
Ware/Core	3.2YR 6.5/6 lt red/reddish yellow; some small–medium white (lime) and many quartz grits
Exterior	Traces of medium thick matt slip 2.5YR 5.5/6 lt red/red
Interior	Slip as ext at rim – 2.5YR 3/4 dk reddish brown at body
Notes	Crowfoot, Crowfoot and Kenyon 1957: fig. (2nd c B.C.); Zayadine 1977–78: fig. 14.146 (E 2nd c B.C.?)

No	3
Site	139
Sample	235
Ware/Core	2.5YR 6/7 lt red; core 10YR 6/1.5 lt grey/lt brownish grey; many small, some medium quartz grits; rare blistering in body
Exterior	Uneven matt slip 10YR 5/1 grey – N 5/0 grey
Interior	Traces of thin faded slip, may be as ext
Notes	Crowfoot, Crowfoot and Kenyon 1957: fig. 55.4 (2nd c B.C.); may belong to same vessel as No 5

No	4
Site	73
Sample	99
Ware/Core	2.5YR 6/6 lt red; few small white (lime) and rare red grits
Exterior	6.2YR 7/6 reddish yellow; traces of thick slightly burnished slip 10R 5/7 red
Interior	6.2YR 7/6 reddish yellow

No	5
Site	139
Sample	235
Ware/Core	As No 3
Exterior	As No 3, slip more uniform; tool trimming marks
Interior	As No 3
Notes	May belong to same vessel as No 3

No	6
Site	155
Sample	256
Ware/Core	2.5YR 6/7 lt red; core 2.5YR 5/2 weak red; some small white and grey grits
Exterior	As ware; reduced bands of N 5/0 grey
Interior	2.5YR 6.5/7 lt red; reduced top of rim N 4/0 dk grey; slightly reduced areas in wheel marks
Notes	[In Nab tradition]

No	7
Site	94
Sample	144
Ware/Core	5YR 6.5/6 reddish yellow; core N 5.5/0 grey; rare small white (lime) and some quartz grits
Exterior	Tool trimming marks lower body; medium thick slip, matt, reduced at rim N 4.5/0 N 4.5/0 dk grey; slightly burnished body; 2.5YR 5/7 red with grey at tool trimming marks
Interior	Uneven matt slip, colours as ext
Notes	Baly 1962: pl. XLIX. 34.C1 (Hell–Rom); Negev 1986: 74.563; [Nab tradition]

No	8
Site	94
Sample	144
Ware/Core	3.2YR 6/8 lt red/reddish yellow; many small quartz grits
Exterior	Uneven thick matt slip N 3.5/0 dk grey/v dk grey where thickest
Interior	8.2YR 7/6 reddish yellow/yellow; medium thick slip 2.5YR 6/7 lt red to within approximately 1.5 cm from top of rim

No	9
Site	94
Sample	144
Ware/Core	3.2YR 6/6 lt red/reddish yellow; core N 5/0 grey; few small white and grey grits
Exterior	Uneven matt slip 2.5YR 4.5/3 weak red/reddish brown extending top of rim
Interior	As ware

No	10
Site	154E
Sample	276
Ware/Core	5YR 6.5/6 reddish yellow; many small, few large white (lime), grey and red grits; many small round
Exterior	Slightly burnished, thin slip (?) 7.5YR 7/5 pink/reddish yellow
Interior	As ext

No	11
Site	237
Sample	404
Ware/Core	2.5YR 5/5 reddish brown/red; some small, few medium white (lime) and black grits
Exterior	As ware
Interior	As ware

No	12
Site	154
Sample	252
Ware/Core	7.5YR 5/3 brown; core 10YR 5.5/1 grey; many small–large white (lime), dk grey (basalt?) and brown (grog) grits; many small–large deep voids; some showing surfaces, giving somewhat pocked appearance
Exterior	10YR 6.5/4 v pale brown/lt yellowish brown
Interior	As ext
Notes	Corbo and Loffreda 1981: fig. 35.14 (before ca. 30 B.C.); McNicoll, Smith and Hennessy 1982: pl 129.2 (Hell, 1st quarter of 1st c B.C.)

No	13
Site	94
Sample	144
Ware/Core	10YR 5.5/2 lt brownish grey/greyish brown; many small–medium white (lime), grey and brown grits; many small–medium round–semiangular voids, deep showing int, giving pocked appearance, some showing ext; hair-line cracking ext and top of rim
Exterior	Medium thick matt slip top of rim 5Y 8/3.5 pale yellow; thinning to 10YR 7/5 v pale brown/yellow
Interior	As ware
Notes	Feel similar to No 14

No	14
Site	94
Sample	144
Ware/Core	3.2Y 6/3 lt brownish grey/lt greyish brown/pale olive; many small–large white (lime) and grey grits; many small–medium, round–semiangular voids, deep showing int; giving pocked appearance; some showing ext
Exterior	Thin matt slip (?) 7.5YR 6/5 lt brown/reddish yellow
Interior	As ware; as ext top of rim curve
Notes	Zayadine 1977–78: fig. 15. 404 (red ware); (Hell, E 2nd c B.C.?)

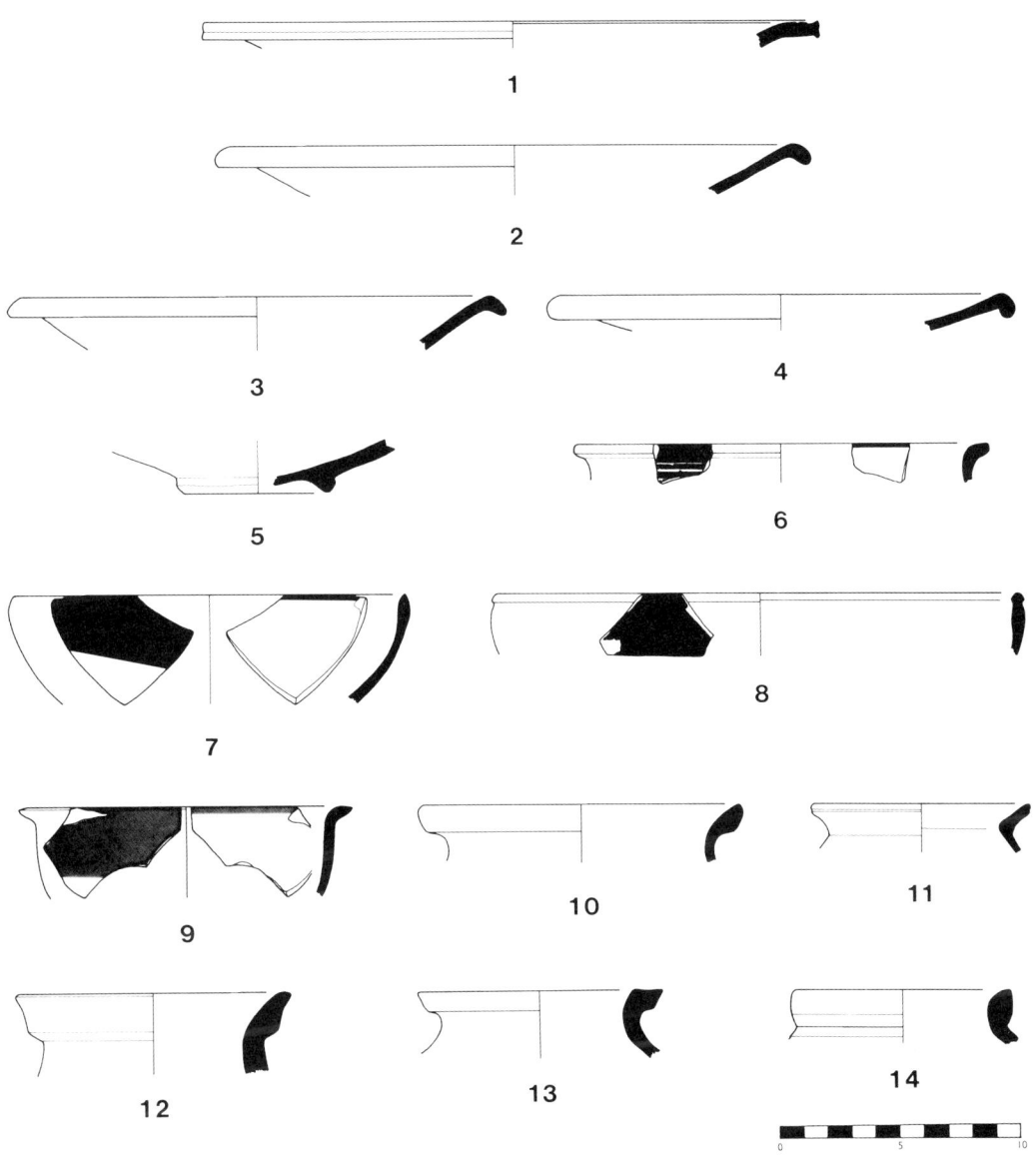

Plate 21 Hellenistic: Sites 73, 94, 139, 154, 155, and 237 (all wheel-made)

Plate 22   'Nabataean' (=LHell): Site 6 (all wheel-made)

No	1
Site	6
Sample	11
Ware/Core	3.2YR 6.5/7 lt red/reddish yellow; core 5YR 5.5/1 grey; few small white, grey and red grits
Exterior	As ware; 'shaved'; matt slip in band at rim N 4.5/0 grey/dk grey
Interior	As ware
Notes	Baly 1962: pl. XLIX. 32.C3 (no slip); (Hell–Rom)

No	2
Site	6
Sample	11
Ware/Core	2.5YR 6/7 lt red; core at rim only, slightly greyer than ware; some small–medium white (lime + quartz), grey and red grits
Exterior	3.2YR 6.5/7 lt red/reddish yellow; shaving resulting in burnished bands of N 5.5/0 grey – 5YR 6/4 lt reddish brown; matt slip in band at rim N 4.5/0 grey/dk grey
Interior	3.2YR 6.5/7 lt red/reddish yellow

No	3
Site	6
Sample	14
Ware/Core	5YR 7/7 reddish yellow; patchy core 5YR 6/2 pinkish grey; few small white (lime) and grey grits, one large lime (0.4 cm) protruding shaved ext
Exterior	3.2YR 6.5/8 lt red/reddish yellow; shaved; uneven wash N 4.5/0 grey/dk grey where thick; matt slip in band at rim N 2.5/0 v dk grey/black
Interior	3.2YR 6.5/8 lt red/reddish yellow; uneven grey wash as ext
Notes	Baly 1962: pl. XLIX. 32.B2 (no slip); (Hell–Rom)

No	4
Site	6
Sample	14
Ware/Core	2.5YR 6/6 lt red; core N 5.5/0 grey; some small–medium white (lime), grey and red grits; some mica flecks
Exterior	As ware; shaving resulting in uneven burnish bands 3.2YR 6/2 pale red/pinkish grey; matt slip in band at rim 10YR 6.5/2 lt grey/lt brownish grey
Interior	Matt uneven slip 10R 5/5 wk red/red in thicker bands

No	5
Site	6
Sample	11
Ware/Core	3.2YR 6.5/6 lt red/reddish yellow; core 7.5YR 6/3 – pinkish grey/lt brown; some small–medium white (lime), grey, red and quartz grits
Exterior	10YR 7.5/2 white/lt grey to within 1.2 cm below rim, rest as ware; shaving resulting in thin burnish band; matt slip in band at rim 2.5YR 4.5/8 red
Interior	Thick matt slip 10R 4/7 red
Notes	Baly 1962: pl. XLIX. 34.B1 (Hell–Rom)

No	6
Site	6
Sample	11
Ware/Core	2.5YR 6/7 lt red; core N 5.5/0 grey; some small white, grey, red and quartz grits
Exterior	As ware; slip in band at rim, very eroded leaving traces of 'cream' and 5YR 6.5/5 pink/lt reddish brown/reddish yellow surface
Interior	As ware
Notes	Baly 1962: pl. XLIX. 34.B6 (Hell–Rom); Tushingham 1972: fig. 4.12; (Nab)

No	7
Site	6
Sample	11
Ware/Core	2.5YR 6/7 lt red; core N 5.5/0 grey; few small white and grey grits
Exterior	Too little left under band for colour determination, as ware (?); shaving resulting in burnished bands

of 5YR 4/2.5 dk reddish grey/reddish brown under matt slip band of 10YR 7.5/2.5 white/lt grey/v pale brown

Interior	5YR 7/7 reddish yellow
Notes	Baly 1962 pl. XLIX. 34.B2–4 (Hell–Rom)

No	8
Site	6
Sample	11
Ware/Core	2.5YR 6/7 lt red; core at rim only N 6/0 grey; some small white, grey and quartz grits
Exterior	Slip band 5YR 6/1 grey/lt grey (worn out 'cream' slip?)
Interior	5YR 7/7 reddish yellow
Notes	Murray and Ellis 1940: fig. XXVII; Baly 1962: pl. L.34. D1,2,5 (red-orange slip) (Hell–Rom); Negev 1986: 74.561

No	9
Site	6
Sample	11
Ware/Core	2.5YR 5.5/6 lt red/red; few small white and grey grits
Exterior	2.5YR 5/7 red; slightly burnished slip in band at rim + darker 7.5YR 7.5/3 bands pinkish white/pinkish grey/pink; reduced surface showing where slip is flaked off 5YR 4.5/1.5 (mainly dk reddish grey)
Interior	Thin uneven slip colour as ext
Notes	As No 8

No	10
Site	6
Sample	14
Ware/Core	2.5YR 6/6 lt red; core N 5/0 grey; some small white, grey and red grits
Exterior	6.2YR 6/6 reddish yellow
Interior	As ext

No	11
Site	6
Sample	11
Ware/Core	10R 6/7 lt red – 5YR 6.5/8 reddish yellow; patchy core 10YR 7/2.5 lt grey/v pale brown; many small white, grey, red and quartz grits
Exterior	10R 6/7 lt red; traces of slip on handle 2.5Y 7.5/2 white/lt grey
Interior	5YR 6.5/8 reddish yellow
Notes	Negev 1986: 84.679

No	12
Site	6
Sample	11
Ware/Core	2.5YR 5.5/4 lt reddish brown/reddish brown; some small–medium white, grey and brown grits; few mica flecks
Exterior	Matt slip extending over rim 2.5Y 8/3 white/pale yellow; traces of deep red paint (?)
Interior	5YR 5.5/6 reddish yellow/yellowish red

No	13
Site	6
Sample	11
Ware/Core	2.5YR 6/7 lt red; core cm 7.5YR 5/5 brown/strong brown; some small white, grey and red grits
Exterior	As ware
Interior	As ware
Notes	Negev 1986: 103.871 (darker colours)

No	14
Site	6
Sample	11
Ware/Core	2.5YR 6/7 lt red; core N 5.5/0 grey; few small white (lime) and grey grits rarely causing blistering
Exterior	As ware
Interior	As ware; paint redder than 10R 4/6 red here thick – redder than 10R 4.5/6 red where thin

No	15
Site	6
Sample	11
Ware/Core	Core filling section N 5/0 grey; some small–medium white, grey and red grits; many small–large voids, on and under base
Exterior	6.2YR 6.5/4 pink/lt reddish brown/lt brown
Interior	As ext; wet smoothed

No	16
Site	6
Sample	11
Ware/Core	2.5YR 6/6 lt red; core 10YR 6/2.5 brownish grey/pale brown; some small white and grey grits
Exterior	As ware
Interior	As ware
Notes	Baly 1962: pl. LVIII. bases.5 (Hell–Rom); Negev 1986: 105.899

No	17
Site	6

Sample	11
Ware/Core	2.5YR 6/8 lt red; core from slightly greyer than ware – 5YR 5/1 reddish grey; few small white, grey and red grits
Exterior	As ware
Interior	As ware; very faint traces of paint slightly redder than ware
Notes	Murray and Ellis 1940: fig. XVII.51; Negev 1986: 57.409

No	18
Site	6
Sample	11
Ware/Core	2.5YR 6/7 lt red; core N 5.5/0 grey; few small white, grey and red grits
Exterior	Body: 1.2YR 6/6 lt red; under base as ware
Interior	5YR 7/3.5 pink; thin somewhat deep, wheel grooves corresponding to joint of ring base
Notes	Baly 1962: pl. LVIII. bases.4 (Hell–Rom)

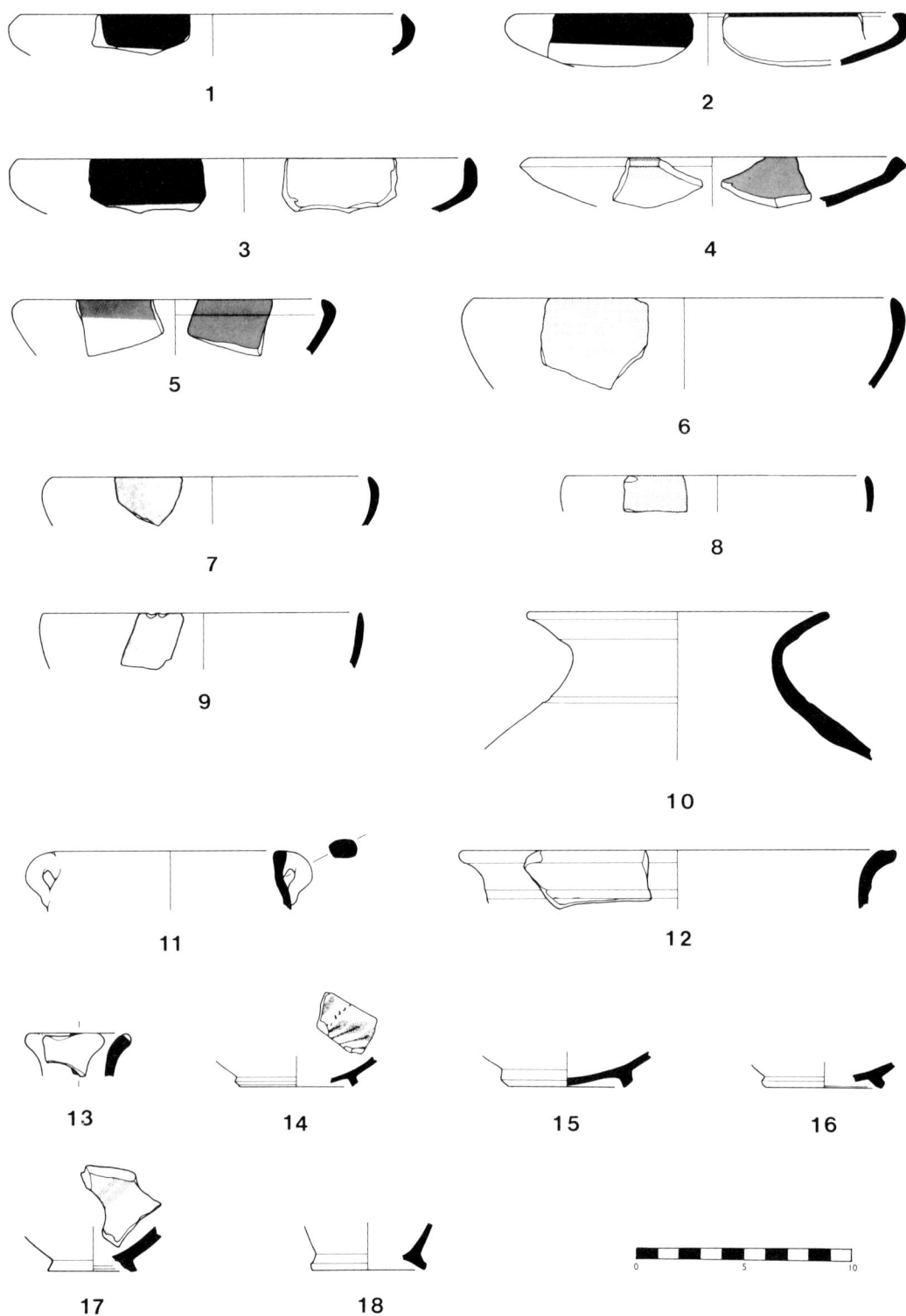

Plate 22   'Nabataean' (=LHell): Site 6 (all wheel-made)

Plate 23   'Nabataean' (=E.Rom): Sites 155, 223, and 229

No   1
Site   229
Sample   337
Ware/Core   Wheel-made; 2.5YR 6/7 lt red; core N 4/0 dk
                grey; few small white (lime) and rare quartz grits
Exterior   As ware; one thin burnish line, may be due to
                trimming tool
Interior   As ware; paint 2.5YR 4/3 weak red/reddish brown
                where thickest
Notes   Murray and Ellis 1940: fig. XXIX.86; Winnett and
                Reed 1964: fig. 68.9; Negev 1986: 50.361;
                51.367; Parker 1987: fig. 92.18 (ERom/Nab=63
                B.C.– A.D. 135)

No   2
Site   223
Sample   403
Ware/Core   Wheel-made; 5YR 6.5/4 pink/lt reddish brown;
                core N 6/0 grey; few small white (lime) grits; rare
                mica flecks
Exterior   As ware; thick matt slip at rim 10R 4.5/4 weak red
Interior   Thick matt slip as ext
Notes   Murray and Ellis 1940: fig. XXVII.61

No   3
Site   155
Sample   254
Ware/Core   Wheel-made; 2.5YR 6/6 lt red; core 7.5YR 7/1 lt
                grey/pinkish grey; few small white (lime) and red
                grits
Exterior   As ware; 'shaved'; uneven worn slip at rim 5YR
                4.5/1 grey/dk grey; 7.5YR 7/7 reddish yellow
                under worn slip
Interior   Uneven matt slip 5YR 4.5/1 grey/dk grey where
                thickest
Notes   Parr 1970: fig. 4:44, Petra Phase VIII (grey slip
                ext only) (1st c B.C.); Negev 1986: 80.624 (grey
                slip ext only)

No   4
Site   229
Sample   378
Ware/Core   Wheel-made; 2.5YR 5.5/8 lt red/red; some small
                white (lime) and grey grits; rare mica flecks
Exterior   1.3YR 5.5/8 lt red/red; patch at rim 7.5YR 7/4
                pink
Interior   As ware

No   5
Site   229
Sample   379
Ware/Core   Wheel-made; 10R 6/5 pale red/lt red; patchy core
                5YR 4.5/3 reddish brown; many small–medium
                white (lime + quartz) and grey grits; rare blistering
                at surfaces
Exterior   Secondary burning; as ware
Interior   As ware

No   6
Site   229
Sample   378
Ware/Core   Wheel-made; 2.5YR 6/7 lt red; some
                small–medium white (lime) and grey grits
Exterior   As ware
Interior   As ware
Notes   Negev 1986: 84.678

No   7
Site   229
Sample   378
Ware/Core   Wheel-made; 2.5YR 6/7 lt red; core N 4.5/0
                grey/dk grey; few small white (lime) and quartz
                grits
Exterior   As ware
Interior   As ware
Notes   Negev 1986: 85.683 (reddish brown)

No   8
Site   229

Sample   377
Ware/Core   Wheel-made; N 3/0 v dk grey; many small white
                (lime), few grey and brown grits; some mica
                flecks; rare spalling int
Exterior   10YR 5/1.5 grey/greyish brown; faint traces of
                worn light brownish grey slip
Interior   10YR 5/1.5 grey/greyish brown with bands of
                5YR 4/3 reddish brown
Notes   Negev 1986: 86.706

No   9
Site   229
Sample   379
Ware/Core   Wheel-made 2.5Y 7.5/4 pale yellow; few small
                white, grey and rare, medium angular light grey
                grits; rare mica flecks
Exterior   Discoloured by many grey spots; 3.2Y 8/2 white
Interior   As ext
Notes   Murray and Ellis 1940: fig. XXV.15 (has
                denticulations at top of rim)

No   10
Site   229
Sample   379
Ware/Core   Wheel-made; 2.5YR 6/7 lt red; some small white
                (lime), grey, red and many fine sand (quartz) grits;
                rare cracking and small lumps of excess clay
                adhering int
Exterior   Fine sharp ribbing; some secondary burning; 10R
                5.5/4 pale red/weak red
Interior   As ware
Notes   Murray and Ellis 1940: fig. XXVIII. 76

No   11
Site   229
Sample   379
Ware/Core   Moulded; 2.5YR 6/6 lt red; few small white and
                red grits; some mica flecks
Exterior   Nozzle blackened; many fingerprint marks;
                piercing tool marks for filling and lighting holes;
                colour as ware
Interior   Nozzle blackened; surfaces flaked off in areas;
                colour as ware
Notes   Zayadine 1982: fig. 4.5; pl. CXXII.5

No   12
Site   229
Sample   378
Ware/Core   Wheel-made; 2.5YR 6/6 lt red to within 0.2 cm
                from ext – 3.2YR 6/4 lt reddish brown towards int;
                many small white, grey (chert) and rare, red and
                quartz grits
Exterior   Knife-parred base; 2.5YR 6/6 lt red; traces of
                medium, thick matt slip 10YR 8/2.5 white/v pale
                brown where thick – 2.5YR 6.5/4 (mainly lt
                reddish brown) where thin
Interior   Sharp wheel-marks 3.2YR 6/4 lt reddish brown
Notes   Negev 1986: 108.940 (brown); 108.942 (no slip)

No   13
Site   229
Sample   377
Ware/Core   Wheel-made; 5YR 5/5 reddish brown/yellowish
                red; few small white (lime) grits
Exterior   Knife-parred and rouletted under base; colour as
                ware
Interior   Uneven thick matt slip 2.5YR 4.5/4 reddish brown
                – 2.5YR 3.5/4 reddish brown/dk reddish brown
Notes   Murray and Ellis 1940: XXVIII. 67

No   14
Site   223
Sample   403
Ware/Core   Wheel-made; 2.5YR 6/8 lt red to within 0.1 cm
                from ext – 2.5YR 6/6 lt red towards int; core N 5/0
                grey; few small white (lime) grits
Exterior   2.5YR 6/8 lt red
Interior   2.5YR 6/6 lt red

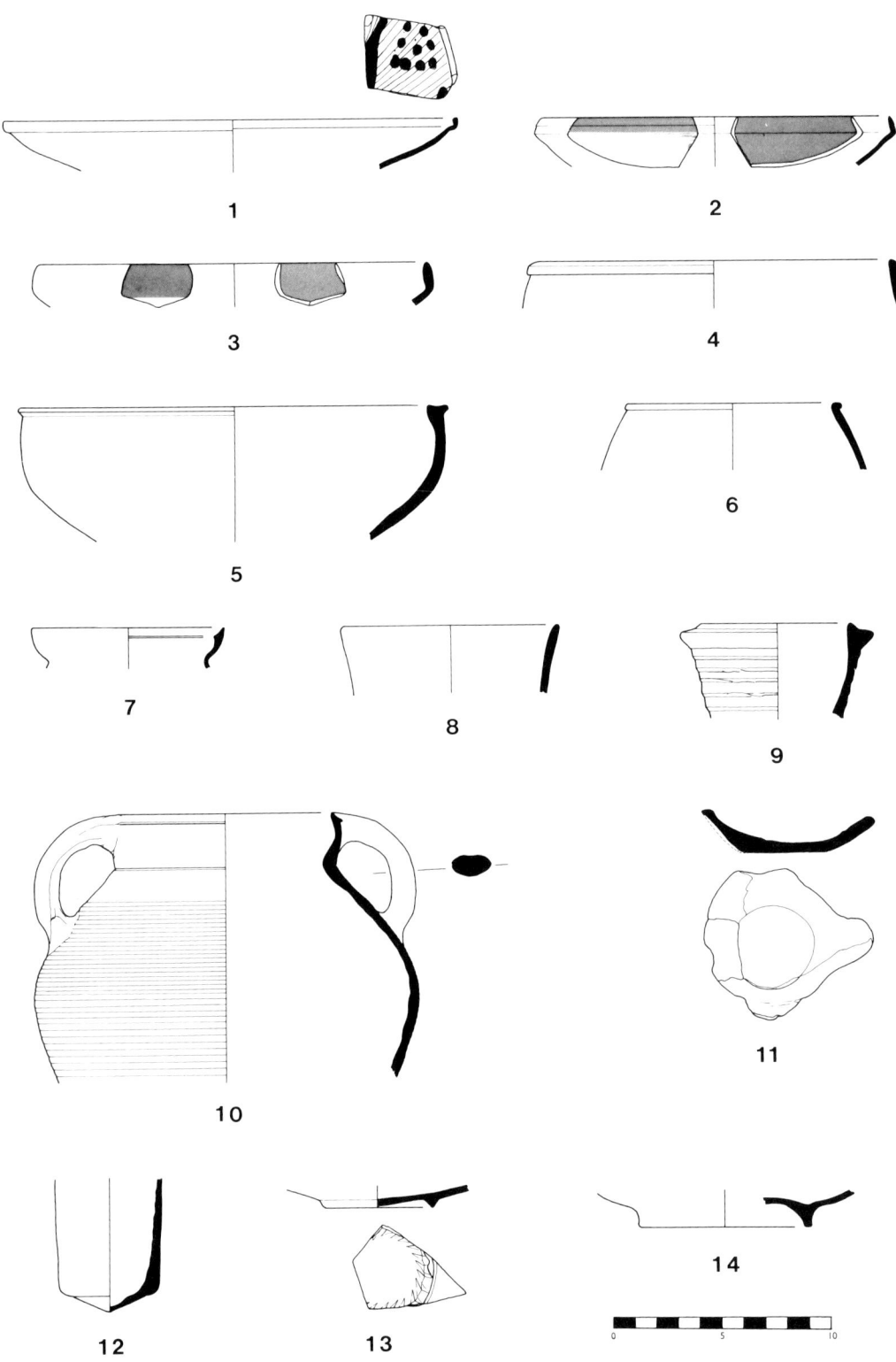

Plate 23   'Nabataean' (=E.Rom): Sites 155, 223, and 229

Plate 24   Roman–Byzantine Sites 28, 30, 73, 94, 155, and 223 (all wheel-made)

No	1
Site	94
Sample	144
Ware/Core	3.2YR 6.5/7 lt red/reddish yellow; few small, white, grey and red grits; many mica flecks; fine compact appearance
Exterior	Lime encrusted; much cracked and worn with areas 'flaked off'; thick glossy slip 10R 4.5/8
Interior	As ext
Notes	Eastern terra sigillata B [ERom]

No	2
Site	223
Sample	400
Ware/Core	10R 4.5/2 weak red; core N 3/0 v dk grey; many small, few medium–large white (lime), grey, dk grey and rare, medium red grits, large lime grits appearing at surfaces have been rubbed level with surfaces; many mica flecks
Exterior	As ware
Interior	As ware
Notes	[ERom]

No	3
Site	73
Sample	99
Ware/Core	2.5YR 6/7 lt red; patchy core showing in patchy bands ext and top of rim N 3.5/0 dk grey/v dk grey; many small–medium quartz grits giving somewhat sandy texture
Exterior	As ware
Interior	As ware
Notes	[LRom–EByz (?)]

No	4
Site	30
Sample	77
Ware/Core	2.5YR 5.5/8 lt red/red; some small–large white (lime + quartz), grey and red grits; rare chaff impressions
Exterior	Much abraded; somewhat deep flattend (angular) ribbing; thick matt slip N 3.5/0 dk grey/v dk grey
Interior	Much abraded; slip as ext
Notes	[LByz]

No	5
Site	30
Sample	77
Ware/Core	2.5YR 6/7 lt red; many small white (lime), black (basalt) and few red grits
Exterior	Traces of thin (slightly burnished?) slip 5YR 7/5 pink/reddish yellow
Interior	As ext
Notes	Bar-Nathan and Adato 1986: fig. 1.14 (2nd–3rd c A.D. =LRom)

No	6
Site	28
Sample	72
Ware/Core	2.5YR 5.5/8 red; core N 4.5/0 grey/dk grey; some small–medium white (lime + quartz) and grey grits
Exterior	Traces of thin slip 3.2YR 4.5/8 red
Interior	As ware
Notes	Negev 1986: 110. 956 [ERom of Nab tradition]

No	7
Site	30
Sample	77
Ware/Core	2.5YR 5/7 red; many small white, grey and quartz grits
Exterior	Much abraded; traces thin slip 2.5YR 4/5 reddish brown/red
Interior	Medium thick matt slip; colour as ext
Notes	Birger 1981: pl. 12.10 (Byz, 5th–6th c A.D.)

No	8
Site	30
Sample	76
Ware/Core	2.5YR 5/7 red; core at handle attachment N 4/0 dk grey; many small quartz grits; rare chaff impressions
Exterior	Secondary burning; deep narrow rounded ribbing; thin matt slip 2.5YR 4/1 dk grey/weak red
Interior	Secondary burning; thin matt slip as ext
Notes	[Byz]

No	9
Site	155
Sample	257
Ware/Core	2.5YR 5.5/8 lt red/red; many small quartz grits
Exterior	Secondary burning; somewhat deep wide rounded ribbing; thin matt slip 2.5YR 4/5 reddish brown/red
Interior	Secondary burning; as ware
Notes	[Byz]

No	10
Site	30
Sample	77
Ware/Core	2.5YR 4/5 reddish brown/red; many small grey and quartz grits
Exterior	Deep narrow rounded ext ribbing; medium thick matt slip 2.5YR 4.5/4 reddish brown
Interior	Slip as Ext
Notes	[Byz]

No	11
Site	94
Sample	144
Ware/Core	5YR 7/4 reddish yellow; some small, few medium grey and quartz grits
Exterior	Uneven slightly burnished slip 1.2YR 5/6 red
Interior	As ext.
Notes	[LRom]

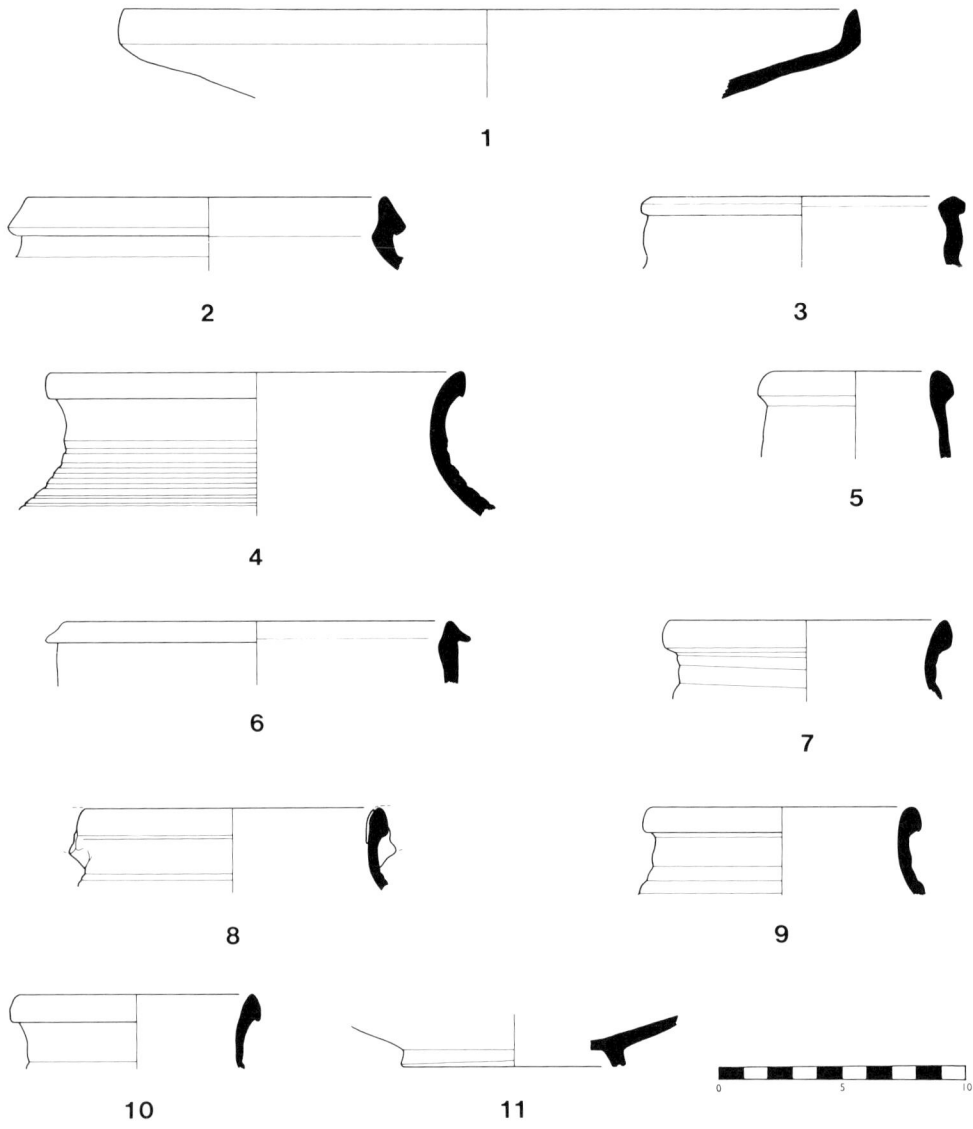

Plate 24 Roman–Byzantine Sites 28, 30, 73, 94, 155, and 223 (all wheel-made)

Plate 25   Roman–Ummayad: Site 211 (all wheel-made)

No	1
Site	211
Sample	353
Ware/Core	Hand-built, wheel finished; 10YR 7.5/4 v pale brown; some small–medium white (lime), grey, and rare medium, angular green (schist?) grits
Exterior	Applied thumb indented decoration; body burnished (trimming of coils?); colour as ware
Interior	As ware
Notes	Tushingham 1972: fig. 8.8 (cream slip int and top rim, two dark matt strokes running top rim); (No date Ayyubid destruction); [Um]

No	2
Site	211
Sample	353
Ware/Core	5YR 7/7 reddish yellow; many small white, grey and quartz grits giving sandy texture
Exterior	Abraded and discoloured; may be as ware
Interior	As ware
Notes	[LByz]

No	3
Site	211
Sample	353
Ware/Core	2.5YR 6/6 lt red; core 10YR 6.5/2 lt brownish grey; many small white, grey and quartz grits giving sandy texture
Exterior	Thin matt slip 5YR 5/1.5 grey/reddish grey
Interior	Wet-smoothed; colour as ware
Notes	[Byz]

No	4
Site	211
Sample	351
Ware/Core	5YR 6.5/6 reddish yellow; some small, white (lime), grey and quartz grits
Exterior	As ware
Interior	As ware
Notes	[Byz]

No	5
Site	211
Sample	353
Ware/Core	2.5YR 5/6 red; core N 4.5/0 grey/dk grey; many small white (lime), grey and quartz grits; rare mica flecks
Exterior	Shallow rounded ribbing, colour as ware
Interior	As ware
Notes	Hennessy 1970: fig. 7.28 (up to 1st c A.D.=ERom)

No	6
Site	211
Sample	352
Ware/Core	2.5YR 5/4 reddish brown; core N 5/0 grey; some small white (lime), grey and quartz grits; few chaff impressions
Exterior	Thick matt slip 3.2Y 7.5/2 white/lt grey extending over rim int; surface reduced where slip is abraded N 5.5/0 grey
Interior	N 4.5/0 grey/dk grey with areas of 2.5YR 5/4 reddish brown (as ware)
Notes	[LByz]

No	7
Site	211
Sample	353
Ware/Core	N 5.5/0 grey; many small–large white (lime), grey and quartz grits; rare spalling int; rare chaff impressions
Exterior	As ware; traces of slightly lighter coloured slip (?)
Interior	As ware
Notes	Tushingham 1972: fig. 7.10 (Byz, probably 3rd quarter of 6 c A.D.); Parker 1987: fig. 119.219; (LByz I–II=A.D. 502–551)

No	8
Site	211

Sample	352
Ware/Core	5YR 7/4 pink; many small white (lime), grey and quartz grits; rare mica flecks; rare chaff impressions
Exterior	As ware
Interior	As ware
Notes	Baly 1962: pl. LV. 130.7 (Byz)

No	9
Site	211
Sample	352
Ware/Core	5YR 5.5/6 reddish yellow/yellowish red; many small white, grey and red grits; rare mica flecks; rare chaff impressions
Exterior	7.5YR 6.5/5 pink/lt brown/reddish yellow
Interior	As ext
Notes	Adan-Bayewitz 1986: fig. 2.13 (LByz, E6th–E7th c A.D.)

No	10
Site	211
Sample	352
Ware/Core	10YR 5/1 grey (core filling section?); many small–medium white, grey (basalt) and few medium red grits; rare mica flecks
Exterior	10YR 5/1.5 grey/greyish brown; traces of matt slip 2.5Y 7.5/2 white/lt grey
Interior	10YR 5/1.5 grey/greyish brown
Notes	[LByz]

No	11
Site	211
Sample	353
Ware/Core	5YR 7/6 reddish yellow; core 10YR 7/1.5 lt grey; many small–medium white (lime) and grey grits
Exterior	Thick matt (self?) slip 5Y 8/2.5 white/pale yellow
Interior	As ext
Notes	Smith 1973: pl. 34.489 (Um)

No	12
Site	211
Sample	351
Ware/Core	5YR 6/6 reddish yellow; many small–medium white (lime + quartz) and black (basalt) grits
Exterior	Thick matt slip, patchy under rim, 5YR 5/1 grey
Interior	Slip as ext at rim thinning to 2.5YR 6/7 lt red
Notes	[LByz]

No	13
Site	211
Sample	352
Ware/Core	5YR 4.5/4 reddish brown; many small white, grey and quartz grits
Exterior	Secondary burning at rim; wide somewhat deep ribbing; thin slightly glossy slip 2.5YR 4.5/4 reddish brown
Interior	Medium thick matt slip; colour as ext
Notes	Birger 1981: pl. 12.10 (Byz, 5th–6th c A.D.)

No	14
Site	211
Sample	350
Ware/Core	2.5YR 5/7 red; patchy core N 3.5/0 dk grey/v dk grey; many small white, grey and quartz grits
Exterior	Abraded and thinly lime encrusted; narrow, somewhat deep, ribbing; may be as int
Interior	Traces of medium thick matt slip 2.5YR 3.5/4 reddish brown/dk reddish brown
Notes	Feels similar to No 13; should be of similar date

No	15
Site	211
Sample	352
Ware/Core	'Clumsy' fast-wheel made, workshop second? 5YR 7/7 reddish yellow; some small–medium white, grey and quartz grits
Exterior	Very deep narrow ribbing, covered with excess cracked clay in areas and wiped off in others; colour as ware

Interior	As ware		quartz grits; rare chaff impressions
Notes	[Byz]	Exterior	Narrow, somewhat deep, ribbing; thin, slightly glossy, slip 2.5YR 4/5 reddish brown/red
No	16	Interior	Wet smoothed or very thin slip; colour as ware
Site	211	Notes	Tushingham 1972: fig. 9. 50 (Byz, probably 3rd quarter of 6th c A.D.); feels similar to No 13
Sample	353		
Ware/Core	2.5YR 4.5/6 red; many small, white, grey and		

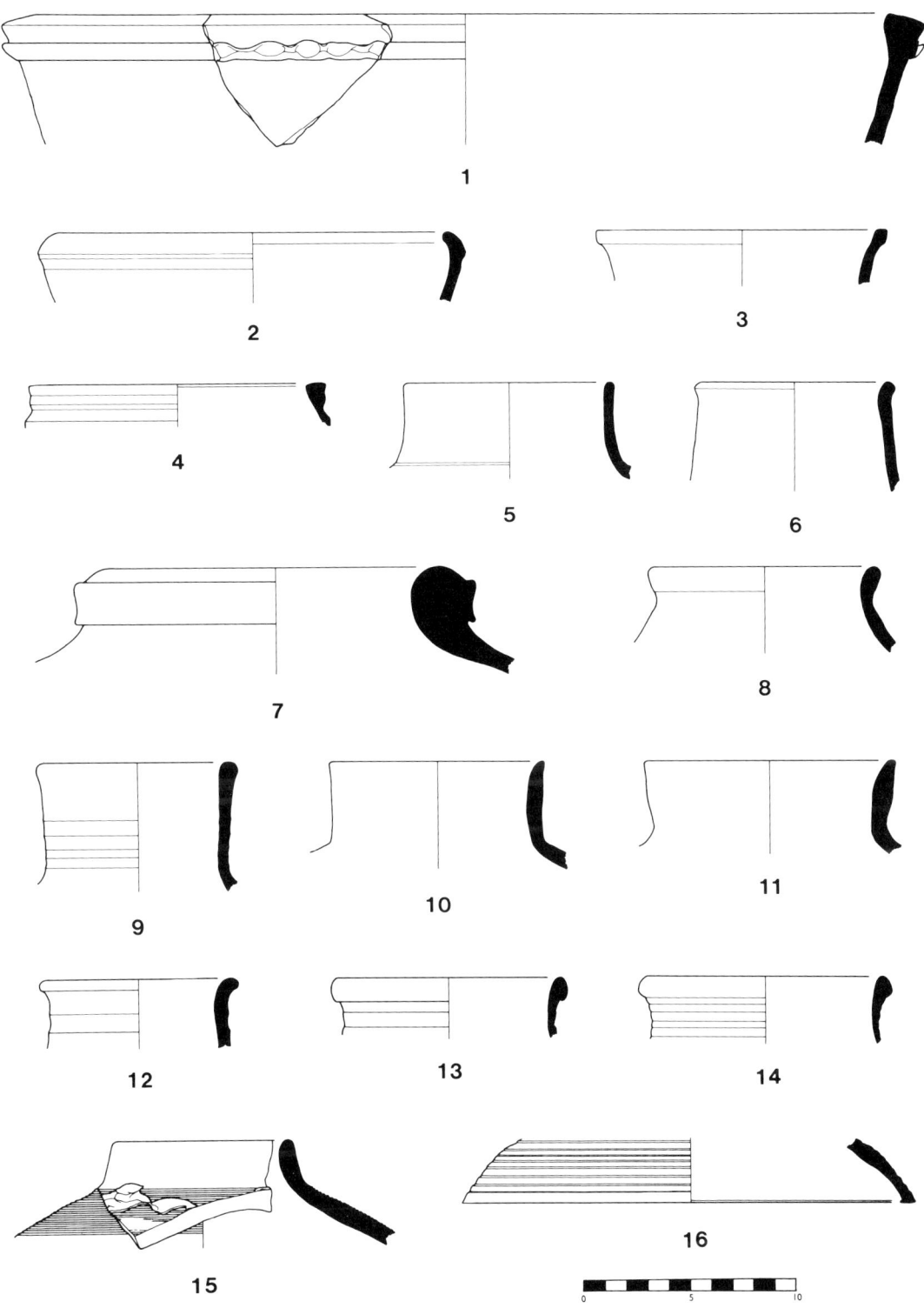

Plate 25   Roman–Ummayad: Site 211 (all wheel-made)

Plate 26 Byzantine: Site 46 (all wheel-made)

No 1
Site 46
Sample 90
Ware/Core 5YR 5.5/2 pinkish grey/reddish grey; core N 4.5/0 grey/dk grey; some small–medium white, grey and black grits, rare large white (lime), causing some spalling and blistering at surfaces
Exterior As ware; slip at rim 10YR 7.5/1 white/lt grey, matt and somewhat thin
Interior As ware

No 2
Site 46
Sample 90
Ware/Core N 6/0 grey; few small white and grey, rare medium white grits
Exterior N 4.5/0 grey/dk grey from top of rim to 0.5–1.0 cm below carination, rest: N 5.5/0 grey
Interior As ware

No 3
Site 46
Sample 90
Ware/Core 5YR 6.5/6 reddish yellow; some small white, grey and red grits
Exterior 10 YR 8/2
Interior As ext white
Notes Zayadine 1977–78: fig. 17.329 (pink-orange) (Byz, end of 5th c)

No 4
Site 46
Sample 408
Ware/Core 7.5YR 5.5/2 brown/pinkish grey; core 10YR 4.5/1 grey/dk grey; many small–medium white, grey, quartz grits
Exterior Thin matt slip 7.5YR 6.5/2 pinkish grey thumb-impressed rope decoration and combing
Interior As ware

No 5
Site 46
Sample 90
Ware/Core 10R 4/6 red; many small–medium white, grey and quartz grits; 'sandy' appearance to surfaces
Exterior N2/0 black
Interior As ext

No 6
Site 46
Sample 90
Ware/Core N6.5/0 grey/lt grey; few small white and grey grits
Exterior N 5/0 grey; trace of slip N 4/0 dk grey; combed
Interior 10YR 6/1.5 grey/lt brownish grey

No 7
Site 46
Sample 408
Ware/Core 10YR 5/1 grey; core 'sandwiching' ware 3.2YR 5.5/6 (mainly yellowish red; some small–medium white and grey grits
Exterior Uneven matt slip 2.5Y 5/2 (greyish brown) – 1.2Y 3.5/1 (mainly dk grey)
Interior Thick matt slip 10YR 3.5/1 dk grey/v dk grey
Notes Tushingham 1972: fig. 5.41 Dhiban Byz Phase B; Parker 1987: fig. 109.154 (EByz II–IV=A.D.

363–502)

No 8
Site 46
Sample 90
Ware/Core 7.5YR 6.5/4 pink/lt brown; some small white, grey and red grits, rare mica
Exterior Much abraded; matt slip 2.5Y 7.5/2 white/lt grey; combed and ribbed
Interior Totally abraded

No 9
Site 46
Sample 90
Ware/Core 6.2YR 7/3.5 pink; few small white and grey grits
Exterior Somewhat thick matt slip; 7.5YR 6/3 pinkish grey/lt brown
Interior 5YR 6/5 lt reddish brown/reddish yellow
Notes Birger 1981: pl. 12:4 (no slip) (Byz, 5th–6th c)

No 10
Site 46
Sample 90
Ware/Core N 6/0 grey; few small white and grey grits
Exterior N 5.5/0 grey
Interior As ext

No 11
Site 46
Sample 90
Ware/Core N 5.5/0 grey; few small white and grey grits
Exterior 10YR 5.5/1 grey/lt greyish brown/greyish brown
Interior As ware
Notes Parker 1987: fig. 107.140 (EByz II–IV=A.D. 363–502)

No 12
Site 46
Sample 409
Ware/Core 2.5YR 5.5/8 red/lt red; core 5YR 5/1.5 grey/reddish grey; many small–large white, grey and quartz grits; 'sandy' appearance to surfaces; rare blistering int
Exterior As ware; sloppy deep angular ribbing
Interior As ware

No 13
Site 46
Sample 409
Ware/Core N 4.5/0 grey/dk grey; some small–medium white (lime) and grey grits causing rare spalling int
Exterior As ware; ribbed
Interior As ware
Notes Parker 1987: fig. 113.178 (LByz I–II=A.D. 502–551)

No 14
Site 46
Sample 409
Ware/Core 5YR 4.5/1 grey/dk grey; core 2.5YR 4.5/4 reddish brown; some small white and grey grits, rare medium white (lime) causing blister
Exterior As ware up to 1.7 cm from rim; rest 5YR 5.5/1 grey
Interior 7.5YR 6.5/2 pinkish grey, uneven bands of 5YR 5.5/1 grey

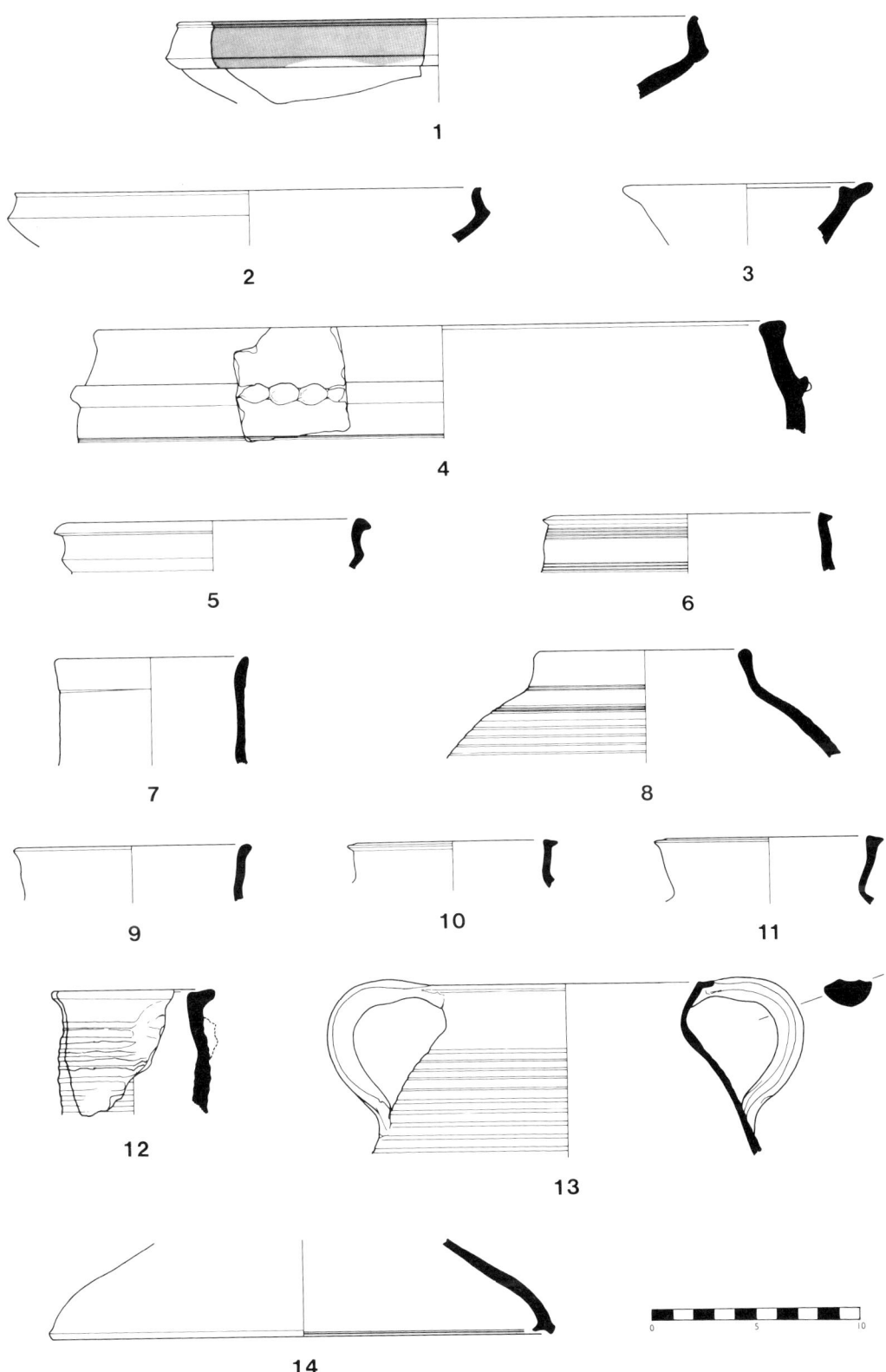

Plate 26   Byzantine: Site 46 (all wheel-made)

Plate 27   Byzantine: Sites 66, 215 and 216 (all wheel-made)

No	1
Site	66
Sample	111
Ware/Core	2.5YR 5.5/8 lt red/red; some small white (lime), grey, red and medium quartz grits
Exterior	As ware; slip around and under flange, narrow horizontal burnish lines 10R 5.5/6 lt red/red
Interior	Thick (abraded) slip, colour as ext
Notes	Hayes 1972, African Red Slip Ware, Form 107 (ca 600–650 A.D.)

No	2
Site	66
Sample	111
Ware/Core	2.5YR 6/6 lt red; some small white (lime), grey and red grits; few mica flecks
Exterior	Tool finished surface on wheel; shallow rouletting, thin slightly lustrous slip on rim 7.5YR 7/6 reddish yellow (thicker in grooves); medium thick, slightly lusterous, slip body 10R 5/4 weak red – 10R 5/8 red in grooves where thicker
Interior	Extensively abraded; thick, slightly lustrous; slip 10R 5.8
Notes	Baly 1962: pl. X.VIII. 14.A3 (Waag's Late Roman C); Tushingham 1972: fig. 11.5 (probably 3rd quarter of 6th c A.D.); Hayes 1972, Late Roman C, Form F (6th c A.D.)

No	3
Site	66
Sample	111
Ware/Core	3.7YR 5/4 reddish brown; some small white and black grits; few mica flecks; very compact
Exterior	'Band smoothed'; thick, slightly lustrous, slip abraded at rim where it is 5YR 4/1 dk grey, body 3.2YR 5/3.5 reddish brown – 2.5YR 5/5 reddish brown/red
Interior	'Band smoothed' slip as ext
Notes	Hayes; 1972, Cypriot Red slip Ware (Late Roman D, Form 1) (late 4th c A.D. or earlier to about 3rd quarter of 5th c)

No	4
Site	216
Sample	392
Ware/Core	2.5YR 6/6 lt red; many small, few medium white (lime), grey and quartz grits; some mica flecks
Exterior	Deep combing; uneven matt slip 2.5Y 8/3 white/pale yellow where thickest
Interior	Thick matt slip; colour as ext

No	5
Site	216
Sample	391
Ware/Core	2.5Y 7/3 lt grey/pale yellow, patches of 7.5YR 7/5 pink/reddish yellow; some small white and grey grits
Exterior	1.2Y 7.5/4 v pale brown/pale yellow
Interior	As ext

No	6
Site	216
Sample	392
Ware/Core	2.5YR 5/6 red; many small white (lime), grey and quartz, rare medium white grits
Exterior	Thick matt slip, excluding patch near applied knob, 5YR 4/1.5 dk grey/dk reddish grey
Interior	As ware; slip as ext extending over rim

No	7
Site	215
Sample	372
Ware/Core	2.5YR 5/6 red to within 0.13–0.17 cm from ext, 6.2YR 5/3 reddish brown/brown towards int; many small white and grey, rare large white grits; some mica flecks
Exterior	2.5YR 5/6 red
Interior	6.2YR 5/3 reddish brown/brown

No	8
Site	216
Sample	392
Ware/Core	2.5YR 6/7 lt red; core N 6.5/0 lt grey/grey few small, white and grey grits
Exterior	Band burnished; 5YR 6/6 reddish yellow, 7.5YR 7/6 pink/reddish yellow at burnished bands
Interior	5YR 6/6 reddish yellow
Notes	Baly 1962: pl. L.36.B15 (Byz–Isl, 7–8th c A.D.); Gichon 1974, Type ß, En Boqeq Phase III (5th–beg. 6 c A.D.)

No	9
Site	216
Sample	391
Ware/Core	2.5YR 6/6 lt red; core 10YR 6.5/2 lt grey/lt brownish grey; some small white, rare medium, white (lime) and grey grits; few mica flecks
Exterior	Thick matt slip, banded 10YR 5/1.5 grey/greyish brown, 7.5YR 5/1 grey/brown in the narrower bands
Interior	As ext

No	10
Site	216
Sample	390
Ware/Core	2.5YR 5.5/8 lt red/red; some small–medium white, grey and quartz grits
Exterior	Thick matt slip 5YR 4/1 dk grey
Interior	As ext

No	11
Site	215
Sample	372
Ware/Core	5YR 4.5/1 grey/dk grey – 10YR 6/1.5 grey/lt brownish grey to within 0.6 cm from ext, 5YR 6/5 lt reddish brown/reddish yellow towards int; few small white, grey and red grits
Exterior	5YR 4.5/1 grey/dk grey – 10YR 6/1.5 grey/lt brownish grey
Interior	5YR 4.5/1 grey/dk grey to within 0.8 cm from rim, 5YR 6/5 lt reddish brown/reddish yellow body

No	12
Site	216
Sample	391
Ware/Core	2.5YR 6/7 lt red; core 5YR 4/1.5 dk grey/dk reddish grey; many small white, grey and quartz grits
Exterior	Thin slip 2.5YR 5/5 reddish brown/red
Interior	As ware
Notes	Baly 1962: pl. LII.75 A6 (Byz +/-); Parker 1987: fig. 114.187 (LByz I–II=A.D.502–551)

No	13
Site	215
Sample	372
Ware/Core	1.2YR 4.5/6 red; core N 2/0 black towards and showing in areas int; many small white, grey, quartz and few medium quartz grits; spalling and cracking int
Exterior	As ware
Interior	As ware; as core to within 0.8 cm from rim plus small patches at neck
Notes	Baly 1962: pl LVI 134.14 (Hell–Byz); Bar-Nathan and Adato 1986: fig. 3.17, (Byz, pre-E 6th c A.D.)

No	14
Site	66
Sample	111
Ware/Core	5YR 7/5 pink/reddish yellow; many small white, brown, quartz and rare medium black (basalt) grits; some mica flecks
Exterior	Deep combing; as ware
Interior	As ware

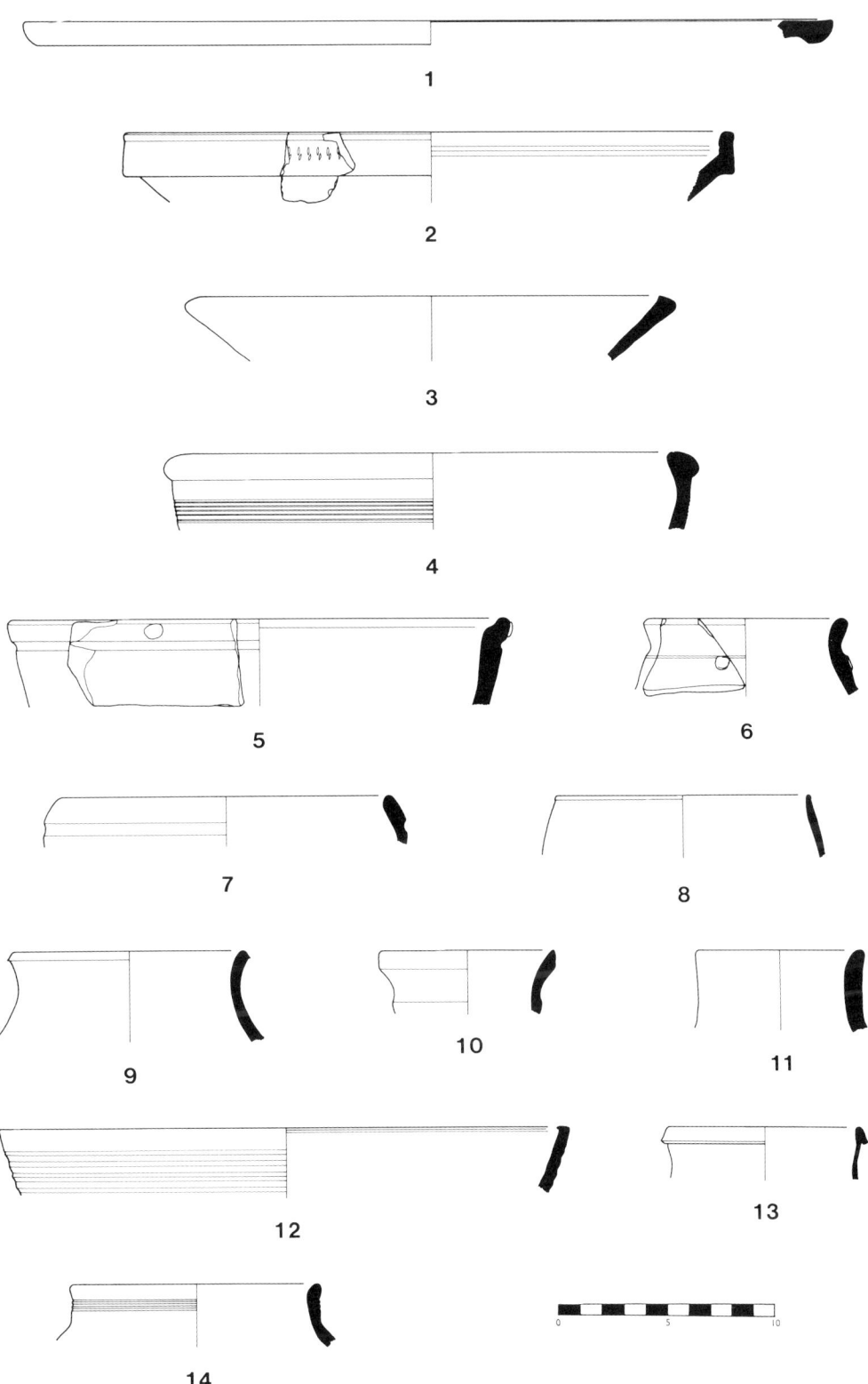

Plate 27   Byzantine: Sites 66, 215 and 216 (all wheel-made)

Plate 28   Late Byzantine: Sites 205 and 206 (all wheel-made)

No 1
Site 205
Sample 355
Ware/Core 7.5YR 7/6 reddish yellow; many small white, red, quartz and rare large angular grey grits; sandy texture]
Exterior 10YR 8/3.5 v pale brown
Interior As ext

No 2
Site 205
Sample 354
Ware/Core 2.5YR 6/7 lt red; core N 5.5/0 grey; few small white (lime) and grey grits; rare blistering under rim ext
Exterior Uneven matt slip in band under rim 5YR 7/5 pink/reddish yellow; burnish bands due to trimming tool at body exposing core; body colour as ware
Interior As ware; slightly more yellow bands at 'lower' body
Notes Baly 1962: pl. LI. 49.C2 (Byz–Arab); Gichon 1974 Type ß, En Boqeq Phase III (5th–beg 6th c A.D.)

No 3
Site 206
Sample 356
Ware/Core 5YR 7/4 pink; some small–medium white and grey grits; compact
Exterior Incised horizontal line; horizontally burnished uneven slip at body 2.5YR 6/7 lt red where thick – 3.2YR 7/8 lt red/reddish yellow where thin; matt thick slip in band at rim 5YR 3/3.5 dk reddish brown
Interior Burnished slip as ext

No 4
Site 205
Sample 355
Ware/Core 5YR 6/7 reddish yellow; rare small white and grey grits
Exterior As ware; 'feathery' bands N 4.5/0 grey/dk grey
Interior As ware; somewhat well-defined, slightly 'feathery' narrow bands near rim, colour as ext
Notes Baly 1962: pl. L.36.B15 Byz–Isl (7–8?c A.D.); Gichon 1974: fig. 3.12 Type ß, En Boqeq Phase III (5th–beg. 6th c A.D.)

No 5
Site 205
Sample 354
Ware/Core 2.5YR 6/7 lt red; few small white and grey grits; rare reed impressions ext
Exterior Tool trimmed on wheel; uneven matt slip 10YR 7.5/3 v pale brown where thick – 5YR 7/5 pink/reddish yellow where thin, in wide bands
Interior As ware

Notes As No 4

No 6
Site 205
Sample 355
Ware/Core 5YR 5/5 reddish brown/yellowish red; some small white, grey and brown grits
Exterior 5YR 6.5/4 pink/lt reddish brown
Interior 5YR 5.5/4 lt reddish brown/reddish brown
Notes Baly 1962: pl. L.36.B15 Byz–Isl (7th–8th c A.D.)

No 7
Site 205
Sample 355
Ware/Core 8.2YR 7/4 pink/v pale brown; some small white, grey and red grits
Exterior Deep angular combing; 10YR 7.5/3 v pale brown
Interior Colour as ext
Notes Tushingham 1972: fig. 5.32, Dhiban Phase A

No 8
Site 205
Sample 354
Ware/Core 2.5Y 6.5/4 pale yellow/lt yellowish brown; many small white, grey and red grits; few mica flecks;
Exterior 5Y 8/2.5 white/pale yellow
Interior As ext

No 9
Site 205
Sample 354
Ware/Core 5YR 6/3.5 lt reddish brown, sandwiched within core at body; core 0.05–0.6 cm 2.5YR 5/7 red; many small, few medium white, grey and red grits; rare reed impressions
Exterior Medium deep combing; 7.5YR 6.5/5 pink/lt brown/reddish yellow
Interior Colour as ext

No 10
Site 205
Sample 354
Ware/Core 3.2YR 6/6 lt red/reddish yellow near surfaces – 7.5YR 6.5/4 pink/lt brown; core 0.03 cm sandwiching second ware colour 10R 6/7 lt red; some small–medium white (lime), dark grey and red grits; rare chaff impressions
Exterior Colours as ware in horizontal bands
Interior As ext

No 11
Site 205
Sample 354
Ware/Core 5Y 7.5/3 pale yellow; some small white, grey and red grits
Exterior Deep narrow combing; colour as ware
Interior As ware

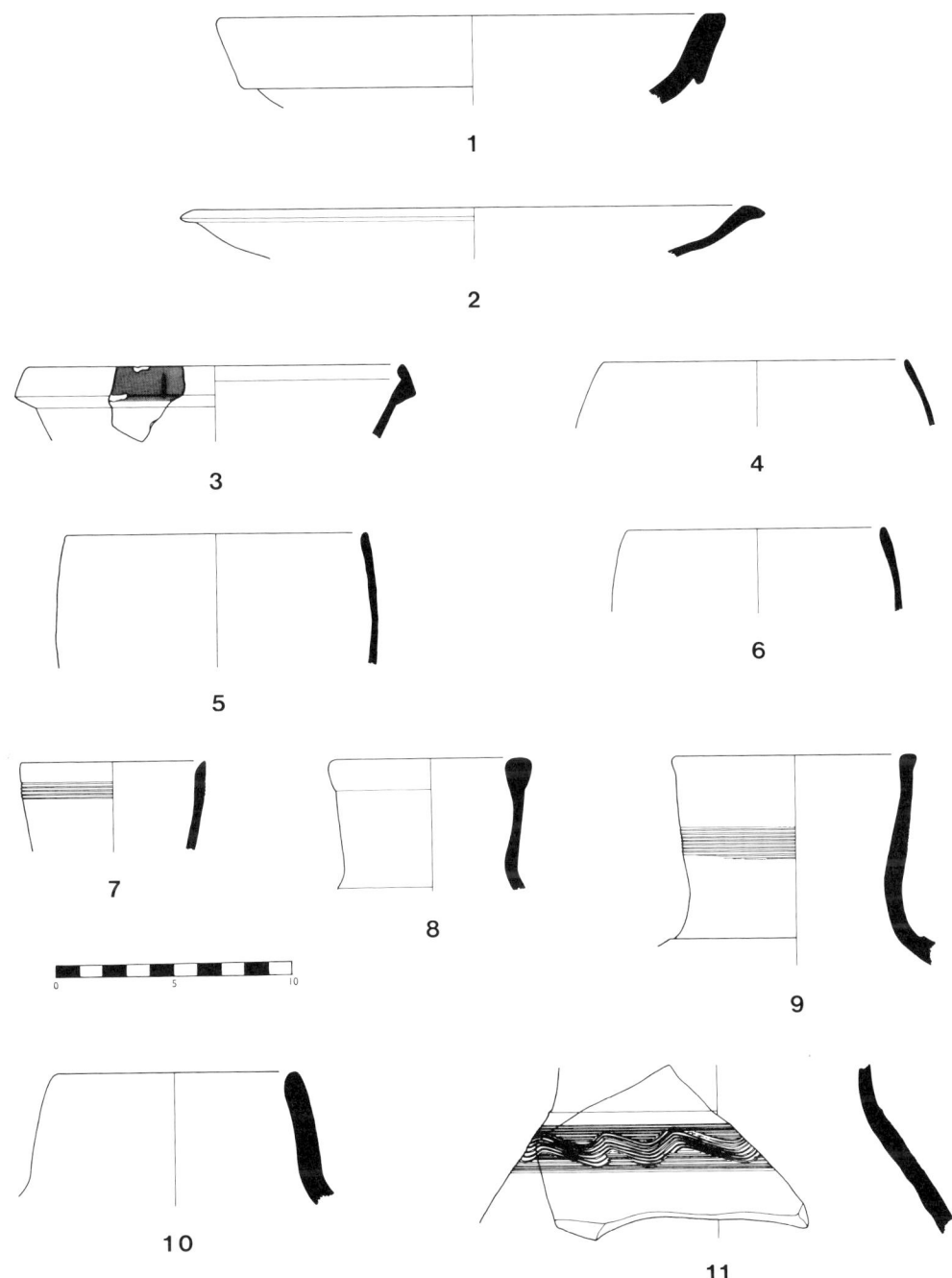

Plate 28   Late Byzantine: Sites 205 and 206 (all wheel-made)

Plate 29   Tawahin al-Sukkar

Tawahin al-Sukkar, Ghor al-Dhra' [+]

a   red, cream slip, yellow, green, brown, clear glaze on interior and exterior, moderate medium sand.
b   buff, cream surfaces, green, brown, clear glaze on interior, common medium sand.
c   buff-cream, cream slip, yellow, clear glaze on interior, common medium sand.
d   cream-buff, cream surfaces, clear, green, brown glaze on interior, moderate medium sand.
e   orange, buff-tan surfaces, dark horizontal lines on interior, fine, diameter unknown.
f   tan-grey, abundant medium sand.
g   dark red, ridged, abundant medium sand.
h   grey, orange-brown surfaces, horizontal burnishing on exterior, fine.
i   orange-buff, brown horizontal streaks on interior, horizontal burnishing on exterior, fine.

Tawahin al-Sukkar, Ghor al-Safi (SGNAS Site 1) [SGNAS Sample No]

j   cream, moderate medium sand. [.2]
k   tan-cream, moderate medium sand. [.1]
l   cream, common medium sand. [.3]
m   brown-tan, moderate medium sand. [.1]
n   cream, light green glaze on interior, dark green on rim and exterior spot, moderate medium sand, diameter unknown. [.1]
o   red-orange, cream surfaces, turquoise, dark brown glaze on interior and rim, moderate medium sand. [.3]
p   brown-red, white slip, clear, black, green glaze on interior, clear on exterior, moderate medium sand, diameter unknown. [.3]
q   cream-buff, moderate medium sand. [.2]
r   cream, moderate medium sand. [.1]
s   cream, moderate medium sand. [2]
t   buff, cream surfaces, moderate medium sand. [.2]

Plate 30   Feifa (SGNAS Site 91) [SGNAS Sample No (where pertinent)]

a   buff, cream slip, green, yellow, clear glaze on interior and exterior, common medium sand, diameter unknown. [+]
b   orange-buff, cream slip, yellow, green, clear glaze on interior, clear glaze on exterior, common medium sand, diameter unknown. [+]
c   red-brown, slip paint and green glaze on interior, common medium sand. [.135]
d   red-brown, cream slip paint, green glaze on interior, common medium sand. [+]
e   cream, white, green, dark yellow-brown, black glaze on interior and exterior, moderate medium sand. [.136]
f   black, light orange surface and dark red paint on exterior, common medium sand and chaff. [+]
g   black, orange surface on exterior, brown surface on interior, white slip, red and black paint on exterior, abundant chaff. [+]
h   red-brown, grey surfaces, cream slip and brown paint on exterior, common medium sand. [+]

i   dark red, clear glaze on interior, exterior surface blackened, moderate medium sand. [.135]
j   black, orange-buff surfaces, red paint on rim, abundant chaff, diameter unknown. [.134]
k   red, light grey core, cream surfaces, common medium sand. [.136]
l   dark grey, red surface on exterior, ridged, common medium sand. [+]
m   black, tan surface on interior, fine. [+]
n   orange, cream surfaces, abundant medium sand. [.136]
o   black, orange-tan surfaces, abundant coarse grit, pebbles and chaff. [+]
p   greenish cream, abundant medium sand. [.136]
q   cream, comb incised on exterior, blackened exterior, moderate medium sand. [.136]
r   orange-red, light grey core, buff surface on exterior, moderate coarse grit, diameter unknown. [.135]

Plate 31   Khirbet Sheikh 'Isa (SGNAS Site 4) [SGNAS Sample No (where pertinent)]

a   red-brown, cream surfaces, moderate medium sand. [.9]
b   buff, buff-cream surfaces, moderate medium sand. [.9]
c   cream, moderate medium sand. [.9]
d   cream, common coarse pebbles, diameter unknown. [.9]
e   buff-tan, fire-blackened interior, moderate medium sand. [.9]
f   buff-tan, cream-buff surfaces, moderate medium sand. [.9]
g   black, buff surfaces, white slip, red and black paint on exterior, common medium sand and chaff. [+]
h   black, buff-orange surfaces, cream slip, brown paint on exterior, common medium sand and chaff, diameter unknown. [+]
i   black, buff surfaces, brown paint, common medium sand and chaff. [+]
j   cream, light orange surfaces, red paint on interior, common medium sand and chaff. [+]
k   cream, brown paint on exterior, common coarse grit,

diameter unknown. [.9]
l   brown, grey core, cream-buff-orange surfaces, red paint, abundant chaff. [.9]
m   cream-buff, orange surfaces, common medium sand and coarse grit. [+]
n   dark grey, buff surfaces, chattering on exterior, fine, diameter unknown. [+]
o   orange, common medium sand. [.9]
p   buff, cream-buff slip, moderate medium sand and chaff. [+]
q   brown-buff, common medium sand and chaff. [+]
r   buff-orange, moulded on exterior, common medium sand. [+]
s   cream, punctate, moderate medium sand. [+]
t   cream-buff, comb incised, moderate medium sand. [+]
u   cream, moderate medium sand. [.9]
v   red-brown, common medium sand. [.9]
w   cream, moderate medium sand. [.9]

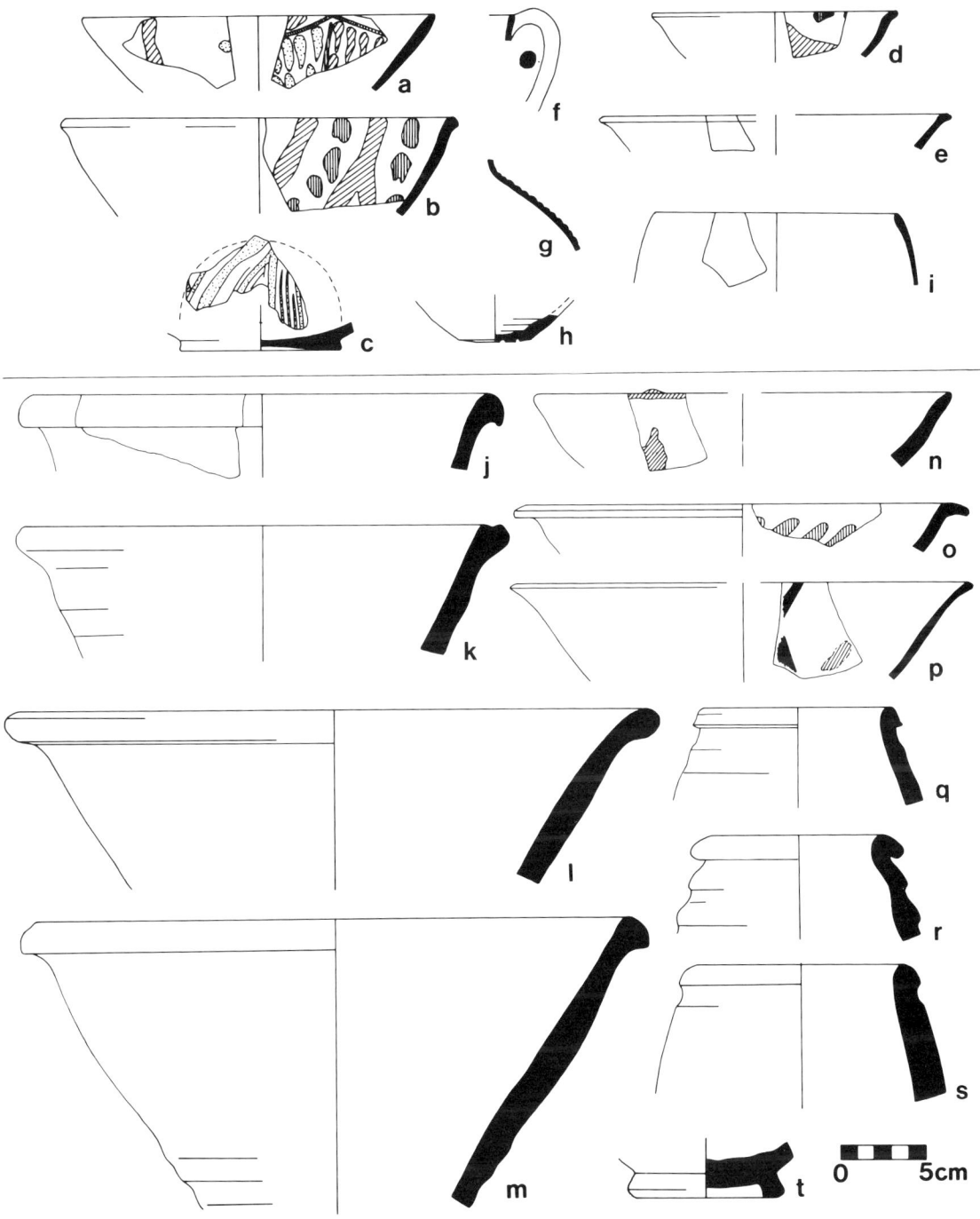

Plate 29   Tawahin al-Sukkar

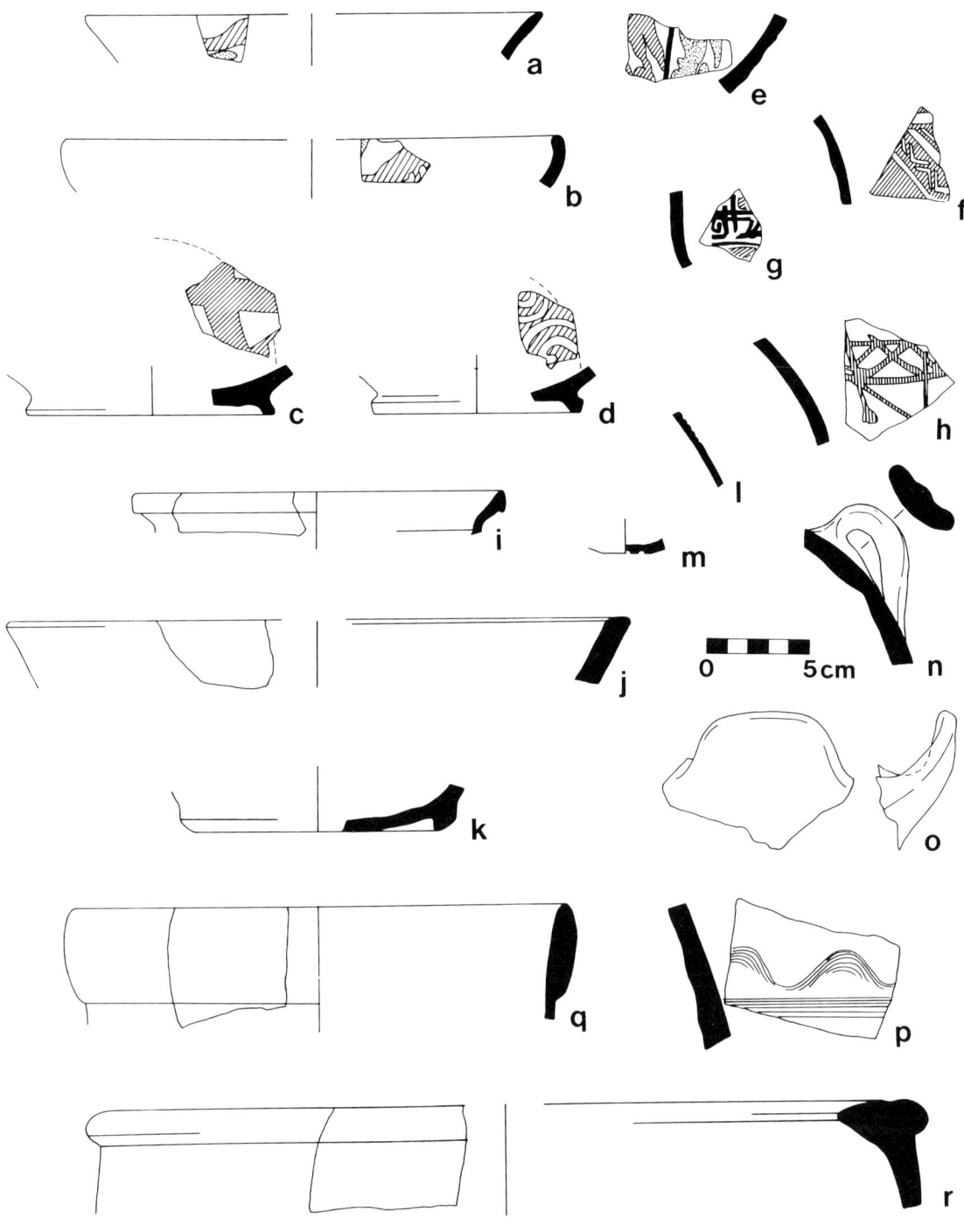

Plate 30 Feifa (SGNAS Site 91) [SGNAS Sample No (where pertinent)]

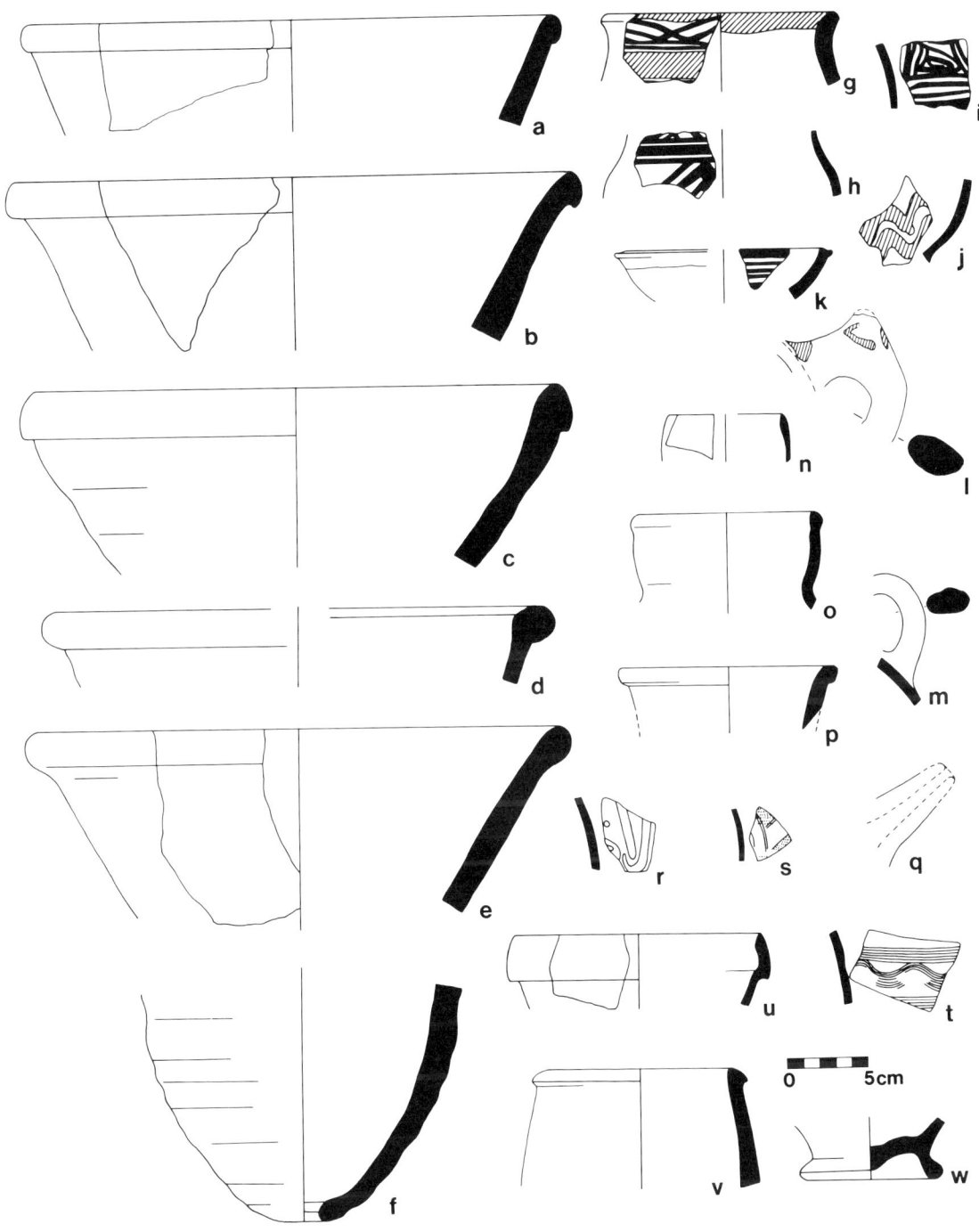

Plate 31   Khirbet Sheikh 'Isa (SGNAS Site 4) [SGNAS Sample No (where pertinent)]

Plate 32   Khirbet Sheikh 'Isa (SGNAS Site 4) [SGNAS Sample No (where pertinent)]

a   orange, cream surfaces, yellow-green glaze on interior and exterior, moderate medium sand. [+]

b   cream, green, yellow, brown, clear glaze on interior, green, clear glaze on exterior, moderate medium sand, diameter unknown. [+]

c   dark red, grey surface on exterior, slip paint and light green glaze on interior and rim, moderate medium sand. [.9]

d   white, turquoise glaze on interior and exterior, black paint under exterior glaze, frit. [.9]

e   white, black paint under blue glaze on exterior, frit. [+]

f   white, black paint under clear glaze on interior and exterior, frit. [.9]

g   white, black paint under bluish clear glaze on exterior, frit. [+]

h   orange, white slip and light green glaze on interior and exterior, moderate medium sand. [.9]

i   dark red, slip paint and clear glaze on interior, fire blackened exterior, moderate medium sand. [.9]

j   orange, cream surfaces, white slip and light green glaze on interior, drips of yellow and green glaze on exterior, moderate medium sand. [.9]

k   dark red, white slip on interior, light yellow glaze on interior and exterior, sgraffiato, moderate medium sand.

l   [.9]
   red-buff, white slip and glossy yellow glaze on interior and exterior, brownish spots on rim, moderate medium sand. [.9]

m   dark red, clear glaze on interior, rim and handle, moderate medium sand, diameter unknown. [.9]

n   red-orange, cream surfaces, glossy yellow glaze on interior and exterior, brownish in grooves, moderate medium sand, diameter unknown. [.9]

o   buff, white slip and glossy yellow glaze on interior and exterior, brownish vertical streaks, moderate medium sand. [.9]

p   orange-brown, impressed rim, moderate medium sand. [.9]

q   buff-orange, black horizontal streaks on exterior, fine, diameter unknown. [+]

r   red-orange, light red slip on interior and exterior, moderate medium sand. [+]

s   brown, buff-tan surfaces, common medium sand and chaff. [+]

t   tan-buff, common medium sand. [.9]

u   brown, tan-buff surfaces, moderate medium sand. [.9]

v   cream-buff, cream slip, common medium sand. [.9]

Plate 33   al-Rujoum   (SGNAS Site 45) [SGNAS Sample No (where pertinent)]

a   greenish cream, tan core, moderate medium sand and chaff (?). [.54]

b   buff, orange core, moderate medium sand. [.53]

c   dark red, moderate medium sand. [+]

d   buff, cream surfaces, common medium sand. [.54]

e   buff, buff-cream surfaces, common medium sand. [.53]

f   black, red surfaces (handle completely red), moderate medium sand. [+]

g   buff, cream surfaces, moderate medium sand. [.54]

h   black, orange surface on interior, buff surface and brown paint on exterior, common coarse grit and pebbles. [+]

i   greenish cream, cream surfaces, moderate coarse grit. [.53]

j   orange-buff, cream surfaces, moderate coarse grit. [.53]

k   orange-tan, cream surfaces, common coarse grit, diameter 42 cm. [.53]

l   black, tan surface on exterior, common medium sand and abundant chaff. [+]

m   brown-grey, buff-red-brown surfaces, abundant coarse pebbles. [.53]

n   tan-grey, orange surface on interior, grey-brown surface on exterior, abundant coarse grit and pebbles. [+]

o   black, orange surface on exterior, cream slip, moderate medium sand and abundant chaff. [+]

Plate 34: al-Rujoum (SGNAS Site 45) [SGNAS Sample No (where pertinent)]

a   buff, buff-tan surfaces, cream-white slip, black and red paint on exterior, common coarse grit and chaff. [.54]

b   brown, orange surface on exterior, abundant coarse pebbles. [.53]

c   black, red-brown surface and red and black paint on exterior, abundant coarse grit and chaff. [.53]

d   black, buff surfaces, red-brown paint on exterior, abundant chaff. [.53]

e   black, buff surfaces, orange-brown paint, moderate medium sand and chaff. [.53]

f   cream, red-brown and black paint on exterior, common coarse grit. [+]

g   grey-brown, buff-orange surfaces, cream slip, red paint on interior, red and dark brown paint on exterior, common coarse grit and chaff, diameter unknown. [+]

h   cream, moderate medium sand. [.53]

i   cream, common medium sand. [+]

j   buff, grey core, red surface and white paint on exterior, moderate medium sand and chaff. [+]

k   black, cream slip, orange surface and red paint on exterior, moderate medium sand and chaff. [+]

l   black, tan surfaces, cream slip, red and black paint on exterior, common medium sand and chaff. [+]

m   buff, buff-orange surfaces, moderate medium sand. [.53]

n   black, orange-buff surfaces, abundant chaff, diameter unknown. [.54]

o   cream, common medium sand. [.53]

p   cream, comb incised, common medium sand, diameter 40 cm. [.53]

q   orange-buff, cream slip on interior and exterior, moderate medium sand. [.54]

r   cream, brown paint on interior and rim, common coarse red grit. [.53]

s   black, tan surfaces, cream slip, brown paint on interior, ledge handle, abundant coarse grit and chaff, diameter unknown. [+]

t   red-brown, cream surface on exterior, moderate medium sand. [.54]

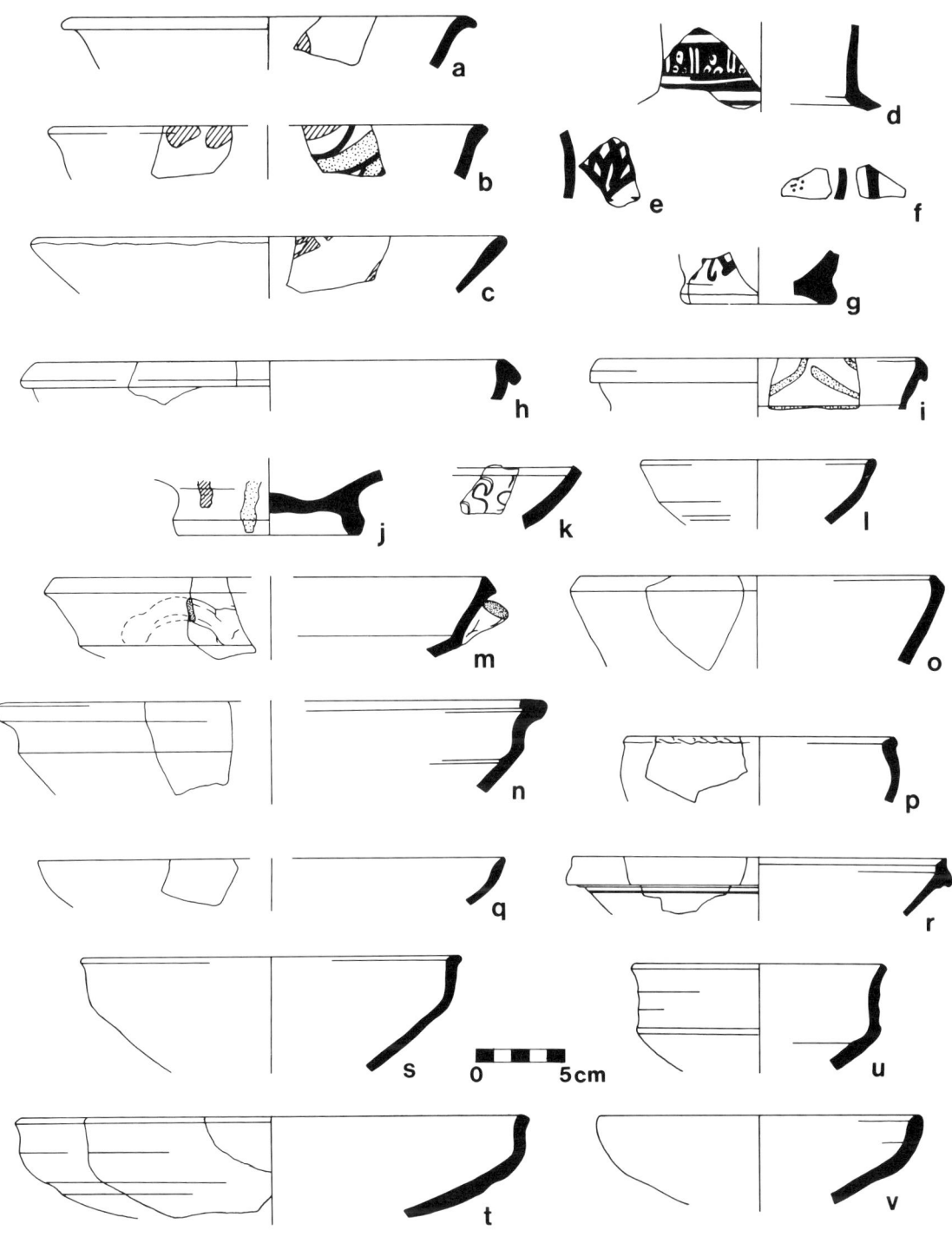

Plate 32 Khirbet Sheikh 'Isa (SGNAS Site 4) [SGNAS Sample No (where pertinent)]

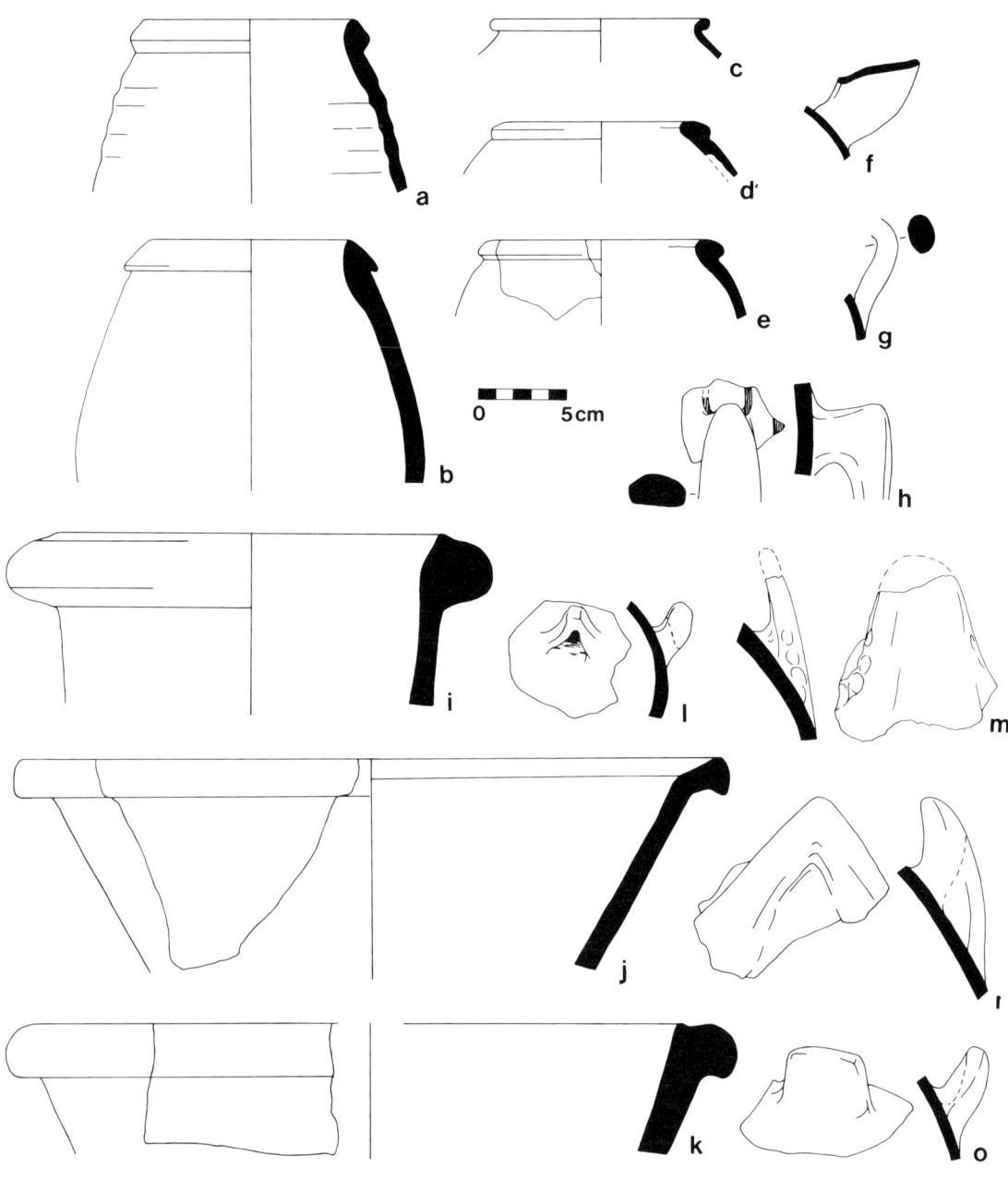

Plate 33   al-Rujoum (SGNAS Site 45) [SGNAS Sample No (where pertinent)]

Plate 34: al-Rujoum (SGNAS Site 45) [SGNAS Sample No (where pertinent)]

Plate 35 al-Rujoum (SGNAS Site 45) [SGNAS Sample No (where pertinent)]

a   white, gold lustre and clear glaze on interior and exterior, frit. [+]

b   white, black and blue paint under clear glaze on interior and exterior, frit, diameter unknown. [+]

c   white, black paint under turquoise glaze on interior and exterior, frit, diameter unknown. [+]

d   white, black paint under turquoise glaze on interior and exterior, frit, diameter unknown. [+]

e   white, black, blue and red paint under clear glaze on interior, clear glaze on exterior (not base), frit. [+]

f   cream, yellow, brown glaze on interior, sgraffiato (?), greenish clear glaze on exterior, common medium sand. [+]

g   cream, clear, brown, green glaze on interior, moderate medium sand. [.53]

h   orange-red, cream slip, brown, yellow glaze on interior, clear glaze on exterior, moderate medium sand. [+]

i   white, porcelain. [.54]

j   buff, light yellow and green glaze on interior and exterior, moderate medium sand. [.54]

k   red, cream slip, green glaze, sgraffiato, moderate medium sand. [+]

l   red, slip painted, green glaze on interior, moderate medium sand. [+]

m   dark red, slip paint on interior, yellow glaze on interior and rim, moderate medium sand. [.54]

n   red, cream slip on interior, yellow glaze on interior and rim, horizontal brownish streaks, moderate medium sand. [.54]

o   buff, light orange surfaces, cream slip, yellow glaze on interior and rim, moderate medium sand, diameter unknown. [+]

p   red, cream slip, yellow glaze on interior, sgraffiato, moderate medium sand. [+]

q   dark red, traces of cream slip, green glaze and sgraffiato on interior, common medium sand, diameter unknown. [.53]

r   red, traces of yellow glaze and sgraffiato, moderate medium sand. [.54]

s   orange-red, cream slip, yellow glaze on interior and exterior, brownish at rim, moderate medium sand. [+]

t   buff, cream slip, green glaze on interior, moderate medium sand. [+]

u   tan, cream slip (?), mottled green glaze on interior and exterior, common medium sand. [+]

v   brown, thick cream slip, green glaze on interior and rim, spots of yellow glaze on exterior, moderate medium sand, diameter unknown. [+]

w   buff-orange, cream slip, streaking yellow glaze on interior and rim, incised line on interior, moderate medium sand. [+]

Plate 36 Glass bracelets from al-Rujoum (SGNAS Site 45) and regional map [SGNAS Sample No (where pertinent)]

a   cobalt blue ca. 6 cm. [.53] (interior diameter a–h)

b   turquoise ca. 4 cm. [+]

c   opaque black, twisted ca. 7–8 cm. [.54]

d   opaque black with white, twisted ca. 8 cm. [.53]

e   amber, orange and yellow marvered sections, turquoise sections ca. 5 cm. [+]

f   greenish clear, red, twisted yellow and green bands ca. 7–8 cm. [.53]

g   greenish clear, red, yellow, twisted black and white bands ca. 5–6 cm. [.53]

h   greenish clear, yellowish green surface, twisted black and white bands ca. 7 cm. [.53]

Regional map showing primary connecting links to Zughar. (Horizontal hatched area is below sea level; dashed lines are 300 m elevation.).

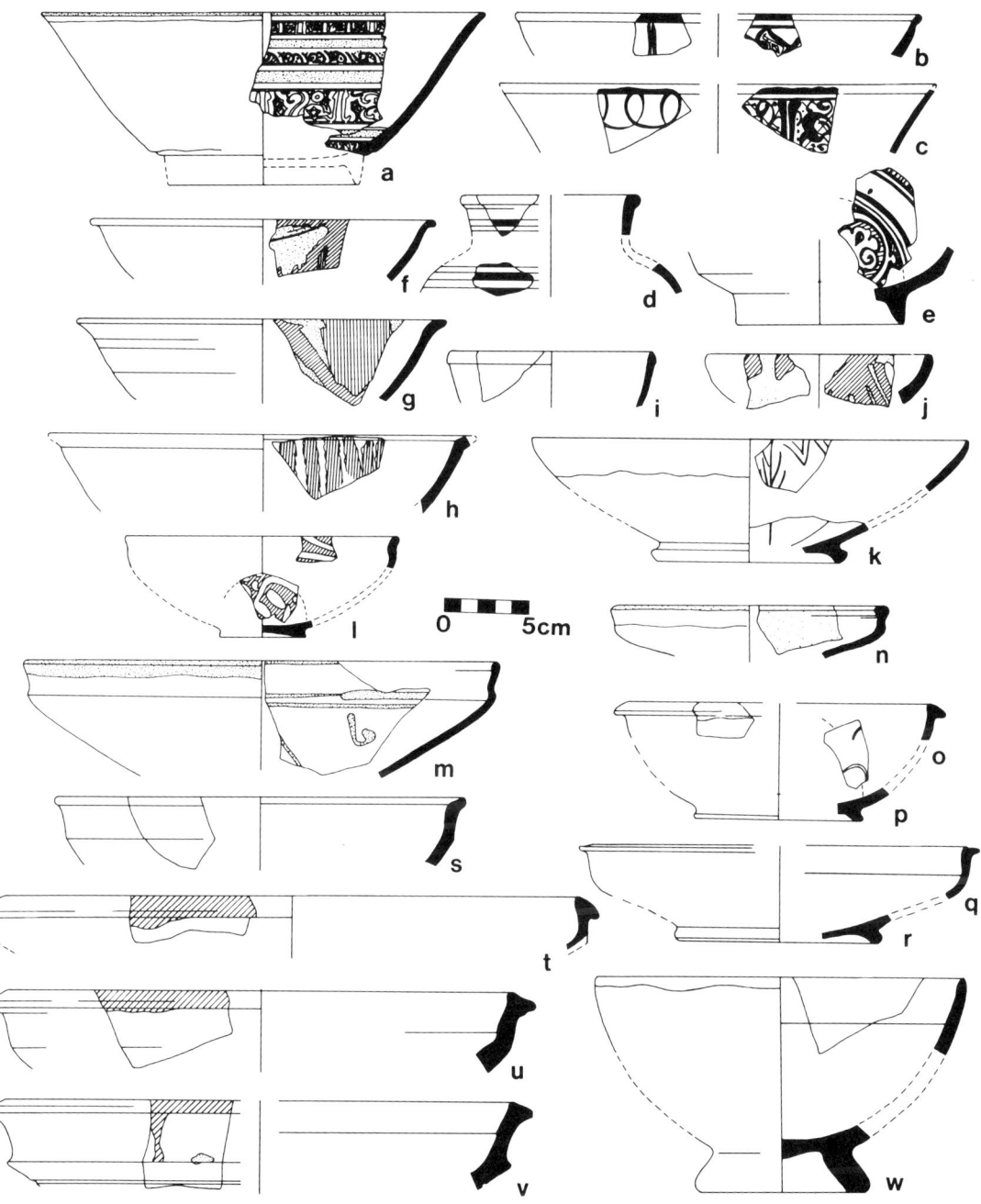

Plate 35   al-Rujoum (SGNAS Site 45) [SGNAS Sample No (where pertinent)]

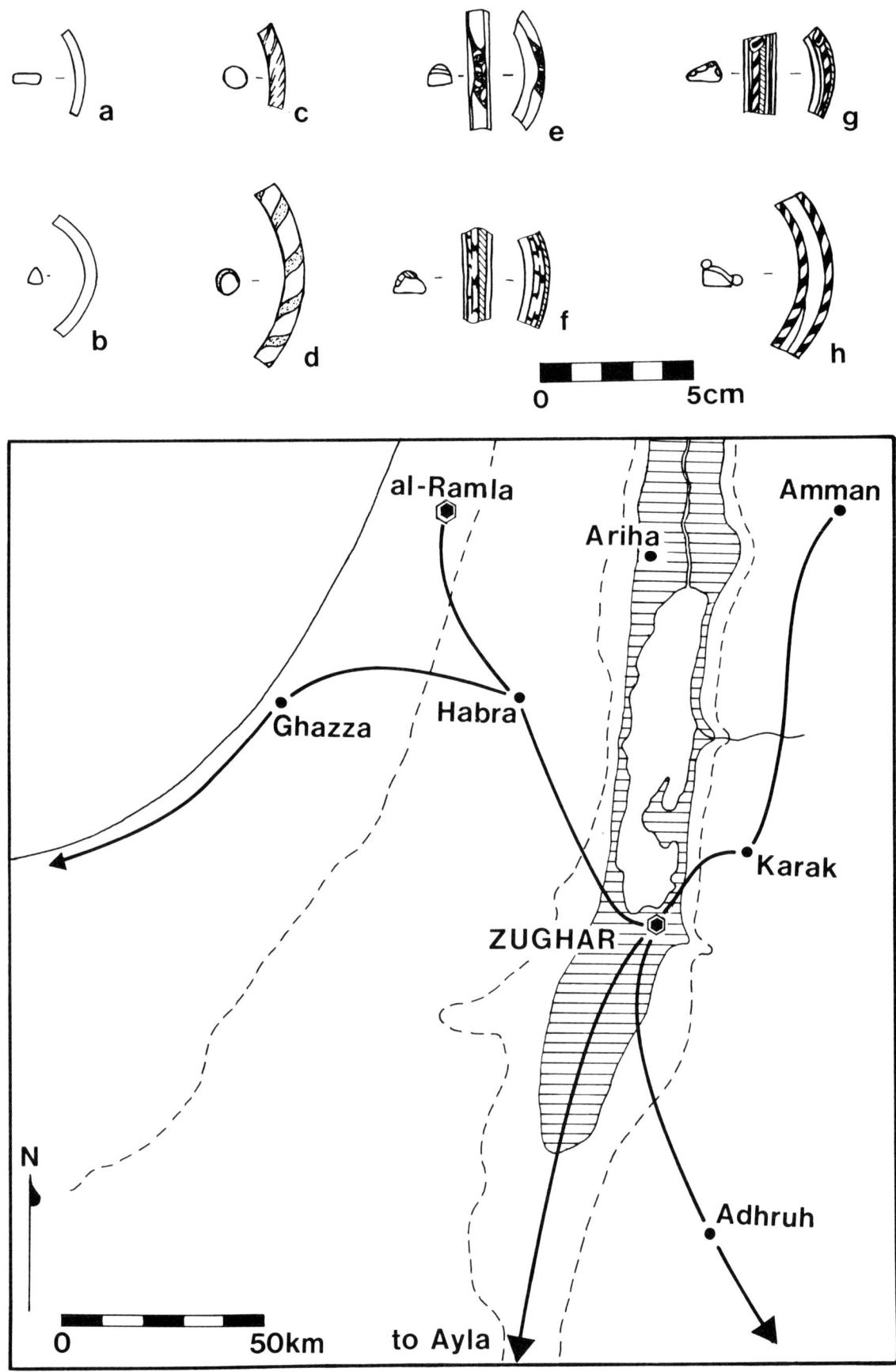

Plate 36   Glass bracelets from al-Rujoum (SGNAS Site 45) and regional map [SGNAS Sample No (where pertinent)]

Plate 37   Glass from Sites 4; 27; 46; 75; 91; 155; 211; 216; and 228

No	a
Site	4
Sample	9
Reg No	19
Colour	Clear w/turq coil marvered in
Surface	Little Y decomp
Comments	lg bowl?

No	b
Site	4
Sample	9
Reg No	18
Colour	Lt blue-gr
Surface	Liitle wt decomp, opal
Comments	Cup/small bowl?

No	c
Site	4
Sample	9
Reg No	9
Colour	V dk purple
Surface	Horiz bubbles
Comments	Bowl

No	d
Site	4
Sample	9
Reg No	13
Colour	Dk Olive w/wt opaque marvered herringbones
Surface	Horiz bubbles
Comments	Bowl, marvered

No	e
Site	4
Sample	9
Reg No	20
Colour	Y-olive?
Surface	Tough Y decomp
Comments	Looped base

No	f
Site	4
Sample	9
Reg No	12
Colour	Lt grey
Surface	Bubbles
Comments	Hollow-stem lamp

No	g
Site	27
Sample	38
Reg No	33
Colour	Lt blue-gr
Surface	Pitted, worn
Comments	Looped-out rim

No	h
Site	46
Sample	90
Reg No	42
Colour	Lt blue-gr
Surface	Dulled, bubbles
Comments	Handle

No	i
Site	46
Sample	90
Reg No	42
Colour	Lt blue-gr
Surface	Few bubbles
Comments	Flaring rim

No	j
Site	46
Sample	408
Reg No	104
Colour	Blue-gr
Surface	Dull
Comments	Pincered dec

No	k
Site	75
Sample	116
Reg No	68
Colour	Lt blue
Surface	Worn, some impurities
Comments	Handle, to looped-out rim

No	l
Site	91
Sample	135
Reg No	66
Colour	V dk purple w/opaque wt coils
Surface	Worn, some opal
Comments	Bottle neck

No	m
Site	91
Sample	135
Reg No	66
Colour	Dk purple w/opaque wt stripes, slight ribs
Surface	Dull
Comments	Marvered and ribbed

No	n
Site	155
Sample	257
Reg No	74
Colour	Lt blue-gr
Surface	Dull
Comments	Small bowl or cup?

No	o
Site	211
Sample	353
Reg No	88
Colour	Dk gr
Surface	Bubbles, impur, little wt decomp
Comments	Unguentarium rim

No	p
Site	216
Sample	392
Reg No	93
Colour	Amber
Surface	Horiz bubbles
Comments	Incurved bowl rim

No	q
Site	216
Sample	392
Reg No	93
Colour	Lt blue-gr
Surface	Dull
Comments	Bowl, looped-out rim

No	r
Site	216
Sample	392
Reg No	93
Colour	Blue-gr
Surface	Impurities
Comments	Rolled-in rim w/handle, dia est

No	s
Site	216
Sample	392
Reg No	93
Colour	Lt blue-gr w/turq threads
Surface	Dull
Comments	Bottle neck, trailed threads

No	t
Site	216
Sample	392
Reg No	93
Colour	Lt Y-gr
Surface	Dull
Comments	Bottle rim and neck

No	u
Site	216
Sample	392
Reg No	93
Colour	Lt blue w/amber handle
Surface	Bubbles
Comments	Handle

No	v
Site	216
Sample	392
Reg No	100
Colour	Lt gr
Surface	Dull
Comments	Coil dec, v lg bottle?

No	w
Site	216
Sample	392
Reg No	93

Colour	Lt blue-gr
Surface	Dull
Comments	Prob bottle neck, dia est 2.5cm

No	x
Site	228
Sample	395
Reg No	92
Colour	Lt Y-gr
Surface	Impurities
Comments	Bowl or cup

No	y
Site	228
Sample	395
Reg No	92
Colour	Lt blue-gr w/Y-gr trail
Surface	Impurities
Comments	Trailed dec

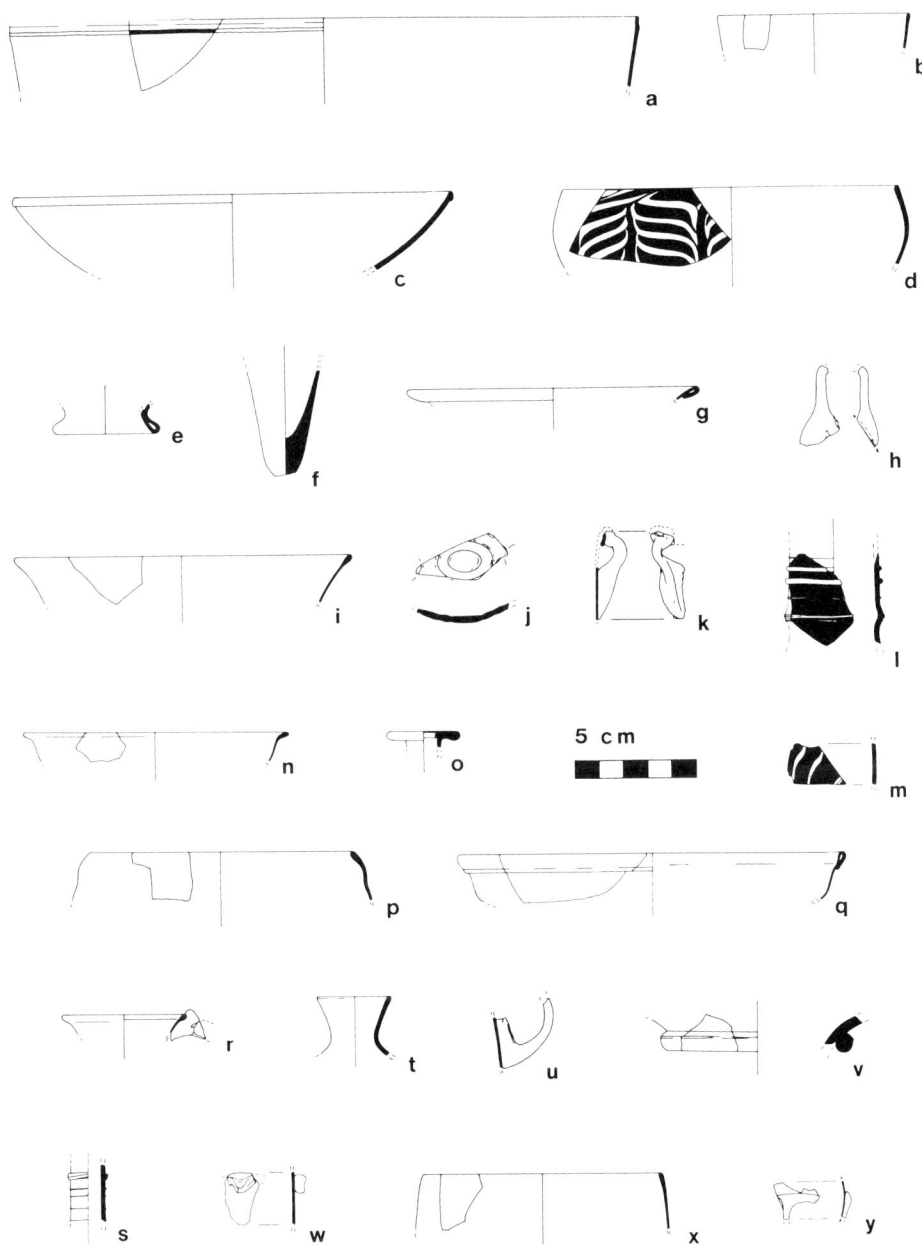

Plate 37   Glass from Sites 4; 27; 46; 75; 91; 155; 211; 216; and 228

Plate 38   Glass and beads from Site 45

No	a
Site	45
Sample	53
Reg No	53
Colour	Lt blue-gr
Surface	Dull
Comments	Ribbed vessel

No	b
Site	45
Sample	53
Reg No	53
Colour	Lt Y-gr
Surface	Dull, bubbly
Comments	Bowl

No	c
Site	45
Sample	54
Reg No	59
Colour	Clear
Surface	Dull, bubbly
Comments	Cup or small bowl

No	d
Site	45
Sample	54
Reg No	50
Colour	Lt purple
Surface	Worn
Comments	Bottle mouth?

No	e
Site	45
Sample	54
Reg No	59
Colour	Dk purple and opaque wt, marvered
Surface	–
Comments	Bowl, marvered dec

No	f
Site	45
Sample	54
Reg No	59
Colour	V dk purple w/opaque lt blue marvered in
Surface	Dull, impur, stone
Comments	Small bowl, v crude, rim uneven, marvered dec

No	g
Site	45
Sample	54
Reg No	59
Colour	Lt blue-gr
Surface	Worn, pitted
Comments	Bottle mouth, rim uneven

No	h
Site	45
Sample	53
Reg No	49
Colour	Deep purple
Surface	Worn
Comments	Vial rim, folded in

No	i
Site	45
Sample	54
Reg No	50
Colour	Lt purple
Surface	Worn, pitted
Comments	Flaring rim

No	j
Site	45
Sample	54
Reg No	59
Colour	Clear
Surface	Dull, bubbly
Comments	Jar mouth and neck

No	k
Site	45
Sample	53
Reg No	53
Colour	V lt Y-gr
Surface	Little wt decomp
Comments	Bottle neck, coil dec

No	l
Site	45
Sample	54
Reg No	50
Colour	Dk blue
Surface	Bubbly
Comments	Hollow-stem lamp

No	m
Site	45
Sample	54
Reg No	50
Colour	Lt blue-gr
Surface	Little wt decomp
Comments	Flat base, prob mould-blown, pontil off centre

No	n
Site	45
Sample	54
Reg No	50
Colour	Lt grey
Surface	Bubbly
Comments	Looped base

No	o
Site	45
Sample	54
Reg No	50
Colour	Lt grey
Surface	Worn
Comments	Looped base

No	p
Site	45
Sample	53
Reg No	53
Colour	Dk purple
Surface	Dull
Comments	Looped base

No	q
Site	45
Sample	54
Reg No	59
Colour	Clear
Surface	Dull
Comments	Base and body in 2 parisons? dia est

No	r
Site	45
Sample	54
Reg No	59
Colour	Blue-gr
Surface	Few bubbles
Comments	Moulded diamond dec

No	s
Site	45
Sample	53
Reg No	46
Colour	Red
Surface	–
Comments	Round bead

No	t
Site	45
Sample	53
Reg No	46
Colour	Lt gr
Surface	Thick wt decomp
Comments	Round, coiled bead

No	u
Site	45
Sample	53
Reg No	46
Colour	Dk gr
Surface	Dull
Comments	Rounded Bead

No	v
Site	45
Sample	53
Reg No	46
Colour	Turquoise
Surface	Worn
Comments	Round bead

No	w
Site	45
Sample	53
Reg No	46
Colour	Dk red w/opaque wt centre
Surface	Dull
Comments	Bead

No	x
Site	45
Sample	53
Reg No	46
Colour	Dk red w/opaque wt centre
Surface	Dull
Comments	Tubular bead

No	y
Site	45
Sample	53
Reg No	46
Colour	Lt yellow
Surface	–
Comments	Barrel bead

No	z
Site	45
Sample	53
Reg No	46
Colour	Blue-gr
Surface	Worn
Comments	Barrel bead, coiled

No	aa
Site	45
Sample	53
Reg No	46
Colour	Lt yellow
Surface	–
Comments	Barrel bead, coiled

No	bb
Site	45
Sample	53
Reg No	46
Colour	Emerald
Surface	–
Comments	Square x-section

No	cc
Site	45
Sample	53
Reg No	46
Colour	Dk blue, opaque
Surface	Worn, bubbly
Comments	Tubular, approx pentagonal

No	dd
Site	45
Sample	53
Reg No	46
Colour	V dk blue, opaque
Surface	Worn
Comments	Tubular bead

No	ee
Site	45
Sample	53
Reg No	46
Colour	Lt amber
Surface	Dull
Comments	Ring bead

No	ff
Site	45
Sample	53
Reg No	46
Colour	Dk turquoise
Surface	Some opal, worn
Comments	Polygonal bead

No	gg
Site	45
Sample	53
Reg No	46
Colour	Red
Surface	Dull
Comments	Capsule-shaped bead, moulded

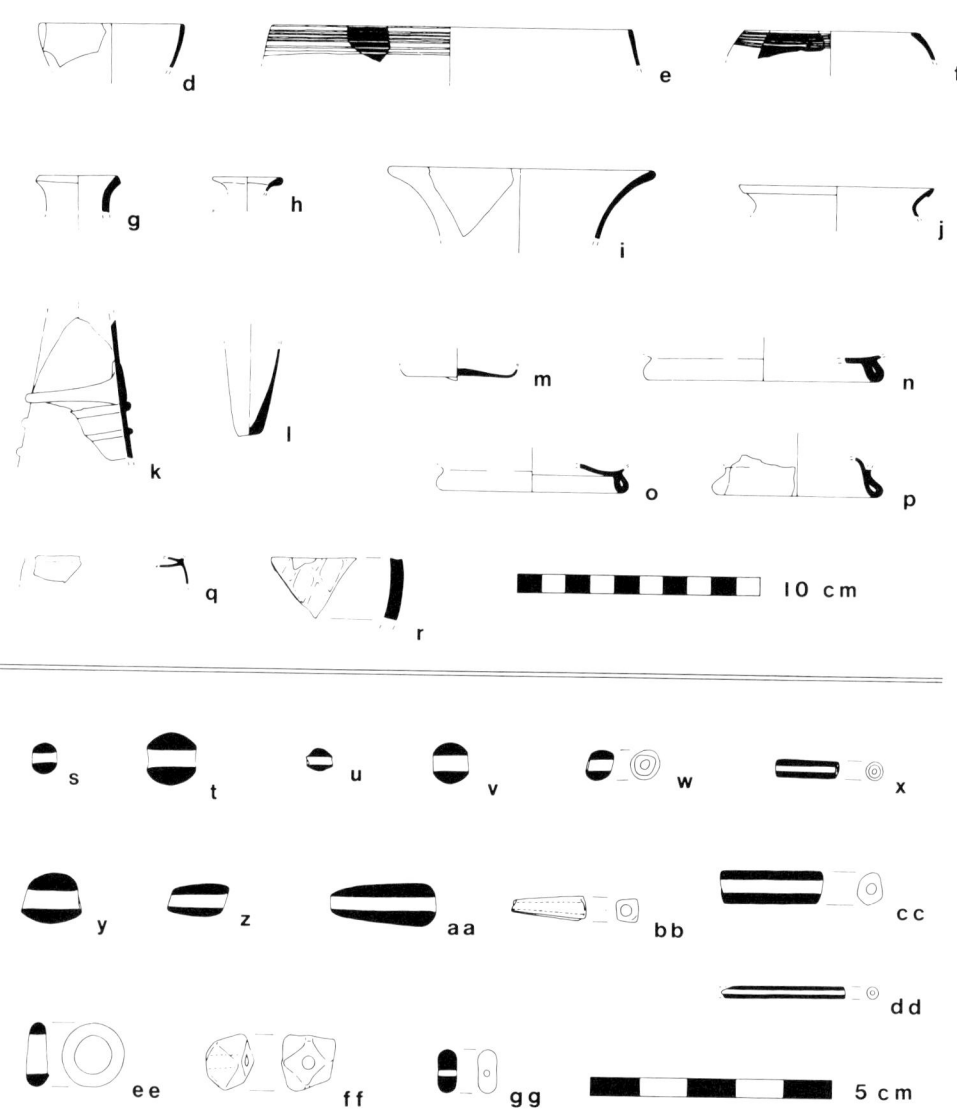

Plate 38   Glass and beads from Site 45

Appendix 1

Description of SGNAS Sites 1–240

* The Periods represented at each site are based on the analyses of the ceramics, glass, and lithic material.

Site No.: 1
Site Name: Tawahin al-Sukkar/Qasr al-Tub(ah)
Map References: 3052 II, 737; 3052/II/C/6 (23)
Location on 1:50,000: 3634/348
Location on 1:10,000: 476/195.3
Elevation: Minus 340 m
Inventory Rating: 93
Periods represented: * EB II–III; Nab; Byz; LByz–Um; LAbb/Fat; Mam; Mod; Ud.
Description: The site is a sugar mill covering an area of ca. 80 x 50 m located immediately E of the large EB cemetery of al-Safi, Site 2. It presently consists of remnants of aqueducts, spillways, and the main buildings used for milling and storing purposes. Segments of mudbrick buildings still stand ca. 3–4 m high. The site is now bordered on the SW by a cemetery, on the N and NE by a midden, and on the E by a paved road. A great deal of bulldozing has been carried out to the SE of the structures. Sherds, especially from sugar pots, are abundant in the midden. The SGNAS collected samples from the midden area, main structures, cemetery, and surrounding area.

Site No.: 2
Site Name: al-Safi
Map References: 3052 II, K737; 3052/II/C/6 (23)
Location on 1:50,000: 365/345
Location on 1:10,000: 474/195
Elevation: Minus 285–240
Inventory Rating: 88
Periods represented: EB IB; EB II–III; EB; Mam; Mod.
Description: The site is primarily an Early Bronze Age cemetery. According to informants, it is also the site of a Byzantine cemetery. However, the ceramics which the SGNAS collected date predominantly to the Early Bronze Age period. The site is located on a ridge just to the south of Wadi al-Hasa. This ridge at one time jutted into agricultural fields. However, through time it was cut by the sugar mill, Site 1, agricultural fields, Site 66, and houses. Today a JVA townsite camp is located at one of the highest points in the cemetery. A modern, military camp is located along the SW segment of the cemetery. A great deal of looting of the tombs, which appear to be all cist tombs built of cobble stones with a large flat stone over the top, has taken place over the years. It is hard to ascertain just when this activity took place and whether or not it is continuing until the present time. Moreover, erosion has exposed many of the tombs. Most of the samples collected came from these looted or eroded tombs. The SGNAS collected a large amount of restorable pottery.

Site No.: 3
Site Name: None
Map References: 3052 II, K737; 3052/II/C/6 (23)
Location on 1:50,000: 369/343
Location on 1:10,000: 473/195.9
Elevation: Minus 280 m
Inventory Rating: 43
Periods represented: EB I; Iron IA; Mam; Ott.
Description: The site consists of one robbed tomb, a line of stones measuring ca. 7 m in length, and a sherd and lithic scatter. It is located SE of the JVA townsite. There may be buried structures at the site.

Site No.: 4
Site Name: Khirbet Sheik 'Isa
Map References: 3052 II, K737; 3052/II/C/6 (23)
Location on 1:50,000: 360/350
Location on 1:10,000: 480/195.2
Elevation: Minus 350 m
Inventory Rating: 60
Periods represented: EB I; EB; Rom; Byz; Um; LByz–Um; Abb; Fat; Ayy–Mam; Ud.
Description: At one time Kh. Sheik 'Isa was an imposing mound. However, it has been bulldozed for agricultural purposes. There are, nonetheless, some wall lines still visible in the bulldozed field. The SGNAS noted in 1986 column base fragments at the SE corner and column drums in the NE corner of the field. The column drums were larger in size than the column base fragments. The SGNAS collected a great deal of pottery in the field along with pottery wasters in a midden deposit in the centre of the field. This is possibly the location of an ancient kiln. A modern road cuts the site on the west. The SGNAS collected a sample from this area as well. Although the entire field has been bulldozed, a small area had not been planted up to 1987. Excavations are possible here. Personnel of the Impresit Construction Co. told the SGNAS that they uncovered columns about 2 m below the surface of the ground when laying irrigation pipes. Thus, there could be a great deal of deposition still at the site.

Site No.: 5
Site Name: None
Map References: 3052 II, K737; 3052/II/C/6 (23)
Location on 1:50,000: 375/341
Location on 1:10,000: 196.5/47.1
Elevation: Minus 270 m
Inventory Rating: 33
Periods represented: Iron IA; Nab; Mam; Ud.
Description: The site consists of what appears to be a Bedouin camp, many graves (some of which are looted), and a sherd scatter on a hill overlooking Wadi al-Hasa to the N and NW. There are indications that the military recently used the area.

Site No.: 6
Site Name: Umm al-Tawabin/Kh. Labrush/al-Ebrosh
Map References: 3052 II, K737; 3052/II/C/6(23)
Location on 1:50,000: 379/337
Location on 1:10,000: 196.9/46.7 (highest segment)
Elevation: Minus 200–130 m
Inventory Rating: 76
Periods represented: Chal/EB; Nab (=LHell–ERom); Rom; Byz; Mam; Ud.
Description: The site is predominantly a large Nabataean (=LHell–ERom) fortress located to the SE of al-Safi and to the E of the Wadi al-Hasa gorge. It is composed of several segments. The lower segment is enclosed by a stone wall, built for the most part on a natural rock ledge, which extends for ca. 2.50 km around the site. The wall does not, however, encircle the northern extremity of the site. The wall ought to be defined as an enclosure wall rather than as a defensive one. On the west side of the site, there are small circular structures both within and outside the wall. These measure ca. 2–3 m in diameter with 'entrances' facing NE. However, several are larger and one measures ca. 5 m in diameter. The walls of some of these structures still stand three to four courses high. They were probably used as locations for tents for soldiers. The remnants of larger structures and at least one reservoir are located within the wall in the lower segment of the site, especially along the W and S sides. One of the larger structures is noted on Kitchener's plan. However, another, located near the southern end of the site but northwest of the southern tower (?), is not noted on the plan. The ridge which leads to the summit of the site is cut in four places. These cuts do not appear to be natural. The 'citadel' segment of the site provides a sweeping panorama of the entire area south of the Dead Sea. There is evidence of a reservoir also in this segment

of the site. Some basalt fragments were noted at the summit of the site. It appears that the summit of the site has been used recently (?) for a military purpose. The SGNAS collected Nabataean pottery from all segments of the site.

Site No.: 7
Site Name: None
Map References: 3052 II, K737; 3052/II/C/6 (23)
Location on 1:50,000: 379/344
Location on 1:10,000: 196.9/47.4
Elevation: Minus 300
Inventory Rating: 63
Periods represented: Byz; Ud.
Description: The site is a Byzantine hermitage consisting of two adjacent, rock-cut chambers and a rock-cut cistern. One chamber, the most westerly located one, measures ca. 4 x 4 m while the other measures ca. 1.5 x 4 metres. The first chamber has what appears to be a tomb cut into the floor. However, this has been disturbed. There is a small niche cut into the right wall of this chamber. The top of the doorway, which measures ca. 55 cm in width, leading into the second chamber has two cuts in the rock which indicate that they served to hang a doorway or a screen between the two chambers. The second chamber has remnants of plaster and paint on the ceiling and walls and possibly on the floor. There is an apse, measuring ca. 1 m in width, cut into the back wall of the second chamber. It is flanked by two small niches which measure ca. 0.50 x 0.50 metres. There is an inscription on the right side of the doorway leading into the first chamber. Each chamber is ca. 2 m high. The cistern is located ca. 5 m SSE of the chambers and about 3 m below them. It measures ca. 2.2 x 3.5 m and plaster can be seen on the side walls. It is now filled in with rubble. There is a large stone wall to the southeast of the cistern. It is probably a retaining wall.

Site No.: 8
Site Name: None
Map Reference: 3051 I, K737
Location on 1:50,000: 363/302
Elevation: Minus 330
Inventory Rating: 40
Periods represented: Ud.
Description: The site consists of what appear to be a number of graves spread over a large area on a terrace overlooking the sand dunes to the W between Wadi al-Hasa to the N and Wadi Madsus al-Shamali to the S. The SGNAS collected neither lithics, sherds, or other artifactual materials in association with the graves.

Site No.: 9
Site Name: None
Map Reference: 3051 II, K737
Location on 1:50,000: 292/959
Elevation: 20 m
Inventory Rating: 50
Periods represented: Chal/EB; EB IVB; EB; Ud.
Description: The site is a cave/rockshelter measuring ca. 9 m wide by 18 m deep with possibly several meters of sediment inside. The cave is formed in granite ridge with interstratified conglomerates (big mass of conglomerate over entrance). The surface of the cave is presently covered with goat dung and ash to an unknown depth. There is evidence of ash and charcoal under the overhang. The cave faces W and, thus, overlooks the bed of Wadi Fidan. There is a spring, 'Ain Fidan, located ca. 1 km to the S. The SGNAS collected a 'thin scatter' of potsherds and big, clunky lithics (crude flakes, blades made by percussion) on the slope in front of the cave leading down to the wadi bed. It seems probable that the artifacts are associated with the cave. Moreover, the SGNAS collected one cowrie shell, one piece of slag, and one piece of copper ore at the site. This is not surprising since there is a smelting site, Site 30, immediately across the wadi to the W. There are a series of smaller rockshelters to the N which also produced small collections of pottery and crude lithics.

Site No.: 10
Site Name: East part of Raikes' site 'E'

Map Reference: 3051 II, K737
Location on 1:50,000: 283/958
Elevation: 0 m
Inventory Rating: 41
Periods represented: Chal; Chal/EB; Ud.
Description: The site consists of a small mound with what appears to be a domestic structure (oval low mound with rock alignments, possible hearths) along the S side of Wadi Fidan. There is a medium scatter of lithics (large, crude flakes and blades) and crude, undecorated pottery at the site. Moreover, there is slag over part of the site. The SGNAS also found one basalt, quern fragment (mortar), at the site.

Site No.: 11
Site Name: None
Map Reference: 3051 II, K737
Location on 1:50,000 287/961
Elevation: 0 m
Inventory Rating: 66
Periods represented: Ud.
Description: This a rockshelter located on the E side of Wadi Fidan and ca. 0.5 km NNE of Site 9. It is ca. 30–40 m from the wadi bed and ca. 3–4 m above it. The opening to the shelter faces SSW. Deposits are not very deep and, currently, it appears that the shelter is being used, at least occasionally, by Bedouin. There is a great deal of goat dung within and in front of the shelter. Several recent (?) campfires are also in evidence. The SGNAS found a few lithics in front of the rockshelter. However, nearby, broken flint nodules are evident. It is not known whether or not these represent cores. There is a small, walled-in storage unit, which appears to be modern, to the S of the shelter.

Site No.: 12
Site Name: Raikes' Site 'A'
Map Reference: 3051 II, K737
Location on 1:50,000 272/963
Elevation: Minus 30 m
Inventory Rating: 67
Periods represented: EB; EB IV (?); EB IVB–MB I(?); Ud.
Description: The site is located on a small island at the mouth of Wadi Fidan. Raikes first discovered it. A scatter of lithics is present on the top and slopes of the hill which form the island. There is a concentration of sherds on a flat surface at the NE end of the site overlooking the wadi to the E. On top of the island to the SSW are the remains of a wall measuring ca. 13 m long. Also on top are 3–4 round walled structures measuring ca. 2–4 m in diameter. There is a pile of stones which may be a later grave at the NNW edge of the site. Some of the shell which the SGNAS found on the SW summit of the site is associated with bone. Whether the bone is animal or human is not known. Many lithics show up in the section along the NE side of the site, where seasonal erosion has exposed 3–4 m of midden deposits. Although the SGNAS collected many small, fine flakes and blades from the section, no sherds were noted.

Site No.: 13
Site Name: Raikes' Site 'B'
Map Reference: 3051 II, K737
Location on 1:50,000: 275/963
Elevation: Minus 30 m
Inventory Rating: 40
Periods represented: Ud.
Description: The site consists of stone walls, possibly retaining/terrace walls for agricultural fields, immediately NE of Site 12, on the N side of Wadi Fidan. Two to three courses of one L-shaped wall measuring ca. 12 x 14 m are still in place.

Site No.: 14
Site Name: Raikes' Site 'D'
Map Reference: 3051 II, K737
Location on 1:50,000 278/960
Elevation: Minus 15 m
Inventory Rating: 70
Periods represented: Chal/EB; EB IVB; Ud.
Description: This is a cemetery site consisting of over

200 graves immediately N of Wadi Fidan. Several of the graves have been looted especially at the W side of the site. There is a medium lithic and a low sherd scatter at the site. On a second visit to the site (10/24/86), the SGNAS noted more graves of the same kind on another plateau immediately to the W. The SGNAS included these graves as part of the site since they are separated from the ones to the E by a small wadi.

Site No.: 15
Site Name: Raikes Site 'C'
Map Reference: 3051 II, K737
Location on 1:50,000: 277/957
Elevation: Minus 20 m
Inventory Rating: 56
Periods represented: Chal/EB; Ud.
Description: This site consists of a lithic and sherd scatter and some architecture. The lithics are similar to those at Site 12. The SGNAS collected the sherds on the NW flank of a hill on the S bank of Wadi Fidan.

Site No.: 16
Site Name: None
Map Reference: 3051 II, K737
Location on 1:50,000: 95.7 to 95.9/27.5 to 28.7
Elevation: Minus 10 to 0 m
Inventory Rating: 51
Periods represented: Ud.
Description: The site consists of traces/remnants of an aqueduct on both sides of the Wadi Fidan gorge in the vicinity of Sites 10–12. The aqueduct is constructed of roughly dressed blocks of stone. The SGNAS found neither lithics nor sherds at the site.

Site No.: 17
Site Name: None
Map References: 3051 I, K737; 3051/I/B/2 (26)
Location on 1:50,000: 378/319
Location on 1:10,000: 196.8/449
Elevation: Minus 210 to 240
Inventory Rating: 60
Periods represented: Ud.
Description: The site consists of a cemetery consisting of several, rock-capped tombs/piles of rock, a cistern, and at least one camp (one rock alignment) with an associated hearth. The graves are scattered over an area between Wadi al-Hasa and Wadi Madsus al-Shamali. The area is bordered to the S by a wadi and the N end of the site is across another wadi.

Site No.: 18
Site Name: None
Map References: 3051 I, K737; 3051/I/B/2 (26)
Location on 1:50,000: 379/315
Location on 1:10,000: 196.8/44.4
Elevation: Minus 260 m
Inventory Rating: 37
Periods represented: Byz; Ud.
Description: The site consists of hearths and stone lines, probably a campsite, located on a small, low terrace between Wadi al-Hasa and Wadi Madsus al-Shamali. It is located on the S side of a small wadi just to the S of Site 17. The SGNAS collected a low, sherd scatter at the site.

Site No.: 19
Site Name: None
Map References: 3051 I, K737; 3051/I/B/2 (26)
Location on 1:50,000: 374/307
Location on 1:10,000: 196.4/438
Elevation: Minus 270
Inventory Rating: 35
Periods represented: Ud.
Description: This site consists of a raised midden within a small enclosure. The ash which is associated with the midden appears to be confined to the enclosure. The site is upstream from Site 23 a distance of ca. 200 m and on the opposite side of the wadi. The SGNAS found neither lithics nor sherds at the site.

Site No.: 20
Site Name: West side of Raikes' Site 'E'
Map Reference: 3051 II, K737
Location on 1:50,000: 282/955
Elevation: 0 m
Inventory Rating: 51
Periods represented: Chal; Chal/EB.
Description: This site is located immediately above and to the W of Site 10, Raikes' Site 'E', on the S side of Wadi Fidan. It could be one with it. It is cut by erosion and extends SE along the ridge. It consists of a cemetery, indications of camping, wall lines, and a heavy lithic and sherd scatter. It could have been used for watching game moving in the wadi as well as for farming the small terraces along the sides of the wadi. The SGNAS noted one robbed tomb and wall lines, which could be remnants of houses, especially at the S side of the site. There are also wall lines of 'houses' (?) visible along the eroded sides of the plateau.

Site No.: 21
Site Name: None
Map Reference: 3051 II, K737
Location on 1:50,000: 290/957
Elevation: 0–20 m
Inventory Rating: 42
Periods represented: PNL; EB; Nab; Ud.
Description: This may be the site of ancient agricultural fields along the S side of Wadi Fidan. What appear to be retaining and/or terrace walls are present. Remnants of an aqueduct may also be present. What could be the remnants of dams were noted in a small side wadi coming from the S. The SGNAS collected a very low ceramic scatter at the site.

Site No.: 22
Site Name: None
Map References: 3051 I, K737; 3051/I/B/2 (26)
Location on 1:50,000: 373/314
Location on 1:10,000: 196.3/444
Elevation: Minus 285
Inventory Rating: 59
Periods represented: Ud.
Description: This site is located to the N of Wadi Madsus al-Shamali. It consists of a circular cleared area with bedrock exposed at the centre. It does not appear that the area was excavated, only the surface rock cleared away. It may be a cleared area for a tent and, thus, a campsite. There is a tomb located ca. 100 m to the SSE of the circular area. The SGNAS found neither lithics nor sherds at the site.

Site No.: 23
Site Name: None
Map References: 3051 I, K737; 3051/I/B/2 (26)
Location on 1:50,000: 373/309
Location on 1:10,000: 196.3/439
Elevation: Minus 290
Inventory Rating: 37
Periods represented: Rom; Ud.
Description: This site consists of what appears to be a camp and at least one grave. There is evidence of some stonewall alignments. There is some fragments of terracing on the N side of an E–W tributary wadi that is part of the Wadi Madsus al-Shamali system. The SGNAS collected a low sherd scatter, possibly all from one vessel, from all over the terrace on which the site is located.

Site No.: 24
Site Name: None
Map References: 3051 I, K737; 3051/I/B/2 (26)
Location on 1:50,000: 373/300
Location on 1:10,000: 196.3/430
Elevation: Minus 255 m
Inventory Rating: 34
Periods represented: Rom.
Description: This site appears to be a potbust. It is located to the N of Wadi Madsus al-Shamali.

Site No.: 25
Site Name: None
Map References: 3051 I, K737; 3051/I/B/2 (26)
Location on 1:50,000: 369/316
Location on 1:10,000 195.9/446
Elevation: Minus 320 m
Inventory Rating: 65
Periods represented: Ud.
Description: The site consists of graves, an oven, a structure (house ?), and a lithic and sherd scatter between Wadi al-Hasa and Wadi Madsus al-Shamali. The structure measures ca. 2–3 x 1.5–2.5 metres. At least one of the graves has been robbed. The sherds could come from this looting.

Site No.: 26
Site Name: None
Map References: 3051 I, K737; 3051/I/B/2 (26)
Location on 1:50,000: 370/319
Location on 1:10,000: 196/449
Elevation: Minus 320 m
Inventory Rating: 63
Periods represented: Ud, prob EB.
Description: The site consists of a tomb located ca. 100 m N of Site 25 between Wadi al-Hasa and Wadi Madsus al-Shamali. At least five more tombs are located ca. 50 m to the NNE.

Site No.: 27
Site Name: Al-Jor
Map References: 3052 II, K737; 3052/II/C/6 (23)
Location on 1:50,000: 358/364
Location on 1:10,000: 194.9/495
Elevation: Minus 320 m
Inventory Rating: 69
Periods represented: Byz–Um; Isl, poss Mam; Mod; Ud.
Description: The site consists of remnants of what appears to have been a reservoir. The N and S walls are partially preserved. The area within is now used as an agricultural field. A modern (?) canal runs immediately E of the site. The SGNAS noted some burials, both of children and adults, in an adjacent mound to the NW.

SiteNo.: 28
Site Name: Raikes' Site 'H' (?)
Map Reference: 3051 II, K737
Location on 1:50,000: 292/960
Elevation: 0 to 20 m
Inventory Rating: 46
Periods represented: Iron I–EIron II; Iron II; Iron Age; Nab (=ERom); Ud.
Description: The site appears to be ancient agricultural fields north of Wadi Fidan. What appear to be retaining/terrace walls can be seen for ca. 200 m (E–W).

Site No.: 29
Site Name: None
Map Reference: 3051 II, K737
Location on 1:50,000: 293/960
Elevation: 0 to 20 m
Inventory Rating: 69
Periods represented: PNL; NL–Chal; Chal; Chal/EB; Iron II; Iron IIA; 'Negevite Ware'; LByz; Isl; Ud.
Description: The site consists of a very heavy sherd concentration on a steep slope immediately south of Site 28. The SGNAS noted what appear to be robbed graves, along with ash and bones, in the rock of the slope. The site is located on a hill and its slopes just where the 'Old Road' meets Wadi Fidan to the N of 'Ain Fidan. The entire site covers an area of ca. 50 (E–W) x 30 (N–S) metres.

Site No.: 30
Site Name: Al-Munbateha/Kh. Hamr Ifdan (Raikes' Site 'F')
Map Reference: 3051 II, K737
Location on 1:50,000: 293/948

Elevation: 20 m
Inventory Rating: 88
Periods represented: Chal; Chal/EB; EB IV; EB IVA and B; EB; Iron II; Rom; LRom; Byz; LByz; Isl; Ud.
Description: The site is located on an 'island' on the W side of Wadi Fidan ca. 1 km N of 'Ain Fidan. Erosion has damaged the path up to the top of the site from the SW. The SE portion of the site consists of a large slag area with small circles of stones. Some of the slag is located inside these circular structures (hearths ?). Immediately to the north is a raised area that looks like a large platform area. Some of the rock alignments here are recent but others appear to be the remains of ancient structures. The NW portion of the site has an extensive area of slag remains in and around a complex of building foundations. The building foundations are on what appears to be a platform which is not unlike the platform structure at the southern segment of the site. The area covered by this complex is ca. 50 m square. There are also several stone circles (hearths ?) here, especially along the east section of the platform. The SGNAS noted a great deal of occupational debris along the NE side of the island where illicit digging has taken place. There is also the remains of what appear to be large retaining walls in this area. The SGNAS noted several basalt querns at the site.

Site No.: 31
Site Name: None
Map Reference: 3051 II, K737
Location on 1:50,000: 285–89/961
Elevation: 20 m
Inventory Rating: 37
Periods represented: Ud.
Description: The site consists of a series of tombs spread over an area of ca. 1 km on a terrace N of Wadi Fidan. The SGNAS found neither lithics nor sherds at the site.

Site No.: 32
Site Name: None
Map Reference: 3051 II, K737
Location on 1:50,000 285/961
Elevation: 20 m
Inventory Rating: 36
Periods represented: Ud.
Description: The site is a lithic scatter of low density covering much of the surface of a small plateau measuring ca. 125 x 70 metres. The plateau is the upper surface of a thick, conglomerate which is full of quartzite, chert, flint, and sandstone cobbles. These are deflated on the surface, forming a flint/gravel, desert pavement.

Site No.: 33
Site Name: None
Map Reference: 3051 II, K737
Location on 1:50,000: 289/961
Elevation: ca. 20 m
Inventory Rating: 38
Periods represented: Ud.
Description: This site is similar to Site 32. It is really an eastward extension of a lithic scatter on a conglomerate terrace.

Site No.: 34
Site Name: None
Map Reference: 3051 II, K737
Location on 1:50,000: 293/960
Elevation: 20 m
Inventory Rating: 65
Periods represented: Iron II; Ud.
Description: The site consists of a domestic-cluster and a sherd scatter. It is located on a conglomerate island between Wadi Fidan to the S and a tributary drainage.

Site No.: 35
Site Name: None
Map Reference: 3051 II, K737
Location on 1:50,000: 291/950
Elevation: 20 m

Inventory Rating: 53
Periods represented: EB; Ud.
Description: The site consists of what may be a farm and/or camp, a lithic and sherd scatter, and terrace walls on a slope and hill to the W of Site 30 and, thus, W of Wadi Fidan. There is a stone platform measuring ca. 18 x 5 m at the summit of the hill. The SGNAS noted walls running up/down (E–W) the hill as well as across the slope (N–S).

Site No.: 36
Site Name: Al-Altiahem
Map References: 3052 II, K737; 3052/II/C/4 (20)
Location on 1:50,000: 372/383
Location on 1:10,000: 196.2/51.3
Elevation: Minus 375 m
Inventory Rating: 63
Periods represented: Isl-glazed ware; Ud, prob Isl.
Description: The site consists of a farm located in agricultural fields to the N of Wadi al-Hasa. The mudbrick, farm building measures ca. 21 x 6 metres.

Site No.: 37
Site Name: None
Map Reference: 3051 II, K737
Location on 1:50,000: 298/972
Elevation: 20 to 40 m
Inventory Rating: 32
Periods represented: Ud.
Description: The site consists of two badly eroded graves and a probable potbust. Other grave were noted to the E.

Site No.: 38
Site Name: Raikes' Site 'I'
Map Reference: 3051 II, K737
Location on 1:50,000: 295/955
Elevation: 0 to 20 m
Inventory Rating: 71
Periods represented: Ud.
Description: The site consists of a rectilinear, two-room structure on an alluvial, W-facing fan 2–3 m above a tributary wadi on the N side of Wadi Fidan. Each room measures ca. 6 x 5 metres.

Site No.: 39
Site Name: None
Map Reference: 3051 II, K737
Location on 1:50,000: 307/969
Elevation: 20 to 40 m
Inventory Rating: 32
Periods represented: Ud.
Description: The site consists of a cemetery, a lithic scatter, and a possible enclosure, which could actually be several graves together, covering an area of ca. 40 x 20 metres. It is located ca. 500 m due E of Site 37 on the edge of a small wadi which flows northward into Wadi al-Ghuweib.

Site No.: 40
Site Name: None
Map Reference: 3051 II, K737
Location on 1:50,000: 304/972
Elevation: 20 to 40 m
Inventory Rating: 30
Periods represented: Ud.
Description: The site consists of at least four graves and a line of stone which could have served as a windbreak for a camp. It is located ca. 750 m E of Site 37. Wadi al-Ghuweib is located to the N. The SGNAS found neither lithics nor sherds at the site.

Site No.: 41
Site Name: None
Map Reference: 3051 II, K737
Location on 1:50,000: 281/960
Elevation: 0 to 20 m

Inventory Rating: 30
Periods represented: Ud.
Description: This is a rectilinear outline of rocks facing S on the N side of Wadi Fidan. It is across the wadi and ca. 120–140 m NW of Sites 10 and 20, Raikes' Site 'E'. The SGNAS found one flake, which it did not collect, at the site.

Site No.: 42
Site Name: None
Map Reference: 3051 II, K737
Location on 1:50,000: 297/977
Elevation: 10 to 20 m
Inventory Rating: 40
Periods represented: Ud.
Description: The site is a camp covering an area of ca. 40 x 40 metres. It consists of an enclosure and several stone structures. The structures do not appear to be recent. Another enclosure or series of structures is located to the SW. Two other enclosures, one measuring ca. 120 m and the other 90–100 m in circumference, are located nearby to the NW. A low lithic scatter is associated with the structures.

Site No.: 43
Site Name: None
Map Reference: 3051 II, K737
Location on 1:50,000: 297/978
Elevation: 10 to 20 m
Inventory Rating: 36
Periods represented: Ud.
Description: The site consists of a cemetery and an enclosure, measuring ca. 17 (N–S) x 12 (E–W) m, to the NW. It probably served as a campsite. There is an associated light lithic scatter.

Site No.: 44
Site Name: None
Map Reference: 3051 II, K737
Location on 1:50,000: 278/956
Elevation: 0 to 20 m
Inventory Rating: 47
Periods represented: Ud.
Description: The site consists of a dense lithic scatter on a hill and its slope. There are two circular structures at the summit. One of the structures has been 'excavated'. This site should be seen in relation to Site 15, Raikes' Site 'C'.

Site No.: 45
Site Name: Al-Rujoum/Kh. Cheikh 'Ali/Kh. es-Safieh
Map References: 3052 II, K737; 3052/II/C/6 (23)
Location on 1:50,000: 358.5/368
Location on 1:10,000: 194.9/49.9
Elevation: Minus 360 to 370 m
Inventory Rating: 81
Periods represented: Rom (?); Abb; Fat; Ayy–Mam; Mam and/or Ott.
Description: The site consists of a low mound to the W and a modern cemetery to the E immediately S of Wadi al-Hasa. Both segments cover an area of at least 100 (N–S) x 200 (E–W) metres. The cemetery could actually be located on the eastern segment of an ancient site. The mound is cut on the east by an unpaved, agricultural road. The entire site is encircled by agricultural fields. The sherd scatter is more abundant in the area of the cemetery than in the area where there are no graves. The area to the west gives the impression of a midden since the soil is dark brown in colour. The people of modern al-Safi refer to this site as ancient al-Safi. Besides sherds, the SGNAS collected glass, a coin fragment, a marine shell, a glass bead, and bracelet fragments at the site.

Site No.: 46
Site Name: Deir 'Ain 'Abata
Map References: 3152 III, K737; 3152/III/D/3 (21)
Location on 1:50,000: 392/385

Location on 1:10,000:   197.98/050.77
Elevation: ca. Minus 300 m
Inventory Rating: 93
Periods represented: Nab; Rom; Byz (E and L); Byz (?); Um (?); Abb; Ott; Ud.
Description: The site appears to be a monastery/church complex located halfway up a hill to the E of the Impresit Construction Co. camp and N of the Wadi al-Hasa gorge. It consists of a number of buildings. The main building is on two levels. The top level of the building measures ca. 18 (N–S) x 7 (E–W) metres. It has the remnants of seven arches interiorly and a single arch is visible against the back or eastern wall. The main arches measure ca. 60 cm wide. There is plaster on the western wall of this building. Many flat stones, which could at one time have formed the arches, were noted within the building where some digging has taken place. The lower level appears to be the main segment of the building. It, too, measures ca. 18 x 7 metres. It is now filled with rubble or fallen stone. The western or exterior wall of the lower level still stands 4–5 m high (16–18 courses). The wall separating the upper and lower segment of the building measures ca. 1.10 m wide while the western exterior wall of the structure measures ca. 1 m wide.Around this structure there are pieces of columns, capitols, and other building materials. The slope in front of the structure appears to be terraced. These walls run E–W as well as N–S. There is a midden located in front of the main structure and another to the N. Rubble from other structures is located for a distance of at least 50 m to the N of the main structure. There is a large retaining wall in a small wadi about 10 m to the S of the main structure. Besides sherds, the SGNAS collected glass, marble, an iron object, and pieces of tile at the site. In the midden to the N, the SGNAS collected one red sherd inscribed with a cross. There are the letters alpha and omega under the arms of the cross. The name of the region in which the monastery/church complex is located is called 'Ain 'Abata.

Site No.:   47
Site Name: None
Map Reference: 3051 II, K737
Location on 1:50,000:   297/972
Elevation: 20 to 40 m
Inventory Rating: 54
Periods represented: Ud.
Description: This is a cemetery measuring ca. 30 x 20 m located on both sides of the 'Old Road' to the S of Wadi al-Ghuweib. It is perched on the W-facing edge of the plateau, no more than 15–20 m from its edge. There are more grave/tombs on the E than on the W side of the road. The SGNAS noted 20–25 graves/tombs. The distinction between grave and tomb: a grave has a head and footstone with smaller rocks piled on the body; a tomb has no head/footstones but has a much more substantial pile of rocks on top. The SGNAS collected a light lithic and sherd scatter at the site.

Site No.:   48
Site Name: None
Map Reference: 3051 II, K737
Location on 1:50,000:   298/970
Elevation: 20 to 40 m
Inventory Rating: 54
Periods represented: LPL/MPL.
Description: This is a lithic scatter, heavily patinated, on the SSE facing slope of the plateau between Wadi al-Ghuweib and Wadi Fidan. The plateau is a finger of land with small drainages running on three sides away from the top of the plateau. The slope is very gentle.

Site No.:   49 'A'–'F'
Site Name: None
Map Reference: 3051 II, K737
Location on 1:50,000:   294–298/961–970
Elevation: 20 to 40 m
Inventory Rating: 39
Periods represented: Iron Age; Ud.
Description: This is a series of tombs located on both sides of the 'Old Road' between Wadi al-Ghuweib and Wadi Fidan. Tomb 'A', located at 297/965, is a circular arrangement of rocks

measuring ca. 4.5 x 2–3 metres. It is disturbed. Tombs 'B' and 'C' are located at 298/963 and 295/962 respectively. Tomb 'D' consists of two circular and three oval graves at 294/964. Tomb 'E' consists of two grave at 295/969. Tomb 'F', located at 296/966, has large stones on top. The ceramics collected are associated with Tomb 'A'.

Site No.:   50
Site Name: None
Map Reference: 3051 II, K737
Location on 1:50,000:   295/964
Elevation: 20 to 40 m
Inventory Rating: 47
Periods represented: Iron IA; Iron II.
Description: This site consists of a medium sherd scatter covering an area of ca. 20 x 20 metres. It is located on a SSW facing drainage slope of the plateau between Wadi al-Ghuweib and Wadi Fidan. It is ca. 100 m SSW of Site 49 'A'.

Site No.:   51
Site Name: None
Map Reference: 3051 II, K737
Location on 1:50,000:   297/963
Elevation: 20 to 40 m
Inventory Rating: 45
Periods represented: Ud.
Description: This is a lithic scatter measuring ca. 25 x 20 m located on the SSE edge of the drainage on the plateau on the S side of Wadi al-Ghuweib. There is a gentle slope to the SSW from which most of the SGNAS' collection came. There is probably a light scatter of flakes across the entire surface of this side of the plateau/interfluve.

Site No.:   52
Site Name: None
Map Reference: 3051 II, K737
Location on 1:50,000:   292/962
Elevation: 15–25 m
Inventory Rating: 40
Periods represented: Ud.
Description: The site consists of a series of small rock alignments which could be no more than a natural alignment of rocks caused by erosion. However, it could be a water control device of some sort. It is located on the S side of the plateau overlooking a tributary wadi emptying into Wadi Fidan. It is W of the 'Old Road' and at the head of a pass. The SGNAS collected neither lithics nor sherds at the site.

Site No.:   53
Site Name: None
Map Reference: 3051 II, K737
Location on 1:50,000:   295/967
Elevation: 20 to 40 m
Inventory Rating: 46
Periods represented: Ud.
Description: This is a lithic scatter, heavily patinated, on the west-central portion of the plateau between Wadi Fidan and Wadi al-Ghuweib. It is located on a gentle slope, dissected by minor drainages, facing SSW. One of these drainages may have deposited the lithics in the area. The whole area has a gentle roll to it. The SGNAS noted a circular outline of stones which is possibly a hearth. It is not likely associated with the scatter. The SGNAS found only one sherd.

Site No.:   54
Site Name: None
Map Reference: 3051 II, K737
Location on 1:50,000:   294/969
Elevation: 20 to 40 m
Inventory Rating: 43
Periods represented: Ud.
Description: This is a sherd scatter. It may be a potbust.

Site No.: 55
Site Name: None
Map Reference: 3051 II, K737
Location on 1:50,000: 297/970
Elevation: 20 to 40 m
Inventory Rating: 54
Periods represented: Ud.
Description: The site consists of a rectilinear alignment of rocks measuring ca. 25 x 6–7 metres. It may have internal dividers. There is a grave measuring ca. 2 m wide at its S end. It is located between Wadi al-Ghuweib and Wadi Fidan. The SGNAS found neither lithics nor sherds at the site.

Site No.: 56
Site Name: None
Map Reference: 3051 II, K737
Location on 1:50,000 290–300/961–973
Elevation: 20 to 40 m
Inventory rating: 36
Periods represented: Iron Age; Byz; Ud.
Description: This is a lithic and sherd scatter located on the plateau between Wadi al-Ghuweib and Wadi Fidan.

Site No.: 57
Site Name: None
Map Reference: 3051 II, K737
Location on 1:50,000: 278/955
Elevation: 0 to 20 m
Inventory Rating: 52
Periods represented: Ud.
Description: The site consists of two possible graves, side-by-side, which appear to be looted, plus rock alignments which may have served as animal pens, a house, or as a check dam, and a lithic scatter in an area ca. 70 x 30 metres. One rectilinear arrangement of rocks is ca. 10 x 5 m and probably served as an animal pen. It appears that some of the other alignments are unconnected which suggests a water-control device or, possibly, terracing. The site is on a terrace on the S side of Wadi Fidan and ca. 2–3 m above its bed.

Site No.: 58
Site Name: None
Map References: 3052 II, K737; 3052/II/C/6 (23)
Location on 1:50,000: 359/358
Location on 1:10,000: 194.9/48.8
Elevation: Minus 355 m
Inventory Rating: 45
Periods represented: Isl, some glazed; Ud.
Description: The site consists of a sherd scatter in agricultural fields immediately S of Wadi al-Hasa.

Site No.: 59
Site Name: None
Map References: 3052 II, K737; 3052/II/C/6 (23)
Location on 1:50,000: 358/355
Location on 1:10,000 194.8/48.45
Elevation: Minus 355 m
Inventory Rating: 71
Periods represented: Mod; Ud.
Description: The site consists of a three-roomed, mudbrick farmhouse, measuring ca. 25 x 6 m, in agricultural fields to the S of Wadi al-Hasa. There are animal pens and/or storage areas attached to the house.

Site No.: 60
Site Name: None
Map Reference: 3051 I, K737
Location on 1:50,000 378/265
Elevation: Minus 200 m
Inventory Rating: 35
Periods represented: Iron Age; Byz; Ud.
Description: This is a low sherd scatter covering an area of ca. 20 x 20 m immediately above and S of 'Ain Umm Jufna. Water pipes and indications of bulldozing are in the area.

Site No.: 61
Site Name: None
Map References: 3052 II, K737; 3052/II/C/6 (23)
Location on 1:50,000: 381/369
Location on 1:10,000: 197.2/49.9
Elevation: Minus 335 m
Inventory Rating: 65
Periods represented: Byz; Isl; Ud.
Description: The site consists of two structures measuring ca. 9 x 5 and 7 x 5 m overlooking modern al-Safi. Each structure has an internal partition and a porch (?) measuring ca. 3 x 1 m on the NE side. There are graves/tombs nearby.

Site No.: 62
Site Name: None
Map References: 3052 II, K737; 3052/II/C/6 (23)
Location on 1:50,000: 375/359
Location on 1:10,000: 196.5/48.9
Elevation: Minus 315 m
Inventory Rating: 52
Periods represented: Iron Age; Ott; Ud.
Description: The site consists of at least six rock-built tombs in an area measuring ca. 50 x 20 metres. It is located N of Wadi Al-Hasa and E of modern al-Safi. Some of the tombs are looted. The SGNAS noted other tombs in the area, especially to the N and W.

Site No.: 63
Site Name: None
Map References: 3052 II, K737; 3052/II/C/6 (23)
Location on 1:50,000: 376/349
Location on 1:10,000: 196.6./47.9
Elevation: Minus 310 m
Inventory Rating: 47
Periods represented: Ud.
Description: The site consists of two rock piles in an area measuring ca. 20 x 10 m just N of Wadi al-Hasa. The piles are graves presently. Many of the graves in the most westerly located of the piles are disturbed. The SGNAS noted many bones, which do not appear to be human, in the area. Some of them appear to be burnt. The SGNAS collected both lithics and sherds at the site.

Site No.: 64
Site Name: None
Map References: 3052 II, K737; 3052/II/C/6 (23)
Location on 1:50,000: 377/347
Location on 1:10,000: 196.7/47.8
Elevation: Minus 290 m
Inventory Rating: 39
Periods represented: Ud.
Description: This is a camp located on marl overlooking Wadi al-Hasa immediately to the S. A possible retaining wall supports the terrace on which the site is located.

Site No.: 65
Site Name: None
Map References: 3052 II, K737; 3052/II/C/6 (23)
Location on 1:50,000: 359/354
Location on 1:10,000: 194.9/48.4
Elevation: Minus 350 to 355 m
Inventory Rating: 48
Periods represented: Byz; Isl–glazed; Ud.
Description: This site is a sherd scatter in an area measuring ca. 15 x 10 metres. It is located in a plowed field just to the N of Kh. Sheikh 'Isa, Site 4. All the superficial material in the field is disturbed.

Site No.: 66
Site Name: None
Map References: 3052 II, K737; 3052/II/C/6 (23)
Location on 1:50,000: 360/345
Location on 1:10,000: 195.0/47.5
Elevation: Minus 355 m

Inventory Rating: 45
Periods represented: Nab; Rom; Byz (E and L); Byz–Um; LByz–Um; Abb–import from Mesopotamia; Isl; Mod; Ud.
Description: This is a sherd scatter located in a plowed field to the SW of Tawahin al-Sukkar, Site 1.

Site No.: 67
Site Name: None
Map Reference: 3051 I, K737
Location on 1:50,000: 364/277
Elevation: Minus 300 m
Inventory Rating: 53
Periods represented: EB.
Description: This is a potbust in an area measuring ca. 7 x 5 m on the S side of Wadi Umm Jufna.

Site No.: 68 'A'–'C'
Site Name: None
Map Reference: 3051 I, K737
Location on 1:50,000: 366–373/269–276
Elevation: Minus 240 to 290 m
Inventory Rating: 40
Periods represented: Ud.
Description: The site consists of a series of tombs/graves along the S side of Wadi Umm Jufna. 'A' consists of two graves, one with a headstone and no cairn and one with a small cairn of rock (possibly a rock-lined, box-tomb). 'B' consists of a cairn of rock 6 m in diameter. There is some disturbance at the top of the tomb. 'C' consists of five graves in a line, covering an area of ca. 16 x 4 m, on the N edge of the interfluve. The graves consist of small cairns of rock without headstones. The SGNAS found neither lithics nor sherds in association with the structures.

Site No.: 69
Site Name: None
Map Reference: 3051 I, K737
Location on 1:50,000: 368/275
Elevation: Minus ca. 270 m
Inventory Rating: 65
Periods represented: Iron II; Ud.
Description: This site consists of two graves and a tower/tomb covering an area of ca. 20 x 10 metres. It is located on an interfluve on the S side of Wadi Umm Jufna and commands a view of the whole area. The tower/tomb measures ca. 8 m in diameter and is the largest feature of the site. A grave is located at its top. The SGNAS collected a moderate density of sherds around the structure.

Site No.: 70
Site Name: None
Map Reference: 3051 I, K737
Location on 1:50,000: 369/275
Elevation: ca. Minus 270 m
Inventory Rating: 63
Periods represented: Mod.
Description: The site consists of a windbreak, a circular alignment of stones, and, to the S and W, irrigated fields in an area measuring ca. 70 x 100 metres on the N side of the interfluve on the S side of Wadi Umm Jufna. Besides ceramics, the SGNAS noted burlap bags, pieces of cloth, a belt, and an irrigation ditch, about 40 cm wide, which is stone lined with cement poured in the bottom.

Site No.: 71
Site Name: None
Map Reference: 3051 I, K737
Location on 1:50,000: 378/265
Elevation: Minus 210 m
Inventory Rating: 48
Periods represented: EB; Iron IA; Ud.
Description: This is a sherd scatter, probably a potbust, in an area of ca. 10 x 6 m along the S side of Wadi Umm Jufna.

Site No.: 72
Site Name: None
Map Reference: 3051 I, K737
Location on 1:50,000: 380/264
Elevation: Minus 190 m
Inventory Rating: 62
Periods represented: Iron II; Nab; Ud.
Description: The site consists of a tomb, a possible caravanserai, and a sherd scatter along the S side of Wadi Umm Jufna. The sherd scatter is located on the N edge of a ridge while the tomb and the possible caravanserai are located to the NNE. The latter consists of large boulders aligned in a arc ca. 12 m long. The tomb may be rock-lined. There are sand dunes to the NNW.

Site No.: 73
Site Name: Rujm Umm Jufna
Map Reference: 3051 I, K737
Location on 1:50,000: 383/264
Elevation: Minus 180 m
Inventory Rating: 60
Periods represented: Iron IC; Iron II; Iron Age; Hell; LRom–Byz; EIsl; Ud.
Description: This is a tower measuring ca. 15 m in diameter and 4–5 m high with a possible grave at its summit. There are two circular alignments on its SSW side. It is located on the S side of Wadi Umm Jufna on the N edge of the interfluve ca. 150 m NNE of Site 72. It commands a good view up the wadi.

Site No.: 74
Site Name: None
Map Reference: 3051 I, K737
Location on 1:50,000: 385/264
Elevation: Minus 200 m
Inventory Rating: 52
Periods represented: Byz.
Description: This is a possible farm located on a terrace on the N side of Wadi Umm Jufna ca. 500 m E of Site 73. One rectilinear alignment of rock, of which only the foundation course is visible, measures ca. 5 x 2 metres. There appear to be other rock alignments nearby. What appears to be a grave is present in the area. If it is a grave, it is a very neat one with no stones capping it. There is an agricultural field located ca. 50 m to the E of the site.

Site No.: 75
Site Name: Feifa – Western Segment
Map References: 3051 I, K737; 3051/I/B/4 (29)
Location on 1:50,000: 345/258
Location on 1:10,000: 193.5/38.9
Elevation: Minus 302 m
Inventory Rating: 84
Periods represented: PNL; NL–Chal; Chal; Chal/EB; EB I; EB IIB; EB IVA; EB; Iron I–II; Iron II; Iron II–Edomite painted; Rom; LByz–Um; Fatt/Ayy–some glazing; Isl; Ott; Ud.
Description: This site consists of the western extremity of a ridge on which there are two distinct mounds separated by a saddle. The SGNAS collected samples from the three segments of the site. One mound, at the western extremity of the ridge, serves as a surveyor's mark. There is a medium scatter of sherds in this area. Sherds continue down the slope to the W. Walls lines, running in a southwesterly direction, are visible in the saddle. There are also possible wall lines along the southern slope of the saddle along with graves in the same region. It appears that the eastern mound is divided into segments. However, recent military activity may be the cause of these divisions. There are graves also on the eastern mound. There is what appears to be a very large wall at the eastern extremity of the site. From the aerial photos, it is evident that this wall forms the eastern wall of a fort (?) measuring ca. 90 (E–W) x 60 (N–S) metres. There is a tower, standing higher than the walls, in the middle of this fort (?). The entire complex seems to be defensive. What appears to be a ramp/roadway, leading up to the fort (?), is visible on the N slope of the ridge. This ramp can be followed to the N, especially on the aerial photos.

Site No.: 76
Site Name: Feifa Cemetery
Map References: 3051 I, K737; 3051/I/B/4 (29)
Location on 1:50,000: 348/258
Location on 1:10,000: 193.8/38.9
Elevation: Minus 270 to 300 m
Inventory Rating: 87
Periods represented: PNL; NL–Chal; Chal; Chal/EB; EB I; EB IV; EB; Isl–painted; Ott; Ud.
Description: This site is the eastern extension of Site 75. It is mainly a cemetery which extends over a southern, central, and western ridge system. It covers an area, dissected by many small wadis, of at least 1 x 0.50 kilometres. The SGNAS collected samples from the southern, central, and northern ridges of the site. Many of the tombs in the cemetery have been looted while others have been disturbed by military trenching. They are built of cobble stones with stone slabs for a covering. They are not unlike the cist tombs at the EB I cemetery at al-Safi, Site 2. The SGNAS noted some walls which are possibly only segments of cist tombs. What appears to be a tower is located at the SE extremity of the cemetery. It is badly eroded by the wadi road which passes just to the south. It could have been associated with the fort (?) at Site 75 rather than with the cemetery. On the aerial photos, what appears to be an L-shaped, stone wall is located on the S side of the cemetery, ca. 150 m SE of the SE corner of the fort (?) at Site 75.

Site No.: 77
Site Name: None
Map References: 3051 I, K737; 3051/I/B/4 (29)
Location on 1:50,000: 359/253
Location on 1:10,000: 194.9/38.4
Elevation: Minus 270 m
Inventory Rating: 57
Periods represented: EB; Isl (?); Ud.
Description: This site consists of two square, stone buildings and an associated aqueduct. The buildings may have been used for milling purposes. There is not much rubble around the buildings. The inside walls of the buildings are plastered and the E building contains a stone ring (hearth ?) which may be recent. The floor of the W building has been 'excavated'. A long aqueduct, measuring 1 m wide, runs from the buildings to the SSE. What appears to be a containing pool is located ca. 500 m to SSE. The aqueduct is thicker where this pool is located and there are walls to the E which may aid in capturing water. The aqueduct continues to the E for a distance of ca. 450 m and ends at a modern dam/spring area. From here it may have continued further to the E. Some slope wash has covered and destroyed parts of the aqueduct and the construction of the modern reservoir may have destroyed more of it. On the W, the aqueduct flows beneath the two, stone buildings. The 'excavated' area in the W building is the place where the aqueduct flows through the building.

Site No.: 78
Site Name: None
Map References: 3051 I, K737; 3051/I/B/4 (29)
Location on 1:50,000: 353/251
Location on 1:10,000: 194.5/38.1
Elevation: ca. Minus 280 m
Inventory Rating: 40
Periods represented: EB; Byz; Ott; Ud.
Description: The site consists of a low sherd and lithic scatter on a terrace, dissected by two small, S-flowing wadis, on the N side of Wadi Feifa. Small stone piles may indicate a cemetery. There are also signs of camping on the terrace.

Site No.: 79 'A–H'
Site Name: None
Map References: 3052 II, K737; 3052/II/C/6 (23)
Location on 1:50,000: 377–381/368–355
Location on 1:10,000: 197.2/49.9 to 196.8/48.5
Elevation: Minus 265 to 350 m
Inventory Rating: 58
Periods represented: EB IV; EB IV (?); EB; Iron II; Iron Age; Nab; Rom; EByz; LByz; Mam; Ott; Isl; Ud.
Description: This site is a series of tombs spread over a terrace to the N of Wadi al-Hasa and E of modern al-Safi. 'A' includes four, widely spaced tombs, forming a triangle, separated from each other by 50–70 metres. They are located on a W-facing slope. They are stone lined with circular alignments. A pile of rock is on each tomb. The tombs are ca. 2 m in diameter. With the rubble around them they measure ca. 6–5 m oval. 'B' consists of ca. 6–10 tombs/graves, in an area of ca. 100 x 100 m, which are similar and probably related to those of 'A'. 'C'–'F' are also similar in structure to those described above. 'F' consists of four tombs and one grave which has no headstone and only a small cairn. 'G' consists of ca. seven graves in an area measuring ca. 15 x 10 m, which have small cairns on their tops.

Site No.: 80
Site Name: None
Map References: 3052 II, K737; 3052/II/C/6 (23)
Location on 1:50,000: 382/361
Location on 1:10,000: 197.3/49.1
Elevation: Minus 275 m
Inventory Rating: 63
Periods represented: Chal; Ud.
Description: This is a possible campsite in a cleared area measuring ca. 22 x 6 metres. It is located on a W-facing slope N of Wadi al-Hasa and in the same general area as Site 79. Rock pebbles cover the surface. However, no large rocks, with the exception of two stones for possible seats, are present. The density of cobbles on the site is much lower than in the surrounding area.

Site No.: 81
Site Name: None
Map References: 3052 II, K737; 3052/II/C/6 (23)
Location on 1:50,000: 377/356
Location on 1:10,000: 196.7/48.6
Elevation: Minus 310 m
Inventory Rating: 60
Periods represented: Ud.
Description: This is the remnants of a conduit, ca. 40 cm wide and spread over an area of ca. 100 m, on a low terrace on the S side of a wadi N of Wadi al-Hasa and E of al-Safi.

Site No.: 82
Site Name: None
Map Reference: 3051 II, K737
Location on 1:50,000: 299/982
Elevation: Minus 10 m
Inventory Rating: 51
Periods represented: Ud.
Description: The site consists of an enclosure measuring ca. 25 x 12 m and a sherd and lithic scatter. The N side of the enclosure is eroded and/or is covered with silt. The site is located W of the 'Old Road' and just S of the Wadi al-Ghuweib.

Site No.: 83
Site Name: None
Map Reference: 3051 II, K737
Location on 1:50,000: 298/986
Elevation: Minus 0 to 10 m
Inventory Rating: 20
Periods represented: Ud.
Description: This is a lithic scatter in an area ca. 20 x 10 m on a terrace W of the 'Old Road' and S of Wadi al-Ghuweib.

Site No.: 84
Site Name: None
Map References: 3051 I, K737; 3051/I/B/4 (29)
Location on 1:50,000: 366/251
Location on 1:10,000: 195.6/38.1
Elevation: ca. Minus 250 m
Inventory Rating: 54
Periods represented: Chal; Chal/EB; Iron II; Ud.
Description: The is a lithic and sherd scatter located on

the SE edge of the upper terrace on the N side of Wadi Feifa. The SGNAS' samples are from an area that is undisturbed. They are not water borne. It seems that the site probably extended to the SW but this area is bulldozed. Erosion of the terrace edge is distributing the materials to the lower terrace. No architectural features are evident but during earlier times the samples were probably associated with architectural features which are now probably destroyed by bulldozing. A segment, ca. 10 m long by 40 cm wide, of an aqueduct is evident at the SW end of the site. Erosion and bulldozing have probably removed the rest of it.

Site No.:   85
Site Name: None
Map Reference: 3051 II, K737
Location on 1:50,000:   299/995
Elevation: 0 m
Inventory Rating: 37
Description: The site consists of about 10 graves, which do not appear to be recent, and a light lithic scatter.
Periods represented: Ud.

Site No.:   86
Site Name: None
Map Reference: 3051 II, K737
Location on 1:50,000:   299/997
Elevation: 0 m
Inventory Rating: 64
Periods represented: Chal/EB; Ud.
Description: The site consists of two stone enclosures, measuring ca. 25 m and 15 m in diameter, S of Wadi al-Ghuweib. The SGNAS collected lithics from the larger and both pottery and lithics from the smaller enclosure.

Site No.:   87
Site Name: None
Map Reference: 3051 II, K737
Location on 1:50,000:   299/998
Elevation: 0 m
Inventory Rating: 45
Periods represented: Byz; Ud.
Description: The site consists of an enclosure, heavily silted, measuring ca. 19 (E–W) x 23 (N–S) m along the S side of Wadi al-Ghuweib and W of the 'Old Road'. A stone pile is located ca. 10 m from the NE corner of the enclosure. The SGNAS collected both lithics and sherds at the site.

Site No.:   88
Site Name: None
Map Reference: 3051 II, K737
Location on 1:50,000:   298/000
Elevation: Minus 5–0 m
Inventory Rating: 38
Periods represented: Ud.
Description: The site consists of two tombs and a small, 5 m square enclosure E of the 'Old Road' between Wadi al-Ghuweib and Wadi Fidan. There is an associated, light lithic scatter.

Site No.:   89
Site Name: None
Map Reference: 3051 II, K737
Location on 1:50,000:   300–310/980–005
Elevation: Minus 20–0 m
Inventory Rating: 39
Periods represented: Ud.
Description: This site includes lithics from the entire E side of Wadi al-Ghuweib surveyed on 11/04/86. It is made up of isolated lithics from terrace tops and eroded deposits.

Site No.:   90
Site Name: None
Map Reference: 3051 I, K737
Location on 1:50,000:   372/249
Elevation: ca. Minus 220 m
Inventory Rating: 16

Periods represented: Byz; Ud.
Description: This site consists of a light sherd scatter and one flake on a terrace on the N side of Wadi Feifa. There is evidence of recent (?) Bedouin camping on the terrace.

Site No.:   91
Site Name: Qasr al-Feifa
Map References: 3051 I, K737; 3051/I/B/4 (29)
Location on 1:50,000:   337/260
Location on 1:10,000:   192.5/38.8
Elevation: Minus 340 m
Inventory Rating: 72
Periods represented: Byz; Um; Abb–Fat; Mam; Isl; Ud.
Description: The site consists of a great deal of midden material in and around the village of Feifa. There are wall lines and remnants of a sugar mill. The milling stone, which measures ca. 1.40 m in diameter, is still in place as are remnants of mudbrick buildings. However, the mill is not as well preserved as is Tawahin al-Sukkar, Site 1. Most of the area of the sugar mill is presently used as a dump and there are modern (?) graves present. The SGNAS collected samples from E of and from around the mill as well as from N of the road that runs through the village. There are indications of recent bulldozing around the remnants of the sugar mill.

Site No.:   92
Site Name: None
Map References: 3051 I, K737; 3051/I/B/4 (29)
Location on 1:50,000:   351/247
Location on 1:10,000:   194.1/37.7
Elevation: Minus 295 m
Inventory Rating: 69
Periods represented: LNL; PNL–Chal; Chal; Ud.
Description: The site consists of a heavy sherd and a light lithic scatter in a plowed field just S of Wadi Feifa and just E of the main Mazra' to 'Aqaba highway. There are small piles of stones which could be graves. Plowing could have destroyed a large portion of the site.

Site No.:   93
Site Name: None
Map References: 3051 I, K737; 3051/I/B/4 (29)
Location on 1:50,000:   351/245
Location on 1:10,000:   194.1/37.5
Elevation: Minus 300–295 m
Inventory Rating: 54
Periods represented: Ott/Mod; Ud.
Description: The site consists of a cemetery (?) and a stone 'platform' at the top of a small hill ca. 0.50 km S of Wadi Feifa and just E of the highway. What appear to be graves are located at the top and on the N and S slopes of the hill.

Site No.:   94
Site Name: Rujm Umruq
Map References: 3051 I, K737; 3051/I/B/6 (32)
Location on 1:50,000:   352.5/228
Location on 1:10,000:   193.9/35.9
Elevation: Minus 305 m
Inventory Rating: 77
Periods represented: Hell; Nab; Nab (=ERom); LRom; Byz; Um (?); Ud.
Description: This is a tower/tomb complex on an isolated island/ridge immediately N of Wadi Umruq and just E of the main highway. The summit of the site, at which there is a probable tower, is at least 4–5 m above the sands that surround it. The tower was reused as a grave. It is now looted. There are more structures and graves, especially on the W side of the ridge. Feifa, Sites 75–76, is visible to the N while Rujm Khuneizir, Site 108, is visible to the S. The site would have served as a good lookout point at the western end of Wadi Umruq. The 1:50,000 map shows a path going along the N side of Wadi Umruq to just S of al-Tafila.

Site No.:   95
Site Name: None

Map References: 3051 I, K737; 3051/I/B/4 (29)
Location on 1:50,000: 353/248
Location on 1:10,000: 194.3/37.8
Elevation: Minus 290 m
Inventory Rating: 45
Periods represented: PNL; Chal/EB; Ud.
Description: The site consists of a sherd and lithic scatter on a gravel terrace, where there are signs of bulldozing, on the S side of Wadi Feifa, ca. 0.40 km from the main highway.

Site No.: 96
Site Name: None
Map Reference: 3051 II, K737
Location on 1:50,000: 304/983
Elevation: 0 m
Inventory Rating: 43
Periods represented: Ud.
Description: This site, on the E side of Wadi al-Ghuweib, consists of an oval alignment of cobbles/boulders which is, for the most part, one course high and one course wide. There is a break in the alignment (an entrance ?) on the W and it is 2–3 courses wide on the N. Its long axis is oriented N–S. The SGNAS collected neither lithics nor sherds at the site.

Site No.: 97 'A'–'N'
Site Name: None
Map Reference: 3051 II, K737
Location on 1:50,000: 302–306/983–005
Elevation: 0 to 25 m
Inventory Rating: 50
Periods represented: Byz; Ud.
Description: The site consists of a series of graves/tombs on the E side of Wadi al-Ghuweib. 'A' is comprised of three graves/tombs. One may be a rock-lined box measuring ca. 2 x 1.5 metres. The other two are ca. 1–2 m in diameter. Both have headstones. 'B', measuring ca. 2 x 1 m, is a small stone cairn, oval in shape, which appears to be rock-lined. In the centre, there are two flat stones with an upright stone, measuring ca. 20–30 cm, between them. 'C' is a possible grave measuring 1 m in diameter. 'D' is a set of 8–10 graves, oval to rectilinear in shape, covering an area of ca. 20 x 10 metres. Some have headstones. One is disturbed. 'F' is located on a hilltop above 'D' and ca. 100 m to the NE. It consists of a large cairn, measuring ca. 3 x 2 m, on bedrock. 'G' consists of a cairn measuring ca. 4 x 2 metres. There is no headstone. 'H' is a cairn, measuring ca. 3 x 2 m which is deflated and somewhat eroded. It is located ca. 100 m SE of 'G'. 'I' consists of a large pile of stones measuring ca. 5 m in diameter. It is located ca. 100 m SSE of 'H'. There are sherds present but it is not known if they are from the grave. 'J' is a series of graves which may be recent. Some appear to be disturbed. There are remnants of a Bedouin camp, covering an area of ca. 40 x 30 m, nearby. 'K' is a circular grave measuring ca. 3 x 2 metres. 'L' consists of two groups of graves separated by ca. 30 metres. The southerly located group consists of 3–4 graves with rather small cairns on top. The graves are ca. 1 m in diameter. The northerly group, covering an area of ca. 20 x 20 m, consists of 11–13 graves. Some have head/footstones. They vary in shape from circular to oval. 'M' may be possible graves, each measuring ca. 1.5 m in diameter. They appear to be undisturbed. 'N' consists of graves which are badly disturbed.

Site No.: 98
Site Name: None
Map Reference: 3051 II, K737
Location on 1:50,000 306/987
Elevation: 0 to 10 m
Inventory Rating: 39
Periods represented: Ud.
Description: This is a campsite consisting of rock alignments on the E side of Wadi al-Ghuweib. The rocks are widely spaced. The SGNAS collected neither lithics nor sherds.

Site No.: 99
Site Name: None
Map Reference: 3051 II, K737
Location on 1:50,000: 306/989

Elevation: 0 to 10 m
Inventory Rating: 55
Periods represented: Ud.
Description: The site consists of a number of rock alignments, tombs/graves, and a lithic scatter located ca. 100 m NW of Site 98 on the E side of Wadi al-Ghuweib. The most easterly alignment of rocks consists of detached rocks ca. 12–13 m long. SW of this, a distance of ca. 15 m, is a cairn grave. SW of the grave are several more cairn graves and a semicircular alignment of rock broken in several places. This alignment is ca. 20 m in arc. It is anchored at one end by a rectilinear pavement of stone about 5 x 3 metres. At the other end, measuring ca. 4 x 3 m, is a similar structure. Beyond this is another cairn grave. To the SW, a distance of ca. 30 m, is yet another cairn grave. The collected lithics are probably not directly associated with the site. At the top of a knoll to the NE, a distance of ca. 10–15 m, the SGNAS collected a few more lithics.

Site No.: 100
Site Name: None
Map Reference: 3051 II, K737
Location on 1:50,000: 304/991
Elevation: Minus 20 m
Inventory Rating: 49
Periods represented: Ud.
Description: The site is a possible camp located on a low terrace on the E side of Wadi al-Ghuweib. All that remain are rock alignments, mostly linear. Most of the alignments are linear. However, one, measuring ca. 1.5 x 0.5 m, is L-shaped. The SGNAS collected neither lithics nor sherds.

Site No.: 101
Site Name: None
Map Reference: 3051 II, K737
Location on 1:50,000: 307/998
Elevation: Minus 10–0 m
Inventory Rating: 51
Periods represented: Ud.
Description: This is a lithic scatter on top of a hill on the E side and ca. 20–30 m above the bed of Wadi al-Ghuweib. The surface is covered with small stones derived from the bedrock, which appears to be some type of volcanic rock, directly under the surface. A shallow erosion channel, midway across the hilltop, has collected some lithics. However, the lithics are all over the S portion of the top while the SGNAS observed few or none on the N end of the hill. It is not known if they represent the remains of a camp. There are two depressions at the S end of the top of the hill which have sediments in them. There are lithics surrounding the depressions. Some probably washed onto the lower areas. There may be more lithics in the depressions.

Site No.: 102
Site Name: None
Map Reference: 3051 II, K737
Location on 1:50,000: 307/994
Elevation: Minus 10 to 0 m
Inventory Rating: 51
Periods represented: Ud.
Description: This is a light lithic scatter on a terrace on the E side of Wadi al-Ghuweib ca. 20–30 m above its bed. A drainage separates it from Site 101 which is ca. 300 m away. There are no erosional channels evident on the terrace which is covered with sediments. The low density is probably due to erosion and deflation processes, or it may be background noise of scattered retouch or tool production in the area.

Site No.: 103
Site Name: None
Map Reference: 3051 I, K737
Location on 1:50,000: 381/246
Elevation: ca. Minus 190 m
Inventory Rating: 36
Periods represented: Ud.
Description: This is a probable potbust on the N side

of Wadi Feifa. The SGNAS noted no associated features.

Site No.: 104
Site Name: None
Map Reference: 3051 I, K737
Location on 1:50,000: 381/246
Elevation: ca. Minus 190 m
Inventory Rating: 47
Periods represented: Byz (?).
Description: This is a cemetery consisting of 6–8 graves, two of which have been looted, along the N side of Wadi Feifa.The graves, which measure ca. 3 x 2, 2 x 2, and 3 x 1 m, are oriented N–S in an area of ca. 20 x 5 metres. There are neither head nor footstones to the graves and their boundaries are not outlined with stones. The sherds, which the SGNAS collected, were near a looted grave. However, they were not on the backfill but on the ground away from the grave. Thus, they need not be associated with the graves.

Site No.: 105
Site Name: None
Map Reference: 3051 I, K737
Location on 1:50,000: 381/246
Elevation: ca. Minus 190 m
Inventory Rating: 50
Periods represented: EB; Byz; Ud.
Description: The site consists of a lithic and sherd scatter on two levels along the N side of Wadi Feifa. The lower level is a ledge that drops down to the wadi. The upper is a plateau top ca. 15–20 m above the ledge. The entire site is above the marls or just at their highest point. There are no features associated with the area except graves, Site 104, and a potbust, Site 103. The upper surface of the plateau is ca. 60–70 m above the wadi bed. There are no visible marls to the E. The site may be, although this is conjecture, a beach deposit. It is not known whether the sample is background noise or transported material.

Site No.: 106
Site Name: None
Map References: 3051 I, K737; 3051/I/B/4 (29)
Location on 1:50,000: 353/247
Location on 1:10,000: 194.4/37.8
Elevation: Minus 280 m
Inventory Rating: 38
Periods represented: Ott/Mod; Ud.
Description: This site consists of a sherd scatter and a possible campsite located ca. 50 m S of Wadi Feifa.

Site No.: 107
Site Name: None
Map References: 3051 I, K737; 3051/I/B/4 (29)
Location on 1:50,000: 355/249
Location on 1:10,000: 194.5/37.9
Elevation: Minus 270 m
Inventory Rating: 49
Periods represented: Ud.
Description: The site is a lithic scatter on the S rim of Wadi Feifa ca. 20 m above its bed. It appears to be on a terrace which has been eroded and dissected by water.

Site No.: 108
Site Name: Rujm Khuneizir
Map References: 3051 I, K737; 3051/I/B/5 (31)
Location on 1:50,000: 326/209
Location on 1:10,000: 191.5/34.0
Elevation: Minus 280 m
Inventory Rating: 79
Periods represented: Chal; EB IV; Iron IA; Iron II; Iron Age; Ud, prob EB IV.
Description: Rujm Khuneizir is located on a high hill overlooking the Southern Ghors. Rujm Umruq, Site 94, and Feifa, Sites 75 and 76, are clearly visible from it. The tower segment of the site stands ca. 5–6 m high. There are walls visible on the NE side of the site where the slope is not eroded. They appear to consist of

three levels progressing in a step-like fashion to the summit. There is a 1 m distance between the first and second steps. There is a platform area, below the summit, from which the SGNAS collected most of the sherds. Moreover, there are wall lines and what appear to be graves here. One wall line measures ca. 3 x 3 metres. There is a grave ca. 5 m to the N and a 5–6 m in diameter pile of stones to the NE. Could this have been a structure at one time? The SGNAS found no sherds on a plateau to the S. There are EB IV graves eroding out of the E-facing side of a small wadi at the base as well as on the slope of the hill on which the site is located. They are cist graves like those at al-Safi, Site 2, and Feifa, Site 76.

Site No.: 109
Site Name: None
Map References: 3051 I, K737; 3051/I/B/5 (31)
Location on 1:50,000: 326/206
Location on 1:10,000: 191.6/33.6
Elevation: Minus 285 m
Inventory Rating: 69
Periods represented: EB IV; EB IVA; EB III; EB; Ud.
Description: This site is probably a cemetery on a terrace on the E side of Wadi Khuneizir. It could be one with Site 119, immediately to the N, but now separated by erosional gullies and/or small wadis. There could have been a village (?) here at one time. The site consists of graves and/or structures. Many distinct wall lines are indicative of this. The SGNAS collected some pottery from the W slope of the ridge on which Rujm Khuneizir is located. There are EB IV cist tombs, similar to those at al-Safi, Site 2, and Feifa, Site 76, in this area. Some of the pottery collected is reconstructible.

Site No.: 110
Site Name: None
Map References: 3051 I, K737; 3051/I/B/5 (31)
Location on 1:50,000: 324/199
Location on 1:10,000: 191.4/32.9
Elevation: Minus 270 m
Inventory Rating: 47
Periods represented: EB IV; EB; Ud.
Description: This site consists of a sherd scatter and a stone fence (?) on a terrace on the W side of Wadi Khuneizir. There is a level area to the S on which the SGNAS noted a wall, measuring ca. 36 x 2 m, cut on the SE side by erosion. Another structure, a platform (?), measuring ca. 5 x 2.50 m, is located ca. 35 m to the S. Most of the sherds which the SGNAS collected came from the slope to the N rather than in association with the two, above-describe features. However, they could be water-borne. There are two stone piles to the W of these structures. However, no pattern could be detected. Since there are EB IV tombs immediately to the W, across erosional gullies, this site could be associated in some way.

Site No.: 111 'A'–'G'
Site Name: None
Map References: 3051 I, K737; 3051/I/B/4 and B/6 (29;32)
Location on 1:50,000: 351/242–336/214
Location on 1:10,000: 192.6–194.2/34.5–37.2
Elevation: Minus 310 to 290 m
Inventory Rating: 14
Periods represented: Iron II; Ott; Ott/Mod; Ud.
Description: This site consists of graves located on the lower slopes between Wadi Feifa and Wadi Khuneizir and immediately E of the highway. The SGNAS found very little pottery in association with the graves. 'A' consists of a number of oval and rectangular graves, measuring ca. 1.5 x 2–2.5 m and spread over an area of ca. 25 x 15 m, outlined with small piles of stones above the graves. The sherds which the SGNAS collected come from 'A'. 'B', which covers an area of ca. 4 x 4 m., is located on an alluvial spur. However, only a 1.5 m length of aligned stones is visible. There are other large rocks located nearby. This may or may not be a grave. 'C' is located on the N side of Wadi Umruq. It includes two graves, measuring ca. 3 x 1.5 m, spaced ca. 20 m apart. The graves run along an alluvial spur. Several other probable graves are located to the N across a drainage on another alluvial spur. They were not investigated. All are probably Bedouin. 'C' consists of graves

outlined in rock. No artifacts are associated with them. 'D' is a grave consisting of a pile of rocks in an area of ca. 3 x 2.5 m and located on an alluvial spur. The cairn is somewhat scattered. It may be disturbed. The SGNAS noted, but did not collect, two possible LPL–MPL artifacts near 'D'. The artifacts are probably water-borne. There is another pile of large rock, ca. 100 m to the NNE, that may be a grave. There is yet another large cairn of rock, across a drainage and ca. 200–225 m to the NNE, that may also be a grave. The SGNAS did not investigated it. All of the above-describe graves are in the dissected slopes stratum. 'E' is a cluster of graves in an area measuring ca. 40 m square on an alluvial fan due N of Wadi Khuneizir. The graves, with head and footstones, appear recent. They average between 1–2 m square. Some of the graves are deflated. 'F' consists of a grave, measuring ca. 1 m square and located on an alluvial spur, with a headstone. More graves may have been present, but if they were, bulldozing activity has destroyed them. 'G' is a disturbed grave, measuring ca. 2.5 x 1.5 metres. It too is located on an alluvial spur. It is ca. 100–120 m SE of 'F'. It is outlined in stone with a small cairn on top.

Site No.:	112
Site Name:	None
Map References:	3051 I, K737; 3051/I/B/5 (31)
Location on 1:50,000:	328/197
Location on 1:10,000:	191.4/32.7
Elevation:	Minus 280 m
Inventory Rating:	82
Description:	The site is a well-built aqueduct which is

now eroded in many places. It begins where the JVA has built its water collecting device in Wadi Khuneizir and can be followed for a distance of ca. 0.60 km to a tributary wadi entering Wadi Khuneizir from the E. Along the way, one arch permits water to enter Wadi Khuneizir from another tributary wadi. The aqueduct still stands ca. 7 m above the wadi bed in places. Its water channel, which is now almost completely silted in, measures ca. 90 cm wide and 75 cm deep. It possibly once brought water to a mill. The construction appears to be similar to that at Site 77 in Wadi Feifa. The SGNAS found neither lithics nor sherds at the site.

Periods represented:	Ud.

Site No.:	113
Site Name:	None
Map References:	3051 I, K737; 3051/I/B/5 (31)
Location on 1:50,000:	328/195
Location on 1:10,000:	191.7/32.5
Elevation:	Minus 210 m
Inventory Rating:	50
Periods represented:	Ud.
Description:	The site consists of three stone structures,

still standing ca. 1.50 m high to the E above Wadi Khuneizir. They appear to be graves. The most easterly located one measures ca. 10 (E–W) x 3 (N–S) meters. All three are looted. The SGNAS found neither sherds nor lithics at the site.

Site No.:	114
Site Name:	None
Map Reference:	3051 II, K737
Location on 1:50,000:	294/002
Elevation:	Minus 40 m
Inventory Rating:	41
Periods represented:	Ud.
Description:	This site is an enclosure, measuring ca. 9

(E–W) x 10 (N–S) m, constructed of unhewn stones which have a heavy patina. There is a great deal of silt within the enclosure. Small stone piles, possibly graves, are located ca. 150 m to the SW. The SGNAS collected the lithic sample both within and around the enclosure.

Site No.:	115
Site Name:	None
Map Reference:	3051 II, K737
Location on 1:50,000:	283/993
Elevation:	Minus 60 m
Inventory Rating:	14

Periods represented:	Byz.
Description:	This site is a sherd scatter.

Site No.:	116
Site Name:	None
Map Reference:	3051 II, K737
Location on 1:50,000:	277/980
Elevation:	Minus 45 m
Inventory Rating:	31
Periods represented:	Nab; Nab (?); LIsl; Ud.
Description:	The site consists of a possible cemetery

and camp in an area measuring ca. 75 x 50 m where there are many stone piles N of the Wade Fidan gorge. The SGNAS collected both lithics and sherds at the site.

Site No.:	117
Site Name:	None
Map Reference:	3051 II, K737
Location on 1:50,000:	276/968
Elevation:	Minus 40 m
Inventory Rating:	41
Periods represented:	Chal/EB.
Description:	The site consists of wall lines, possibly

for houses and/or retaining walls, in an area which measures ca. 150 (N–S) x 75 (E–W) metres. It could have been a farm or hamlet. There are also signs of graves in the area. The two, however, need not be contemporaneous. The SGNAS collected both lithics and sherds at the site.

Site No.:	118
Site Name:	None
Map Reference:	3051 II, K737
Location on 1:50,000:	272/959
Elevation:	Minus 30 m
Inventory Rating:	34
Periods represented:	EB; Byz; Ud.
Description:	The site consists of a light lithic and

sherd scatter, possibly water-borne, in a gravel pit immediately S of Wadi Fidan. The gravel was used for the construction of the asphalt road from Mazra' to 'Aqaba. There are wall lines but it is impossible to determine if they are ancient.

Site No.:	119
Site Name:	None
Map References:	3051 I, K737; 3051/I/B/5 (31)
Location on 1:50,000:	325/208
Location on 1:10,000:	191.6/33.8
Elevation:	Minus 300 m
Inventory Rating:	54
Periods represented:	EB IV; EB IVB; Nab; Ud.
Description:	The site consists of a cemetery and a

lithic and sherd scatter on a terrace, dissected by several erosional channels, on the E side of Wadi Khuneizir just to the S of the main highway and just W of Site 108. It could be one with Site 109 which is located immediately to the S and separated by erosional gullies. It is located in a greatly disturbed area measuring ca. 200 (E–W) x 100 (N–S) m where there are traces of bulldozing. Many of the graves, which probably date to the EB IV period, have been disturbed by erosion, looting, or bulldozing. The SGNAS found the heaviest concentration of sherds at the S end of the site and the lithics, in small numbers, throughout the area. There is what appears to be a wall, ca. 5 m long, of large stones at the base of a spur at the SE corner of the site. It may be a retaining wall and have graves above it. The SGNAS covered the area completely by walking transects.

Site No.:	120 'A'–'E'
Site Name:	None
Map References:	3051 I, K737; 3051/I/B/5 (31)
Location on 1:50,000:	324/200
Location on 1:10,000:	191.3/32.9
Elevation:	Minus 275–270 m
Inventory Rating:	49
Periods represented:	EB IV; EB IVA; Ud.
Description:	This is a cemetery located on a terrace on

the W side of Wadi Khuneizir. Most of the graves appear to EB IV cist tombs. The construction of the graves is not unlike the cist tombs observed at al-Safi, Site 2; Feifa, Site 76; and on the slopes of Rujm Khuneizir, Site 108. 'A' is a grave, measuring ca. 3 x 1.5 m, which appears to be outlined with rock with more rocks on top. 'B' consists of at least three graves, possibly undisturbed, in a linear arrangement (E–W) covering an area of ca. 10 x 4 m at the base of the foothills. The graves appear to be outlined in rock with more rock on top. 'C' is a large cairn of stones, measuring ca. 5 x 3 m, with two, robber pits dug into it. The SGNAS noted large numbers of sherds in the area. 'D' consists of two graves, one of which is presently robbed, in close proximity. Each grave measures ca. 3 x 2 metres. 'E' consists of two, widely spaced graves at the base of the escarpment. They are disturbed. The most easterly located one measures ca. 2 x 1.5 m while the other, to the W, measures ca. 3.5 x 1.5–2 metres.

Site No.: 121
Site Name: None
Map References: 3051 I, K737; 3051/I/B/5 (31)
Location on 1:50,000: 323/201
Location on 1:10,000: 191.3/33.1
Elevation: Minus 280–275 m
Inventory Rating: 55
Periods represented: EB, painted sherds; Ud.
Description: This site is a lithic and sherd scatter, of low density, in an area measuring ca. 200 x 150 m on a terrace, dissected by at least three channels, on the W side of Wadi Khuneizir. The SGNAS found the highest density of artifacts closest to the wadi. It is difficult to say if they are background noise or are washed/eroded into the area. There may be graves in the area.

Site No.: 122 'A' and 'B'
Site Name: None
Map References: 3051 I, K737; 3051/I/B/5 (31)
Location on 1:50,000: 325/194
Location on 1:10,000: 191.5/32.4
Elevation: Minus 230–220 m
Inventory Rating: 45
Periods represented: EB IV; Ud, prob EB.
Description: This site appears to consist of EB IV cist tombs on the W side of Wadi Khuneizir ca. 80 m above the wadi bed. 'A' is a looted grave, measuring ca. 3 x 2 m, outlined with rock with more rock on top. 'B' is a another looted grave, measuring ca. 5 x 1.5–2.0 m, located ca. 50 m NW of 'A' and ca. 40–30 m below it.

Site No.: 123
Site Name: None
Map Reference: 3051 II, K737
Location on 1:50,000: 295/948
Elevation: ca. 50 m
Inventory Rating: 63
Periods represented: Nab; Ud.
Description: This site consists of a lithic and sherd scatter in association with a cave measuring ca. 7 (N–S) x 10 (E–W) m just above the bed of Wadi Fidan. The cave has both a front and back entrance. A retaining wall, three course high, is downslope from the mouth of the cave. There are storage areas set off by stones within the cave and evidence of burning inside and out. There may be ancient deposits within the cave. It is worth investigating. It is presently used as an animal pen. The SGNAS found slag ca. 30–40 m behind the cave. This is not unusual since there is a large smelting site, Site 30, almost directly W of the cave across the wadi.

Site No.: 124
Site Name: None
Map Reference: 3051 I, K737
Location on 1:50,000: 377/249
Elevation: ca. Minus 190 m
Inventory Rating: 45
Periods represented: EB; Iron II; Iron Age; Nab; Nab (?); Byz; LByz, poss; Ud.
Description: The site consists of a lithic and sherd scatter on a large plateau measuring ca. 1 (E–W) x 0.50 (N–S) km N

of Wadi Feifa. There is what looks like a series of 'platforms', each measuring ca. 10 x 3 m, located at the western extremity of the plateau. There also appear to be graves in the same area. There are more isolated graves throughout the plateau.

Site No.: 125
Site Name: None
Map References: 3051 I, K737; 3051/I/B/4 (29)
Location on 1:50,000: 356/247
Location on 1:10,000: 194.6/37.8
Elevation: Minus 280 m
Inventory Rating: 29
Periods represented: Rom; Mam; Ud.
Description: This site consists of two sherd scatters. One is in an area ca. 40 x 25 m on a small terrace, disturbed by erosion, S of Wadi Feifa (behind the first ridge). The area may have been a campsite (there are other campsites nearby). The scatter extends S of a small hill. The SGNAS noted no architectural features. There is a jumble of rock, a distance of ca. 20 m, to the W with a possible wall on its S side. The second scatter of sherds is located ca. 30 m to the W of the first. It too is on a low terrace between the ridge and the jumble of rocks (wall ?).

Site No.: 126
Site Name: None
Map Reference: 3051 I, K737
Location on 1:50,000: 383/257
Elevation: ca. Minus 190 m
Inventory Rating: 24
Periods represented: EB IV; Iron I (?); Iron Age; Rom; LRom–Byz; Ud.
Description: This site is a heavy sherd scatter located between Wadi Feifa and Wadi Umm Jufna.

Site No.: 127
Site Name: None
Map Reference: 3051 II, K737
Location on 1:50,000: 295/946
Elevation: ca. 50 m
Inventory Rating: 43
Periods represented: Iron II; Iron Age; Ud.
Description: This site is a looted grave, somewhat oval in shape, located on the upper terrace on the E side of Wadi Fidan.

Site No.: 128
Site Name: None
Map Reference: 3051 I, K737
Location on 1:50,000: 379/256
Elevation: ca. Minus 190 m
Inventory Rating: 21
Periods represented: Nab; Nab (?); Byz; Ud.
Description: The site consists of graves and a lithic and sherd scatter in an area measuring ca. 800 (E–W) x 500 (N–S) m on the plateau between Wadi Umm Jufna and Wadi Feifa. There are indications of camping and possible stone lines, retaining or terrace walls (?), in the central segment of the plateau.

Site No.: 129
Site Name: None
Map Reference: 3051 I, K737
Location on 1:50,000: 376/254
Elevation: ca. Minus 190 m
Inventory Rating: 44
Periods represented: Chal; EB; Ud.
Description: The site consists of the remnants of two circular, stone structures, measuring ca. 12 and 8 m in diameter, and a lithic and sherd scatter between Wadi Umm Jufna and Wadi Feifa. There are two terraces, ca. 50 cm high, adjoining the larger structure.

Site No.: 130
Site Name: None
Map Reference: 3051 I, K737
Location on 1:50,000: 383/248

Elevation: ca. Minus 175 m
Inventory Rating: 25
Periods represented: Iron II (?); Ud.
Description: This is a sherd scatter, probably mainly a potbust, in an area measuring ca. 5 x 5 metres.

Site No.: 131
Site Name: None
Map Reference: 3051 I, K737
Location on 1:50,000: 384/256
Elevation: ca. Minus 190 m
Inventory Rating: 23
Periods represented: EB.
Description: This is a heavy concentration of very small body sherds and a light lithic scatter in an area ca. 30 x 25 m just to the NW of Site 128 on the plateau between Wadi Umm Jufna and Wadi Feifa. The SGNAS noted at least one grave in the area. There are more graves and/or a camp in a small valley a distance of ca. 75 m away.

Site No.: 132
Site Name: None
Map References: 3051 I, K737; 3051/I/B/6 (32)
Location on 1:50,000: 352/225
Location on 1:10,000: 194.1/35.7
Elevation: Minus 300 m
Inventory Rating: 27
Periods represented: Rom; Byz; Ud.
Description: This is a sherd scatter on a low terrace on the S side of Wadi Umruq. The terrace has been bulldozed and is dissected by erosion. Remnants of a small aqueduct, showing signs of recent use, cut the terrace in several places.

Site No.: 133
Site Name: None
Map References: 3051 I, K737; 3051/I/B/6 (32)
Location on 1:50,000: 364/222
Location on 1:10,000: 195.4/35.1
Elevation: Minus 190 m
Inventory Rating: 59
Periods represented: Chal.
Description: This is a very well preserved 'domestic' cluster consisting of an enclosure measuring ca. 16 m in diameter, a rectangular building measuring ca. 17 x 4 m, and several smaller structures on a plateau S of Wadi Umruq. The enclosure is constructed of two lines of stones filled with smaller stones. There is rubble around the enclosure and what appear to be at least two small, semi-circular structures on the north and east sides. There is a cairn and a rectangular outline of stones between the enclosure and the rectangular building. The latter is located ca. 55 m south of the enclosure and has an entrance-way which faces it.

Site No.: 134
Site Name: None
Map References: 3051 I, K737; 3051/I/B/6 (32)
Location on 1:50,000: 364/221
Location on 1:10,000: 195.4/35.1
Elevation: Minus 190 m
Inventory Rating: 29
Periods represented: PNL–Chal; Iron Age (Iron I ?); Ud.
Description: The site consists of a poorly preserved enclosure, measuring ca. 8 (E–W) x 5 (N–S) m, built of unhewn stone, on a plateau along the S side of Wadi Umruq.

Site No.: 135
Site Name: None
Map Reference: 3051 I, K737
Location on 1:50,000: 376/252
Elevation: ca. Minus 190 m
Inventory Rating: 33
Periods represented: Ud.
Description: This is a lithic scatter in an area ca. 60 (N–S) x 35 (E–W) m on the plateau N of Wadi Feifa. There is a drainage channel to the N and a slope, with outcropping sandstone,

covered in places by alluvial sediment, to the S. The density of lithics is lower on the ESE than on the WNW.

Site No.: 136
Site Name: None
Map Reference: 3051 I, K737
Location on 1:50,000: 384/247
Elevation: ca. Minus 155 m
Inventory Rating: 27
Periods represented: Iron II; Byz; Ud.
Description: This is a sherd scatter a trail leading away to the E from the plateau between Wadis Umm Jufna and Feifa.

Site No.: 137
Site Name: None
Map References: 3051 I, K737; 3051/I/B/6 (32)
Location on 1:50,000: 370/217
Location on 1:10,000: 196.0/34.7
Elevation: Minus 135 m
Inventory Rating: 28
Periods represented: Chal; Chal/EB; Ud.
Description: The site consists of a lithic and sherd scatter on a plateau just N of Wadi Umruq. It is just above an open area in the wadi where there is much vegetation and water.

Site No.: 138
Site Name: None
Map References: 3051 I, K737; 3051/I/B/6 (32)
Location on 1:50,000: 369/219
Location on 1:10,000: 195.9/34.8
Elevation: Minus 150 m
Inventory Rating: 24
Periods represented: Chal/EB; Ud, probably EB.
Description: This is a lithic and sherd scatter, W of Site 137 a distance of ca. 100 m, along the N side of Wadi Umruq.

Site No.: 139
Site Name: None
Map References: 3051 I, K737; 3051/I/B/6 (32)
Location on 1:50,000: 359/222
Location on 1:10,000: 194.9/35.2
Elevation: Minus 200 m
Inventory Rating: 23
Periods represented: EB IVB; Iron Age (Iron I ?); Hell; Ud.
Description: This is a sherd scatter on a plateau below a high mountain S of Wadi Umruq.

Site No.: 140
Site Name: None
Map References: 3051 I, K737; 3051/I/B/5 (31)
Location on 1:50,000: 331/196
Location on 1:10,000: 191.8/32.4
Elevation: Minus 200 m
Inventory Rating: 30
Periods represented: Ud.
Description: This is a lithic scatter in an area measuring ca. 100 (E–W) x 75 (N–S) m on a plateau above and to the E of Wadi Khuneizir. The SGNAS collected most of the sample from the centre of the plateau where there is water runoff.

Site No.: 141
Site Name: Abu Ishariebeh
Map References: 3051 I, K737; 3051/I/B/6 (32)
Location on 1:50,000: 333/199
Location on 1:10,000: 191.8/32.6
Elevation: Minus 190 m
Inventory Rating: 85
Periods represented: EB IV; EB IVA and B; EB III(?); EB II–III; Byz; Ud.
Description: The site consists of at least 50 structures, tombs and/or houses (?), located at the base of a high mountain to the E and high above Wadi Khuneizir. The structures are spread over an area of ca. 2 km in a very well protected area. They vary in size from ca. 7–14 x 2.5–3 metres. They do not appear to have any

definite orientation. Some of the structures have been dug into but many of them are still preserved with walls still standing 2–5 courses or 1 m high. The SGNAS could not locate 'entrances' into the structures. Some of the structures appear to be 'long' walls. They are built of unhewn stone taken from the nearby mountain slope. The pottery which the SGNAS collected at the site indicates that the structures belong to the EB IV period. The SGNAS also collected a light lithic scatter in the area.

Site No.: 142
Site Name: None
Map References: 3051 I, K737; 3051/I/B/5 (31)
Location on 1:50,000: 328/196
Location on 1:10,000: 191.5/32.6
Elevation: Minus 245 m
Inventory Rating: 23
Periods represented: EB IV; Nab–painted; Ud, prob EB IV.
Description: The site is a light sherd scatter in an area measuring ca. 20 x 10 m along a path to Sites 140 and 141.

Site No.: 143
Site Name: None
Map References: 3051 I, K737; 3051/I/B/5 (31)
Location on 1:50,000: 324/191
Location on 1:10,000: 191.4/33.1
Elevation: Minus 285 m
Inventory Rating: 69
Periods represented: EB; Hell; Ud, prob EB.
Description: The site is a tomb and sherd scatter, in an area measuring ca. 10 x 10 m, on a spur W of Wadi al-Nukhbar.

Site No.: 144
Site Name: None
Map Reference: 3051 I, K737
Location on 1:50,000: 322–335/172–180
Elevation: ca. Minus 190 to 160 m
Inventory Rating: 37
Periods represented: Ud.
Description: The site is a lithic scatter in an area measuring ca. 1000 (N–S) x 800–900 (E–W) m on the plateau between Wadis Khuneizir and al-Nukhbar. The lithic sample is represented by isolated finds of five or fewer lithics. The majority of the lithics which the SGNAS collected came from three areas: the NW corner; the N end; and the SW portion.

Site No.: 145 'A'–'B'
Site Name: None
Map References: 3051 I, K737; 3051/I/B/6 (32)
Location on 1:50,000: 355/227
Location on 1:10,000: 194.5/35.7
Elevation: Minus 270 m
Inventory Rating: 47
Periods represented: Ud.
Description: The site consists of two graves N of Wadi Umruq. 'A' is undisturbed. It measures ca. 4 m in diameter and has a substantial cairn of rock on it (ca. 1 m high). It is located on a ridge crest. 'B', measuring ca. 2 x 1 m, is on a low hill. It is probably a recent Bedouin burial. There are no cairn, head, nor footstones present. The SGNAS found neither lithics nor sherds in association with the graves.

Site No.: 146
Site Name: None
Map References: 3051 I, K737; 3051/I/B/6 (32)
Location on 1:50,000: 359/228
Location on 1:10,000: 194.9/35.8
Elevation: Minus 220 m
Inventory Rating: 37
Periods represented: EB; Byz; Ud.
Description: This is a light lithic and sherd scatter on a plateau N of Wadi Umruq. The plateau, which faces W, is a skirt around a sandstone mountain. It is dissected by many erosional channels. Large areas of the plateau are clear of rock as if they had been intentionally cleared, perhaps as Bedouin campsites. However,

the SGNAS observed no alignments of rocks nor piles of stones. Sheet wash, erosion, and wind deflation have probably influenced the ground surface. The lithics which the SGNAS collected were in an area measuring ca. 150 x 100 m in the SW portion of the plateau only. More time here may produce a larger collection. However, the worth of the activity is probably pointless given the nature of the surface and density of the lithics.

Site No.: 147
Site Name: None
Map References: 3052 II, K737; 3052/II/C/4 (20)
Location on 1:50,000: 386/373
Location on 1:10,000: 197.6/50.4
Elevation: Minus 300 m
Inventory Rating: 57
Periods represented: Ud.
Description: The site consists of a series of tombs/graves (4–5) and a circular structure located on the upper terrace on the slope behind modern al-Safi. The graves are circular to oval and measure ca. 3–2 x 2 m in diameter. There are mounds of rock (cairns), to a height of ca. 50–70 cm, on them. Some of the graves/tombs have been disturbed either by looting or erosion. The circular structure is composed of two ovals sharing a common wall. The eastern most oval is ca. 4 x 3 m while the western one is ca. 9 x 4 metres. The smaller one is filled with dirt and is slightly raised above the larger. The SGNAS collected neither lithics nor sherds at the site.

Site No.: 148
Site Name: None
Map Reference: 3051 I, K737
Location on 1:50,000: 321/200
Elevation: Minus 200 m
Inventory Rating: 30
Periods represented: EB IV; EB; Iron Age; Nab; Byz; Isl; Ott; Ott/Mod; Ud.
Description: The site consists of a moderate sherd scatter, spread over a distance of ca. 1.50 km with few interruptions, on a plateau immediately W of Wadi al-Nukhbar.

Site No.: 149
Site Name: None
Map Reference: 3051 I, K737
Location on 1:50,000: 324/198
Elevation: ca. Minus 190 m
Inventory Rating: 56
Periods represented: Nab–painted; Rom; Isl; Ud.
Description: The site is a tower/tomb complex and a well-built 'platform' measuring at least 6 x 6 m overlooking Wadi Khuneizir to the NE. It could have been used originally as a tower and then reused as a tomb. The centre of the complex has been looted either by grave robbers or construction workers. What appear to be graves are located to the NE. Rujm Khuneizir, Site 108, can be clearly seen to the NE. This would have been a good watchtower location.

Site No.: 150
Site Name: None
Map Reference: 3051 I, K737
Location on 1:50,000: 327/178
Elevation: ca. Minus 160 m
Inventory Rating: 31
Periods represented: Byz; Ud.
Description: The site consists of rock alignments and a sherd scatter on the SW corner of the plateau between Wadis Khuneizir and al-Nukhbar. The scatter represents at least two potbusts. There is a circular alignment of rock, one course high and one course wide, with charcoal associated on its N side, ca. 30 m to the E. It may be recent or ancient.

Site No.: 151
Site Name: None
Map Reference: 3051 I, K737
Location on 1:50,000: 331/178

Elevation: ca. Minus 160 m
Inventory Rating: 31
Periods represented: Byz; Ud.
Description: This site is probably a potbust. It is on a very gentle slope on the S side of Wadi Khuneizir in the NE corner of a plateau.

Site No.: 152 'A' and 'B'
Site Name: None
Map Reference: 3051 I, K737
Location on 1:50,000: 325/175
Elevation: Ca. Minus 160 m
Inventory Rating: 36
Periods represented: Ud.
Description: The site consists of several campsites on the plateau between Wadis Khuneizir and al-Nukhbar. 'A' is located on a small drainage on the SW portion of the plateau. It consists of two rock alignments, separated by ca. 3 m: one is 2 m in diameter while the other is ca. 5 x 4 m and is oval. There is charcoal associated with the smaller alignment. 'B' is on a terrace that runs along the base of a higher plateau on the SW part of the main plateau. It faces NE. It has a slightly raised mound, with charcoal on top, with some rocks loosely placed around it. There is a possible windbreak measuring ca. 6–7 m long ca. 20 m to the SE. It is one course high and wide. There are other camps, which have not been given a letter, located in the same general area. The SGNAS collected neither lithics nor sherds at the site.

Site No.: 153 'A' and 'B'
Site Name: None
Map Reference: 3051 I, K737
Location on 1:50,000: 323/172
Elevation: ca. Minus 160 m
Inventory Rating: 53
Periods represented: Ud.
Description: This site consists of several camps and graves/tombs on the plateau between Wadis Khuneizir and al-Nukhbar. 'A' is three possible, undisturbed graves oriented in a N–S line. The largest measures 2.5 m in diameter and may have a rock outline or cairn on top. The smallest two are ca. 1.5–2.0 m in diameter and may not be graves but outcroppings. It appears that these two have very small cairns placed on their tops. The three are located on the E side of a raised plateau on the larger plateau. They are located on the SE side of this larger plateau. There is a circle of stones ca. 5 m in diameter to the E. It is probably a camp. It is about 10 m below the graves. 'B' consists of 20–25 graves whose dimensions range from 1 x 1 to 2.5 x 2 metres. The shapes of the graves vary. One or two have head and footstones. They are outlined in rock with rocks on top. They are all located on the SW side of the large plateau. There are several more possible graves to the SE. One measures ca. 3 x 1.5 and is oval in shape. It is also outlined in rock with one course on the long axis and courses making up the short axis. It has a possible headstone. To the W, a distance of ca. 20 m, is a possible camp. There is a rectangular arrangement of rock with a break in the rock outline also in this area. There is another possible camp with a 5 x 5 m circle of stones to the SSE. There is charcoal within the circle. To the NW is another oval measuring ca. 3 x 1.5 metres. The SGNAS collected neither lithics nor sherds at the site.

Site No.: 154 'A'–'H'
Site Name: None
Map Reference: 3051 I, K737
Location on 1:50,000: 317/173
Elevation: ca. Minus 175 m
Inventory Rating: 49
Periods represented: EB IV; EB IIIA; EB–red painted; Hell; Rom (?); Byz; Ud.
Description: This site is a series of graves/tombs (?) and stone piles on the plateau immediately W of Wadi al-Nukhbar. 'A' consists of a line of stones, measuring ca. 40 m in length, going in a SE–NW. It could be a series of graves. There are many stone piles in the area. Some of these could be the result of bulldozing activity. 'B' is a large pile of stones, possibly graves. It may, however, be something other since wall lines can be seen, especially

on the E side. It measures ca. 13 (N–S) x 5 (E–W) m and is located ca. 160–180 m SW of 'A'. The SGNAS found no associated artifacts. 'C' is a third, very large structure, measuring ca. 17 x 5 m, located ca. 250 m to the SE of 'B'. It also could be a burial. The foundation walls can be followed, for the most part, on all sides. It still stands ca. 2 m high. The SGNAS found no artifacts around it. There are many other stone piles, also possible graves, to the W of 'C' as well as between 'C' and 'B'. 'D' consists of stone piles, a distance of ca. 150–200 m, to the W of 'C'. The SGNAS collected two ceramic and one lithic samples here. There are signs of bulldozing activity here as well. 'E' is comprised of a sherd scatter and graves (?). 'F' is another grave complex (?) at a higher elevation, ca. 200 m SE of 'E'. One structure measures ca. 20 (N–S) x 5 (E–W) metres. It still stands at least 1 m high in places and is of the same general construction as previously-described large structures on this plateau. The SGNAS collected no artifacts here. 'G' is another stone pile, possibly graves, ca. 200 m SW of 'F'. 'H' is yet another stone pile, possibly serving the same function as the others. The SGNAS collected no artifacts here either.

Site No.: 155
Site Name: Qasr al-Tilah
Map Reference: 3051 I, K737
Location on 1:50,000: 306/134
Elevation: Minus 140 m
Date Surveyed: 11/17/86
Inventory Rating: 75
Periods represented: Iron II; Hell; Nab–painted; Nab (=ERom); Rom; Byz; Um; Mod; Ud.
Description: This site is a caravanserai at the mouth of Wadi al-Tilah. There are extensive agricultural fields associated with the reservoir and fort. Many of the terracing walls, which range from 50–100 cm in thickness, are still clear. In places, they have been destroyed either by human or natural causes. In other places, they extend for 50 m without a break and then extend an additional 50 m in broken segments for a total of ca. 100 m. There is a fort located to the SE of the fields and SSW of a reservoir. It has been partially destroyed by bulldozing activity by construction workers seeking rock. Some internal partitions are still visible. The reservoir is still in a fairly good state of repair. In antiquity, it was filled by water which was brought to it by an aqueduct running along the N side of Wadi al-Tilah. The aqueduct can be followed up the wadi for several hundred meters. It appears that a possible mill was located at the SW corner of the reservoir. Now, however, it has fallen away and only its outlines remain. The SGNAS collected samples from the different segments of the site.

Site No.: 156
Site Name: None
Map Reference: 3051 I, K737
Location on 1:50,000: 323/134
Elevation: ca. Minus 90 m
Inventory Rating: 37
Periods represented: Nab, poss; Ud.
Description: This is a campsite on the S side of Wadi al-Tilah at a point where a tributary drainage enters the wadi. It consists of stone circles measuring ca. 1 m in diameter with a possible hearth and possible graves, eight in all. The grave-like alignments are oval and rectangular. They range in size from 2 x 1.5 m (rectangular) to 1.5 m in diameter, to 1.5 x 0.75 m (oval). Some of the graves have small cairns on top and one may have a head or footstone. To the S and up a hill, there are numerous camps that are recent. To the W, over the ridge, on the NW face of the spur, there is part of a retaining wall measuring ca. 2 m long, 1 m high, and ca. 0.50–0.75 m wide. It is 2–3 courses high and one course wide. It is constructed of cut stone.

Site No.: 157
Site Name: None
Map References: 3051 I, K737; 3051/I/B/4 (29)
Location on 1:50,000: 343/258
Location on 1:10,000: 193.3/38.8
Elevation: Minus 320 m
Inventory Rating: 59
Periods represented: Chal/EB; EB IV; EB; Nab; Rom; Ud.

Description: This is a sherd scatter in an agricultural field ca. 100 m W of the main highway and Feifa, Sites 75 and 76.

Site No.: 158
Site Name: None
Map References: 3051 I, K737; 3051/I/B/4 (29)
Location on 1:50,000: 347/247
Location on 1:10,000: 193.7/37.7
Elevation: Minus 310 m
Inventory Rating: 47
Periods represented: Ud.
Description: The site consists of many stone piles, possibly graves, in a sandy area W of the main highway and S of Wadi Feifa. The SGNAS found neither lithics nor sherds there.

Site No.: 159
Site Name: Khirbet al-Nahas
Map Reference: 3051 II, K737
Location on 1:50,000: 334/969
Elevation: 80 m
Inventory Rating: 70
Periods represented: Iron IA; Iron IC; Iron I–II; Iron IIA, B, and C; Iron II; Iron Age; 'Negevite' ware; Ud.
Description: This is an important smelting site on the S side of Wadi al-Ghuweib. It has been visited and studied by several surveyors. The SGNAS sampled, by means of transects, three different segments of the site.

Site No.: 160
Site Name: None
Map Reference: 3051 II, K737
Location on 1:50,000: 347/977
Elevation: 100 m
Inventory Rating: 40
Periods represented: Byz; Iron Age, prob Iron I.
Description: This is mound/structure and sherd scatter in an area measuring ca. 40 x 30 m along Wadi al-Ghuweib. The mound/structure measures ca. 12 x 4 metres. It may be a grave. The site is located ca. 1.50 km NE of Site 159.

Site No.: 161
Site Name: Khirbet al-Ghuweib
Map Reference: 3051 II, K737
Location on 1:50,000: 362/982
Elevation: 140 m
Inventory Rating: 43
Periods represented: Iron IA; Iron I–II; Iron II; Iron Age; Byz; Ud.
Description: This is a very large smelting and village site located on both sides of Wadi al-Ghuweib. There are many wall lines and piles of stones visible at the site. There are graves located at the NE segment of the site. They are located in a pile of stones which measures ca. 4 x 4 m and still stands ca. 1 m high. The pile is divided into two main segments each measuring ca. 2 x 4 metres. There is another possible grave ca. 20 m to the S. There are more graves, evidence of smelting, and stone alignments, which may be the remnants of house walls, on the S side of the wadi. There is presently some land under cultivation near a spring at the SW corner of the site. The SGNAS collected samples from both sides of the wadi.

Site No.: 162
Site Name: None
Map Reference: 3051 I, K737
Location on 1:50,000: 310/111
Elevation: Minus 90 m
Inventory Rating: 45
Periods represented: Iron I (?); Iron Age; Ud.
Description: This is a cemetery and lithic and sherd scatter above the bed and on the S side of Wadi al-Dahal.

Site No.: 163 'A'–'C'
Site Name: None

Map Reference: 3051 I, K737
Location on 1:50,000: 314/200
Elevation: ca. Minus 205 m
Inventory Rating: 51
Periods represented: LRom–Byz; Ott; Ott/Mod; Ud.
Description: The site consists of a series of sherd scatters and/or potbusts. 'A' is a sherd scatter, comprised of one or possibly two vessels, in an area covering ca. 20 (E–W) x 10 (N–S) metres. It is ca. 30 m S of the JVA camp on the plateau just W of Wadi Khuneizir. 'B' is a sherd scatter and two potbusts in an area measuring ca. 40 x 15 m just SW of Site 148 'B'. The area has been influenced by sheetwash. However, one potbust was very restricted in area. The other potbust was surrounded by the sherd scatter. 'C' is the remains of a potbust in an area measuring ca. 10 x 5 m ca. 150–200 m SW of Site 148 'C'. Some of the collected material may be water-borne since it is located on a slight slope.

Site No.: 164
Site Name: None
Map Reference: 3051 I, K737
Location on 1:50,000: 314/113
Elevation: Minus 85
Inventory Rating: 40
Periods represented: Ott; Mod; Ud.
Description: This is a cemetery and lithic and sherd scatter in an area measuring ca. 100 (E–W) x 20 (N–S) m on a terrace on the N side of Wadi al-Dahal.

Site No.: 165
Site Name: None
Map Reference: 3051 I, K737
Location on 1:50,000: 331/106
Elevation: Minus 10 m
Inventory Rating: 48
Periods represented: Iron II; Rom; Ott/Mod; Ud.
Description: This is a cemetery and sherd scatter on a terrace on the N side of Wadi al-Dahal.

Site No.: 166
Site Name: None
Map Reference: 3051 I, K737
Location on 1:50,000: 307/141
Elevation: Minus 160 m
Inventory Rating: 38
Periods represented: Ud.
Description: This is a light lithic scatter on a slope just to the NE of the agricultural fields at Qasr al-Tilah.

Site No.: 167
Site Name: None
Map Reference: 3051 I, K737
Location on 1:50,000: 324/134
Elevation: ca. Minus 90 m
Inventory Rating: 32
Periods represented: Iron II; Iron Age; Byz; Ud.
Description: This is a light sherd scatter among stone piles, possibly graves, along the S side of Wadi al-Tilah.

Site No.: 168
Site Name: None
Map Reference: 3051 I, K737
Location on 1:50,000: 340/101
Elevation: 15 m
Inventory Rating: 39
Periods represented: Iron Age; Byz; Ud.
Description: This is a cemetery and sherd scatter on a terrace above and on the N side of Wadi al-Dahal. There are 20–30 graves, some looted, in an area measuring ca. 100 (N–S) x 100 (E–W) metres. Some of the graves appear to be recent.

Site No.: 169
Site Name: None
Map Reference: 3051 I, K737
Location on 1:50,000: 339/100

Elevation: 10 m
Inventory Rating: 26
Periods represented: Chal/EB; Byz; Ud.
Description: This is a cemetery, campsite, and sherd scatter on the N side of Wadi al-Dahal.

Site No.: 170
Site Name: None
Map Reference: 3051 I, K737
Location on 1:50,000: 339/099
Elevation: 10 m
Inventory Rating: 34
Periods represented: Ud.
Description: This is a light lithic scatter on a terrace on the N side of Wadi al-Dahal just S of Sites 168 and 169.

Site No.: 171
Site Name: None
Map Reference: 3051 I, K737
Location on 1:50,000: 341/098
Elevation: 15 m
Inventory Rating: 44
Periods represented: Chal/EB; Iron Age; Ud.
Description: This is a very dense lithic and sherd scatter along the N side of Wadi al-Dahal just to the E of Sites 168–170. There is a sharp drop from the site to the wadi bed.

Site No.: 172 'A'–'B'
Site Name: None
Map Reference: 3051 I, K737
Location on 1:50,000: 321/179
Elevation: ca. Minus 200 m
Inventory Rating: 47
Periods represented: Chal/EB; Byz; Isl; Ud.
Description: The site consists of graves and sherd scatters on a terrace within Wadi al-Nukhbar. 'A' is a sherd scatter and two graves in an area measuring ca. 25 (N–S) x 15 (E–W) metres. The grave are circular and ca. 2.50 m in diameter. The southern most grave is pretty diffused as its rock cairn has been scattered, probably by natural forces. The other grave, which is intact, is outlined with rock and covered by a low cairn. The collected sherds may be water-borne. However, there are no sherds on the slope. 'B', located ca. 300 m N of 'A', is a sherd scatter that covers an area of ca. 25 (N–S) x 15 (E–W) metres. No features are associated with it. The sherds do not seem to have washed down from above.

Site No.: 173 'A'–'B'
Site Name: None
Map Reference: 3051 I, K737
Location on 1:50,000: 322/180
Elevation: ca. Minus 200 m
Inventory Rating: 41
Periods represented: Iron II; Byz; Ott/Mod.
Description: The site consists of potbusts close to Wadi al-Nukhbar. 'A' is the remains of one vessel in an area ca. 2 m square on the road between the wadi bed and a ridge to the E. 'B' consists of two potbusts, ca. 100 m apart, on a terrace on the E side of the wadi, ca. 40–100 m SSW of 'A'. There is a possible grave, ca. 1 m in diameter, located ca. 20 m to the E. The collected sherds are possibly not directly associated with this feature.

Site No.: 174 'A'–'H'
Site Name: None
Map Reference: 3051 I, K737
Location on 1:50,000: 322/178
Elevation: Ca. Minus 180 m
Inventory Rating: 80
Periods represented: EB IV; Ud.
Description: This site consists for the most part of a series of cobble 'platforms' to the E of Wadi al-Nukhbar. 'A' measures ca. 8 x 3 m and is oriented N–S. It is elevated, ca. 30–40 cm, above the ground. It is not lined with rock but with fill. It is at the base of a ridge just before the ridge drops off several 10's of m

to a tributary drainage. 'B', located ca. 75–85 m NW of 'A', measures ca. 18 x 5 m and is oriented N–S. It has more rock on and about it than 'A'. It is elevated ca. 50–75 cm above the gravel surface. The SGNAS collected lithics around and ceramics both around and on the 'platform'. 'C' is oval and measures ca. 21 x 5 metres. It is oriented N–S on the far N end of the site. It rises to a heights of 2 m and 1 m at its S end its N end respectively. The SGNAS collected sherds on as well as to the W and N of it and lithics to the E. It is ca. 200 m N of 'B'. 'D' consists of three piles of rock. The southern most pile measures ca. 9 x 5 m and rises 20–50 cm above the gravel surface. It is on the plateau, across a drainage, a distance of ca. 30 m from 'C'. The most northerly situated of the three measures ca. 14 x 5 m and is 1 m high. It is somewhat mounded, i.e., with rocks on top. There were no sherds but the SGNAS collected a few lithics around it. To the N is a diffused line of rock, measuring ca. 10–15 m, which may be a series of graves. The most westerly located of the three is actually a raised pile of rock forming an oval. It measures ca. 6 x 5 m and is ca. 50–75 cm high. The SGNAS collected a substantial number of sherds to its N and W. One density probably represents a reconstructible vessel. There are other possible graves, outlined and topped with cobbles, nearby. 'E' measures ca. 13 x 6 m and ca. 30–50 cm high. The SGNAS found sherds on, as well as W, of it and lithics nearby. It too is made of cobbles. It has not been disturbed but erosion may begin to cut away at its E side. 'F', measuring ca. 11 x 5 m and ca. 1–1.5 m at its highest point, is oriented N–S along the ridge. It is disturbed by erosion on its E side. The SGNAS found sherds both within and around it. There is a possible circular area, measuring ca. 2 m in diameter, between 'E' and 'F' that may have been cleared by humans. Nearby are what appear to be a series of graves or a disturbed rock alignment. 'G' is a structure which appears to be built upon a mound. Whether the mound is natural or artificial is unknown. There is what appears to be a wall measuring several meters along its E side. The entire mound is ca. 10 m in diameter and is the highest of all the features recorded for the site. 'H' is yet another 'platform' at the end of the ridge and oriented N–S. It is ca. 17 x 5 m and stands ca. 1.5–2 m high. It is located ca. 100 m S of 'A' and 'G'. About 80 m W of 'H', on the next ridge, there are seven rock piles that range in size from 1–1.5 m in diameter. Many of these consist of large boulders with smaller pebbles placed on top. They are ca. 1 m high. They are oriented N–S up a slope that may be part of an old track. Only excavations will determine the nature of the 'platforms'. They are similar in many ways to those at Site 141.

Site No.: 175
Site Name: None
Map Reference: 3051 I, K737
Location on 1:50,000: 314–324/156–201
Elevation: ca. Minus 180 m
Inventory Rating: 49
Periods represented: Ud.
Description: This site is a domestic (?) cluster, tombs (?), and a lithic scatter. The latter is really isolated finds (five or fewer specimens found together) from an area measuring ca. 45 (N–S) x 100–300 (E–W) m between the Mazra'–'Aqaba highway and Wadi al-Nukhbar. The SGNAS noted lithics in association with 'buildings' and tombs but not in densities sufficient to make a sample. Therefore, all lithics collected were made into one general collection.

Site No.: 176
Site Name: None
Map Reference: 3051 I, K737
Location on 1:50,000: 345/098
Elevation: 25 m
Inventory Rating: 30
Periods represented: Ud.
Description: This is a light lithic scatter on a rocky slope along the N side of Wadi al-Dahal. The lithics appear to be coming from the rocky hill. However, no direct source could be found. One cave in the rock is still used at least for storage. The SGNAS collected additional lithics further to the N on the opposite side of the hill.

Site No.: 177
Site Name: None
Map Reference: 3151 IV, K737
Location on 1:50,000: 415/271 (?)
Elevation: 400 m (?)
Inventory Rating: 38
Periods represented: NL–Chal; Chal.
Description: This is an enclosure high in the mountains between Wadi Madsus al-Shamali and Wadi Umm Jufna.

Site No.: 178
Site Name: None
Map Reference: 3051 I, K737
Location on 1:50,000: 348/097
Elevation: 40 m
Inventory Rating: 37
Periods represented: Ud.
Description: This is a lithic scatter among graves on a terrace on the N side of Wadi al-Dahal.

Site No.: 179
Site Name: None
Map References: 3051 I, K737; 3051/I/B/6 (32)
Location on 1:50,000: 336/197
Location on 1:10,000: 192.2/32.9
Elevation: ca. Minus 120 m
Inventory Rating: 3
Periods represented: Ud, poss Nab (?).
Description: This is a potbust in a 5 m square area on a peak above Site 141 which is high above and to the E of Wadi Khuneizir. No features were observed in the area.

Site No.: 180 'A'–'B'
Site Name: None
Map References: 3051 I, K737; 3051/I/B/4 (29)
Location on 1:50,000: 345/253
Location on 1:10,000: 193.5/38.3
Elevation: Minus 310 m
Inventory Rating: 52
Periods represented: Byz; Mod; Ud.
Description: The site consists of two sherd scatters. 'A' is in an area measuring ca. 5 m square on the alluvial plain W of Wadi Feifa. It is ca. 40 m W of the Mazra'–'Aqaba highway and ca. 250 m N of a dam. 'B' covers an area of ca. 150 (N–S) x 60 (E–W) m in an agricultural field ca. 20 m SE of the road leading into the village of Feifa. It is ca. 80–90 m NW of 'A'.

Site No.: 181
Site Name: None
Map References: 3051 I, K737; 3051/I/B/4 (29)
Location on 1:50,000: 342/261
Location on 1:10,000: 193.2/39.1
Elevation: Minus 325 m
Inventory Rating: 50
Periods represented: Chal/EB; EB; Nab; Nab/Rom; Ayy/Mam, prob Mam; Isl; Ott; Ud.
Description: This is a sherd scatter in an agricultural field ca. 700–800 m NW of Wadi Feifa and ca. 50 m W of the highway.

Site No.: 182
Site Name: None
Map References: 3051 I, K737; 3051/I/B/2 (26)
Location on 1:50,000: 338/282
Location on 1:10,000: 192.8/41.2
Elevation: Minus 370 m
Inventory Rating: 46
Periods represented: NL–Chal; Ud.
Description: This is a sherd scatter W of the Mazra'–'Aqaba highway a distance of ca. 35–40 m.

Site No.: 183
Site Name: None
Map Reference: 3051 I, K737

Location on 1:50,000: 352/096
Elevation: ca. 60 m
Inventory Rating: 27
Periods represented: Ud.
Description: This is a lithic scatter on the N side of the Wadi al-Dahal.

Site No.: 184
Site Name: None
Map Reference: 3051 I, K737
Location on 1:50,000: 356/092
Elevation: ca. 50 m
Inventory Rating: 38
Periods represented: Ud.
Description: This is a cemetery and lithic scatter at the confluence of Wadi al-Dahal and a tributary wadi coming from the NE. There is one large grave at the northern end of a spur with other smaller graves along the spur.

Site No.: 185
Site Name: None
Map Reference: 3051 I, K737
Location on 1:50,000: 356/093
Elevation: ca. 50 m
Inventory Rating: 62
Periods represented: Iron Age; Byz; Ud.
Description: This is a lithic and sherd scatter as well as a 'domestic-cluster' along the N side of Wadi al-Dahal. The latter consists of a stone circle and other structures.

Site No.: 186
Site Name: None
Map Reference: 3051 I, K737
Location on 1:50,000: 357/093
Elevation: ca. 50 m
Inventory Rating: 36
Periods represented: Ud.
Description: This is a lithic scatter. It is located on a spur directly N of Wadi al-Dahal.

Site No.: 187
Site Name: None
Map Reference: 3051 I, K737
Location on 1:50,000: 309/114
Elevation: Minus 90 m
Inventory Rating: 45
Periods represented: Chal/EB; Iron IA; Iron II.
Description: This is a cemetery consisting of ca. 20 graves, most of which are rectangular and measure from 2 x 1–1.5 x 1 m, scattered over an area of ca. 40 square m on the N side of Wadi al-Dahal. The graves are both individual and in clusters. They are rock outlined with gravel fill. They look very recent. The SGNAS noted modern artifacts nearby.

Site No.: 188
Site Name: None
Map Reference: 3051 I, K737
Location on 1:50,000: 327/108
Elevation: ca. Minus 60 m
Inventory Rating: 45
Periods represented: Iron IA; Ud.
Description: This is a cemetery and a sherd scatter on a terrace along the S side of Wadi al-Dahal and ca. 10–15 m above the bed of the wadi. The cemetery consists of more than 20 graves. The main concentration is to the E where about 18 are clustered. Two have been robbed. Two graves are isolated to the W, separated from each other by ca. 30 metres. Their shapes vary from rectangular to oval. The rectangular ones measure ca. 2 x 1 m; the oval 1.5 x 1 metres.

Site No.: 189
Site Name: None
Map Reference: 3051 I, K737
Location on 1:50,000: 333/104

Elevation: Minus 20 m
Inventory Rating: 41
Periods represented: Chal/EB; Rom; Ud.
Description: This is a lithic and sherd scatter as well as graves and a rock alignment along both a lower and upper terrace on the S side of Wadi al-Dahal. The SGNAS collected the lithics and a potbust at the western end and at eastern most edge respectively of the site on the upper terrace. There is a possible grave associated with the potbust. It collected the ceramics, along with a couple of lithics, on the lower terrace, mainly to the E. The few lithics on the lower terrace are 15–20 m below the upper terrace. The wadi bed is ca. 5 m below the lower terrace. The SGNAS noted one grave measuring ca. 3 x 2 m on the lower terrace. It does not appear to be recent. The lower terrace also appears to have been used in the past as a camping area. Cleared areas are evident along with rock alignments.

Site No.: 190
Site Name: None
Map Reference: 3051 I, K737
Location on 1:50,000: 343/095
Elevation: ca. 20 m
Inventory Rating: 44
Periods represented: Iron Age; Byz; Ud.
Description: This is a lithic and sherd scatter along with a tomb/grave on the upper terrace ca. 150 m S of Wadi al-Dahal and ca. 10–15 m above the wadi bed. There are two possible graves at the E-central area of the site. However, their outline is somewhat different from what has been seen previously. The most easterly located is D-shaped with the N end open. It is outlined in stone and measures ca. 2.5 x 2 metres. There is no cairn present. The grave (?) to its W, a distance of ca. 10 m, is horseshoe shaped with a platform (?) connected to its W side. The platform (?), which measures ca. 1.5 x 1 m, is constructed of undressed cobbles. The grave is outlined in rock with the N end left open. There is no cairn present. This, however, could be a Bedouin camp. The only certain grave, oval and measuring ca. 2.5 x 2 m, is at the W end of the terrace. It is topped with stones. Around 120 m to the E of the grave is a concentrated sherd scatter ca. 2 m in diameter. Several vessels are represented. It is in a cleared area. There are stone alignments ca. 100 m to the E. There is a terrace below the site that appears to have been used for camping. The SGNAS found only two lithics and no ceramics here. It did not give the lithics a sample number. Some rock alignments in the area may be a series of graves. However, this is uncertain. There are 2–3 possible grave, oval in shape and measuring ca. 1.5–2 x 1 m, on the hill/ridge to the S, behind the terrace. One is located at its W end; the other is located at the opposite end. Both are capped by cairns.

Site No.: 191
Site Name: None
Map Reference: 3051 I, K737
Location on 1:50,000: 354/092
Elevation: ca. 30 m
Inventory Rating: 29
Periods represented: Iron IA; Iron II; Ud.
Description: This is a sherd scatter immediately N of Wadi al-Dahal. There is evidence of camping and graves in the area which covers ca. 200 x 60 metres.

Site No.: 192
Site Name: None
Map Reference: 3051 I, K737
Location on 1:50,000: 353/092
Elevation: ca. 30 m
Inventory Rating: 45
Periods represented: Iron Age; Byz; Ud.
Description: This is a very large cemetery measuring ca. 500 x 500 m at the confluence of Wadi al-Dahal and another smaller wadi coming from the NE. It is spread over at least five terraces. The graves do not all appear to be from the same period. There is also evidence of camping throughout the terraces. The SGNAS noted a few, water-borne sherds and collected the NE extremity of the cemetery.

Site No.: 193
Site Name: None
Map Reference: 3051 I, K737
Location on 1:50,000: 305–358/080–114
Elevation: Minus 100 to Plus 60 m
Inventory Rating: 28
Periods represented: Ud.
Description: This is actually a lithic sample which includes the entire Wadi al-Dahal from its mouth up to a second spring to the E. The lithics are isolated finds from both side of the wadi. Thus, they are only general samples.

Site No.: 194
Site Name: None
Map Reference: 3051 I, K737
Location on 1:50,000: 277/140
Elevation: Minus 190 m
Inventory Rating: 51
Periods represented: EB IV; Rom; Byz; Ud.
Description: This site consists of a lithic and sherd scatter among stone piles and a stone scatter along the E side of the main Mazra'–'Aqaba highway and W of Wadi al-Tilah. The material could be water-borne. The stone piles could be graves.

Site No.: 195
Site Name: None
Map Reference: 3051 I, K737
Location on 1:50,000: 271/134
Elevation: Minus 180 m
Inventory Rating: 43
Periods represented: Ott/Mod; Ud.
Description: This site consists of a lithic and sherd scatter in an area which is badly eroded. It is located immediately W of the main Mazra'–'Aqaba highway and N of the present, Dahal Police Post. The SGNAS collected the sherds and lithics among stone piles. However, it could detect no definite alignment. The lithics, for the most part, come from an area measuring ca. 5 x 5 metres. The sherds could be a potbust.

Site No.: 196
Site Name: None
Map Reference: 3151 IV, K737
Location on 1:50,000: 436/286 (?)
Elevation: ca. Plus 750 m (?)
Inventory Rating: 55
Periods represented: Iron Age; Nab (?); Ud.
Description: This site was surveyed on the day that the SGNAS made its transects from the 'Edomite' plateau to the Southern Ghors. It is located on the western edge of the plateau overlooking the Ghors. It consists of four graves, some rock alignments that look like possible field foundations, and some windbreaks/structures. The graves measure ca. 2 x 3 m in diameter with a cairn on top. The possible wall alignment is ca. 10 m long. The windbreak/structure is two rooms, measuring ca. 5 x 5 m, sharing a common dividing wall. There are two circular outlines of rock, measuring ca. 2.5 m in diameter and two courses wide, to the NE. The site commands a view to the E, W, and S. Wadi al-Hasa is to the N. The 'Arabah and the Southern Ghors are visible from this site.

Site No.: 197
Site Name: None
Map Reference: 3051 I, K737
Location on 1:50,000: 345/093
Elevation: ca. 30 m
Inventory Rating: 33
Periods represented: Rom; Byz; Ud.
Description: This is a potbust on a terrace ca. 30–40 m S of Wadi al-Dahal.

Site No.: 198 'A'–'D'
Site Name: None
Map Reference: 3051 I, K737

Location on 1:50,000: 347/095
Elevation: 30 m
Inventory Rating: 36
Periods represented: EB IV; EB IVB; EB IV/MB I (?); Ud.
Description: This site consists of several features S of Wadi al-Dahal. 'A' is a disturbed grave on a plateau/terrace. It consists of a large cairn of rock, oval in shape, and ca. 3 m in diameter. There is bone associated with it. Another possible grave may be located ca. 20–25 m to the E. 'B' is a possible grave, oval and measuring ca. 3 x 2 m, located ca. 200–250 m E of 'A'. It is ca. 30–35 m from the edge of the terrace. A cairn of rock is on its top. However, this may be nothing more than a natural piling of rock due to erosional activity. 'C' consists of three graves, two of which are robbed, along with one possible structure. The graves are located ca. 250 m SE of 'A'. The SGNAS found ceramics at two of the graves. What appears to be a rock alignment, ca. 2.5–3 m long with a corner, is located to the E. Around 10–12 m to the W is another rock alignment, measuring ca. 2.5 m, running parallel to it. All of the graves have a large cairn on top. 'D' is an oval grave measuring ca. 3 x 2–2.5 metres. It has a fairly large cairn on top. It is ca. 300–350 m from 'A'. The SGNAS found neither lithics nor sherds in association. There may be additional graves/tombs on the plateau/terrace.

Site No.: 199
Site Name: None
Map Reference: 3051 I, K737
Location on 1:50,000: 349/094
Elevation: ca. 40 m
Inventory Rating: 31
Periods represented: Ud.
Description: This is a sherd scatter ca. 60–70 m S of Wadi al-Dahal. Cleared areas nearby could be campsites.

Site No.: 200
Site Name: None
Map Reference: 3051 I, K737
Location on 1:50,000: 348/093
Elevation: ca. 50 m
Inventory Rating: 31
Periods represented: Ud.
Description: This is a potbust on a plateau ca. 120 m S of Wadi al-Dahal.

Site No.: 201
Site Name: None
Map Reference: 3051 I, K737
Location on 1:50,000: 347/091
Elevation: ca. 40 m
Inventory Rating: 31
Periods represented: Rom; Ott/Mod; Ud.
Description: This is a sherd scatter and potbust at the southern most edge of the plateau ca. 400–500 m S of Wadi al-Dahal. They are at the base of small hills leading up to higher ones. Sheetwash is probably great here. The sherd scatter and potbust are separated by ca. 10 m. The SGNAS collected them separately.

Site No.: 202
Site Name: None
Map Reference: 3051 I, K737
Location on 1:50,000: 354/087
Elevation: ca. 60 m
Inventory Rating: 40
Periods represented: Ud.
Description: This site consists of about three graves/tombs and a camp (?) on the S side of Wadi al-Dahal. It is located on the upper terrace at the base of a ridge and looks N. The graves are oval and range in size from 1–2 x 1 metres. They are ca. 2 m W of a camp (?) which consists of a structure, measuring ca. 3 m square, which is one course wide and high except at the ends where it is two courses wide. No entrance is evident but the alignments are diffused. The alignment is not of solid rock. The rocks have spaces between them.

Site No.: 203
Site Name: None
Map Reference: 3051 I, K737
Location on 1:50,000: 357/082
Elevation: ca. 80 m
Inventory Rating: 38
Periods represented: Ott; Ud.
Description: This is a campsite and potbust in an area measuring ca. 35–40 x 20–25 m on a terrace above and ca. 40 m S of Wadi al-Dahal. There are rock-free areas which appear to have been cleared for camping. There are also rock alignments, measuring ca. 3–3.5 x 1.5–2 m and forming three-sided rectangles, in the area. It is not known if the collected sherds are directly associated with the camps.

Site No.: 204
Site Name: None
Map Reference: 3051 I, K737
Location on 1:50,000: 358/080
Elevation: ca. 80 m
Inventory Rating: 40
Periods represented: Ud.
Description: This appears to be a campsite, with a northern exposure, on the S side of Wadi al-Dahal. There is at least one circular alignment of rock, measuring ca. 4 m in diameter, present. It has sediment built up in it. There is ash within the sediment. There is a semicircular, possibly circular, alignment of rock measuring ca. 5 m in diameter ca. 3 m to the E. It has neither ash nor sediment within it.

Site No.: 205
Site Name: Sammar
Map References: 3052 II, K737; 3052/II/C/6 (23)
Location on 1:50,000: 359/325
Location on 1:10,000: 194.6/45.6
Elevation: Minus 380 m
Inventory Rating: 69
Periods represented: Nab; Nab (?); Rom; LByz; LByz–Um; Abb (?); Ud.
Description: This is a midden located ca. 50 m S of the a drainage canal. It is 0.60 km E of the Mazra'–'Aqaba highway and ca. 7.5 km N of the Wadi Feifa bridge. There is a heavy concentration of sherds and some glass in what is essentially a sandy area measuring ca. 75 (N–S) x 25 (E–W) metres. There is much ash in the area. The site of a kiln?

Site No.: 206
Site Name: None
Map Reference: 3051 I, K737
Location on 1:50,000: 275/123
Elevation: Minus 170 m
Inventory Rating: 41
Periods represented: LByz; Ud.
Description: This is a sherd scatter of low density, covering an area of ca. 20 x 30 m, on the S slope of a small wadi directly E of the old, Dahal Police Post. Wadis al-Tilah and al-Dahal are to the NE and E respectively.

Site No.: 207
Site Name: None
Map Reference: 3051 I, K737
Location on 1:50,000: 275/122
Elevation: Minus 170 m
Inventory Rating: 36
Description: This is a cemetery (?) and sherd scatter. Wadis al-Tilah and al-Dahal are to the NE and E respectively.
Periods represented: Ud.

Site No.: 208
Site Name: None
Map Reference: 3051 I, K737
Location on 1:50,000: 274/118
Elevation: Minus 170 m
Inventory Rating: 29

Periods represented: Chal/EB; Ud.
Description: This is a lithic and sherd scatter, in an area of ca. 100 (E–W) x 50 (N–S) m, along the N side of Wadi Madsus.

Site No.: 209
Site Name: None
Map Reference: 3051 I, K737
Location on 1:50,000: 273–283/118–127
Elevation: Minus 170 to 160 m
Inventory Rating: 37
Periods represented: Ud.
Description: This site represents a large tract of survey area measuring ca. 2000 (N–S) x 150 (E–W) m between Wadis al-Dahal and Madsus. The lithic sample represents isolated finds (five or fewer lithics over a restricted area). The area is flat but dissected by erosional and drainage channels.

Site No.: 210
Site Name: None
Map Reference: 3051 I, K737
Location on 1:50,000: 282/136
Elevation: Minus 180 m
Inventory Rating: 39
Periods represented: Nab/Rom (?); LRom–Byz; Ud.
Description: This is a lithic and sherd scatter in a campsite area on the E side of the Mazra'–'Aqaba highway NW of Wadi al-Tilah. A tributary wadi/drainage runs along the S side of the site. Rocks have been cleared away and put into piles. There are some rock alignments but their function is unknown. The age(s) of the camp(s) is unknown. The lithics are probably background noise. The sherds may or may not be directly associated with the camps. Actually, the site is in a small depression caused by erosion.

Site No.: 211
Site Name: Khirbet al-Dahal
Map Reference: 3051 I, K737
Location on 1:50,000: 277/138
Elevation: Minus 190 m
Inventory Rating: 66
Periods represented: Nab (=ERom); Rom; LRom; Byz; LByz; Um; Mod; Ud.
Description: This is a major village site along the western extremity of Wadi al-Dahal and to the E of the Mazra'–'Aqaba highway. It is located in a wash area measuring ca. 200 (N–S) x 150 (E–W) m and below the surface of the plain into which the channel is cut. It consists of several multiroom and one room structures. They are probably houses. All the structures are made from cobble stones. Both the exterior and partition walls within the larger structures are two courses wide and still stand one to two courses high. The larger, multiroomed structures measure as much as ca. 17–18 x 7–8 metres. The room sizes are not uniform. The smaller, singled room structures measure ca. 4.0–3.5 m square. There are other structures which appear to be platforms (?). Both type of structures are on both sides of the wadi. The SGNAS collected five samples at the site. The pottery, which may be described as dense, was predominantly Byzantine. A walk in the vicinity of the site revealed many Byzantine, sherd scatters. The SGNAS also collected a general lithic sample in the vicinity of the site.

Site No.: 212
Site Name: None
Map Reference: 3051 I, K737
Location on 1:50,000: 298/110
Elevation: Minus 100 m
Inventory Rating: 44
Periods represented: Byz; Ud.
Description: This is a cemetery and a lithic and sherd scatter on an island in the Wadi al-Dahal floodplain. The SGNAS collected most of the sherds among graves at the summit of the site and the lithics, for the most part, on the E slope. There are also possible graves on a small terrace on the S slope of the hill.

Site No.: 213
Site Name: None
Map References: 3051 I, K737
Location on 1:50,000: 299/102
Elevation: Minus 100 m
Inventory Rating: 52
Periods represented: Ud.
Description: The site consists of a cemetery and a light, lithic scatter on a hill/island in the Wadi al-Dahal floodplain. Graves are located on almost every segment of the site. A large, robbed grave is located at the summit.

Site No.: 214
Site Name: None
Map Reference: 3051 I, K737
Location on 1:50,000: 308/107
Elevation: ca. Minus 100 m
Inventory Rating: 35
Periods represented: Nab; Byz; Ud.
Description: This is a very light sherd scatter immediately S of Wadi al-Dahal where there is abundant evidence of modern (?), Bedouin camps. There are stone piles (graves ?) nearby.

Site No.: 215
Site Name: Rechemat el-bed (?)
Map Reference: 3051 II, K737
Location on 1:50,000: 308/001
Elevation: Minus 20 m
Inventory Rating: 39
Periods represented: Nab (?); Byz; Byz–Um; Ud.
Description: The site appears to be the remnants of a village on a terrace between Wadis al-Mahash to the N and Wadi al-Ghuweib to the S. The 'Old Road' is immediately to the W. There are wall lines, stone piles, and what could be graves present. The impression is of a domestic unit. Some of the walls are two courses wide and are made of cobble stones. The site is cut by a small, N–S running wadi. The SGNAS took samples from both sides of this wadi. It collected basalt, grinding stone fragments and pieces of glass from the W segment of the site. It noted a number of grinding stone fragments on the E but collected none. One of the structures is divided into partitions here.

Site No.: 216
Site Name: None
Map Reference: 3051 II, K737
Location on 1:50,000: 315/013
Elevation: 0 m
Inventory Rating: 64
Periods represented: Byz; LByz; LByz/Um; Mam; Ud.
Description: This is a village site consisting of many structures along a dissected ridge located ca. 1.5 km E of the 'Old Road' and ca. 0.50 km N of Wadi al-Mahash. For sampling purposes, the SGNAS divided the site into three segments. The SGNAS observed sherds from the top of the ridge, down the slope, to its base. The density of sherds varies from area to area. However, overall it is medium to high. The structural remains vary from 1–2 courses wide by 1–4 courses high. Some buildings are constructed of sandstone cobbles while others are of tabular sandstone. The area has been robbed but only to a minor degree. The SGNAS collected a fragment of a grinding stone from the W end of the site. It noted other fragments in the area but they were not collected. Some areas of the site have been disturbed by pothunters (?), although given the size of the site, this activity may be thought to be minimal. The eastern third of the site is cut off from the remaining segments by a drainage channel which has cut through the ridge. A large structure, with partitions, is located here that has a wall two courses wide filled with rubble/small cobbles. A doorway is located at the NE corner of the structure. Several other small structures are to the E of this large structure. The hill to the S has an L-shaped, structure/stone pile. Several meters away is a square area that is raised ca. 1 m above the ground. It may be a platform (?). This hill was sampled as part of the site.

Site No.: 217
Site Name: None
Map Reference: 3051 II, K737
Location on 1:50,000: 317/014
Elevation: 0 m
Inventory Rating: 48
Periods represented: Chal/EB; Ud, prob EB body sherds.
Description: The site consists of two, interconnected enclosures, each measuring ca. 10 x 13 m, just to the N of Site 216. There appears to be an opening at the E and W end of the more northerly located enclosure. The SGNAS collected both lithics and sherds at the site.

Site No.: 218
Site Name: None
Map Reference: 3051 I, K737
Location on 1:50,000: 283/127
Elevation: Minus 170 m
Inventory Rating: 33
Periods represented: Byz; Ud.
Description: This is a sherd scatter in an area measuring ca. 5 x 5 m on a small drainage between Wadi al-Dahal and Wadi Madsus. The area has small erosional channels cutting it.

Site No.: 219
Site Name: None
Map Reference: 3051 I, K737
Location on 1:50,000: 280/124
Elevation: Minus 170 m
Inventory Rating: 49
Periods represented: Iron II; Byz; Ud.
Description: This site consists of oval rock alignments S, a distance of ca. 75–85 m, of Wadi al-Dahal. One rock alignment measures ca. 10 (N–S) x 6 (E–W) m and is three courses high and one or two courses wide. It is partitioned. Sediments have build up inside it giving it the appearance of a platform. Rocks, in the form of an arc ca. 6–7 m long, are located ca. 60 m to the NW. The SGNAS noted no artifacts associated with it. It is running approximately parallel to the drainages. It does not appear to be a retaining wall or terrace. Sherds from here are being washed to the NNE by erosion. This is where the SGNAS collected most of them.

Site No.: 220
Site Name: None
Map Reference: 3051 I, K737
Location on 1:50,000: 279/118
Elevation: Minus 165
Inventory Rating: 34
Periods represented: Ud.
Description: This is a cemetery of circular cairns ranging from 1–2 m in diameter between Wadi al-Dahal and Wadi Madsus. Some of the cairns are heavily deflated. The SGNAS found neither lithics nor sherds at the site.

Site No.: 221
Site Name: None
Map Reference: 3051 I, K737
Location on 1:50,000: 307/116
Elevation: ca. Minus 90 m
Inventory Rating: 48
Periods represented: Iron II–Edomite; Mod; Ud.
Description: This is a cemetery, camp, and sherd scatter N of Wadi al-Dahal. The west component of the site is a potbust, the middle is a cleared area for a campsite, while the east component is a cemetery consisting of 15 or more graves. Some of the graves are large rectangles, measuring ca. 1 x 2 m, outlined by large stones with pebbles on top; others are mounded with large stone and are 1–1.5 m in diameter. A fourth component to the site is another camp to the E of the cemetery. It has two 'paved' areas measuring ca. 5 m square. One has two partitions in it. To the E is another area outlined in rock but not 'paved'. Their function is unknown. Some military trenches and tent platforms are located to the W and SW. Another Bedouin camp is located to the N. Recent artifacts are associated with it.

Site No.: 222
Site Name: None
Map Reference: 3051 I, K737
Location on 1:50,000: 308/116
Elevation: ca. Minus 190 m
Inventory Rating: 48
Periods represented: Chal.
Description: This is a cemetery and sherd scatter located N of Wadi al-Dahal and Site 221. The two sites are separated by a minor drainage and a hill. The SGNAS noted approximately 10–15 graves in the area. They appear to be recent and undisturbed. Most measure ca. 1–1.5 m in diameter and are capped with a stone but several measure roughly 2–2.5 x 1–1.5 metres. There is one and perhaps more camping areas located around the graves. These too appear to be recent. An area to the E has a rectilinear outline of rock which measures ca. 8 x 4 metres. The sherd scatter appears to be a potbust.

Site No.: 223
Site Name: None
Map References: 3051 I, K737; 3051/I/B/4 (29)
Location on 1:50,000: 330/260
Location on 1:10,000: 1920.5/0389.5
Elevation: Minus 350 m
Inventory Rating: 51
Periods represented: Nab (=ERom); Rom; Byz; Mod; Ud.
Description: This is a sherd scatter among remnants of walls in the bed of Wadi Feifa just to the SW of Feifa, Site 91. The walls are located in an area where there is very dark-coloured, organic-looking soil. There is one large stone wall, possibly the foundation of a building, in the wadi where water presently runs. About 100 m NW, but still in the wadi bed, there are more wall lines and indications of building stones from structures. The stones look Nabataean in cut. The site is located in such an unlikely area! It is possible that it was once on one of the banks of the wadi.

Site No.: 224
Site Name: None
Map Reference: 3051 I, K737
Location on 1:50,000: 308/113
Elevation: ca. Minus 80 m
Inventory Rating: 40
Periods represented: Ud.
Description: This is a lithic scatter at the top of a ridge and its W slope above and to the N of Wadi al-Dahal. There is some evidence of digging at the top (military trenching ?). The site is on the highest point at the mouth of the wadi.

Site No.: 225
Site Name: None
Map Reference: 3051 I, K737
Location on 1:50,000: 309/117
Elevation: ca. Minus 190 m
Inventory Rating: 37
Periods represented: Ud.
Description: This is a potbust N of Wadi al-Dahal.

Site No.: 226
Site Name: None
Map Reference: 3051 II, K737
Location on 1:50,000: 297/026
Elevation: Minus 50 m
Inventory Rating: 49
Periods represented: Byz.
Description: This is a cemetery and sherd scatter NW of Wadi al-Ghuweib and E of the 'Old Road'. The cemetery, which is badly disturbed by robbing, consists of some very large rectangular tombs encircled by walls measuring ca. 7 x 5 metres. The bottom course of these walls is formed of stones dressed on three sides. The inner-facing side is undressed. Fields stones are piled above this foundation course. All three large graves which the SGNAS examined are robbed. There are more graves to the E. Some of these look recent.

Site No.: 227
Site Name: None
Map Reference: 3051 II, K737
Location on 1:50,000: 293/025
Elevation: Minus 60 m
Inventory Rating: 26
Periods represented: Chal/EB; Iron Age; Byz; Ud.
Description: This site consists of two robbed tombs and a light lithic and sherd scatter NE of Wadi al-Ghuweib and W of the 'Old Road'. The tombs are constructed of large, flat stones which have probably been quarried nearby. They are located at the summit of a hill. The SGNAS found most of the lithics on the E and S slopes of the hill. It found a lithic and sherd scatter E, a distance of ca. 100 m, of the summit. There are also small graves (?) in this area.

Site No.: 228
Site Name: Tell Rabet ed-dschamuse (?)
Map Reference: 3051 II, K737
Location on 1:50,000: 308/025
Elevation: Minus 10 m
Inventory Rating: 66
Periods represented: Byz; Abb; Isl; Ud.
Description: This is a series of what appear to be domestic dwellings to the E of the 'Old Road' and Wadi al-Ghuweib. One of the structures measures ca. 2.5 x 3.5 m interiorly. Its walls are ca. 50 cm thick and stand three course high. They are made of undressed stone. The doorway is clearly visible. A second structure is somewhat larger and has a large courtyard, actually larger than the building itself. There is a larger building to the SE with a larger courtyard. The SGNAS noted a very large, basalt, grinding stone. It collected glass, as well as sherds, and noted some 'digging' at two places. Could this site be related to Site 226?

Site No.: 229
Site Name: Khirbet al-Hassiya North
Map Reference: 3051 I, K737
Location on 1:50,000: 304/047
Elevation: Minus 30 m
Inventory Rating: 73
Periods represented: Nab (=LHell–ERom); Nab (=ERom).
Description: This is probably a Nabataean caravanserai. It is located on the N side of Wadi al-Hassiya and just N of the 'Old Road'. It is comprised, for the most part, of a large rectangular structure with rooms on at least the S and W sides. There could also be rooms on the E side. One room, on the W side, is robbed. There is much pottery lying where the digging took place. The walls of the structure, which are made of unhewn stone, are at least 1 m thick. There is a great deal of silt within the structure. There are graves to the N. They are probably recent. There is black-brown soil along Wadi al-Hassiya nearby. It could indicate a midden.

Site No.: 230
Site Name: None
Map Reference: 3051 I, K737
Location on 1:50,000: 303/048
Elevation: Minus 30 m
Inventory Rating: 46
Periods represented: Ud.
Description: This is a cemetery located to the N of Wadi al-Hassiya. One grave measures ca. 1 x 2 m while another measures ca. 1.50 x 1.00 metres. The largest grave is robbed. There is much bone, some burnt, in the excavated material as well as burnt wood. There is also evidence of burning within the robbed grave. The SGNAS noted neither lithics nor sherds at either grave. The graves could be associated with the cemetery to the S mentioned in relation to Site 229.

Site No.: 231
Site Name: None
Map Reference: 3051 I, K737
Location on 1:50,000: 311/049

Elevation: Minus 15 m
Inventory Rating: 45
Periods represented: Rom; Byz; Ott; Ud.
Description: This is a cemetery and sherd scatter N of Wadi al-Hassiya.

Site No.: 232
Site Name: None
Map Reference: 3051 I, K737
Location on 1:50,000: 312/049
Elevation: Minus 15 m
Inventory Rating: 52
Periods represented: Nab–painted; Rom; Byz; Isl; Mod; Ud.
Description: The site is comprised of five structures, some partitioned, N of Wadi al-Hassiya. Some of the stones constituting the walls, which are ca. 75 cm thick, appear to be dressed. The walls of the largest structure still stand five courses high. There are courtyards, facing east. One structure has been 'excavated'. This digging indicates that there is some deposition at the site. The SGNAS noted another structure on the N side of a small tributary wadi to the E of the five main structures. There were very few sherds at the site which leads to the question as to its function. The SGNAS noted a grinding stone at the eastern extremity of the site and many graves, some seemingly modern, to the N and E.

Site No.: 233
Site Name: Khirbet al-Hassiya South
Map Reference: 3051 II, K737
Location on 1:50,000: 313/041
Elevation: Minus 10 m
Inventory Rating: 50
Periods represented: Chal/EB; Byz; Ud.
Description: This is another village/hamlet site consisting of many houses and courtyards, built of unhewn stone, on a plateau immediately S of Wadi al-Hassiya. The courtyards face E. The structures are not as well built as those at Sites 232 and 229. Some of the walls of the structures still stand 4–5 courses high. There appears to be some deposition and some of the interior walls are in good shape. One building has a robbed grave inside. The SGNAS found glass and a piece of bronze in the backfill. Downslope from the structures, a distance of ca. 40 m, the SGNAS collected a medium, Chal/EB sherd scatter in an area measuring ca. 5 x 5 metres.

Site No.: 234
Site Name: None
Map Reference: 3051 II, K737
Location on 1:50,000: 310/043
Elevation: Minus 20 m
Inventory Rating: 42
Periods represented: Ud.
Description: This is a small, stone structure measuring ca. 3 x 3 m in the floodplain of Wadi al-Hassiya to the NW of Site 233. What appears to be an entrance into the structure faces N. There is a great deal of silt within the structure. The SGNAS found neither lithics nor sherds nearby.

Site No.: 235
Site Name: None
Map Reference: 3051 II, K737
Location on 1:50,000: 310/035
Elevation: Minus 20 m
Inventory Rating: 24
Periods represented: Byz.
Description: This is a light sherd scatter in an area measuring ca. 5 x 5 m S of Wadi al-Hassiya and E of the 'Old Road'.

Site No.: 236
Site Name: None
Map Reference: 3051 II, K737
Location on 1:50,000: 314/036
Elevation: 0 m
Inventory Rating: 35

Periods represented: Byz, prob.

Description: This is a circular enclosure measuring ca. 15 m in diameter at the base of a hill with an open view to the W. It is located S of Wadi al-Hassiya and E of the 'Old Road'. The walls of the enclosure measure ca. 50 cm wide and appear to be 4–5 courses high. The stones are undressed and are, for the most part, 20–30 cm in size. There is another enclosure (or arc) to the W which appears to be interconnected but incomplete. There is a pile of stone, a grave (?), to the W.

Site No.:   237
Site Name: None
Map References: 3051 I, K737; 3051/I/B/4 (29)
Location on 1:50,000:   345/262
Location on 1:10,000:   1935.5/0392
Elevation: Minus 305 m
Inventory Rating: 51
Periods represented: Iron I; Hell; Nab/Rom; Ud.
Description: The site consists of large tombs and a sherd scatter on a spur ca. 200 m N of Feifa, Sites 75 and 76, and ca. 200 m E of the highway. The tombs extend to the E and S.

Site No.:   238
Site Name: None
Map Reference: 3051 I, K737
Location on 1:50,000:   360/301.5
Elevation: Minus 320 m
Inventory Rating: 35
Periods represented: EB.
Description: This is probably only a potbust in an area measuring ca. 10 x 10 m S of Wadi Madsus al-Shamali.

Site No.:   239
Site Name: None
Map Reference: 3051 I, K737
Location on 1:50,000:   371/300
Elevation: Minus 275 m
Inventory Rating: 30
Periods represented: Isl; Ud.
Description: This is a light lithic and sherd scatter and an enclosure, measuring ca. 10 (E–W) x 15 (N–S) m, in an area ca. 30 x 30 m immediately to the N of Wadi Madsus al-Shamali. The SGNAS noted many graves, some possibly recent in the area. There is also evidence of camping, some recent, nearby.

Site No.:   240
Site Name: None
Map Reference: 3051 I, K737
Location on 1:50,000:   369.9/299.7
Elevation: Minus 280 m
Inventory Rating: 48
Periods represented: Iron II (?); Nab (?); Ud.
Description: This is an enclosure measuring ca. 17 m in diameter on the N side of Wadi Madsus al-Shamali. The walls of the structure, of unhewn stone, are in good shape. They still stand ca. 50 cm high, especially on the E side. There is a great deal of silt within the structure. There is what appears to be an entrance, measuring ca. 2 m wide, in its N wall. The SGNAS collected most of the sherds N of this entrance (?). It found very few sherds within the enclosure itself. The site provides an excellent view to the S, W, and N. The view to the E is blocked by a slight rise.

Appendix 2

Samples of SGNAS Data Collection Sheets

Site Sheet

Ceramic Sample Sheet

Lithic Sample Sheet

Inventory Rating Sheet

SGNAS SITE SHEET

SITE NO: SITE NAME:
DATE: COORDINATES:
MAP REF: AIR PHOTO REF:
ELEVATION: INVENTORY RATING:
TIME SPENT: RECORDER:

Dimensions: L   W   A   H   C   D   D   Dep.

SITE:	City	Mill	Tower	Village	Factory-Site	Stone-Fence
	Camp	Dam	Mound	Fort	Tower/Tomb	Terrace-Site
	Qsar	Road	Hamlet	Quarry	Kill-Site	Butchering-Site
	Cemetery	Cave	Tomb	Petroglyph	Sherd-Scatter	Lithic-Scatter
	Farm	Bridge	Rock-Shelter	Other		

Comments:

CLUSTER:	Citadel	Villa	Temple-C	Residential-Ward	Domestic-Cluster	Courtyard
	Factory	Lower-Town	Forum	Other		

Comments:

FEATURE:	Kiln	Cave	Temple	Def.Wall	Magazine	Slag/Ore
	Scatter	Road	Tomb	House	Paddock	Monument
	Altar	Grave	Stable	Hearth	Bone-Scatter	Debitage-Sc
	Midden	Boulder/PebbleSc		Other		

Comments:

WATER:	Stream	Spring	Well	Cistern	Aqueduct	Dam
	Other					

Comments:

TERRAINE:	Plain	Plateau	Hill	Slope	Terrace	Pos-Lake
	Dune	Alluvial-Fan	Ridge	Spur	Valley	Levee
	Oasis	Pos-Beach	Sabkha	Cliff	Saddle	Other

Comments:

SURFACE:	BareRock	Barren	Cultivation	Sand	Swamp	Agricultural

Other Comments:

PERIOD:	LPL	MPL	UPL	EPL	PPNL	PNL	CHAL
	EB	MB	LB	IRON	IRONI	IRONII	PER
	HELL	NAB	ROM	BYZ	EISL	LISL	MOD
	UD						

CATCHMENT:	r=1 km	r=2 km	r=3 km	r=4 km	r=5 km	r=? km

STRATIFICATION:	None	Unknown	Prob Disturbed	Prob Intact	Observed	Sketch

Comments:

PHOTOGRAPHS:	Time	B/W	Color	Dir	Staff

SAMPLE NO (S):	Ceramic:	Purposive	Random	Total
	Lithic:	Purposive	Random	Total

Other (Please Specify)

Comments:

COMMENTS AND SKETCH (use back of sheet):

SGNAS CERAMIC SHEET

SITE NO: SAMPLE NO:
DATE: NO OF BAGS:
MAP REF: COORDINATES:
TIME SPENT: RECORDER:

COLLECTION: Purposive   Randon   Total   Other

                   Comments:

FIELD READING

PNL	CHAL	CHAL-EB	EBI	EBI-II	EBII	EBII-III	EBIII
EBIII-IV	EBIV	EB	MBI	MBII	MB	MB-LB	LBI
LBI-II	LBII	LB	LB-IRON	LB-IRONIA	LB-IRONI	IRONIA	IRONIC
IRONI	IRONI-II	IRONI-IIA	IRONIC-IIA	IRONIIA	IRONIIB	IRONIIC	IRONII
IRON	PER	HELL	NAB	NAB-ROM	EROM	LROM	ROM
LROM-BYZ	EBYZ	LBYZ	BYZ	BYZ-UM	UM	EISL	LISL
AYY-MAM	MAM	OTT	OTT-MOD	LOTT-MOD	MOD	UD	

DISTURBANCE:

        None   Eroded Slope   Water-Borne   Deflated   Plowed   Excavated   Other

        Comments:

DENSITY: High   Medium   Low   Other

PHOTOGRAPHS: In Situ   Laboratory

REF PAGES: Site   Lithic   Inventory

REGISTERED:

DRAWN:

STORAGE:

COMMENTS (use back of sheet if necessary)

SGNAS LITHIC SHEET

SITE NO: SAMPLE NO:
DATE: NO OF BAGS:
MAP REF: COORDINATES:
TIME SPENT: RECORDER:

COLLECTION: Purposive   Random   Total   Other

                                Comments:

FIELD READING

LPL   LPL-MPL   MPL   MPL-UPL   UPL   UPL-EPL   PL
EPL   EPL-PPNL   PPNL   PNL   PNL-CHAL   CHAL   CHAL-EB
EB   LATE   UD

DISTURBANCE: None   Eroded Slope   Water-Borne   Deflated   Plowed
                                Excavated   Other

                                Comments:

DENSITY: High   Light   Medium   Other

PHOTOGRAPHS: In Situ   Laboratury

REFERENCE PAGES: Site   Ceramic   Inventory

REGISTERED:

DRAWN:

STORAGE:

COMMENTS:

SGNAS INVENTORY RATING

SITE NO: SITE NAME:
DATE: RECORDER:

1.   ARCHAEOLOGICAL IMPORTANCE OF SITE (55):

        Rarity (15)   _____
        Preservation (15)   _____
        Stratification (10)   _____
        Context (15)   _____
        IMPORTANCE   _____

2.   URGENCY FOR EXCAVATION (20):

        Natural Threat   _____
        Human Interference   _____
        URGENCY   _____

3.   EXCAVATION PRACTICABILITY (20):

        Accessibility (5)   _____
        Accommodations (5)   _____
        Labour (5)   _____
        Food, Water, Electricity, etc. (5)
        EXCAVATION   _____

4.   TOURISTIC POTENTIAL (5):

        Touristic (5)   _____

        INVENTORY RATING   _____

        TOTAL RATING (100)   _____

References

Abbott, R. T. 1979 *Kingdom of the Seashell.* New York: Crown.

Abel, F.-M. 1931 Inscription Chrétienne du Ghôr es-Sâfi. *Revue Biblique* 40: 95–98.

    1967 *Géographie de la Palestine.* Tome 2. *Géographie Politique. Les Villes.* Troisième Edition. Paris: J. Gabalda et Cie.

Adams, R.B. 1991 The Wadi Fidan Project, Jordan, 1991. *Levant* 23: 181–83.

Adan-Bayewitz, D. 1987 The Pottery from the Late Byzantine Building and its Implications (Stratum 4). Pp. 92–129 in *Excavations at Caesarea Maritima 1975, 1976, 1979 – Final Report,* eds. L. I. Levine and E. Netzer. *Qedem* 21. Jerusalem: The Hebrew University.

Albright, W. F. 1924 The Archaeological Results of an Expedition to Moab and the Dead Sea. *Bulletin of the American Schools of Oriental Research* 14: 2–12.

    1926 The Jordan Valley in the Bronze Age. Pp. 13–74 in *The Annual of the American Schools of Oriental Research* 6 (1924–1925), ed. B. W. Bacon. New Haven, CT: American Schools of Oriental Research.

Aldred, C. 1978 *Jewels of the Pharaohs.* New York: Ballantine.

Alt, A. 1935 Aus der 'Araba II. Römische Kastelle und Strassen. *Zeitschrift des Deutschen Palästina-Vereins* 58: 1–59.

Alt, A., and Wickert, L. 1935 Aus der 'Araba III. Inschriften und Felszeichnungen. *Zeitschrift des Deutschen Palästina-Vereins* 58: 60–74.

Anonymous
    1965 *East Bank Jordan Water Resources.* The Hashemite Kingdom of Jordan Central Water Authority. Report by Sir M. Macdonald and Pts. 4 vols.

    1973 *Mujib and Southern Ghors Irrigation Project Updated Report,* March 1973. Hunting Technical Services LTD, 6 Elstree Way, Boreharn Wood, Hertfordshire, England. Mimeo.

    1977 *Mujib and Southern Ghors Irrigation Project, Preliminary Review Report, Water Resources Supplement.* Binnie and Jouzy Arup Bookers, consultants. Mimeo.

Ashtor, E. 1977 Levantine Sugar Industry in the Later Middle Ages – An Example of Technological Decline. *Israel Oriental Studies* 7: 226–80.

Avi-Yonah, M. 1954 *The Madaba Mosaic Map: With Introduction and Commentary.* Jerusalem: The Israel Exploration Society.

    1977 Medeba (Madaba). Pp. 819–23 in vol. 3 of *Encyclopedia of Archaeological Excavations in the Holy Land,* eds. M. Avi-Yonah and E. Stern. Jerusalem: The Israel Exploration Society and Massada Press.

Bachmann, H.-G., and Hauptmann, A. 1984 Zur alten Kupfergewinnung in Fenan und Hirbet en-Nahas im Wadi Arabah in Südjordanien. Ein Vorbericht. *Der Anschnitt (Zeitschrift für kunst und kultur im Bergrau)* 36.4: 110–23.

Baly, T. J. C. 1962 Pottery. Pp. 270–303 in *Excavations at Nessana (Auja Hafir, Palestine).* Vol. 1, ed. H. D. Colt. London: British School of Archaeology in Jerusalem.

Banning, E. B. 1988 Methodology. Pp. 13–25 in *The Wadi el Hasa Archaeological Survey 1979–1983, West-Central Jordan,* ed. B. MacDonald. Waterloo: Wilfrid Laurier University Press.

Bar-Adon, P. 1962 Expedition C-The Cave of the Treasure. *Israel Exploration Journal* 12.3–4: 215–26.

Barag, D. 1967 The Glass. Pp. 65–72 in *Excavations at Shavei Zion: The Early Christian Church,* ed. M. W. Prausnitz. Rome: Centro per le Antichità e la Storia dell'arte del Vicino Oriente.

    1974 A Tomb Cave of the Byzantine Period Near Netiv ha-Lamed He. *Atiqot* (Hebrew Series) 7:13 and 81–87.

Bar-Nathan, R., and Adato, M. 1986 B. Pottery. Pp. 160–75 in *Excavations at Caesarea Maritima 1975, 1976, 1979 – Final Report,* eds. L. I. Levine and E. Netzer. *Qedem* 21. Jerusalem: The Hebrew University.

Bartlett, J. R. 1972 The Rise and Fall of the Kingdom of Edom. *Palestine Exploration Quarterly* 104: 26–37.

    1979 From Edomites to Nabataeans. *Palestine Exploration Quarterly* 111: 53–66.

    1989 *Edom and the Edomites.* (Journal for the Study of the Old Testament, Supplement Series 77). Sheffield: Sheffield Academic Press.

Bar-Yosef, O. 1981 The 'Pre Pottery Neolithic' Period in the Southern Levant. Pp. 555–69 in *Prehistoire du Levant* (CNRS Colloque 598), eds. J. Cauvin and P. Sanlaville. C.N.R.S.: Paris.

Bar-Yosef, O., *et al.* 1977 The Nawamis Near 'Ein Huderah (Eastern Sinai). *Israel Exploration Journal* 27.2–3: 65–88.

Bass, G. F. 1984 The Nature of the Serçe Limani Glass. *Journal of Glass Studies* 26: 64–69.

Baur, P. V. C. 1938 Other Glass Vessels. Pp. 513–46 in *Gerasa: City of the Decapolis,* ed. C. H. Kraeling. New Haven, CT: American Schools of Oriental Research.

Beck, H. C. 1928 Classification and Nomenclature of Beads and Pendants. *Archaeologia* 87. (Reprinted as a book in 1981 by George Shumway, York, PA.)

Begin, Z., Ehrlich, A. and Nathan, Y. 1974 Lake Lisan: The Pleistocene Precursor of the Dead Sea. *Bulletin of the Geological Survey of Israel* 63: 1–30.

Beit Arieh, I. 1981 An Early Bronze Age II Site Near Sheikh 'Awad in Southern Sinai. *Tel Aviv* 8.2: 95–127.

    1982 An Early Bronze Age II Site Near the Feiran Oasis in Southern Sinai. *Tel Aviv* 9.2: 146–56.

    1988 New Light on the Edomites. *Biblical Archaeology Review* 14.2: 28–41.

Beit Arieh, I., and Cresson, B. 1985 An Edomite Ostracon from Horvat 'Uza. *Tel Aviv* 12.1: 96–101.

Beit Arieh, I., and Gophna, R. 1977 A Note on a Chalcolithic Site in Wadi Araba. *Tel Aviv* 4.3–4: 105–09.

Bennett, C.-M. 1971 An Archaeological Survey of Biblical Edom. *Perspective* 12: 35–44.

    1973a Excavations at Buseirah, Southern Jordan, 1971: A Preliminary Report. *Levant* 5: 1–11.

    1973b The Third Season of Excavations at Buseirah. *Annual of the Department of Antiquities of Jordan* 18: 85.

    1974 Excavations at Buseirah, Southern Jordan, 1972:

Preliminary Report. *Levant* 6: 1–24.

1975   Excavations at Buseirah, Southern Jordan, 1973: Third Preliminary Report. *Levant* 7: 1–19.

1976   Edom. Pp. 251–52 in *The Interpreter's Dictionary of the Bible*, Supplementary Volume, ed. L. R. Bailey. Nashville: Abingdon.

1977   Excavations at Buseirah, Southern Jordan, 1974: Fourth Preliminary Report. *Levant* 9: 1–10.

1980   Soundings at Dhra', Jordan. *Levant* 12: 30–39.

1984   Excavations at Tawilan in Southern Jordan, 1982. *Levant* 16: 1–23.

Benvenisti, M. 1970 *The Crusaders in the Holy Land.* Jerusalem: Israel Universities Press.

Betts, A. V. G. 1988 The Black Desert Survey. Prehistoric Sites and Subsistence Strategies in Eastern Jordan. Pp. 369–91 in *The Prehistory of Jordan*, eds. A. N. Garrard and H. G. Gebel. B.A.R. International Series 396 (i,ii): Oxford.

Birger, R. 1981 Pottery and Miscellaneous Finds of the Byzantine Period. Pp.75–77 in *Greater Herodium*, ed. E. Netzer. *Qedem* 13. Jerusalem: The Hebrew University.

Bodenheimer, F. S. 1960 *Animal and Man in Bible Lands.* Collection de Travaux de l'Académie Internationale d'Histoire des Sciences 10. Leiden: E. J. Brill.

Bottema, S., and Van Zeist, W. 1981 Palynological Evidence for the Climate History of the Near East. Pp. 111–32 in *Préhistoire du Levant* (CNRS Colloque 598), eds. J. Cauvin and P. Sanlaville. C.N.R.S.: Paris.

Boucharlat, R., and Labrousse, A. 1979 Une Sucrerie d'époque islamique sur la rive droite du Chaour à Suse, I: Description et Essai d'interpretation des structures. *Cahiers de la Délegation Archéologique française en Iran* 10:155–76.

Brill, R. H. 1963 Ancient Glass. *Scientific American* 209.5.

Brosh, N. 1986 Pottery of the 8th–13th Centuries C.E. (Strata 1–3). Pp. 66–89 in *Excavations at Caesarea Maritima 1975, 1976, 1979 – Final Report*, eds. L. I. Levine and E. Netzer. *Qedem* 21. Jerusalem: The Hebrew University.

Brown, R. M. 1987 A 12th Century A.D. Sequence from Southern Transjordan: Crusader and Ayyubid Occupation at el-Wu'eira. *Annual of the Department of Antiquities of Jordan* 31: 267–88.

1988a 'Report of the 1987 Excavations at Kerak Castle: The Mamluk Palace Reception Hall.' Unpublished report submitted to the Department of Antiquities of Jordan.

1988b Summary Report of the 1986 Excavations: Late Islamic Shobak. *Annual of the Department of Antiquities of Jordan* 32: 225–46.

Brünnow, R. E., and Domaszewski, A. von 1904 *Die Provincia Arabia: Auf grund zweier in den Jahren 1897 und 1898 unternommenen Reisen und der Berichte früherer Reisender. Erster Band: Die Römerstrasse von Madeba über Petra und Odruh bis el-'Akaba.* Strassburg: Karl J. Trübner.

Brunton, G. 1927 *Qau and Badari I.* London: British School of Archaeology in Egypt and Bernard Quaritch.

1928   *Qau and Badari II.* London: British School of Archaeology in Egypt and Bernard Quaritch.

Burckhardt, J. L. 1822 *Travels in Syria and the Holy Land.* London: John Murray.

Burian, F., and Friedman, E. 1979 A Typology of Arrowheads and Sickle Blades and its Chronological Implications. *MeT'kufat haEven*

16:1–16.

Callaway, J. A. 1972 *The Early Bronze Age Sanctuary at Ai (et Tell)*, No. I. London: Bernard Quaritch.

Canova, R. 1954 *Iscrizioni e Monumenti Protocristiani del Paese di Moab.* Roma: Pontificio Istituto di Archeologia Cristiana.

Da Costa, K. 1989 'The Lamps from Deir 'Ain 'Abata: 1988 Season.' Unpublished report submitted to the Department of Antiquities of Jordan.

Clark, G. A. 1984 The Negev Model for Paleoclimatic Change and Human Adaptation in the Levant. *Annual of the Department of Antiquities of Jordan* 28: 225–48.

1986   *Symbols of Excellence.* Cambridge: Cambridge University Press.

1988   Some Thoughts on the Southern Extent of the Lisan Lake as seen from the Jordan side. *Bulletin of the American Schools of Oriental Research* 272: 42–43.

1992   Wadi Hasa Paleolithic Settlement Patterns: Ethnography-Based Transhumance Models Generalized and Tested. *Studies in the History and Archaeology of Jordan IV*, ed. G. Bisheh. Amman: Department of Antiquities.

Clark, G. A., *et al.* 1988 Excavation at Middle, Upper and Epipaleolithic Sites in the Wadi Hasa, West-Central Jordan. Pp. 209–85 in *The Prehistory of Jordan*, eds. A. N. Garrard and H. G. Gebel. B.A.R. International Series 396 (i,ii): Oxford.

Clermont-Ganneau, C. 1886 Segor, Gomorrah, and Sodom. *Palestine Exploration Fund, Quarterly Statement,* 19–21.

Cleveland, R. L. 1960 The Excavation of the Conway High Place (Petra) and Soundings at Khirbet Ader. Pp. 55–97 in *The Annual of the American Schools of Oriental Research* 34–35 (1954–1956). New Haven, CT: American Schools of Oriental Research.

Cohen, R., and Dever, W. G. 1978a H. Be'er Resisim. *Israel Exploration Journal* 28.4: 263–64.

1978b Preliminary Report of the Pilot Season of 'Central Negev Highlands Project'. *Bulletin of the American Schools of Oriental Research* 232: 29–45.

1979   Preliminary Report of the Second Season of the 'Central Negev Highlands Project'. *Bulletin of the American Schools of Oriental Research* 236: 41–60.

1981   Preliminary Report of the Third and Final Season of the 'Central Negev Highlands Project'. *Bulletin of the American Schools of Oriental Research* 243: 57–77.

Coinman, N.; Clark G. A.; and Lindly, J. 1986 Prehistoric Hunter-Gatherer Settlement in the Wadi Hasa, West-Central Jordan. Pp. 129–69 in *The End of the Paleolithic in the Old World*, ed. L. G. Strauss. B.A.R. International Series 284: Oxford.

Coogan, M. D. 1984 Numeira 1981. *Bulletin of the American Schools of Oriental Research* 255: 75–81.

Corbo, V., and Loffreda, S. 1981 Nuove scoperte alla Fortezza di Macheronte. Rapporta preliminare alla quarta campagna di scavo: 7 settembre–10 ottobre 1981. *Liber Annuus* 31: 257–86.

Crowfoot, G. M. 1932 Pots, Ancient and Modern. *Palestine Exploration Fund, Quarterly Statement* 64: 179–87.

1957   Glass. Pp. 403–22 in *Samaria-Sebaste: The*

Objects from Samaria. Reports of the Work of the Joint Expedition in 1931–1933 and of the British Expedition in 1935, No. 3, by J. W. Crowfoot; G. M. Crowfoot; and K. M. Kenyon. London: Palestine Exploration Fund.

Crowfoot, J. W.; Crowfoot, G. M.; and Kenyon, K. M. 1957 *Samaria-Sebaste: The Objects from Samaria.* Reports of the Work of the Joint Expedition in 1931–1933 and of the British Expedition in 1935, No. 3. London: Palestine Exploration Fund.

Crowfoot Payne, J. 1983 The Flint Industries of Jericho. Pp. 622–759 in *Excavations at Jericho V*, eds. K. M. Kenyon and T. A. Holland. British School of Archaeology in Jerusalem: Jerusalem.

Dale, G. 1986 London Correspondence. *The Bead Forum* 8: 4–7.

Dana, E. S., and Ford, W. E. 1932 *A Textbook of Mineralogy.* 4th edition. New York: John Wiley and Sons.

Danin, A. 1985 Palaeoclimates in Israel: Evidence from Weathering Patterns of Stones in and near Archaeological Sites. *Bulletin of the American Schools of Oriental Research* 259: 33–43.

Davidson, G. R. 1940 A Mediaeval Glass-Factory at Corinth. *American Journal of Archaeology* 44: 297–324.

1952 *Corinth: The Minor Objects.* Vol. 12. Princeton, NJ: The American School of Classical Studies at Athens.

de Contenson, H. 1956 La céramique chalcolithique de Beersheba; étude typologique. *Israel Exploration Journal* 6.3: 163–79; 6.4: 226–38.

Delougaz, P., and Haines, R. C. 1960 *A Byzantine Church at Khirbat al-Karak.* Oriental Institute Publications 85. Chicago: The University of Chicago Press.

Dever, W. G. 1973 The EB IV–MB I Horizon in Transjordan and Southern Palestine. *Bulletin of the American Schools of Oriental Research* 210: 37–63.

1975 A Middle Bronze I Cemetery at Khirbet el-Kirmil. Pp. 18–33 in Nelson Glueck Memorial Volume. *Eretz-Israel*, Vol. 12, ed. B. Mazar. Jerusalem: The Israel Exploration Society.

1976 Gezer. Pp. 428–43 in vol. 2 of *Encyclopedia of Archaeological Excavations in the Holy Land*, ed. M. Avi-Yonah. Jerusalem: The Israel Exploration Society and Massada Press.

1980 New Vistas on the EB IV ('MB I') Horizon in Syria-Palestine. *Bulletin of the American Schools of Oriental Research* 237: 35–64.

Dollfus, G., *et al.* 1988 Abu Hamid, an Early Fourth Millennium Site in the Jordan Valley. Preliminary Results. Pp. 567–601 in *The Prehistory of Jordan*, eds. A. N. Garrard and H. G. Gebel. B.A.R. International Series 396 (i, ii): Oxford.

Donner, H., and Cüppers, H. 1977 *Die Mosaikkarte von Madeba, I, Tafelband.* Wiesbaden: Otto Harrassowitz.

Donner, H., and Knauf, E. A. 1985 Ghor es-Safi et Wadi el-Kerak (1983). *Revue Biblique* 92: 429–30.

1986 Ghor as-Safi – Wadi al-Karak 1983. Archiv für Orientforschung 33: 266–67.

Donahue, J., and Beynon, D. E. 1988 Geologic History of the Wadi el Hasa Survey Area. Pp. 26–39 in *The Wadi el Hasa Archaeological Survey 1979–1983, West-Central Jordan*, ed. B. MacDonald. Wilfrid Laurier University Press: Waterloo.

Dubin, L.S. 1987 *The History of Beads.* New York: Harry N. Abrams.

Dunand, M. 1945 *Byblia Grammata: Documents et recherches sur le developpement de l'écriture en Phénicie.* Beyrouth.

1973 *Fouilles de Byblos Tome V: L'Architecture, les tombes, le matériel domestique, des origines néolitiques à l'avenement.* Paris. Librairie d'Amérique et d'Orient, Adrièn Maissoneuve.

Dussart, O. 1986 Analyse du matériel de verre. Pp. 74–76 in *Jerash Archaeological Project* 1981–1983. Vol. 1, ed. F. Zayadine. Amman: Department of Antiquities.

Edwards, I. E. S.; Gadd, C. J.; and Hammond, N. G. L., eds. 1970 Prolegomena and Prehistory. Vol. 1, Part 1 in *The Cambridge Ancient History.* Third Edition. Cambridge: Cambridge University Press.

Edwards, P. C., *et al.* 1988 Late Pleistocene Prehistory in the Wadi al-Hammeh, Jordan Valley. Pp. 525–65 in *The Prehistory of Jordan*, eds. A. N. Garrard and H. G. Gebel. B.A.R. International Series 396 (i, ii): Oxford.

Epstein, C. 1984 A Pottery Neolithic Site near Tel Qatif. *Israel Exploration Journal* 34.4: 209–19.

Erdmann, E. 1977 Die Glasfunde von Mezad Tamar (Kasr Gehainije). *Saalburg-Jahrbuch* 34: 98–146.

Feig, N. 1985 Pottery, Glass, and Coins from Magen. *Bulletin of the American Schools of Oriental Research* 258: 33–40.

Feinberg, H. S., ed. 1979 *Guide to Shells.* New York: Simon and Schuster.

Fitzgerald, G. M. 1931 *Beth-Shan Excavations 1921–1923: The Arab and Byzantine Levels.* Philadelphia: The University of Pennsylvania Museum.

Fleischer, M. 1987 *Glossary of Mineral Species.* Bowie, MD: Mineralogical Record.

Fontaine, A.-L. 1952 Enquête sur Péluse. *Bulletin de la Société d'Etudes historiques de l'Isthme de Suez*, 4. Cairo: Imprimerie le Scribe Egyptien S.A.E.

Forbes, R. J. 1964 *Studies in Ancient Technology.* Vol. 1. Second Edition. Leiden: E. J. Brill.

Francis, P. 1982 Bead Report Part VII: When India Was Beadmaker to the World. *Ornament* 6/2.

1987 Some Comments on Mulberry and Twisted Square Beads. *The Bead Forum*, 11: 8–12.

Frank, F. 1934 Aus der 'Araba I: Reiseberichte. *Zeitschrift des Deutschen Palästina-Vereins* 57: 191–280.

Franken, H. H. 1969 *Excavations at Tell Deir 'Alla. I: A Stratigraphical and Analytical Study of the Early Iron Age Pottery.* Leiden: E. J. Brill.

Frolich, B., and Lancaster, W. J. 1985 'Archaeological Survey in Wadi al 'Arabah, Jordan.' Unpublished report submitted to the Assistant Secretary for Science, Smithsonian Institution, Washington, D.C..

Garrard, A. N., *et al.* 1985 Prehistoric Environment and Settlement in the Azraq Basin. A Report on the 1982 Survey Season. *Levant* 17: 1–28.

1988 Summary of Palaeoenvironmental and Prehistoric Investigations in the Azraq Basin. Pp. 311–37 in *The Prehistory of Jordan*: The State of Research in 1986, eds. A. N. Garrard and H. G. Gebel. B.A.R. International Series 396 (i,ii): Oxford.

Gawlikowski, M., and Musa, A. 1986 The Church of Bishop Marianos. Pp. 137–62 in *Jerash Archaeological Project 1981–1983.* Vol. 1, ed. F. Zayadine. Amman: Department of Antiquities.

Gebel, H. G., *et al.* 1988 Preliminary Report on the First Season of Excavations at the Late Aceramic

Neolithic Site of Basta. Pp. 101–34 in *The Prehistory of Jordan*, eds. A. N. Garrard and H. G. Gebel. B.A.R. International Series 396 (i,ii): Oxford.

Gemological Institute of America 1980 Glass Imitations. *Colored Stones* 37.

Gichon, M. 1974 Fine Byzantine Wares from the South of Israel. *Palestine Exploration Quarterly* 106: 119–39.

Gilead, I. 1988 The Chalcolithic Period in the Levant. *Journal of World Prehistory* 2.4: 397–443.

Gitin, S. 1975 Middle Bronze I 'Domestic' Pottery at Jebel Qa'aqir – A Ceramic Inventory of Cave G23. Pp. 46–62 in Nelson Glueck Memorial Volume. *Eretz-Israel*, Vol. 12, ed. B. Mazar. Jerusalem: The Israel Exploration Society.

Glueck, N. 1935 *Explorations in Eastern Palestine, II*. The Annual of the American Schools of Oriental Research 15 (1934–1935). New Haven, CT: American Schools of Oriental Research.

1937 An Aerial Reconnaissance in Southern Transjordan. *Bulletin of the American Schools of Oriental Research* 67: 19–26.

Gold, V. R. 1958 The Mosaic Map of Madeba. *The Biblical Archaeologist* 23: 50–71.

Goldberg, P. 1981 Late Quaternary Stratigraphy of Israel: An Eclectic View. Pp. 55–66 in *Préhistoire du Levant* (CNRS Colloque 598), eds. J. Cauvin and P. Sanlaville. C.N.R.S.: Paris.

Goldberg, P., and Bar-Yosef, O. 1982 Environmental and Archaeological Evidence for Climatic Change in the Southern Levant. Pp. 399–414 in *Paleoclimates, Paleoenvironments, and Human Communities in the Eastern Mediterranean in Later Prehistory*, eds. J. L. Bintliff and W. Van Zeist. B.A.R. International Series 133: Oxford.

Goldberg, P., and Rosen, A. M. 1987 Early Holocene Paleoenvironments of Israel. Pp. 23–33 in *Shiqmim I*, ed. T. E. Levy. B.A.R. International Series 356 (i,ii): Oxford.

Grose, D. F. 1977 Early Blown Glass: The Western Evidence. *Journal of Glass Studies* 19: 9–29.

1979 The Syro-Palestinian Glass Industry in the Later Hellenistic Period. *MUSE* 13: 54–67.

1984 Glass Forming Methods in Classical Antiquity: Some Considerations. *Journal of Glass Studies* 26: 25–34.

Guy, P. L. O., and Engberg, R. M. 1938 *Megiddo Tombs*. Oriental Institute Publications Vol. 33. Chicago: The University of Chicago Press.

Hackin, J. 1939 Recherches archéologiques à Begram. Mémoires de la Délégation *Archéologique Française en Afghanistan* 9. Paris: Les Editions d'Art et d'Histoire.

Hamarneh, S. 1977–78 Cultivation of Sugar Cane and Its Manufacture Among the Muslim Arabs. *Annual of the Department of Antiquities of Jordan* 22: 12–19 (in Arabic).

al-Hamdani 1884 *Géographie der Arabischen Halbinsel*, ed. D. H. Müller. Leiden: E. J. Brill.

Hammond, P. C. 1959 The Nabataean Bitumen Industry at the Dead Sea. *The Biblical Archaeologist* 22: 40–48.

Hanbury-Tenison, J. W. 1986 *The Late Chalcolithic to Early Bronze I Transition in Palestine and Transjordan*. B.A.R. International Series 311: Oxford.

Harden, D. B. 1934 Glass from Kish. *Iraq* 1: 131–36.

1936 Roman *Glass from Karanis*. Ann Arbor:

University of Michigan Press.

1955 The Glass Found at Soba. Pp. 60–76 in *Excavations at Soba*, eds. P. L. Shinnie and D. B. Harden. Sudan Antiquities Service Occasional Papers 3. Khartoum (reprinted 1961).

1962 Glass. Pp. 76–91 in *Excavations at Nessana (Auja Hafir, Palestine)*. Vol. 1, ed. H. D. Colt. London: British School of Archaeology in Jerusalem.

1971 Ancient Glass, III: Post Roman. *Archaeological Journal* 128: 78–117.

1978 Glass. Pp. 83–89 in *Debira West*, eds. P. L. Shinnie and M. Shinnie. Warminster, England: Aris and Philips.

Harding, G. L. 1953 *Four Tomb Groups from Jordan*. Palestine Exploration Fund Annual 6. London: The Palestine Exploration Fund.

Harlan, J. R. 1981 Natural Resources of the Southern Ghor. Pp. 155–64 in *The Southeastern Dead Sea Plain Expedition: An Interim Report of the 1977 Season*, eds. W. E. Rast and R. T. Schaub. The Annual of the American Schools of Oriental Research 46 (1979). Cambridge, MA: American Schools of Oriental Research.

1982 The Garden of the Lord: A Plausible Reconstruction of Natural Resources of Southern Jordan in Early Bronze Age. *Paléorient* 8.1: 71–78.

1985 The Early Bronze Age Environment of the Southern Ghor and the Moab Plateau. Pp. 125–29 in *Studies in the History and Archaeology of Jordan II*, ed. A. Hadidi. Amman: Department of Antiquities.

1988 Natural Resources. Pp. 40–47 in *The Wadi el Hasa Archaeological Survey, 1979–1983, West-Central Jordan*, ed. B. MacDonald. Waterloo: Wilfrid Laurier University Press.

Hart, H. C. 1885 A Naturalist's Journey to Sinai, Petra, and South Palestine. *Palestine Exploration Fund, Quarterly Statement*, 231–86.

Hart, S. 1986 Some Preliminary Thoughts on Settlement in Southern Edom. *Levant* 18: 51–58.

1987 Five Soundings in Southern Jordan. *Levant* 19: 33–47.

Hauptmann, A. 1986 Archaeometallurgical and Mining-Archaeological Studies in the Eastern 'Arabah, Feinan Area, 2nd Season. *Annual of the Department of Antiquities of Jordan* 30: 415–19.

1989 The Earliest Periods of Copper Metallurgy in Feinan. In *Archäometallurgie der Alten Welt/Old World Archaeology*, eds. A. Hauptmann; E. Pernicka; and G. A. Wagner. *Der Anschnitt*, Beiheft (in press).

Hauptmann, A., and Weisgerber, G. 1987 Archaeometallurgical and Mining-Archaeological Investigations in the Area of Feinan, Wadi 'Arabah (Jordan). *Annual of the Department of Antiquities of Jordan* 31: 419–37.

Hauptmann, A.; Weisgerber, G.; and Knauf, E. A. 1985 Archäometallurgische und bergbauarchäologische Untersuchungen im Gebiet von Fenan, Wadi Arabah (Jordanien). *Der Anschnitt (Zeitschrift für kunst und kultur im Bergbau)* 37.5–6: 163–95.

Hayes, J. W. 1972 *Late Roman Pottery*. London: The British School at Rome.

1975 *Roman and Pre-Roman Glass in the Royal Ontario Museum: A Catalogue*. Toronto: Royal Ontario Museum.

Hayne, W. A. 1873 On the Flora of Moab. Pp. 400–10

(Appendix C) in H.B. Tristram, *The Land of Moab: Travels and Discoveries on the East Side of the Dead Sea and the Jordan*. New York: Harper.

Hennessy, J. B. 1969 Preliminary Report on a First Season of Excavations at Teleilat Ghassul. *Levant* 1: 1–24.

1970 Excavations at Samaria-Sebaste, 1968. *Levant* 2: 1–21.

Henry, D. O. 1982 The Prehistory of Southern Jordan and Relationships with the Levant. *Journal of Field Archaeology* 9.4:417–44.

1986 The Prehistory and Paleoenvironments of Jordan: An Overview. *Paléorient* 12.2: 5–26.

1988 Summary of Prehistoric and Palaeoenvironmental Research in the Northern Hisma. Pp. 7–37 in *The Prehistory of Jordan*, eds. A. N. Garrard and H. G. Gebel. B.A.R. International Series 396 (i,ii): Oxford.

Henry, D. O., *et al.* 1981 An Investigation of the Prehistory and Paleoenvironments of Southern Jordan (1979 Field Season). *Annual of the Department of Antiquities of Jordan* 5: 113–46.

Hester, T. R.; Heizer, R. F.; and Graham, J. A. 1975 *Field Methods in Archaeology*. Sixth Edition. Palo Alto: Mayfield.

Hill, G. 1896 A Journey East of the Jordan and the Dead Sea, 1895. *Palestine Exploration Fund, Quarterly Statement*, 24–46.

Hoffman, M. A. 1979 *Egypt Before the Pharaohs: The Prehistoric Foundations of Egyptian Civilization.* New York: Alfred A. Knopf.

Homès-Fredericq, D., and Hennessy, J. B., eds. 1986 *Archaeology of Jordan. I. Bibliography*. Leuven: Peeters.

Horowitz, A. 1979 *The Quaternary of Israel*. New York: Academic Press.

Hurlbut, C. S., Jr., and Switzer, G. S. 1979 *Gemology*. New York: John Wiley. Ibn Hauqal

1873 *Kitab Surat al-Ard*, ed. M. de Goeje. Leiden: E. J. Brill (Bibliotheca Geographorum Araborum III).

Ingholt, H. 1940 *Rapport préliminaire sur sept campagnes de fouilles à Hama en Syrie (1932–1938)*. Copenhagen: Ejnar Munksgaard.

Irby, C. L., and Mangles, J. 1823 *Travels in Egypt and Nubia, Syria, and Asia Minor; During the Years 1817 and 1818*. London: Darf (new impression 1985).

1844 *Travels in Egypt and Nubia, Syria, and the Holy Land, Including a Journey Round the Dead Sea, and Through the Country East of the Jordan.* London: John Murray.

Isings, C. 1957 *Roman Glass From Dated Finds*. Academiae Rheno-Traiectinae Instituto Archaeologico II. Groningen: J. B. Wolters. al-Istakhri

1927 *Kitab al-Masalik wa'l-Mamalik*, ed. M. de Goeje. Leiden: E. J. Brill (Bibliotheca Geographorum Araborum I).

Jacobs, L. K. 1983 Survey of the South Ridge of the Wadi 'Isal, 1981. *Annual of the Department of Antiquities of Jordan* 27: 245–74.

Johnston, R. H., and Schaub, R. T. 1978 Selected Pottery from Bâb edh-Dhrâ', 1975. Pp. 33–49 in *Preliminary Excavation Reports: Bâb edh-Dhrâ', Sardis, Meiron, Tell el-Hesi, Carthage (Punic)*, ed. D. N. Freedman. The Annual of the American Schools of Oriental Research 43 (1976). Cambridge, MA: American Schools of Oriental Research.

Kafafi, Z. A. 1982 'The Neolithic of Jordan (East Bank).'

Unpublished Ph.D. Thesis, Freien Universität Berlin.

Karklins, K. 1983 Dutch Trade Beads in North America. Pp. 111–26 in *Proceedings of the 1982 Glass Trade Bead Conference = Rochester Museum and Science Center Research Records No. 16*, ed. C. F. Hayes III. Rochester, NY: Research Division, Rochester Museum and Science Center.

Kehrberg, I. 1986 Summary Report on Glass. Pp. 375–84 in *Jerash Archaeological Project 1981–1983*. Vol. 1, ed. F. Zayadine. Amman: Department of Antiquities.

Kenyon, K. M. 1956 Tombs of the Intermediate Early Bronze–Middle Bronze Age at Tell Ajjul. *Annual of the Department of Antiquities of Jordan* 3: 41–55.

1960 *Excavations at Jericho*. Vol. 1: The Tombs Excavated in 1952–4. London: British School of Archaeology in Jerusalem.

1965 *Excavations at Jericho*. Vol. 2: The Tombs Excavated in 1955–8. London: British School of Archaeology in Jerusalem.

Kenyon, K. M., and Holland, T. A. 1982 *Excavations at Jericho*. Vol. 4: The Pottery Type Series and Other Finds. London: British School of Archaeology in Jerusalem.

1983 *Excavations at Jericho*. Vol. 5: The Pottery Phases of the Tell and Other Finds. London: British School of Archaeology in Jerusalem.

Kervran, M.1984 Les niveaux islamiques du secteur oriental du Tépé de l'Apadana. *Cahiers de la Délégation Archéologique Française en Iran* 14: 211–35.

Khader, B., and Badran, A., eds.1987 *The Economic Development of Jordan*. London: Croom Helm.

Khouri, R. G. 1981 *The Jordan Valley: Life and Society below Sea Level*. London and New York: Longman.

Kidd, K. E., and Kidd, M. A. 1983 A Classification System for Glass Beads for the Use of Field Archaeologists. Pp. 219–82 in *Proceedings of the 1982 Glass Trade Bead Conference = Rochester Museum and Science Center Research Records 16*, ed. C. F. Hayes III. Rochester, NY: Research Division, Rochester Museum and Science Center.

Kiener, L. C. 1834 *Spécies général et iconographie des coquilles vivantes*. Paris: B. Bailliére.

King, G. R. D. 1985 A Survey of the Southern Ghawr, the Wadi 'Araba and Western Trans-Jordan, 1981–2. *Proceedings of the Seminar for Arabian Studies* 15: 41–47.

1986 A Survey of Byzantine and Islamic Sites in Jordan. The Third and Fourth Seasons (1982, 1983). *Archiv für Orientforschung* 33: 251–52.

King, G. R. D., *et al.* 1987 Survey of Byzantine and Islamic Sites in Jordan: Third Season Preliminary Report (1982), The Southern Ghor. *Annual of the Department of Antiquities of Jordan* 31: 439–59.

1989 Survey of Byzantine and Islamic Sites in Jordan. Third Preliminary Report (1982): The Wadi 'Arabah (Part 2). *Annual of the Department of Antiquities of Jordan* 33: 199–215.

Kitchener, H. H. 1884 Major Kitchener's Report. *Palestine Exploration Fund, Quarterly Statement*, 202–21.

Klein, F. A. 1880 *Notes on a Journey to Moab. Palestine Exploration Fund, Quarterly Statement*, 249–55.

Knauf, E. A., and Lenzen, C. J. 1987 Edomite Copper Industry. Pp. 83–88 in *Studies in the History and Archaeology of Jordan III*, ed. A. Hadidi. Amman:

Department of Antiquities of Jordan.

Koeppel, R. 1940 *Teleilat Ghassul II: Compte rendu des fouilles de l'Instiut Biblique Pontifical 1932–1936*. Rome: Institut Biblique Pontifical.

Koucky, F. L., and MacDonald, B. 1985 The Northeast 'Araba Archaeological Reconnaissance Survey, 1985. *Annual of the Department of Antiquities of Jordan* 29: 293–94.

Kunz, G. F. 1971 *The Curious Lore of Precious Stones*. New York: Dover. (Originally published by J. B. Lippincott Company in Philadelphia [1913]).

Kyle, M. G. 1924 The Story of Ancient Sodom in the Light of Modern Science. *Bibliotheca Sacra* 81: 262–91.

1928 *Explorations at Sodom*. New York: Fleming H. Revell.

Lamb, H. H. 1982 *Climate, History and the Modern World*. New York: Methuen.

Lamm, C. J. 1929 *Mittelalterliche Gläser und Steinschnittarbeiten aus dem Nahen Osten*. Berlin: Verlag Dietrich Reimer/Ernst Vohsen.

1935 *Glass from Iran*. London: Kegan Paul, Trench, Trubner.

Lapp, N. L., ed. 1983 *The Excavations at Araq el-Emir*, Vol. 1. The Annual of the American Schools of Oriental Research 47 (1980). Cambridge, MA: American Schools of Oriental Research.

Le Strange, G. 1896 *Description of Syria, including Palestine, by Muqaddasi (circ. 985 A.D.)*. London (reprint New York: AMS press, 1971).

Levy, T. E., and Alon, D. 1987 Settlement Patterns along the Nahal Beersheva – Lower Nahal Besor: Models of Subsistence in the Northern Negev. Pp. 45–138 in *Shiqmim I*, ed. T. E. Levy. B.A.R. International Series 356 (i,ii): Oxford.

Levy, T. E., and Rosen, S. A. 1987 The Chipped Stone Industry at Shiqmim: Typological Considerations. Pp. 281–94 in *Shiqmim I*, ed. T. E. Levy. B.A.R. International Series 356 (i,ii): Oxford.

Lewarch, D., and O'Brien, M. 1981 The Expanding Role of Surface Assemblages in Archaeological Research. Pp. 297–34 in *Advances in Archaeological Method and Theory* Vol 4, ed. M. Schiffer. Academic Press: New York.

Loffreda, S. 1974 *Cafarno. II. La Ceramica*. Jerusalem: Franciscan Printing Press.

1976 Stampi su terre sigillate del IV–VI secolo in Palestina. Pp. 177–96 in *Studia Hierosolymitana in onore del P. Bellarmino Bagatti. I. Studi Archeologici*, eds. E. Testa; I. Mancini; and M. Piccirillo. Jerusalem: Franciscan Printing Press.

Lucas, G. 1934 *Ancient Egyptian Materials and Industries*. London: Edward Arnold.

Luynes, Duc de 1874 *Voyage d'exploration à la Mer Morte, à Petra et sur la rive gauche du Jourdain*. 2 vols. Paris.

Lynch, W. F. 1849 *Narrative of the United States' Expedition to the River Jordan and the Dead Sea*. London: Richard Bentley.

MacDonald, B. 1980 The Hermitage of John the Abbot at Hammam 'Afra, Southern Jordan. *Liber Annuus* 30: 351–64.

1986 Southern Ghors and Northeast 'Araba Archaeological Survey, Jordan, 1986. *Annual of the Department of Antiquities of Jordan* 30: 407–9.

1988a The Pottery Neolithic and Chalcolithic Periods. Pp. 128–378 in *The Wadi el Hasa Archaeological Survey 1979–1983, West-Central Jordan*, ed. B.

MacDonald. Wilfrid Laurier University Press: Waterloo.

1988b The Early to Late Bronze Periods. Pp. 155–70 in *The Wadi el Hasa Archaeological Survey West-Central Jordan*, ed. B. MacDonald. Wilfrid Laurier University Press: Waterloo.

MacDonald, B.; Clark, G. A.; and Neeley, M. P. 1988 Southern Ghors and Northeast 'Araba Archaeological Survey 1985 and 1986, Jordan: A Preliminary Report (with an Appendix by G. A. Clark). *Bulletin of the American Schools of Oriental Research* 272: 23–45.

MacDonald, B., and Koucky, F. L. 1986 The Northeast 'Araba: An Archaeological Reconnaissance Survey in May–June 1985. *Archiv für Orientforschung* 33: 273–75.

MacDonald, B., and Politis, K. D. 1988 Deir 'Ain 'Abata: A Byzantine Church/Monastery Complex in the Ghor Es-Safi. *Liber Annuus* 38: 287–96.

MacDonald, B., *et al.* 1983 The Wadi el Hasa Archaeological Survey 1982: A Preliminary Report. *Annual of the Department of Antiquities of Jordan* 27: 311–23.

1987 Southern Ghors and Northeast 'Arabah Archaeological Survey 1986, Jordan: A Preliminary Report. *Annual of the Department of Antiquities of Jordan* 31: 391–418.

1988 The Wadi el Hasa Archaeological Survey, 1979–1983, West-Central Jordan. Waterloo: Wilfrid Laurier University Press.

Mallon, A. 1924 Voyage d'exploration au sud-est de la Mer Morte. *Biblica* 5: 413–55.

Marks, A. E., ed. 1976 *Prehistory and Paleoenvironments in the Central Negev, Israel I*. SMU Press: Dallas.

1977 *Prehistory and Paleoenvironments in the Central Negev, Israel II*. SMU Press: Dallas.

1983 *Prehistory and Paleoenvironments in the Central Negev, Israel III*. SMU Press: Dallas.

McCreery, D. W. 1979 'Initial Report of the Archaeological Survey of the Southern Ghors and Wadi Araba.' Unpublished report submitted to the Department of Antiquities of Jordan.

1980 'The Nature and Cultural Implications of Early Bronze Age Agriculture in the Southern Ghor of Jordan – An Archaeological Reconstruction.' Unpublished Ph.D. Dissertation, University of Pittsburgh.

McNicoll, A.; Smith, R. H.; and Hennessy, J. B. 1982 *Pella in Jordan 1*: Plates and Illustrations. An Interim Report on the Joint University of Sydney and The College of Wooster Excavations at Pella 1979–1981. Canberra: Australian National Gallery.

Meyer, C. 1984 Byzantine and Umayyad Glass from Jerash: Battleship Curves. Paper delivered at the Annual Meetings of the American Schools of Oriental Research, Chicago, Illinois, December 1984.

1987 Glass from the North Theater Byzantine Church, and Soundings at Jerash, Jordan, 1982–1983. *Bulletin of the American Schools of Oriental Research* Supplement 25: 175–222.

1989 Crown Window Panes: Constantinian or Justinian? Pp. 213–19 in *Essays in Ancient Civilization Presented to Helene J. Kantor*, eds. A. Leonard, Jr. and B. B. Williams. Studies in Ancient Oriental Civilization 47. Chicago: Oriental Institute of the University of Chicago.

Mintz, E., and Ben-Ami, D. 1977 Neolithic Occurrences. Pp. 219–244 in *Prehistoric Investigations in Gebel Maghara, Northern Sinai*, eds. O. Bar-Yosef and J. Phillips. *Qedem* 7. Monographs of the Institute of Archaeology, Hebrew University: Jerusalem.

Moore, A. M. T. 1973 The Late Neolithic in Palestine. *Levant* 5: 36–68.

1982　A Four-Stage Sequence for the Levantine Neolithic, ca. 8500–3750 B.C. *Bulletin of the American Schools of Oriental Research* 246: 1–34.

Morey, G. 1954 *The Properties of Glass*. New York: Reinhold.

Munsell, A. H.1975 *Soil Color Charts*. Baltimore: Macbeth.

1981　*A Color Notation*. Baltimore: Macbeth.

al-Muqaddasi 1906 *Kit-ab Ahsan al-Taq-as-im f-i Ma'rifat al-Aq-al-im*, ed. M. de Goeje. Second edition. Leiden: E. J. Brill (Bibliotheca Geographorum Araborum III).

Murray, M. A., and Ellis, J. C. 1940 *A Street in Petra*. London: British School of Archaeology in Egypt and Bernard Quaritch.

Musil, A. 1907 *Arabia Petraea. I. Moab; II. Edom: Topographischer Reisebericht*. Wien: Alfred Hölder.

Neeley, M. P. 1989 'The Late Pleistocene and Early Holocene Prehistory in the Southern Ghor and Northeast Araba, Jordan.' Unpublished Master's Thesis. Department of Anthropology, Arizona State University.

Neev, D., and Emery, K. 1967 The Dead Sea: Depositional Processes and Environments of Evaporites. *Bulletin of the Geological Survey of Israel* 41: 1–147. Negev, A.

1986　The Late Hellenistic and Early Roman Pottery of Nabatean Oboda, Final Report. *Qedem* 22. Jerusalem: The Hebrew University.

Noy, T.; Friedman, E.; and Burian, F. 1981 Nahal Lavan 108: A Pre-Pottery Neolithic A Site in the Western Negev, Israel. *Palestine Exploration Quarterly* July–December 113: 81–88.

Noy, T.; Schuldenrein, J.; and Tchernov, E. 1980 Gilgal, a Pre-Pottery Neolithic A Site in the Lower Jordan Valley. *Israel Exploration Journal* 30: 63–82.

Oakeshott, M. F. 1978 'A Study of the Iron II Pottery of East Jordan with Special Reference to Unpublished Material from Edom'. Unpublished Ph.D. Thesis, Institute of Archaeology, University of London.

O'Callaghan, R. T. 1953　Madaba (Carte de). Cols. 627–704, figs. 514–36 in vol. 5 of *Supplément au Dictionnaire de la Bible*. Paris.

Olavarri, E. 1969 Fouilles à 'Aro'er sur l'Arnon. Les niveaux bronze intermédiaire. *Revue Biblique* 76: 230–59.

Olszewski, D. 1986 *The North Syrian Late Epipaleolithic*. B.A.R. International Series 309: Oxford.

Oren, E. D., and Gilead, I. 1981 Chalcolithic Sites in Northeastern Sinai. *Tel Aviv* 8.1: 25–44.

Palmer, E. H. 1871 *The Desert of the Exodus: Journeys on Foot in the Wilderness of the Forty Years' Wanderings*. Part II. Cambridge: Deighton, Bell.

Parker, S. T. 1987 'The Pottery'. Pp. 525–619 in *The Roman Frontier in Central Jordan: Interim Report on the Limes Arabicus Project, 1980–1985*, ed. S. T. Parker. Oxford: B.A.R. International Series 340.

Parr, P. J. 1970 A Sequence of Pottery from Petra. Pp. 348–81 in *Near Eastern Archaeology in the Twentieth Century: Essays in Honor of Nelson Glueck*, ed. J. A. Sanders. Garden City, NY: Doubleday.

Perrot, J. 1955 The Excavations at Tell Abu Matar, near Beersheba. *Israel Exploration Journal* 5.3: 167–89.

1975 Beersheba. Pp. 153–58 in vol. 1 of *Encyclopedia of Archaeological Excavations in the Holy Land*, ed. M. Avi-Yonah. Jerusalem: The Israel Exploration Society and Massada Press.

Petrie, F. 1931 *Ancient Gaza I, Tell el Ajjul*. London: British School of Archaeology in Egypt and Bernard Quaritch.

Pfeiffer, R. 1982 'A Study of the Bead Corpus Found at Caesarea Maritima, Israel, 1971–1980.' Madison, NJ: Unpublished Master of Arts Thesis, Drew University.

1983　Glass Trade Beads from Caesarea Maritima, Israel. Pp. 205–12 in *Proceedings of the 1982 Glass Trade Bead Conference = Rochester Museum and Science Center Research Records* 16, ed. C. F. Hayes III. Rochester, NY: Research Division, Rochester Museum and Science Center.

Poidebard, A. 1934 *La Trace de Rome dans le désert de Syrie. Le Limes de Trajan à la conquête Arabe. Recherches Aériennes (1925–1932)*. Texte and Atlas. (Bibliotheque Archéologique et Historique, Tome 18). Paris: Paul Geuthner.

Politis, K. D. 1988 Deir 'Ain 'Abata Excavations, 1988. *Liber Annuus* 38: 461–62.

1989　Excavations at Deir 'Ain 'Abata, 1988. *Annual of the Department of Antiquities of Jordan* 33: 227–33.

1990　'Excavations at Deir 'Ain 'Abata 1990.' *Annual Report of the Department of Antiquities of Jordan*. 34: 377–88.

Prag, K. 1971 'A Study of the Intermediate Early Bronze –Middle Bronze Age in Transjordan, Syria and Lebanon.' Unpublished D. Phil. Thesis, St. Hugh's College, Oxford.

Pringle, D. 1986 *The Red Tower (al-Burj al-Ahmar): Settlement in the Plain of Sharon at the Time of the Crusaders and Mamluks A.D. 1099–1516*. London: British School of Archaeology in Jerusalem.

Pritchard, J. B. 1963 *The Bronze Age Cemetery at Gibeon*. Philadelphia: The University Museum, University of Pennsylvania.

1985　*Tell es-Sa'idiyeh: Excavations on the Tell, 1964–1966*. Philadelphia: The University Museum, University of Pennsylvania (Monograph 41).

Raikes, T. D. n.d. 'Ancient Sites in the Wadi Araba and Nearby.' Unpublished list of sites deposited by the author in the library of the British School at Amman for Archaeology and History.

1980　Notes on Some Neolithic and Later Sites in the Wadi Araba and the Dead Sea Valley. *Levant* 12: 40–60.

1985　The Character of the Wadi Araba. Pp. 95–101 in *Studies in the History and Archaeology of Jordan II*, ed. A. Hadidi. Amman: Department of Antiquities.

Rast, W. E. 1978 *Taanach I: Studies in the Iron Age Pottery*. Cambridge, MA: American Schools of Oriental Research.

1981　Patterns of Settlement at Bab edh-Dhra. Pp. 7–34 in *The Southeastern Dead Sea Plain Expedition: An Interim Report of the 1977 Season*, eds. W. E. Rast and R. T. Schaub. The Annual of the American Schools of Oriental Research 46 (1979).

Cambridge, MA: American Schools of Oriental Research.

Rast, W. E., and Schaub, R. T. 1974 Survey of the Southeastern Plain of the Dead Sea, 1973. *Annual of the Department of Antiquities of Jordan* 19: 5–53.

1978 A Preliminary Report of Excavations at Bab edh-Dhra', 1975. Pp. 1–32 in *Preliminary Excavation Reports: Bab edh-Dhra', Sardis, Meiron, Tell el-Hesi, Carthage (Punic)*, ed. D.N. Freedman. The Annual of the American Schools of Oriental Research 43 (1976). Cambridge, MA: American Schools of Oriental Research.

1980 Preliminary Report of the 1979 Expedition to the Dead Sea Plain, Jordan. *Bulletin of the American Schools of Oriental Research* 240: 21–61.

1981 The 1977 Expedition to the Southeastern Dead Sea Plain, Jordan. Pp. 1–5 in *The Southeastern Dead Sea Plain Expedition: An Interim Report of the 1977 Season*, eds. W. E. Rast and R. T. Schaub. The Annual of the American Schools of Oriental Research 46 (1979). Cambridge, MA: American Schools of Oriental Research.

Redman, C. L. 1978 *The Rise of Civilization: From Early Farmers to Urban Society in the Ancient Near East*. San Francisco: W. H. Freeman.

Reese, D. S. 1982 Marine and Fresh-Water Molluscs from the Epipaleolithic Site of Hayonim Terrace, Western Galilee, Northern Israel, and Other East Mediterranean Sites. *Paléorient* 8.2: 83–90.

1983 Marine Shells. Pp. 224–26 in *Ergebnisse der Ausgrabungen auf der Hirbet el-Msas (Tel Masos) 1972–1975*, eds. V. Fritz and A. Kempinski. Wiesbaden: Otto Harrassowitz.

1984 Strange and Wonderful: Exotic Fauna from Sanctuary Sites. *Newsletter of Athens: the American School of Classical Studies at Athens.* Fall, 13.

1985 The Kition Ostrich Eggshells. Pp. 341–82 Appendix VIII(B) in V. Karageorghis, *Excavations at Kition V/II.* Nicosia: Department of Antiquities.

1986 'The Marine and Freshwater Shells.' Pp. 320–32 in *The Late Bronze and Early Iron ges of Central Transjordan: The Baq'ah Valley Project, 1977–1981*, ed. P. E. McGovern. Philadelphia: The University Museum, University of Pennsylvania (Monograph 65).

1989 On Cassid Lips and Helmet Shells. *Bulletin of the American Schools of Oriental Research* 275: 33–39.

Reese, D. S.; Mienis, H. K.; and Woodward, F. R. 1986 On the Trade of Shells and Fish from the Nile River. *Bulletin of the American Schools of Oriental Research* 264: 79–84.

Rhoads, D. C., and Lutz, R. A. 1980 *Skeletal Growth of Aquatic Organisms.* New York: Plenum.

Riis, P. J., and Poulsen, V. 1957 *Hama: Fouilles et recherches de la Fondation Carlsberg 1931–1938. IV, 2: Les verreries et poteries médiévales.* Copenhagen: Fondation Carlsberg.

Roberts, N. 1982 Lake Levels as an Indicator of Near Eastern Palaeo-Climates: A Preliminary Appraisal. Pp. 235–67 in *Palaeoclimates, Palaeo-environments and Human Communities in the Eastern Mediterranean Region in Later Prehistory*, eds. J. L. Bintliff and W. Van Zeist. B.A.R. International Series 133 (i,ii): Oxford.

Rodziewicz, M. 1984 *Alexandrie III: Les habitations romaines tardives d'Alexandrie à al lumière des fouilles polonaises à Kôm el-Dikka.* Warsaw: Editions scientifiques de Pologne.

Rollefson, G. O. 1983 Ritual and Ceremony at Neolithic Ain Ghazal. *Paléorient* 9/2: 29–38.

1986 Neolithic 'Ain Ghazal (Jordan): Ritual and Ceremony, II. *Paléorient* 12/1: 45–52.

Rollefson, G. O., and Simmons, A. H. 1988 The Neolithic Settlement at 'Ain Ghazal. Pp. 393–421 in *The Prehistory of Jordan*, eds. A. N. Garrard and H. G. Gebel. B.A.R. International Series 396 (i,ii): Oxford.

Rosen, S. A. 1984 Kvish Harif: Preliminary Investigation at a Late Neolithic Site in the Central Negev. *Paléorient* 10(2): 111–21.

1985 The En Shadud Lithics. Pp. 153–67 in *En Shadud: Salvage Excavations at a Farming Community in the Jezreel Valley, Israel*, ed. E. Braun. B.A.R. International Series 249: Oxford.

1987 The Potentials of Lithic Analysis in the Chalcolithic of the Northern Negev. Pp. 295–313 in *Shiqmim I*: Studies Concerning Chalcolithic Societies in the Northern Negev Deserts, Israel (1982–1984), ed. T. E. Levy. B.A.R. International Series 356 (i,ii): Oxford.

Roth, A. M. 1979 Glass. Pp. 144–81 in *Quseir al-Qadim 1978: Preliminary Report*, eds. D. S. Whitcomb and J. H. Johnson. Cairo: American Research Center in Egypt.

Rothenberg, B. 1971 The Arabah in Roman and Byzantine Times in the Light of New Research. Pp. 211–23 in *Roman Frontier Studies 1967. Proceedings of the 7th International Congress*, ed. S. Applebaum. *Tel Aviv*: Tel Aviv University.

Saller, S. J. 1941 *The Memorial of Moses on Mount Nebo.* Jerusalem: Franciscan Press.

Saller, S. J., and Bagatti, B. 1949 *The Town of Nebo (Khirbet el-Mekhayyat) with a Brief Survey of Other Ancient Christian Monuments in Transjordan.* Jerusalem: Franciscan Press.

Saulcy, F. de 1853 *Voyage autour de la Mer Morte et dans les terres bibliques, exécuté de décembre 1850 à avril 1851.* 2 vols. Paris: Gide et J. Baudry.

Schaub, R. T. 1973 An Early Bronze IV Tomb from Bâb edh-Dhrâ'. *Bulletin of the American Schools of Oriental Research* 210: 2–19.

1981 Ceramic Sequences in the Tomb Groups at Bâb edh-Dhra. Pp. 69–118 in *The Southeastern Dead Sea Plain Expedition: An Interim Report of the 1977 Season*, eds. W. E. Rast and R. T. Schaub. The Annual of the American Schools of Oriental Research 46 (1979). Cambridge, MA: American Schools of Oriental Research.

Schaub, R. T., and Rast, W. E., eds. 1989 *Bâb edh-Dhra': Excavations in the Cemetery Directed by Paul W. Lapp (1965–67).* Winona Lake: Eisenbrauns.

Schick, T. 1978 Flint Implements. Pp. 58–63 in *Early Arad*, ed. R. Amiran. Israel Exploration Society: Jerusalem.

Schienerl, P. W. 1985 Cornerless Cube Stone Beads in Egypt and Palestine. *The Bead Forum*, 7: 8–9.

Schuldenrein, J. 1983 'Late Quaternary Paleo-Evnironments and Prehistoric Site Distributions in the Lower Jordan Valley'. Unpublished Ph.D. Dissertation, Department of Anthropology, University of Chicago.

Schuldenrein, J. and Goldberg, P. 1981 Late Quaternary

Paleoenvironments and Prehistoric Site Distributions in the Lower Jordan Valley: A Preliminary Report. *Paléorient* 7: 57–72.

Seetzen, U. J. 1854–55 *Reisen durch Syrien, Pälestina, Phönicien, die Transjordan-Länder, Arabia Patraea und Unter-Aegypten.* 3 vols. Berlin: G. Reimer.

Serjeant, R. B. 1972 *Islamic Textiles: Materials for a History up to the Mongol Conquest.* Beirut: Librairie du Liban.

Shalev, S. and Northover, P. J. 1987 Chalcolithic Metal and Metalworking from Shiqmim. Pp. 357–71 in *Shiqmim I: Studies Concerning Chalcolithic Societies in the Northern Negev Deserts, Israel (1982–1984),* ed. T. E. Levy. B.A.R. International Series 356 (i,ii): Oxford.

Shinnie, P. L., and Harden, D. B. 1955 *Excavations at Soba.* Sudan Antiquities Service Occasional Papers 3. Khartoum (reprinted 1961).

Shinnie, P. L., and Shinnie, M. 1978 *Debira West.* Warminster, England: Aris and Philips.

Smith, R. H. 1973 *Pella of the Decapolis.* Vol. 1: The 1967 Season of the College of Wooster Expedition to Pella. Wooster, Ohio: The College of Wooster.

Solecki, R. L. 1985 A Note on the Dating of Choppers, Chopping Tools, and Related Flake Tool Industries from Southwest Asia. *Paléorient* 11(1): 103–5.

Spaer, M. 1988 The Pre-Islamic Glass Bracelets of Palestine. *Journal of Glass Studies* 30: 51–61.

Sperber, D. 1976 Objects of Trade Between Palestine and Egypt in Roman Times. *Journal of the Economic and Social History of the Orient* 19(II): 113–47.

Starcky, S. L., and Harding, L. 1932 *Beth-Pelet II.* London: British School of Archaeology.

Stekelis, M. 1972 *The Yarmoukian Culture of the Neolithic Period.* The Magnes Press, The Hebrew University: Jerusalem.

Tait, H. 1976 *Jewellery Through 7000 Years.* London: British Museum.

Tatton-Brown, V. A. 1984 The Glass. Pp. 194–212 in *Excavations at Carthage: The British Mission,* Vol. 1, pt. l. Sheffield: J. R. Collis Publications.

Tristram, H. B. 1866 *The Land of Israel: A Journal of Travels in Palestine Undertaken with Special Reference to its Physical Characters.* Second Edition. London: Society for Promoting Christian Knowledge.

1873 *The Land of Moab: Travels and Discoveries on the East Side of the Dead Sea and the Jordan.* New York: Harper.

Tubb, M. 1985 Preliminary Report on the 'Ain Ghazal Statues. *Mitteilungen der Deutschen Orient Gesellschaft* 117: 117–34.

Tufnell, O., and Ward, W. A. 1966 Relations Between Byblos, Egypt, and Mesopotamia at the End of the Third Millenniun B.C.: A Study of the Montet Jar. *Syria* 43: 165–241.

Tushingham, A. D. 1972 The Excavations at Dibon (Dhiba^n) in Moab: The Third Campaign 1952–53. *The Annual of the American Schools of Oriental Research* 40. Cambridge, MA: American Schools of Oriental Research.

Tylecote, R. F. 1976 *A History of Metallurgy.* London: The Metals Society.

Ussishkin, D. 1971 The 'Ghassulian' Temple in Ein Gedi and the Origin of the Hoard from Nahal Mishmar. *The Biblical Archaeologist* 34: 23–39.

1980 The Ghassulian Shrine at En-Gedi. *Tel Aviv* 7.1–2: 1–44.

De Vaux, R. 1961 *L'archéologie et les manuscripts de las Mer Morte.* London: Oxford University Press.

Vessberg, O. 1952 Roman Glass in Cyprus. Pp. 109–65 in *Opuscula Archaeologica* 7. Skrifter Utgivna av Svenska Institutet i Rom 16, No. 4. Lund: C. W. K. Gleerup.

von Saldern, A. 1980 *Ancient and Byzantine Glass from Sardis.* Cambridge, MA: Harvard University Press.

von Wartburg, M.-L. 1983 The medieval cane sugar industry in Cyprus: Results of recent excavation. *Antiquaries Journal* 63: 298–314.

Wagner, R. J. L., and Abbott, R. T., eds. 1967 *Van Nostrand's Standard Catalog of Shells.* Second Edition. New York: D. Van Nostrand.

Walmsley, A. G. 1986 The Abbasid Occupation in Area XXIX (part of the Preliminary Report on the University of Sydney's Seventh Season of Excavations at Pella [Tabaqat Fahl] in 1985). *Annual of the Department of Antiquities of Jordan* 30: 182–95

1987 'The Administrative Structure and Urban Geography of the Jund of Filastin and the Jund of al-Urdunn: The Cities and Districts of Palestine and East Jordan during the Early Islamic.' Unpublished Ph.D. dissertation, University of Sydney.

Watson, A. M. 1983 *Agricultural Innovation in the Early Islamic World: The Diffusion of Crops and Farming Techniques, 700–1100.* Cambridge: Cambridge University Press.

Webster, R. 1983 *Gems: Their Sources, Descriptions, and Identification.* London: Butterworth.

Weinberg, G. D. 1973 Notes on Glass from Upper Galilee. *Journal of Glass Studies* 15: 35–51.

Weinberg, G. D., and Barag, D. 1974 Glass Vessels. Pp. 103–5 in *Discoveries in the Wadi ed-Dâliyeh,* eds P. W. Lapp and N. L. Lapp. The Annual of the American Schools of Oriental Research 41. Cambridge, MA: American Schools of Oriental Research.

Wheeler, R. E. M.; Ghosh, A.; and Deva, K. 1946 Arikamedu: An Indo-Roman Trading Station on the East Coast of India. *Ancient India* 2: 17–124.

Whitcomb, D. 1982 Islamic Glass. Pp. 233–41 in *Quseir al-Qadim 1980: Preliminary Report,* eds. D. S. Whitcomb and J. H. Johnson. Malibu: Undena Publications.

1982 *Quseir al-Qadim 1980: Preliminary Report* (with Janet H. Johnson). Malibu, American Research Center in Egypt Reports, vol. 7.

1983 Islamic Glass from Quseir al-Qadim, Egypt. *Journal of Glass Studies* 25: 101–8.

1985 *Before the Roses and Nightingales: Excavations at Qasr-i Abu Nasr, Old Shiraz.* New York: The Metropolitan Museum of Art.

1987 Excavations in 'Aqaba: First Preliminary Report. *Annual of the Department of Antiquities of Jordan* 31: 247–66.

1988 Khirbet al-Mafjar Reconsidered: The Ceramic Evidence. *Bulletin of the American Schools of Oriental Research* 271: 51–67.

Wigley, T. M. L.; Ingram, M. J.; and Farmer, G. 1981 *Climate and History: Studies in Past Climate and Their Impact on Man.* Cambridge: Cambridge University Press.

Wilbur, K. M., and Saleuddin, A. S. M. 1983 *Shell Formation. The Mollusca, Vol. 4. Physiology, Part 1*, eds. A. S. M. Saleuddin and K. M. Wilbur. New York: Academic Press.

Winnett, F. V., and Reed, W. L. 1964 *The Excavations of Dibon (Dhibân) in Moab*. The Annual of the American Schools of Oriental Research 36–37 (1957–1958). New Haven, CT: American Schools of Oriental Research.

Woolley, C. L. 1934 *Ur Excavations*. Vol. 2: A Report of the Predynastic and Sargonid Graves Excavated between 1926 and 1931. London: The British Museum and the Museum of the University of Pennsylvania to Mesopotamia.

al-Ya'qubi 1892 *Kitab al-Buldan*, ed. M. de Goeje. Leiden: E. J. Brill (Bibliotheca Geographorum Araborum VII).

Yassine, K. 1984 *Tell el Mazar I: Cemetery A*. Amman: The University of Jordan.

1988 *Archaeology of Jordan: Essays and Reports*. Amman: The University of Jordan.

Zaghloul, M., ed. 1988 General Index (Authors of Sites) I–XXX 1951–1986. *Annual of the Department of Antiquities of Jordan*.

Zayadine, F. 1977–78 Excavations on the Upper Citadel of Amman – Area A (1975 and 1977). *Annual of the Department of Antiquities of Jordan*, 22: 20–56.

1982 Recent Excavations at Petra (1979–81). *Annual of the Department of Antiquities of Jordan* 26: 365–93.

Zohary, M. 1962 *Plant Life of Palestine*. New York: The Ronald Press.

1982 *Vegetation of Israel and Adjacent Areas*. Wiesbaden: Reichert.